Intelligent Scheduling

Contributors:

M. Aarup
M.M. Arentoft
John Bresina
Peter Burke
Michael Carpenter
Stephen E. Cross
Brian Daun
Eugene Davis
Michael Deale
Roberto V. Desimone
Jürgen Dorn
Brian Drabble
Mark Drummond
Hugh E. Fargher
Kenneth Fordyce
Khosrow C. Hadavi
Othar Hansson
Wen-Ling Hsu
Mark D. Johnston
Donna Kautz
Karl G. Kempf
Richard Kirby
Claude Le Pape
Andrew Mayer
Glenn E. Miller

Steven Minton
Nicola Muscettola
Kazuo Miyashita
Masayuki Numao
Peng Si Ow
Y. Parrod
Michael J. Prietula
Patrick Prosser
Norman Sadeh
Danielle Schnitzius
Wolfgang Slany
Richard A. Smith
Stephen F. Smith
J. Stader
I. Stokes
Gerald Sullivan
Keith Swanson
Katia Sycara
Austin Tate
Gerald L. Thompson
H. Vadon
Pascal Van Hentenryck
Edward Walker
David E. Wilkins
Mark Yvanovich

Editors:

Monte Zweben
Red Pepper Software Company

Mark S. Fox
University of Toronto

MORGAN KAUFMANN PUBLISHERS
SAN FRANCISCO, CALIFORNIA

Editor and Publisher   *Michael B. Morgan*
Project Management   *Professional Book Center*
Electronic Composition   *Professional Book Center*
Cover Design   *Melanie Smith*

Library of Congress **Cataloging-in-Publication Data**
is available for this title.

Printed in the United States of America

10   9   8   7   6   5   4   3   2

MORGAN KAUFMANN PUBLISHERS, INC.
340 Pine St., Sixth Floor
San Francisco, California 94104
415-392-2665

CONTENTS

PREFACE

Intelligent Scheduling is a collection of chapters, spanning a decade of research and development, written by experts in the field of artificial intelligence (AI) planning and scheduling. AI planning systems automatically determine a course of action (i.e., a plan) from a set of objectives or goals. AI scheduling systems assign times and resources to a plan, subject to resource limitations, precedence relationships, due dates, and other constraints. Practical AI planning and scheduling systems also attempt to optimize objectives in addition to satisfying hard constraints. Usually these objectives relate to economic variables, such as overtime costs and profit, but sometimes they relate to intangible measures, such as the degree of change in one schedule from another. All of the chapters in this book describe implemented AI planning and scheduling systems. While theory is an important foundation for these systems, we focus here on practical solutions that demonstrate results on realistic problems.

Scheduling is a ubiquitous activity in everyday life affecting both the private and public sectors. In the private sector, scheduling is key to manufacturing, distribution, transportation, engineering maintenance, entertainment production, and construction. It is a mission-critical activity that can separate corporate success from financial disaster. In government, scheduling is also mission critical. All of NASA's spacecraft operations, both in space and on the ground, are meticulously scheduled. Department of Defense missions, both peaceful and in confrontation, are repeatedly planned and scheduled. In the current atmosphere of government budget cuts, agencies must perform more work for less money. Thus operations must be accomplished in less time with fewer resources, creating great planning and scheduling challenges.

The book is organized into two sections: scientific methodologies and case studies. This organization attempts to bridge the gap between the state-of-the-science and the state-of-the-practice. The methodologies section contains highly technical chapters that describe implemented scheduling systems. Each chapter presents a comprehensive overview of a system and the problems it can solve. The chapters do not report detailed incremental research results, which are better suited for journals or conferences, and they do not require much background preparation. The case studies are real-world applications of AI scheduling methods. These applications span many topics in both government and industry. The case studies are less technical in nature and focus on operational improvements and practical challenges.

The chapters of the book are not organized according to any rule of importance or significance. In most cases, they are chronologically ordered. We expect readers to use the text in a directed manner but those with little background in the area can use the introduction as a guide. Government and industry managers can use this text as a guide to operations planning and scheduling systems. The case studies describe the trials and tribulations of others who have already embarked on this path. The methodology section provides a glimpse of the next generation of scheduling systems.

We hope that the book serves both academics and practitioners. The methodologies section provides the scientific community with a central repository for the major efforts in this area. It also provides AI researchers in the areas of search and reasoning a rich collection of practical problems to serve as domains for their general methods. We are frustrated by experimental research on standard AI "toy problems" and hope this book will facilitate the use of scheduling problems to guide fundamental work in representation and reasoning. We urge AI researchers to help extend the methods described in this volume or to invent new methods to solve these real-world problems.

INTRODUCTION

Since the 1960s, the problem of planning has captured the interest of many AI researchers. Planning is the process of selecting and sequencing activities such that they achieve one or more goals and satisfy a set of domain constraints. For the most part, planning research has focused on finding a feasible set of actions that accomplish one or more goals.

In 1982, a paper by Fox, Allen, and Strohm, titled "Job-Shop Scheduling: An Investigation in Constraint-Directed Reasoning," appeared in the *Proceedings of the Second Annual National Conference on Artificial Intelligence.* This paper introduced the scheduling problem to the artificial intelligence community. Scheduling is the process of selecting among alternative plans and assigning resources and times to the set of activities in the plan. These assignments must obey a set of rules or constraints that reflect the temporal relationships between activities and the capacity limitations of a set of shared resources. The assignments also affect the optimality of a schedule with respect to criteria such as cost, tardiness, or throughput. In summary, scheduling is an optimization process where limited resources are allocated over time among both parallel and sequential activities.

The event that led to this scheduling paper was a visit to a Westinghouse turbine component manufacturing plant where it was discovered that *scheduling,* not *planning,* was the significant problem. It is surprising that the AI community did not recognize the importance of scheduling sooner, because one of the earlier papers on planning explicitly pointed out the problem of allocating resources over time (Simon 1972). The blocks-world problem used by planning researchers never forced the issues that arise in scheduling—it took a return to the "real world" for these issues to reappear.

Scheduling is known to be NP-complete and has proven to be a difficult task for human planners and schedulers. The 1982 paper proposed a new outlook on the scheduling problem, namely that the generation of a schedule is a constraint-directed search process. Since the appearance of that paper, scheduling as a topic of research has garnered the attention of a significant number of AI researchers. Much of the successful work to date has been based on the use of constraints to guide the search process.

This book provides a sampling of what we believe are some of the significant works in the artificial intelligence approach to scheduling. The book is divided into two parts. The first part focuses on scheduling methodologies; the second part describes case studies of real-world applications.

SCHEDULING METHODOLOGIES

Scheduling methodologies generally fall into two camps: constructive methods and repair methods. The constructive approach incrementally extends a partial schedule until it is complete. The repair-based methods iteratively modify a complete schedule to remove conflicts or to further optimize the solution. While each method has its strengths and weaknesses, there has been little thorough analysis of their performance on different classes of problems. We encourage the research community to actively compare and constrast these methods empirically and theoretically.

Constructive methods were the basis of the pioneering research at Carnegie Mellon University (CMU). Chapter 1, "ISIS: A Retrospective" by Mark Fox, describes the first constraint-based scheduling system. The ISIS paper provides a detailed account of constraint-directed scheduling from an order perspective; i.e., iteratively selecting and scheduling one order at a time. One of the important contributions of this work that persists in future work is the representation of constraints. Up to this point the AI community used constraints to prune search—ISIS used constraints to intelligently generate, filter, and quantitatively score search states. ISIS also uses abstraction to reduce the complexity of search.

Chapter 2, "OPIS: A Methodology and Architecture for Reactive Scheduling" by Stephen Smith, describes the successor to ISIS. This chapter introduces the opportunisitc selection of scheduling and rescheduling methods. Using a blackboard, OPIS can identify bottlenecks and switch from an order perspective (as in ISIS) to a resource perspective where a subset of activities that need to use the bottleneck resource are scheduled. OPIS can also select among a few rescheduling methods based on the state of the schedule.

Chapter 3, "Scheduling as Intelligent Control of Decision-Making and Constraint Propagation" by Claude Le Pape, builds on the OPIS model of scheduling. (Le Pape spent a year with the CMU scheduling group.) This chapter provides a more formal interpretation of constraint propagation in addition to an empirical analysis of the SONIA scheduling system. In this chapter, Le Pape shows that SONIA is a valid and complete scheduling system.

Chapter 4, "Micro-Opportunistic Scheduling: The Micro-Boss Factory Scheduler" by Norman Sadeh, also describes an opportunistic scheduler. Micro-Boss takes a microscopic view of opportunism by iteratively selecting and scheduling one activity at a time (in contrast with the macro-opportunism of OPIS, which scheduled entire resources or orders). Micro-Boss focuses its search by evaluating "textures" of the constraint graph. These textures measure graph properties such as contention and reliance of variables on values.

Though the majority of the AI approaches to scheduling have been constraint-based, it is only in the last seven years that we have seen the emergence of constraint-based programming languages that simplify the construction of constraint-directed schedulers. In Chapter 5, "Scheduling and Packing in the Constraint Language cc(FD)," Pascal Van Hentenryck of Brown University, provides a detailed description of how constraint logic programming combines nondeterministic goal-directed programming with constraint satisfaction to solve scheduling problems. These languages have been widely used in Europe and in Japan and are garnering an increasing following in North America.

Chapter 6, "HSTS: Integrating Planning and Scheduling" by Nicola Muscettola, describes a unique knowledge representation that can specify complex behavioral constraints. HSTS combines planning and scheduling by instantiating interval-based state variables in a temporal database.

Tate, Drabble, and Kirby (University of Edinburgh) describe another approach to combining planning and scheduling in Chapter 7, "O-Plan2: an Open Architecture for Command, Planning, and Control." O-Plan2 uses a blackboard architecture to manage the opportunistic application of planning, scheduling, and execution monitoring knowledge sources.

Around 1986, the NASA Ames Artificial Intelligence Research Branch started to investigate a number of NASA scheduling problems. This work led to an alternative approach to scheduling called *iterative repair*. The Ames researchers pursued this path for a number of reasons including a frustration with the performance of backtracking search on real-world problems, a need for incremental rescheduling that minimizes change to an original schedule, and an analysis of a particularly powerful neural network approach to scheduling (built at the Space Telescope Science Institute). Two important algorithms resulted from this research, which are presented in Chapters 8 and 9.

Chapter 8, "Scheduling and Rescheduling with Iterative Repair" by Zweben et al., describes an extensible system that combines the use of constraints (for generating, filtering, and scoring search alternatives like ISIS) with a repair-based search. This system exploits constraint knowledge in the repair process to converge to near-optimal schedules. It represents state constraints in addition to typical scheduling constraints and minimizes perturbation to the original schedule when rescheduling.

In Chapter 9, "Analyzing a Heuristic Strategy for Constraint-Satisfaction and Scheduling," Johnston and Minton describe a different repair-based method that uses lookahead search instead of heuristic constraint knowledge to guide the repair process. This general heuristic, named MIN-CONFLICTS, is widely applicable and performs remarkably well on some large-scale problems. The authors present a theoretical analysis of MIN-CONFLICTS to characterize its performance. MIN-CONFLICTS is similar to the contention texture found in Sadeh's work.

At Carnegie Mellon University, Miyashita and Sycara combine case-based reasoning, constructive methods, and repair methods in their CABINS scheduling system. Chapter 10, "Adaptive Case-Based Control of Schedule Revision," describes how case-based reasoning can be used to further optimize schedules derived by the Micro-Boss scheduler. CABINS uses cases to modify the problem constraints thereby forcing the scheduler to generate a new solution in the direction suggested by the case.

Chapter 11, "The Distributed Asynchronous Scheduler" by Burke and Prosser of the University of Strathclyde, examines how a distributed set of scheduling agents, operating at three levels of control, coordinate their decision making.

Chapter 12, "Robust Scheduling and Execution for Automatic Telescopes" by Drummond, Swanson, and Bresina, presents the CERES system, which is unique in its use of "situated control rules" and contingency planning. Situated control rules are condition/action representations that allow for the automatic execution of a schedule. CERES explicitly represents the uncertainty of action outcomes and performs contingency planning to prepare proactively for execution failures.

Chapter 13, "DTS: A Decision-Theoretic Scheduler for Space Telescope Applications" by Hansson and Mayer, describes a method that improves a heuristic search process by correlating the performance of the search mechanism with its hard-coded heuristics. DTS uses probabilistic inference to aggregate these statistics and therefore form more accurate heuristics that better direct the search process.

APPLICATION CASE STUDIES

This section contains case studies of intelligent scheduling applications that generally fall into four categories: (1) space applications, (2) semiconductor manufacturing, (3) heavy manufacturing, and (4) defense logistics. These systems range from advanced prototypes that operate on real-world data to actual operational deployments. The space applications include both ground and space-borne systems. These systems have drawn insights, techniques, and inspiration from the projects defined in the methodologies section.

Space Applications

Chapter 14, "SPIKE: Intelligent Scheduling of Hubble Space Telescope Observations" by Johnston and Miller, describes a system that uses the lookahead methods from Chapter 9 to operationally solve the telescope scheduling problem.

SPIKE uses "suitability functions" to allow the system to efficiently propagate preferences through a constraint network.

Chapter 15, "The Space Shuttle Ground Processing Scheduling System" by Deale et al., describes an application of the iterative repair methods from Chapter 8 to schedule the repair and refurbishment of the NASA Space Shuttle fleet. This system uniquely focuses on optimization and rescheduling. It also has a rich modeling language for reasoning about the physical state of the Space Shuttle. The Red Pepper Software Company is now commercializing this technology to other industrial problems such as airline maintenance and manufacturing.

Chapter 16, "Optimum-AIV: A Knowledge-Based Planning and Scheduling System for Spacecraft AIV" by Aarup et al., describes a system developed for the European Space Agency. It combines planning and scheduling methods with a rich plan representation language. Optimum-AIV has sophisticated tools that assist the user in manually adjusting the schedule for both planning and plan repair.

Semiconductor Manufacturing

Semiconductor manufacturing is a very complex process rife with uncertainty. The chapters in this section all use different methodologies to attack similar problems. Each system tries to meet due dates, reduce cycle time, reduce work-in-process inventory, and increase throughput. One common message in these chapters is that is is very difficult to integrate an intelligent scheduling system into both an existing information system infrastructure and an existing operational process.

Chapter 17, "Logistics Management System (LMS): Integrating Decision Technologies for Dispatch Scheduling in Semiconductor Manufacturing" by Fordyce and Sullivan, describes an operational system at IBM's Burlington Vermont facility. This expert system dispatches work to the shop-floor based on a voting process. A set of heuristic advocates score each lot, and the overall winner is subsequently dispatched to the floor.

Chapter 18, "Intelligently Scheduling Semiconductor Wafer Fabrication" by Karl Kempf, describes a set of modules that together decompose scheduling problems into subproblems, sort those problems in importance orderings, propose subproblems to focus on and finally place the subproblems onto the schedule. This chapter also describes some of the "cultural" frustrations experienced during the project. This work has its roots in the OPIS system of Chapter 2.

Chapter 19, "Planning in a Flexible Semiconductor Manufacturing Environment" by Fargher and Smith, describes the Microelectronics Manufacturing Science and Technology planning system developed by Texas Instruments. This system uses fuzzy logic representations to handle the inherent uncertainty in modeling cycle times. Their system uses constructive search to plan the release of work to the shop floor.

Chapter 20, "ReDS: A Real Time Production Scheduling System from Conception to Practice" by Khosrow Hadavi, describes an operational production scheduler installed in three Siemens VLSI plants. ReDS is a distributed system of planning agents; these agents are continually updated by shop-floor data and by a statistical analysis component that monitors execution trends. These agents work independently with the goal of releasing orders to the shop-floor effectively.

Heavy Manufacturing

The heavy manufacturing case studies include two steelmaking applications and one glass windshield operation. In two of these applications, the human plays an integral role because the systems do not completely automate the scheduling process.

Chapter 21, "Development of a Cooperative Scheduling System for the Steel-Making Process" by Masayuki Numao, describes SCHEPLAN, a system developed jointly by IBM and the Nippon Kokan company. This system introduces the concept of cooperative scheduling where the user makes manual schedule refinements and the system then fixes any conflicts introduced by the user with a rule-based expert system.

Chapter 22, "A Flow Shop with Compatibility Constraints in a Steelmaking Plant" by Dorn and Slany, describes an application to an Austrian steelmaking plant. There are physical constraints in this domain that can only be roughly described. For example, the compatibility between any two consecutive jobs in a furnace is constrained by the residual elements left on the walls of the furnace by the first job. These constraints are represented by fuzzy sets and are satisfied with a repair-based search method.

Chapter 23, "MacMerl: Mixed-Initiative Scheduling with Coincident Problem Spaces" by Prietula, Hsu, Ow, and Thompson, describes a system that schedules the production of windshields for automobiles, trucks, and recreational vehicles. MacMerl was built by studying the human experts with the goal of creating schedules in a manner analogous to the human approach while simultaneously exploiting the computational power of the computer. MacMerl can generate schedules using a dispatch method that minimizes set-ups but allows the human to intervene at any point.

Defense Logistics

The final application chapters describe work in crisis action planning and scheduling funded by the Defense Advanced Research Projects Agency (DARPA), Rome Laboratories (RL) and the United States Transportation Command (USTRANSCOM). Chapter 24, "Applying an AI Planner to Military Operations Planning" by Wilkins and Desimone, describes SOCAP, an extension of the SIPE planning system. This chapter describes how SIPE's hierarchical plan decomposition is well suited to building crisis action plans. Chapter 25, "DART: Applying Knowledge Based Planning and Scheduling to Crisis Action Planning" by Cross and Walker, describes a system that played a critical role in the Persian Gulf crisis. This system was integrated with many operational databases and applications to provide operational assistance during the crisis.

Reference

Simon, H. A. (1972). On Reasoning About Actions. *Representation and Meaning: Experiments with Information Processing Systems*. Englewood Cliffs: Prentice Hall, Inc., pp. 414–430.

PART

ONE

SCHEDULING
METHODOLOGIES

1

ISIS:

A Retrospective

Mark S. Fox
(University of Toronto)

1.1 INTRODUCTION

Since the 1960s, planning has captured the interest of many AI researchers. *Planning selects and sequences activities such that they achieve one or more goals and satisfy a set of domain constraints.* For the most part, planning research has focused on finding a feasible chain of actions that accomplish one or more goals. Even though Simon pointed out in 1972 the problem of allocating resources over time (Simon, 1972), it was not until the early 1980s that scheduling came under serious scrutiny. More recently, it has garnered the attention of a significant number of AI researchers, primarily in the domains of manufacturing, military transportation, and space.[1] *Scheduling selects among alternative plans and assigns resources and times for each activity so that the assignments obey the temporal restrictions of activities and the capacity limitations of a set of shared resources.* Scheduling is an optimization task where limited resources are allocated over time among both parallel and sequential activities such that measures such as tardiness, work-in-process inventory, and makespan are minimized. Both problems have been proven to be NP-Hard (Chapman, 1987; Garey & Johnson, 1979).

Thirteen years ago, the "real world" foisted our group at Carnegie Mellon University into the midst of the scheduling problem. The work that followed ultimately led to the creation of the ISIS system. This chapter reviews the ISIS series

---

[1] There is even a conference on the topic, "Expert Systems in Production Operations and Management," and workshops on the topic have held at the AAAI conference.

Figure 1-1:   Turbine blade

of systems, examines the ideas those systems introduced, and reflects upon their
relevance today.

1.2 PROBLEM DEFINITION

In 1980, we were asked to explore the application of AI techniques to a
turbine component plant's job-shop scheduling problem. The primary product of
the plant was steam turbine blades. A turbine blade (Figure 1-1) is a complex three
dimensional object produced by a sequence of forging, milling, grinding, and finishing operations to tolerances of a thousandth of an inch. Thousands of different
styles of blades were produced in the plant; many were used as replacements in
turbines in service.

The plant continuously received orders for one to a thousand blades at a time.
Orders fell into at least six categories:

1. **Forced outages** are orders to replace blades that malfunctioned during operation. It is important to ship these orders as soon as possible, no matter what
   the cost.

2/3. **Critical replacement and ship direct** are orders to replace blades during
   scheduled maintenance. Advance warning is provided, but the blades must
   arrive on time.

4/5. **Service and shop orders** are orders for new turbines. Lead times of up to
   three years are known.

6. **Stock orders** are orders for blades to be placed in stock for future needs.

The portion of the plant studied has from 100 to 200 orders in process at any time.

Parts are produced according to a process routing. A routing specifies a sequence of operations on the part. An operation is an activity that defines

- resources required such as tools, materials, fixtures, and machines
- machine setup and run times
- labor requirements

In the plant, each part number has one or more process routings containing 10 or more operations.[2] Process routing variations can be as simple as substituting a different machine or as complex as changing the manufacturing process. Furthermore, the resources needed for an operation might also be needed by other operations in the shop. The flow diagram in Figure 1-2 shows the path that different parts take through the factory. Many of the areas and machines are contended for by different parts.

In AI terms, job-shop scheduling is a planning problem with the following characteristics:

- It is a *time-based* planning problem (i.e., scheduling) in which activities must be selected, sequenced, and assigned resources and time of execution.
- It is a *multi-agent* planning problem. Each order represents a separate agent for which a plan/schedule is to be created. The number of agents to be scheduled is in the hundreds and sometimes thousands.
- The agents are *uncooperative*. Each is attempting to maximize its own goals.
- *Resource contention* is high, hence closely coupling decisions.
- Search is *combinatorially explosive*. Eighty-five orders move through 10 operations without alternatives, with a single substitutable machine for each operation, and no machine idle time has over 10^{1000} possible schedules.

An expert systems approach was used to construct the scheduler. This approach assumed that one or more experts could be interviewed to acquire the rules that govern their decision process. During our discussions, we found that orders were not scheduled in a uniform manner. Each scheduling choice entailed side effects whose importance varied by order. One factor that continuously appeared was the reliance of the scheduler on information other than due dates, process routings, and machine availability. The types and sources of this information were found by examining the documents issued by the scheduler. A schedule was distributed to persons in each department in the plant. Each recipient could provide information that could alter the existing schedule. In support of this observation, we

---

[2]Multiple process routings correspond to a network of activities, each path representing a separate plan.

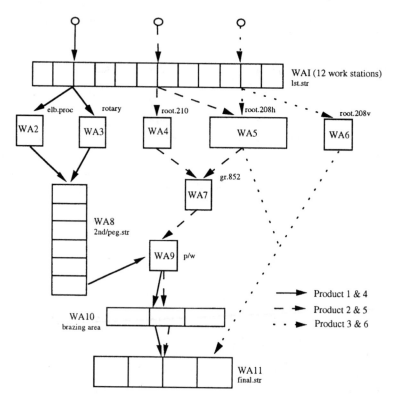

Figure 1-2:   Product/process flow

found that the scheduler was spending 10%–20% of the time scheduling and 80%–90% of the time communicating with other employees to determine what additional "constraints" could affect an order's schedule. These constraints included operation precedence, operation alternatives, operation preferences, machine alternatives and preferences, tool availability, fixture availability, NC program availability, order sequencing, setup time reduction, machine breakdowns, machine capabilities, work-in-process time, due dates, start dates, shop stability, cost, quality, and personnel capabilities/availability.

From this analysis, we concluded that the object of scheduling is not only meeting due dates but also satisfying the many constraints found in various parts of the plant. Scheduling is not a distinct function, separate from the rest of the plant, but is highly connected to, and dependent upon, decisions being made elsewhere in the plant. The added complexity imposed by these constraints leads schedulers to produce poor schedules. Indicators such as high work-in-process, tardiness, and low machine utilization support this conclusion.[3] Hence, any solution to the job-shop scheduling problem must identify the set of scheduling constraints and their affect on the scheduling process.

Once the issue of designing a constraint-directed scheduling system was identified, we decided to solve the problem by constructing a family of systems. Our purpose was to investigate the performance of successively more sophisticated search architectures. At each stage, experiments were run to measure the effectiveness of the architecture.

In the remaining sections, we review the evolution of ISIS, at each stage identifying the key ideas of each version. Last, we reflect upon the long term impact of ISIS.

1.3 ISIS-0

In the fall of 1980, work began on ISIS-0. Realizing that the number and variety of constraints are what make scheduling difficult, we set out to identify the types of constraints used by schedulers and the extent to which they could prune the space of alternative schedules using a simple search method.

1.3.1 Architecture

ISIS-0 employed a simple best-first, backtracking approach using constraints as a dynamically defined evaluation function (Figure 1-3). The salient points of the search architecture include the following:

- Each order was scheduled separately, in priority order, as determined by a combination of order category and due date.
- Search could be performed forward from the order's start date or backward from the order's due date.
- Operators would generate alternative operations, machines, and operation times. The shop was loaded; hence, the availability of resources at a particular time was restricted.
- States represent partial schedules. A path through the network determines a complete schedule.

---

[3] It is unfair to measure a scheduler's performance based on the above measures alone. Our analysis has shown that scheduling is a complex constraint satisfaction problem, where the above indicators illustrate only a subset of constraints that the scheduler must consider. Schedulers are expert in acquiring and "juggling" the satisfaction of constraints.

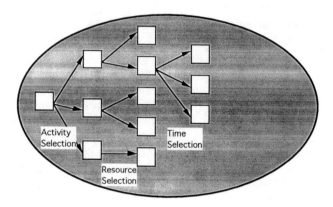

Figure 1-3:   Incremental generation of partial schedules for a single order

- Constraints were either imposed exogenously by the scheduling person upon the system or were already embedded in the factory model and their applicability determined at each point in the search space.
- Propagation of constraints was performed when scheduling decisions early in the search path restricted decisions further on.

Research on version 0 of ISIS yielded five broad categories of constraints. The first category encountered is what we called an *Organizational Goal*. Part of the organization planning process is the generation of measures of how the organization is to perform. These measures act as constraints on one or more organization variables. An organizational goal constraint can be viewed as an expected value of some organization variable; for example:

Due dates: A major concern of a factory is meeting due dates. The lateness of an order affects customer satisfaction.

Work-in-process: Work-in-process (WIP) inventory levels are another concern. WIP inventory represents a substantial investment in raw materials and added value. These costs are not recoverable until delivery. Hence, reducing WIP time is desirable.

Resource levels: Another concern is maintaining adequate levels of resources necessary to sustain operations. Resources include personnel, raw materials, and tools. Each resource will have associated constraints. For example, labor size must be smoothed over a month's interval, or raw materials inventory might have to be limited to a two-day supply.

Costs: Cost reduction can be another important goal. Costs can include material costs, wages, and lost opportunity. Reducing costs might help achieve other goals such as stabilization of the work force.

Production levels: Advance planning also sets production goals for each cost center in the plant. This serves two functions: it designates the primary facilities of the plant by specifying higher production goals and also specifies a preliminary budget by predicting how much the plant will produce. One outcome of this activity is a forecast of the work shifts that will be run in various areas of the plant.

Shop stability: Shop stability is a function of the number of revisions to a schedule and the amount of disturbance in preparation caused by these revisions. It is an artifact of the time taken to communicate change in the plant and the preparation time.

One can view all organizational goal constraints as being approximations of a simple profit constraint. The goal of an organization is to maximize profits. Scheduling decisions are then made on the basis of current and future costs incurred. For example, not meeting a due date might result in the loss of a customer and, in turn, erosion of profits. The longer the work-in-process time, the greater the carrying charge will be for raw materials and value-added operations. Maintaining a designated production level might distribute the cost of the capital equipment in a uniform manner. In practice, most of these costs cannot be determined accurately and must, therefore, be estimated.

Physical constraints determine a second category of constraint. Physical constraints specify characteristics that limit functionality. For example, the length of a milling machine's workbed might limit the types of turbine blades for which it can be used. Similarly, there are specific machine setup and processing times associated with different manufacturing operations.

Causal restrictions constitute a third category of constraint. They define what conditions must be satisfied before initiating an operation. Examples of causal constraints include the following:

- **Precedence** is a process routing that is a sequence of operations. A precedence constraint on an operation states that another operation must take place before (or after) it. There can be further modifiers on the constraint in terms of minimum or maximum time between operations, product temperature to be maintained, etc.

- **Resource requirements** are another causal constraint that is the specification of resources that must be present before or during the execution of a process. For example, a milling operation requires the presence of certain tools, an operator, fixtures, etc.

A fourth category of constraint is concerned with the **availability** of resources. As resources are assigned to specific operations during the production of a schedule, constraints declaring the resources unavailable for other uses during the

Table 1-1: Manufacturing constraints

Constraint	Organization Goal	Physical	Causal	Preference	Availability
Operation alternatives			X		
Operation preferences				X	
Machine alternatives			X		
Machine preferences				X	
Machine physical constraints		X			
Setup times	X	X			
Machine queue ordering pref.				X	
Machine queue stability	X				
Due date	X				
Work-in-process	X				
Tool requirement			X		
Material requirement			X		
Personnel requirement			X		
Resource reservation					X
Shifts					X
Down time					X
Cost	X				
Productivity goals	X				
Quality	X	X			
Inter-operation transfer time			X		

relevant time periods must be generated and associated with these resources. Resource availability is also constrained by the work shifts designated in the plant, machine maintenance schedules, and other machine down times (e.g., breakdowns).

A fifth category of constraint is **preference** or what has come to be known as a "soft" constraint. A preference constraint can also be viewed as an abstraction of other types of constraints. Consider a preference for a machine. It expresses a floor supervisor's desire that one machine be used instead of another. The reason for the preference can be due to cost or quality, but sufficient information does not exist to derive actual costs. In addition to machine preferences, operation preferences and order sequencing preferences exemplify this type of constraint.

Constraints shown in Table 1-1 are those we have identified as well as the categories we have used to classify them.

1.3.2 Performance

ISIS-0 was completed in December 1980 and partially demonstrated, bugs and all, at the sponsoring plant. Although it demonstrated that schedules could be constructed by generating alternative process plans and resource assignments and pruned using constraints, its knowledge was not strong enough to deal with the complexity of the problem.

1.3.3 Constraint-directed Search Concepts

Constraint-Directed Evaluation. ISIS-0 dynamically constructed a different evaluation function for each state in the search space. It constructed the evaluation function out of the constraints that were resolved to be applicable to the state under consideration. Each constraint contributed both an importance (i.e., weight) and a utility. Constraints were resolved by extracting them from the resources and operations defined in the particular state.

1.4 ISIS-1: CONSTRAINT-DIRECTED SCHEDULING

ISIS-0 identified the broad categories of constraints, but more work on the representation and search architecture was required. In January 1981, work on the second version of ISIS began. The purpose of this system was twofold. Given the central role of constraints to determine a job shop schedule, a major focus of our research was to identify and characterize the constraint knowledge required to support an effective constraint-directed search. Consider the imposition of a due date: In its simplest form, this constraint would be represented by a date alone, implying that the job be shipped on that date. In actuality, however, due dates might not always be met, and such a representation provides no information as to how to proceed in these situations. An appropriate representation must include the additional information about the due date that might be necessary in constructing a satisfactory schedule; for example:

- How important is the constraint relative to the other known constraints? Is it more important to satisfy the cost constraint than the due date?
- If I cannot find a schedule that satisfies the constraint, are there relaxations of the constraint that can be satisfied? (i.e., is there another due date that is almost as good?)
- If there are relaxations available for the constraint, are any more preferred? Perhaps I would rather ship the order early rather than late.
- If I chose a particular relaxation, how will it affect the other constraints I am trying to satisfy? Will meeting the due date negatively or positively affect the cost of the order?
- Under what conditions am I obliged to satisfy a constraint? What if there are two constraints specified for the same variable? (i.e., two different due dates for the same lot or two different due dates depending on the time of year.)

In essence, a constraint is not simply a restriction on the value of a slot, for example, but the aggregation of a variety of knowledge used in the reasoning process.

The second goal was to measure the effectiveness of a modified beam search (Lowerre & Reddy, 1990) architecture that uses constraints.

1.4.1 Constraint Representation

Given the importance of constraints in the construction of schedules, we first examine the types of constraint knowledge needed to be represented and then give an example of one constraint: a due date.

One of the central issues that must be addressed by the constraint representation is *conflict*. Consider cost and due date constraints. The former might require reduction of costs, but the latter might require shipping the order in a short period of time. To accomplish the latter, faster, more expensive machines might be required, thereby causing a conflict with the former. In short, it might not be possible to satisfy both constraints; in which case, one or both must be relaxed. This is implicitly accomplished in mathematical programming and decision theory by means of utility functions and the specifications of relaxation through bounds on a variable's value. In AI, bounds on a variable are typically specified by predicates (Stefik, 1981; Brown, 1986), or choice sets (Waltz, 1975; Sussman & Steele, 1980).

Given the diversity of constraints in the job-shop scheduling domain, it is necessary to provide a variety of forms for specifying *relaxations* (i.e., alternative values) of constraints (Figure 1-4). Accordingly, relaxations can be defined within the ISIS constraint representation as either predicates or choice sets, which, in the latter case, are further distinguished as discrete or continuous. However, the simple specification of bounds on a variable provides no means of differentiating between the values falling within these bounds, a capability that is required by ISIS both for generating plausible alternative schedules for consideration and for effectively discriminating among alternative schedules that have been generated to resolve a given conflict. The necessary knowledge is provided by associating a *utility* with

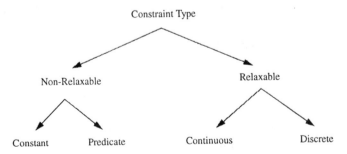

Figure 1-4:   Constraint taxonomy

each relaxation specified in a constraint, indicative of its preference among the alternatives available. The utility of a relaxation might have more than one interpretation, which can be problematic. In the case of a due date constraint, it represents a preference for shipping on time rather than late. In the case of shifts, it represents the degree of difficulty with which another can be added. In both cases, the focus is on the difference in utility between alternative relaxations. This difference is called the *elasticity* of the relaxation. The greater the decrease in utility, the lower the elasticity is. If the information were available, the utility measure would reduce to a cost function.[4]

The relative influence to be exerted by a given constraint, i.e., its *importance*, is a second aspect of the constraint representation. Not all constraints are of equal importance. The due date constraint associated with high priority orders, for example, is likely to be more important than an operation preference constraint. Moreover, the relative importance of different types of constraints can vary from order to order. In one order, the due date might be important, and in another, cost might be important. Both of these forms of differentiation are expressible within the ISIS constraint representation, the former through the association of an absolute measure of importance with each constraint and the latter by the use of *scheduling goals* that partition the constraints into importance classes and assign weights to be distributed among each partition's members. This knowledge enables ISIS to base its choices of which constraints to relax on the relative influence exerted by various constraints.

A third form of constraint knowledge explicitly represented is constraint *relevance*, which defines the conditions under which a constraint should be applied. Given that constraints are attached directly to the schemata, slots, and/or values they constrain, constraint relevance can be determined to a large degree by the proximity of constraints to the portion of the model currently under consideration. A finer level of discrimination is provided by associating a specific procedural test with each constraint. However, there are situations in which problems arise if the applicability of constraints is based solely on their context sensitivity to the current situation. First, many constraints tend to vary over time. The number of shifts, for example, fluctuates according to production levels set in the plant. Consequently, different variants of the same constraint type can be applicable during different periods of time. Within the ISIS constraint representation, these situations are handled by associating a *temporal scope* with each variant, organizing the collection of variants according to the temporal relationships among them and providing a resolution mechanism that exploits the organization. A second problem involves inconsistencies that might arise with respect to a given constraint type. Because ISIS is

---

[4] The use of constraints as a means of ordering relaxtions has been explored by Sadeh (1991).

intended as a multiple user system, different variants of the same constraint type could quite possibly be created and attached to the same object in the model. For example, both the material and marketing departments might place different and conflicting due date constraints on the same order. In this case, a first step has been taken to exploit an authority model of the organization in order to resolve such inconsistencies.

A fourth aspect of the constraint representation concerns the *interactions* amongst constraints. Constraints do not exist independently of one another, but rather, the satisfaction of a given constraint will typically have a positive or negative effect on the ability to satisfy other constraints. For example, removing a machine's second shift might decrease costs but might also cause an order to miss its due date. These interdependencies are expressed as relations within the ISIS constraint representation, with an associated *sensitivity* measure indicating the extent and direction of the interaction. Knowledge of these interactions is used to diagnose the causes of unsatisfactory final solutions proposed by the system and to suggest relaxations to related constraints which may yield better results.

A final concern is that of constraint *generation*. Many constraints are introduced dynamically as production of the schedule proceeds. For example, a decision to schedule a particular operation during a particular interval of time imposes bounds on the scheduling decisions that must be made for other operations in the production process. The dynamic creation and propagation of constraints is accomplished by attaching constraint generators to appropriate relations in the model.

The basic due date constraint is a continuous value constraint that constrains the due date slot of an order. The choice of a due date has a utility specified by the piece-wise-linear utility function. An example of its use is a due date for forced outage orders. The tester for due date constraints takes the search state and the constraint as parameters; retrieves the due date being considered in the state; or predicts one if the final operation has yet to be scheduled and applies the value of the utility function slot to the due date. The utility function uses the piece-wise-liner utility value to interpolate and return a utility.

This example (Figure 1-5) specifies that the utility of the due date chosen is 1.0 if the date chosen is 24-July-91. Otherwise, it has a linearly decreasing utility that bottoms out to zero if the scheduling decision is today or earlier or after 31-Dec-92.

1.4.2 Constraint-directed Scheduling

Search is divided into three levels: order selection, resource analysis, and resource assignment (Figure 1-6). Each level is composed of three phases: a pre-search analysis phase that constructs the problem, a search phase that solves the problem, and a post-search analysis phase that determines the acceptability of the

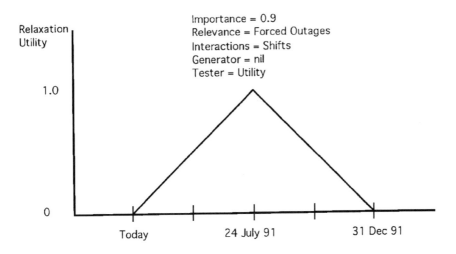

Figure 1-5:   Range of acceptable dates

solution. In each phase, ISIS-1 uses constraints to bound, guide, and analyze the search.

The *order selection level* is responsible for selecting the next unscheduled order to be added to the existing shop schedule. Its selection is made according to a prioritization algorithm that considers order type and requested due dates. The selected order is passed to the resource analysis level for scheduling.

The *resource analysis level* selects a particular routing for the order and assigns reservation time bounds to the resources required to produce it. Pre-search analysis begins with an examination of the order's constraints, resulting in the determination of the scheduling direction (either forward from the start date or backward from the due date), the creation of any missing constraints (e.g., due dates, work-in-process), and the selection of the set of search operators that will generate the search space. A beam search (Figure 1-7) is then performed using the selected set of search operators. The search space to be explored is composed of states that represent partial schedules. The application of operators to states results in the creation of new states that further specify the partial schedules under development. Depending on the results of pre-search analysis, the search proceeds either forward or backward through the set of allowable routings for the order. An operator that generates states that represent alternative operations initiates the search, in this case generating alternative initial (or final) operations.

Once a state specifying an operation has been generated, other operators extend the search by creating new states that bind a machine and/or execution time

ORDER SELECTION

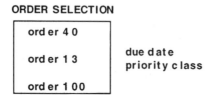

RESOURCE SELECTION

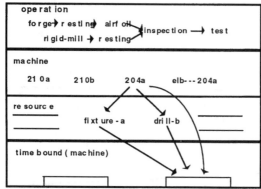

operation precedence
operation preferences
direction

alternative machines
machine preferences
product attributes

resource availability

start date
due date
productivity
sequencing preferences

RESERVATION SELECTION

resource time bounds
(from resource level)
shop stability

work-to-process
destructive possession

Figure 1-6: ISIS-1 architecture

to the operation. A variety of alternatives exist for each type of operator. For example, two operators were tested for choosing the execution time of an operation. The *eager reserver* operator chose the earliest possible reservation for the operation's required resources, and the *wait and see* operator tentatively reserved as much time as available, leaving the final decision to resource selection level. This enabled the adjustment of reservations in order to reduce work-in-process time. Alternative resources (e.g., tools, materials) are generated by other operators.

Each state in the search space is rated by the set of constraints found (resolved) to be relevant to the state and its ancestors. This set is determined by collecting the constraints attached to each object (e.g., machine, tool, order) speci-

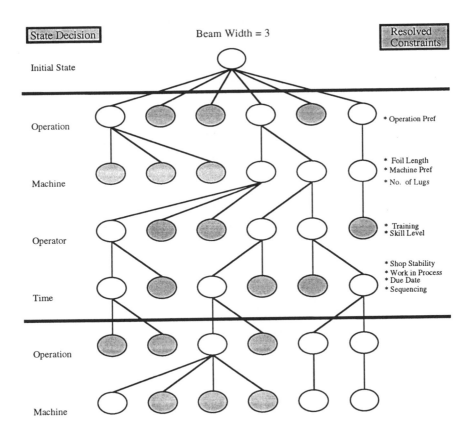

Figure 1-7:   Beam search

fied by the state and applying resolution mechanisms. Each constraint assigns a utility to a state. The rating of a state with multiple constraints is the mean of the utilities assigned by the constituent constraints, each weighted by the importance of the assigning constraint.

Once a set of candidate schedules has been generated, a rule-based post-search analysis examines the candidates to determine if one is acceptable (a function of the ratings assigned to the schedules during the search). If no acceptable schedules are found, then diagnosis is performed. First, the schedules are examined to determine the types of scheduling error and the appropriate repairs. Intra-level repair can result in the re-instantiation of the level's search. For example, if the order was of high priority and was scheduled backward from its due date and if its start date turned out to be earlier than "today," then the order would be rescheduled

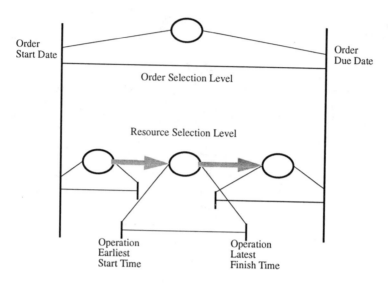

Figure 1-8:   Inter-level temporal constraints

at high priority in the forward direction from "today." Pre-analysis is performed again to alter the set of operators and constraints for rescheduling the order.

This level outputs reservation time bounds for each resource required for the operations in the chosen schedule. A time bound is a time interval in which an operation should be scheduled at the next level. Figure 1-8 depicts how one level constrains the temporal decisions of another. The Order Selection Level constrains the Resource Selection Level by providing a time bound for the first operation of the Order Start Date and the Order Due Date for the last operation. The Resource Selection Level then refines the order time bound to individual time bounds for each of the operations. Note that time bounds might overlap because of resource availability.

The *resource selection level* establishes actual reservations for the resources required by the selected operations that minimize the work-in-process time. The algorithm takes the time bounds for each resource and proceeds to shift the availability of the resources within the bounds so that a schedule is produced that minimizes work-in-process time.

1.4.3 Performance

Experiments were performed with a real plant model and order data. In each experiment, an empty job shop was loaded with a representative set of 85 orders with arrival times distributed over a period of two years. The various types of constraint knowledge influencing the development of schedules in these experi-

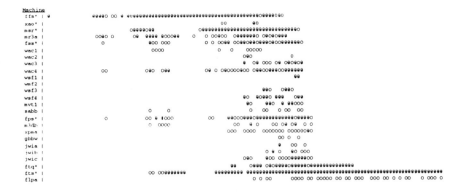

Figure 1-9:   Gantt chart depicting schedule created by ISIS-1

ments included alternative operations, alternative machines, requested due dates, requested start dates, operation time bounds, order priority classification (with orders falling into 4 priority classes), work-in-process restrictions, queue ordering constraints to reduce setup time, machine constraints on product form and length, resource availability, and shop stability (minimizing preemption).

A number of experiments were performed. These experiments explored the effects of alternative constraints, alternative search operators, and beam width size. A detailed discussion of all experiments can be found in Fox (1983, 1987).

The Gantt chart in Figure 1-9 depicts a schedule created by ISIS-1. Each row represents a machine and each column a week. If a position in the Gantt chart is empty, then the machine is idle for that week. If a position contains an "o," then it is utilized for less than 50% of its capacity. If the position contains a "@," then over 50% of its capacity is utilized. Machines that are encountered earlier in the process routings appear closer to the top of the chart.

The schedule is a poor one; 65 of the 85 orders scheduled were tardy. To compound the problem, order tardiness led to high work-in-process times (an average of 305.15 days), with an overall makespan[5] of 857.4 days. These results stem from the inability of the beam search to anticipate the bottleneck in the "final straightening area" of the plant (the fts* machine on the Gantt chart) during the early stages of its search. Had the bottleneck operation been known in advance, orders could have been started closer to the time they were received by the plant and scheduled earlier through the bottleneck operation.

Beam search sizes between 5 and 20 were tested. Sizes greater than 10 had little affect on the outcome, and sizes less than 10 performed more poorly.

---

[5] Makespan is the time taken to complete all orders.

1.4.4 Search Concepts

Constraints as Generators. Constraints that specify precedence between operations and requirements for resources can be interpreted as search operators. For example, a constraint that specifies that drilling must follow milling can be interpreted as an operator that extends a state for which milling is defined to be the operation into a new state for which drilling is the successor operation. Some of the constraints in ISIS-1 have code that interprets the constraint as an operator to be used in search. ISIS-1's pre-search analysis selects the operators from a subset of available constraints.

Constraints Bound the Search Space. The omission of constraints by pre-search analysis (e.g., not including an operator that generates alternative shifts) when selecting operators results in a bounding of the search space. This restriction on the size of the search space is intentional but can be relaxed by post-search analysis.

Generative Constraint Relaxation. The joint satisfaction of all constraints simultaneously is impossible because of conflict among constraints. Relaxation is the process by which alternative solutions are explored by considering values for variables that are relaxations of their corresponding constraints. Generative relaxation is one type of relaxation process. Relaxations of constraints are generated during the search process by extending the code that interprets a constraint as an operator. It uses the specified relaxations to generate alternative successor states that define alternative bindings of variables. In some cases, the number of relaxations are large (e.g., a continuous constraint such as start time of an operation), requiring the code to use a relaxation's utility to determine whether it is good enough to be generated.

Constraint Resolution and Dynamic Evaluation. ISIS-1 extends the concept of dynamic evaluation function construction by utilizing a more sophisticated form of constraint resolution. *Local Resolution* is the process by which ISIS-1 dynamically resolves the set of applicable constraints at each search state. Resolution is performed by examining each schema (i.e., operation, machine, etc.) in the current state description. The contents of any constraint slots or constraints attached to any slots that enable the object are added to the local resolution set. Constraints can originate from four sources:

- **Model-based:** Constraints can be embedded in any resource or activity in the factory model. For example, there can be physical constraints associated with a machine, sequencing constraints associated with an operation, and queue ordering constraints associated with certain work centers.
- **Lateral imposition:** Constraints can also be propagated laterally during the search. A decision made earlier in the elaboration of a schedule can result in a

constraint being attached to the lot that restricts a choice point further on in the search. For example, the selection of one operation over another early in the process plan might preclude other operations later in the process plan.

- **Exogenous imposition:** The user can also create and implant constraints. These constraints can be attached to anywhere in the model or be attached globally so that it is considered at each search state.

Global Resolution.   The rating of a state is a rating of the partial schedule up to the current state and not the single choice represented by the state. Hence, the rating of a state must include not only the local constraints but also the constraints applied to all the states along the partial schedule ending at the current state. Not all the constraints locally resolved at each state along the path are globally resolved. Consider the due date constraint. It is a classic evaluation function as defined in heuristic search. Part of the constraint calculates the work-in-process time of the lot to the current state, and the other part predicts the remaining work-in-process time to the end state. Each time the constraint is applied, it is a better estimator of the work-in-process time and should override applications of the same constraint earlier in the partial schedule. On the other hand, the queue stability constraint is applied at each state that reserves a machine. It rates the state by how much it destabilizes existing machine reservations. The greater the destabilization, the lower the rating is. This constraint measures a decision made at that state and remains invariant over future states because any future states will not affect an earlier state.

Constraints are classified into two categories: *invariant* and *transient*. All invariant constraints participate in the globally resolved constraint set, and only the most recent version of transient constraints participates.

Relative Resolution.   All constraints are not created equal. Relative resolution differentially interprets the resolved constraints by partitioning the constraint set according to the applicable scheduling goal. A scheduling goal partitions the constraint set and defines an importance for each partition. The importance is then uniformly divided amongst the constraints in the partition.

Analytic Relaxation via Constraint Diagnosis and Repair.   The completion of the beam search can result in schedules that are not acceptable because of the poor satisfaction of many of its important constraints. Analytic relaxation is defined to be the process by which the results of the search are examined to determine which "peep hole" repair of a constraint will generate a significant increase in the overall constraint rating of a schedule. In addition to the procedural embedding of situational knowledge in the form of rules (e.g., IF you cannot meet the due date THEN relax the start date constraint by starting earlier), a declarative approach is taken. Each constraint can have a "constrains" relation that links it to another constraint.

If the first constraint was not acceptably satisfied (e.g., due date), then by searching along the "constrains" relation, another constraint could be found (e.g., shifts) whose further relaxing or strengthening could impact the first constraint. Consequently, post-analysis could suggest the increase in number of shifts to pre-search analysis and have the search rerun.

1.5 ISIS-2: HIERARCHICAL CONSTRAINT-DIRECTED SCHEDULING

ISIS-1 identified the representational requirements of constraints and their use in directing search. Neither changes in beam width nor alterations to existing constraints were able to significantly affect the degree to which due date and work-in-process constraints were optimized. Simply stated, ISIS-1 schedules were bad. The cause of this problem lay with the combinatorics of the search space combined with the horizon effect. ISIS-2 was designed to reduce the impact the horizon effect had on the quality of the schedules (Fox, 1983, 1987). ISIS-2 constructs schedules by performing a hierarchical, constraint-directed search in the space of alternative schedules.

1.5.1 Architecture

An analysis of the schedules produced by ISIS-1 led to the conclusion that orders were spending too much time waiting for bottlenecked resources, i.e., machines. Given that demand for capacity exceeded availability, if an order was to be completed on time, it should either avoid the bottlenecks by choosing an alternative path in their process routing or reach the bottleneck earlier. The question was how to do this.

Given the anchoring of ISIS-1's search (i.e., it searched forward from the first operation or backward from the last operation but not opportunistically), how could we provide information that would allow the resource selection level search evaluation function to ascertain the probable impact of its decision? If we could determine the latest start time for each operation in an order's process plan that would allow it to complete by its due date, then we could provide this to the beam search in the form of a constraint. Then any state whose start time was later than specified by the "time bound" constraint would receive a low rating.

The calculation of these time bounds could be done efficiently by ignoring constraints and resources that had little impact on the bottleneck problem. That is, the computation could be done on an *abstraction* of the original problem. The latest start time of an order's final operation would be determined by an analysis of the available capacity of all the machines an operation might use prior to the order's due date. Once the latest start time of the final operation is determined, the earlier operations' latest start times could be determined in a similar manner, assuming their subsequent operation provides them with a finish time (i.e., using dynamic

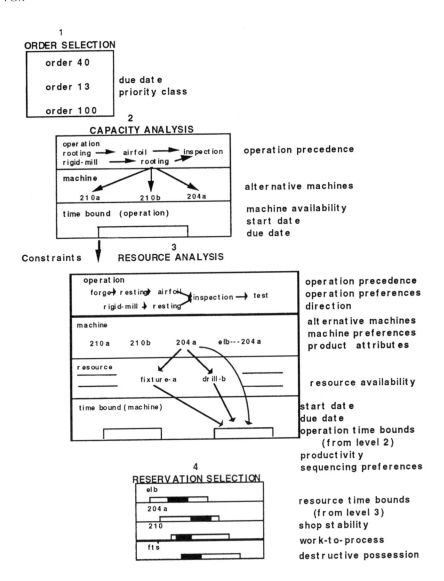

Figure 1-10:   ISIS-2 architecture

programming). To achieve this, an additional level was added between order selection and resource selection: *capacity analysis* (Figure 1-10). This level considers a subset of the more important constraints in order to "look ahead" so that capacity bottlenecks could be identified in a smaller search space.

Capacity analysis takes as input the selected order from the order selection level and uses the following subset of constraints in its search: due date, start date, operation precedence and alternatives, machine requirements, and machine reservations. All other constraints are ignored. The capacity analysis level performs a dynamic programming analysis (i.e., critical path analysis, of the plant based on current resource capacity constraints and existing resource reservations). It determines the earliest start time and latest finish time for each operation of the selected order as bounded by the order's start and due date. The times generated at this level are codified as operation time bound constraints that hierarchically propagated to the resource analysis level.

Post-analysis of search was extended to include "inter-level repair." It is initiated when diagnosis determines that the poor solutions were caused by constraint satisfaction decisions made at another level. Inter-level diagnosis can be performed by analyzing the interaction relations linking constraints. A poor constraint decision at a higher level can be determined by the utilities of constraints affected by it at a lower level, and an alternative value can be chosen.

1.5.2 Performance

ISIS-2's inclusion of a level of abstraction in the top down search hierarchy had a significant impact on the results, evidenced by the increased satisfaction of the due date constraints (Figure 1-11).

The average utility assigned by the due date constraint to lower priority "service orders," for example, almost doubled, rising from a value of 0.46 in the first experiment to a value of 0.80. The total number of tardy orders was reduced to 14.

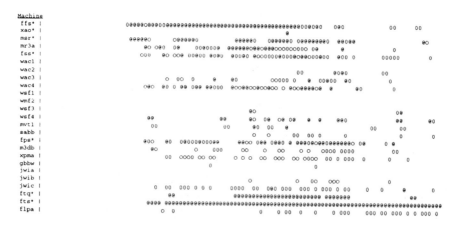

Figure 1-11:   Gantt chart depicting schedule generated by ISIS-2

Moreover, a much lower average work-in-process time of 186.73 days was achieved, resulting in an overall makespan of 583.25 days. In this case, inadequate machine capacity in the "final straightening area" (fts*) appeared to be the principal limitation affecting order tardiness.

1.5.3 Search Concepts

Periscoping. The improved performance of ISIS-2 rests on the ability of the capacity analysis level to identify bottlenecks and encode their effect in the form of operation time bound constraints. At the resource selection level, whenever alternatives are generated for the time to perform a particular operation, the operation time bound constraint is resolved and evaluated. The effect is what we call *periscoping.* It is as if the evaluation of the state looked "up above" the local situation to see what problems lay further down the search path it has yet to explore. If there was a bottleneck, the operation time bound constraint would lower the utility of times that do not provide enough time to get through the bottleneck.

Constraint-Directed Focus of Attention. The hierarchical imposition of constraints of one level onto the next results in the lower level's focusing of its search on the "better" parts of the search space, reducing the complexity of the search and increasing the utility of the outcome.

Constraint Stratification. Constraints appear to fall naturally into a partial ordering in this domain according to the degree of difficulty with which they can be relaxed. For example, it is easier to alter a due date by a day than it is to add another shift. Consequently, a level of the search hierarchy, in addition to constraining the search of the next level via periscoping, can determine the values of a subset of constraints that are more difficult to change than constraints at a lower level. This concept will be elaborated in the next section.

Interlevel Analytic Relaxation. The concept of analytic relaxation is extended to work across levels. If a constraint is identified as needing to be relaxed, and it is bound at a higher level, then post-search analysis could re-invoke the higher level. The level will either alter the constraint and/or perform the search again at that level.

1.5.4 Reactive Scheduling in ISIS-2

From early in the project, the issue of being able to respond to dynamic changes on the factory floor was recognized as an important part of a scheduling system. Machine breakdowns, material shortages, unavailable tooling and personnel illness all conspired to make any scheduling generated by ISIS invalid within hours. Although much of our effort was focused elsewhere, we did implement a schedule repair method:

1. Whatever the source of change, the final impact was to invalidate one or more activity reservations.

2. ISIS then identified the activities affected by the change.

3. For each activity, ISIS identified the order it was associated with and retracted the reservation and the remaining downstream reservations for that order.

4. ISIS then turned each of the retracted reservations into a preference constraint.

5. It then rescheduled each affected order.

With this approach, only the affected reservations and those subsequent to them were rescheduled. By turning the retracted reservations into preferences, the scheduler attempted to construct a schedule as close to the initial schedule as possible. We did not run any experiments to ascertain how well this method performed.

1.6 CONCLUSION

The ISIS constraint-directed scheduling system was designed to provide intelligent support in the domain of job-shop scheduling. Job-shop scheduling is an "uncooperative" multiagent (i.e., each job is to be "optimized" separately) planning problem in which activities must be selected, sequenced, and assigned resources and times of execution. Resource contention is high, causing scheduling decisions to be coupled closely. Search is combinatorially explosive; for example, 85 orders moving through 10 operations without alternatives, with a single machine substitution for each and no machine idle time, has over 10^{1000} possible schedules. The selection of a schedule is influenced by such diverse factors as due date requirements, cost restrictions, production levels, machine capabilities and substitutability, alternative production processes, order characteristics, resource requirements, and resource availability.

At the core of the ISIS family of systems is an approach to automatic scheduling that provides a framework for incorporating the full range of real-world constraints. Given the conflicting nature of the domain's constraints, the problem differs from typical constraint satisfaction problems. One cannot rely solely on propagation techniques to arrive at an acceptable solution because no feasible solution might exist. Instead, constraints must selectively be *relaxed*; the problem solving strategy becomes one of finding a solution that best satisfies the constraints. Second, scheduling is an optimization problem where we seek to find the best schedule. Thus, the design of ISIS has focused on

- constructing a knowledge representation that captures the requisite knowledge of the job shop environment and its constraints to support constraint-directed search
- developing a search architecture capable of exploiting this constraint knowledge to effectively control the combinatorics of the underlying search space but, at the same time, finding the best solution possible

This results in a system that can generate detailed production schedules that accurately reflect the current status of the shop floor, distinguishing ISIS from traditional scheduling systems that are more myopic.

The perspective that ISIS introduced—that scheduling is a constraint-directed search process—has been embraced within AI and outside it. A recent paper by McKay (1993) documents the plethora of constraints in the "factory from hell" from an Operations Research perspective. Even Goldratt, the creator of OPT, publishes a journal on "constraints." The methods of reasoning about constraints have grown more sophisticated since ISIS was completed (Ow & Smith, 1987; Fox, Sadeh, & Baykan, 1989; Keng & Yun, 1989; Sadeh, 1991; Zweben, Deale, & Gargan, 1990); however, ISIS's ability to represent and use all a domain's constraints still endures.

ACKNOWLEDGMENTS

The work reported in this chapter represents the effort of many of my colleagues who were at CMU at the time—Steve Smith, Brad Allen, Ranjan Chak, Lin Chase, Steve Miller, Tom Morton, Peng Si Ow, Ram Rachamadugu, Gary Strohm, Ari Vepsalainen, Mark Wright, Doug Zimmerman—as well as colleagues at Westinghouse—Bob Baugh, Jose Isasi, and Dwight Mize.

This research was supported by numerous agencies and companies, including the Air Force Office of Scientific Research under contract F49620-82-K0017, the Defense Advanced Research Projects Agency under contract #F30602-88-C-0001, Westinghouse Electric Corporation, International Business Machines, Schlumberger Co., Boeing Computer Services Co., and McDonnell Douglas Corporation.

References

Brown, R. 1986. A Solution to the Mission Planning Problem. *Proceedings of the Second Aerospace Applications of Artificial Intelligence*.

Chapman, D. 1987. Planning for Conjunctive Goals. *Artificial Intelligence*, 32:333–377.

Fox, M.S. 1983. Constraint-Directed Search: A Case Study of Job-Shop Scheduling. Ph.D. Thesis, Carnegie Mellon University, CMU-RI-TR-85-7, Intelligent Systems Laboratory, The Robotics Institute.

Fox, M.S. 1987. *Constraint-Directed Search: A Case Study of Job-Shop Scheduling.* Morgan Kaufmann, San Francisco, Calif.

Fox, M.S., N. Sadeh, and C. Baykan. 1989. Constrained Heuristic Search. *Proceedings of the International Joint Conference on Artificial Intelligence*, 309–316, AAAI Press, Menlo Park, Calif.

Garey, M.R., and D.S. Johnson. 1979. *Computers and Intractability: A Guide to the Theory of NP-Completeness,* W.H. Freeman and Co., New York.

Keng, N.P., and D.Y.Y. Yun. 1989. A Planning/Scheduling Methodology for the Constrained Resource Problem. *Proceedings of the Eleventh International Joint Conference on Artificial Intelligence*, 998–1003, AAAI Press, Menlo Park, Calif.

Lowerre, B.T., and R. Reddy. 1990. The HARPY Speech Understanding Systems. *Trends in Speech Recognition*, Lea, W.A., ed. Prentice-Hall, Englewood Cliffs, N.J.

McKay, K.N. 1993. The Factory from Hell—A Modelling Benchmark. *Proceedings of the NSF Workshop on Intelligent, Dynamic Scheduling*, 97–113.

Ow, P-S., and S.F. Smith. 1987. Two Design Principles for Knowledge-Based Systems. *Decision Sciences* 18(3):430–447.

Sadeh, N. 1991. Look-Ahead Techniques for Micro-Opportunistic Job Shop Scheduling, Ph.D. Thesis, School of Computer Science, Carnegie Mellon University.

Simon, H.A. 1972. On Reasoning about Actions. *Representation and Meaning: Experiments with Information Processing Systems*, 414–430, H.A. Simon & L. Siklossy (eds.) Prentice-Hall, New York.

Stefik, M. 1981. Planning with Constraints (MOLGEN: Part 1). *Artificial Intelligence*, 16(2):111–140.

Sussman, G.J. and G.L. Steele, Jr. 1980. CONSTRAINTS: A Language for Expressing Almost-Hierarchical Descriptions. *Artificial Intelligence*, 14(1):1–39.

Waltz, D. 1975. Understanding Line Drawings of Scenes with Shadows. *The Psychology of Computer Vision*, Winston P.H., ed., McGraw-Hill, New York.

Zweben, M., M. Deale, and R. Gargan. 1990. Anytime Rescheduling. *Proceedings of the Annual Conference of the American Association for Artificial Intelligence*, AAAI Press, Menlo Park, Calif.

2

OPIS:

A Methodology and Architecture for Reactive Scheduling

Stephen F. Smith
(Carnegie Mellon University)

2.1 INTRODUCTION

The broad goal of manufacturing production management, like other resource-constrained, multi-agent planning problems, is to produce a coordinated behavior where demands are serviced in a timely and cost-effective manner. In most manufacturing environments, the construction of advance schedules is recognized as central to achievement of this goal; it enables anticipation of potential performance obstacles (e.g., resource contention) and provides opportunities to minimize their harmful effects on overall manufacturing system behavior. In practice, however, two factors confound the use of schedules as operational guidance. The first is the inability to extract useful guidance from generated schedules in any effective, systematic manner; most existing production planning and scheduling systems operate with models that ignore important operating constraints and conditions, and the correspondence of generated schedules to factory floor operations is missing. The second confounding factor is the dynamically changing nature of the production environment. Machines break down, materials fail to arrive on time, changing market conditions present unexpected production demands, etc., all of which work against attempts to follow prescriptive plans. In fact, the performance of the manufacturing organization ultimately hinges on an ability to rapidly adapt schedules to fit changing circumstances over time. In this respect, production planning/scheduling is not a static optimization problem but an ongoing reactive process. Optimization objectives (assuring a good global manufacturing behavior) must continually be balanced with concerns of continuity in operations (because execution of a schedule sets a large number of interdependent processes in motion) and responsiveness (to keep the manufacturing system moving).

In this chapter, we present an approach to incremental reactive management of schedules based on a view of scheduling as an iterative, constraint-directed process. Under this view, schedule revision/adaptation is driven by detection and analysis of conflicts and opportunities that are introduced by changes to current solution constraints. Constraint analysis is used to prioritize outstanding problems in the current schedule, identify important modification goals, and estimate the possibilities for efficient and non-disruptive schedule modification. This information, in turn, provides a basis for selecting among a set of alternative modification actions, which differ in conflict resolution and schedule improvement capabilities, computational requirements, and expected disruptive effects. This approach to reactive scheduling is implemented in OPIS (OPportunistic Intelligent Scheduler), a knowledge-based system developed originally for manufacturing production scheduling. OPIS combines a modeling framework suitable for capturing essential operational constraints and objectives with a blackboard-based control architecture to provide a general infrastructure for configuring constraint-based schedule revision methods and strategies. The current OPIS manufacturing scheduler instantiates this infrastructure with a specific set of methods and a constraint-based model for directing their application in responding to reactive scheduling problems. Experimental studies have demonstrated the viability and effectiveness of the scheduler in both generative and reactive scheduling contexts in a variety of complex manufacturing scheduling domains.

To provide a context for discussion, we first examine the characteristics and complexities of the reactive scheduling problem in practical domains. We then sketch the origins and evolution of the current OPIS scheduler, highlighting the basic concepts that underlie the approach and summarizing the results obtained. Next, we describe the principal components of the current OPIS scheduling architecture. This provides a basis for summarizing the heuristic methodology defined in the current OPIS manufacturing scheduler and illustrating its operation in responding to reactive scheduling problems. The approach is then summarized and contrasted with other recent work in reactive scheduling, and we conclude with a brief discussion of various ways in which the OPIS approach has been and is currently being extended and generalized for use in other application domains.

2.2 THE REACTIVE SCHEDULING PROBLEM

The general problem of interest in this chapter is that of managing prescriptive solutions to scheduling problems. In brief, scheduling problems involve allocation of resources to the activities of multiple independent processes over time to achieve a targeted global behavior. Coordination of production in a factory, management of space missions, and transportation scheduling to support crisis management are representative examples. To be viable as operational guidance, a solution—or schedule—must first be *feasible*; i.e., it must satisfy the physical constraints in the domain relating to usage of resources and execution of processes. In practical domains, these constraints are often wide ranging and complex in nature. In manufacturing production environments, for example, resource allocation decisions must be consistent with capacity limitations, machine setup requirements, batching constraints on parallel use, work shift times, etc. Similarly, production activities have associated duration and precedence constraints and may require the availability of multiple resources (e.g., machines, operators, tooling, raw materials).

However, feasibility alone is rarely the goal of scheduling; typically, the task is one of optimizing (to the extent possible) a set of objectives and preferences. For example, processes to be coordinated typically have requested start and due dates, and one scheduling objective is to attend to these constraints. Because it may not be possible to satisfy all these constraints (nor is it generally computationally feasible to determine precisely whether this is the case), the common operational objective is minimizing tardiness. Other global objectives (often conflicting) relate to the efficiency with which the processes are executed and resources are utilized: minimizing wait time between constituent process activities, maximizing resource utilization, etc. In some cases, performance objectives can be approximated by tactical operating biases (or preferences). In a manufacturing context, for example, there might be a preference for a new machine over an older machine with overlapping capabilities because of reliability considerations. The *quality* of a schedule is a function of the extent to which it achieves (or effectively balances) stated objectives and preferences.

Scheduling research has traditionally focused on generating optimal solutions to classes of problems that make specific assumptions about the nature of domain constraints and objectives (e.g., Graves, 1981). Unfortunately, practical scheduling domains rarely meet these assumptions. More generally, scheduling can rarely be treated as a static optimization problem. Aside from unpredictability in the execution environment, schedule generation in practice also tends to be a dynamic reactive process (particularly when multiple decision-makers are involved). An initial schedule is built, problematic or unsatisfactory aspects of the result are identified, requirements are relaxed or strengthened, schedule modifications are made, and so on. Here, the current schedule provides the context for identifying and negotiating constraint changes (with the user or other scheduling agents). Although the focus is on improving the acceptability/quality of the solution, there is considerable pragmatic value placed on maintaining continuity in the schedules produced across iterations. Likewise, once execution begins, it is important to preserve continuity in domain activity while those changes are made that are necessary to ensure continued feasibility and attendance to overall performance objectives.

These pragmatic requirements argue strongly for approaches to scheduling based on incremental revision/adaptation of an existing schedule. It is this net change perspective that leads to what we refer to as the reactive scheduling problem. We assume that a schedule consists of a set of constraints that delineate (1) start time, end time, and resource assignments for each activity of each process and (2) available resource capacity over the scheduling horizon. The need for schedule revision arises in response to the introduction of new constraints or the removal of existing constraints, which might reflect the receipt of status/requirements updates from the environment or might be the result of prior modification actions. Schedule modification can be initiated for two purposes: (1) to restore the feasibility of a schedule now known to be infeasible because of the introduction of new conflicting constraints or (2) to attempt to produce a higher quality solution if one or more constraints respected by the current schedule have been relaxed. In the first case, modification is necessary to ensure continued executability. In the second case, the potential gain in schedule quality can be weighed against its likelihood.

There are several characteristics of the schedule revision problem that influence the approach taken in OPIS toward its solution:

- It is generally not possible to bound the scope of change required to the current schedule in advance. Given the tightly coupled nature of scheduling decisions, changes to one portion of the schedule often have ripple effects. Heuristic guidance can minimize this phenomenon, but problem combinatorics prevent its elimination. Schedule modification must necessarily proceed *opportunistically* (i.e., with the understanding that revision actions may have unforseen interactions with other portions of the schedule that must subsequently be resolved).

- Striking an appropriate balance between attending to various scheduling objectives, minimizing disruption, and being computationally efficient when reasoning about possible modifications is a difficult task. There are often simple, fairly non-disruptive changes that can restore schedule feasibility. For example, if resource capacity is suddenly lost, affected activities could simply be delayed until a time in the schedule when required resource capacity is available (disregarding implications with respect to scheduling objectives such as minimizing tardiness). At the same time, however, it is not possible to enforce rigid bounds on schedule quality (e.g., degree of tardiness allowed) with assurance that a solution actually exists.

- What about exploiting the expertise of human schedulers? Although we do not discount the experience accumulated by veteran human schedulers, our experience in many manufacturing environments is that schedulers often fall prey to the complexity of interacting constraints and decisions and tend to adopt myopic "fire-fighting" tactics (where extinguishing one fire ignites the next). Such tactics keep execution moving, but global system behavior deteriorates rapidly. In OPIS, use of knowledge about current problem structure (i.e., properties of current solution constraints) is advocated as an alternative basis for directing the schedule revision process.

2.3 ORIGINS AND EVOLUTION OF APPROACH

The approach to the reactive scheduling problem taken in the OPIS scheduler is rooted in earlier work with the ISIS job-shop scheduling system (Fox, 1983; Fox & Smith, 1984). The ISIS scheduler was the first attempt to formulate and operationalize the view of scheduling as a heuristic, constraint-directed activity. ISIS emphasized complete representation of all constraints that impact operational decision-making and a representational framework that recognized the conflicting and negotiable nature of many of these constraints. A representation of preference (i.e., relaxable) constraints was defined to encode knowledge relating to various factory objectives and operating preferences, including their relative importance, possible relaxations of preferred choices, the utility of each alternative, and the types of decisions that the constraint impacts. This knowledge about preferences was embedded in a larger relational framework for modeling the entities and physical constraints of the production environment. The OPIS modeling framework was built directly on these representational concepts.

ISIS also introduced a heuristic search framework for using constraints to guide the scheduling process. At the core of the ISIS approach was a beam search strategy for adding a new job (order) into the developing shop schedule (or alternatively revising the schedule of a job previously added to the schedule). Within this search, physical constraints (i.e., operation precedence constraints, resource requirements, and availability) were used as a basis for generating alternative sets of decisions. Relevant preference constraints provided the basis for evaluation and pruning of alternatives at each step of the search, thus implementing a generative approach to constraint relaxation. This core search process was augmented in two ways to define the overall scheduling procedure. First, it was bracketed by rule-based analysis steps. Domain specific rules were applied both prior to any invocation of the search to fix specific relaxable constraints (e.g., specify "backward" scheduling to ensure satisfaction of due date) and after the search to assess results and propose constraint relaxations if appropriate (e.g., relax the due date and attempt "forward" scheduling if a feasible schedule cannot be found during backward scheduling). Second, this extended beam search procedure was embedded in an iterative, hierarchical control regime where additional types of constraints were considered at each successive level. After selecting the next job to schedule (or reschedule) on each iteration, a high level analysis of remaining resource availability was used to emphasize specific allocation intervals (through the introduction of additional preferences). After detailed forward or backward beam search scheduling, which incorporated these additional preferences, final local optimization to minimize WIP time was performed.

One difficulty encountered with this search architecture was its inflexibility with respect to strategic problem decomposition. Although the kernel heuristic beam search procedure provided a flexible basis for local search in the presence of diverse constraints and objectives, its placement within an overall decomposition framework based rigidly on relative job priority and stepwise construction of job schedules was found to impose significant limits on the system's ability to achieve a good compromise with respect to conflicting global objectives (Smith & Ow, 1985). The problem can simply be seen by considering two common factory scheduling objectives: minimizing work-in-process (WIP) time and maximizing resource utilization. The job-oriented problem decomposition framework of ISIS provides an opportunity to minimize WIP time because subproblems are solved that contain all constraints involved in optimizing this objective. At the same time, a job-oriented decomposition works against the objective of optimizing resource usage because the constraints relevant to this trade-off are spread across subproblems. A resource-oriented decomposition strategy alternatively provides the complementary opportunity to optimize resource usage (at the expense of leverage in minimizing WIP). The subproblems solved in this case contain the competing requests of multiple jobs for a given resource, enabling resource setups to be minimized. Similar arguments against a fixed decomposition strategy can be made in reactive scheduling contexts. Localized revision of individual job schedules (the reactive strategy in ISIS) can provide a direct basis for resolving operation precedence violations (e.g., resulting from quality control failures and the subsequent introduction of "part repair" operations) with continued attendance to WIP minimization but provides only indirect leverage, at best, in rearranging resource assignments to maximize throughput in response to an unexpected loss in resource capacity.

To broaden the range of constraints and objectives that could effectively be dealt with, the OPIS scheduler adopts a more flexible approach to problem structuring, referred to as *multi-perspective scheduling*. The concept of multi-perspective scheduling, as originally conceived, advocated the selective use of a complementary set of local scheduling methods, each conducting its search under different problem decomposition assumptions. An initial implementation (OPIS 0) focused on integrating use of the job-oriented beam search procedure of ISIS with a resource-oriented search procedure built around the "idle time" priority rule (Ow, 1985) and designed to maximize usage of substitutable resource groups. Schedules were generated according to a predefined strategy, first constructing a schedule for a predesignated bottleneck resource group and then completing the shop schedule on a job-by-job basis. Comparative experimental analysis carried out in the context of a specific Westinghouse job shop environment convincingly demonstrated the power of this configuration over both ISIS and a well-regarded resource-centered dispatch scheduling method in balancing weighted tardiness and WIP minimization goals over a broad range of factory conditions (Ow & Smith, 1988).

Although OPIS 0 experiments confirmed the utility of incremental schedule construction from both resource-centered and job-centered decomposition perspectives, it did so under rigid and simplifying control assumptions. By presuming a static problem structure comprised of a single pre-identified bottleneck resource group, it was possible to perform the necessary computation to ensure feasibility of the partial schedule each step of the way (and avoid the complications of backtracking). However, dependence on any static assumptions about problem structure is ultimately confining (this was the original criticism of the ISIS search architecture). Resource bottlenecks are typically not stationary but float over time according to production characteristics (e.g., job mix, shop load); attendance to primary resource bottlenecks can lead to the emergence of secondary bottlenecks; and in some cases, there is no dominant locale of resource contention in the overall manufacturing system. Each of these circumstances suggests different problem decomposition/structuring decisions and indicates the need for dynamically determined schedule building strategies.

To dynamically control the use of local search methods oriented around job and resource loci, respectively, the OPIS 1 scheduler (Smith, 1987) introduced the concept of *constraint-based control*. The general idea here is that monitoring and analysis of characteristics of the evolving structure of solution constraints (in particular, flexibilities and inflexibilities in the solution space) can provide useful problem structuring knowledge. As foreshadowed in the design of the initial hardwired, multi-perspective strategy of OPIS 0, resource contention was incorporated in OPIS 1 as the essential aspect of current solution structure upon which to focus the schedule building process. A resource capacity analysis procedure was defined and used in conjunction with the heuristic that decisions at "bottleneck" resources are the most critical to the overall quality of the solution and should be considered first (Ow, 1985; Meleton, 1986). In moving to this *opportunistic* scheduling strategy, the OPIS 0 assumption of a guaranteed feasible partial solution at each intermediate solution state was also abandoned, giving rise to the possibility of inconsistent decisions. It was felt that repeated generation of "throw away" schedule extensions to ensure feasibility (as was done in OPIS 0) would not only become computationally overbearing but would also add undesirable bias to the opportunistic scheduling strategy (because of the influence of the heuristics used to generate extensions). In OPIS, inconsistent intermediate solution states are seen as equivalent to inconsistencies arising from unexpected external events. They are reactive scheduling problems to be solved. In the OPIS 1 scheduler, a simple "schedule shifting" method was added to reconcile all detected conflicts and allow the schedule building process to proceed.

This opportunistic approach to schedule building was supported by an underlying system architecture based on standard principles of blackboard systems (Erman et al., 1980). The OPIS 1 architecture reflected the central role of constraint management in the scheduling process and the constraint-based approach to coordinating local search. The design anticipated a wider array of solution constraint metrics upon which to base strategic control decisions and a larger repertoire of potential scheduling actions. Constraint analysis routines and scheduling methods were encapsulated as knowledge sources that, when triggered, operated on a globally accessible representation of the current solution. Strategic decision making was localized within a single controller that maintained and executed an explicit plan (i.e., an agenda of analysis and scheduling tasks) for solving the problem. The OPIS 1 architecture provided an initial infrastructure for investigating constraint-based, multi-perspective approaches to reactive schedule revision and adaptation.

Focus on the reactive scheduling problem necessitated a shift in perspective with respect to strategic control. Whereas problem solving in generative contexts can be driven top-down from global analysis of problem requirements and identification of critical decisions, the situation is different in reactive contexts. Here the starting point is a set of identified problems in the current solution (e.g., constraint conflicts), and focusing heuristics must be based on localized solution analysis. Moreover, control decisions must balance pressing (re)optimization needs with potential opportunities to make revisions with limited non-local impact. Investigation of reactive scheduling strategies also sharpened understanding with respect to scheduling architecture requirements and highlighted problems in some of the assumptions made in the OPIS 1 scheduler. Most important was recognition of the inappropriateness of attempting to maintain a strategic control plan for solving a reactive scheduling problem. Because it is generally not possible to predict the non-local effects of a given conflict-resolving action (e.g., the number and types of conflicts, if any, that will be introduced as a result of applying the action, the potential serendipitous effects of this action on other currently pending conflicts), it was rarely the case that an initially formulated control plan could be carried out to completion. Reassessment and revision of the agenda of pending tasks was typically required at each strategic step.

These considerations and experiences contributed to development of the OPIS 2 scheduler (Smith et al., 1990). Work in reactive scheduling led to expansion of the set of scheduling methods, extending the search-based methods utilized in OPIS 1 to provide schedule revision capabilities and incorporating additional, more specialized repair actions. The underlying scheduling architecture was revised to provide a more reactive, blackboard-based control framework. Within the OPIS 2 architecture, schedule generation and revision is uniformly cast as an iterative process of subproblem formulation and subproblem solution, opportunistically directed by analysis of current problem structure. A specific heuristic model, which maps the optimization needs and opportunities implied by specific reactive scheduling states to the differential capabilities of the expanded set of revision methods, was developed and implemented as a means of validating the approach (Ow, Smith, & Thiriez, 1988). A series of experiments carried out in the context of an IBM computer board assembly and test line demonstrated the comparative advantage of this reactive model over several less flexible revision strategies as well as a random selection model biased by the choice percentages observed using the model across all experiments (to verify that the model did, in fact, encode useful knowledge) (Smith, 1990). Performance was evaluated in this study with respect to weighted criteria reflecting optimization, stability, and efficiency objectives across a diverse range of reactive problems involving unexpected resource loss and job delays because of quality control failures. More recent experimental analysis has evaluated this reactive model in support of generative decision making (Amiri & Smith, 1992); reruns of the original multi-perspective job shop experiments with the OPIS 2 scheduler, using dynamic, bottleneck-based problem decomposition and the reactive model to resolve conflicts introduced along the way, yielded significant further improvements in schedule quality over the original hard-wired multi-perspective strategy.[1]

In the next few sections, we summarize the organization and operation of the OPIS 2 scheduling system (referred to hereafter simply as OPIS). We first describe the infrastructure for constraint-based, reactive scheduling provided by the OPIS scheduling architecture. We then turn attention to the methods and heuristics implemented within this architecture in the current OPIS reactive scheduler.

2.4 THE OPIS SCHEDULING ARCHITECTURE

Figure 2-1 schematically depicts the blackboard-based control architecture defined in OPIS. The architecture presumes a collection of base scheduling methods (or knowledge sources) that carry out designated *scheduling tasks* and make changes to a commonly accessible representation of the current solution. An additional "model update" knowledge source is invoked upon receipt of external notification of constraint changes (e.g., new requirements, execution status updates) to reflect their consequences on the current solution. The introduction of changes to the current schedule (whether they are externally imposed or the result of execution of a scheduling task) results in the posting of *control events* in a global description of the system's current control state. The control state at any point characterizes the

---

[1] The reader is referred to Ow & Smith (1988), Ow, Smith, & Thiriez (1988), Smith (1990), and Amiri & Smith (1992) for details of the experimental results obtained with variants of the OPIS scheduler.

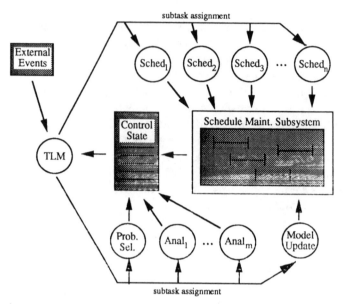

Figure 2-1:   The OPIS scheduling architecture

set of outstanding problems that remain (i.e., current conflicts in the schedule, set of commitments that remain to be made, unexplored opportunities for improving the solution). A separate set of analysis knowledge sources extends this control description to provide the information necessary to support the formulation of subsequent scheduling tasks.

Two additional system components provide the distinguishing characteristics of the OPIS architecture and the infrastructure for opportunistic, multi-perspective scheduling: a *schedule maintenance* subsystem, which incrementally maintains a representation of current solution constraints, and *a top level manager (TLM)*, which holds responsibility for coordinating the use of scheduling, analysis, and model update methods and implements an event-driven control cycle. The former provides both a basis for analyzing aspects of the current scheduling state and a means for communicating scheduling constraints among different formulated subproblems. The latter defines a structure for specifying and a mechanism for applying the control knowledge necessary to implement constraint-based scheduling strategies.

Both the representation of the schedule maintained within OPIS and the methods incorporated to analyze and modify this schedule are defined relative to an underlying domain model, which contains a specification of the constraints and objectives on process execution and resource allocation that must be accounted for in the target environment. Before considering the schedule management subsystem and the TLM in more detail, we first summarize the structure of domain models constructed within the OPIS modeling framework.

2.4.1 Modeling Framework

Within an OPIS domain model, prototype process descriptions (e.g., manufacturing production plans for various part types) are represented as hierarchies of operations, with aggregate operations designating either more detailed sub-processes (i.e., sequences of operations) or sets of exclusive alternatives. Operation descriptions at any level specify precedence relations (predecessor and successor operations), duration constraints, and resource capacity and setup requirements. Resources are correspondingly represented hierarchically, with atomic resources grouped into increasingly larger resource pools, to provide a description of resource allocation constraints (e.g., available capacity, hours of operation) at each level of abstraction in the prototype plans. Thus, for example, if a disjunctive leaf operation specifies usage of a particular manufacturing machine as a resource requirement, the aggregate operation to which it is related at the next level specifies usage of capacity in an encompassing machine group as a resource requirement. This hierarchical domain model provides a structure for representing and maintaining solution constraints at different levels of precision; in reactive contexts, this hierarchical model provides one basis for reasoning about the scope of potential schedule modifications.

The OPIS modeling framework provides an extensible set of primitives for specifying a wide range of constraints on resource allocation. Resource representations enable specification of unit capacity resources, which must be allocated exclusively to a given process (e.g., a machine); batch capacity resources, which can simultaneously be allocated to multiple processes over the same interval (e.g., an oven); and a variety of disjunctive and conjunctive aggregate capacity resources, where capacity can simultaneously be allocated to multiple processes without temporal synchronization (e.g., machine, operator groups). Resource setup constraints can be modeled as temporal delays, expressed as arbitrary functions of the operations that consecutively utilize a given resource. Operation durations similarly can be expressed as functions of work content (e.g., the number of parts in the batch being processed). Work shift constraints can additionally be imposed on resource availability, with allowance for preemption of process execution across nonworking hours. Priorities and priority classes can be associated with process requests (e.g., orders for manufactured parts) in addition to requested release and due dates. The utility-based representation of preferences originally developed in ISIS provides a basis for specifying idiosyncratic biases with respect to choice sets defined in the domain model (e.g., preferences over substitutable resource groups). Details of the OPIS representational framework can be found in Smith (1989).

2.4.2 Schedule Maintenance

To provide a representation of the current schedule, an appropriate prototype plan in the domain model is instantiated for each job or process to be accomplished in the current scheduling horizon. These instantiated plans designate the set of process operations that must be scheduled to obtain a complete solution (actually a superset because some instantiated operations designate alternatives that will become undefined as choices are made). Given these instantiated plans and the resource hierarchy defined in the domain model, the schedule maintenance subsystem incrementally maintains the following solution constraints:

- the current time bounds (an earliest start time, latest end time pair) on the execution of each instantiated operation that has been or might be scheduled
- a specification of the current available capacity of resources at each level of the hierarchy over time at each level in the hierarchy (represented as an ordered sequence of intervals of the form *(st, et, capacity available)* that covers the scheduling horizon)

As additional scheduling decisions are made or the constraints implied by external status updates are introduced, the schedule maintenance system combines these new constraints with the constraints on process execution and resource utilization defined in the underlying domain model and specified problem constraints (e.g., job release and due dates). This results in an updating of the time bounds and available capacity representations, respectively, of related operations and resources at all defined levels of abstraction. Thus, an unscheduled operation's time bounds at any point reflect the set of allocation decisions compatible with domain and problem constraints and any scheduling decisions that have been made.

Constraint propagation in response to schedule changes can lead to the detection of two types of conflicts:

- time conflicts—situations where either the time bounds or scheduled execution times of two operations belonging to the same process instantiation violate a defined temporal precedence constraint, or the time bounds of a single operation violate a rigid absolute bound on process execution[2]
- capacity conflicts—situations where the resource requirements of a set of currently scheduled operations exceed the available capacity of a specific resource over some interval of time

---

[2] Some types of imposed time constraints, in particular due date constraints, are specified as relaxable instead of rigid. Violations of such relaxable constraints are not seen as conflicts but are instead interpreted as relaxation decisions made by the originator of the change. In such cases, time bounds of other temporally related operations belonging to the same process are updated to reflect this newly determined end time bound.

The recognition of conflicts signals the need for schedule revision. Detected conflicts are posted in the current control state as *elementary conflict events* that require subsequent scheduling attention.

Constraint propagation can also lead to detection of rescheduling *opportunities*, situations where time and capacity constraints are loosened by introduced schedule changes. In the current implementation, such situations are treated in a somewhat specialized manner; *opportunity events* are posted only in response to changes originating from external events that imply additional resource capacity (e.g., cancellation of a process request) to ensure that a rescheduling process is triggered. The final type of control event that can be posted by the schedule management subsystem is an *incomplete hypothesis event*, signifying that some set of scheduling decisions still remains to be made. Details of this approach to schedule maintenance can be found in LePape & Smith (1987).

2.4.3 Strategic Control

Events posted by the schedule management subsystem are responded to within a control cycle defined by the TLM. The TLM control cycle identifies four stages of control decision-making that must occur in specifying the next scheduling action to perform and, correspondingly, four types of knowledge sources necessary to support the process:

- *Event aggregation*—The first decision-making step contributes to selection of the particular control event (or events) of those currently posted to serve as the focal point of reaction on the current cycle. It is often the case that individual events are related in some manner and would be better addressed simultaneously. During event aggregation, knowledge of such relationships is applied to the set of posted events. In cases where specific relationships are detected, *aggregate* events are created and added to the list of posted events in the current control state.

- *Event prioritization*—After this preprocessing of posted control events, prioritization heuristics are applied to select the specific event to be responded to in the current cycle. All events other than the highest priority event are left pending until the next cycle.

- *Event analysis*—Having identified a focal point for problem solving, the next step in the control cycle is problem analysis. The goal of this step is to summarize essential aspects of the current solution state (e.g., the relative looseness or tightness of current time and capacity constraints), providing a basis for determining how to best respond to the event. Analysis results are appended to the event description in the current control state.

- *Subproblem formulation*—During the last step, subproblem formulation knowledge is applied to the results of problem analysis, resulting in genera-

tion of a particular *scheduling task* to execute. A scheduling task designates
(1) a particular component of the overall schedule to extend or revise; (2) a
particular scheduling method to apply; and (3) depending on the KS selected,
appropriate parameterization of the solution procedure.[3]

Once an appropriate scheduling task has been determined, it is carried out, the
results are introduced into the current solution, and the TLM control cycle repeats.
When, on any given cycle, the set of posted events becomes empty, a complete and
consistent solution has been obtained, and the process terminates.

2.5 CONSTRAINT-BASED SCHEDULE REPAIR IN OPIS

The OPIS scheduling architecture allows specification of a range of methods
and heuristics for addressing the reactive scheduling problem. The current OPIS
manufacturing scheduler implements one such configuration of methods and heuristics, emphasizing principles of constraint-based focus of attention and multi-perspective scheduling discussed earlier in the chapter. In this section, we examine the
various heuristic components of this constraint-based repair methodology. We start
with an overview of the base methods defined as strategic schedule revision alternatives.

2.5.1 Strategic Alternatives

The set of possible modification actions available in the current OPIS scheduler range from general heuristic search procedures oriented toward generating and
revising sets decisions associated with a specific process or resource to more specialized revision procedures for sliding schedule components forward or backward
in time and performing pairwise resource assignment exchanges. In describing
these methods below, we restrict attention to describing revision capabilities and
characterizing their differential behavioral characteristics.

The **Order Scheduler (OSC)** provides a method for revising the schedule of
some contiguous sequence of operations in the plan of a given process (e.g., the
plan associated with a given manufacturing order). Revision of a designated process (or subprocess) schedule is accomplished by first retracting the current time
and resource assignments of each constituent operation (i.e., releasing previously
allocated intervals of resource capacity) and then applying the augmented beam
search strategy of ISIS (see Section 2.3) to determine new resource assignments
and execution intervals for the operation sequence. In addition to identifying the

---

[3] It is possible in some circumstances for the subproblem formulation step to produce a sequence of
scheduling tasks. In this case, all specified tasks will be executed before further consideration of the
current control state.

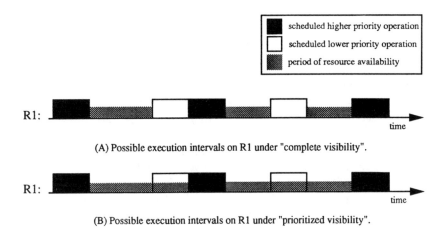

Figure 2-2:   OSC visibility of allocation decisions

specific subprocess to be revised, an OSC scheduling task also designates a level of "visibility" with respect to resource availability. The search can be constrained to consider only execution intervals for which resource capacity currently exists, which we designate as the complete visibility (CV) OSC, or can be allowed to consider capacity allocated to lower priority jobs as available, which we designate as the prioritized visibility (PV) OSC. These two modes of operation are illustrated in Figure 2-2. Because prioritized visibility search admits the possibility of introducing additional capacity conflicts into the schedule (leading to "bumping" of lower priority processes), a decision to invoke the PV-OSC trades off potential additional disruption for some ability to perform resource-based optimization.

The **Resource Scheduler (RSC)** provides a second general revision method, in this case for resequencing operations on a designated resource (or substitutable resource group) from a specified point in time onward to consistently accommodate a designated set of conflicting operations. Schedule revision is accomplished by "assuming" that the schedule must be completely regenerated from the revision start time onward and applying an iterative forward-dispatch search procedure to accomplish this goal. However, the decisions in the current schedule are not actually retracted prior to invoking this procedure; rather, operations in the current schedule are only retracted when they are chosen to be "dispatched on a resource" on a given dispatch cycle. After all designated conflict operations have been rescheduled, the procedure terminates on the first cycle where retraction and reinsertion of the chosen operations leave the overall resource schedule consistent. Thus, RSC attempts to preserve as much of the original resource schedule as possible while it resolves the problem at hand. The dispatch cycle itself makes selective use of a collection of priority rules to balance weighted tardiness and setup minimization concerns when selecting among alternative resource assignment and operation dispatch decisions. A detailed description of these heuristics can be found in Ow & Smith (1988). The RSC method is designed from the assumption that contention for the resource(s) to be rescheduled is high; use of a dispatch-based search framework presumes that it is not necessary to consider insertion of resource idle time and places emphasis instead on efficient resource utilization. Because revision of the schedule of a resource (or resource group) by RSC typically results in some amount of resequencing of scheduled operations (forcing some to be scheduled later than before), it is possible that its application will introduce new time conflicts with downstream process operations into the overall schedule.

The **Right Shifter (RSH)** implements a considerably less sophisticated reactive method that resolves conflicts by simply "pushing" the scheduled execution times of designated operations forward in time ("jumping" over any scheduled operation on the same resource whose end time falls before the end of the shift). Execution of these designated shifts can introduce both time conflicts (with downstream operations belonging to the same process) and capacity conflicts (with operations scheduled downstream on the same resource). However, these conflicts are internally resolved by recursively propagating the shifts through resource and process schedules to the extent necessary. Thus, the RSH will not introduce any new conflicts into the overall schedule. Figure 2-3 shows the result of an RSH action to resolve a time conflict involving $op - a1$ by shifting its scheduled start time on $R1$. In this example, each process i follows the operation sequence $op - i1 \rightarrow op - i2$ on resources $R1$ and $R2$, respectively.

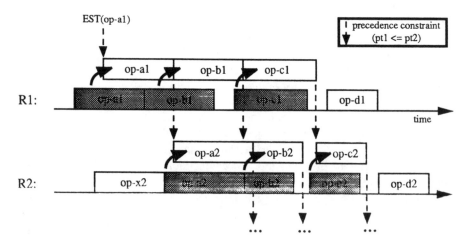

Figure 2-3: Application of RSH to $op - a1$ on $R1$

The **Left Shifter (LSH)** provides a similar but totally nondisruptive reactive method that "pulls" operations backward in time (i.e., closer to execution) to the extent that current resource availability and temporal process constraints will permit. The method proceeds by sliding operations on a designated resource R to exploit an identified interval of available resource capacity (and any capacity intervals created by this sliding) and then recursively applying the procedure to the resources associated with the successor operations of processes who have had their scheduled execution interval on R changed. The recursion terminates whenever a downstream resource schedule is encountered that does not provide opportunities for left shifting or when process schedules have been completely traversed. Within the current implementation, LSH is used exclusively for responding to opportunity events. Figure 2-4 shows the result of an LSH action invoked on resource $R1$ upon indication that $R1$ has become available earlier than expected. In this case, $op - a1$ is first rescheduled to start as soon as $R1$ is available; $op - c1$ is then shifted into the time interval vacated by $op - a1$ (because $op - b1$'s earliest start time constraint does not allow it to be moved); and, finally, $op - d1$ is shifted left as far as possible.

The **Demand Swapper (DSW)** implements a final revision method based on pairwise exchange of the respective resource assignments and execution intervals of two similar processes. It is applicable in situations where a given process has unexpectedly been delayed and is now expected to be tardy. When invoked, DSW first identifies a set of suitable candidate processes for exchange (i.e., similar processes that are currently scheduled to complete ahead of their due dates). If at least one candidate is found, then an exchange of the remaining unexecuted portion of the problematic process's schedule with the corresponding portion of the schedule of another is made to minimize their combined tardiness. In essence, this action has the effect of redirecting the pair of processes to fulfill each other's respective

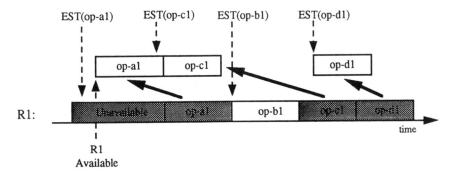

Figure 2-4: LSH revision in response to unexpected resource availability

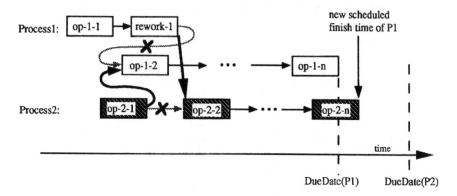

Figure 2-5: DSW revision in response to an unexpected process delay

demands. Note that the DSW is not necessarily a conflict resolution strategy. It is more appropriately viewed as a scheduling action that improves the character of the conflict. Figure 2-5 illustrates the result of applying a DSW action, in this case in response to the insertion of an extra "rework" operation into *Process*1's operation sequence and the subsequent detection of a precedence violation between operations *rework* − 1 and *op* − 1 − 2. The depicted exchange of downstream execution intervals leaves the schedule of *Process*1 conflict free and ending with a small amount of tardiness. The precedence violation has moved to *Process*2's schedule, but given that *Process*2 was originally scheduled to finish well ahead of its due date, there is now additional slack available for resolution of the conflict.

2.5.2 Responding to Conflicts

The above revision methods provide a range of capabilities for responding to reactive scheduling problems, and the strategic control problem faced by the scheduler is that of intelligently mapping relevant capabilities to detected problems. As indicated in Section 2.4, three general sources of knowledge are required by the TLM to solve this control problem: the first supporting selection of the particular conflict or set of conflicts to focus on next, the second providing characteristics of essential aspects of the current solution state, and the third concerning formulation of the most appropriate revision action to take to resolve this conflict (or set of conflicts).

2.5.2.1 Conflict Selection

Posted conflict descriptions provide basic characterizations of problems indicating the type of conflict (time or capacity), the operation(s) whose current commitments are in conflict, the resource (or resources) involved, the processes (or

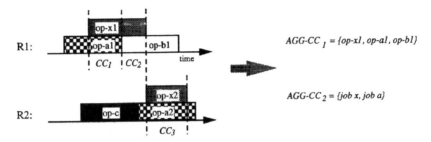

Figure 2-6:   Aggregation of conflicts

jobs) involved, the start time of the conflict, and its temporal magnitude. Given this information, a variety of criteria can be defined for aggregating and prioritizing the current set of posted conflicts on any given revision cycle. The heuristics incorporated in the current scheduler reflect our experiences to date.

With respect to aggregation of posted elementary conflicts for simultaneous consideration, the heuristics currently utilized emphasize recognition of two types of relationships in posted elementary capacity conflicts that have been observed to occur with some regularity in specific reactive contexts.[4] The first relationship that triggers aggregation is based on *commonality in the resources involved* in elementary capacity conflicts. It is often the case that two or more capacity conflicts involving the same resource have intersecting sets of conflicting operations. For example, in the simple case of a unit capacity resource, if a given operation is scheduled over an interval that spans the scheduled execution times of several other operations previously allocated to that resource, individual capacity conflicts will be detected for each pair of operations. This situation is illustrated in Figure 2-6, which depicts (in Gantt chart form) portions of the schedules of two unit capacity resources $R1$ and $R2$ and indicates two capacity conflicts CC_1 and CC_2 in $R1$'s schedule that involve $op - x1$. Because problems of over-allocation often require resource resequencing, it makes little sense to consider these conflicts individually.

The second situation under which elementary capacity conflicts are aggregated is based on *commonality in the processes involved* in the conflicts. This aggregation is motivated by a type of situation that can result from execution of a PV-OSC revision task (the only modification action that can introduce additional capacity conflicts). If PV-OSC determines new scheduling decisions for a given process that bump a lower priority process with a similarly structured plan (as is common in manufacturing environments with flow shop characteristics), then it is

---

[4] We have experimented with various relationships for aggregating time conflicts but have as yet found none that add substantial value to rescheduling performance.

quite possible for capacity conflicts to be introduced on several resources that involve operations belonging to these same two processes. This situation is also depicted in Figure 2-6, where it is assumed that jobs are processed first on $R1$, then on $R2$. Conflicts CC_1 and CC_3 involve the same two jobs at two consecutive process steps. Because multiple components of the same process schedule now require revision, it is natural to consider the aggregate problem.

Recognition of either relationship leads to the generation of aggregate events (as depicted in Figure 2-6) and their introduction into the list of currently posted events. Note that distinct aggregate events are not necessarily mutually exclusive groupings of elementary events. Any created aggregate event that is not selected as the current focal point for reaction is discarded.

Within the current scheduler, events are selected (prioritized) first as a function of event type. Aggregate conflicts are higher priority than elementary conflicts, and process-based aggregations (by their linkage to an ongoing reactive strategy) are higher priority than resource-based aggregations. Elementary time and capacity conflicts are of equal priority. Opportunity events are lowest priority and are only selected in conflict free situations (because conflict resolution may actually exploit any posted opportunities). The second selection criteria applied (in situations where event type does not identify a unique event) is the urgency of the event (i.e., temporal proximity to execution).

2.5.2.2 Conflict Analysis

Determination of the most appropriate revision action to undertake to resolve a given conflict requires knowledge about the continued validity of various scheduling decisions, pressing (re)optimization needs, and current sources of rescheduling flexibility. The base assumption underlying the OPIS scheduler is that analysis of current problem structure can provide this knowledge. In this section, we describe the set of metrics that are currently computed for this purpose. These metrics summarize various characteristics of current solution constraints, and computations are confined to a local region of the solution containing the focal point conflict. A *conflict horizon*, defined as an interval that temporally spans the conflict by a pre-specified margin, restricts attention to a subset of operations in addition to those directly involved in the conflict.[5]

Two metrics are defined to estimate the severity of conflict itself, and five others are defined to characterize the tightness or looseness of current time and capacity constraints in the schedule. Several are defined with respect to a particular resource involved in the conflict, designated R_C. For all types of capacity conflicts

---

[5] This use of metrics is quite similar to the concept of "textures" described in Fox, Sadeh, & Baycan (1989), although the focus there is in generating schedules.

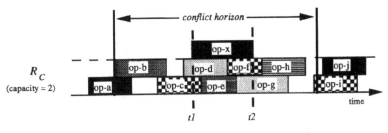

$$Confl_C = \{op\text{-}c, op\text{-}d, op\text{-}e, op\text{-}f, op\text{-}g, op\text{-}x\}$$

Figure 2-7: A capacity conflict

except process-based aggregate conflicts, R_C is the single resource that is over-allocated (which might well be an aggregate capacity resource representing a pool of more atomic resources). Unless otherwise stated, we will assume that relevant metrics are computed relative to each constituent $<conflict,R_C>$ pair in the case of a process-based aggregate conflict. In the case of a time conflict, which designates a precedence violation between two consecutive process operations, we assume that R_C is the resource assigned to the downstream operation. We also designate $Confl_C$ as the set of operations whose commitments are in conflict (the union over all constituent conflicts in the case of all aggregate conflicts). Figure 2-7 graphically depicts a portion of a schedule for aggregate resource R_C that contains a capacity conflict, identifying both the conflict horizon and $Confl_C$.

Conflict Duration is defined as the temporal magnitude of the inconsistency (e.g., $t2 - t1$ in Figure 2-7) normalized with respect to the average duration of all operations scheduled on R_C within the conflict horizon (e.g., the average duration of operations $op - b$ through $op - h$ in Figure 2-7). This metric provides one indicator of the continuing validity of R_C's schedule. Based on sensitivity analysis (Johnson & Montgomery, 1974; Bean & Birge, 1985), if the duration is low, then it is reasonable to assume that the sequencing decisions previously made at R_C remain valid. The problem lies only in the timing details. If the duration is high, however, this assumption is not valid.

Conflict Size is defined as $|Retract_C|$, where $Retract_C$ is an identified (minimal) set of operations in $Confl_C$ that must be retracted (and hence rescheduled) to restore consistency (in the case of process-based aggregate conflicts, $Retract_C$ is computed for each constituent capacity conflict, and conflict size is the average size of these sets). $Retract_C$ is constructed with the assumption that the operation whose commitment created the conflict will not be moved, and this set is retained for later use in formulating revision tasks. In Figure 2-7, for example, $Retract_C = \{op - d, op - f\}$ and $|Retract_C| = 2$ if we assume all operations are of equal priority. If the conflict size is low, then it is reasonable to assume that most

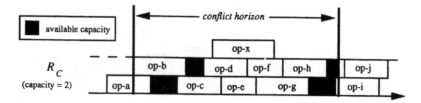

Figure 2-8: Periods of idle time within the conflict horizon

sequencing decisions relative to R_C are valid. For example, if the conflict size is 1, then the operation in $Retract_C$ might be the only one out of sequence. If the number is high, then sequence optimization at R_C is an important concern.

Resource Idle Time is defined as the average amount of capacity available at R_C over the conflict horizon (recall we are typically speaking of an aggregate resource). Figure 2-8 indicates periods of available capacity (or resource idle time) in the case of the conflict contained in Figure 2-7. If average idle time is low, indicating a bottleneck situation, then optimization of R_C's schedule to achieve maximum throughput is a primary concern. If average idle time is high, then resource-based optimization is unimportant. Resource Idle time is also computed for any disjunctive aggregate capacity resource that contains R_C in the underlying hierarchical model. An increase in resource idle time moving upward in the resource hierarchy indicates flexibility to assign alternative resources to operations in $Confl_C$.

Local Upstream Slack measures the flexibility in the scheduled start times of the operations scheduled on R_C. The upstream slack of a given job is defined simply as the difference between the scheduled start time of its operation on R_C and the scheduled (or actual) end time of its immediately preceding operation, and local upstream slack is the average slack over all jobs scheduled on R_C within the con-flict horizon. Figure 2-9 expands the schedule given in Figure 2-7 to include por-tions of the upstream and downstream schedule (on resources R_i and R_j, respec-tively) and indicates the upstream slack associated with jobs c, e, g, and h (in this figure, the operation sequence $op - i' \rightarrow op - i \rightarrow op - i''$ is assumed for each job i). If the local upstream slack of operations requiring R_C is high, then there are opportunities for resequencing on R_C. It might be possible to place operations into the "holes" of available capacity that will be vacated by operations in $Confl_C$.

Local Downstream Slack, alternatively, captures the local flexibility in the scheduled end times of operations currently scheduled on R_C. In defining this mea-sure, we appeal to an assumption concerning characteristics of a good schedule, namely, that good schedules will exhibit queue times only before bottleneck

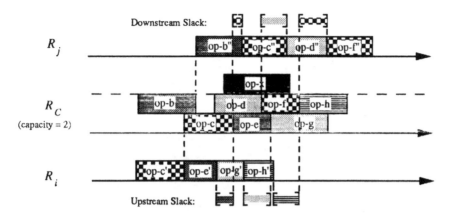

Figure 2-9: Upstream and downstream slack

resources. Given this assumption, we define local downstream slack to be the average of the durations of the first scheduled delay in the downstream schedules of each process/job scheduled on R_C within the conflict horizon. If there are no scheduled delays in the schedule of a given process, then there is no local slack. Figure 2-9 (top) indicates the downstream slack for jobs b, c, d, and f scheduled on R_C in the simple case where there is only one successor operation. If downstream slack is low, then downstream resource contention is not likely to be severe (i.e., there are no apparent downstream bottlenecks). If downstream slack is high, there is evidence of at least one downstream bottleneck, and optimization of resource schedules further downstream can be important.

Projected Lateness defines another average measure of temporal flexibility, this time relative to the operation(s) in $Confl_C$. The projected lateness of an operation is defined similarly to local downstream slack, except now we are interested in the difference between the earliest time that the process/job can arrive at the downstream bottleneck and its scheduled start time on that resource. If there is no downstream bottleneck, then we are interested in the difference between the earliest the process can finish and its due date. If the projected lateness of an operation in $Confl_C$ is negative (i.e., the operation is still "early" relative to its current deadline), then resource-based optimization is unimportant. If the lateness is positive, then resource-based optimization is important.

Variance in Projected Lateness is defined with respect to all operations scheduled on R_C within the conflict horizon. This provides an indication of the opportunities for pairwise optimization of process/job schedules. If the variance is high, then it might be possible to trade off positive and negative projected latenesses of specific processes by swapping demands.

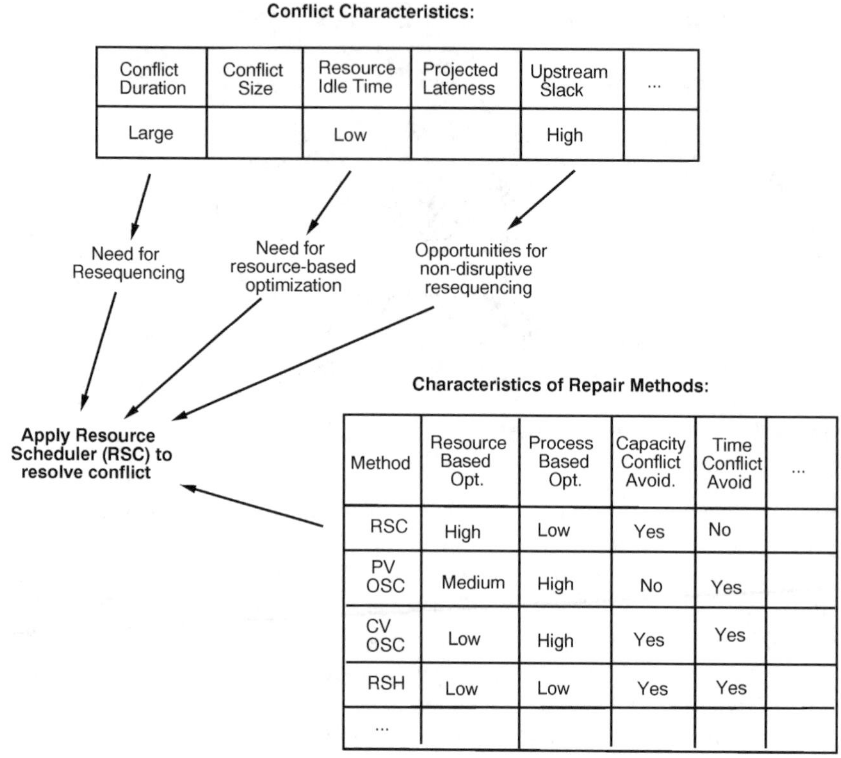

Conflict Characteristics:

Conflict Duration	Conflict Size	Resource Idle Time	Projected Lateness	Upstream Slack	...
Large		Low		High	

Need for Resequencing

Need for resource-based optimization

Opportunities for non-disruptive resequencing

Apply Resource Scheduler (RSC) to resolve conflict

Characteristics of Repair Methods:

Method	Resource Based Opt.	Process Based Opt.	Capacity Conflict Avoid.	Time Conflict Avoid	...
RSC	High	Low	Yes	No	
PV OSC	Medium	High	No	Yes	
CV OSC	Low	High	Yes	Yes	
RSH	Low	Low	Yes	Yes	
...					

Figure 2-10:   Mapping analysis results to repair actions

2.5.2.3 Subtask Formulation

Determination of how to best resolve a given conflict is based on a qualitative model that combines the above stated implications of computed analysis metrics with knowledge of the differential optimization and conflict resolution capabilities of alternative revision actions. Given the results of conflict analysis, the model yields the revision method whose behavioral characteristics best match recognized revision needs and opportunities. The reasoning process underlying construction of the model is illustrated in Figure 2-10. In this case, the presence of a "large" conflict duration indicates the need for some amount of resequencing at R_C. Because resource idle time at R_C is "low," efficient utilization of R_C to maximize throughput is needed. RSC is the strongest candidate from the standpoint of these needs, with the potential disadvantage of introducing time conflicts with down-stream process operations. However, because upstream slack is "high," there are

Table 2-1: Action selection model

Conflict Dur.	Conflict Size	Idle Time	Upstream Slack	Proj. Lateness	σ^2(Pr. Late.)	Action
small						RSH
large		high		negative		CV-OSC
large		high		positive	high	DSW, PV-OSC
large		high		positive	low	PV-OSC
large	large	low				RSC
large	small	low	high			RSC
large	small	low	low			PV-OSC

opportunities for non-disruptive sequence changes at R_C. Hence, RSC is selected as the method to apply.[6]

The set of rules that make up the constructed model is given in Table 2-1. Only one rule does not specify a unique choice. In this case, DSW is always selected first (because it typically acts to improve the character of the conflict) and then removed from consideration on the next cycle. As indicated previously, handling of opportunity events is restricted to those reflective of unexpected gains in available resource capacity. Such events are responded to only after a feasible schedule has been obtained and always by applying LSH.

Formulation of a scheduling task involving the selected action requires determination of scope (i.e., what particular set of scheduling decisions is to be revised). This decision is also based on information provided by conflict analysis as well as knowledge relating to prior modification actions. Because revision methods differ in the types of schedule components they manipulate, decisions about scope depend on the specific method selected. If either OSC and RSH actions are to be applied to resolve a capacity conflict, then the process (or processes) to be rescheduled must be selected. Here the operation whose commitments originally introduced the conflict are left intact; scheduling tasks are created for the processes associated with each operation contained in the set $Retract_C$ (computed during conflict analysis).[7] For OSC actions, it is also necessary to delineate which portion of its downstream schedule to revise. If downstream slack is high (indicating the presence of downstream bottleneck resources), then scope is limited to the portion of the process's plan that precedes the downstream bottleneck operation.

---

[6] Currently, simple thresholds on conflict analysis metric values are used to produce qualitative interpretations.

[7] Given the current action selection model, |$Retract_C$| is rarely > 1 when OSC or RSH is selected.

In the case of RSC actions, decisions about scope concern the level of aggregation of the focal point resource (or, equivalently, how large a set of substitutable resource schedules to revise). This decision is a function of the increased rescheduling flexibility that can be gained by broadening scope. If a disjunctive aggregate resource is found moving upward the hierarchical model with significantly higher estimated resource idle time than that of R_C, then that resource is selected as the focal point of the RSC action; otherwise, scope is restricted to R_C. DSW tasks, finally, require designation of a set of processes to consider, which is taken to be the set of operations scheduled on R_C over the conflict horizon.

2.5.3 An Example

To illustrate the behavior of the OPIS reactive scheduler, we consider a sample reactive scenario involving response to an unexpected loss in resource capacity. Figure 2-11 graphically depicts (again in Gantt chart form) the current schedule for a portion of a hypothetical factory. The diagram indicates machine and time assignments of operations for nine jobs (or orders) covering three stages of the manufacturing process. The operations associated with each particular job are related by temporal precedence constraints that are designated by directed arcs in the diagram. The pattern used to designate the operations of a job reflects the job's "part type," which has implications with respect to machine setup requirements at different stages of the manufacturing process (there are four types of parts being manufactured in this example). We assume in this example that all assigned machines are

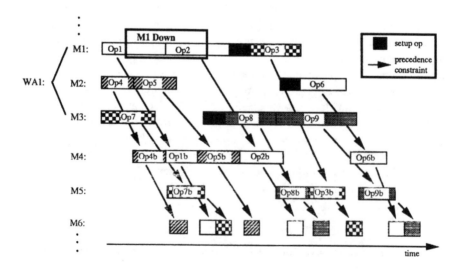

Figure 2-11:   Unexpected machine breakdown

unit-capacity resources (i.e., capable of servicing only one job at a time); thus, the time line associated with a given machine in the diagram indicates either a scheduled operation, a scheduled setup operation (represented as a black rectangle), or a period of availability (represented as blank space).

The three stages of the manufacturing process covered in the diagram impose the following allocation constraints. Machines *M1, M2,* and *M3* are organized into work area *WA1* and are utilized in the first stage of the process. Each of these machines is capable of manufacturing any of the four part types; however, a machine setup must be incurred in switching from one part type to another. Machines *M4* and *M5* are used in the second stage of the process. Each of these machines is specialized to the manufacture of two unique part types, and there is no setup required for part changeovers. Machine *M6,* finally, is used in the third stage for all part types (again with no setup requirements).

As indicated in Figure 2-11, machine *M1* is expected to be down for an interval that overlaps the ongoing execution of *Op1* and the scheduled execution of *Op2*. In this case, the already completed portion of *Op1* is salvageable. Introduction of these newly known constraints into the current solution (via execution of a model update task) results in (1) a split of *Op1* into a two operation sequence *(Op1 Op1*)* reflecting completed and uncompleted portions of the original *Op1,* (2) allocation of a "machine repair" operation for the designated interval, and (3) subsequent detection and posting of two capacity conflicts. Because both conflicts involve the same resource, they are aggregated for simultaneous consideration. Analysis of this aggregate event indicates high resource contention over the conflict horizon, positive projected lateness in the jobs involved in the conflict, and a large conflict size, all leading to formulation of an RSC revision task. Given that resource contention is lower at the aggregate *WA1* level in the hierarchical model (suggesting resequencing flexibility if alternative machine assignments are considered), *WA1* is chosen as the focal point of the RSC task. The revisions made by the RSC in this step are indicated in Figure 2-12. The resulting solution state is given in Figure 2-13.

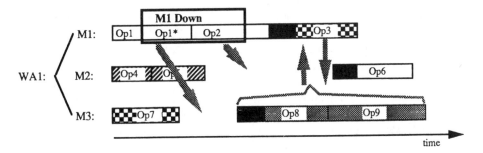

Figure 2-12:   Action of RSC in revising *WA1* schedule

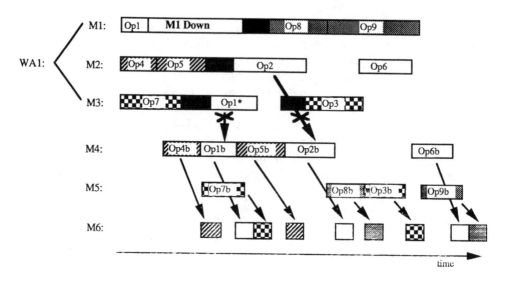

Figure 2-13: Solution state after revision of *WA1* schedule

Execution of the RSC scheduling task introduces two new time conflicts, reflecting precedence violations between operation pairs *(Op1* Op1b)* and *(Op2 Op2b)*, respectively. On the basis of conflict urgency, problem selection determines an initial focus on the conflict involving *Job1*. Analysis of this conflict indicates relatively low resource contention on *M4* over the conflict horizon but positive projected lateness in the job involved in the conflict. Accordingly, a PV-OSC scheduling task is formulated to provide an aggressive approach to revising the downstream portion of *Job1*'s schedule. Figure 2-14 indicates the result of this action. Because weighted tardiness prioritization favors *Job1* over both *Job5* and *Job2*, decisions are made to utilize machine capacity currently allocated to both of these jobs. Upon commitment to these decisions, the depicted capacity conflicts are detected and posted. The previously detected precedence violation between the operation pair *(Op2 Op2b)* persists also (the earliest feasible start time of *Op2b* is indicated by the "[" in Figure 2-14).

In this case, commonality in the jobs involved in each capacity conflict results in creation of an aggregate conflict event. Subsequent conflict analysis again indicates relatively low contention at resource focal points as well as the presence of rescheduling flexibility in the form of upstream slack. A CV-OSC scheduling task is formulated to reschedule the downstream operations of *Job5* from *Op5b* forward using existing intervals of available capacity. The results of this action are indicated in Figure 2-15.

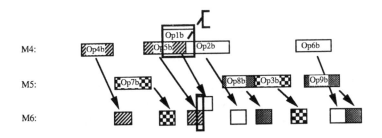

Figure 2-14:   Scheduling state after PV-OSC (init-op = Op1b)

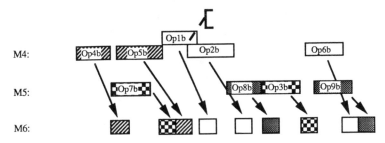

Figure 2-15:   Solution state after CV-OSC (init-op = Op5b)

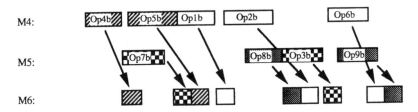

Figure 2-16:   Final solution

The final remaining conflict is also resolved using CV-OSC because of absence of significant downstream resource contention and negative projected job lateness. The final revised schedule is shown in Figure 2-16.

2.5.4 Characteristics of the Approach

The OPIS scheduling methodology makes several pragmatic assumptions to deal with the special characteristics and complexities of the schedule modification task pointed out in Section 2.2. Each of these assumptions involves compromise in some respect, but it is also these assumptions that make the approach viable in practical scheduling domains. In this section, we examine these assumptions in relation to the issues previously raised.

Bounding the Scope of a Given Reaction. On each cycle of the repair process, OPIS makes heuristic decisions as to the scope of the next schedule modification action. These decisions are based on implications of the structure of current solution constraints as encoded in its subproblem formulation model. However, the conflict analysis metrics on which these implications are founded are, by computational necessity, aggregate and interpreted qualitatively. There is no guarantee that solution of the delineated subproblem (which limits visibility to a subset of the current solution constraints) will not introduce additional constraint conflicts into the schedule, and there are accordingly no a priori bounds that can be placed on the extent to which change will ripple through the solution. The expectation is that on average, the heuristic model will limit the amount of revision performed to what is required (given expected performance biases—see below). Experimentation has borne out this expectation. Although missed opportunities for more localized change have been observed in specific reactive circumstances (e.g., when the current state falls at the boundaries of the model), overall results indicate that on average, this model significantly outperforms other more rigid and less informed schedule revision strategies (Smith et al., 1990). Moreover, because the model is based on generic properties of the underlying solution constraint graph, it is applicable across a range of scheduling domains (and certainly generalizable to others).

Trading Off Attending to Scheduling Objectives for Being Nondisruptive.
The degree of emphasis given to either of these concerns is also a function of the heuristic subproblem formulation model employed. Abstract characterizations of the current solution state have implications with respect to both optimization needs and opportunities for nondisruptive modification, and these implications are not always synergistic. In such circumstances, the current OPIS subproblem formulation model is biased toward modification actions that preserve schedule quality. Other models are of course possible. For example, within the NEGOPRO software project scheduler (Safavi & Smith, 1990), which adopts a similar constraint-directed, multi-perspective approach, a subproblem formulation model biased in the opposite direction is employed (in this domain, continuity of resource assignments is preferred even at the expense of acquiring more resources when milestones slip).

"Time to Execution" Bias. Although the above trade-off has implications with respect to computational efficiency, the iterative nature of the modification process allows the need for responsiveness in reactive situations to be treated separately. On any given cycle of the iterative process, constraint propagation produces descriptions of the currently pending set of constraint conflicts and improvement opportunities. If prioritization of this set is based first on the temporal proximity of these problems to the current time, then it can be ensured that conflicts blocking execution are attended to in bounded time. Moreover, because new external

updates are imported on each cycle, focus can shift to more pressing problems as they arise.

Guarantee of a Feasible Solution. The existence of a feasible solution is guaranteed in any modification context by assuming that constraints are "infinitely relaxable" along at least one dimension (e.g., activities can always be delayed, additional resource capacity can always be acquired, processes can always be dropped from the schedule). This flexibility is counterbalanced by the inclusion of corresponding scheduling objectives to minimize relaxation to the extent possible (e.g., minimize tardiness) and the subproblem formulation model's overall bias toward maintaining solution quality.

2.5.5 Performance

Experimental studies with the OPIS reactive scheduling model have been carried out with realistically sized problems taken from distinctly different manufacturing environments. For the most part, these studies have sought to validate the comparative advantage of the underlying opportunistic, multi-perspective methodology in building and maintaining good quality solutions. At the same time, these studies also demonstrate the approach's viability and generality across different classes of manufacturing environments. In this section, we briefly summarize the problems that have been studied and give an indication of the scheduler's operational performance characteristics in these experiments.[8]

As indicated in Section 2.3, a systematic evaluation of reactive scheduling performance was conducted with a model of the IBM Computer Board assembly and test line at Poughkeepsie, NY. This domain can broadly be characterized as a generalized, flow shop with re-entrant processes. The line is structured into 11 "sectors," and all products (boards) follow a nominal linear process routing through these sectors that includes some amount of sector revisiting. However, because of inherent unpredictability in the process, a variable amount of additional looping through various sectors (for rework activities) is necessary for any given board. Each individual sector can be seen as a sub-facility (in most cases, consisting of machines physically connected with automated material handling systems) with a

---

[8]The running times given below were obtained on a TI Explorer. These numbers should be taken as loose indicators because the CommonLisp/KnowledgeCraft version of the scheduler utilized in these experiments has evolved over time in response to ongoing, exploratory research and often with only secondary consideration of computational efficiency. In conjunction with current research in applying the approach to logistics scheduling problems (see Section 2.7), we have constructed a more streamlined and better engineered implementation built strictly on CommonLisp and CLOS. Preliminary testing of this rebuilt system on some of the problems to be discussed below indicates roughly an order of magnitude speedup in computational performance. For example, reruns of selected job-shop scheduling experiments, which originally required about an hour for solution, are now solved in 2-3 minutes..

similar, more detailed linear process flow through constituent workstations (dependent on the manufacturing stage in the case of sectors that are visited more than once). The problem naturally decomposes into a 2- to 3-week horizon "line" scheduling problem (corresponding to the average cycle time of boards through the facility) and a set of shorter-term (1–2 days) intra-sector scheduling problems.

In the experimental study reported in Smith et al., (1990), attention was restricted to the "line level" scheduling problem. Board processes were modeled as sequences of operations requiring capacity in specific sectors. To provide greater control in experimental design, sector processing capacities were variably scaled, on average to about 10% of the actual capacity of the facility. A base schedule for the 11 aggregate capacity resources consisting of approximately 700 total operations and spanning a 3 week horizon was used as a starting context, and a set of 26 reactive problems were posed for solution. This problem set was designed to cover a range of reactive circumstances and included both unexpected losses of resource capacity (of varying amounts) and process delays (of varying lengths because of the unexpected need for rework operations). As suggested by the above discussion of the performance biases inherent in the reactive model, the time required for solution of a given problem varied considerably over the problem set. Elapsed time from input of the problem until a feasible final schedule was obtained ranged from about 15 seconds (in situations where simple nondisruptive repairs were found) to about 20 minutes (where the problem involved a substantial loss of resource capacity during a period of high contention, and model responses led to major revision of the initial schedule), with an average response time of 2–3 minutes. Similarly, the number of iterations (or revision actions applied) before a feasible final schedule was obtained ranged from 1 to 30, with slightly greater than 3 cycles required on average. Despite the reduction in overall line capacity assumed in these experiments, these performance characteristics can be seen to be quite reasonable in relation to the time scales of individual process operations at this level, which range from 4 hours to 3 days in this case.

A second experimental study evaluated the utility of the reactive model in support of an opportunistic schedule building process (Amiri & Smith, 1992). This study was carried out with the model of a Westinghouse turbine components manufacturing facility in Winston-Salem, NC, that was used in the initial OPIS 0 experiments in schedule generation (see Section 2.3). In contrast to the board line, this domain is representative of more of a job-shop environment. Different product types follow different routings through the factory and utilize overlapping sets of resources that are physically grouped according to capabilities. In this domain, consecutive processing of different product types on a given machine often requires significant resource reconfiguration, and minimization of setup time is fundamental to achieving adequate throughput. The factory model utilized consisted of 30 machines organized into 7 distinct work areas, differing from the actual facility in that a linear sequence of operations common to all products and presenting no resource capacity problems was collapsed into a single production step, and the set of resources utilized in this common subprocess was correspondingly reduced. Six different product types were defined in this model, with linear production plans ranging from 4 to 6 operations.

This model is fully documented in Chiang (1990), along with the set of scheduling problems originally solved in Ow & Smith (1988) with a backtrack-free, multi-perspective strategy that assumed a single pre-identified bottleneck work area (see Section 2.3). This problem set was re-solved using a capacity analysis procedure to dynamically identify and focus attention on bottleneck resources and applying the reactive model to resolve constraint conflicts introduced along the way. Each problem solved involved the production of 120 orders of some mix of 6 different product types over a 2- to 3-month scheduling horizon (representative of the actual load of the facility); problem parameters (e.g., product mix, level of resource contention, tightness, and spread of due dates) were varied to cover a range of manufacturing circumstances. As reported in Amiri & Smith (1992), use of the more flexible scheduling strategy in conjunction with the reactive scheduling model led to a 25% reduction in tardiness cost over the original results at the expense of a 5% increase in work-in-process time. Elapsed time required for solution on average was twice the time required by the static decomposition scheme, increasing from 30 minutes to about an hour.

Less systematic reactive scheduling experiments performed with the Westinghouse model relative to an initial 120-order schedule (approximately 650 total operations) have yielded performance numbers comparable to those obtained in the board line experiments (i.e., several seconds to several minutes). In this case, the expected leverage, from a reactive efficiency standpoint, of a somewhat more decoupled problem structure, where different processes require overlapping but distinct sets of resources (as opposed to a single overall process flow), is counterbalanced by the added complexity of dealing with both resource reassignment and resequencing decisions in the presence of resource setup constraints.

2.6 RELATIONSHIP TO OTHER WORK

Work in reactive scheduling and schedule revision techniques has gained considerable prominence within the field of knowledge-based scheduling in recent years. Relative to manufacturing scheduling, several alternative constraint-based approaches have appeared. In Collinot, LePape, & Pinoteau (1988), a blackboard-based system for generating and revising factory schedules based fairly directly on the concepts of OPIS (although employing different revision operators) is described. One interesting aspect of this work, from an architectural perspective, was its use of a decomposable framework for temporal constraint propagation that provided a basis for explicitly controlling the amount of constraint propagation performed in different problem-solving circumstances and, thus, an ability to trade off the time spent revising the schedule for the quality of the reaction.

In Burke & Prosser (1989), a distributed constraint satisfaction problem-solving (CSP) approach to reactive scheduling based on a hierarchically organized set of scheduling agents is defined. Each agent is given responsibility for making and retracting specific commitments (time assignments on a particular machine, machine assignments in a given work area, due dates of current jobs). Schedule revision proceeds as a collective activity based on dependency-directed backtracking search, with the single strategic agent bearing responsibility trading off global objectives when it has been established that current constraints cannot be met. From a behavioral standpoint, the interaction protocols employed give rise to a reactive strategy where scope is systematically enlarged from individual machine schedules; to groups of substitutable machines; and, finally, to consideration of process due date relaxation. The real issue here is scalability given the reliance on systematic backtrack search.

Recent work in iterative repair scheduling approaches (Biefeld & Cooper, 1990; Johnston, 1990; Minton et al., 1990; Zweben, Deale, & Gargan, 1990) shares the same incomplete search assumption as OPIS in approaching conflict resolution. However, this work has principally focused on a different class of scheduling problems (e.g., space mission scheduling) where absolute temporal constraints are not relaxable, and there is generally less temporal structure to the processes. The optimization problem here can be seen as minimizing the number of capacity conflicts (because any conflicts that cannot be resolved will require processes to be dropped from the schedule), and thus, the trade-offs emphasized in the OPIS reactive model concerning tardiness and WIP minimization are not relevant. One exception is the space shuttle processing domain of Zweben, Deale & Gargan (1990), which presents a complex "project scheduling" problem that is much closer in character to manufacturing scheduling problems. However, the approach taken here treats due dates as non-relaxable and attempts to minimize the number of capacity conflicts in the final schedule.

Work in iterative repair scheduling also differs in the approach taken to control of the revision process. Whereas OPIS relies on knowledge about problem structure to direct application of sophisticated local search methods, most of this work has instead emphasized more extensive global search with simpler (typically smaller granularity) repair heuristics. In Johnston (1990) and Minton et al. (1990), a "min-conflict" heuristic, which revises a single conflicting commitment with bias toward minimizing the number of new conflicts introduced, is repeatedly applied to attempt to find a conflict-free schedule from an initial randomly generated set of commitments (using periodic restarts as a hedge against local minima traps). In Zweben, Deale & Gargan (1990), a more complex heuristic that ensures continued consistency of relative temporal process constraints it moves a conflicting operation is repeatedly applied within a simulated annealing search framework. In this case, provisions are provided for introduction of additional repair heuristics to deal with constraint violations other than capacity conflicts, and utility-based penalty functions associated with constraints and objectives are used to evaluate alternative solutions. The approach taken in Biefeld & Cooper (1990) is perhaps the closest in concept to the OPIS methodology. Here, extensive initial global search, which randomly shuffles activities to other regions on the time line to relieve capacity conflicts, is used as a basis for discovering inherent bottleneck regions in the space, and this information is used to direct the application of more informed schedule revision operators.

2.7 EXTENSIONS AND CURRENT FOCUS

Subsequent research in manufacturing scheduling domains has explored frameworks for distributing and refining variants of the scheduling methodology employed by OPIS. In Smith & Hynynen (1987) and Hynynen (1988), a structural decomposition of the factory, employing hierarchical descriptions of time and resource capacity constraints, was used as a basis for extending the OPIS framework to manage schedules at different levels over different time horizons. The CSS scheduler (Ow, Smith, & Howie, 1988), alternatively explored a decomposition of scheduling responsibility among a set of "resource broker agents" (each concerned with efficient utilization of a specific set of resources) and a single "work order manager" agent (concerned with process oriented constraints and objectives). In Smith, Keng, & Kempf (1992), a framework for partitioning responsibility between a global scheduler and a set of local "dispatching" agents was defined, emphasizing exploitation of existing temporal flexibility in the global schedule as a means for localized, execution-time schedule repair as circumstances warrant. This framework is currently being further developed for operational use in real-time control of an INTEL wafer fabrication facility.

One area of current research is investigating the broader applicability of these results and the basic OPIS schedule repair methodology to the problem of distributed management of large-scale transportation schedules. Work here has led to development of the DITOPS (DIstributed Transportation Scheduling in OPIS) system (Smith & Sycara, 1993), which is currently being applied to problems in military crisis-action deployment logistics. Generalizations and extensions have been made to the original OPIS representational framework, the repertoire of revision methods available, and the heuristic subproblem formulation model to better reflect the character of the important constraints in this domain and the dimensions along which constraint relaxation and schedule modification should proceed. We have demonstrated capabilities to intelligently respond to a range of reactive problems (e.g., port closings, unexpected unavailability of transport vehicles, changes to material movement requirements) and are currently engaged in integrating DITOPS with other, complementary transportation planning technologies to support a large-scale demonstration in an operational scenario.

Current research is also exploring the use of constraint-based schedule revision strategies with more flexible "temporal data base" representations of current solution constraints (e.g., Dean & McDermott, 1987), where start and end times are not fixed but constrained to intervals that satisfy posted temporal constraints. This work is being carried out with the HSTS system (Muscettola et al., 1992), an integrated planning and scheduling architecture that provides such a representational framework.

ACKNOWLEDGMENTS

The OPIS scheduler is the result of the contributions of many individuals spanning a period of many years. Peng Si Ow provided inspiration for many of the ideas underlying the approach and was a research partner throughout the original system development. Discussions with Mark Fox have also had a major influence in shaping the OPIS approach. Other individuals who have made valuable contributions include Gilad Amiri, Dina Berkowitz, Casper Cheng, Geir Hasle, Juha Hynynen, Ora Lassila, Claude LePape, Jyi-Shane Liu, Dirk Matthys, Bruce McLaren, Pedro Muro, Nicola Muscettola, Kevin Neel, Kikuo Ogaki, Jean-Yves Potvin, Ali Safavi, Toshihiro Satomi, Katia Sycara, and Christopher Young.

This research has been sponsored in part by the Air Force Office of Scientific Research under contract F49620-82-K-0017, International Business Machines Inc. under contract number 71223046, DARPA under contract F30602-90-C-0119, and the CMU Robotics Institute.

References

Amiri, G., and S.F. Smith. 1992. "A Comparative Analysis of Constraint-Based Scheduling Strategies," Working Paper, Carnegie Mellon University, The Robotics Institute, September.

Bean, J.C., and J.R. Birge. 1985. "Match-Up Real-Time Scheduling," Technical Report 85-22, University of Michigan, Department of Industrial and Operations Engineering, June.

Biefeld, E. and L. Cooper. 1990. "Operations Mission Planner: Final Report," Technical Report 90-16, Jet Propulsion Laboratory, March.

Burke, P., and P. Prosser. 1989. "A Distributed Asynchronous System for Predictive and Reactive Scheduling," Technical Report AISL42, University of Strathclyde, Department of Computer Science.

Chiang, W.Y., M.S. Fox, and P.S. Ow. 1990. "The OPIS Test Experiments," Technical Report CMU-RI-TR-90-05, Carnegie Mellon University, The Robotics Institute, January.

Collinot, A., C. LePape, and G. Pinoteau. 1988 "SONIA: A Knowledge-Based Scheduling System," *Artificial Intelligence in Engineering*, 2(2), pp. 86–94.

Dean, T.L., and D.V. McDermott. 1987. "Temporal Data Base Management," *Artificial Intelligence*, 32(1), pp. 1–56.

Erman, L.D., F. Hayes-Roth, V.R. Lesser, and D.R. Reddy. 1980. "The Hearsay-II Speech Understanding System: Integrating Knowledge to Resolve Uncertainty," *Computing Surveys*, 12(2), pp. 213–253.

Fox, M.S. 1983. "Constraint-Directed Search: A Case Study in Job Shop Scheduling," Ph.D. Thesis CMU-CS-RT-83-22, Carnegie Mellon University, Department of Computer Science.

Fox, M.S., and S.F. Smith. 1984. "ISIS: A Knowledge-Based System for Factory Scheduling," *Expert Systems*, 1(1), pp. 25–49.

Fox, M.S., N. Sadeh, and C. Baycan. 1989. "Constrained Heuristic Search," *Proceedings IJCAI-89*, pp. 309–315, AAAI Press, Menlo Park, Calif.

Graves, S.C. 1981. "A Review of Production Scheduling," *Operations Research*, 29(4), pp. 646–675.

Hynynen, J. 1988. "A Framework for Coordination in Distributed Production Management," Ph.D. Thesis, Helsinki University of Technology, Laboratory of Information Processing Science, Mathematics and Computer Science Series, No. 52.

Johnson, L.A., and D.C. Montgomery. 1974. *Operations Research in Production Planning, Scheduling and Inventory Control*, John Wiley, New York.

Johnston, M. 1990. "SPIKE: AI Scheduling for NASA's Hubble Space Telescope," *Proceedings 6th IEEE Conference on Artificial Intelligence Applications*, pp. 184–190, IEEE Computer Society Press, Los Alamitos, Calif.

LePape, C., and S.F. Smith. 1987. "Management of Temporal Constraints for Factory Scheduling," Technical Report TR-CMU-RI-87-13, Carnegie Mellon University, The Robotics Institute.

Meleton, M.P. 1986. "OPT: Fantasy or Breakthrough," *Production and Inventory Management*, Second Quarter, pp. 13–21.

Minton, S., M.D. Johnston, A.B. Phillips, and P. Laird. 1990. "Solving Large-Scale Constraint Satisfaction and Scheduling Problems Using a Heuristic Repair Method," *Proceedings AAAI-90*, pp. 17–24, AAAI Press, Menlo Park, Calif.

Muscettola, N., S.F. Smith, A. Cesta, and D. D'Aloisi. 1992. "Coordinating Space Telescope Operations in an Integrated Planning and Scheduling Framework," *IEEE Control Systems*, 12(1), pp. 28–37.

Ow, P.S. 1985. "Focused Scheduling in Proportionate Flowshops," *Management Science*, 31(7), pp. 852–869.

Ow, P.S., and S.F. Smith. 1988. "Viewing Scheduling as an Opportunistic Problem Solving Process," *Annals of Operation Research*, Vol. 12, (ed.) R. Jareslow, Baltzer Scientific Publishing Co., Basel, Switzerland.

Ow, P.S., S.F. Smith, and R.E. Howie. 1988. "CSS: A Cooperative Scheduling System," *Expert Systems and Intelligent Manufacturing*, (ed.) M.D. Oliff, pp. 43–56, Elsevier Science Publishing Co., New York.

Ow, P.S., S.F. Smith, and A. Thiriez. 1988. "Reactive Plan Revision," *Proceedings AAAI-88*, pp. 77–82, AAAI Press, Menlo Park, Calif.

Safavi, A., and S.F. Smith. 1990. "A Heuristic Search Approach to Planning and Scheduling of Software Projects," *Advances in Artificial Intelligence, Natural Language, and Knowledge-Based Systems*, (ed.) M. Golumbic, pp. 247–268, Springer-Verlag Publishers, New York.

Smith, S.F. 1987. "A Constraint-Based Framework for Reactive Management of Factory Schedules," *Intelligent Manufacturing*, (ed.) M.D. Oliff, pp. 113–130, Benjamin-Cummings Publishers, Menlo Park, Calif.

Smith, S.F. 1989. "The OPIS Framework for Modeling Manufacturing Systems," Technical Report TR-CMU-RI-89-30, Carnegie Mellon University, The Robotics Institute.

Smith, S.F., and J.E. Hynynen. 1987. "Integrated Decentralization of Production Management: An Approach for Factory Scheduling," *Intelligent and Integrated Manufacturing Analysis and Synthesis*, (eds.) C.R. Liu, A. Requicha, and S. Chandrasekar, ASME PED-Vol. 25, pp. 427–440, American Society of Manufacturing Engineers, New York.

Smith, S.F., and P.S. Ow. 1985. "The Use of Multiple Problem Decompositions in Time-Constrained Planning Tasks," *Proceedings IJCAI-85*, pp. 1013–1015, AAAI Press, Menlo Park, Calif.

Smith, S.F., and K.P. Sycara. 1993. "Distributed, Multi-Level Management of Transportation Schedules," Technical Report CMU-RI-TR-93-17, Carnegie Mellon University, The Robotics Institute.

Smith, S.F., N. Keng, and K. Kempf. 1992. "Exploiting Local Flexibility during Execution of Pre-Computed Schedules," *Applications of AI in Manufacturing* (eds.) D. Nau and C. Tong, pp. 277–292, MIT Press, Cambridge, Mass.

Smith, S.F., P.S. Ow, N. Muscettola, J.Y. Potvin, and D. Matthys. 1990. "An Integrated Framework for Generating and Revising Factory Schedules," *Journal of the Operational Research Society*, 41(6), pp. 539–552.

Zweben, M., M. Deale, and R. Gargan. 1990. "Anytime Rescheduling," *Proceedings 1990 DARPA Workshop on Innovative Approaches to Planning, Scheduling, and Control*, (ed.) K.P. Sycara, pp. 251–259, Morgan Kaufmann Publishers, San Francisco, Calif.

3

SCHEDULING AS INTELLIGENT CONTROL OF DECISION-MAKING AND CONSTRAINT PROPAGATION

Claude Le Pape
(ILOG S.A., France)

3.1 INTRODUCTION

Important features of factory scheduling problems vary from one shop to the other. In the same shop, they also vary from one situation to the other. For example, the variation of the duration of operations depends on the manufactured products, and the importance of bottleneck resources varies with the global load of the shop. The existence of such disparities implies that rigid scheduling procedures, designed to provide optimal or near-optimal schedules in particular circumstances, are in general not satisfactorily applicable in other circumstances. A natural reaction to this situation is to involve artificial intelligence (AI) techniques in the scheduling process. There are three main reasons for this:

1. AI techniques facilitate the expression and the application of expert and factory dependent knowledge together with theoretical and empirical knowledge coming from other fields (operations research). In scheduling as in many other domains, the distinction between the problem-solving knowledge and the control structure of the problem-solving system facilitates the adaptation of the system to different environments.

2. AI techniques are useful for analyzing scheduling problems and determining which pieces of knowledge and which parts of the schedule are the most important in a given situation. This includes, for example, the determination of the most critical manufacturing orders and resources, the evaluation of the

effects of unexpected events (such as delays or machine breakdowns), and the analysis of problem-solving failures.

3. AI techniques facilitate the management of interactions between the scheduling system and the system user on the shop floor. The user can understand the scheduling decisions made by the system and override them when necessary.

A large number of techniques and applications are reported in the literature along these lines. (See Steffen [1986]) for a review of scheduling systems developed before 1986 with AI techniques and Kempf [1989] for a more recent bibliography.) Nevertheless, a few architectural issues of great complexity remain in the process of designing and implementing flexible scheduling software usable in many environments (Le Pape, 1991a):

- *What is a suitable architecture to integrate in the same system (1) mathematical algorithms, (2) expert and factory-dependent knowledge, and (3) interactive capabilities allowing the user to make and cancel decisions?* There are many reasons to believe that, when appropriately applied (Kempf & Le Pape, 1991; Kempf & Russell, 1991), mathematical, knowledge-based, and interactive methods can all contribute to a better resolution of scheduling problems. Consequently, the integration of these methods within the same scheduling tool is an important problem to address.

- *What is a suitable relation between predictive and reactive scheduling and a suitable architecture to balance these activities with respect to the characteristics of each scheduling problem?* Predictive reasoning activities are usually performed under no significant time stress, but reactive activities are subjected to either *hard real-time constraints*, indicating that reactive decisions must be made within strict delays, or *soft real-time constraints*, indicating that the utility of a given decision varies not only with the quality of the decision per se but also with the time at which the decision is made. In a sense, the uncertainty in the environment suggests the maintenance of many ordering possibilities, allowing a reactive system to cope easily with unexpected events during execution. However, the extreme solution that consists in predictively assessing all possible execution-time contingencies and plan responses to them is in general impossible to implement: there are too many non-similar possible situations to determine in advance how to react to all of them. In most cases, the best solution is to get a schedule that covers the most likely possible situations and revise it in response to conflicting contingencies. This suggests the design of a generic scheduling model that allows the definition of predictive and reactive scheduling activities with respect to the uncertainty of the information available in the manufacturing environment.

- *Is it possible to define a generic architecture configurable to perform either centralized or distributed scheduling?* Experimental results such as those reported in Smith, Fox, & Ow, (1986) and Le Pape (1991) suggest that the appropriate intermediate strategy between fully centralized and fully distributed scheduling varies from one scheduling problem to the other. An important question is, therefore, to determine whether we can design a scheduling tool configurable either to solve a complete scheduling problem (at some level of abstraction) or to solve a partial problem and communicate with other schedulers to identify interactions and solve them.

• *Can we define the suitable relations of the scheduling system with other software systems and anticipate the architectural requirements for the establishment of these relations?* The current separation between scheduling and other functions is in a sense a necessity to master complexity. However, more and more integration will become possible and desirable in the future. From the viewpoint of designing a scheduling system, this does not only imply the existence of communication means (e.g., through databases) between the scheduling system and the rest of the factory. It does mean that the scheduling system must be designed carefully to make the system usable in many possible ways, together with many other systems.

The following sections argue that a decomposition of scheduling activities into "constraint propagation," "decision-making," and "intelligent control of constraint propagation and decision-making" enables an appropriate investigation of the above questions. Section 3.2 presents the principles of decomposition and delimits the scheduling problems that it enables to address. Section 3.3 deals with constraint propagation and Section 3.4 with decision-making. Section 3.5 discusses the integration of decision-making modules with constraint propagation and proposes the consideration of four points of flexibility to define the control strategy of the overall system. The use of these "points of flexibility" is illustrated in Sections 3.6 through 3.8, which present a flexible scheduling system, SONIA (Collinot & Le Pape, 1991).

3.2 DECOMPOSITION PRINCIPLES

Basically, scheduling is the allocation of resources over time to perform a collection of tasks. It is a decision-making process—the process of determining a schedule. A variety of constraints affect this process: release dates, operation durations and precedences, transfer and setup times, resource availability, (shifts, downtime) and resource sharing. These constraints define the space of admissible solutions. In addition, relaxable preference constraints characterize the quality of scheduling decisions. These preferences are related to due dates, productivity, frequency of tool changes, inventory levels, and shop stability. They lead to priority relations between manufacturing orders, alternative production routings, manufacturing operations, and alternative resources. Because preference constraints can conflict with one another, the scheduling problem also consists of deciding which preferences should be satisfied and to what extent others should be relaxed.

There are mainly two ways to consider preference constraints. The first is to combine preferences into a unique evaluation (or cost) function to maximize (or minimize); then the scheduling system attempts to generate an optimal schedule in the sense of the given evaluation function. The second is to compile preferences into evaluation heuristics to favor candidate solutions that satisfy (or are likely to satisfy) the preferences; then the scheduling system attempts to generate a satisfactory schedule without considering the issue of optimality. None of these two possibilities is really satisfactory: on the one hand, it is not easy to define a unique evaluation function that truly accounts for the realities of the manufacturing environment; on the other hand, the absence of a unique evaluation function prevents a complete assessment of the quality of a given schedule. Fortunately (or unfortunately), the complexity of scheduling problems often forces one to implement optimization as an iterative improvement of more and more satisfactory solutions. Given a solution S_0 to a scheduling problem P_0, one can define a new scheduling problem P_1 as the problem of determining a solution S_1 with a cost smaller than the cost of S_0. Repeating this operation until P_{n+1} is unsolvable suffices to establish that S_n is an optimal schedule.

On the assumption that absolute optimization is either unnecessary or recast in terms of iterative improvement of more and more satisfactory solutions, a scheduling problem is definable as a set of constraints to satisfy. A solution to the scheduling problem is a set of compatible scheduling decisions (such as "perform operation O_2 as soon as possible after operation O_1 on machine M") that guarantee the satisfaction of the constraints. The aim of each scheduling decision is, therefore, to guarantee the satisfaction of some constraints without contradicting either the other constraints or the other decisions. A simple step further from this perspective is to consider each decision as a new constraint d that (maybe temporarily because a decision is generally defeasible) modifies the scheduling problem from P_0 to the problem of "finding a solution to P_0 that satisfies d." Hence, a scheduling problem is a set of constraints P_0; a partial solution is a set of constraints P_i; some of which are decisions; and a complete solution is a set of compatible constraints P_n such that the satisfaction of every constraint in P_n is guaranteed by any execution following the decisions in P_n.

To sum up, what is needed is (1) a constraint language L to define the scheduling problem and (2) a sublanguage S of L to represent the scheduling decisions (a priori any sublanguage comprehensible to manage schedule execution on the shop floor). The constraints in S can be said to be "in solved form" because they are directly interpretable on the shop floor. The role of decision-making is to refine the scheduling problem through the addition of new constraints and to guarantee that the satisfaction of every constraint necessarily follows from the satisfaction of those constraints that belong to S. An important advantage of this view of the decision-making process is that it allows any number of decision makers. For example, the scheduling system can include any number of mathematical, knowledge-based, and interactive decision-making modules, which can intervene in any order. The system can also integrate a module reporting the events that occur on the shop floor, provided that these events are expressible in the form of new constraints. An assumption made below is that a blackboard (or a similar) architecture (Hayes-Roth, 1985; Nii, 1986) is adopted to organize the contributions of the various modules that make up the whole system.

Two difficult tasks remain. The first is to guarantee the compatibility of the decisions made. This is the role of constraint propagation (cf. Section 3.3). More precisely, constraint propagation must allow the detection of any incompatibility among constraints in S to guarantee that only admissible schedules are accepted by the system: whenever decisions are incompatible, one of them must be withdrawn. In addition, constraint propagation can prevent the making of incompatible decisions by informing the decision-making modules of the consequences of problem constraints and already-made decisions. Even though it is not absolutely necessary, this additional capability can have significant effects because it allows decision-making modules to make choices with respect to much more information.

The second difficult task is to decide in which order decisions must be made. The order in which to apply distinct modules to different parts of the problem is important to converge rapidly to satisfactory solutions of the problem. Micro-opportunistic and macro-opportunistic approaches are worth distinguishing in this respect:

- In a micro-opportunistic approach, each decision-making module makes one decision at a time (e.g., schedules one operation each time it applies [Sadeh & Fox, 1990; Sadeh, 1991]). The control problem consists of determining which decision to make at each step of the problem-solving process and how far to propagate the consequences of this decision. The control problem is, in this case, fully external to the decision-making module per se.

- In a macro-opportunistic approach, each module makes a collection of decisions each time it applies. For example, an application of the module might consist of scheduling a complete manufacturing order or a complete set of resources (Smith et al., 1986). In this case, the control problem consists both of ordering the contributions of the various modules and controlling the behavior of each module each time it applies. As these two subproblems relate, this induces a need to provide the decision-making module with relevant control information (e.g., global importance of each preference constraint) or, equivalently, to control the module "from the outside."

The basic principles discussed in Sections 3.3 through 3.5 apply to both micro-opportunistic and macro-opportunistic approaches. Macro-opportunistic approaches are even easier to analyze when recast as micro-opportunistic approaches allowing only specific types of control strategies. On the other hand, macro-opportunistic approaches can be easier to implement and use, depending on the available control knowledge.

The SONIA system, presented in Sections 3.6 through 3.8, relies on a macro-opportunistic approach that allows the selection and adaptation of the behavior of "macro" scheduling "knowledge sources" with respect to the situation at hand. In theory, it is applicable to any predictive and reactive scheduling problem definable in the available constraint language (cf. Section 3.3.2). In practice, it has been applied to non-preemptive predictive and reactive job-shop scheduling problems involving release dates and due dates, operation precedences, duration constraints, transfer and setup times, shift specifications, and disjunctive resource sharing constraints. By disjunctive, it is meant that the system must allocate a precise machine to an operation prior to scheduling it. (The constraint language accepts cumulative resource sharing constraints, but no knowledge source was developed to guarantee their satisfaction.) By non-preemptive, it is meant that the system never considers the possibility of interrupting an operation unless the operation is effectively interrupted on the shop floor or explicitly preempted by the system user.

3.3 CONSTRAINT PROPAGATION

3.3.1 Introduction

Constraint propagation is a deductive activity performed by a constraint propagation system for a problem-solver (Figure 3-1) or for several problem-solvers operating in sequence or in parallel. It enables the problem-solver to decompose a problem without neglecting interactions between subproblems, determine which subproblems are the most constrained, and focus attention accordingly. The constraint propagation system derives new constraints from existing constraints. It also detects inconsistencies between several types of constraints, for example (in the planning and scheduling domain), goals, decisions, preferences, and occurring or expectable events.

Mathematically speaking, the main concept in constraint propagation is the concept of a variable "held constant" "with a conditional interpretation" (Kleene, 1967; Le Pape, 1988):

- "Held constant" means that a variable x stands for the same object throughout all the constraint statements.

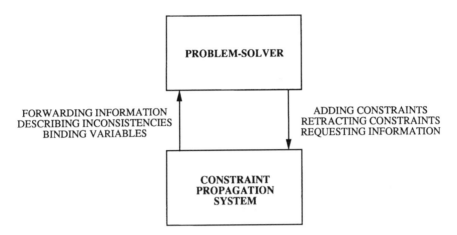

Figure 3-1: Constraint propagation

- "With a conditional interpretation" means that every statement containing a free variable x expresses a condition on x or—more precisely—on the object that x stands for.

In other terms, a constraint set $C = \{P(x)\ P(y)\ Q(x\ y)\}$, where P and Q are predicates and x and y variables, is used when one wants to determine (or prove the existence of) two values v and w such that $P(v)$, $P(w)$, and $Q(v\ w)$ hold.

Constraints provide a specification of admissible assignments of values to variables. Domain constraints such as $x \in \{2\ 4\ 8\ 16\}$ and $y \in \{2\ 4\ 8\ 16\ 32\ 64\}$ describe domains over which variables can vary. Variable relations such as $(x + 1) \geq (2 * y * y)$ define a subset of the Cartesian product of these domains. Variables and constraints are often represented in a hypergraph whose vertices are the variables (with the associated domains) and whose hyperedges correspond to the variable relations. In particular, constraints involving two variables are often organized in a graph, as shown in Figure 3-2.

Different types of constraint propagation steps are useful depending on the domains and relations: for Boolean variables, each constraint propagation step consists of deducing a formula in propositional logic; when domains are Euclidean spaces and relations refer to Euclidean properties, theorems of Euclidean geometry are put into use; etc. More generally, combinatorial and algebraic approaches to constraint propagation are distinguishable (Dechter, 1989):

- A combinatorial approach consists of performing operations concerning the possible values of variables. For example, if x equals 1, and y is constrained to be greater than x, only values greater than 1 are candidates for y.

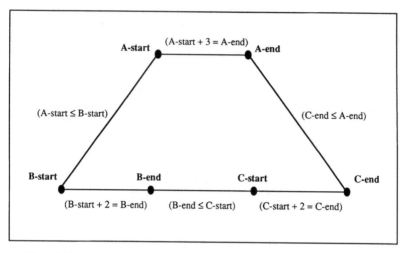

Figure 3-2:   A binary constraint network

- An algebraic approach consists of performing operations concerning relations between the unknown values of variables. For example, if x is constrained to be greater than y, and y is constrained to be greater than z, then x is constrained to be greater than z.

Combinatorial approaches are often applied in finite domains (Shenoy & Shafer, 1988; Van Hentenryck, 1989; Hower, 1990; Kumar, 1992), but algebraic approaches are often applied in infinite but homogeneous structured domains. In particular, algebraic approaches are often used to reason about time (Allen, 1983; Ladkin & Maddux, 1988).

When constraints are not compatible, it is useful to provide the user of the constraint propagation system (human user or computer system) with a description of the detected conflicts. For example, such a description allows a problem-solver to perform "relevant" backtracking (Stallman & Sussman, 1977; Latombe, 1979; Codognet, Fages, & Sola, 1991; Havens, 1991) and to avoid recreating the conditions of a failure. To provide such a description, the constraint propagation system must remember which constraints have been derived from which other constraints. This leads to the use of techniques similar to those used in assumption-based truth maintenance systems (De Kleer, 1986; Kelleher, 1990). Conversely, truth maintenance problems have been mentioned as particular constraint satisfaction problems (Dechter, 1989). The two research domains (truth maintenance and constraint propagation) are consequently very close to each other. In particular, the same complexity problem arises from the use of disjunctions in the two domains.

When disjunctive constraints (or constraints with an intrinsic disjunctive nature) are considered, the problem of determining whether a given set of constraints is consistent is "NP-hard." Informally, this means that no algorithm is known to detect contradictions between n disjunctive constraints in an amount of time bounded by a polynomial function of n (see Garey and Johnson, 1979 for a more precise definition). This leads to the design of incomplete constraint propagation systems through the establishment of a trade-off between the detection of contradictions and the computational time spent in constraint propagation. When a constraint propagation algorithm is not complete, some interactions among constraints are not detectable. The problem-solver must explore possible refinements of the constraints (e.g., choose a disjunct for each disjunction) to guarantee constraint satisfaction.

Most constraint propagation systems perform a fixed amount of propagation: the trade-off between the anticipation of interactions and the amount of computational effort spent in constraint propagation is set once for all. More flexible systems allow their user to reduce or extend propagation with respect to a predetermined set of particular parameters (e.g., reference intervals in Allen [1983]) or include a small programming language to control constraint propagation (Le Pape, 1988; Van Hentenryck, 1989). Results of experiments with such systems (Van Hentenryck, 1989; Collinot & Le Pape, 1991) show that one should carefully consider the control of constraint propagation to improve the efficiency of the resolution of constraint satisfaction problems: the amount of constraint propagation that enables a problem-solver to be the most efficient varies with the problem-solver, with the application (e.g., in job-shop scheduling, the appropriate amount of propagation varies from one shop to another), and with the problem-solving context (e.g., in case of urgency, propagation can be restricted to constraints relating to imminent manufacturing operations). In the following, we consequently adopt an explicit definition of the constraint propagation system as a controllable inference system. This means that we distinguish (1) a set of **deduction rules** that determine what inferences *might* be drawn from a set of premises and (2) a set of **control rules** that specify what inferences *must* be drawn at each point in the problem-solving process.

3.3.2 The Constraint Language of SONIA

In the context of the SONIA scheduling system, three constraint propagation activities (types of deduction rules) are distinguished:

- **Constraint combination** consists of building new constraints from existing constraints. A typical constraint combination rule is the generalized resolution rule: "if g follows from e_i and f, then ($or \, e_1 \ldots e_{i-1} \, g \, e_{i+1} \ldots e_n$) follows from ($or \, e_1 \ldots e_{i-1} \, e_i \, e_{i+1} \ldots e_n$) and f."
- **Constraint subsumption** consists of hiding constraints, the satisfaction of which results from the satisfaction of other constraints. A typical subsumption

rule is the disjunction subsumption rule: "if e subsumes e_i for some i in $\{1 \ldots n\}$, then e subsumes $(or\ e_1 \ldots e_n)$."

- **Constraint rewriting** consists of writing constraints in normal forms or translating constraints from one representation to another. For example, "$(not\ (x \leq_E y)) \Rightarrow (y <_E x)$" is a rewriting rule that applies when $(E \leq_E)$ is defined as a totally ordered set.

A set of deduction rules is **valid** if and only if whenever it allows the deduction of a new constraint c from a set of constraints C, $C \cup \{(not\ c)\}$ is inconsistent. It is **refutation-complete** for a set of constraints S (usually the complete constraint language) that if a set of constraints $C \subseteq S$ is inconsistent, the deduction rules allow the derivation of a conflict from C. It is **refutation-decidable** for a set of constraints S if there exists a finite propagation procedure (implementable in the form of control rules) that, whenever a set of constraints $C \subseteq S$ is inconsistent, generates a derivation of a conflict from C. The constraint propagation procedure is then said to be "refutation-complete for S." (By finite, it is meant that the procedure always terminates. A similar definition exists for semi-decidability, for which the procedure is not constrained to terminate.)

The implementation of a constraint propagation system equivalent to first-order logic (refutation-complete but not decidable as a consequence of Church's theorem [Kleene, 1967]) is possible. However, the expressive power of first-order logic is generally not needed as far as constraint propagation is concerned. Introducing convenient sets of deduction rules through more specific axiomatizations and using them when necessary is much more efficient. The constraint propagation system of SONIA gathers a number of "specialized" subsystems:

- A refutation-complete and decidable system for propositional logic is the first subsystem.
- A refutation-complete and decidable system for point ordering relations in infinite totally ordered sets: The system also accepts disjunctive, conjunctive, and negative formulas of ordering constraints (e.g., $(or\ (x \leq y)\ (not\ (z \leq y))))$; it is refutation-complete and decidable for these constraints. In addition, the user of the system can commit to a particular totally ordered set $(E \leq_E)$ and manipulate constants from this set as soon as he or she provides a definition of the ordering relation over E and indicates which elements of E are immediate predecessors or successors of other elements of E.
- A refutation-complete and decidable system for James Allen's interval relations (Allen, 1983) and disjunctions of interval relations: The system also accepts disjunctive, conjunctive, and negative formulas of interval relations; it is refutation-complete and decidable for these constraints.
- A refutation-complete and decidable system for duration constraints (minimal, maximal, and known distances between time points): The only assumption

about durations is that they belong to the positive part of a totally ordered Abelian group (e.g., the set of integers Z, the set of rationals Q, etc.) defined by the user of the system in the form of a few functions $(+, -, \leq$, etc.). The system also accepts disjunctive, conjunctive, and negative formulas of duration constraints; it is refutation-complete and decidable for these contraints.

- A refutation-complete and decidable system for reservation constraints: Basically, each reservation constraint (*reserve G t_1 t_2 n motives*) states that n individual resources from the group G are unavailable throughout the interval of time $(t_1$ $t_2)$. The list of motives explains why they are unavailable (i.e., what they are used for). Constraint propagation enables the maintenance of accurate time-tables and the detection of capacity conflicts (overloads). The system also accepts disjunctive and conjunctive formulas of reservation constraints; it is refutation-complete and decidable for these constraints.

- Last is a refutation-complete and decidable system for several families of domain constraints such as $(x \in \{a_1 \dots a_n\})$, together with equalities such as $(x = y)$ and $(x = 2)$ and inequalities such as $(x \leq y)$, $(x < y)$, and $(2 < x)$ when the overall domain (defined by the user of the system) is totally ordered.

For each subsystem, a refutation-complete constraint propagation procedure is available. The overall system is refutation-complete and decidable (Le Pape, 1988). The first implementation was made in COMMON-LISP in "Laboratoires de Marcoussis" to support the SONIA reactive scheduling system. In this implementation, each deduction rule is available as a set of "propagation functions" or "demons." Each propagation function defines the reaction of a certain type of constraint to a certain type of event. For example, the reaction of a disjunction to one of its disjuncts being contradicted is the elimination of the disjunct from the disjunction. Hence, whenever a disjunct e_i of a disjunctive constraint (*or* $e_1 \dots e_{i-1}$ $e_i e_{i+1} \dots e_n$) is found incompatible with another constraint c, (*or* $e_1 \dots e_{i-1} e_i e_{i+1} \dots e_n$) and c combine to provide (*or* $e_1 \dots e_{i-1} e_{i+1} \dots e_n$) in replacement of (*or* $e_1 \dots e_{i-1} e_i e_{i+1} \dots e_n$). The constraint propagation system automatically records justifications for the new constraint in order to retract it when one of its origins is retracted (e.g., when the user retracts c or (*or* $e_1 \dots e_{i-1} e_i e_{i+1} \dots e_n$)) and reinstate the complete disjunction if c (and consequently (*or* $e_1 \dots e_{i-1} e_{i+1} \dots e_n$)) is retracted. Control rules are attached to each propagation function to specify whether and under which conditions the propagation function must intervene in the constraint propagation process. Static and dynamic control rules are distinguished as follows:

- The user of the constraint propagation system can define static control rules at compile-time to enforce the application of the propagation functions considered as absolutely necessary and to eliminate the propagation functions considered as totally useless (or much too expensive) in the context of the final application.

- A simple inference engine applies dynamic control rules at run-time to determine whether to apply the corresponding propagation function or not. In the context of the SONIA system, a "constraint propagation controller" (cf. Section 3.7.2) dynamically updates the set of dynamic control rules, thereby allowing the adaptation of the constraint propagation procedure to the problem-solving context.

A variant of this implementation was made, also in COMMON-LISP, at Stanford University to serve in robotic applications. A few papers provide implementation details and results of experiments with the two versions (Collinot, 1988; Le Pape, 1988, 1991b, 1992a; Lemoine, 1991). Another completely different implementation of some of the subsystems above is also available at ILOG as a set of specialized cooperating constraint solvers using the PECOS (Puget & Albert, 1991, 1992) object and constraint programming tool.

3.4 DECISION MAKING

A constraint propagation system facilitates the integration of multiple decision-making modules within a blackboard-like architecture. The aim of this section is to present the principles underlying a blackboard architecture and provide a simple example of how the overall system runs.

A **blackboard system** consists of three major components (Hayes-Roth, 1985; Nii, 1986):

- **The knowledge sources:** The knowledge needed to solve the problem is partitioned into "knowledge sources," which are kept separate and independent.

- **The blackboard data structure:** The problem-solving state data are kept in a global database, the "blackboard." Knowledge sources produce changes to the blackboard that lead incrementally to a solution to the problem. Communication and interaction among the knowledge sources take place solely through the blackboard.

- **The control cycle:** There is no control component specified in the basic blackboard model. The knowledge sources are self-activating and respond opportunistically to changes on the blackboard. In most cases, however, a control component is required to decide which of the knowledge source instances to execute at each point in the problem-solving process. For example, when all the knowledge sources rely on a single processor, control knowledge allows the execution sequencing of knowledge source instances in an appropriate fashion (i.e., to execute the most important actions first).

Figure 3-3 presents a possible control cycle (Hayes-Roth, 1985). Modifications of the blackboard data are called **events**. Each event can trigger knowledge

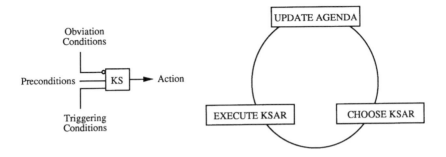

Figure 3-3: The structure of a knowledge source—the control cycle

sources. Both triggering conditions and execution preconditions are attached to knowledge sources. Each triggered knowledge source gives rise to a **ksar** (knowledge source activation record) available for execution as soon as its preconditions are satisfied. The basic control cycle consists of the following steps:

- Update the agenda of pending actions (ksars) according to the occurrence of new events.
- Choose a ksar in the agenda with respect to a set of control policies.
- Execute the selected ksar (the execution produces new events considered on the next cycle).

In addition, one can attach obviation conditions to a knowledge source: a ksar that satisfies its obviation condition is removed from the agenda. The first step includes removing from the agenda the ksars that are no longer applicable.

Here, each knowledge source adds or retracts constraints in reaction to the presence of other constraints on the blackboard. Changes on the blackboard trigger the constraint propagation system. This allows the derivation of new constraints from existing constraints, the detection of contradictions, and the description of the origins of each constraint. For example, if the constraints resulting from the execution of two ksars are conflicting, an explanation of the conflict is made available in the form of a list of conflicting constraints together with identifiers of the ksars from which these constraints originate. Then at least one of the knowledge sources is able to retract one of the conflicting constraints (in general, this implies the replacement of this constraint with other constraints), or the system is unable to solve the problem.

Figure 3-4 illustrates the behavior of such a system on a simple example. We assume that a solution to the given constraint satisfaction problem consists of a set of compatible (temporal) inequalities that guarantee the satisfaction of the other constraints (inequalities and disjunctions of inequalities); as a result, knowledge

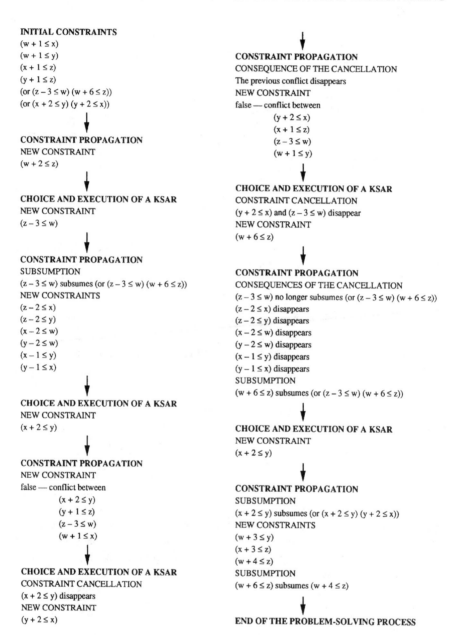

INITIAL CONSTRAINTS
(w + 1 ≤ x)
(w + 1 ≤ y)
(x + 1 ≤ z)
(y + 1 ≤ z)
(or (z − 3 ≤ w) (w + 6 ≤ z))
(or (x + 2 ≤ y) (y + 2 ≤ x))

↓

CONSTRAINT PROPAGATION
NEW CONSTRAINT
(w + 2 ≤ z)

↓

CHOICE AND EXECUTION OF A KSAR
NEW CONSTRAINT
(z − 3 ≤ w)

↓

CONSTRAINT PROPAGATION
SUBSUMPTION
(z − 3 ≤ w) subsumes (or (z − 3 ≤ w) (w + 6 ≤ z))
NEW CONSTRAINTS
(z − 2 ≤ x)
(z − 2 ≤ y)
(x − 2 ≤ w)
(y − 2 ≤ w)
(x − 1 ≤ y)
(y − 1 ≤ x)

↓

CHOICE AND EXECUTION OF A KSAR
NEW CONSTRAINT
(x + 2 ≤ y)

↓

CONSTRAINT PROPAGATION
NEW CONSTRAINT
false — conflict between
          (x + 2 ≤ y)
          (y + 1 ≤ z)
          (z − 3 ≤ w)
          (w + 1 ≤ x)

↓

CHOICE AND EXECUTION OF A KSAR
CONSTRAINT CANCELLATION
(x + 2 ≤ y) disappears
NEW CONSTRAINT
(y + 2 ≤ x)

↓

CONSTRAINT PROPAGATION
CONSEQUENCE OF THE CANCELLATION
The previous conflict disappears
NEW CONSTRAINT
false — conflict between
          (y + 2 ≤ x)
          (x + 1 ≤ z)
          (z − 3 ≤ w)
          (w + 1 ≤ y)

↓

CHOICE AND EXECUTION OF A KSAR
CONSTRAINT CANCELLATION
(y + 2 ≤ x) and (z − 3 ≤ w) disappear
NEW CONSTRAINT
(w + 6 ≤ z)

↓

CONSTRAINT PROPAGATION
CONSEQUENCES OF THE CANCELLATION
(z − 3 ≤ w) no longer subsumes (or (z − 3 ≤ w) (w + 6 ≤ z))
(z − 2 ≤ x) disappears
(z − 2 ≤ y) disappears
(x − 2 ≤ w) disappears
(y − 2 ≤ w) disappears
(x − 1 ≤ y) disappears
(y − 1 ≤ x) disappears
SUBSUMPTION
(w + 6 ≤ z) subsumes (or (z − 3 ≤ w) (w + 6 ≤ z))

↓

CHOICE AND EXECUTION OF A KSAR
NEW CONSTRAINT
(x + 2 ≤ y)

↓

CONSTRAINT PROPAGATION
SUBSUMPTION
(x + 2 ≤ y) subsumes (or (x + 2 ≤ y) (y + 2 ≤ x))
NEW CONSTRAINTS
(w + 3 ≤ y)
(x + 3 ≤ z)
(w + 4 ≤ z)
SUBSUMPTION
(w + 6 ≤ z) subsumes (w + 4 ≤ z)

↓

END OF THE PROBLEM-SOLVING PROCESS

Figure 3-4:   A constraint satisfaction example

sources must intervene as long as there are disjunctive constraints or conflicts. We also assume that static control rules disallow the propagation of disjunctive constraints.

The resolution consists of 12 problem-solving steps:

1. An initialization knowledge source makes a statement of the problem, which results in the posting of six constraints: $(w + 1 \leq x)$ ... $(or\ (x + 2 \leq y)\ (y + 2 \leq x))$.

2. The constraint propagation system processes these constraints and deduces a new constraint $(w + 2 \leq z)$. It automatically records justifications for the new constraint. Here, there are two possible justifications: $\{(w + 1 \leq x)\ (x + 1 \leq z)\}$ and $\{(w + 1 \leq y)\ (y + 1 \leq z)\}$.

3. A problem-solving knowledge source applies and submits a new constraint $(z - 3 \leq w)$ to guarantee the satisfaction of the disjunction $(or\ (z - 3 \leq w)\ (w + 6 \leq z))$.

4. The constraint propagation system processes this constraint, deduces new constraints (for which it records justifications), and notes that $(z - 3 \leq w)$ subsumes the disjunction $(or\ (z - 3 \leq w)\ (w + 6 \leq z))$. The main effect of the subsumption is that the disjunction $(or\ (z - 3 \leq w)\ (w + 6 \leq z))$ is no longer visible as a constraint. The constraint propagation system records the subsumption: should $(z - 3 \leq w)$ be retracted, the system will automatically reinstate $(or\ (z - 3 \leq w)\ (w + 6 \leq z))$.

5. A problem-solving knowledge source applies and selects $(x + 2 \leq y)$, guaranteeing the satisfaction of $(or\ (x + 2 \leq y)\ (y + 2 \leq x))$.

6. The constraint propagation system processes this constraint and detects a contradiction.

7. A problem-solving knowledge source applies, cancels $(x + 2 \leq y)$, and submits the new constraint $(y + 2 \leq x)$.

8. The constraint propagation system propagates these modifications and detects a new contradiction.

9. A problem-solving knowledge source applies, cancels $(y + 2 \leq x)$ and $(z - 3 \leq w)$, and submits the new constraint $(w + 6 \leq z)$. Note that the cancellation of $(y + 2 \leq x)$ is not necessary and depends on the knowledge sources and the control strategy of the blackboard system.

10. The constraint propagation system propagates these modifications.

11. A problem-solving knowledge source applies and reinstates $(x + 2 \leq y)$.

12. The constraint propagation system propagates this constraint.

Then the process stops. A solution is available as a set of compatible inequalities that guarantee the satisfaction of the disjunctive constraints of the initial problem.

3.5 PROPERTIES OF THE OVERALL SYSTEM

We say that the overall system (constraint propagation system + set of knowledge sources + control strategy) is **valid** if and only if for every initial set of constraints, the following conditions are met:

- The system does not stop in a state that contains a conflict unless the initial set of constraints is inconsistent.
- The system does not stop in a state that contains no conflict unless the initial set of constraints is consistent.

We say that the overall system is **complete** for S if and only if it necessarily stops in a state that either (1) contains a conflict or (2) is such that for every initial constraint c_i, there is a constraint s_i both on the blackboard and in S such that the satisfaction of s_i guarantees the satisfaction of c_i.

The following theorem shows how the properties of the overall system derive from the properties of its parts.

Theorem. The satisfaction of the following conditions is sufficient to guarantee that the overall system is **valid** and **complete** for S:

1. The constraint propagation procedure is valid and refutation-complete for S.
2. Knowledge sources do not retract initial constraints.
3. Whenever a constraint c on the blackboard does not logically follow from another constraint both on the blackboard and in S, at least one knowledge source is applicable to produce such a constraint s.
4. Whenever the blackboard contains the description of a conflict involving a set of constraints $s_1 \ldots s_n$ (posted to solve $c_1 \ldots c_n$), either a knowledge source is able to replace a constraint s_i with another constraint t_i (such that c_i logically follows from t_i), or the initial constraints $c_1 \ldots c_n$ are inconsistent.
5. The control strategy guarantees that the system stops.

A direct consequence of this theorem (demonstrated and applied to a concrete example in Le Pape [1992c]) is that it is possible to design/implement/modify the constraint propagation system and the decision-making modules independently: the correctness of the complete system follows from the correctness of its parts. This allows the implementation of precise, flexible, efficient, and extendable scheduling systems: precise and flexible because the system can account for any constraint expressible in the constraint language; efficient because highly optimized constraint propagation procedures are now available, and extendable because the consideration of a new type of constraint might require only an extension to the constraint propagation system or the implementation of additional decision-making modules—without necessitating any modification of the existing code (Le Pape, 1992b). Also the theorem generalizes to the case of dynamic problems and knowledge sources applicable in parallel (Le Pape, 1992b, 1992d, 1992e). This means that in the absence of *hard real-time constraints*, the integration of decision-making modules with the constraint propagation system gives rise to reactive and distributed systems, the properties of which follow from the properties of their parts.

However, it should be clear that the efficiency of the scheduling process highly depends on the definition of an appropriate control strategy. For a distributed system, the definition of this strategy is a very complex issue because it includes decisions about which problem-solving actions to execute in parallel. An important amount of parallelism can even impact the guarantee that the system stops, even if the probability that the system stops usually remains 1. For a centralized system, the guarantee that the system stops is much easier to obtain. The definition of an efficient control strategy is then split up into the consideration of four points of flexibility:

1. The set of heuristics allowing the system to choose among possible decisions can vary with the problem-solving context.

2. The flexibility of the constraint propagation system enables some adjustment (through control rules) of the amount of propagation performed in evaluating the consequences of scheduling decisions.

3. When a knowledge source fails (i.e., some of the previous decisions are inconsistent), various strategies from "naive" chronological backtracking to sophisticated analyses of the failure (enabling the system to avoid further failures and to cancel not the most recent decision but the relevant decision) can be considered.

4. Knowledge sources can consider a quality criterion either as a preference constraint or as a restriction. In the first case, the preference constraint is relaxed if necessary. In the second case, the knowledge source fails if the restriction cannot be satisfied.

Sections 3.6 through 3.8 illustrate the use of these "points of flexibility" in the case of the SONIA predictive and reactive scheduling system.

3.6 AN APPLICATION: THE SONIA SCHEDULING SYSTEM

SONIA is a knowledge-based job-shop scheduling system designed to detect and react to inconsistencies between a schedule and the actual events on a shop floor. The system is built on a BB1-like blackboard architecture (Hayes-Roth, 1985). It is provided with both predictive and reactive "macro" knowledge sources, which are used to build and modify schedules. Analyzing knowledge sources can be employed to evaluate both predictive and reactive problem-solving contexts. Control knowledge sources can use analysis results to choose the most appropriate knowledge sources to execute and determine which "behavior" the scheduling knowledge sources should adopt (e.g., which heuristics they should use). A schedule management system (built on the flexible constraint propagation system presented in Section 3.3.2) is used to update schedule descriptions and detect inconsistencies as scheduling knowledge sources make decisions and unexpected events happen on the shop floor.

In Section 3.6.1, we first call attention to the management of schedule descriptions. An overview of the various knowledge sources that make up the SONIA system follows: predictive and reactive scheduling knowledge sources (Section 3.6.2), analyzing knowledge sources (Section 3.6.3), knowledge sources constituting interfaces between SONIA and the real-world (Section 3.6.4), and control knowledge sources (Section 3.6.5).

3.6.1 Management of Schedule Descriptions

Within SONIA, a shop schedule is represented as a set of resources, manufacturing orders, and operations to which various kinds of constraints are attached. As in the ISIS (Fox, 1983; Fox & Smith, 1984) and OPIS (Smith et al., 1986; Smith, 1987) scheduling systems, resources are described at various levels of abstraction. At each level, time-tables composed of reservation constraints (including shift specifications: a particularity of the SONIA system is that it schedules a given set of work shifts with operations selected from a given set of operations) are associated with resources. To each manufacturing order are associated a release date, a due date, and a production plan represented as a hierarchy of operations. An *actual-status* and a *schedule-status* are defined for each operation: they indicate whether the operation is *completed*, *in-process*, or *ignored* (i.e., not started) on the shop floor and whether it is *scheduled*, *selected*, or *ignored* by SONIA. Temporal constraints are generated in accordance with the status information.

The schedule management system is responsible for evaluating the consequences of both decisions and unexpected events happening on the shop floor. Decisions are related to status of operations, release dates, due dates, and resource capacity (e.g., work shifts, resource sharing). Unexpected events are machine breakdowns and delays. The schedule management system is used to create reservation constraints or temporal constraints (e.g., temporal inequalities or disjunctions of temporal inequalities) according to the type of scheduling decisions or shop floor events. These constraints are then passed to the constraint propagation system that derives new constraints from existing ones and detects inconsistencies.

When an inconsistency is detected, an appropriate description of the conflict is built. Depending on the conflicting constraints, a conflict belongs to one or more of the following categories: the *delays* category gathers all the conflicts that result from unexpected delays (for example, a *global tardiness conflict* states that because some operations have begun or ended later than expected on the shop floor, it is impossible to perform all the selected operations during the open work shifts), the *capacity conflicts* category gathers all the conflicts involving reservation constraints (for example, an *out-of-shift conflict* means that a resource is allocated to an operation outside its work shifts), and the *breakdowns* category is composed of *delays* and *capacity conflicts* caused by machine breakdowns.

3.6.2 Predictive and Reactive Scheduling Knowledge Sources

SONIA is able to perform five distinct scheduling tasks. Each of them corresponds to the implementation of a scheduling knowledge source. This section briefly presents these scheduling knowledge sources.

Global Selection. The *Selection* knowledge source is used to choose a set of operations to perform during the open work shifts and to assign resources to them. More precisely, this knowledge source is employed when resources are underloaded. Operations that require the use of such resources are then selected. Operations are selected with respect to the capacity of these resources. Heuristics are used to determine which operations should be performed. These heuristics can vary with both the shop and the problem-solving contexts. For example, it might be interesting to give priority to manufacturing orders for which the remaining processing time required for achievement is important compared to the remaining time made acceptable by the due date of the order. In some cases, it might be more profitable to take into account other scheduling criteria such as minimizing tool changes. When an operation is selected, its *schedule-status* is modified, and the relevant constraints are created and propagated by the schedule management system.

Order Selection. The *Order Selection* knowledge source is employed to select operations that belong to the same production plan. It selects operations one after the other and stops as soon as an operation cannot be selected within the open work shifts. This component is often used when operations have been discarded by the *Rejection* knowledge source. This allows improvement of the schedule.

Ordering. The *Ordering* knowledge source is used to make ordering decisions when disjunctive constraints (e.g., resource sharing) must be satisfied. It consists of an iterative constraint satisfaction process: disjunctive constraints that characterize the various orders in which operations can be performed are satisfied by choosing underlying temporal inequalities. At each iteration, heuristics are used to make ordering decisions that are propagated through the schedule management system. Various backtracking procedures can be invoked when some ordering *free decisions* (as opposed to *imperative decisions*) conflict with other constraints. These procedures select one of the conflicting *free decisions* to be rejected; the effects of this decision are undone by means of the schedule management system, and the reverse ordering decision is made as an *imperative decision* (forced by the other conflicting decisions); then the process re-starts. The constraint satisfaction process fails when a conflict is derived from *imperative decisions*. When the *Ordering* knowledge source fails (for instance, when too many operations have been selected by the *Selection* knowledge source), some of the less important operations are rejected by the *Rejection* knowledge source.

Rejection. The *Rejection* knowledge source is responsible for rejecting selected operations. It is employed when the *Ordering* knowledge source fails or when unexpected events prevent the whole predictive schedule from executing. It uses heuristics to choose the operations to be rejected from among the operations involved in conflicting situations. When an operation is *rejected*, its *schedule-status* is set back to *ignored*. Consequently, constraints and conflicts concerning this operation are removed by the schedule management system.

Global Re-scheduling. The *Global Re-scheduling* knowledge source is used in order to process and modify the whole plan forward from the current date. Its process rests upon the fact that any deviation can eventually be expressed by precise delays associated with resources. The forward propagation of these delays results in conflicts relating to due dates or to end of work shifts, which can be solved by relaxing due dates, extending work shifts, or rejecting operations. However, if processing time is available (i.e., if it is not necessary to correct the plan in a few seconds), it is worth reducing idle times of resources by permuting operations. Consequently, two strategies are available. The first one consists of a simple right shifting strategy: for each resource, the operations to be performed remain in the same order, and the schedule is moved forward from the current date. The other strategy allows permutations in order to optimize the plan and reduce the effects of the original delay. In any case, when an operation cannot be performed within a shift, heuristics are used to determine whether the shift is extended or whether the operation is discarded or postponed until the next shift.

3.6.3 Analyzing Knowledge Sources

Analyzing tasks has been proved useful for improving scheduling problem-solving (Descotte & Delesalle, 1986; Smith et al., 1986; Le Pape, 1988). For example, the detection of bottleneck and under-loaded resources (capacity analysis) enables improvement of the problem-solving task achieved by the *Ordering* knowledge source (cf. Section 3.7.1). Similarly, an analysis of conflicts detected by the schedule management system allows improving the use of reactive scheduling knowledge sources to correct the current schedule. This section briefly presents two knowledge sources responsible for achieving each of these analyzing tasks.

Capacity Analysis. The *Capacity Analyzer* is used to detect both bottleneck and under-loaded resources. As the shop-level capacity analyzer of the OPIS system (Smith et al., 1986), it divides the time-line into time periods and determines both the available capacity and the demand over each period for each considered resource. Capacity and demand are computed from the existing reservations and by building a rough predictive schedule (which is discarded once the analysis is achieved) for selected operations.

Analysis of Conflicts. The *Analyzer of Conflicts* is used to examine in details a set of conflicts in order to determine appropriate reactions. The analysis results in various proposals in order to solve all or some of the contemplated conflicts. Very simple rules are applied in order to determine which and how available reactive components should be used. For example, when several *global tardiness conflicts* are to be solved, using the *Global Re-scheduler* knowledge source is recommended. Conversely, it is more appropriate to use the *Rejection* knowledge source for the resolution of an isolated *global tardiness conflict*. (Of course, the default strategy that consists of using the *Global Re-scheduler* is always applicable.) In addition, heuristics can be used to focus the analysis on a particular category of conflicts or on conflicts related to a given work-area or manufacturing order.

3.6.4 Interfaces

Three knowledge sources are used as interfaces between SONIA and the shop floor.

User Interface. The *User Interface* allows the user of the system to build and update schedules. More precisely, the system allows the user to select and reject operations, to order and permute operations, to cut operations (explicit pre-emption), to allocate a resource to an operation over an interval of time, to add and delete work shifts, to update release dates and due dates, and to add and delete constraints expressible in the available constraint language (cf. Section 3.3.2). After each decision (or modification of original data), the user can activate the constraint propagation system and visualize the results in the form of a Gantt chart.

Schedule Application. The *Schedule Application* knowledge source provides the user of the system (e.g., the shop floor manager) with a schedule generated or corrected by the predictive and reactive scheduling knowledge sources of SONIA. It is called each time a new (updated) schedule is considered acceptable.

Execution Controller.   The *Execution Controller* informs the schedule management system about the actual course of events on the shop floor (i.e., the schedule execution with regard to unexpected events).

3.6.5 Control Knowledge Sources

SONIA is built upon a BB1-like blackboard architecture for both coordinating the contribution of the various knowledge sources and adjusting their behavior according to the problem-solving context. Each time a knowledge source is involved in the problem-solving process, it generates events that are posted on the *domain* blackboard or on the *control* blackboard (or on both). The domain blackboard collects events related to the actual state and progress of the scheduling decision-making process. The control blackboard collects events related to the control process.

As in Hayes-Roth (1985), three basic control knowledge sources are used to implement the basic control loop that runs the SONIA system (cf. Section 3.4). In addition, two high-level control knowledge sources (a *Controller of Heuristics* and a *Constraint Propagation Controller*) are employed to update the set of heuristics used by scheduling knowledge sources (cf. Section 3.7.1) and to control the propagation of the consequences of scheduling decisions (cf. Section 3.7.2).

3.7 CONTROLLING THE BEHAVIOR OF KNOWLEDGE SOURCES WITHIN SONIA

As mentioned in Section 3.2, the adoption of "macro" knowledge sources induces a need to control their behavior from the outside. Within SONIA, a knowledge source is considered a three-part knowledge component (Figure 3-5):

- The *condition* part allows the knowledge source to know whether it can be active.
- The *action* part determines the events the knowledge source is going to produce. It is defined as a partial procedure (i.e., a procedure where there still are choices to be made).
- The *behavior* part defines flexible points that can dynamically be set to complete the partial procedure.

Four control issues are considered: (1) adjusting the set of heuristics used by a knowledge source (Section 3.7.1), (2) controlling constraint propagation (Section 3.7.2), (3) choosing among various backtracking strategies (Section 3.7.3), and

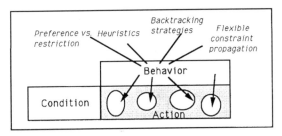

Figure 3-5:   A knowledge source as a three-part knowledge component

(4) considering scheduling criteria as preference constraints or as restrictions (Section 3.7.4).

3.7.1 Adjusting Heuristics

Calling attention to the heuristics, a knowledge source can use leads to consider a knowledge source as a search procedure (Ow, 1984; Le Pape, 1988). Obviously, the search procedure varies with the heuristics: adjusting heuristics to encountered problem-solving contexts improves problem-solving. For example, the EDD (Earliest Due Date) priority rule, which consists of selecting and scheduling operations of the most urgent orders first, produces satisfactory results with respect to due-date constraints, *provided that the shop is not over-loaded*. When the shop *is* over-loaded (i.e., when one cannot prevent the relaxation of many due-dates), this priority rule is known to provide poor results and *should not* be applied. Similarly, the heuristic that recommends scheduling the most critical resources first is more or less relevant, depending on the irregularities in resource loading (bottleneck and under-loaded resources). Information about irregularities in resource loading is produced by the *Capacity Analyzer*. The *Controller of Heuristics* can use this information to activate or de-activate heuristics accordingly. This makes the behavior of the *Selection* and *Ordering* knowledge sources more appropriate.

3.7.2 Controlling Constraint Propagation

The flexibility of the constraint propagation system enables adjustment of the amount of propagation performed in evaluating the consequences of scheduling decisions. When the amount of propagation is reduced, a knowledge source has either to explore the search space in order to find a satisfactory solution or to run the risk of introducing un-detected conflicts (which will be detected later by other knowledge sources). When the amount of propagation is extended, a knowledge source can drastically prune the search space. The search procedure that the knowledge source applies varies—from purely heuristic search to a least-commitment approach (Stefik, 1980)—with the amount of propagation. As shown in the following examples, the amount of propagation can be adapted according to a particular problem-solving task or to more general purposes.

- The set of control rules used by the constraint propagation system can be modified by the *Constraint Propagation Controller* before the *Capacity Analyzer* knowledge source is activated. When the *Capacity Analyzer* builds its rough predictive schedule in order to evaluate the demand for each resource, it is not necessary to take into account constraints related to the use of resources. Similarly, the decisions that the *Capacity Analyzer* makes do not need to be confronted to order due-dates or to end-of-work-shift constraints. The analysis is therefore more rapid when constraint propagation is reduced to the miminum required for a significant evaluation.

- Conversely, it is worth increasing the amount of propagation before the *Order Selection* knowledge source is called. Indeed, this knowledge source only makes a few decisions related to a few operations. An extended propagation of the consequences of selection decisions virtually ensures (if no inconsistency is detected) that the selected operations can be scheduled.

- In case of emergency (e.g., when conflicts arising from unexpected delays are related to very important and urgent manufacturing orders), reactive decisions must be made without evaluating all their consequences. Such an emergency context can be detected by the *Analyzer of Conflicts*. Then, the *Constraint Propagation Controller* can be activated in order to specify (through the control rules of the constraint propagation system) that only constraints concerning "imminent" events need to be combined.

- Propagating disjunctive constraints is time consuming and generally avoided. However, it might be worth taking a closer look at operations that require the use of a scarce resource. When scarce resources are identified by the *Capacity Analyzer*, the *Constraint Propagation Controller* can specify that disjunctive constraints (e.g., resource sharing) need to be combined only if they relate to these resources.

3.7.3 Choosing Backtracking Strategies

When decisions (typically ordering decisions made by the *Ordering* knowledge source) lead to an inconsistency, various strategies can be considered, from "naive" chronological backtracking to sophisticated analyses of the failure.

- The *chronological backtracking strategy* allows immediate backtracking (without analyzing the failure). It recommends considering decisions in reverse chronological order and canceling all the decisions until the most recent decision involved in the inconsistency is removed.

- The *selective backtracking strategy* recommends the cancellation of an ordering decision if and only if the cancellation is absolutely necessary (in order to remove the inconsistency). This strategy prevents the system from cancelling (and further re-making) ordering decisions that are not directly responsible for the inconsistency. However, these decisions might have been made to satisfy a preference constraint in a context involving some of the inconsistent decisions. The selective backtracking strategy is often more rapid at the expense of the homogeneity (with regard to various scheduling criteria) of the solution. This means the selective backtracking strategy can be more or less relevant depending on the problem-solving context (importance of scheduling criteria, emergency, problem size).

Furthermore, possibilities of analyzing conflicts in order to gain information can be considered. The *Ordering* knowledge source can invoke an inconsistency processing procedure in order to record incompatibilities detected by the schedule management system. This avoids making the same mistake twice. When some decisions $d_1 \dots d_n$ conflict with regard to a set of constraints $\{c_1 \dots c_m\}$, it is possible to create a new constraint $(or\ (not\ d_1) \dots (not\ d_n))$ and maintain it as long as $c_1 \dots c_m$ are considered. The creation of such a constraint guarantees that the same inconsistency resulting from the constraints c_i and the decisions d_j will not be met again (provided that the amount of constraint propagation is sufficient). However, it is worth noting that the cost of storing and exploiting incompatibilities can be more important than the resulting gain in search processing time.

3.7.4 Considering Quality Criteria as Preferences or Restrictions

A knowledge source can consider a quality criterion as a preference or as a restriction. When the criterion is considered a restriction, the knowledge source makes a decision to respect the criterion and carries on searching without relaxing this decision (the knowledge source fails if the criterion cannot be satisfied). This conveys a very high importance to the criterion. Conversely, when the criterion is considered as a preference, it is used merely as a heuristic to guide search.

For example, the *Global Re-scheduler* can decide to systematically ignore schedules that cannot be obtained without cancelling previous ordering decisions. This means that a stability criterion is now considered as a restriction used to discard potential schedules as opposed to a preference used to compare potential schedules. When the *Global Re-scheduler* allows cancellation of ordering decisions, the re-scheduling process is less rapid but enables optimization of resource schedules.

3.8 EXPERIMENTS

SONIA can be used with a simulator to investigate various reactive scheduling strategies.

- Given a description of a shop-floor, we can measure the utility of reactive scheduling compared to the use of classical dispatching rules.
- We can investigate the relevance and the efficiency of each knowledge source in various contexts (e.g., over-loaded shop, highly disrupted shop).
- The behavior of scheduling and analyzing knowledge sources can be adjusted with respect to several control issues.

This section describes some of our experiments regarding the use of various backtracking strategies and the control of constraint propagation. Collinot & Le Pape (1988) provide a detailed description of the results and also discuss both the global utility of reactive scheduling and the efficiency of reactive methods implemented in the SONIA system.

3.8.1 Description of the Experiments

Experiments regarding backtracking strategies and constraint propagation have been made (using a LISP-machine SYMBOLICS-3600) for three shop-floors: an actual sheet-iron shop (23 machines, 100 to 150 operations per shift), a bottleneck area of this shop (6 machines, about 30 operations per shift), and a hypothetical shop obtained by doubling the capacity of this bottleneck area (12 machines, about 60 operations per shift). Figure 3-6 shows, for each workshop, the number of tests made, the number of shifts per test, and the number of operations per shift. Shifts are 7 to 12 hours long. The demand/capacity ratio in the sheet-iron shop

Workshop	Sheet-Iron Workshop	Bottleneck Area	Hypothetical Workshop
Number of Machines	23	6	12
Number of Tests	15	100	100
Number of Shifts	3.5	2.5	2.5
Number of Operations	100 to 150	30	60

Figure 3-6:   Experiments with three workshops

varies from 30% for under-loaded machines to 90% for bottleneck machines. In the two other shops, machines are equally loaded. The duration of operations varies from a few minutes to a few hours in the sheet-iron shop and from 45 minutes to 3 hours in the two other shops. Tool setups are costly (10 to 40 minutes). Unexpected events are delays, operation interruptions, and mainly machine breakdowns. For each machine, breakdowns are generated with respect to a Poisson law, the parameter of which is 2,000 minutes. In most cases, the machine is unavailable for 90 minutes or less.

Two backtracking issues are considered: (1) chronological or selective (dependency-directed) backtracking and (2) recording or not recording incompatibilities detected by the constraint propagation system. Consequently, four backtracking strategies are available.

Similarly, a series of constraint propagation "scenarios" are defined with respect to the following issues:

- Constraint propagation can be restricted to the determination of critical paths in a PERT-like graph. This means disjunctive constraints are not considered by the constraint propagation system. On the contrary, the constraint propagation system can eliminate contradicted disjuncts from disjunctive constraints, as shown in Section 3.3.2. For example, if a machine is planned to be unavailable throughout the interval of time (6 8) and if an operation op must be performed on this machine without interruption, the system can deduce $start(op) \geq 8$ from $end(op) \geq 7$ and $(or \ (start(op) \geq 8) \ (end(op) \leq 6))$.

- The constraint propagation system can either ignore or detect re-scheduling opportunities. For example, $end(op) \geq 7$ might disappear in the course of the simulation (because an operation preceding op ends earlier than expected, thereby enabling op to start earlier than expected). If no other constraint prevents op from ending before 6, the constraint propagation system can then discard $start(op) \geq 8$ and signal an opportunity for re-scheduling op.

- Two well-known methods were considered (and implemented in the form of control rules) for updating critical paths as scheduling decisions are made. The first method involves exploring the graph forward from j and backward from i, using a variant of Ford's algorithm (cf. Gondran and Minoux, 1984; Le Pape, 1988), whenever a new arc $(i \ j \ v)$ (representing the inequality $i + v \leq j$ where i and j are time points and v a constant) is added. This allows the deduction of new constraints $k + w \leq l$ when paths exist from k to i and from j to l. The complexity of this method is $O(n^3)$ in the worst case if n denotes the number of manufacturing operations considered within a shift. The second method consists of maintaining a matrix M such that $M(i \ j)$ denotes the length of the longest path from node i to node j in the graph.

When a new inequality $i + v \leq j$ with $v > M(i\,j)$ is added, and $w = M(k\,i) + v + M(j\,l) > M(k\,l)$, $M(k\,l)$ becomes w. The complexity of this method is $O(n^2)$.

- When disjunctions of temporal inequalities are considered, subsumption rules might or might not always be used to "hide" disjunctions, the satisfaction of which results from the satisfaction of other constraints.

- For two knowledge sources of the SONIA system (*Order Selection* and *Capacity Analyzer*), we were able to design appropriate constraint propagation procedures that were more efficient than others.

3.8.3 Results

As expected, selective backtracking strategies are in most cases more efficient than chronological backtracking strategies. However, extended constraint propagation often leads to a significant decrease in the number of backtracks. Consequently, the utility of selective backtracking is reduced (and sometimes reversed) when constraint propagation is extended. Similarly, the recording of incompatibilities is all the more useful as constraint propagation is reduced.

The system reacts more quickly to unexpected events when constraint propagation is restricted to the determination of critical paths. Globally, the quality of the schedule eventually executed is not significantly altered by the absence (because of reduced propagation) of both early detection of conflicts and detection of scheduling opportunities. On the other hand, for predictive scheduling, the cost of an extended constraint propagation is balanced by a reduction of search in nearly 50% of the cases. In 90% of the cases, the exploration of the PERT-like graph is much more efficient than the matrix-based method (although it is $O(n^3)$ against $O(n^2)$ in the worst case). The cost of subsuming disjunctive constraints is hardly balanced by the resulting reduction of search: in 80% of the cases, subsumption does not enable saving more than 10% of the total (search + constraint propagation) time.

Providing propagation scenarios dedicated to two knowledge sources of the SONIA system turned out to be very worthwhile. By performing reduced propagation, the *Capacity Analyzer* was able to save 18% to 78% of its computational time and produce equivalent results. By performing extended propagation, the *Order Selection* knowledge source was able to detect immediately cases in which several operations of the same order could not be performed during the same shift without re-scheduling operations of other orders—thereby enabling the whole system to prune the search space.

The existing implementation (in COMMON-LISP on a SYMBOLICS 3600) is nevertheless not very efficient compared to what we can expect today with better hardware and highly optimized constraint programming tools. For a scheduling problem with 23 machines and 100 to 150 operations per shift, the system generates a predictive schedule in 5 to 10 iterative improvements per shift (each involving the *Capacity Analyzer*; *Selection*; *Ordering*; and, possibly, the *Rejection* and *Order Selection* knowledge sources), representing a total of 20 to 30 minutes of computational time. Reactive scheduling is more efficient: 10% of the schedule execution time is spent propagating events occurring on the shop-floor, with an average re-scheduling time of 2 to 3 seconds when the *Global Re-scheduler* applies and about 10 seconds when a more intelligent reaction (involving every other knowledge source) is carried out. Drastic improvements (more than 1 to 10 on the same hardware) have been obtained on an industrial version of SOJA (Le Pape, 1988), the predictive part of SONIA marketed in France by GSI-Industrie. Even more drastic improvements are expected from a PECOS (Puget & Albert, 1991; Puget, 1992) implementation of a system with similar functionalities.

3.9 CONCLUSION

The SONIA system is a valid and complete scheduling system. It generates correct schedules, reacts whenever an unexpected event prevents schedule execution, and reaches quiescence when a new (updated) correct schedule is available. In terms of optimization, the system is not complete because it cannot be used to minimize or maximize the value of a given cost or evaluation function. Nevertheless, the use of appropriate heuristics and the fact that the system can apply some of its knowledge sources to improve a given schedule (e.g., the *Capacity Analyzer* knowledge source to detect under-loads and the *Selection* knowledge source to repair under-loads) enable the generation and the maintenance of satisfactory solutions to the scheduling problem. With respect to classical optimization criteria, the improvements made possible by SONIA compared to a simple due-date oriented dispatching rule are of the order of 5% for the number of setups, 10% for setup costs, 5% for machine idleness, 10% (more than 20% in some cases) for the number of tardy orders, and −5% (a negative figure that reflects the specialization of the dispatching rule) for average tardiness.

The main difficulties that remain in using such a system are the identification of control knowledge and the expression of this knowledge in the current control language. Customizing a controllable constraint system is not an impossible task for a computer science researcher accustomed to describing complex procedures in abstract mathematical terms. However, the current systems do not enable a human problem-solver to make his or her own applications as efficient as possible without the help of a specialist. An interesting prospect is to make the adaptation of a controllable system manageable by its users. Another is to provide a system with the ability to gain control knowledge from its experience and adapt its own process to the type of problems it encounters.

References

Allen, James F. 1983. "Maintaining Knowledge about Temporal Intervals." *Communications of the ACM*, **26**(11): 832–843.

Codognet, Philippe, François Fages, and Thierry Sola. 1988. *A Cheap Implementation of CLP(F) and Its Combination with Intelligent Backtracking.* Technical Report, Laboratoire Central de Recherches Thomson-CSF.

Collinot, Anne. 1988. *Le problème du contrôle dans un système flexible d'ordonnan cement.* Ph.D. Thesis, University Paris VI.

Collinot, Anne, and Claude Le Pape. 1988. *Comparaison de plusieurs modes d'utilisation d'un système d'ordonnancement flexible.* Technical Report, Laboratoires de Marcoussis.

Collinot, Anne, and Claude Le Pape. 1991. "Adapting the Behavior of a Job-Shop Scheduling System." *International Journal for Decision Support Systems*, **7**(3): 341–353.

Dechter, Rina (editor). 1989. *Proceedings of the AAAI Workshop on Constraint Processing.* AAAI Press, Menlo Park, Calif.

De Kleer, Johan. 1986. "An Assumption-Based TMS. Extending the ATMS. Problem Solving with the ATMS." *Artificial Intelligence*, **28**(2): 127–224.

Descotte, Yannick, and Hervé Delesalle. 1986. "Une architecture de système expert pour la planification d'activité." *Proceedings of the Sixth International Workshop on Expert Systems and Applications*, EC2, Nanterre, France, pp. 903–916.

Fox, Mark S. 1983. *Constraint-Directed Search: A Case Study of Job-Shop Scheduling.* Ph.D. Thesis, Carnegie Mellon University.

Fox, Mark S., and Stephen F. Smith. 1984. "ISIS: A Knowledge-Based System for Factory Scheduling." *Expert Systems*, **1**(1): 25–49.

Garey, Michael R., and David S. Johnson. 1979. *Computers and Intractability. A Guide to the Theory of NP-Completeness.* W. H. Freeman and Company, New York.

Gondran, Michel, and Michel Minoux. 1984. *Graphs and Algorithms.* John Wiley and Sons.

Havens, William S. 1991. *Intelligent Backtracking in the Echidna CLP Reasoning System.* Technical Report, Simon Fraser University.

Hayes-Roth, Barbara. 1985. "A Blackboard Architecture for Control." *Artificial Intelligence*, **26**(3): 251–321.

Hower, Walter. 1990. *A Novel Algorithm for Constraint Satisfaction.* Technical Report, University of Koblenz-Landau.

Kelleher, Gerald. 1990. *Extending the Expressive Power of de Kleer's ATMS.* Technical Report, University of Leeds.

Kempf, Karl. 1989. "Manufacturing Planning and Scheduling: Where We Are and Where We Need To Be." *Proceedings of the IEEE International Conference on Artificial Intelligence Applications*, IEEE Computer Society Press, Los Alamitos, Calif.

Kempf, Karl, Claude Le Pape, Stephen F. Smith, and Barry R. Fox. 1991. "Issues in the Design of AI-Based Schedulers: A Workshop Report." *AI Magazine*, **11**(5): 37–46.

Kempf, Karl, Bruce Russell, Sanjiv Sidhu, and Stu Barrett. 1991. "AI-Based Schedulers in Manufacturing Practice: Report of a Panel Discussion." *AI Magazine*, **11**(5): 46–55.

Kleene, Stephen C. 1967. *Mathematical Logic*. John Wiley and Sons, New York.

Kumar, Vipin. 1992. "Algorithms for Constraint Satisfaction: A Survey." *AI Magazine*, **13**(1): 32–44.

Ladkin, Peter B., and Roger D. Maddux. 1988. *On Binary Constraint Networks*. Technical Report, Kestrel Institute.

Latombe, Jean-Claude. 1979. "Failure Processing in a System for Designing Complex Assemblies." *Proceedings of the Sixth International Joint Conference on Artificial Intelligence*. AAAI Press, Menlo Park, Calif., pp. 508–515.

Lemoine, Philippe, and Claude Le Pape. 1991. "Simulating Actions and Perceptions of Autonomous Mobile Robots in a Multi-Agent Indoor Environment." Working Paper, Stanford University.

Le Pape, Claude. 1988. *Des systèmes d'ordonnancement flexibles et opportunistes*. Ph.D. Thesis, University Paris XI.

Le Pape, Claude. 1991. "Architectural Issues in the Design of (Future) AI-Based Schedulers." *Proceedings of the Tenth UK Planning SIG*, Logica, Cambridge, U.K., pp. 1–9.

Le Pape, Claude. 1991. *Constraint Propagation in Planning and Scheduling*. CIFE Technical Report, Stanford University.

Le Pape, Claude. 1992a. "Coupling Predictive Scheduling and Execution Monitoring." *Proceedings of the Twelfth International Workshop on Expert Systems and Applications*, EC2, Nanterre, France, pp. 225–234.

Le Pape, Claude. 1992b. "Programmation par contraintes et ordonnancement: réalités et perspectives." *Deuxième congrès "Systèmes Experts en Informatique de Gestion*, University of Nice, France, pp. 7–15.

Le Pape, Claude. 1992c. "Solving Scheduling Problems with Constraint Propagation and a Blackboard System." *Information Technology Journal*, Vol. 5, No. 2, pp. 19–26.

Le Pape, Claude. 1992d. "Using Constraint Propagation in Blackboard Systems: A Flexible Software Architecture for Reactive and Distributed Systems." *IEEE Computer*, **25**(5): 60–62.

Le Pape, Claude. 1992e. "Validity and Completeness Properties of Blackboard Systems Using Constraint Propagation." Jayantha Herath (editor), *Readings in Computer Architectures for Intelligent Systems*, IEEE Computer Society Press.

Nii, H. Penny. 1986. "Blackboard Systems Part One: The Blackboard Model of Problem Solving and the Evolution of Blackboard Architectures." *AI Magazine*, **7**(2): 38–53.

Ow, Peng Si. 1984. *Heuristic Knowledge and Search for Scheduling*. Ph.D. Thesis, Carnegie Mellon University.

Puget, Jean-François. 1992. "Programmation par contraintes orientée objet." *Proceedings of the Twelfth International Workshop on Expert Systems and Applications*. EC2, Nanterre, France.

Puget, Jean-François, and Patrick Albert. 1991. "PECOS: programmation par contraintes orientée objets." *Génie logiciel et systèmes experts*, (23):100–105.

Sadeh, Norman. 1991. *Look-Ahead Techniques for Micro-Opportunistic Job-Shop Scheduling*. Ph.D. Thesis, Carnegie Mellon University.

Sadeh, Norman, and Mark S. Fox. 1990. "Variable and Value Ordering Heuristics for Activity-Based Job-Shop Scheduling." *Proceedings of the Fourth International Conference on Expert Systems in Production and Operations Management*, pp. 134–144.

Shenoy, Prakash P., and Glenn R. Shafer. 1988. "Constraint Propagation." Working Paper, University of Kansas.

Smith, Stephen F. 1987. "A Constraint-Based Framework for Reactive Management of Factory Schedules." In M.D. Oliff (editor), *Intelligent Manufacturing*, Benjamin Cummings Publishers, Redwood City, Calif.

Smith, Stephen F., Mark S. Fox, and Peng Si Ow. 1986. "Constructing and Maintaining Detailed Production Plans: Investigations into the Development of Knowledge-Based Factory Scheduling Systems." *AI Magazine*, **7**(4): 45–61.

Smith, Stephen F., Peng Si Ow, Claude Le Pape, Bruce McLaren, and Nicola Muscettola. 1986. "Integrating Multiple Scheduling Perspectives to Generate Detailed Production Plans." *Proceedings of the SME Conference on Artificial Intelligence in Manufacturing. Society of Manufacturing Engineers*, New York.

Stallman, Richard M., and Gerald J. Sussman. 1977. "Forward Reasoning and Dependency-Directed Backtracking in a System for Computer-Aided Circuit Analysis." *Artificial Intelligence*, **9**(2): 135–196.

Steffen, Mitchell S. 1986. "A Survey of Artificial Intelligence-Based Scheduling Systems." *Proceedings of the Fall Industrial Engineering Conference*.

Stefik, Mark. 1980. *Planning with Constraints*. Ph.D. Thesis, Stanford University.

Van Hentenryck, Pascal. 1989. *Constraint Satisfaction in Logic Programming*. MIT Press, Cambridge, Mass.

4

MICRO-OPPORTUNISTIC SCHEDULING:

The Micro-Boss Factory Scheduler

Norman Sadeh
(Carnegie Mellon University)

4.1 INTRODUCTION

In a global market economy, the need for cost-efficient production manage-ment techniques is becoming more critical every day. In contrast with this need, current production management practice is too often characterized by low levels of due date satisfaction; high levels of inventory; and, more generally, a state of chaos in which the computer systems that are used to provide managerial guidance do not accurately reflect the current state of affairs because they rely on oversimplified and rigid models of the production environment. A major challenge for research in this area is to develop new production management techniques and tools that (1) can account more precisely for actual production management constraints and objectives, (2) are better suited for handling production contingencies, and (3) allow the user to interactively manipulate the production schedule to reflect idio-syncratic constraints and preferences not easily amenable to representation in the computer model. This chapter describes Micro-Boss, a decision-support system for factory scheduling currently under development at Carnegie Mellon University. Micro-Boss aims at generating and maintaining high-quality realistic production schedules by combining powerful predictive, reactive, and interactive scheduling capabilities. Specifically, the system relies on new *micro-opportunistic* search heu-ristics that enable it to constantly revise its scheduling strategy during the construc-tion or repair of a schedule. These search heuristics are shown to be more effective than less flexible scheduling techniques proposed in the operations research and artificial intelligence literature.

4.1.1 The Production Scheduling Problem

Production scheduling requires allocating resources (e.g., machines, tools, human operators) over time to a set of jobs while attending to a variety of constraints and objectives.

Typical constraints include

- *functional constraints* limiting the types of operations that a specific resource can perform
- *capacity constraints* restricting the number of jobs a resource can process at any given time
- *availability constraints* specifying when each resource is available (e.g., number of shifts available on a group of machines)
- *precedence constraints* existing between operations in a job, as specified in the job's process routing
- *processing time constraints* specifying how long it usually takes to perform each operation
- *setup constraints* requiring that each machine be in the proper configuration before performing a particular task (e.g., proper sets of fixtures and tools)
- *time-bound constraints* specifying for each job an earliest acceptable release date before which the job cannot start (e.g., because its raw materials cannot arrive earlier) and a due date by which ideally it should be delivered to a customer

Some of these constraints must be satisfied for a schedule to be valid (so-called non-relaxable or hard constraints). For instance, milling operations can only be performed on milling machines. Other groups of constraints are not always satisfiable and might need to be relaxed (so-called relaxable or soft constraints). For instance, due date constraints often need to be relaxed for a couple of jobs because of the limited capacity of the production facility. Availability constraints are another example of constraints that can be relaxed, by either working overtime or adding extra shifts. A good schedule is one that satisfies all hard constraints while selectively relaxing soft constraints to maximize performance along one or several metrics.

Two factors that critically influence the quality of a schedule are due date satisfaction and inventory levels. Missing a customer due date can result in tardiness penalties, loss of customer orders, delayed revenue receipts, etc. Inventory costs include interests on the costs of raw materials, direct inventory holding costs, interests on processing costs, etc. One often distinguishes between in-process inventory costs (also referred to as work-in-process inventory costs) and finished-goods inventory costs. Work-In-Process (WIP) inventory costs account for inventory costs resulting from orders that have not yet been completed, and finished-goods inventory costs result from completed orders that have not yet been shipped to customers.

Manufacturing contingencies such as machine breakdowns, late arrivals of raw materials, and variations in operation durations and yields further complicate production scheduling. In the face of contingencies, schedules need to be updated to reflect the new state of affairs. The sheer size of most factory scheduling problems precludes the generation of new schedules from scratch each time an unanticipated event occurs. In fact, most contingencies do not warrant such extreme actions and are best handled by repairing a portion of the existing schedule (Bean *et al.*, 1991).

As schedules are optimized at a more detailed level, they can also become more sensitive to disruptions and require more frequent repairs. In general, there is a limit to the amount and detail of information that one can reasonably expect to represent in a computer model. For instance, a worker's preference for performing more demanding tasks in the morning might not be worth storing in the computer model and, instead, might be best accounted for by allowing the end-user to interactively manipulate the schedule.

Even under idealized conditions such as simplified objectives (e.g., minimizing total tardiness or maximizing throughput) and deterministic assumptions, scheduling has been shown to be an NP-hard problem (Garey & Johnson, 1979; Graves, 1981; French, 1982). Uncertainty further adds to the difficulty of the problem and makes it even more impractical to look for optimal solutions. Instead, practical approaches to production scheduling are heuristic in nature. The next subsection briefly reviews earlier approaches to production scheduling; identifies some of their shortcomings; and introduces a new search paradigm, called micro-opportunistic search, that shows promise for addressing some of these shortcomings.

4.1.2 A Micro-Opportunistic Approach to Production Scheduling

To this date, the most widely used computer-based approach to production scheduling remains by far the Material Requirements Planning (MRP) or Manufacturing Resource Planning (MRP-II) approach developed in the 1970s (Orlicky, 1975; Wight, 1981; Wight, 1984). In this approach, demand for end-products, as specified in a Master Production Schedule, is exploded into time-phased requirements for component items (subassemblies, parts, raw materials, etc.) required for the production of these end-products.[1] Because their time-phasing logic relies on

---

[1] For instance, if an end-product required by the end of week 2 is obtained by assembling two sub-components, and the assembly process typically takes a week to be completed, both sub-components will be required by the end of week 1.

standard operation leadtimes that do not account for the actual load of the production facility, MRP systems often fail to produce realistic schedules. They sometimes overload the facility, thereby causing orders to be delivered late. In an attempt to alleviate this problem, MRP systems often pad the schedule by inserting generous "safety" leadtimes. These safety leadtimes tend to be rather arbitrary and produce unnecessarily large amounts of inventory. In fact, because they are often unrealistic and are not meant to be updated in real-time,[2] MRP schedules are not directly used to schedule production but, rather, to assign priorities to jobs (Panwalkar & Iskander, 1977; Vollmann, Berry & Whybark, 1988). These priorities in turn determine the order in which jobs are actually processed at each work center.

Shortcomings of the traditional MRP approach reflect limitations of computing technologies available in the 1970s. In the 1980s with the advent of more powerful computers, several more sophisticated techniques emerged (Goldratt, 1980; Fox, 1983; Ow, 1985; Adams, Balas, & Zawack, 1988; Morton *et al.*, 1988; Ow & Smith, 1988). The first and by far most publicized of these techniques is the one developed by Goldratt and his colleagues within the context of the OPT factory scheduling system (Goldratt, 1980; Jacobs, 1984; Fox, 1987). OPT demonstrated the benefits of building detailed production schedules that account for the actual load of the plant and the finite capacity of its resources ("finite scheduling" approaches). This system also underscored the potential benefits of distinguishing between bottleneck and non-bottleneck resources (Jacobs, 1984; Fox, 1987). In OPT, bottlenecks are scheduled first to optimize the throughput of the plant. Later, the production schedule is completed by compactly scheduling non-bottleneck operations to reduce inventory. The distinction between bottleneck and non-bottleneck machines was pushed one step further in the OPIS system (Smith, Fox, & Ow, 1986; Ow & Smith, 1988), as it was recognized that new bottlenecks can appear during the construction of the schedule. The OPIS scheduler combines two scheduling perspectives: a resource-centered perspective for scheduling bottleneck resources and a job-centered perspective to schedule non-bottleneck operations on a job-by-job basis. Rather than relying on its initial bottleneck analysis, OPIS typically repeats this analysis each time a resource or a job has been scheduled. This ability to detect the emergence of new bottlenecks during the construction of the schedule and revise the current scheduling strategy has been termed *opportunistic scheduling* (Ow & Smith, 1988). Nevertheless, the opportunism in this approach remains limited in the sense that it typically requires scheduling an entire bottleneck (or at least a large chunk of it) before being able to switch to another one. For this reason, we actually refer to these techniques as *macro-opportunistic*.

---

[2]MRP systems are generally run on a weekly, possibly even a monthly, basis.

In fact, variations in the job mix over time often cause different machines (or groups of machines) to be bottlenecks over different time intervals. Bottlenecks are sometimes said to "wander over time." Also, as a schedule is constructed for a bottleneck machine, a new machine can become more constraining than the original bottleneck. For instance, scheduling decisions on a bottleneck machine might require that a large number of jobs be processed on a preceding machine over a short period of time. At some point during the construction of the schedule, contention for the preceding machine might become higher than that for the original bottleneck. A scheduling technique that can only schedule large resource/job subproblems will not be able to take such considerations into account. It will overconstrain its set of alternatives before having worked on the subproblems that will most critically affect the quality of the entire schedule. This, in turn, will often result in poorer solutions. A more flexible approach would stop scheduling operations on a resource as soon as another resource is identified as more constraining. In the presence of multiple bottlenecks, such a technique would be able to shift attention from one bottleneck to another during the construction of the schedule rather than focus on the optimization of a single bottleneck at the expense of others. This chapter presents such a flexible approach to scheduling. We call it *micro-opportunistic* scheduling. In this approach, resource contention is continuously monitored during the construction of the schedule, and the problem solving effort is constantly redirected toward the most serious bottleneck resource. In its simplest form, this micro-opportunistic approach results in an *operation-centered* view of scheduling, in which each operation is considered an independent decision point and can be scheduled without requiring that other operations using the same resource or belonging to the same job be scheduled at the same time.[3]

Experimental results presented at the end of this chapter indicate that micro-opportunistic scheduling procedures often yield better schedules than less flexible bottleneck-centered approaches. Because of their flexibility, micro-opportunistic scheduling heuristics also seem particularly well suited to solving problems in which some operations have to be performed within non-relaxable time windows (Sadeh & Fox, 1991; Sadeh, Sycara, & Xiong, 1992) as well as repairing schedules in the face of contingencies. Finally, we find that they can easily be integrated in interactive systems in which manual and automatic scheduling decisions can be

---

[3] An alternative approach in which resources can be resequenced to adjust for resource schedules built further down the road is described in Adams, Balas, & Zawack (1988) and Dauzere-Peres & Lasserre (1990). This approach has been very successful at minimizing *makespan*, namely, the total duration of the schedule. This measure is closely related to the throughput of the plant but does not account for individual job due dates, tardiness costs, or inventory costs. Attempts to generalize the procedure to account for due dates seem to have been less successful so far (Serafini *et al.*, 1988). It should be pointed out that the idea of continuously reoptimizing the current partial schedule is compatible with a micro-opportunistic approach.

interleaved, thereby allowing the user to incrementally manipulate and compare alternative schedules (e.g., "What-if" type of analysis).

4.1.3 Chapter Outline

The remainder of this chapter successively reviews the predictive, reactive, and interactive capabilities of the Micro-Boss scheduling system.

Section 4.2 describes the micro-opportunistic search procedure implemented in Micro-Boss, focusing on look-ahead techniques used to measure contention and heuristics to identify and schedule critical operations. A small example illustrating the use of these techniques is provided in Section 4.3. Section 4.4 describes the reactive and interactive components of the system. Section 4.5 reports the results of an experimental study comparing Micro-Boss with several popular scheduling approaches, including coarser opportunistic schedulers, under a wide range of simulated situations. Finally, Section 4.6 briefly reviews current research efforts and summarizes the impact of this work.

4.2 A MICRO-OPPORTUNISTIC SEARCH PROCEDURE

In this section, a deterministic scheduling model is assumed in which all jobs to be scheduled are known in advance. Issues pertaining to reactive scheduling and control in the face of manufacturing contingencies such as machine breakdowns are addressed in a later section.

4.2.1 A Deterministic Scheduling Model

For the time being, we consider a deterministic scheduling problem in which a set of jobs $J = \{j_1, ..., j_n\}$ has to be scheduled on a set of physical resources $RES = \{R_1, ..., R_m\}$. Each job j_l consists of a set of operations $O^l = \{O^l_1, ..., O^l_{n_l}\}$ to be scheduled according to a process routing that specifies a partial ordering among these operations (e.g., O^l_i BEFORE O^l_j). We further assume scheduling problems with in-tree process routings, namely, process routings in which operations can have one or several direct predecessors but at most one direct successor (e.g., assembly process routings). This is by far the most common type of process routing encountered in manufacturing.

Additionally, each job j_l has an earliest acceptable release date, erd_l, a due-date, dd_l, and a latest acceptable completion date, lcd_l, where $lcd_l \geq dd_l \geq erd_l$. All jobs need to be scheduled between their earliest acceptable release date and latest acceptable completion date.[4] The earliest acceptable release date might correspond

---

[4] Notice that this formulation does not exclude infeasible problems.

to the earliest possible arrival date of raw materials. It is assumed that the actual release date (or job start date) will be determined by the schedule that is constructed. The latest acceptable completion date might correspond to a date after which the customer will refuse delivery. If such a date does not actually exist, it can always be chosen far enough in the future so that it is no longer a constraint.

Each operation O_i^l has an expected duration, du_i^l, and a start time, st_i^l (to be determined), whose domain of possible values is delimited by an earliest start time, est_i^l, and a latest start time, lst_i^l (initially derived from the job's earliest acceptable release date erd_l and latest acceptable completion date lcd_l). We assume that each operation O_i^l requires a single resource R_i^l for which there might be several alternatives in RES. The model further allows for resource availability constraints that specify the times when each resource is normally available (e.g., what the number of shifts is and whether the resource is available over the week-end). Finally, setup operations might be required before an operation can start on a machine. Examples of setup operations include changing the fixtures holding a part, loading a new part, cleaning a painting station when switching from one color to another, etc.

The objective of the scheduling system, under deterministic assumptions, is to build a schedule that satisfies the above constraints and minimizes (as much as possible) the costs incurred for missing due dates or carrying overhead inventories. These costs are briefly described below.

Costs.

Each job j_l has

- A **marginal tardiness cost, *tard$_l$*** : This is the cost incurred for each unit of time that the job is tardy (i.e., finishes past its due date). Marginal tardiness costs generally include tardiness penalties, interests on delayed profits, loss of customer goodwill, etc.[5] The tardiness cost of job j_1 in a given schedule is

$$TARD_l = tard_l \times Max(0, C_l - dd_l) \tag{1}$$

  where $C_l = st_{n_l}^l + du_{n_l}^l$ is the completion date of job j_1 in that schedule, assuming that $O_{n_l}^l$ is the last operation in job j_l.

- **Marginal in-process and finished-goods inventory costs**: In our model, each operation O_i^l can incrementally introduce its own non-negative marginal inventory cost, inv_i^l. Typically, the first operation in a job introduces marginal inventory costs that correspond to interest on the costs of raw materials, interest on processing costs (for that first operation), and marginal holding costs.

---

[5] In this model, inventory costs incurred after the due date are not included in the tardiness costs but, rather, in the inventory costs described below.

Downstream operations[6] introduce additional marginal inventory costs, such as interest on processing costs or interest on the costs of additional raw materials required by these operations. The total inventory cost for a job j_l in a given schedule is

$$INV_l = \sum_{i=1}^{n_l} inv_i^l \times [Max(C_l, dd_l) - st_i^l]$$

(2)

This cost accounts for both work-in-progress and finished-goods inventory costs.[7]

The total cost of a schedule is obtained by summing the cost of each job schedule:

$$Schedule\ Cost = \sum_{l=1}^{n} (TARD_l + INV_l)$$

(3)

A Small Example Figure 4-1 depicts a small scheduling problem with four jobs that will be used in this section to illustrate the behavior of the micro-opportunistic scheduling heuristics implemented in Micro-Boss. Each square box represents an operation and is labeled by the name of this operation (e.g., O_1^1), its (expected) duration (e.g., $du_1^1 = 2$), and the resource it requires (e.g., $R_1^1 = R_1$). In this simple example, each operation is assumed to require a single resource, for which there are no substitutes. The arrows represent precedence constraints. For instance, job j_1 has five operations $O_1^1, O_2^1,..., O_5^1$. O_1^1 has to be performed before O_2^1, O_2^1 before O_4^1, etc. The other arcs in the graph represent capacity constraints that require that each resource be allocated to only one operation at a time. There is a capacity constraint between each pair of operations that require the same resource. Notice that R_2 is the only resource required by four operations (one from each job). Notice also that in three out of four jobs (namely, j_1, j_3, and j_4), the operation requiring R_2 is one of the job's longest operations. Consequently, resource R_2 can be expected to be the main bottleneck of the problem. We will see that to some extent, resource R_1 constitutes a secondary bottleneck.

The earliest acceptable release dates, due dates, and latest acceptable completion dates of the jobs are provided in Table 4-1 along with the marginal tardiness and inventory costs of these jobs.

---

[6] An operation O_i^k is said to be downstream (upstream) of another operation O_j^k within its job if O_i^k is a direct or indirect successor (predecessor) of O_j^k in that job, as defined by the job's process routing.

[7] Note that in this deterministic model, minimizing work-in-progress inventory costs is equivalent to minimizing job leadtimes or flowtimes.

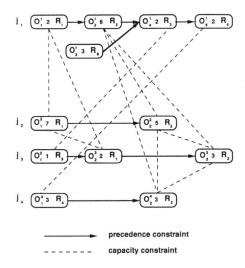

Figure 4-1: A simple job shop problem with four jobs. Each node is labeled by the operation that it represents, its duration, and the resource that it requires. Solid lines indicate precedence constraint; dashed lines indicate capacity constraint.

Table 4-1: Earliest acceptable release dates, due dates, latest acceptable completion dates, and marginal costs.

Job j_l	erd_l	dd_l	lcd_l	$tard_l$	inv_1^l	inv_2^l	inv_3^l	inv_4^l	inv_5^l
j_1	0	12	20	20	2	1	2	0	0
j_2	0	14	20	20	5	0	-	-	-
j_3	0	9	20	5	1	0	0	-	-
j_4	0	18	20	10	1	0	-	-	-

4.2.2 Overview of the Search Procedure

In Micro-Boss, each operation is considered an independent decision point. Any operation can be scheduled at any time if deemed appropriate by the system. There is no obligation to simultaneously schedule other operations upstream or downstream within the same job, nor is there any obligation to schedule other operations competing for the same resource.

Micro-Boss proceeds by iteratively selecting an operation to be scheduled and a reservation (i.e., a resource/time interval) to be assigned to that operation. Every time an operation is scheduled, a new *search state* is created, where new constraints are added to account for the reservation assigned to that operation. A consistency enforcing procedure then takes care of updating the set of remaining possible reservations of each unscheduled operation. If an unscheduled operation is found to have no possible reservations left, a *deadend state* has been reached, in which case the system needs to *backtrack* (i.e., it needs to undo some earlier reservation assignments to be able to complete the schedule). If the search state does not appear to be a deadend, the system moves on and looks for a new operation to schedule and a reservation to assign to that operation.

To enhance search efficiency[8] and positive high-quality schedules, Micro-Boss interleaves search with the application of consistency-enforcing mechanisms and a set of look-ahead techniques that help decide which operation to schedule next (*operation ordering heuristic*) and which reservation to assign to that operation (*reservation ordering heuristic*).

1. **Consistency Enforcing/Checking:** Consistency enforcing techniques prune the search space by inferring new constraints resulting from earlier reservation assignments (Mackworth & Freuder, 1985; Sadeh, 1991). By constantly accounting for earlier scheduling decisions, these techniques reduce the chances of reaching a deadend (i.e., a partial schedule that cannot be completed without backtracking). Simultaneously, by allowing for the early detection of deadend states, these techniques limit the amount of work wasted in the exploration of fruitless alternatives.

2. **Look-Ahead Analysis**: A two-step look-ahead procedure is applied in each search state, which first optimizes reservation assignments within each job and then, for each resource, computes contention between jobs over time. Resource/time intervals where contention is the highest help identify the critical operation to be scheduled next (*operation ordering heuristic*). Reservations for that operation are then ranked according to their ability to minimize the costs incurred by the jobs contending for the critical resource (*reservation ordering heuristic*). By constantly redirecting its effort toward the most serious conflicts, the system is able to build schedules that are closer to the global optimum. Simultaneously, because the scheduling strategy is aimed at reducing job contention as rapidly as possible, chances of reaching deadend states tend to quickly subside too.

The opportunism in Micro-Boss results from the ability of the system to constantly *revise its search strategy and redirect its effort toward the scheduling of the operation that appears to be the most critical in the current search state*. This degree of opportunism differs from the one displayed by earlier approaches where scheduling entities were large resource/job subproblems (Ow & Smith, 1988; Col-

---

[8]We define search efficiency as the ratio of the number of operations to be scheduled over the number of search states generated. If the number of search states generated to build the schedule is equal to the number of operations, search efficiency is equal to 1.

linot, Le Pape, & Pinoteau, 1988), i.e., where large resource/job subproblems had to be scheduled before the system could revise its scheduling strategy.

Concretely, given a scheduling problem such as the one described in Figure 4-1, Micro-Boss starts in a search state in which no operation has been scheduled yet[9] and proceeds according to the following steps:

1. If all operations have been scheduled, then stop; else go on to 2.

2. Apply the **consistency enforcing** procedure.

3. If a deadend is detected, then **backtrack**; else go on to 4.

4. If one or more operations were found to have only one possible reservation left, then schedule these operations (creating a new search state for each one). If all operations have been scheduled, then stop; else go on to 5.

5. Perform a **look-ahead** analysis: Rank the possible reservations of each unscheduled operation according to how well they minimize the costs of the job to which the operation belongs (step 1), and evaluate resource contention over time (step 2).

6. Select the next operation to be scheduled (i.e., **operation ordering** heuristic).

7. Select a reservation for that operation (i.e., **reservation ordering** heuristic).

8. Create a **new search state** by adding the new reservation assignment to the current partial schedule. Go back to 1.

As in other constraint-directed scheduling systems (LePape & Smith, 1987), the consistency enforcing procedure used in Micro-Boss (1) maintains for each unscheduled operation a pair of earliest/latest possible start times and (2) marks as unavailable those resource/time intervals allocated to already scheduled operations. Additionally, the consistency-enforcing procedure used in Micro-Boss accounts for resource/time intervals that are absolutely needed by unscheduled operations. Figure 4-2 displays an example of an unscheduled operation O_i^k whose earliest and latest possible reservations overlap. Whichever reservation this operation is ultimately assigned, it will always need time interval $[lst_i^k, eft_i^k]$. Accordingly, the Micro-Boss consistency procedure prunes the set of remaining possible reservations of other unscheduled operations requiring that resource by removing all those reservations that overlap with time interval $[lst_i^k, eft_i^k]$.[10]

---

[9] Alternatively, Micro-Boss can also complete a partial schedule; in which case, the initial search state corresponds to the initial partial schedule. A description of reactive and interactive capabilities of the system is provided in Section 4.4.

[10] This differs from an earlier version of the system (Sadeh, 1991) in which resource/time intervals needed by unscheduled operations were only used to detect conflicts. In this earlier version, a conflict would be detected when two or more unscheduled operations needed overlapping resource/time intervals. Rather than waiting for such conflicts to arise, our new consistency procedure efficiently prevents

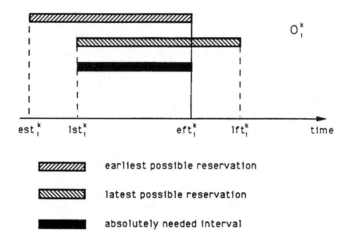

$$O_i^k$$

est$_i^k$ lst$_i^k$ eft$_i^k$ lft$_i^k$ time

earliest possible reservation

latest possible reservation

absolutely needed interval

Figure 4-2:   An example of an unscheduled operation that absolutely needs a resource/time interval.

Results presented in this chapter were obtained using a simple chronological backtracking scheme. Experimentation with more sophisticated backtracking schemes is described in Sadeh, Sycara, & Xiong (1992).

The remainder of this section gives a more detailed description of the look-ahead analysis and the operation/reservation ordering heuristics used in Micro-Boss. Further details on these techniques, as well as other aspects of the system, can be found in Sadeh (1991).

4.2.3 Look-Ahead Analysis in Micro-Boss

4.2.3.1 Optimizing Critical Conflicts First

If all jobs could be scheduled optimally (i.e., just-in-time), there would be no scheduling problem. Generally, this is not the case. Jobs typically have conflicting resource requirements. The look-ahead analysis carried out by Micro-Boss in each search state aims at helping the scheduling system focus its effort on those conflicts that currently appear most critical. A critical conflict is one that will require an important trade-off, i.e., a trade-off that will significantly impact the quality of the *entire* schedule. By first focusing on critical conflicts, Micro-Boss ensures that it has as many options as possible to optimize these conflicts. As illustrated by a trace provided in the next section, once critical trade-offs have been worked out, the remaining unscheduled operations tend to become more decoupled and, hence,

---

such conflicts from occurring, thereby further reducing backtracking. A generalized version of this procedure is used for parallel machines.

easier to optimize.[11] As contention subsides, so does the chance of needing to backtrack. In other words, by constantly redirecting search toward those trade-offs that appear most critical, Micro-Boss is expected to produce better schedules and simultaneously keep backtracking at a low level.

More specifically, a two-step look-ahead procedure is applied to each search state. This procedure first optimizes reservation assignments within each job and then, for each resource, computes contention between jobs over time. The so-called *demand profiles* produced by these computations help identify operations whose good reservations (as identified in the first step) conflict with the good reservations of other operations. These operations define the critical conflicts on which Micro-Boss works first.

This two-step look-ahead analysis is further detailed below.

4.2.3.2 Step 1: Reservation Optimization within a Job

In order to measure contention between the resource requirements of unscheduled operations, Micro-Boss keeps track of the best start times that remain available to each unscheduled operation within its job. Additionally, the system implicitly maintains, for each remaining possible start time τ of each unscheduled operation O_i^k, a function $mincost_i^k(\tau)$ that indicates the minimum additional costs that would be incurred by job j_k (the job to which O_i^k belongs) if O_i^k were to start at $st_i^k = \tau$ rather than at one of its best possible start times. By definition, if $st_i^k = \tau$ is one of the best start times that remain available to O_i^k within its job, then $mincost_i^k(\tau) = 0$. Rather than explicitly maintaining *mincost* functions, Micro-Boss simply maintains for each unscheduled operation O_i^k (1) an apparent marginal tardiness cost, $app-bid_i^k$, that approximates the cost incurred by *job j_k* for each unit of time that O_i^k starts past its latest best start time and (2) an apparent marginal inventory cost, $app-inv_i^k$, that approximates the cost incurred by *job j_k* for each unit of time that O_i^k starts before its earliest best start time. These costs are updated in each search state to account for earlier scheduling decisions, using a set of efficient propagation procedures described in Sadeh (1991).

4.2.3.3 Step 2: Building Demand Profiles to Identify Critical Resource/Time Intervals

In Micro-Boss, critical conflicts are identified as groups of operations whose good reservations (within their jobs) conflict with each other. The importance of a conflict depends on the number of operations that are competing for the same resource, the amount of temporal overlap between the requirements of these operations, the number of alternative reservations still available to each of these conflict-

---

[11] This is similar to the way bottleneck schedules drive other scheduling decisions in OPT.

ing operations and their costs, as determined by the *mincost* functions computed in step 1.

To identify critical conflicts, Micro-Boss uses a probabilistic framework in which each remaining possible start time τ of an unscheduled operation O_i^l is assigned a *subjective probability* $\sigma_i^l(\tau)$ to be selected for that operation in the final schedule. Possible start times with lower *mincost* values are assigned a larger probability, thereby reflecting our expectation that they will yield better schedules. Given these start time probability distributions, the probability that an unscheduled operation O_i^l uses its resource[12] at time t, which is referred to as the *individual demand* of O_i^l for R_i^l, is

$$D_i^l(t) = \sum_{t - du_i^l < \tau \leq t} \sigma_i^l(\tau)$$

$$(4)$$

where du_i^l is the duration of O_i^l. $D_i^l(t)$ is also a (subjective) measure of the reliance of operation O_i^l on the availability of its resource at time t. By adding the individual demands of all unscheduled operations requiring a given resource, say R_k, the system obtains an *aggregate demand profile*, $D_{R_k}^{aggr}(t)$, that indicates contention between (all) unscheduled operations for that resource R_k as a function of time:

$$D_{R_k}^{aggr}(t) = \sum D_i^l(t)$$

$$(5)$$

where the summation is carried over all unscheduled operations that need resource R_k.

Figure 4-3 displays $\sigma_2^2(\tau)$, the start time distribution of operation O_2^2 in the problem defined in Figure 4-1. This start time distribution is depicted in the initial search state, where all operations still have to be scheduled. In this search state, start time $st_2^2 = 9$ is the best possible start time for O_2^2: it corresponds to a just-in-time schedule of job j_2. Later start times have a lower subjective probability because they would force the job to finish after its due date. Earlier start times are also suboptimal because they would produce additional inventory. In this example, the marginal tardiness cost of job j_2, $tard_2 = 20$, is four times larger than the marginal inventory cost introduced by operation O_1^2, $inv_1^2 = 5$. Accordingly, $\sigma_2^2(\tau)$ decreases faster for $\tau > 9$ than $\tau < 9$.

---

[12] For the sake of simplicity, we assume here that each operation requires a single resource for which there are no alternatives. The construction of demand profiles can easily be generalized to deal with parallel machines by building profiles for entire groups of machines and normalizing them based on their remaining available capacities over time.

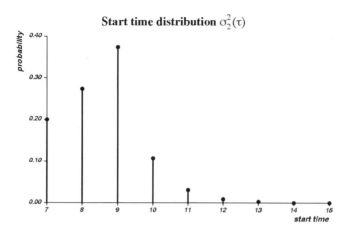

Figure 4-3: Start time distribution $\sigma_2^2(\tau)$ for operation O_2^2 in the initial search state for the problem defined in Figure 4-1.

Figure 4-4 displays the individual demand profiles of the four operations requiring resource R_2. These demand profiles represent the subjective probability that each one of these operations uses resource R_2 as a function of time. The aggregate demand for resource R_2 is obtained by summing these four individual demands over time. The individual demands of operations O_3^3 and O_2^4 are quite uniform because these two operations have relatively low apparent marginal costs (see the marginal tardiness and inventory costs of job j_3 and job j_4 in Table 4-1). In contrast, operations O_2^1 and O_2^2, which have larger apparent marginal costs, have individual demands that are concentrated around their best reservations.

Similar computations can be performed for each of the five resources in the problem. The resulting aggregate demands (in the initial search state) are displayed in Figure 4-5. As expected, resource R_2 appears to be the most contended for. The aggregate demand for that resource is well above 1.0 over a large time interval, with a peak at 1.79. Resource R_1 appears to be a potential bottleneck at the beginning of the problem, with a demand peaking at 1.52. Whether R_1 will actually be an auxiliary bottleneck or not cannot be determined directly from the curves displayed in Figure 4-5. Instead, the system needs to update these curves in each search state to account for earlier decisions. It could be the case that as operations requiring R_2 are scheduled, the aggregate demand for R_1 becomes smoother. In this example, this is not the case. On the contrary, as operations are scheduled on resource R_2, some operations on resource R_1 end up with only one possible reservation and need to be immediately scheduled, as indicated by the trace provided in Section 4.4.

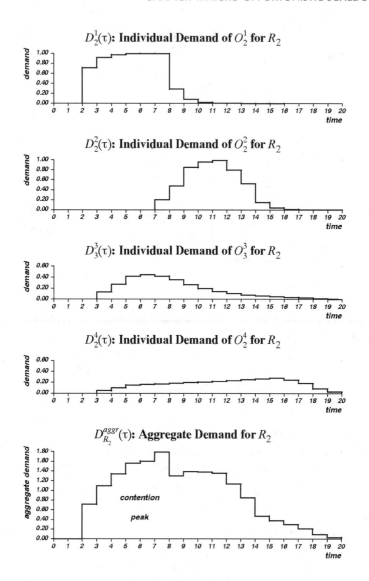

Figure 4-4:   Building R_2's aggregate demand profile in the initial search state.

4.2.4 Operation Selection

Critical operations are identified as operations whose good reservations (as identified in the first step of the look-ahead analysis) conflict with the good reservations of other operations. The largest peak in the aggregate demand profiles

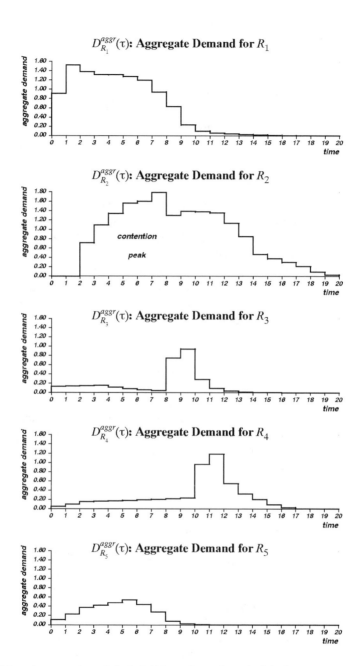

Figure 4-5: Aggregate demands in the initial search state for each of the five resources.

determines the next conflict (or micro-bottleneck) to be optimized; the operation with the largest reliance on the availability of the corresponding resource/time interval (i.e., the operation with the largest individual contribution to the peak) is selected to be scheduled next. Indeed, this operation is the one whose good reservations are the most likely to become unavailable if other operations contending for the current micro-bottleneck were scheduled first.

In the example introduced earlier, the largest demand peak is the one for resource R_2 over interval [4, 8]. Figure 4-6 displays the aggregate demand for resource R_2 together with the individual demands of the four operations requiring this resource. The operation with the largest contribution to the demand peak is O_2^1. Therefore, this operation is selected to be scheduled next. This is no real surprise: O_2^1 belongs to one of the two jobs in the problem that have a high marginal tardiness cost ($tard_1 = 20$). While any delay in starting job j_1 will result in large tardiness costs, job j_3 (i.e., the job with the next highest contribution) can tolerate a small delay and is subject to lower tardiness penalties.

The computation of demand profiles, as described in Section 4.2.3.3, can be quite expensive when performed for each resource in each search state over the entire scheduling horizon. Micro-Boss can avoid this problem by incrementally maintaining a set of *rough* demand profiles for each resource (or group of identical resources). These rough demand profiles use a much coarser time granularity and are obtained by splitting the demand of each unscheduled operation into two components. One component (50% of the operation's total demand in the current implementation[13]) is evenly spread between the start and end times of the latest best reservation of the operation, while the second component (the remaining 50% of the operation's demand) is evenly spread between the earliest start time and latest finish time of the operation. Rough demand profiles can be quickly updated as the system moves from one search state to the next and are used in each search state to identify a small number of critical resource/time intervals over which the more detailed demand profiles described in Section 4.2.3.3 are then constructed.

4.2.5 Reservation Selection

To schedule the critical operation identified in Section 4.2.4, the system attempts to identify a reservation (for the critical operation) that will reduce as much as possible the costs incurred by the job to which that operation belongs and the other jobs with which that operation competes. This is approximated as a single-machine or *parallel-machine* early/tardy scheduling problem in which operations scheduled past their best start times incur penalties determined by their apparent marginal tardiness costs, while operations scheduled before their best start

---

[13] The total demand of an operation is equal to its duration.

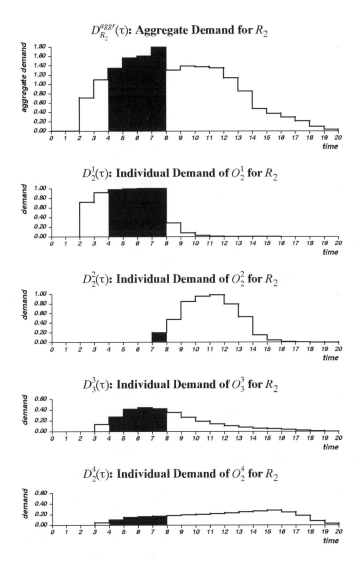

Figure 4-6: Operation selection in the initial search state.

times incur earliness penalties as determined by their apparent marginal inventory costs (Baker & Scudder, 1990; Sadeh, 1991). In the experiments reported at the end of this chapter, several variations of a single-machine early/tardy procedure developed by Ow and Morton (Ow & Morton, 1989; Sadeh, 1991) were successively run, and the single-machine schedule with the lowest cost was used to determine the reservation assigned to the critical operation. More recently, a new scheduling heuristic has been developed to solve problems with setups (Li & Sadeh, 1993).

4.3 A SMALL EXAMPLE

Micro-Boss is implemented in C++ with an X^{TM}/Motif^{TM} interface. The small example used throughout this chapter requires less than 0.1 CPU seconds on a DECstation^{TM} 5000/200 running under UNIX^{TM}.[14] An edited trace of this example is given in Figure 4-7.

In this example, the scheduling procedure first focuses on the scheduling of the main bottleneck resource, R_2. However, as it schedules operations on this resource, the system can also jump to other resources and consolidate the schedule by allocating reservations to critical operations requiring these other resources. In this small example where operations have a small number of possible reservations, this is mainly accomplished through the identification of operations that have only one possible reservation left (e.g., the scheduling of O_1^1 or O_1^2). In general, this can be done based on the contention analysis performed by Micro-Boss (e.g., the identification of a critical conflict on resource R_4 at depth 6). As a result, the system jumps back and forth between several resources, always trying to focus on what appears to be the most critical decision.

The *average expected demand* displayed in each search state is the average demand for the critical demand peak; and the *average contribution* is the percentage of the total demand for the peak that comes from the critical operation. When search starts, contention is relatively high, as illustrated by the average expected demand for the critical peak (1.58 at depth 0; 1.73 at depth 2, and 1.50 at depth 4) and the relatively low contribution of the critical operation to the demand for the peak (e.g., O_2^1 contributes only 63% of the total demand for the peak in the initial search state, O_2^2 57% at depth 2, etc.) indicating that the resource requirements of the critical operation compete with those of several other operations. During construction of the schedule, the average demand for the critical peak progressively decreases[15] and the critical operation progressively contributes a larger percentage of the demand for the critical peak. This indicates that contention between unscheduled operations decreases. After half of the operations have been scheduled (depth 7), contention has totally disappeared: the critical operation is the only one to contribute to the demand for the peak. The resource requirements of the operations

---

[14] X-Window System is a registered trademark of the Massachusetts Institute of Technology. Motif is a registered trademark of the Open Software Foundation, Inc. UNIX is a registered trademark of UNIX Systems Laboratories, Inc. DECstation is a registered trademark of the Digital Equipment Corporation.

[15] Remember that the demand peak corresponds to the interval of highest contention in the current search state.

>> Depth: 0, Number of states visited: 0
Critical demand peak:
R_2 between 4 and 8, Avg. expected demand: 1.58
Critical Operation: O_2^1, Avg. contrib.: 63%
O_2^1 is scheduled between 2 and 8 on R_2

>> Depth: 1, Number of states visited: 1
O_1^1 has only one possible reservation left
and is scheduled between 0 and 2 on R_1

>> Depth: 2, Number of states visited: 2
Critical demand peak:
R_2 between 10 and 14, Avg. expected demand: 1.73
Critical Operation: O_2^2, Avg. contrib.: 57%
O_2^2 is scheduled between 9 and 14 on R_2

>> Depth: 3, Number of states visited: 3
O_1^2 has only one possible reservation left
and is scheduled between 2 and 9 on R_1

>> Depth: 4, Number of states visited: 4
Critical demand peak:
R_2 between 14 and 18, Avg. expected demand: 1.50
Critical Operation: O_2^4, Avg. contrib.: 50%
O_2^4 is scheduled between 14 and 17 on R_2

>> Depth: 5, Number of states visited: 5
O_3^3 has only one possible reservation left
and is scheduled between 17 and 20 on R_2

>> Depth: 6, Number of states visited: 6
Critical demand peak:
R_4 between 10 and 12, Avg. expected demand: 1.12
Critical Operation: O_5^1, Avg. contrib.: 73%
O_5^1 is scheduled between 10 and 12 on R_4

>> Depth: 7, Number of states visited: 7
O_4^1 has only one possible reservation left
and is scheduled between 8 and 10 on R_3

Figure 4-7:   An edited trace.

```
>> Depth: 8, Number of states visited: 8
   Critical demand peak:
```
R_5 between 5 and 8, Avg. expected demand: 0.95

Critical Operation: O_3^1, Avg. contrib.: 100%

O_3^1 is scheduled between 5 and 8 on R_5

```
>> Depth: 9, Number of states visited: 9
   Critical demand peak:
```
R_4 between 7 and 9, Avg. expected demand: 0.96

Critical Operation: O_1^4, Avg. contrib.: 100%

O_1^4 is scheduled between 7 and 10 on R_4

```
>> Depth: 10, Number of states visited: 10
   Critical demand peak:
```
R_1 between 14 and 17, Avg. expected demand: 0.65

Critical Operation: O_2^3, Avg. contrib.: 100%

O_2^3 is scheduled between 15 and 17 on R_1

```
>> Depth: 11, Number of states visited: 11
   Critical demand peak:
```
R_3 between 13 and 15, Avg. expected demand: 0.52

Critical Operation: O_1^3, Avg. contrib.: 100%

O_1^3 scheduled between 14 and 15 on R_3

```
>> Depth: 12, Number of states visited: 12
   Schedule Completed
   Total Cost: 180
   Total Tardiness Cost: 55
   Total Inventory Cost: 125
   Avg. Weighted Tardiness: 1.0
   Avg. Weighted Flowtime (WIP): 10.33
   Avg. Weighted Inventory (Flowtime + Earliness): 10.42
   CPU time: 0.067 seconds
```

Figure 4-7:   (concluded)

that still need to be scheduled no longer compete with each other. This is not particular to this example: The same has been observed on all the problems we have run and suggests that the operation ordering heuristic implemented in Micro-Boss is indeed very effective at redirecting search towards the most serious conflicts.

Notice also that no backtracking was necessary to schedule this problem. The resulting schedule is displayed in Figure 4-8.

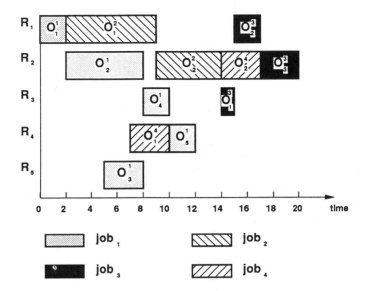

Figure 4-8: Gantt chart of the final schedule produced by Micro-Boss.

4.4 REACTIVE AND INTERACTIVE SCHEDULING IN MICRO-BOSS

Manufacturing is a process often fraught with contingencies and subject to a multitude of constraints and preferences that are not always easily amenable to representation in a computer model.

Operation durations tend to vary, machines break down, raw materials fail to arrive on time, new customer orders arrive, others get cancelled, etc. Many ad hoc constraints and preferences that vary over time, such as the preference of a worker on a specific day to perform more demanding tasks in the morning, might be best accounted for via interactive manipulation of the schedule. This section briefly outlines reactive and interactive scheduling capabilities currently under development in the Micro-Boss decision support system.

4.4.1 Reactive Scheduling and Control Issues

Small disruptions, such as minor deviations in operation durations, often do not warrant major modifications to the schedule. However, as the effects of small disruptions accumulate or as more severe disruptions occur, such as long machine breakdowns, it is sometimes desirable to reoptimize the schedule from a more global perspective. Accordingly, in Micro-Boss, schedule disruptions can be handled at two levels based on their severity and the required response time:

1. **Control level**: Small disruptions that require fast responses are handled by simple control heuristics such as *"process the operation with the earliest scheduled start time first"* or *"when a machine is down, reroute critical jobs to equivalent machines, if any."*

2. **Scheduling level**: In the face of more severe deviations from the schedule, the control level calls upon the Micro-Boss scheduling module to repair/reoptimize the schedule from a more global perspective, while possibly continuing to attend to immediate decisions.

Determining when disruptions should be handed over to the scheduling level can be tricky. Decisions at the control level tend to be rather fast because they are based on local heuristics with a very restricted view of the problem. Decisions at the scheduling level tend to produce better repairs but take longer because they are based on more global considerations. There is generally a trade-off between the responsiveness of the overall system and the amount of reoptimization that can be performed. In manufacturing environments where disruptions are very frequent, a large number of disruptions might need to be handled at the control level, whereas in less chaotic environments, a larger proportion of disruptions might be processed at the scheduling level. A similar two-tier approach to handling schedule disruptions was first proposed by Smith, Keng, & Kempf (1990). Within this approach, the scheduling level restricts the set of alternatives to be considered at the control level by imposing a legal temporal window of execution on each operation. If the controller cannot respect an operation's window of execution, it has to request a new schedule (and a new set of execution windows) from the scheduler. One objective of ongoing research in reactive scheduling and control within Micro-Boss is to assess the merits of different coordination regimes between the scheduling and control levels.

Schedule repair in Micro-Boss differs from recent approaches that emphasized the use of iterative repair heuristics (Minton *et al.*, 1990; Smith *et al.*, 1990; Zweben, Davis, & Deale, 1991). In the process of resolving schedule conflicts, iterative repair heuristics are allowed to introduce new conflicts, which, in turn, require more repairs. This iterative behavior can sometimes lead to myopic decisions and can potentially become expensive. In contrast to these approaches, schedule repair in Micro-Boss attempts to take a more global view of the repair problem and capitalize on the strengths of the micro-opportunistic search procedures in the system. Concretely, schedule repair in Micro-Boss is performed in two phases: (1) a set of operations that need to be rescheduled is identified and all the operations in this set are unscheduled, and (2) the scheduling problem consisting of all these unscheduled operations and the constraints imposed on them by operations that have already been executed or have not been unscheduled is passed to the micro-opportunistic scheduling module described in the previous sections. The set of operations unscheduled in the first phase is selected in such a way that the resulting scheduling problem (i.e., the one solved in phase 2) generally admits a solution. In the event that a feasible schedule could not be built in phase 2, the system needs to return to phase 1 and undo a larger number of operations. In practice, this situation can generally be avoided by unscheduling slightly more operations than apparently required. Although the resulting search space is slightly larger and, hence, might require longer to be explored, it might also contain better repair solutions. Details of conflict propagation heuristics used in Micro-Boss to determine which (and how many) operations to reschedule in the presence of contingencies such as machine breakdowns can be found in Sadeh, Otsuka, & Schnelbach (1993).

4.4.2 Interactive Scheduling with Micro-Boss

Although the combinatorial complexity of factory scheduling problems is best handled by automatic scheduling procedures such as the ones described earlier in this chapter, ad hoc scheduling constraints and preferences that occur very infrequently or change over time are often best accounted for through interactive manipulation of the schedule. Interactive user support should also include mechanisms that help the user identify sources of inefficiency in the schedule (e.g., tardy orders, overloaded resources, etc.) and ways of correcting these inefficiencies (e.g., adding overtime on the set of resources, rerouting some orders, etc.). Through interaction with the system, the user should be able to explore "what-if" scenarios and weigh different alternatives (e.g., decide whether to complete some jobs past their due dates or work overtime).

The Micro-Boss decision support system enables the end-user to interleave both manual and automatic (micro-opportunistic) scheduling decisions, analyze, edit, save, and compare complete and partial schedules.

Interactive schedule manipulation is performed using an interactive Gantt chart that displays each resource along with the operations to which that resource has been allocated over time (Figure 4-9). Schedule manipulation is performed under the supervision of the Micro-Boss consistency enforcing module, which enforces consistency with earlier scheduling decisions (manual and automatic). Partial or complete schedules can be saved and compared against each other along different metrics, including total schedule cost, average weighted tardiness, average weighted earliness, Work-In-Process, and Work-In-System (which accounts for both Work-In-Process inventory and finished goods inventory). Optimistic estimates are used for partial schedules for which these metrics cannot be computed exactly. By interleaving both manual and automatic scheduling decisions and saving/restoring partial and complete schedules, the user can compare the impact of alternative scheduling decisions and perform "what-if" analyses.

Figure 4-9 shows a typical view of the Micro-Boss user interface. In this example, the user is getting ready to modify the working schedule displayed in the

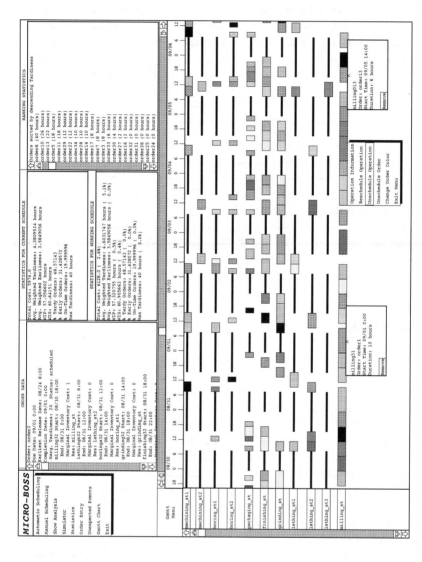

Figure 4-9: The Micro-Boss user interface allows for interactive manipulation of schedules. By interleaving both manual and automatic scheduling decisions, saving and comparing alternative schedules, the user can easily assess different trade-offs and locally impose ad hoc constraints or preferences that are not easily amenable to representation in the computer model.

Gantt chart by manually unscheduling an operation on which he/she just clicked. Statistics for the working schedule are compared with statistics for the "current" schedule, namely, the schedule currently in force in the system. These statistics are continuously updated as the user edits the schedule. In another window, the user can check information about specific orders (*order2* in this example). In yet another window, he/she has elected to rank orders based on their tardiness in the working schedule. Alternative metrics to rank jobs or resources can be selected in the statistics menu (e.g., cost, tardiness, flowtime, resource utilization, etc.). By clicking on boxes displayed in the Gantt chart, the user can directly obtain information on specific operations (e.g., information on operation *milling31*), manually unschedule and reschedule operations (by moving the corresponding box in the Gantt chart), unschedule jobs, or highlight a job by changing its color. The Gantt menu also allows for zooming in and out of the Gantt chart, unscheduling specific resource/time intervals, displaying contention measures over time for different resources, etc.

4.5 PERFORMANCE EVALUATION

Experimental studies performed with an initial version of Micro-Boss implemented using Knowledge Craft[TM] [16] were reported in Sadeh (1991). These experiments studied the performance of the system under a variety of scheduling conditions and different cost assumptions. They included comparisons with combinations of popular priority dispatch rules and release policies advocated in the Operations Research literature, comparisons with coarser bottleneck-centered approaches to scheduling described in the Artificial Intelligence literature, and a comparison with a variation of Micro-Boss in which resource contention was measured using unbiased demand profiles.

In this chapter, we report the results of a similar study performed on the same set of scheduling problems with a more recent version of the system written in C++. At the present time (January 1994), the new version of Micro-Boss is two orders of magnitude faster than the version described in Sadeh (1991) on this set of problems, mainly because of the C++ reimplementation of the system and the use of rough demand profiles to identify small areas of high contention over which more detailed profiles are then constructed (see Section 4.2.4). The new system also uses a more powerful consistency enforcing procedure (see Section 4.2.2) than the original version, which almost eliminates the need for backtracking on the experiments reported in this chapter. Finally, the new system also produces sched

---

[16] Knowledge Craft is a registered trademark of Carnegie Group, Inc.

Table 4-2:   Characteristics of the eight problem sets.

Problem Sets			
Problem Set	**Number of Bottlenecks**	**Avg. Due Date**	**Due Date Range**
1	1	Loose	Wide
2	1	Loose	Narrow
3	1	Tight	Wide
4	1	Tight	Narrow
5	2	Loose	Wide
6	2	Loose	Narrow
7	2	Tight	Wide
8	2	Tight	Narrow

ules that are significantly better than those obtained with the earlier version. This improvement in schedule quality is mainly attributed to the use of a more accurate set of propagation heuristics to update the best remaining start time(s) of unscheduled operations during construction of the schedule and the use of a stronger bias in the construction of demand profiles.

The results reported in Table 4-2 were obtained on a suite of 80 scheduling problems initially described in Sadeh (1991). The suite is made of eight sets of scheduling problems obtained by adjusting three parameters to cover a wide range of scheduling conditions. The three parameters are the following: an average due date parameter (tight versus loose average due date), a due date range parameter (narrow versus wide range of due dates), and a parameter controlling the number of major bottlenecks (in this case, one or two). For each parameter combination, a set of 10 scheduling problems was randomly generated (see Table 4-2), thereby resulting in a total of 80 scheduling problems (10 problems × 2 average due date values × 2 due date ranges × 2 bottleneck configurations). Each problem requires scheduling 20 jobs on 5 resources for a total of 100 operations. Marginal tardiness costs in these problems were set to be, on the average, five times larger than marginal inventory costs to model a situation where tardiness costs dominate but inventory costs are non-negligible.[17] A comprehensive description of these scheduling problems can be found in Sadeh (1991).

Micro-Boss required between 10 and 15 CPU seconds to schedule each problem on a DECstation[TM] 5000/200. Nearly all problems were solved without any backtracking.

---

[17] Experiments under different cost assumptions were also reported in Sadeh (1991).

4.5.1   Comparison against Combinations of Priority Dispatch Rules and Release Policies

In a first set of experiments, Micro-Boss was compared with the best of a set of 39 combinations of popular priority dispatch rules and release policies. The priority dispatch rules used in these experiments were of two types:

1. a set of five priority dispatch rules that have been reported to be particularly good at reducing tardiness under various scheduling conditions (Vepsalainen & Morton, 1987): the Weighted Shortest Processing Time (WSPT) rule; the Earliest Due Date (EDD) rule; the Slack per Remaining Processing Time (S/RPT) rule; and two parametric rules, the Weighted Cost OVER Time (WCOVERT) rule and the Apparent Tardiness Cost (ATC) rule

2. an exponential version of the parametric early/tardy dispatch rule recently developed by Ow and Morton (Ow & Morton, 1989; Morton *et al.*, 1988) and referred to below as EXP-ET (this rule differs from the other five in that it can explicitly account for both tardiness and inventory costs)

EXP-ET was successively run in combination with an immediate release policy (IM-REL) that allows each job to be released immediately and with an intrinsic release policy that only releases jobs when their priorities become positive, as suggested in Morton *et al.* (1988). The other five dispatch rules were successively run in combination with two release policies: an immediate release policy (IM-REL) and the Average Queue Time release policy (AQT) described in Morton *et al.* (1988). AQT is a parametric release policy that estimates queuing time as a multiple of the average job duration (the look-ahead parameter serving as the multiple). The release of a job is determined by offsetting the job's due date by the sum of the job's total duration and the estimated queuing time. Combinations of release policies and dispatch rules with a look-ahead parameter were successively run with four different parameter values that generally appeared to produce the best schedules. By combining these different dispatch rules, release policies, and parameter settings, a total of 39 heuristics[18] was obtained. On each problem, the best of the 39 schedules produced by these heuristics was compared with the schedule obtained by Micro-Boss. Among the 39 scheduling heuristics (i.e., excluding Micro-Boss),

----

[18] The 39 combinations were as follows: EXP-ET and its intrinsic release policy (times four parameter settings), EXP-ET/IM-REL (times four parameter settings), EDD/AQT (times four parameter settings), EDD/IM-REL, WSPT/AQT (times four parameter settings), WSPT/IM-REL, S/RPT/AQT (times four parameter settings), S/RPT/IM-REL, WCOVERT/IM-REL (times four parameter settings), WCO-VERT/AQT (times four parameter settings), ATC/IM-REL (times four parameter settings), and ATC/AQT (times four parameter settings).

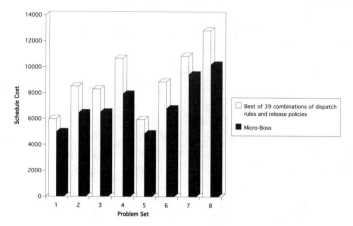

Figure 4-10:   Comparison of Micro-Boss and the best of 39 combinations of priority dispatch rules
and release policies under 8 different scheduling conditions (10 problems were generated under each condition).

each of the 6 dispatch rules (WSPT, EDD, S/RPT, WCOVERT, ATC, and EXP-ET)
and each of the 3 release policies (IM-REL, AQT, and EXP-ET's intrinsic release
policy) performed best on at least one problem out of the 80, and 12 combinations
out of the 39 performed best on at least one problem.

Figure 4-10 compares the average cost of the schedules produced by Micro-
Boss with the average cost obtained by the best of the 39 combinations of dispatch
rules and release policies on each problem set. Schedule cost was computed as the
sum of tardiness and inventory costs, as specified in Equation 3. The results indicate that Micro-Boss consistently outperformed the combination of 39 heuristics
under all 8 conditions of the study.

Overall Micro-Boss yielded reductions of 20% in schedule cost over the 39
heuristics. A more detailed analysis indicates that this reduction in schedule cost
corresponds to a reduction of about 20% in tardiness costs and about 23% in
inventory costs (combined work-in-progress and finished goods inventory costs).

4.5.2 Comparison against Coarser Opportunistic Scheduling Procedures

Micro-Boss was also compared with several coarser opportunistic schedulers
that dynamically combine a resource-centered perspective and a job-centered perspective, such as in the OPIS scheduling system (Ow & Smith, 1988). Although
OPIS relies on a set of repair heuristics to recover from inconsistencies (Ow, Smith,
& Thiriez, 1988), the macro-opportunistic schedulers of this study were built to use
the same consistency enforcing techniques and the same backtracking scheme as

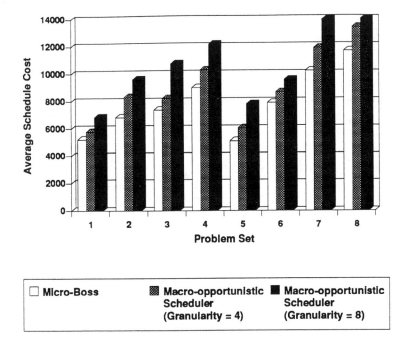

Figure 4-11:   Comparison of Micro-Boss and two coarser opportunistic schedulers.

Micro-Boss.[19] The macro-opportunistic schedulers also used the same demand profiles as Micro-Boss. When average demand for the most critical resource/time interval was above some threshold level (a parameter of the system that was empirically adjusted), the macro-opportunistic scheduler focused on scheduling the operations requiring that resource/time interval; otherwise, it used a job-centered perspective to identify a critical job and schedule some or all of the operations in that job. Each time a resource/time interval or a portion of a job was scheduled, new demand profiles were computed to decide which scheduling perspective to use next.

Figure 4-11 summarizes the results of a comparison between Micro-Boss[20] and two macro-opportunistic schedulers that differed in the number of operations

---

[19] An alternative would have been to implement a variation of Micro-Boss using the same repair heuristics as OPIS. Besides being time-consuming to implement, such a comparison would have been affected by the quality of the specific repair heuristics currently implemented in the OPIS scheduler.

[20] These experiments, as well as the ones presented in the next subsection, were performed in 1993 with an earlier version of Micro-Boss than the one used for the comparison with dispatch rules.

that they were allowed to schedule at once in their resource-centered perspective (referred to below as the granularity of the scheduler). The macro-opportunistic scheduler with granularity 4 was allowed to schedule as many as 4 operations in its resource-centered perspective, after which it had to compute new demand profiles and decide which subproblem (job-centered or resource-centered) to focus on next. The macro-opportunistic scheduler with granularity 8 was allowed to schedule at once as many as 8 operations in its resource-centered perspective. The results in Figure 4-11 indicate not only that Micro-Boss consistently produced better schedules than the two macro-opportunistic schedulers but also that schedule performance degraded as the granularity of the macro-opportunistic scheduler was increased, namely, as the search procedure became less flexible. More detailed performance measures not presented here indicate that the reductions in schedule cost achieved by Micro-Boss correspond to reductions in both tardiness and inventory costs.

Overall, these results strongly suggest that the additional flexibility of a micro-opportunistic scheduling procedure over coarser opportunistic procedures generally yields important improvements in schedule quality.

4.5.3 Evaluating the Impact of Using Biased Demand Profiles

A third set of experiments was carried out to test the effect of using biased demand profiles to guide the micro-opportunistic scheduler. A variation of Micro-Boss using unbiased demand profiles was run on the same set of 80 scheduling problems.

Figure 4-12 compares the average schedule costs obtained by both variations of Micro-Boss. In 7 out of the 8 scheduling situations of the study, biasing the demand profiles produced reductions in schedule cost ranging from 3 to 22 percent, including an impressive 20 percent in the most difficult scheduling situation (Problem Set 8 with two bottlenecks, a tight average due date, and a narrow range of due dates). In the one case (out of eight) where the unbiased version produced better schedules, the biased version was only 5% worse. A more detailed analysis of the results indicates that overall, the biased version of Micro-Boss performed 30% better with respect to tardiness while incurring a slight increase of 0.6% in inventory costs. Altogether, biasing the demand profiles reduced schedule costs by more than 15%. These results validate both the idea of building biased demand profiles to guide the micro-opportunistic search procedure and the particular technique used in Micro-Boss to operationalize this idea (namely, the use of the *mincost* functions). In general, it should be possible to obtain even better results by varying the bias according to specific problem characteristics. One could also consider fine-tuning the bias during the construction of the schedule.

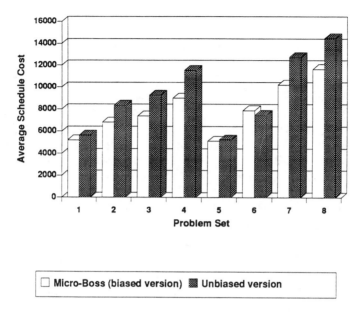

Figure 4-12: Comparison of the cost of the schedules produced by Micro-Boss and a variation of the system that used unbiased demand profiles.

4.6 CONCLUDING REMARKS

Current computer solutions to production management such as the one implemented in MRP/MRP-II systems are of limited help because they rely on oversimplified models of the plant and only provide weak feedback loops to update the production schedule during execution (typically, complete updates of the schedule are only performed on a weekly basis). A major challenge for researchers in production scheduling is to come up with new techniques that can account more precisely for actual manufacturing objectives and constraints, including execution contingencies such as machine breakdowns, new job arrivals, variations in processing times, yields, etc. New production scheduling tools should also enable the user to interactively perform "what-if" analysis and account for ad hoc constraints and/or preferences that are not easily amenable to representation in the computer model.

In this chapter, we presented Micro-Boss, a decision support system for factory scheduling. Micro-Boss aims at combining powerful predictive, reactive, and interactive scheduling capabilities. To this end, the system relies on a new micro-opportunistic search procedure that enables the scheduling system to continuously track the evolution of micro-bottlenecks (or conflicts) during the construction or repair of the schedule and to refocus its optimization effort on those micro-bottlenecks that appear most critical. This approach differs from earlier opportunistic approaches (Ow & Smith, 1988; Collinot, Le Pape, & Pinoteau, 1988) because it does not require scheduling large resource subproblems or large job subproblems before revising the current scheduling strategy. The results of an experimental study comparing Micro-Boss with combinations of popular priority dispatch rules and release policies advocated in the Operations Research literature, as well as coarser opportunistic scheduling approaches proposed in the Artificial Intelligence literature, suggest that the flexibility of this new search procedure can often yield important improvements in schedule quality. We find that because of their flexibility, micro-opportunistic scheduling procedures are also particularly well suited for repairing schedules in the face of execution contingencies and can easily be integrated in interactive decision support systems that enable the user to incrementally manipulate and compare alternative schedules.

Although our work on Micro-Boss has focused on generalized versions of the job shop scheduling problem, micro-opportunistic scheduling techniques have been applied to other manufacturing problems and other classes of problems such as transportation scheduling. Rautaruukki Oy, a large Finnish steel manufacturer, and researchers at the Helsinki University of Technology have reported adapting an earlier version of our micro-opportunistic scheduling heuristics to schedule a steel rolling mill (Torma, Lassila, & Syrjanen, 1991). Variations of the Micro-Boss scheduling heuristics are also used in the Knowledge Based Logistics Planning Shell (KBLPS) developed by Carnegie Group, Inc. (CGI), and LB & M Associates to solve U.S. army transportation scheduling problems and ammunition distribution planning problems (Dunmire et al., 1990; Camden et al., 1990; Saks, Kepner, & Johnson, 1992). Other efforts using variations of the micro-opportunistic techniques developed in the context of Micro-Boss are described in Berry (1991), Linden (1991), Paolucci et al. (1991), and Winklhofer, Maierhofer, & Levi (1992).

Current research efforts within our project aim at applying and extending the existing approach to solve both manufacturing and transportation scheduling problems.

ACKNOWLEDGMENTS

I want to thank Mark Fox for his help and support during the initial development of the system. Special thanks to Bob Schnelbach for his help designing and implementing the Micro-Boss user interface and reactive scheduling component and to Shinichi Otsuka for his help with the C++ reimplementation of the system.

Recent research efforts have also benefited from the participation of Bryan Lewis, Gang Li, Yoichiro Nakakuki, Katia Sycara, Joe Toomey, Sam Thangiah, and Yalin Xiong.

This research was supported in part by the Defense Advanced Research Projects Agency under contract #F30602-91-F-0016 and in part by grants from McDonnell Aircraft Company and Digital Equipment Corporation.

References

Adams, J., E. Balas, and D. Zawack. 1988. The Shifting Bottleneck Procedure for Job Shop Scheduling. *Management Science* 34(3):391–401.

Baker, K.R., and G.D. Scudder. 1990. Sequencing with Earliness and Tardiness Penalties: A Review. *Operations Research* 38(1):22–36.

Bean, J.C., J.R. Birge, J. Mittenthal, and C.E. Noon. 1991. Matchup Scheduling with Multiple Resources, Release Dates, and Disruptions. *Operations Research* 39(3):470–483.

Berry, P.M. 1991. *The PCP: A Predictive Model for Satisfying Conflicting Objectives in Scheduling Problems.* Technical Report, Centre Universitaire d'Informatique, Universite de Geneve.

Camden, R., C. Dunmire, R. Goyal, N. Sathi, B. Elm, and M. Fox. 1990. Distribution Planning: An Integration of Constraint Satisfaction and Heuristic Search Techniques. *Proceedings of the Conference on AI Applications in Military Logistics*

Collinot, A., C. Le Pape, and G. Pinoteau. 1988. SONIA: A Knowledge-based Scheduling System. *International Journal of Artificial Intelligence in Engineering* 2(4):86–94.

Dauzere-Peres, S., and J.B. Lasserre. 1990. *A Modified Shifting Bottleneck Procedure for Job Shop Scheduling.* Technical Report LASS 90106, Laboratoire d'Automatique et d'Analyse des Systemes, Toulouse Cedex, France.

Dunmire, C., N. Sathi, R. Goyal, M. Fox, and A. Kott. 1990. Ammunition Inventory Planning: An Integration of Configuration and Resource Allocation Techniques. *Proceedings of the Conference on AI Applications in Military Logistics.*

Fox, M.S. 1983. *Constraint-Directed Search: A Case Study of Job-Shop Scheduling.* Ph.D. thesis, Department of Computer Science, Carnegie Mellon University.

Fox, R.E. 1987. OPT: Leapfrogging the Japanese. *Just-in-time Manufacture*, ed. C.A. Voxx, Springer Verlag, New York.

French, S. 1982. *Sequencing and Scheduling: An Introduction to the Mathematics of the Job-Shop.* John Wiley & Sons, New York.

Garey, M.R., and D.S. Johnson. 1979. *Computers and Intractability: A Guide to the Theory of NP-Completeness.* W. H. Freeman and Co., New York.

Godratt, E.M. 1980. Optimized Production Timetable: Beyond MRP: Something Better Is Finally Here. Speech to APICS National Conference, Los Angeles, CA.

Graves, S.C. 1981. A Review of Production Scheduling. *Operations Research* 29(4):646–675.

Jacobs, F.R. 1984. OPT Uncovered: Many Production Planning and Scheduling Concepts Can Be Applied with or without the Software. *Industrial Engineering* 16(10):32–41.

Le Pape, C., and S.F. Smith. 1987. *Management of Temporal Constraints for Factory Scheduling.* Technical Report, The Robotics Institute, Carnegie Mellon University. Also in 1987. *Proceedings IFIP TC 8/WG8.1. Working Conference on Temporal Aspects in Information Systems (TAIS 87),* May, pp. 165–176, North Holland Publishers, New York.

Li, G., and N. Sadeh. 1992. *Single-machine Early/Tardy Scheduling Problem with Setups: A Hybrid Heuristic Approach.* Technical Report, Robotics Institute, Carnegie Mellon University, Pittsburgh, PA 195213. Also 1992. Presented at the Joint National ORSA/TIMS Meeting, San Francisco.

Linden, T.A. 1991. *Preference-Directed, Cooperative Resource Allocation and Scheduling.* Technical Report, Advanced Decision Systems, Mountain View, CA.

Mackworth, A.K. and E.C. Freuder. 1985. The Complexity of Some Polymnomial Network Consistency Algorithms for Constraint Satisfaction Problems. *Artificial Intelligence* 25(1):65–74.

Minton, S., M.D. Johnston, A.B. Philips, and P. Laird. 1990. Solving Large-scale Constraint Satisfaction and Scheduling Problems Using a Heuristic Repair Method. *Proceedings of the Eighth National Conference on Artificial Intelligence,* 17–24. AAAI Press, Menlo Park, CA.

Morton, T.E., S.R. Lawrence, S. Rajagopolan, and S. Kekre. 1988. SCHED-STAR: A Price-based Shop Scheduling Module. *Journal of Manufacturing and Operations Management,* 131–181.

Orlicky, J. 1975. *Materials Requirement Planning.* McGraw-Hill, New York.

Ow, P.S. 1985. Focused Scheduling in Proportionate Flowshops. *Management Science* 31(7):852–869.

Ow, P.S., and T. Morton. 1989. The Single-Machine Early/Tardy Problem. *Management Science* 35(2):177–191.

Ow, P.S., and S.F. Smith. Viewing Scheduling as an Opportunistic Problem-Solving Process. *Annals of Operations Research* 12:85–108.

Ow, P.S., S.F. Smith, and A. Thiriez. 1988. Reactive Plan Revision. *Proceedings of the Seventh National Conference on Artificial Intelligence,* 77–82, AAAI Press, Menlo Park, CA.

Panwalkar, S.S., and W. Iskander. 1977. A Survey of Scheduling Rules. *Operations Research* 25(1):45–61.

Paolucci, E., E. Patriarca, M. Sem, and G. Gini. 1992. Predit: A Temporal Predictive Framework for Scheduling Systems. *Proceedings of the AAAI Spring Symposium on Practical Approaches to Scheduling and Planning,* 150–154, AAAI Press, Menlo Park, CA.

Sadeh, N. 1991. *Look-ahead Techniques for Micro-opportunistic Job Shop Scheduling.* Ph.D. Thesis, School of Computer Science, Carnegie Mellon University.

Sadeh, N. and M.S. Fox. 1991. *Variable and Value Ordering Heuristics for Hard Constraint Satisfaction Problems: An Application to Job Shop Scheduling.* Technical Report CMU-RI,TR-91-23, The Robotics Institute, Carnegie Mellon University.

Sadeh, N., K. Sycara, and Y. Xiong. 1992. *A Comparative Study of Backtracking Techniques for Hard Scheduling Problems.* Technical Report CMU-RI-TR-92-06, The Robotics Intsitute, Carnegie Mellon University.

Sadeh, N.M., S. Otsuka, and R. Schnelbach. 1993. Predictive and Reactive Scheduling with the Micro-Boss Production Scheduling and Control System. *Proceedings of the IJCAI-93 Workshop on Knowledge-based Production Planning, Scheduling, and Control,* Chambery, France.

Saks, V., A. Kepner, and I. Johnson. 1992. *Knowledge Based Distribution Planning.* Technical Report, Carnegie Group, Inc., Pittsburgh, PA.

Serafini, P., W. Ukovich, H. Kirchner, F. Giardina, and F. Tiozzo. 1988. Job-shop Scheduling: A Case Study. *Operations Research Models in FMS,* eds. F. Archetti, M. Lucertini, and P. Serafini, Springer, Vienna.

Smith, S., M. Fox, and P.S. Ow. 1986. Constructing and Maintaining Detailed Production Plans: Investigations into the Development of Knowledge-Based Factory Scheduling Systems. *AI Magazine* 7(4):45–61.

Smith, S.F., N. Keng, and K. Kempf. 1990. *Exploiting Local Flexibility during Execution of Pre-computed Schedules.* Technical Report CMU-TR-RI-90-13, The Robotics Institute, Carnegie Mellon University.

Smith, S.F., P.S. Ow, N. Muscettola, J.-Y. Potvin, and D. Matthys. 1990. An Integrated Framework for Generating and Revising Factory Schedules. *Journal of the Operational Research Society* 41(6):539–552.

Torma, S., O. Lassila, and M. Syrjanen. 1991. Adapting the Activity-Based Scheduling Method to Steel Rolling. *Proceedings of the Fourth IFIP Conference on Computer Applications in Production and Engineering (CAPE'91),* eds. G. Doumeingts, J. Browne, and M. Tomljanovich, pp. 159–166. Elsevier Science Publishers, New York.

Vepsalainen, A., and T.E. Morton. 1987. Priority Rules for Job Shops with Weighted Tardiness Costs. *Management Science* 33(8):1035–1047.

Vollmann, T., W. Berry, and C. Whybark. 1988. *Manufacturing Planning and Control.* Second Edition. Dow Jones-Irwin, Homewood, IL.

Wight, O. 1981. *MRP I: Unlocking America's Productivity Potential.* Oliver Wight Limited Publications, Williston, VT.

Wight, O. 1984. *Manufacturing Resource Planning: MRPII.* Oliver Wight Limited Publications, Essex Junction, VT.

Winklhofer, A., M. Maierhofer, and P. Levi. 1992. Efficient Propagation and Computation of Problem Features for Activity-Based Scheduling. *Proceedings of the Seventh Symposium on Information Control Problems in Manufacturing Technology (INCOM-92).* Toronto, Canada.

Zweben, M., E. Davis, and M. Deale. 1991. *Iterative Repair for Scheduling and Rescheduling.* Technical Report, NASA Ames Research Center, Moffett Field, CA.

5

SCHEDULING AND PACKING IN THE CONSTRAINT LANGUAGE CC(FD)

Pascal Van Hentenryck
(Brown University)

5.1 INTRODUCTION

Constraint Logic Programming (CLP) is a new class of declarative programming languages combining nondeterminism and constraint solving. The fundamental idea behind these languages, to use constraint solving instead of unification as the kernel operation of the language, was elegantly captured in the CLP scheme (Jaffar & Lassez, 1987). The CLP scheme can be instantiated to produce a specific language by defining a constraint system (i.e., defining a set of primitive constraints and providing a constraint solver for the constraints). For instance, CHIP contains constraint systems over finite domains (Van Hentenryck, 1989a), Booleans (Buttner & Simonis, 1987), and rational numbers (Graf, 1987; Van Hentenryck & Graf, 1992). Prolog III (Colmerauer, 1990) is endowed with constraint systems over Booleans, rational numbers, and lists; and CLP(R) (Jaffar & Michaylov, 1987) solves constraints over real numbers. The CLP scheme was further generalized into the cc framework of concurrent constraint programming (Saraswat, 1989; Saraswat & Rinard, 1990; Saraswat, Rinard, & Panangaden, 1991) to accommodate additional constraint operations (e.g., constraint entailment [Maher, 1987]) and new ways of combining them (e.g., implication or blocking ask [Saraswat, 1989] and cardinality [Van Hentenryck & Deville, 1991]).

CLP languages[1] support, in a declarative way, the solving of combinatorial search problems using the global search paradigm. The global search paradigm amounts to dividing recursively a problem into subproblems until the subproblems

---

[1] In the following, I use the term *CLP languages* generically to denote both CLP and cc languages.

are simple enough to be solved in a straightforward way. The paradigm includes, as special cases, implicit enumeration, branch and bound, and constraint satisfaction. It is best contrasted with the local search paradigm, which proceeds by modifying an initial configuration locally until a solution is obtained. These approaches are orthogonal and complementary. The global search paradigm has been used successfully to solve a large variety of combinatorial search problems with reasonable efficiency (e.g., scheduling [Carlier & Pinson, 1986], graph coloring [Kubale & Jackowski, 1985], Hamiltonian circuits [Christofides, 1975], microcode labeling [Dincbas, Simonis, & Van Hentenryck, 1990]) and provides, at the same time, the basis for exact methods as well as approximate solutions (giving rise to the so-called "anytime algorithms" [Dean & Boddy, 1988]).

The purpose of this chapter is to demonstrate the use of CLP languages for solving discrete combinatorial search problems such as assignment, scheduling, and packing problems by showing the solutions of two problems.

The CLP language used in the above problems is cc(FD), an instance of the cc framework over finite domains that is best seen as a successor to the finite-domain part of CHIP. Both languages support the use of consistency techniques and local propagation in conjunction with don't-know nondeterminism approximated by backtracking. In addition, they support depth-first branch and bound for combinatorial optimization problems. The novel aspects of cc(FD) include the definition of new general-purpose combinators (such as cardinality, implication, and constructive disjunction) and the availability of constraint entailment and constraint generalization as primitive operations on constraints. cc(FD) generalizes in an elegant way (and thus makes unnecessary) several features and constraints of CHIP that were difficult to justify theoretically. As a consequence, it provides additional operational expressiveness, flexibility, and efficiency and lets us tackle problems such as disjunctions of constraints and the definition of primitive constraints.

The two applications chosen to illustrate the language are the perfect square problem and a Digital Signal Processing (DSP) application. The perfect square problem amounts to packing a number of small squares in a larger square without leaving any empty space. We show a rather short and natural cc(FD) program packing 21 or 24 squares in about 60 seconds on a SUN 4/60. The DSP application consists of scheduling tasks on a number of processors in order to minimize the total delay of the DSP function. The complexity of the DSP application comes from the various types of constraints, including precedence constraints, capacity constraints, and non-uniform communication delays. We show a cc(FD) program that is about four pages long and compares well with a specific branch and bound algorithm especially designed for the task. Other applications of CLP languages over finite domains to similar problems can be found in (Dincbas, Simonis, & Van Hentenryck (1988a, 1988b, 1990) and Van Hentenryck (1989a, 1989b).

The rest of the chapter is organized as follows. The next section gives an overview of the features of cc(FD) used in the applications and provides the necessary background for the two applications. Each feature is illustrated using scheduling examples. The next two sections describe the applications. The last two sections discuss the limitations of cc(FD) and further research and contain the conclusion of the chapter.

5.2 OVERVIEW OF CC(FD)

Here we give an informal overview of the relevant parts of cc(FD). Section 5.2.1 sketches the syntax of the language; Section 5.2.2 introduces the CLP scheme; and Sections 5.2.3, 5.2.4, and 5.2.5 discuss the details of constraint solving in cc(FD), the cardinality combinator, and the meta-level predicates for optimization.

5.2.1 Syntax

Figure 5-1 shows an outline of the syntax of cc(FD) programs as relevant to this chapter. A cc(FD) is a set of clauses in which each clause has a head and a body. A head is an atom, i.e., an expression of the form $p(t_1,...,t_n)$, where $t_1,...,t_n$ are terms. A term is a variable (e.g., X) or a function symbol of arity n applied to n terms (e.g., f(X,g(Y))). A body is either true (the empty body), a goal (procedure call), a constraint (constraint solving), or a cardinality combinator. In this chapter, variables are denoted by uppercase letters, constraints by the letter c, conjunctions of constraints by the letter σ, terms by letters t, s, atoms by letters H, B, goals by the letter G, and integers by the letters l, u, v, all possibly subscripted or superscripted. We also use C to denote a constraint system and D, possibly subscripted, to denote a finite domain. To illustrate the operational semantics of (part of) cc(FD), we use the simple program depicted in Figure 5-2.

5.2.2 The CLP Scheme

At least from a conceptual standpoint, the operational semantics of the CLP scheme is a simple generalization of the semantics of logic programming. It can be

```
Program    ::=    Clauses
Clauses    ::=    Head :- Body | Clauses Clauses
Head       ::=    Atom
Goal       ::=    Atom
Body       ::=    true | Goal | c | Body , Body | #(l,u,[c₁,...,cₙ])
```

Figure 5-1:   An outline of the syntax.

```
p(X,Y,X) :-                    q(X,Y,Z) :-
    X ∈ 0..10,                     r(X,Y).
    Y ∈ 0..10,                 q(X,Y,Z) :-
=   Z ∈ 0..10,                     Z ≥ Y + 2.
    X ≥ Z + 3,
    Y ≤ Z,                     r(X,Y) :-
    q(X,Y,Z).                      X ≤ Y + 2.
```

Figure 5-2:   A simple program.

described as a goal-directed derivation procedure from the initial goal using the program clauses. A *computation state* is best described by

1. *a goal part*, the conjunction of goals to be solved

2. *a constraint store*, the set of constraints accumulated so far

Initially, the constraint store is empty, and the goal part is the initial goal. In the following, we denote the computation state by pairs $\langle G \ \blacksquare \ \sigma \rangle$, where G is the goal part, and σ is the constraint store. We use ε to denote an empty goal part or constraint store. An example computation state is

$\langle$ **q(X,Y,Z)** $\blacksquare$ **X,Y,Z** $\in \{0,\ldots,10\}$ & **X** $\geq$ **Z** + 3 & **Y** $\leq$ **Z** $\rangle$

A *computation step* (i.e., the transition from one computation state to another) can be of two types depending upon the selection of an atom or a constraint in the goal part. In the first case, a computation step amounts to

1. selecting an atom in the goal part

2. finding a clause that can be used to resolve the atom (this clause must have the same predicate symbol as the atom, and the equality constraints between the goal and head arguments must be consistent with the constraint store)

3. defining the new computation state as the old one where the selected atom has been replaced by the body of the clause, and the equality constraints have been added to the constraint store

In the second case, a computation step amounts to

1. selecting a constraint in the goal part that can be satisfied with the constraint store

2. defining the new computation state as the old one where the selected constraint has been removed from the goal part and added to the constraint store

For instance, given a computation state

$\langle$ **q(X,Y,Z)** $\blacksquare$ **X,Y,Z** $\in \{0,\ldots,10\}$ & **X** $\geq$ **Z** + 3 & **Y** $\leq$ **Z** $\rangle$

a computation step can be performed using clause 2 of **q** to obtain a new computation state:

$$\langle\ \text{Z} \geq \text{Y} + 2\ \blacksquare\ \text{X,Y,Z} \in \{0,\ldots,10\}\ \&\ \text{X} \geq \text{Z} + 3\ \&\ \text{Y} \leq \text{Z}\ \rangle$$

Another computation step leads to the configuration

$$\langle\ \varepsilon\ \blacksquare\ \text{X,Y,Z} \in \{0,\ldots,10\}\ \&\ \text{X} \geq \text{Z} + 3\ \&$$
$$\text{Y} \leq \text{Z}\ \&\ \text{Z} \geq \text{Y} + 2\ \rangle$$

because the resulting constraint store is satisfiable. Note that, strictly speaking, equations should have appeared between the variables in the above example; they were omitted for clarity because the variables have the same names in the program.

As should be clear, the basic operation of the language amounts to deciding the satisfiability of a conjunction of constraints. Note also that each computation state has a satisfiable constraint store. This property is exploited inside CLP languages to avoid solving the satisfiability problem from scratch at each step. Instead, CLP languages keep a reduced (e.g., solved) form of the constraints and transform the existing solution into a solution, including the new constraints. Hence, the constraint solver is made incremental. For instance, the last constraint store can be represented as

$$\langle\ \varepsilon\ \blacksquare\ \text{X} \in \{5,\ldots,10\}\ \&\ \text{Y} \in \{0,\ldots,5\}\ \&$$
$$\text{Z} \in \{2,\ldots,7\}\ \&\ \text{X} \geq \text{Z} + 3\ \&\ \text{Y} \leq \text{Z}\ \&\ \text{Z} \geq \text{Y} + 2\ \rangle$$

A computation state is *terminal* if

- The goal part is empty.
- No clause can be applied to the selected atom to produce a new computation state, or the selected constraint cannot be satisfied with the constraint store.

A *computation* is simply a sequence of computation steps that either ends in a terminal computation state or diverges. A finite computation is *successful* if the final computation state has an empty goal and *fails* otherwise.

To illustrate computations in a CLP language, consider our simple program again. The program has only one successful computation, namely,

```
⟨ p(X,Y,Z) ■ ε ⟩
        ↓                  (selecting the first constraint)
  ...
        ↓                  (selecting the last constraint)
⟨ q(X,Y,Z) ■ X,Y,Z ∈ {0,...,10} & X ≥ Z + 3 & Y ≤ Z ⟩
        ↓                  (using clause 2 of q)
⟨ Z ≥ Y + 2 ■ X,Y,Z ∈ {0,...,10} & X ≥ Z + 3 & Y ≤ Z ⟩
        ↓                  (selecting the constraint)
⟨ ε ■ X,Y,Z ∈ {0,...,10} & X ≥ Z+3 & Y ≤ Z & Z ≥ Y+2 >
```

The program also has one failed computation:

⟨ p(X,Y,Z) ■ ε ⟩
    ↓   (selecting the first constraint)

. . .

    ↓   (selecting the last constraint)

⟨ q(X,Y,Z) ■ X,Y,Z ∈ {0,...,10} & X ≥ Z + 3 & Y ≤ Z ⟩
    ↓   (using clause 1 of q)

⟨ r(X,Y,Z) ■ X,Y,Z ∈ {0,...,10} & X ≥ Z + 3 & Y ≤ Z ⟩
    ↓   (using clause 1 of r)

⟨ X ≤ Y + 2 ■ X,Y,Z ∈ {0,...,10} & X ≥ Z + 3 & Y ≤ Z ⟩

The last computation state is terminal because the conjunction of constraints

$$X ≥ Z + 3 \; \& \; Y ≤ Z \; \& \; X ≤ Y + 2$$

is not satisfiable.

Note that the results of the computation are the constraint stores of the successful computations. Also, nothing has been said so far on the strategy used to explore the space of computations. Most CLP languages use a computation model similar to Prolog: atoms are selected from left to right in the clauses, clauses are tried in textual order, and the search space is explored in a depth-first manner with chronological backtracking in case of failures.[2] For instance, on the simple program, a CLP language typically uses clause 1 for p; uses clause 1 for q; and, finally, encounters a failure when trying to solve r. Execution then backtracks to clause 2 of q, giving the successful computation.

5.2.3 The Constraint Solver

In this section, we consider the finite domain part of cc(FD) in isolation (i.e., without discussing first-order terms). cc(FD) works on variables ranging over a finite set of natural numbers (e.g., positive integers that can fit in a memory word). In the following, these variables are called *domain variables*. A finite domain term can then be built using the traditional operations on integers.

Definition 1. An FD-term is defined inductively as follows:

1. A domain variable is an FD-term.

2. A natural number is an FD-term.

3. If t_1 and t_2 are FD-terms, so are

$$t_1 + t_2, t_1 - t_2, t_1 * t_2, t_1 \; div \; t_2, t_1 \; mod \; t_2$$

The operators have their standard semantics on integers: in particular, *div* denotes the integer division, and *mod* is the remainder of the division.

---

[2] Several combinators of cc(FD) permit more sophisticated search procedures.

The constraints on finite terms can now be defined in a simple way.

Definition 2. An FD-constraint is a constraint

$$x \in \{v_1, \ldots, v_n\}$$
$$x \in min..max,$$
$$x \notin \{v_1, \ldots, v_n\}$$
$$x \notin min..max,$$
$$t_1 > t_2, \quad t_1 \geq t_2, \quad t_1 = t_2, \quad t_1 \neq t_2, \quad t_1 \leq t_2, \quad t_1 < t_2$$

where x is a domain variable; $v_1, \ldots, v_n, min, max$ are positive integers; and t_1, t_2 are FD-terms. Once again, the semantics of the relations are the standard.

Because deciding FD-constraints is NP-complete, the constraint solver in cc(FD) is incomplete and enforces arc-consistency (Mackworth, 1977) on the constraints (instead of full consistency).[3]

Definition 3. Let $x_1, \ldots, x_n$ be variables with domains $D_1, \ldots, D_n$. A constraint $c(x_1, \ldots, x_n)$ is arc-consistent wrt $D_1, \ldots, D_n$ iff for each variable x_i and value $v_i \in D_i$, there exist values $v_1 \in D_1, \ldots, v_{i-1} \in D_{i-1}, v_{i+1} \in D_{i+1}, \ldots, v_n \in D_n$ such that $c(v_1, \ldots, v_n)$ holds.

Definition 4. Let $x_1, \ldots, x_n$ be domain variables with domains $D_1, \ldots, D_n$. A set S of constraints over $x_1, \ldots, x_n$ is arc-consistent wrt $D_1, \ldots, D_n$ iff each constraint $c \in S$ over $x_{i_1}, \ldots, x_{i_m}$ is arc-consistent wrt $D_{i_1}, \ldots, D_{i_m}$.

Similarly, cc(FD) does not use full entailment but the weaker notion of arc-entailment.

Definition 5. A constraint $c(x_1, \ldots, x_n)$ is arc entailed by $D_1, \ldots, D_n$ iff for all values $v_1, \ldots, v_n$ in $D_1, \ldots, D_n$, $c(v_1, \ldots, v_n)$ holds.

The constraint solver of cc(FD) is based on AC-5 (Van Hentenryck, Deville, & Teng, 1992), a generic arc-consistency algorithm that can be specialized to AC-4 (Mohr & Henderson, 1986) and AC-3 (Mackworth, 1977). In addition, AC-5 can be instantiated to produce an $O(cd)$ algorithm, where c is the number of constraints, and d is the size of the largest domain, for many classes of binary constraints, including functional and monotone constraints and their piecewise generalizations.

Example 6. The constraint solver of cc(FD) can be applied naturally to solve PERT problems. Consider the following program:

---

[3] The presentation of CC(FD) here is somewhat simplified for clarity. CC(FD) actually contains two versions of each constraint, one enforcing arc consistency and the other interval consistency. In this chapter, only arc consistency is used, but $t_1 = t_2$ must be viewed as an abbreviation of $t_1 \geq t_2$, $t_1 \leq t_2$.

```
stateConstraint([Sa,Sb,Sc,Sd,Se,Sf,Sg,Sh,Sj,Sk,Send],Send) :-
    stateDomain([Sa,Sb,Sc,Sd,Se,Sf,Sg,Sh,Sj,Sk,Send]),
    Sb ≥ Sa + 7,  Sd ≥ Sa + 7,  Sc ≥ Sb + 3,
    Se ≥ Sc + 1,  Se ≥ Sd + 8,  Sg ≥ Sc + 1,
    Sg ≥ Sd + 8,  Sf ≥ Sd + 8,  Sf ≥ Sc + 1,
    Sh ≥ Sf + 1,  Sj ≥ Sh + 3,  Sk ≥ Sg + 1,
    Sk ≥ Se + 1,  Sk ≥ Sj + 2,  Send ≥ Sk + 1.

stateDomain([]).
stateDomain([F|T]) :-
    F ∈ 0..30,
    stateDomain(T).
```

Each variable corresponds to the start date of a task, and each of the constraints expresses a precedence constraint between two tasks (e.g., the first constraint expresses that task b must be scheduled after task a whose duration is 7). The predicate stateConstraint reduces, by constraint propagation, the domains of the variables to $Sa \in 0..8$, $Sb \in 7..19$, $Sc \in 10..22$, $Sd \in 7..15$, $Se \in 15..27$, $Sf \in 15..23$, $Sg \in 15..18$, $Sh \in 15..27$, $Sj \in 19..27$, $Sk \in 21..29$, and $Send \in 22..30$. In addition, the assignment of the minimum possible value to the end task would automatically solve the PERT problem.

Note, however, that constraints are not generally stated so explicitly; they are often generated dynamically by a recursive predicate to guarantee the generality of the program. For instance, precedence constraints can be enforced by a predicate of the form

```
statePrecedence([]).
statePrecedence([precedence(Start1,Start2,Duration2)|Prec]) :-
        Start1 ≥ Start2 + Duration2,
        statePrecedence(Prec).
```

The predicate StatePrecedence receives a list of terms describing the precedence constraints and enforces the associated constraints.

5.2.4 The Cardinality Combinator

In this section, we discuss the cardinality operator, an important abstraction used in the two applications described later. The syntax of the cardinality operator is

$$\#(l,[c_1, \ldots ,c_n],u)$$

where l,u are integers or domain variables, and $c_1, \ldots ,c_n$ are constraints or cardinality combinators. The declarative semantics of the cardinality operator is as follows: the number of true formulae in $[c_1, \ldots ,c_n]$ is no less than l and no more than *u*. Note that the cardinality operator generalizes many other logical connectives, as shown by the following equivalences:

$c_1 \wedge \ldots \wedge c_n$ is equivalent to $\#(n,[c_1, \ldots ,c_n],n)$.
$c_1 \vee \ldots \vee c_n$ is equivalent to $\#(1,[c_1, \ldots ,c_n],n)$.
$\neg c$ is equivalent to $\#(0,[c],0)$.

Implication and equivalence can now be obtained in a straightforward way. cc(FD) allows the programmer to use the standard logical connectives ($\wedge$, $\vee$, $\Leftrightarrow$, $\Rightarrow$, $\neg$) as abbreviations for cardinality formulas.

The main interest of the cardinality combinator lies in its operational semantics. The combinator implements a principle well known in operations research and artificial intelligence: "infer simple constraints from difficult ones." The intuitive idea is to make sure that the cardinality combinator can be satisfied in some way. Moreover, if there is only one way to satisfy it, then the constraints necessary to satisfy it are introduced in the constraint store. Constraint entailment, i.e., checking if a constraint is implied by a set of constraints, is used to check if there is a way to satisfy the constraints. In cc(FD), the cardinality operator is often used to define new (non-primitive) constraints, which are transformed into primitive constraints as soon as possible.

Example 7. In scheduling applications, disjunctive constraints arise when two tasks cannot be scheduled at the same time because, for instance, they use the same resource. In Van Hentenryck (1989b) and Dincbas, Simonis, & Van Hentenryck (1990), disjunctive constraints were expressed through a non-deterministic procedure, as follows:

```
disjunctive(S1,D1,S2,D2) :-
    S1 ≥ S2 + D2.
disjunctive(S1,D1,S2,D2) :-
    S2 ≥ S1 + D1.
```

where S1, S2 are the starting dates of two tasks and D1, D2 their respective durations. Operationally, executing such a procedure amounts to creating a choice point: the first task is chosen to be scheduled after the second task. If backtracking occurs later on, the second alternative (i.e., the first task is scheduled before the second one) is selected. The cardinality operator offers another possibility for expressing disjunctive constraints:

```
disjunctive(S1,D1,S2,D2) :-
    #(1, [ S1 ≥ S2 + D2, S2 ≥ S1 + D1 ], 2).
```

The cardinality formula expresses the fact that the first task is scheduled after the second task or vice-versa. Operationally, the cardinality formula makes sure that at least one of the possibilities is (arc-)consistent with the constraint store. If one possibility is ruled out, the other possibility is automatically enforced. For instance, the predicate show defined as follows:

```
show(S1,S2) :-
    S1 ∈ 1..5,
    S2 ∈ 1..2,
    #(1, [ S2 ≥ S1 + 4, S1 ≥ S2 + 4 ], 2).
```

automatically assigns S2 to 1 and S1 to 5 without any backtracking. The main reason is that the negation of S2 ô S1 + 4 is entailed by the constraint store because S2 ∈ 1..2 and S1 + 4 ranges over 5..9. Hence, the only way to satisfy the cardinality formula is to enforce S1 ≥ S2 + 4. This last constraint requires S1 to be 5 and S2 to be 1.

More sophisticated handlings of disjunctions, taking, for instance, several tasks simultaneously, are possible in cc(FD) using, for instance, the cardinality combinator in conjunction with the implication combinator (Van Hentenryck, Simonis, & Dincbas, 1992). Note also that in the perfect square problem, the above handling of disjunctions is generalized to 2 dimensions.

Example 8.   The cardinality combinator also enables the linking of Boolean variables (i.e., 0-1 domain variables) with a constraint in the following way:

```
B ∈ 0..1, #( B, [C], B )
```

The above expression makes sure that

1. The Boolean B is instantiated to 1 (respectively 0) when the constraint C (respectively its negation) is entailed by the constraint store.
2. The constraint C (respectively its negation) is added to the constraint store when B is instantiated to 1 (respectively 0).

This technique is used in the perfect square problem and in the DSP applications to implement various forms of capacity constraints.

5.2.5 Optimization

cc(FD) contains several meta-level predicates to optimize an objective function. Two common forms are

```
minof(Goal,Function,Res)
maxof(Goal,Function,Res)
```

The predicates expect a goal as first argument, an FD-term as second argument, and a variable as third argument. The predicate minof (resp. maxof) searches for a solution to Goal that minimizes (resp. maximizes) the objective function `function`; the variable `Res` is instantiated to such a solution. Operationally, the implementation uses a depth-first branch and bound algorithm. The idea is to search for a first solution. Each time a solution with cost `C` is obtained, a constraint `Function` `<` `C` (resp. `Function` `>` `C`) is generated dynamically. The search is completed when the search space has been explored implicitly.

Example 9. Reconsider, for instance, the PERT problem discussed previously. A minimal solution instantiating all variables can be obtained by the following program:

```
solvePert(ResStartDates) :-
    stateConstraint(StartDates,EndDate),
    minof(labeling(StartDates),EndDate,ResStartDates).

labeling([]).
labeling([F|T]) :-
    indomain(F),
    labeling(T).
```

The key idea here is to state all constraints in a deterministic way and to enclose the nondeterministic part (i.e., the predicate making choices) in the meta-level predicate for optimization. The `labeling` predicate in the above program simply instantiates all variables using the `indomain` predicate. The `indomain` predicate is a nondeterministic predicate trying all possible values for the variable. Note that in the above program, `cc(FD)` finds the optimal solution without any backtracking. For disjunctive scheduling, the labeling generally also contains a procedure to choose the ordering between the tasks (Dincbas, Simonis, & Van Hentenryck, 1990; Van Hentenryck, 1989b).

5.2.6 The Magic Series Example

We now illustrate, using a small example, how constraint propagation and nondeterminism interact in `cc(FD)`. The problem is the magic series problem whose specification is the following. Let $S = (s_0, s_1, \ldots, s_n)$ be a non-empty finite series of non-negative integers. The series is said to be *magic* if and only if there are s_i occurrences of i in S for each integer i ranging from 0 to n. For instance, for $n = 3$, the series $(1,2,1,0)$ is magic.

The `cc(FD)` program to solve the magic series problem is shown in Figure 5-3. The series is represented as a list, and the ith element of the list is the element indexed by $i - 1$ in the series. The top-level predicate is `magic(N,L)` if the list represents a magic series of length $N + 1$.

The key idea behind the program is to associate a variable O_i with each element i in the series. The predicate `state_domains` simply creates these vari-

```
magic(Nb,L) :-                          collect([],_,[]).
   Nb1 := Nb + 1,                       collect([F|T],V,[F = V|Eqs]) :-
   state_domains(Nb1,L,0,Nb),              collect(T,V,Eqs).
   occurrences(L,0,L),
   state_sum(L,Nb1),                    state_sum(L,N) :-
   state_product(L,Nb1),                   collect_sum(L,Sum),
   labeling(L).                            Sum = N.

state_domains(0,[],L,U).                collect_sum([],0).
state_domains(N,[F|T],L,U) :-           collect_sum([O|Os], O + Rest) :-
   N > 0,                                  collect_sum(Os,Rest).
   F ∈ L..U,
   N1 := N - 1,                         state_product(L,N) :-
   state_domains(N1,T,L,U).                collect_product(L,0,Sum),
                                           Sum = N.
occurrences([],_,_).
occurrences([F|T],V,L) :-               collect_product([],N,0).
   occur(F,V,L),                        collect_product([O|Os],N, N * O + Rest) :-
   V1 := V + 1,                            N1 := N + 1,
   occurrences(T,V1,L).                    collect_product(Os,N1,Rest).

occur(Nb,Val,L) :-                      labeling([],L).
   collect(L,Val,Eqs),                  labeling([F|T],L) :-
   #(Nb,Eqs,Nb).                           indomain(F),
                                           labeling(T,L).
```

Figure 5-3:   The magic series program

ables and constrains them to range in $0..N$. The predicate occurrence (L, O, L) generates the constraints to be satisfied by the magic series, i.e., a set of cardinality constraints of the form

$$\#(O_i, [\; O_0 = i, O_1 = i, \ldots, O_n = i \;], O_i)$$

for $0 \le i \le n$. The next two predicates, state_sum and state_product, generate surrogate constraints. Surrogate constraints state properties that have to be satisfied by the solutions. They are semantically redundant, but operationally, they often prune substantial parts of the search space. The predicate state_sum states a constraint

$$O_0 + , \ldots , + O_n = n + 1$$

but the predicate state_product states a constraint

$$0 * O_0 + 1 * O_1 + \ldots + n * O_n = n + 1$$

The last goal of the program simply assigns values to the variables.

The search space of the magic series program is depicted in Figure 5-4 for $n = 6$. After stating all constraints, the domains of the variables are respectively

$$O_0 \in 0..6, O_1 \in 0..6, O_2 \in 0..3, O_3 \in 0..2, O_4 \in 0..1, O_5 \in 0..1, O_6 \in 0..1$$

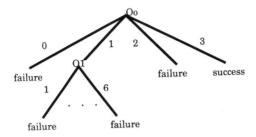

Figure 5-4:   The magic series search space

The first choice tried by the system is $O_0 = 0$. This choice is immediately rejected by the first cardinality constraint

$$\#(O_0 , [\ O_0 = 0,\ O_1 = 0,\ \ldots,\ O_n = 0\ ],\ O_0)$$

because the first constraint is entailed, and hence, the cardinality formula cannot be satisfied. The system then tries the assignment $O_0 = 1$. This assignment leads to the state

$$O_0 = 1,\ O_1 \in 1..6,\ O_2 \in 0..3,\ O_3 \in 0..2,\ O_4 \in 0..1,\ O_5 \in 0..1,\ O_6 \in 0..1$$

The system will not be able to assign O_1 successfully. The value 1 is rejected immediately by its associated cardinality constraint. The value 2 is rejected immediately because the second surrogate constraint requires O_6 to be zero, and the first cardinality formula then forces all the other variables to be at least 1, violating the second surrogate constraint. Similar reasoning is used to reject the values 3 to 6 for O_1. The system then backtracks on the choice of O_0. The value 2 is rejected immediately using the cardinality constraints and the second surrogate constraint. The value 3 directly leads to the solution without any other choice.

5.3 THE PERFECT SQUARE PROBLEM

5.3.1 Problem Statement

The problem amounts to packing a number of squares, all of different sizes, in a larger square, called the master square, in such a way that the squares do not overlap and leave no empty space. Placing 21 squares in a master square is of particular interest because 21 is the smallest number of squares that can fit in a square. This problem and its variations have attracted much attention in the CLP community. Colmerauer (1990) presents a program to fill a rectangle with squares of different sizes using linear equations, inequalities, and disequations over rational numbers. Aggoun and Beldiceanu (1992) present a finite domain program that can solve large instances (e.g., 21 and 24) of the perfect square problem when the sizes of the squares are given. The program uses a specialized cumulative constraint and exploits the link between cumulative constraints and packing in two dimensions. We propose a simple cc(FD) program implementing a natural problem formulation that can solve large instances (e.g., 21 and 24) in about 60 seconds on a SUN 4/60.

5.3.2 Problem Solution

The main idea behind the program consists of creating the squares (i.e., creating variables for their coordinates), expressing the non-overlapping constraints, and assigning values for the coordinates in a nondeterministic way. Moreover, redundant capacity constraints are generated to speed up the computation by pruning the search space early.

5.3.2.1 Problem Data

The program is generic and receives as data the size of the master square and the sizes of the squares. For instance, the data for 21 squares are as follows:

```
sizeMaster(112).
sizeSquares([50,42,37,35,33,29,27,25,24,19,18,17,16,15,11,9,8,7,6,4,2]).
```

5.3.2.2 Program Variables

Each square i is associated with two variables X_i and Y_i representing the coordinates of the bottom-left corner of the square. Each of these variables ranges between 1 and $S - S_i + 1$, where S is the size of the master square, and S_i is the size of square i. The following procedure describes the creation of the two lists of variables as well as the list of the sizes.

```
generateSquares(Xs,Ys,Sizes,Size) :-
    sizeMaster(Size),
    sizeSquares(Sizes),
    generateCoordinates(Xs,Ys,Sizes,Size).

generateCoordinates([],[],[],_).
generateCoordinates([X|Xs],[Y|Ys],[S|Ss],Size) :-
    Sdate := Size - S + 1,
    X ∈ 1..Sdate,
    Y ∈ 1..Sdate,
generateCoordinates(Xs,Ys,Ss,Size).
```

5.3.2.3 The Non-Overlapping Constraint

The non-overlapping constraint between two squares (X1,Y1,S1) and (X2,Y2,S2), where (X1,Y1) and (X2,Y2) are the positions of the squares and S1 and S2 are their respective durations, can be expressed using the cardinality constraint

```
nooverlap(X1,Y1,S1,X2,Y2,S2) :-
    #(1,[X1 + S1 ≤ X2, X2 + S2 ≤ X1, Y1 + S1 ≤ Y2, Y2 + S2 ≤ Y1],2).
```

The cardinality constraint simply expresses that the first square is on the left, on the right, below, or above the second square. It makes sure that as soon as three possibilities are ruled out (i.e., they are not consistent with the constraint store), the last option is automatically enforced. As mentioned previously, the definition simply generalizes the traditional disjunctive constraints to two dimensions.

5.3.2.4 The Capacity Constraints

A traditional technique to improve efficiency in a combinatorial search problem amounts to exploiting properties of all solutions by adding redundant or surrogate constraints. As mentioned previously, these constraints are redundant semantically; i.e., they do not remove any solution but express some important properties of the solutions. Operationally, well chosen surrogate constraints can result in substantial pruning. In the perfect square problem, the summation of the sizes of all squares containing a point with a given x-coordinate (respectively y-coordinate) must be equal to S, the size of the master square, because no empty space is allowed. These surrogate capacity constraints can be stated using cardinality and linear equations. For a given position P, the idea is to associate with each square i a Boolean variable Bi (i.e., a 0-1 domain variable) that is true iff square i contains a point with x-coordinate (resp. y-coordinate) P. The Boolean variable is obtained using the cardinality constraint

```
#(Bi,[Xi ≤ P & P ≤ Xi + Si − 1 ],Bi).
```

The surrogate constraint can now be stated as a simple linear equation:

```
B1 * S1 +...+ Bn * Sn = Size.
```

The program to generate a surrogate constraint is as follows:

```
capacity(Position,Coordinates,Sizes,Size) :-
    accumulate(Coordinates,Sizes,Position,Summation),
    Summation = Size.
accumulate([],[],_,0).
accumulate([C|Cs],[S|Ss],P,B*S + Summation) :-
    B ∈ 0..1,
    #(B,[ C ≤ P & P ≤ C + S − 1],B),
    accumulate(Cs,Ss,P,Summation).
```

5.3.2.5 The Labeling Procedure

The generation of positions for the squares requires giving values to the coordinates of all squares. We use the labeling procedure of Aggoun & Beldiceanu (1992), which exploits the fact that no empty space is allowed. At each step, the program identifies the smallest possible coordinate and selects a square to be placed at this position. On backtracking, another square is selected for the same position. The labeling is as follows:

```
labeling([]).
labeling([Sq|Sqs]) :-
   minlist([Sq|Sqs],Min),
   selectSquare([Sq|Sqs],Min,Rest),
   labeling(Rest).

selectSquare([Sq|Sqs],Min,Sqs) :-
   Sq = Min.
selectSquare([Sq|Sqs],Min,[Sq|Rest]) :-
   Sq > Min,
   selectSquare(Sqs,Min,Rest).
```

The first goal in the labeling finds the smallest position for the remaining squares, and the second goal chooses a square to assign to the position. Because no empty space is allowed, such a square must exist.

5.3.2.6 The Overall Program

Figures 5-5 and 5-6 show the overall program for the perfect square problem. As should be clear, the program is rather small. It packs 21 or 24 squares in a master square in about 60 seconds on a SUN 4/60, illustrating the expressiveness and efficiency of the language.

5.4 THE DIGITAL SIGNAL PROCESSING APPLICATION

5.4.1 Problem Statement

The availability of programmable digital processors at low cost has raised much interest in DSP and its applications such as speech, image processing, and noise and echo cancellation. Moreover, the design of multiprocessor DSP systems has emerged as one of the most promising directions. Recently, Chinneck et al. (1990) and Lavoie (1990) have proposed a new approach to the design of DSP applications that couples an extensible architecture with an automatic task to a processor scheduling method. This approach is suitable for many complex DSP applications because it combines some of the advantages of specialized systems (often efficient but not flexible) with those of general-purpose systems (often flexi-

```
packSquares(Xs,Ys) :-
    generateSquares(Xs,Ys,Sizes,Size),
    stateNoOverlap(Xs,Ys,Sizes),
    stateCapacity(Xs,Sizes,Size),
    stateCapacity(Ys,Sizes,Size),
    labeling(Xs),
    labeling(Ys).

generateSquares(Xs,Ys,Sizes,Size) :-
    sizeMaster(Size),
    sizeSquares(Sizes),
    generateCoordinates(Xs,Ys,Sizes,Size).

generateCoordinates([],[],[],_).
generateCoordinates([X|Xs],[Y|Ys],[S|Ss],Size) :-
    Sdate := Size - S + 1,
    X ∈ 1..Sdate,
    Y ∈ 1..Sdate,
    generateCoordinates(Xs,Ys,Ss,Size).

stateNoOverlap([],[],[]).
stateNoOverlap([X|Xs],[Y|Ys],[S|Ss]) :-
    stateNoOverlap(X,Y,S,Xs,Ys,Ss),
    stateNoOverlap(Xs,Ys,Ss).

stateNoOverlap(X,Y,S,[],[],[]).
stateNoOverlap(X,Y,S,[X1|Xs],[Y1|Ys],[S|Ss]) :-
    nooverlap(X,Y,S,X1,Y1,S1),
    stateNoOverlap(X,Y,S,Xs,Ys,Ss).
nooverlap(X1,Y1,S1,X2,Y2,S2) :-
    #(1,[X1 + S1 ≤ X2, X2 + S2 ≤ X1, Y1 + S1 ≤ Y2, Y2 + S2 ≤ Y1],2).
```

Figure 5-5:   The perfect square program: Part I.

ble but much less efficient). In addition, it provides a real-time simulation tool for systems that will eventually be implemented on a VLSI chip. In the rest of this section, we review the key ideas behind the architecture and introduce the main combinatorial search problems. The presentation is based on Chinneck et al. (1990) and Lavoie (1990), where complete information on the approach can be found.

5.4.1.1 The Architecture

The extensible architecture is depicted in Figure 5-7, from Lavoie (1990). It captures two common paradigms of DSP applications: pipelined processing and master-slave processing. The master (processor 0) has a direct communication link

```
stateCapacity(Cs,Sizes,Size) :-
    stateCapacity(1,Size,Cs,Sizes).

stateCapacity(Pos,Size,Cs,Sizes) :-
    Pos > Size.
stateCapacity(Pos,Size,Cs,Sizes) :-
    capacity(Pos,Cs,Sizes,Size),
    Pos1 := Pos + 1,
    stateCapacity(Pos1,Size,Cs,Sizes).

capacity(Position,Coordinates,Sizes,Size) :-
    accumulate(Coordinates,Sizes,Position,Summation),
    Summation = Size.

accumulate([],[],_,0).
accumulate([C|Cs],[S|Ss],P,B*S + Summation) :-
    B ∈ 0..1, #(B,[ C ≤ P & P ≤ C + S - 1],B),
    accumulate(Cs,Ss,P,Summation).

labeling([]).
labeling([Sq|Sqs]) :-
    minlist([Sq|Sqs],Min),
    selectSquare([Sq|Sqs],Min,Rest),
    labeling(Rest).
selectSquare([Sq|Sqs],Min,Ss) :- Sq = Min.
selectSquare([Sq|Sqs],Min,[Sq|Rest]) :-
    Sq > Min,
    selectSquare(Sqs,Min,Rest).
```

Figure 5-6:   The perfect square program: Part II.

with all processors in the pipeline, whereas processor i in the pipeline can read from its predecessor (processor $i - 1$) and write to its successor (processor $i + 1$). Some redundant links are included in this architecture to simplify programming of the applications.

The processors are synchronized by a clock corresponding to the sampling rate of the incoming signal (or data) of the system. The clock cycle is divided into a *read* part, during which a processor copies its input buffers into local memory, and a *write* part, during which the processor is allowed to write in its output buffers. As a consequence, all tasks must be performed during the clock cycle, and data to be transferred must be available at the clock edge.

Each processor in the architecture is identical; has its own local memory; and is characterized by its limits on the data memory, the code memory, and the processing time in a synchronization cycle.

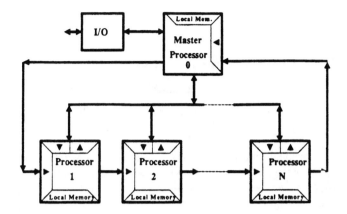

Figure 5-7:   The extensible architecture

The main features of the architecture are

1. *Extensibility*: More processors can be added to accommodate the need for more processing power.

2. *Bounded Communication Delay:* The communication delay between two processors is at most 2.

In the following, we assume that the DSP application is deterministic wrt the data stream, and the task-to-processor scheduling can be performed once in the life time of the system for fixed systems or once for each configuration for reconfigurable systems.

5.4.1.2 The Task Graph

The DSP application is described by a task graph where each node represents a DSP function, and an arc denotes a data flow path between two functions. Each task is characterized by its demand in processing time (e.g., 80 μs), in data memory (e.g., 50 bytes), and in code memory (e.g., 10 bytes). The data flow path expresses precedence constraints between the tasks.

The communication delay between two successive tasks depends on which processors the tasks are assigned to. If the two tasks are assigned to the same processor, the communication delay is zero. If the two tasks are assigned to adjacent processors (e.g., i for the origin task and $i + 1$ for the destination task), the communication delay is one clock cycle; i.e., the destination task can proceed at the next clock cycle. Otherwise, the communication is two clock cycles because the data transfer must go through the master.

In the following, we assume that the whole task graph includes two fictitious tasks: an input task and an output task. Both tasks are assigned to the master processor and have no requirement. The total delay of the application is the time in clock cycles between the input and output tasks.

5.4.1.3 The Combinatorial Search Problems

There are two orthogonal problems that need to be solved:

1. minimizing the number of processors for a task graph
2. minimizing the total delay for a given number of processors

The first problem is a generalization of the well known bin-packing problem for which there exist very good approximation algorithms (e.g., first-fit decreasing). Our cc(FD) program uses such an algorithm to obtain a solution to the first problem. The second problem (i.e., finding the minimum total delay given the number of processors given by the first problem) is more difficult and is the topic of the remaining part of this section.

5.4.2 Problem Solution

5.4.2.1 Overview of the Program

The program is once again a typical finite domain program. The key idea is to create the problem variables (i.e., those variables on which the constraints will be imposed), to state the constraints, and to generate values for the variables with a labeling procedure. Because it is an optimization problem, the labeling procedure, together with an objective function, is enclosed inside a meta-predicate for finding the optimal solution. The main predicate of the program is as follows:

```
scheduleDsp(ResTasks)  :-
    createTasks(Tasks,Nbprocs),
    statePrecedence(Tasks),
    stateCapacity(Tasks,Nbprocs),
    stateDelay(Tasks),
    stateSurrogate(Tasks),

    findEndTask(Tasks,EndTask),
    getCycle(EndDate,EndCycle),

    minof(labeling(Tasks),EndCycle,ResTasks).
```

The first goal creates the tasks Tasks; the next four goals state the constraints, including some "semantically" redundant constraints; the next two goals retrieve the variable expressing the total delay (i.e., the cycle of the end task); and the last goal is the meta-predicate for optimization, receiving the labeling procedure and the variable EndCycle as objective functions. In the rest of this section, the above steps are explained in detail.

5.4.2.2 Problem Variables

Each task in the DSP application is associated with two variables:

- P_i, the processor to which task i is assigned
- S_i, the starting cycle of task i

In the following, we refer to the first type of variable as `processor` variables and the second type of variable as `cycle` variables.

The key problem to be solved is the assignment of processors to the tasks. Once this assignment is completed, it is a simple matter to find a solution to the overall problem. Indeed, the problem is then reduced to a simple PERT problem that is solved automatically through constraint propagation, as mentioned previously. A solution can then be obtained by assigning the earliest starting cycle to each task.

Our `cc(FD)` program creates a term `task(Number,Name,P,S,Time,Memory, Code)` for each task, where `number` is the number of the task; `name` its name; `P` its processor; `S` its starting cycle; and `Time, Memory, Code` its demands in computing time, data memory, and code memory. All components of the term are ground (i.e., fully instantiated) except `P`, which is constrained to range between 0 and the number of processors available minus 1, and `S`, which is required to take a value between 0 and the maximum delay (which can be computed easily by assuming the worst communication delays).

5.4.3 Precedence Constraints

As mentioned previously, the task graph implies a number of precedence relationships between the tasks. The precedence constraints only affect the cycle variables and are stated in the standard way:

```
precedence(Task1,Task2) :-
    getCycle(Task1,C1),
    getCycle(Task2,C2),
    C1 ≤ C2.
```

5.4.4 Capacity Constraints

Because the capacity of each processor is limited, it is necessary to make sure that the tasks assigned to a processor do not exceed its resources. The capacity constraints for the DSP application are closely related to the capacity constraints of the perfect square problem but use inequalities instead of equations. The `cc(FD)` program associates a Boolean variable with each task and each processor. The Boolean variable is true iff the task is assigned to the processor and is obtained through a cardinality formula

```
#(Bi, [ Pi = P ], Bi)
```

where B_i is the Boolean variable associated with task i, P_i is the processor variable of task i, and P is a processor number. The inequalities can now be stated as follows:

```
Ti1 * B1 + ... + Tin * Bn ≤ MaxTime,
Me1 * B1 + ... + Men * Bn ≤ MaxMem,
Ti1 * B1 + ... + Tin * Bn ≤ MaxCode,
```

where $B_1,...,B_n$ are the Boolean variables associated with all tasks for processor P, and Ti_k, Me_k, Ce_k are the demands of each task k in time, data memory, and code memory.

The program for generating a capacity constraint is as follows:

```
capacity(Tasks,Proc,MaxTime,MaxMemory,MaxCode) :-
    collectCapacity(Tasks,Proc,Time,Memory,Code),
    Time ≤ MaxTime,
    Memory ≤ MaxMemory,
    Code ≤ MaxCode.

collectCapacity([],Proc,0,0,0).
collectCapacity([Task|Tasks],Proc,T * B + Ts,
        M * B + Ms, C * B + Cs) :-
    getTime(Task,T),
    getMemory(Task,M),
    getCode(Task,C),
    getProc(Task,P),
    B ∈ 0..1,
    #( B, [ P = Proc ], B ),
    collectCapacity(Tasks,Proc,Ts,Ms,Cs).
```

The predicate `collectCapacity` collects linear terms for the data memory, the code memory, and processing time. Those terms are then used in predicate `capacity` to state the capacity constraints. Collecting the linear terms is performed in a way similar to the capacity constraints for the perfect square problem.

5.4.4.1 The Delay Constraints

The total communication delay depends on the delay between every two successive tasks in the task graph. The cc(FD) program generates delay constraints between the cycle variables of the tasks. If C_1, C_2 are cycle variables of two successive tasks, the idea is to generate a constraint

```
C2 ≥ C1 + Delay
```

where `Delay` is the communication delay between the two tasks. The communication delay can be expressed as a constraint involving the processor variables P_1, P_2 of the tasks using cardinality formulas:

```
delay(P1,P2,S1,S2) :-
    Delay ∈ 0..2,
    Delay = 0 ⇔ P1 = P2,
    Delay = 1 ⇔ P1 ≠ P2 & (P1 = 0 ∨ P2 = 0 ∨ P2 = P1 + 1),
    C2 ≥ C1 + Delay.
```

The first goal expresses that the delay is at most 2, and the second goal states that the delay is 0 whenever the tasks are allocated to the same processor. The third goal imposes the delay to be 1 whenever the tasks are not allocated to the same processor and either one of them is assigned to the master processor, or the second task is allocated to a processor on the right of the processor of the first task. The third case can be omitted because the first two cases are expressed as equivalences, and the delay is at most 2. Note that the distance constraints preclude the need for the precedence constraints that can now be omitted. Finally, note the simplicity of the implementation that follows closely from the definition.

5.4.4.2 Surrogate Constraints

The cycle variable of the end task provides an optimistic evaluation of the minimum delay of the DSP problem. Indeed, this variable is constrained by all the delay constraints, and its minimum value provides the optimistic evaluation. It is, however, possible and desirable to improve this evaluation by stating some properties of the solutions. This helps pruning the search space during the search for the optimal solution. The key idea is to exploit the resource constraints jointly with the precedence constraints. Consider, for instance, a precedence path $t_1, t_2, \ldots, t_n$ and a resource r (e.g., computing time, data memory, code memory). If the tasks $t_1, \ldots, t_i$ ($1 \leq i \leq n$) have resource requirements for resource r exceeding the capacity of the processor, it follows that the delay between tasks t_1 and t_i is at least 1. A constraint

$$C_i > C_1$$

where C_i, C_1 are the cycle variables of tasks t_i and t_1, can then be generated without removing any of the solutions.

Our cc(FD) program systematically generates all such surrogate constraints for all resources. Note that it is sufficient to consider for each task the smallest subpath exceeding the capacity of the resources.

5.4.4.3 The Labeling Procedure

We now consider the labeling procedure for the DSP application. As mentioned previously, the key issue is the assignment of a processor to each task. It is a simple matter to complete the solution by assigning the earliest values to the cycle variables. Hence, we focus on the first part of the labeling.

As is typical with constraint satisfaction problems, two decisions need to be made:

1. which variable should be instantiated first
2. which value should be given to the selected variable

For the first decision, two strategies have been included in the cc(FD) program:

1. a depth-first labeling
2. a breadth-first labeling

The depth-first labeling proceeds by assigning processor variables in a depth-first traversal of the task graph starting with the start task, and the breadth-first labeling uses a breadth-first traversal. The motivation behind the depth-first strategy is to obtain quickly an accurate evaluation of the total delay. The motivation behind the breadth-first strategy is to exploit the locality of the tasks and to schedule closely related tasks together. Both strategies have systematically been evaluated, and experimental results are discussed in the next section.

As far as the second decision is concerned, the cc(FD) program uses the following heuristics: if p is the value of the previously assigned variable,

- First try p.
- Next try $p + 1$.
- Next try the master processor.
- Finally, try all other values.

The heuristics are motivated by the desire to minimize the total communication delay. The first choice guarantees a communication delay of 0 between the last two tasks, the second and third choices ensure a communication delay of 1, and the last choice imposes a communication delay of 2. The implementation of this heuristics is based on the following procedure:

```
assign(P,Previous) :-
    P = Previous.
assign(P,Previous) :-
    P = Previous + 1.
assign(P,Previous) :-
    P ≠ Previous,
    P = 0.
assign(P,Previous) :-
    P ≠ Previous,
    P ≠ Previous + 1,
    P ≠ 0,
    indomain(P).
```

5.4.4.4 Exploiting Symmetries

In general, DSP applications have many symmetrical solutions, and it would be of great advantage if the program could exploit them in order to prune the search space. Consider, for instance, the computation step where the program tries to assign a processor to a task. If there are several processors unused at this computation step, it would be convenient to restrict attention to only one of them. It turns out that this idea is only applicable under restricted circumstances, namely, when all tasks that are on a parallel pipeline with the task being considered have been assigned already (Chinneck et al., 1990).

To evaluate the possible gain of symmetries in the DSP applications, our program also includes an *incomplete* labeling procedure that systematically performs the above pruning at the risk of missing the optimal solution. The labeling procedure needs to keep track of the used processors and is based on the following procedure:

```
assign(P,Previous,MaxUsed,MaxUsed) :-
  P = Previous.
assign(P,Previous,MaxUsed,P) :-
  P = MaxUsed + 1.
assign(P,Previous,MaxUsed,MaxUsed) :-
  P ≠ Previous,
  P = 0.
assign(P,Previous,MaxUsed,MaxUsed) :-
  P ≠ Previous,
  P ≠ 0,
  P ≤ MaxUsed,
  indomain(P).
```

In this procedure, the third argument is the maximum number of the used processors. The fourth argument is the new maximum number. The last clause only considers the previously used processors. Hence, only one new processor can be used (i.e., in the second clauses).

5.4.5 Experimental Results

In this section, we summarize the experimental results obtained by the cc(FD) program on actual DSP applications and compare them with a specialized branch and bound algorithm (written in C).

First, note that the overall cc(FD) program is about four pages long. This obviously comes from the fact that the search tree management and the constraint propagation are automatically taken care of by the programming language. The programming task consisted of stating the constraints and coming with a suitable labeling procedure. Note also the adequacy of the cardinality operator to express sophisticated constraints such as the capacity and delay constraints.

Table 5-1: Description of actual DSP applications.

Problem	Size	Processors	Topology
RDAD01	9	3	Pipeline
RDAD02	9	3	Pipeline
RDAD03	6	5	Architecture-like
RDAD04	19	6	Parallel pipelines
RDAD05	12	4	Pipeline
RDAD06	16	5	Parallel pipelines
RDAD07	12	4	Parallel pipelines
RDAD08	15	5	Merging tasks
RDAD09	9	6	Many generators
RDAD10	15	5	Parallel pipelines
RDAD20	13	5	Architecture-like
RDAD40	25	8	Parallel pipelines
RDAD41	25	8	Parallel pipelines

Table 5-1 presents a description of actual DSP applications taken from Lavoie (1990). The first column describes the name of the applications, the second column the size of the task graph, the third column the number of processors available, and the last column the topology of the applications. The first problems are small, the last ones being much larger. For instance, the potential search space of RDAD40 is 8^{25}, which is 2^{75}.

Table 5-2 presents the results of the complete cc(FD) algorithm. The second column gives the total delay of the optimal solution, the third column the times of the cc(FD) program with the depth-first labeling strategy, the fourth column the times of the cc(FD) program with the breadth-first labeling strategy, and the fifth column the times of the specialized branch and bound of Lavoie (1990). All times are given in seconds for a SUN 4/60. On these actual applications, the cc(FD) program behaves much better in general with the depth-first strategy than with the breadth-first strategy. In particular, it is about 14, 2230, 59 times faster on RDAD04, RDAD08, and RDAD40. The cc(FD) program also compares well with the specific branch and bound algorithm. In particular, the DF program is 31 and 298 times faster on RDAD04 and RDAD08. The specific branch and bound algorithm also could not find a solution for RDAD40 but is faster in general on the problems requiring less computing time.

Table 5-3 presents the results of the incomplete cc(FD) algorithm, i.e., the algorithm systematically exploiting symmetries. Delay-DF and Time-DF give the best total delay found and the computation time for the cc(FD) program with the depth-first search strategy, and Delay-BF and Time-BF give the total delay and the computation time for the cc(FD) program with the breadth-first search

Table 5-2:   Results on actual DSP applications.

Problem	Total Delay	cc(FD): DF	cc(FD): BF	Specialized BB
RDAD01	3	0.78	0.31	0.016
RDAD02	3	0.72	0.32	0.016
RDAD03	5	0.22	0.11	0.000
RDAD04	3	1.66	24.14	51.700
RDAD05	3	1.12	5.29	0.016
RDAD06	3	2.68	18.31	6.300
RDAD07	2	0.56	5.19	0.050
RDAD08	3	3.23	7202.00	963.130
RDAD09	2	0.18	0.20	0.016
RDAD10	4	3.90	1.80	0.033
RDAD20	3	0.99	0.78	0.016
RDAD40	5	54.40	3216.70	?????
RDAD41	4	4.24	3.16	0.100

strategy. The first point to notice is that on those problems, the optimal solution is always found by both programs. The computation time can also drastically be reduced, as illustrated by the problems RDAD40 and RDAD08. To compare the results with the specialized branch and bound, we give in Table 5-4 the results with the same exploitation of the heuristics and, in addition, a dynamic clustering of tasks. The dynamic clustering groups together tasks on a pipeline and, thus, substantially reduces the search space. The results indicate that the cc(FD) program, even without dynamic task clustering, still performs well. It is faster on RDAD08

Table 5-3:   Results with symmetries on actual DSP applications.

Problem	Delay-DF	Time-DF	Delay-BF	Time-BF
RDAD01	3	0.78	3	0.26
RDAD02	3	0.74	3	0.27
RDAD03	5	0.18	5	0.11
RDAD04	3	1.25	5	4.61
RDAD05	3	0.92	5	1.62
RDAD06	3	2.12	3	5.88
RDAD07	2	0.56	2	1.83
RDAD08	3	1.86	3	359.69
RDAD09	2	0.16	3	0.15
RDAD10	4	3.03	4	1.13
RDAD20	3	0.79	3	0.52
RDAD40	5	16.55	5	150.16
RDAD41	4	3.45	4	1.46

Table 5-4: Results of the specialized branch and bound with symmetries and clustering.

Problem	Delay-SBB	Time-SBB
RDAD01	3	0.016
RDAD02	3	0.000
RDAD03	5	0.000
RDAD04	3	0.000
RDAD05	3	0.016
RDAD06	3	0.033
RDAD07	2	0.000
RDAD08	3	29.067
RDAD09	2	0.000
RDAD10	5	0.000
RDAD20	3	0.000
RDAD40	5	1.733
RDAD41	4	0.033

and less than 10 times slower on RDAD40 where many task clusterings can take place. These results indicate clearly that a language such as cc(FD) can be competitive for industrial applications and provide a short development time.

5.5 LIMITATIONS AND FURTHER WORK

The last sections have discussed two applications of cc(FD). cc(FD) has also been applied to many other problems, including disjunctive scheduling, Hamiltonian circuits, graph coloring, frequency allocation, and cutting-stock problems to name a few. In many cases, cc(FD) can be used to provide compact and declarative descriptions of traditional global search algorithms. For instance, it is natural to express the multi-path method for Hamiltonian circuits in cc(FD). One of the limitations of cc(FD) for this class of algorithms is the lack of support for relaxation techniques. Relaxation is a process that consists mainly of three steps:

- relaxing the original problem by removing some (implicit or explicit) constraints
- solving the relaxed problem
- using the solution to the relaxed problem to help solve the original problem

Many relaxation techniques have been studied, such as the relaxation to linear programming for integer programming, the relaxation to preemptive scheduling in disjunctive scheduling, and the relaxation to minimum spanning tree in the travelling salesman problem. It is an open issue to design declarative combinators supporting naturally a variety of relaxations.

Another important issue is how to use local search in constraint languages. As mentioned previously, the global and local search paradigms are orthogonal and complementary, and it would be appealing to have a constraint language based on local search. This, however, raises some difficult semantic and implementation problems.

Finally, cc(FD) is mainly appropriate for off-line algorithms, and little research has been devoted to on-line algorithms and problems such as reactive scheduling and planning. Current research avenues in this area range from incremental constraint solving, where constraints can be deleted and modified, to incremental search, where one tries to exploit the pruning of previous searches when constraints are dynamically added and deleted.

5.6 CONCLUSION

In this chapter, we have described the application of cc(FD) to two applications: the perfect square problem and a digital signal processing application. cc(FD) is a declarative constraint logic programming language over finite domains, offering a short development time and a competitive efficiency for many discrete combinatorial search problems. The cc(FD) program for the perfect square problem is about a page long, is conceptually simple, and packs 21 or 24 squares in about 60 seconds on a SUN 4/60. The cc(FD) program for the DSP applications is about 4 pages long and is competitive in efficiency with a specialized branch and bound algorithms developed for the task. Both programs make use of advanced features of cc(FD) (e.g., the cardinality operator) and exploit the integration of constraint solving in a declarative language, e.g., by using sophisticated choice procedures and generating surrogate constraints. Both applications illustrate the potential benefit of constraint languages such as cc(FD).

ACKNOWLEDGMENTS

Michel Van Caneghem and Alain Colmerauer suggested the perfect square application and the approach taken in the cc(FD) program and pointed out the reference Aggoun & Beldiceanu (1992). Gerald Karam provided the DSP applications and gave us the benchmarks to test our programs. We would like to thank them, as well as Yves Deville and Vijay Saraswat, for the work on the design of cc(FD). This research was partly supported by the National Science Foundation under grant number CCR-9108032 and the Office of Naval Research under grant N00014-91-J-4052 ARPA order 8225.

References

Aggoun, A., and N. Beldiceanu. 1992. "Extending CHIP to Solve Complex Scheduling and Packing Problems." *Journées Francophones de Programmation Logique*, Lille, France.

Buttner, W., and H. Simonis. 1987. "Embedding Boolean Expressions into Logic Programming." *Journal of Symbolic Computation*, 4:191–205.

Carlier, J., and E. Pinson. 1986. *Une Méthode Arborescente pour Optimiser la Durée d'un JOB-SHOP*. Technical Report ISSN 0294-2755, I.M.Angers.

Chinneck, J.W., R.A. Goubran, G.M. Karam, and M Lavoie. 1990. *A Design Approach for Real-Time Multiprocessor DSP Applications*. Report SCE-90-05, Carleton University, Ottawa, Canada.

Christofides, N. 1975. *Graph Theory: An Algorithmic Approach*. Academic Press, New York.

Colmerauer, A. 1990. "An Introduction to Prolog III." *CACM*, 28(4): 412–418.

Dean, T., and M. Boddy. 1988. "An Analysis of Time-Dependent Planning." *Proceedings of the Seventh National Conference on Artificial Intelligence*, pages 49–54, AAAI Press, Menlo Park, CA.

Dincbas, M., H. Simonis, and P. Van Hentenryck. 1988a. "Solving a Cutting-Stock Problem in Constraint Logic Programming." Presented at Fifth International Conference on Logic Programming, Seattle, WA.

Dincbas, M., H. Simonis, and P. Van Hentenryck. 1988b. "Solving the Car Sequencing Problem in Constraint Logic Programming." Presented at European Conference on Artificial Intelligence (ECAI-88), Munich, Germany.

Dincbas, M., H. Simonis, and P. Van Hentenryck. 1990. "Solving Large Combinatorial Problems in Logic Programming." *Journal of Logic Programming*, 8(1–2): 75–93.

Graf, T. 1987. *Extending Constraint Handling in Logic Programming to Rational Arithmetic*. Internal Report, ECRC, Munich.

Jaffar, J., and J-L. Lassez. 1987. "Constraint Logic Programming." *POPL-87*, pp. 111–119.

Jaffar, J., and S. Michaylov. 1987. "Methodology and Implementation of a CLP System." Presented at Fourth International Conference on Logic Programming, Melbourne, Australia, MIT Press, Cambridge, Mass., pp. 196–218.

Kubale, M., and D. Jackowski. 1985. "A Generalized Implicit Enumeration Algorithm for Graph Coloring." *CACM*, 28(4): 412–418.

Lavoie, Marco. 1990. *Task Assignment in a DSP Multiprocessor Environment*. Master's thesis, Department of Systems and Computer Engineering, Carleton University, Ottawa, Ontario.

Mackworth, A.K. 1977. "Consistency in Networks of Relations." *Artificial Intelligence*, 8(1): 99–118.

Maher, M.J. 1987. "Logic Semantics for a Class of Committed-Choice Programs." *Proceedings of Fourth International Conference on Logic Programming*, MIT Press, Cambridge, Mass., pp. 858–876.

Mohr, R., and T.C. Henderson. 1986. "Arc and Path Consistency Revisited." *Artificial Intelligence*, 28:225–233.

Saraswat, V.A. 1989. *Concurrent Constraint Programming Languages*. Ph.D. Thesis, Carnegie Mellon University.

Saraswat, V.A., and M. Rinard. 1990. "Concurrent Constraint Programming." Presented at Seventeenth ACM Symposium on Principles of Programming Languages, San Francisco, CA.

Saraswat, V.A., M. Rinard, and P. Panangaden. 1991. "Semantic Foundations of Concurrent Constraint Programming." Presented at Ninth ACM Symposium on Principles of Programming Languages, Orlando, FL.

Van Hentenryck, P. 1989a. "A Logic Language for Combinatorial Optimization." *Annals of Operations Research*, 21:247–274.

Van Hentenryck, P. 1989b. *Constraint Satisfaction in Logic Programming*. Logic Programming Series. The MIT Press, Cambridge, MA.

Van Hentenryck, P., and Y. Deville. 1991. "The Cardinality Operator: A New Logical Connective and Its Application to Constraint Logic Programming." Presented at Eighth International Conference on Logic Programming (ICLP-91), Paris, France. Also in *Constraint Logic Programming: Selected Research*, The MIT Press, Cambridge, Mass., 1993.

Van Hentenryck, P., and T. Graf. 1992. "Standard Forms for Rational Linear Arithmetics in Constraint Logic Programming." *Annals of Mathematics and Artificial Intelligence*, 5(2–4): 303–370.

Van Hentenryck, P., Y. Deville, and C.M. Teng. 1992. "A Generic Arc Consistency Algorithm and Its Specializations." *Artificial Intelligence*, 57(2–3): 291–321.

Van Hentenryck, P., H. Simonis, and M. Dincbas. 1992. "Constraint Satisfaction Using Constraint Logic Programming." *Artificial Intelligence*, 58: 113–159.

6

HSTS:

Integrating Planning and Scheduling

Nicola Muscettola
*(RECOM Technologies
NASA Ames Research Center)*

6.1 INTRODUCTION

In the traditional approach to managing complex systems, planning and scheduling are two very distinct phases. Planning determines how the system achieves different types of goals. The process consists of concatenating elementary transformations (or actions) to move the world into a state that satisfies the goal. The result is a library of plans. Scheduling takes responsibility for day to day operations. After receiving a set of goals, a scheduler instantiates plan templates contained in the library and assigns to each action a time slot for the exclusive use of the needed resources. The result is the prediction of a specific course of action that, if followed, ensures the achievement of all goals within the system's physical constraints.

A typical case is the management of a manufacturing facility. Planning develops processes to manufacture given product types (e.g., transforming a raw block of metal into a widget). Scheduling receives a number of orders to produce widgets of given types with known release dates for raw materials and due dates for finished products. In both phases, costs should be kept as low as possible; this might require generating processes with a minimum number of steps or scheduling the last action in each order as close as possible to the due date.

This strict separation between planning and scheduling does not match the operating conditions of a wide variety of complex systems. Even in cases where separation is viable, it might be overly restrictive. A more flexible adaptation to the structure of the problem might yield better solutions. For example, during the scheduling phase, it is often necessary to expand setup activities; these are not justified by the achievement of a primary goal but depend exclusively on how other activities are sequenced on a resource. Consider an instance where two sequential operations require drilling holes of different diameters using the same drilling machine; the schedule must allocate time for the substitution of the drill bit. In other situations, planning might profitably be delayed into the scheduling phase. This allows the expansion of courses of action that, although a priori sub-optimal, are clearly convenient when considering expected resource usage. The number of possible alternatives might make the management of a complete plan library impractical as required by the traditional approach.

A major obstacle to more integrated and flexible planning and scheduling is the lack of a unified framework. This should support the representation of all aspects of the problem in a way that makes the inherent structure of the domain evident. When dealing with large problems and complex domains, a framework with strong structuring devices facilitates the decomposition of system models and the consequent management of the combinatorics of search.

In planning, most Artificial Intelligence research adopts the classical representational assumption proposed by the STRIPS planning system (Fikes, Hart, & Nilsson, 1972). In this view, action is essentially an instantaneous transition between two world states of undetermined durations. The structural complexity of a state is unbound, but the devices provided for its description, such as complete first order theories or lists of predicates, are completely unstructured. Some frameworks (Wilkins, 1988; Currie & Tate, 1991) have demonstrated the ability to address practical planning problems. However, the classical assumption lacks balance between generality and structure; this is a major obstacle in extending classical planning into integrated planning and scheduling. Past research has attempted partial extensions in several important directions: processes evolving over continuous (Allen & Koomen, 1983) and metric time (Vere, 1983; Dean, Firby, & Miller, 1988), parallelism (Lansky, 1988), and external events (Forbus, 1989). However, no comprehensive view has yet been proposed to address the integration problem.

Classical scheduling research has always exploited much stronger structuring assumptions (Baker, 1974). Domains are decomposed into a set of resources whose states evolve over continuous time. This facilitates the explicit representation of resource utilization over extended periods of time. Several current scheduling systems exploit reasoning over such representations (Fox & Smith, 1984; Smith et al., 1990; Zweben, Deale, & Gargan, 1990; Biefeld & Cooper, 1991; Sadeh, 1991; Minton et al., 1992). Empirical studies have demonstrated the superiority of this approach (Ow & Smith, 1988; Sadeh, 1991) with respect to dispatching scheduling (Panwalker & Iskander, 1977), where decision making focuses only on the immediate future. However, the scheduling view of the world has very strong limitations. No information is kept about a resource state beyond its availability. Additional state information (e.g., which bit is mounted in a drill at a given time) is crucial to maintain causal justifications and to dynamically expand support activities during problem solving.

In this chapter, we describe HSTS (Heuristic Scheduling Testbed System), a representation and problem solving framework that aims at unifying planning and scheduling. Similar to classical scheduling, HSTS decomposes a domain into a vector of state variables continuously evolving over time. Similar to planning, HSTS provides general devices for representing complex states and causal justifications. Within this framework, we have developed and experimentally tested planning/scheduling systems for several unconventional domains. These domains include short term scheduling for the Hubble Space Telescope (Muscettola et al., 1992) and "bare base" deployment for transportation planning (Frederking & Muscettola, 1992). Several constraint propagation mechanisms support the richness of domain representation at any problem solving stage.

Schedules developed in HSTS implicitly identify a set of legal system behaviors. This is an important distinction with respect to classical approaches that, instead, specify all aspects of a single, nominal system behavior. During execution, a nominal behavior is interpreted as an ideal trajectory to be followed as closely as possible. However, because the schedule does not explicitly represent feasible alternatives, it is difficult to have a clear picture of the impact of the unavoidable deviations from the desired course of action. HSTS, instead, advocates schedules as envelopes of behavior within which the executor is free to react to unexpected events and still maintain acceptable system performance. Viewing scheduling as the manipulation of behavior envelopes has potential advantages during plan/schedule construction. In this chapter, we will discuss a heuristic scheduling methodology, Conflict Partition Scheduling (CPS), that operates on a temporally flexible network of constraints under the guidance of statistical estimates of the network's properties. We will show experimental evidence of CPS's superiority with respect to other intelligent scheduling approaches.

The chapter is organized as follows. In Section 6.2, we briefly describe two unconventional application domains that require integrated planning and scheduling. We then introduce the basic HSTS modeling principle that allows such integration (Section 6.3). A detailed description of the features of HSTS follows in Sections 6.4 and 6.5. Special attention is given to the wide variety of resource capacity constraints supported by the framework (Section 6.6). The rest of the chapter describes two problem solvers implemented in HSTS: a short-term scheduler for Hubble Space Telescope observation scheduling (Section 6.7) and a scheduling methodology for job-shop scheduling (Section 6.8). In the conclusions (Section 6.9), we summarize the status of the project and discuss future research directions.

6.2 TWO APPLICATION DOMAINS

6.2.1 Space Mission Scheduling

Space mission scheduling problems include managing orbiting astronomical observatories, coordinating the execution of activities aboard the space station, and generating detailed command sequences for automated planetary probes. These apparently diverse applications share two main sources of complexity. The first is the need to use the space facility with high efficiency in the presence of a very large number of diverse usage requests. Much of the international scientific community is eager to take advantage of the unique conditions found in space (e.g., weightlessness, extreme vacuum, exposure to radiation that does not reach the surface of the earth). For example, in the case of the Hubble Space Telescope, the number of individual observations requested over a year is on the order of several tens of thousands. Consequently, the time requested by the experiments deemed worth pursuing exceeds the lifetime of any given mission. To maximize return, the final schedule must accommodate as many of these experiments as possible. The second source of complexity is the need to ensure a safe operation of the space facility. It is not enough to allocate exclusive time for the execution of main activities; the schedule must contain enough detail to explicitly ensure that auxiliary reconfigurations and intermediate states of the various subsystems do not interact in a harmful way.

A typical space mission scheduling problem is the generation of short-term schedules for the Hubble Space Telescope (HST). Astronomers formulate observation programs according to a fairly sophisticated specification language (Space, 1986). The basic structure of each program is a partial ordering of observations. Each observation specifies the collection of light from a celestial object with one of the telescope's scientific instruments. A program can contain a diverse set of temporal constraints, including precedences, windows of opportunity for groups of observations, minimum and maximum temporal separations, and coordinated parallel observations with different viewing instruments. When executing an observation, HST gathers light from celestial objects called targets and communicates scientific data back to earth through one of two TDRSS communication satellites (Figure 6-1). Given the telescope's low altitude orbit, the earth periodically occludes virtually any target and communication satellite. The fraction of orbit during which each of them is available for observation or communication depends on their position.

The telescope subsystems must be operated paying continuous attention to several stringent constraints. These include limited available electric power and maintenance of acceptable temperature profiles on the telescope structure. The pointing subsystem is responsible for orienting HST toward a target and locking it at the center of the field of view of the designated scientific instrument. HST has

Hubble Space Telescope

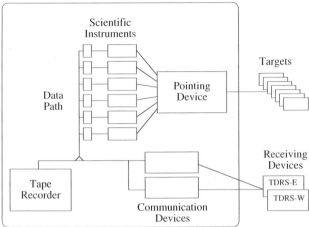

Figure 6-1: The Hubble Space Telescope domain

six different scientific instruments, but available electric power does not allow all of them to be operational simultaneously. Moving an instrument between operation and quiescence requires complex reconfiguration sequences that must be coordinated among various instrument components. Reconfigurations must also be synchronized appropriately among different instruments. Data can be read from the instruments and directly communicated to earth through one of two links operating at different communication rates; it can also be stored temporarily on an on-board tape recorder and communicated to earth at a later time.

In summary, solving the HST observation scheduling problem requires generating command sequences to accommodate as many observations as possible while maintaining telescope integrity and satisfying constraints and preferences imposed by the scientists.

6.2.2 Transportation Planning

Disaster relief operations or other large-scale responses to international crises require the coordination of the transportation of a large number of people, goods, and other facilities. For example, transportation plans to support military operations are very large and involve the movement of tens of thousands of individual units. These units span a diverse range of size and composition, from a single person or piece of cargo to an entire division (Hanes, 1988). The timely execution of a well-coordinated transportation plan is crucial for the success of an operation.

Units can use transportation resources (e.g., planes, ships) depending on their original location, their intended destination, and the time at which they are needed at the destination. Therefore, it is not sufficient for a unit to find a resource with enough transportation capacity at the appropriate time; the resource's route must also match the unit's source and destination locations. Units can be assigned to transportation flows already established. In case their arrival at the destination is extremely critical, transportation resources can be diverted from other less critical uses or temporarily acquired from other sources (e.g., planes chartered from commercial airlines). Justification information includes mutual dependency among different unit deployments and intended effects of a unit becoming operational at the destination. Keeping track of this information is essential in order to adapt the plan to unexpected execution conditions or to partially reuse it in other situations.

Often the primary goal served by a unit is to augment the facilities available at the destination so as to increase its throughput and to allow a higher rate of delivery. Typical examples of these facilities are air traffic control, aircraft refueling, and personnel or cargo unloading. Aggregate capacity resources are often an appropriate representation for these facilities. The state of an aggregate resource represents capacity in use or still available at any point in time. To make a more concrete example, let us consider a "bare base" scenario, where the goal is to turn a bare runway at the destination into a fully functioning airport. The number of planes that can be refueled in parallel at the destination can be represented as an aggregate refueling capacity. Bringing in one or more refueling units permanently increases refueling capacity. Because planes use this facility immediately after arrival, increasing refueling capacity increases the plane arrival rate at the destination. This, in turn, increases the arrival rate of additional refueling units, resulting in a quick amplification of the capabilities of the airport. Increasing the number of units at a site also increases the demand for other supporting functions (such as sleeping space, food, and fuel) that are provided by other units. The arrival of these additional units must be coordinated carefully to avoid chaotic situations and negative consequences on the overall outcome of the mission.

In conclusion, the salient factors in transportation planning are time, dynamic generation and consumption of several types of aggregate capacity, state information, and causal relations. This domain is a primary candidate for the application of integrated planning and scheduling.

6.3 INTEGRATION OF PLANNING AND SCHEDULING

To deal effectively with complex domains, we need a synthesis of the problem solving capabilities currently split between classical planning and classical scheduling. To this end, it is crucial to recognize that a domain can always be described as a dynamical system (Kalman, Falb, & Arbib, 1969). A dynamical system is a formal structure that gives the relationship between exerted actions (*input*) and observed behaviors over time, taking into account the internal memory of past history (*state*).[1] Planning and scheduling are in fact complementary aspects of the process of step-by-step construction of consistent dynamical system behaviors (Muscettola, 1990; Dean & Wellman, 1991). To build a problem solving framework capable of easily accommodating this process, we must choose an appropriate structuring principle for the description of the dynamical system.

In domains such as space mission scheduling and transportation planning, we can accurately describe the system's instantaneous situation with the value of a handful of its properties (e.g., the operative state of each component of the space telescope, the usage of different airport facilities). Therefore, we adopt the fundamental structuring principle of describing both input and state as finite dimensional vectors of values evolving over continuous time. The same principle is adopted by approaches that deal with continuous value dynamical systems (e.g., linear systems) (Kalman, Falb, & Arbib, 1969) and with the temporal specification of reactive software systems (Manna & Pnueli, 1991).

The input and state vector assumption promotes a more general view of the domain than those allowed by classical scheduling and planning.

Classical scheduling requires the representation of resources. A vector component can directly model a single capacity resource because it can assume one and only one value at any point in time. In this case, the range of possible values is essentially binary (e.g., *processing* or *idle*). However, in our representation, the range of vector component values can be wider than binary, allowing the inclusion of more complex state information into the representation of resources. This extends the restrictive assumptions made in classical scheduling.

In classical planning, the evolution of a domain strictly alternates between a stage of change (*action*) and a period of static persistence (*state*). A representation based on input and state vectors promotes a different view. The input vector identifies those system properties directly controlled by an external agent, and the state vector refers to those that can only be influenced indirectly. Values representing change and persistence can appear in any order in any vector component. For example, it is possible to have static values one immediately after the other (when transitions have infinitesimal durations) or changes following one another (when a process is divided into two or more contiguous phases). This facilitates reasoning over parallel processes evolving over continuous time.

In the rest of the chapter, we will discuss only state vectors, assuming that for the domains of interest, the synthesis of the input is straightforward (e.g., sending the signal to start an operation on a resource at a time determined by the schedule).

These modeling premises also support the formulation of a broader class of problems than those usually expressible in classical planning and scheduling. A

---

[1] In the following, we will identify the observable behavior of the system with the evolution of its state over time.

planning/scheduling problem is simply a set of constraints and preferences on state vector values; their satisfaction identifies a desired plan/schedule among all possible consistent behaviors. Constraints can specify both the execution of actions, as in classical scheduling, and the request for stationary states, as in classical planning. Evaluation functions can impose preference on the possible behaviors of the system (e.g., execute as many observations as possible out of a pool submitted to HST). A good planner/scheduler will try to construct behaviors with a high (possibly globally maximal) level of satisfaction for these preferences.

6.4 THE FUNDAMENTAL COMPONENTS OF HSTS

The HSTS framework makes coherent use of the previous representational principle. The two core components are the Domain Description Language (HSTS-DDL) and the Temporal Data Base (HSTS-TDB). HSTS-DDL allows the specification of the static and dynamic structure of a system. It supports the expression of a model as a modular set of constraint templates satisfied by any legal system behavior. HSTS-TDB supports the construction of such legal behaviors. It provides facilities to ensure a strict adherence of its content to an HSTS-DDL system model and to any requirement stated in a problem. By posting assertions and constraints among assertions in the database, a planner/scheduler sets goals, builds activity networks, commits to the achievement of intermediate states, and synchronizes system components. The tight connection between the entities that can be specified in HSTS-DDL and those that can be represented in HSTS-TDB provides a strong basis for exploiting domain structure during problem solving.

6.4.1 Domain Description Language

An HSTS-DDL system model is organized as a set of **system components**, each with an associated set of **properties**. Each property represents an entry of the state vector; it can therefore assume one and only one **value** at any point in time. Properties whose value does not change over time (also called **static properties**) typically represent system parameters. The behavior of the system is determined by the value of its **dynamic properties**, those that change over time; in the rest of the chapter we will refer to them as the **state variables** of the system.

HSTS-DDL gives special emphasis to the specification of state variables. A system model must explicitly declare the set of all possible values for each state variable. A value is expressed as a predicate $R (x_1, x_2, ..., x_n)$, where $< x_1, x_2, ..., x_n >$ is a tuple in the relation R. The model must give a domain for each predicate's argument; currently, HSTS-DDL allows sets of symbols, sets of system components, and numeric quantities (either discrete or continuous).

To illustrate these points, we give an example from HST. The system component POINTING-DEVICE has several properties. One of them is the telescope's average slewing rate, described as a constant value of a static property. The pointing direction of the telescope and the state of target tracking is determined by a single state variable, **state**(POINTING-DEVICE). Its possible values are

- *UNLOCKED* (*?T*): The telescope is pointing in the generic direction of target *?T*.
- *LOCKED* (*?T*): The telescope is actively tracking target *?T*.
- *LOCKING* (*?T*): The tracking device is locking onto target *?T*.
- *SLEWING* (*?T1, ?T2*): The telescope changes its direction from target ?T1 to target ?T2.

The domain of each of the variables *?T, ?T1,* and *?T2* is the set of all known targets, each represented as a separate system component in the HST model.

The specification of each state variable value is incomplete without its temporal characteristics. For a system behavior, each value extends over a continuous time interval or *occurrence*. A value's occurrence depends in part on the value's intrinsic characteristic and in part on its interaction with other values. For example, the duration of a slewing operation is entirely determined by intrinsic parameters, such as the angle between the two targets and the telescope's slewing rate. On the other hand, the only cause for the telescope to exit an unlocked state is the occurrence of either a slewing or a locking operation, i.e., the interaction with other values.

In HSTS-DDL, each value has a **duration constraint** that expresses the intrinsic range $[d, D]$ of its possible durations($D \geq d \geq 0$); d and D are, respectively, the duration's lower and upper bounds. The bounds are specified as functions of the value's arguments; their tightness depends on the binding status of the value's arguments. For example, during problem solving, ?T1 and ?T2 in *SLEWING* (?T1, ?T2) might be restricted to specific sets of targets. The lower bound of the duration constraint would return the slewing time between the closest pair of targets, each selected from a different set; the upper bound would refer to the farthest pair of targets. If each of ?T1 and ?T2 are restricted to a single target, both the lower and upper bounds will assume the slewing time between the two targets.

For any system, it is possible to identify constraining patterns of value occurrences. In any legal behavior, when a value occurs, other values must also occur to match the pattern. Such patterns describe the dynamic characteristics of the system and have a function similar to state operators in classical planning. In HSTS-DDL, each value is constrained by a **compatibility specification** that consists of a set of **compatibilities** organized as an AND/OR graph. Each compatibility represents the request for an elementary temporal constraint between the value and an appropriate segment of behavior. More precisely, a compatibility has the form

[*temp–rel* < *comp–class, st–var, type* >]

The tuple < *comp–class*, *st–var*, *type* > specifies the characteristics of a constraining segment of behavior; *temp–rel* is the temporal relation requested between the constrained value and the constraining segment of behavior. The temporal relations known to HSTS-DDL are equivalent to all combinations of interval relations (Allen, 1983) with metric constraints that can be expressed in continuous endpoint algebra (Vilain, Kautz, & van Beek, 1990). For example, *before* ([d, D]) indicates that the end of the constrained value must precede the start of the constraining behavior segment by a time interval δ, such that $d \leq \delta \leq D$; its inverse is *after* ([d, D]). The relation *contained–by* ([d_1, D_1], [d_2, D_2]) says that the constrained value must be contained within the constraining behavior segment; [d_1, D_1] defines the distance between the two start times, and [d_2, D_2] refers to the two end times. HSTS-DDL restricts the constraining behavior segment to occur on a single state variable, *st–var*. The identifier *comp–class* can be one of two symbols, ν or σ, depending on the nature of the behavior segment. The symbol ν stands for a single value occurrence (**value compatibility**), and σ refers to a sequence of values occurring contiguously on the same state variable (**sequence compatibility**). In this section, we describe value compatibilities; Section 6.5.1 will discuss sequence compatibilities. The behavior segment must consist of values extracted from the set specified in *type*.

To draw an illustrative example from the HST domain, let us consider the dynamic state of the telescope's pointing device (state variable **state**(POINTING-DEVICE)). The possible value transitions are shown in Figure 6-2. Each node represents one of the possible values, and an arc between two nodes represents two compatibilities. More precisely, an arc from node n_i to node n_j is equivalent to a [*before* ([0, 0]) < ν, **state** (*POINTING–DEVICE*), $\{n_j\}$ >] compatibility associated to n_i and to a symmetric *after* ([0,0]) compatibility associated to n_j. Multiple arcs exiting or entering a node correspond to alternative transitions (OR node in the compatibility specification). Some of the values can persist indefinitely (highlighted nodes in Figure 6-2) and, therefore, have an indeterminate duration constraint ([0, +∞]

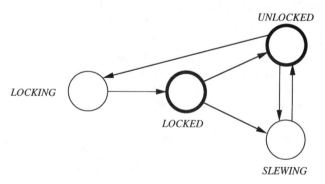

Figure 6-2:   Value transition graph for **state**(POINTING-DEVICE)

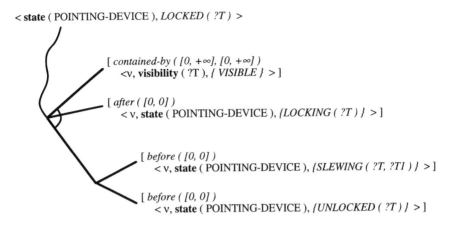

< **state** (POINTING-DEVICE), *LOCKED (?T)* >

[*contained-by ([0, +∞], [0, +∞])*
  <v, **visibility** (?T), *{ VISIBLE }* >]

[*after ([0, 0])*
  < v, **state** (POINTING-DEVICE), *{LOCKING (?T)}* >]

[*before ([0, 0])*
  < v, **state** (POINTING-DEVICE), *{SLEWING (?T, ?T1)}* >]

[*before ([0, 0])*
  < v, **state** (POINTING-DEVICE), *{UNLOCKED (?T)}* >]

Figure 6-3:   Compatibilities for the value *LOCKED* (*?T*).

bound); all other values have a determined duration constraint. To precisely specify the physically consistent patterns of behavior, we must also consider synchronization with other state variables. For example, locking the telescope on a target and keeping the lock requires target visibility. This imposes an additional compatibility

([*contained–by* ([0, +∞], [0, +∞]) < v, **visibility** (*?T*), $\{VISIBLE\}$>])

on each of the values *LOCKING* (*?T*) and *LOCKED* (*?T*). Figure 6-3 lists the complete compatibility specification for *LOCKED* (*?T*) .

HSTS-DDL allows the specification of system models at different levels of abstraction. System components and state variables at abstract levels aggregate those at more detailed levels. The relationship among the levels is established by **refinement descriptors**; these map some of the abstract values into a network of values associated with the immediately more detailed layer. The mapping also specifies the correspondence between the start and end times of each abstract value and those of the corresponding detailed values.

6.4.2 Temporal Data Base

HSTS-TDB shares the basic representational principles of a Time Map temporal database (Dean & McDermott, 1987; Schrag, Boddy, & Carciofini, 1992) but provides additional constructs to support the satisfaction of conditions imposed by an HSTS-DDL system model.

The primitive unit of temporal description is the **token**, a time interval, identified by its *start time* and *end time*, over which a specified condition, identified by a *type*, holds. HSTS-TDB modifies the original Time Map token in two main ways. The first modification is designed to strictly adhere to the state vector assumption:

in HSTS-TDB, each token can only represent a segment of the evolution of a single state variable. The second modification supports the incremental construction of system behaviors: HSTS-TDB allows different kinds of tokens, depending on the level of detail of the corresponding segment of behavior.

The general format of an HSTS-TDB token is a 5-tuple:

$< token–class, st–var, type, st, et, >$

token–class determines the kind of behavior segment described by the token. It can assume three different values: VALUE-TOKEN, CONSTRAINT-TOKEN, and SEQUENCE-TOKEN. In this section, we discuss value and constraint tokens; Section 6.5.1 will describe sequence tokens. *st–var* specifies the state variable on which the token occurs. *type* is a subset of the possible values of *st–var* specified in the HSTS-DDL system model. Depending on *token–class*, the behavior segment consists of one or more values belonging to *type*. *st* and *et* represent the token's start and end times; their nature will be discussed in Section 6.5.2.

The kind of token most directly related to the Time Map token is the VALUE-TOKEN. A value token identifies a behavior segment consisting of a single uninterrupted value. Taking an example from the HST domain to assert the occurrence of a telescope slew from target *NGC4535* to target *3C267*, we can post the token

$<VALUE–TOKEN,$ **state**$(POINTING–DEVICE), \{SLEWING\ (NGC4535, 3C267)\}, t_1, t_2>$

Because the token's type consists of a single ground predicate, this expresses a definite fact. HSTS-TDB can also support decision making with a level of commitment appropriate to the current state of knowledge. During the construction of an HST plan/schedule, we might want to require a slewing operation with a specific destination target, but it might be too early to select the most convenient slew origin (e.g., because of the lack of strong indications on how to sequence a set of observations). This can be done with the token

$<VALUE–TOKEN,$ **state**$(POINTING–DEVICE), \{SLEWING\ (?T, 3C267)\}, t_1, t_2>$

where its type is the set of values obtained by binding *?T* to all possible targets. Further refinement of the token's characteristics depends on additional decisions and constraint propagation throughout the temporal database (see Section 6.5.2).

Asserting a value token does not guarantee that it will eventually be included in an executable plan. An executable token has to also find a time interval over which no other value token can possibly occur on the same state variable. HSTS-TDB supports the satisfaction of this condition with a specific device: the **time line**. This is a generalization of resource capacity profiles as used in classical scheduling. A time line is a linear sequence of tokens that completely covers the scheduling horizon for a single state variable. In a completely specified plan/sched-

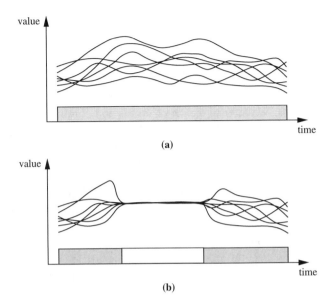

Figure 6-4:   Insertion of a value token into a time line.

ule, the time line consists of a sequence of value tokens with ground predicate types. However, at the beginning of the planning/scheduling process, there is little or no knowledge of the number and nature of these tokens. Constraint posting might allow different degrees of refinement of this knowledge in different time line sections. To express this situation, HSTS-TDB provides a different kind of token, the CONSTRAINT-TOKEN. A constraint token can appear only in a state variable's time line and represents a sequence of values of indefinite length (possibly empty); each value must belong to the token's type.

The principal means to refine a behavior segment is the insertion of a value token into a compatible constraint token. Token insertion generalizes reservation of capacity to an activity, the main decision making primitive in classical scheduling. Figure 6-4 graphically describes the consequences of the insertion of a value token with a single ground predicate into a time line consisting of a single constraint token. The graph in Figure 6-4(a) symbolizes all different evolutions of the state variable values that can possibly substitute for the initial constraint token. The insertion partitions the time line into three sections. The first and third sections consist of constraint tokens that inherit all characteristics of the original constraint token; the inserted value token covers the middle section. All legal refinements of the time line must now assume the specified value throughout the occurrence of the inserted token (Figure 6-4(b)).

Tokens are restricted by the problem statement and by the HSTS-DDL system model. For example, a problem might require the satisfaction of a release date on the occurrence of activity, but compatibility specifications might require the occurrence of a related pattern of support activities and states. The means to assure the satisfaction of these conditions is the posting of temporal and type constraints among pairs of tokens. We refer to the set of tokens and constraints among tokens in the database as the **token network**. In HSTS-TDB, an absolute temporal constraint relates a token τ to a special "reference token" *past*; the end time of *past* is by convention the origin of the temporal axis, or time 0. To enforce a release date on token τ, for example, we can post the constraint ⟨*past* *before* $([r, +\infty])$ τ⟩, which says that τ must start at least r units of time after the time origin. To support the satisfaction of constraints intrinsic to the domain, HSTS-TDB automatically associates to each value token an instance of its type's compatibility specification tree. During the planning/scheduling process, this data structure maintains the current state of the token's causal justification. When the planner/scheduler decides to satisfy a compatibility, it posts a temporal relation between two tokens. HSTS-TDB marks as achieved the appropriate leaves in the causal justification trees of the two tokens and propagates the marking throughout each tree. If the root of a tree is marked as achieved, the corresponding value token is sufficiently justified; the planner/scheduler can therefore remove it from the list of tokens (subgoals) still to achieve. Compatibility implementation corresponds to precondition and postcondition satisfaction in classical planning. Figure 6-5 summarizes the process of implementing a *contained-by* compatibility in the HST domain; the compatibility specifies that while the telescope is locked on target 3C267, the target must be visible.

HSTS-TDB also supports problem solving at multiple levels of abstractions. This is obtained by subdividing a token network into a number of communicating layers, each corresponding to a level of abstraction in the HSTS-DDL system model. If the type of a value token has a refinement specification in the system model, an instance of the refinement specification is automatically associated with the token.

HSTS-TDB provides primitives to allow the creation and insertion of tokens and the creation of instances of temporal relations. Each primitive has an inverse that allows the undoing of previous commitments. HSTS does not impose any particular constraint on the order in which these primitives can be used; this is completely left to the search method and the domain knowledge of the planner/scheduler. Through a context mechanism, a planner/scheduler can also access different alternative database states. Mechanisms are provided to localize tokens that satisfy given conditions (e.g., all tokens on a state variable time line that can be used to implement a given compatibility).

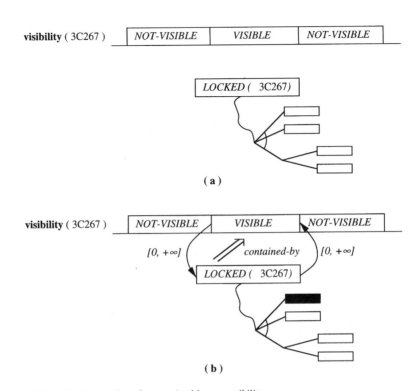

Figure 6-5:   Implementation of a *contained-by* compatibility.

6.5 ADDITIONAL HSTS FEATURES

6.5.1 Sequence Constraints

The primitives introduced in Section 6.4 can express synchronization constraints between "constant" segments of state variable behavior, i.e., time intervals
during which a state variable does not change its value. However, in complex
domains, it might be necessary to synchronize more complex behavior segments. A
typical case involves several sequential values. For example, in the HST domain
when the Wide Field detector (WF) of the Wide Field/Planetary Camera is in an
intermediate reconfiguration state, the instrument platform (WFPC) can be in any of
a number of states that are neither too "cold" nor too "warm." In terms directly
derived from the HSTS-DDL model of HST, we need to express that during the
time when the state variable **state**(WF) has value $s(3n)$, **state**(WFPC) must remain in
a value range within $s(3n)$ and $s(4n)$. Transition among values is allowed, and no
preferences are given on which specific sequence of values to use.

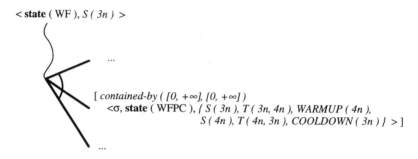

$< \mathbf{state}\ (\ WF\ ),\ S\ (\ 3n\ )\ >$

[*contained-by* (*[0, +∞], [0, +∞]*)
  $<σ, \mathbf{state}\ (\ WFPC\ ),\ \{\ S\ (\ 3n\ ),\ T\ (\ 3n,\ 4n\ ),\ WARMUP\ (\ 4n\ ),$
                              $S\ (\ 4n\ ),\ T\ (\ 4n,\ 3n\ ),\ COOLDOWN\ (\ 3n\ )\ \}\ >\ ]$

Figure 6-6:   A sequence compatibility.

To express these kinds of condition, HSTS-DDL provides a special type of compatibility, the **sequence compatibility** (*comp–class* = σ). If the value's compatibility specification contains a sequence compatibility

$[temp–rel < σ, st–var, type >]$,

a value's occurrence requires a contiguous sequence of values from *type* on state variable *st–var*; moreover, the constrained value must be in the temporal relation *temp–rel* with the overall interval of occurrence of the sequence. Figure 6-6 shows the sequence compatibility for the WF/WFPC example described before.

A planner/scheduler can impose sequence synchronization constraints by using a special kind of HSTS-TDB token, the **sequence token** (*tok–class* = *SEQUENCE-TOKEN*). A sequence token

$< SEQUENCE\text{-}TOKEN,\ st–var,\ type,\ st,\ et >$

represents a time interval during which the state variable *st–var* can assume an indefinite number of sequential values belonging to the set *type*. As for a value token, asserting a sequence token does not automatically imply inclusion into the plan/schedule. This requires the insertion of the token into the time line. Figure 6-7 shows the implementation of the compatibility in Figure 6-6. Notice that the sequence token encompasses several value tokens (in white) and constraint tokens (in gray); each represents a segment of behavior with a different level of refinement.

Sequence compatibilities specify synchronization among "processes" within a single level of abstraction; this makes them different from traditional approaches to hierarchical planning (Knoblock, 1991). A sequence compatibility might not provide the primary justification for the constraining process. In this case, the sequence compatibility merely adds constraints (e.g., on the overall length of the process) that new goal expansions will have to satisfy.

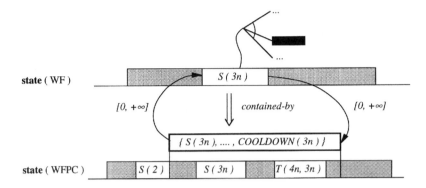

Figure 6-7:   Implementation of a sequence compatibility.

6.5.2 Time and Type Consistency

HSTS-TDB maintains token network consistency through auxiliary constraint networks. Constraint propagation procedures allow the evaluation of the current flexibility of the possible value assignments for time and type.

Temporal constraints are organized in a graph, the **time point network** (Dechter, Meiri, & Pearl, 1991). Each token start or end constitutes a node in the graph, or **time point**; arcs between time points are metric interval distances derived from the temporal relations posted in the database. Drawing an example from the HST domain, Figure 6-8 shows a portion of the time point network underlying a plan/schedule for taking an image of target NGC288 with the WF detector of the Wide Field/Planetary Camera; the black token represents the actual exposure. HSTS-TDB provides a single-source constraint propagation procedure to compute the range of possible times for each time point. If the propagation finds some time point with an empty range, the token network is inconsistent. An all-pairs constraint propagation procedure is also available to determine ranges of temporal distances between pairs of tokens. This is useful when minimizing the token network (e.g., find tokens whose duration is effectively [0, 0] and that can therefore be deleted). The all-pairs procedure also allows the localization of inconsistent distance constraint cycles. Both constraint propagation procedures are incremental; if no constraints are deleted from the network, the time ranges are updated by considering only the additional effects of the new constraints.

To provide a more localized structural analysis of the token network, it is possible to apply temporal propagation to portions of the time point network. This feature is useful when the planner/scheduler can take advantage of a limited amount of look-ahead. For example, during the implementation of a sequence compatibility, the planner/scheduler needs to determine where to insert a sequence token without provoking inconsistencies. If propagation is limited to the subgraph

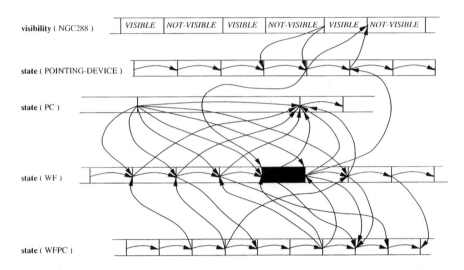

Figure 6-8: A time point network.

of all time points lying on one of the two state variables involved, the planner/scheduler can evaluate in a short time the temporal consistency of a high number of alternative token subsequences. Local consistency does not grant global consistency; however, the amount of pruning obtained is still extremely effective in reducing overall problem solving cost (Haralick & Elliot, 1980).

Maintaining a time point network encompassing the entire token network (irrespective of a token being inserted in a time line or not) encourages a problem solving style that keeps substantial amounts of temporal flexibility at any stage. Although it is certainly possible to make classical scheduling decisions (i.e., post absolute temporal constraints to fix a token start time and/or end time), one could ask if additional leverage could not derive from making decisions with lower levels of commitment. This issue is discussed in more depth in Section 6.8.

A limited constraint propagation among token types keeps track of the possible time line refinements in view of the currently inserted value and sequence tokens. Figure 6-9, for example, represents the consequence of the insertion of a sequence token overlapping a pre-existing one. Type propagation updates the type of each time line token to the intersection of its type with those of all encompassing sequence tokens. The initial type of a free constraint token is represented as { * }, meaning the set of all possible values for the state variable. If type propagation associates an empty type to some time line tokens, the token network is inconsistent. Similar to temporal propagation, type propagation is incremental.

Unlike other approaches (Dean & McDermott, 1987), HSTS-TDB propagation procedures limit their action to the verification and, possibly, localization of

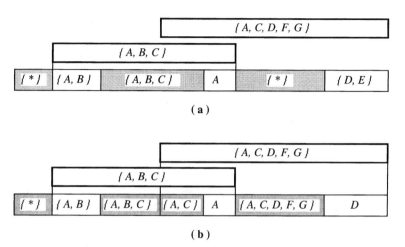

Figure 6-9:   Type propagation on a time line.

inconsistencies; no attempt is made to automatically recover to a consistent state. The problem solver must take full responsibility for the recovery process because different responses might be needed in different situations. For example, if a state variable is over-subscribed, we might either delete tokens that have not yet been inserted (goal rejection) or cancel the insertion of some tokens (resource dealloca-tion). A planner/scheduler implemented in HSTS can operate on inconsistent token networks, adding and retracting tokens and constraints with no need to ensure consistency at each intermediate step. Planning/scheduling algorithms can reach a final consistent plan/schedule with trajectories that lie partially or entirely in the space of inconsistent database instantiations. Therefore, HSTS supports a wide variety of problem solving methods, including search in the space of incremental consistent plan/schedule extensions (Sadeh, 1991), reactive opportunistic scheduling (Smith et al., 1990), and purely repair-based approaches (Minton et al., 1992; Zweben, Deale, & Gargan, 1990; Biefeld & Cooper, 1991).

6.6 MANAGING RESOURCES

To provide a general representation framework for several types of resource, it is important to take into account several features. First is the amount of capacity available for consumption; in general, a resource can be either *single capacity* or *multiple capacity*. A second dimension concerns the number of requests that the resource can service at the same time; we can distinguish between *single user* and *multiple user* resources. Finally, resources differ with respect to what happens to capacity after usage; they can be *renewable* or *not renewable*. HSTS supports the representation and manipulation of all these resource features. By making appropriate use of compatibility and duration constraints, an HSTS-DDL system model can represent various kinds of synchronization with capacity requests and various kinds of resource renewability. For example, we can express a compatibility that requests a human operator to attend to a machine only during the initial part of a machining process. We can also impose a duration constraint to make capacity consumption by an activity permanent. To represent multiple user resources, however, we need an extension of the basic state variable model: the aggregate state variable. In this section, we give examples of resource modeling within HSTS.

6.6.1 Atomic State Variables

The kind of state variable discussed so far (called from now on **atomic state variable**) can model different types of single user resources. The examples given so far are essentially generalized single capacity resources; however, atomic state variables can also cover multiple capacity resources, renewable or not renewable. In the HST domain, the on-board tape recorder is an example of such a resource. Only one instrument at a time can dump data on it, making it single user; the tape has a finite amount of storage, measured in bytes (multiple capacity), that can be cleared by communication to earth (renewable capacity). The state of the tape recorder is tracked by the atomic state variable **state**(TAPE-RECORDER). Each of its values keeps track of the amount of data stored in the tape with a numeric argument, $?C$. The possible values for **state**(TAPE-RECORDER) are $READ-OUT$ ($?I$, $?D$, $?C$), the process of reading $?D$ bytes from instrument $?I$ on the tape already containing $?C$ bytes; $STORED$ ($?C$), when the tape recorder is not in use and is storing $?C$ bytes; and $DUMP-TO-EARTH$ ($?C$), the communication of $?C$ bytes from the tape recorder to earth and the resetting of the tape to empty. The total capacity of the tape, $MAX-C$, determines if it is possible to schedule the transfer of data from an instrument to the tape. More precisely, it is not possible to insert a value token of type $READ-OUT$ ($?I$, $?D$, $?C$) in a position such that $?D + ?C > MAX-C$, for any value that can be assigned to $?D$ and $?C$ in that position. If no position is legal, we need to insert a $DUMP-TO-EARTH$ token to renew the tape capacity, after which the $READ-OUT$ can legally occur. Single user, multiple capacity, not renewable resources can be modeled like the tape recorder, the only exception being the lack of a capacity renewal operation analogous to $DUMP-TO-EARTH$; an example of such a resource is fuel in the propulsion system for a planetary probe's attitude adjustment.

6.6.2 Aggregate State Variables

In principle, we could represent multiple user resources as a collection of atomic state variables, each corresponding to a quantum of individually usable capacity. However, in most cases, this solution is overly cumbersome. For example, to reason about the allocation of cargo to available space on a plane, we would have to subdivide both space and cargo into "units of space" and allocate each unit of cargo space to a free unit of plane space. This might be necessary to yield detailed maps of plane space allocation, but it is inappropriate when we only need an aggregate characterization. In these situations, HSTS provides a different representation primitive: the **aggregate state variable**. The value of an aggregate state variable is a summary of the values of a set of atomic state variables. Electric power in HST and refueling capacity in transportation planning fall into this category.

Consider, for example, the aggregation of classical scheduling resources, i.e., resources that can be either in use (value $OPER$) or idle (value $IDLE$). The state of a pool of resources POOL can be given by an aggregate state variable, **Capacity** ($POOL$), whose possible values have the form

$$(\langle OPER, n_1 \rangle, \langle IDLE, n_2 \rangle)$$

indicating that n_1 atomic resources in POOL are in an $OPER$ state, and those of n_2 are in an $IDLE$ state. During the time when **Capacity** ($POOL$) assumes this value, POOL contains $n_1 + n_2$ atomic resources. In general, a value for an aggregate state variable is a list of such entries $\langle value, counter \rangle$.

When declaring compatibilities, a value might require that some atomic state variables in a pool assume another specified value. The effect of several atomic compatibilities can be aggregated into an **aggregate compatibility**; this will specify how to increment or decrement the counter of each entry of an aggregate state variable value. For example, assuming that activity OP_i requires the use of c_i atomic resources, the value $\langle \mathbf{st}\ (?j), OP_i \rangle$ will have the following compatibility:

[$contains$ ([0, 0], [0, 0])
   $\langle \sigma, \mathbf{Capacity}(POOL),$
   $\{(\langle OPER, INC\ (+c_i) \rangle, \langle IDLE, INC(-c_i) \rangle)\}]$

This means that whenever OP_i of job $?j$ is in progress (state variable $\mathbf{st}\ (?j)$ has value OP_i), there must be an appropriate sequence of values on **Capacity** ($POOL$), starting and ending together with OP_i. The type in the compatibility describes that for each value in the sequence, the number of $OPER$ atomic resources increases by c_i units, and the number of $IDLE$ resources decreases by c_i units.

After having implemented a number of aggregate compatibilities, the value assumed by an aggregate state variable at a given point in time can be obtained by type propagation. Suppose that after having gathered all types of the sequences insisting on a time line token, we have n_{opr} entries of type $\langle OPER, INC\ (c_i) \rangle$ and n_{idle} entries of type $\langle IDLE, INC\ (c_j) \rangle$. The resulting type for the time line token is $(\langle OPER, n_1 \rangle, \langle IDLE, n_2 \rangle)$ with

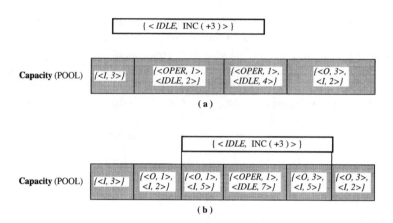

Figure 6-10:   Posting a sequence constraint on an aggregate state variable.

$$n_1 = \sum_{i=1}^{n_{opr}} c_i \qquad n_2 = \sum_{j=1}^{n_{idle}} c_j$$

where c_i and c_j can be both positive (capacity creation) or negative (capacity consumption). Figure 6-10 shows the effect of the insertion of a request of aggregate capacity on the aggregate state variable time line. Checking type consistency requires the computation of the balance between positive and negative requests for each time line segment where a set of capacity requests overlap. The database is inconsistent when an aggregate value contains a negative counter. Notice, however, that in case the system model allows the generation of capacity (i.e., contains aggregate compatibilities with $INC(x)$ entries), inconsistencies can be resolved without backtracking by posting additional compatibilities that provide the missing capacity.

As with atomic state variables, each transition between time line tokens belongs to the HSTS-TDB time point network. Therefore, the synchronization of the requests for capacity allows a certain degree of flexibility regarding the actual start and end of the use of a resource. However, testing that the requested amount does not exceed available capacity still requires a total ordering of start and end times on the time line. One way to obtain a higher degree of flexibility is to statistically estimate resource usage over time, even without committing to a specific total order (see Section 6.8).

6.7 SCHEDULING THE HUBBLE SPACE TELESCOPE

Within HSTS, we have developed and experimentally tested planning/scheduling systems for several domains, including short term scheduling for HST

(Muscettola et al., 1992) and "bare base" deployment for transportation planning (Frederking & Muscettola, 1992). In this section, we describe experience in the HST domain, and we highlight some favorable characteristics of the HSTS framework.

For HST, the problem size and the variety of constraint interactions suggest that complexity should be managed by staging problem solving. This consists of first making decisions concentrating only on some important aspects of the problem and then further refining the intermediate solution to include the full range of domain constraints. Therefore, our model of the HST domain has two levels of abstraction. At the *abstract level*, the generation of initial observation sequences takes into account telescope availability, overall telescope reconfiguration time, and target visibility windows. The model contains one state variable for the visibility of each target of interest and a single state variable representing telescope availability. The *detail level* generates plans/schedules that are directly translatable into spacecraft commands. Abstract decisions are expanded and adapted to a domain model that includes one state variable for each telescope subsystem.

Initially, the temporal database contains the candidate observation programs at the abstract level and an empty time line for each state variable. Each program is a token network, with a value token for each observation request. None of the tokens are inserted into a state variable time line. Two tokens cover each state variable time line: a value token representing the value of the state variable in the telescope's initial state followed by a constraint token with unrestricted type.

At both levels of abstraction, the planner/scheduler uses the same decision making cycle:

1. **Goal selection**: Select some goal tokens.
2. **Goal insertion**: Insert each selected token into the corresponding state variable time line;

Repeat

3. **Compatibility selection**: Select an open compatibility for an inserted token.
4. **Compatibility implementation**: Implement the selected compatibility

until no more tokens in any time line have open compatibilities.

The **Compatibility Implementation** step consists of finding a behavior segment on the time line (either a value token or a sequence of tokens) that is compatible with the conditions on type and time imposed by the compatibility. If such a behavior segment does not exist, a new value or sequence token with the required type is created, inserted in the time line in an appropriate position, and connected to the constrained token with the appropriate temporal relation. This process of token creation and insertion corresponds to subgoal sprouting in classical planning.

The basic cycle is repeated until it is determined that it is not possible to insert another observation token into the abstract time line.

Each of the four steps in the basic decision making cycle requires choosing among alternatives. For example, we can implement a compatibility in different ways, depending on which section of time line we select as the constraining segment of behavior. When different choices are possible, they are separately explored through a heuristic search procedure.

Heuristics at the abstract level must address the trade-off between two potentially conflicting objectives: the maximization of the time spent collecting science data and the maximization of the number of scheduled observation programs. Different sequencing rules have been proposed and evaluated (Smith & Pathak, 1992). A first strategy addresses the first part of the trade-off. The strategy builds a sequence of observations by dispatching forward in time. The observation that minimizes the reconfiguration time and causes the fewest rejections of open requests (i.e., does not use time that was the only one available for the execution of some observations) is appended at the end of the current partial sequence. A second strategy concentrates on the second part of the trade-off. It consists of maintaining a set of possible start times for each open observation and selecting the observation with the fewest alternatives for scheduling. The placement on the time line does not necessarily proceed by building a linear sequence; if the time is available, an observation can be inserted amid previously scheduled observations. A third, more balanced strategy yields better results than the preceding two. At each problem solving cycle, it selects one of the two previous scheduling strategies as a function of problem characteristics dynamically discovered during problem solving.

Heuristics at the detail level ensure the correct synchronization of the reconfiguration of different components; the primary goal is to minimize reconfiguration time (Muscettola et al., 1992). We will describe the nature of these heuristics when discussing the scalability of HSTS.

During planning/scheduling, the two layers of abstraction exchange information. Observations sequenced at the abstract level are communicated to the detail level for insertion in the detail plan/schedule. The request has the form of a token subnetwork that is obtained from the expansion of the abstract token's refinement specification. Preferences on how the goals should be achieved (e.g., "achieve all goals as soon as possible") are also communicated. The detail level communicates back to the abstract level information resulting from detail problem solving; these include additional temporal constraints on abstract observations to more precisely account for the reconfiguration delays.

In developing the planner/scheduler for the HST domain, we followed an incremental approach. We decomposed the problem into smaller sub-problems, we solved each sub-problem separately, and then we assembled the sub-solutions. It is natural to try to apply this methodology when dealing with large problems and complex domains. However, to do so, the representation framework must effectively support modularity and scalability. In particular, a modular and scalable framework should display the following two features:

- The search procedure for the entire problem should be assembled by combining heuristics independently developed for each sub-problem, with little or no modification of the heuristics.
- The computational effort needed to solve the complete problem should not increase with respect to the sum of the efforts needed to solve each component sub-problem.

Experiments on three increasingly complex and realistic models of the HST domain indicate that HSTS displays both of the previously mentioned features. The experiments serve as a framework to test the interaction between abstract and detail level planning and scheduling; therefore, unlike in Smith & Pathak (1992), they pay little attention to the optimization of the main mission performance criteria.

We identify the three models as SMALL, MEDIUM, and LARGE. All share the same abstract level representation. At the detail level, the three models include state variables for different telescope functionalities. The SMALL model has a state variable for the visibility of each target of interest; a state variable for the pointing state of the telescope; and three state variables to describe a single instrument, the Wide Field/Planetary Camera (WFPC). The MEDIUM model includes SMALL and two state variables for an additional instrument, the Faint Object Spectrograph (FOS). Finally, the LARGE model extends MEDIUM with eight state variables accounting for data communication. The LARGE model is representative of the major operating constraints of the domain.

For each model, we use the same pattern of interaction between problem solving at the abstract and at the detail levels. At the abstract level, observations are selected and dispatched using a greedy heuristic to minimize expected reconfiguration time. The last dispatched observation is refined into the corresponding detail level token network; control is then passed to planning/scheduling at the detail level. This cycle is repeated until the abstract level sequence is complete.

The detail planner/scheduler for SMALL is driven by heuristics that deal with the interactions among its system components. A first group ensures the correct synchronization of the WFPC components; one of them, for example, states that when planning to turn on the WF detector, preference should be given to synchronization with a PC behavior segment already constrained to be off. A second group deals with the pointing of HST; for example, one of them selects an appropriate target visibility window to execute the locking operation. A final group manages the interaction between the state of WFPC and target pointing; an example from this group states a preference to observe during the time when the telescope is already scheduled to point at the required target. To solve problems in the contest of MEDIUM, additional heuristics must deal with the interactions within FOS components, between FOS and HST pointing state, and between FOS and WFPC. However, the nature of these additional interactions is very similar to those found in SMALL. Consequently, it is sufficient to extend the domain of applicability of SMALL's heuristics to obtain a complete set of heuristics for MEDIUM. For example, the heuristic excluding WF and PC from being both in operation can easily be modified to ensure the same condition among the two FOS detectors. Finally, for LARGE, we have the heuristics used in MEDIUM with no change plus heuristics that address data communication and interaction among instruments and data communication; an example of these prevents scheduling an observation on an instrument if data from the previous observation have not yet been read out of their data buffer. By making evident the decomposition in modules and the structural similarities among different sub-models, HSTS makes possible the reuse of heuristics and their extension from one model to another. We therefore claim that HSTS displays the first feature of a modular and scalable planning/scheduling framework.

In order to determine the relationship between model size and computational effort, we ran a test problem in each of the SMALL, MEDIUM, and LARGE models. Each test problem consisted of a set of 50 observation programs; each program consisted of a single observation with no user-imposed time constraints. The experiments were run on a TI Explorer II+ with 16 Mbytes of RAM memory.

As required by the second feature of a scalable framework, the results in Table 6-1 indicate that the computational effort is indeed additive. In the table, the measure of model size (number of state variables) excludes visibilities for targets and communication satellites because these can be considered as given data. The time edges are links between two time points that lie on different state variables; the number of these links gives an indication of the amount of synchronization needed to coordinate the evolution of the state variables in the schedule.

Table 6-1:   Performance results to measure scalability. The times are reported in hours, minutes, seconds, and fraction of second.

	Small	Medium	Large
No. state variables	4	6	13
No. tokens	587	604	843
No. time points	588	605	716
No. time edges	1296	1328	1474
CPU time per observation	11.62	12.25	21.74
CPU time per compatibility	0.29	0.29	0.33
Total CPU time	9:41.00	10:11.50	18:07.00
Total elapsed time	1:08:36.00	1:13:16.00	2:34:07.00
Schedule horizon	41:37:20:00	54:25:46.00	52:44:41.00

Because the detail level heuristics exploit the modularity of the model and the locality of interactions, the average CPU time (excluding garbage collection) spent implementing each compatibility remains relatively stable. In particular, given that the nature of the constraints included in SMALL and MEDIUM is very similar, the time is identical in the two cases. The total elapsed time to generate a schedule is an acceptable fraction of the time horizon covered by the schedule during execution. Even if this implementation is far from optimal, nonetheless it shows the practicality of the framework for the actual HST operating environment.

6.8 EXPLOITING TEMPORAL FLEXIBILITY IN SCHEDULING

As we mentioned in Section 6.4.2, HSTS puts special emphasis on temporal database flexibility along several dimensions. For example, temporal information in plan/schedules is uniformly represented as a time point network. One might wonder if this flexibility gives, in fact, any leverage during problem solving. In the following, we will discuss this issue with respect to the classical scheduling problem.

Classical scheduling can be viewed as a process of constructively proving that the initial activity network contains at least one consistent behavior. Such behavior is completely determined by giving a complete assignment of resources and start and end times to each request of capacity originated by some activity. Several scheduling systems actually operate by binding values to variables corresponding to resources and time; a consistent total value assignment can be reached by either incrementally extending a consistent partial assignment (Sadeh, 1991) or repairing a complete but inconsistent total assignment (Zweben, Deale, & Gargan, 1990; Biefeld & Cooper, 1991; Minton et al., 1992). Our alternative to binding exact values to variables is to add sequencing constraints among tokens that request the same resource. In HSTS-TDB, such constraints assume the form $\tau_i \text{ before}$ $([0, +\infty])\tau_j$. The goal is to post enough constraints to ensure that at any point in time, the requested capacity does not exceed the available capacity.

The final result of the two previous approaches is potentially quite similar. In fact, it is straightforward to "relax" a total time value commitment into a network of constraints by introducing a temporal precedence whenever two activities occur sequentially on the same resource. Vice-versa, it is straightforward to generate total time value commitments from a constraint network that satisfies all resource capacity limitations (Dechter, Meiri, & Pearl, 1991). However, there is quite a difference in the way in which the two approaches explore the scheduling search space. When reasoning about sets of possible assignments of start and end times for the remaining unscheduled activities, the flexible time approach shows potential advantages over the value commitment approach. We can illustrate this point with a very simple example. Consider two activities that require the same single capacity resource, each having a duration of one time unit and each having identical time bounds allowing n possible start times. Without considering the resource capacity limitation, there are n^2 possible start time assignments for the pair of activities. If we fix the start time of one activity to a given time, there are $n-1$ possible assignments for the start time of the other activity that do not violate the resource constraint. Instead, if we introduce a precedence constraint between the two activities, the total number of consistent start time assignments is $\frac{(n-1)n}{2}$. Therefore, the size of the remaining search space after a scheduling decision is $O(n)$ in the value commitment approach and $O(n^2)$ in the flexible time approach. In general, every time the value of a problem variable is fixed, the search space loses one dimension. Alternatively, posting a constraint only restricts the range of the problem variables without necessarily decreasing dimensionality. This has the potential of leaving a greater number of variable assignment possibilities and suggests a lower risk of the scheduler "getting lost" in blind alleys.

6.8.1 Conflict Partition Scheduling

Based on these principles, we have developed a constraint-posting scheduling procedure: Conflict Partition Scheduling (CPS) (Muscettola, 1992, 1993b). The initial HSTS-TDB state for CPS is a token network; each request of capacity from some activity corresponds to a token. Initially, no token is inserted into the corresponding resource time line. The goal of CPS is to add constraints to the token network so that the insertion of all tokens according to the final network will not generate any capacity conflicts. To achieve this goal, CPS repeatedly identifies bottleneck sets of tokens, i.e., tokens that have a high likelihood of being in competition for the use of a resource. It then adds precedence constraints to ensure that no conflict will actually arise. In order to identify bottleneck conflicts and decide which constraints are most favorable, CPS uses a search space analysis methodology based on stochastic simulation.

In the following, we will identify T as the set of all tokens, R as the set of all resources, and H as the scheduling horizon. H is an interval of time that is guaranteed to contain the occurrence of any token in the final schedule. We will also identify $EST(\tau)$ and $LFT(\tau)$, respectively, as the earliest start and the latest finish times of token τ.

The outline of the basic CPS procedure is the following:

1. **Capacity analysis**: Estimate token demand and resource contention.

2. **Termination test**: If the resource contention for each resource is zero over the entire scheduling horizon, then exit. The current token network is the solution.

3. **Bottleneck detection**: Identify the resource and time with the highest contention.
4. **Conflict identification**: Select the tokens that are most likely to contribute to the bottleneck contention.
5. **Conflict partition**: Sort the set of conflicting tokens according to the token demand by inserting appropriate temporal constraints.
6. **Constraint propagation**: Update the time bounds in the time point network as a consequence of the introduction of the new temporal constraints.
7. **Consistency test**: If the time point network is inconsistent, signal an inconsistency and exit.
8. Go to 1.

The basic CPS procedure is strictly monotonic. If it generates an inconsistency, the token network is reset to the initial state, and the procedure is repeated. The stochastic nature of CPS's capacity analysis allows each repetition to explore a different path in the problem solving space and to therefore potentially succeed after backtracking. If after a fixed number of repetitions a solution has not been found, CPS terminates with an overall failure. The general structure of the problem solving cycle is similar to that of other heuristic scheduling approaches (Adams, Balas, & Zawack, 1988; Smith et al., 1990; Sadeh, 1991): analyze the problem space (step 1), focus on a set of critical decision variables (steps 3 and 4), and make decisions concerning the critical variables (step 5).

The stochastic Capacity Analysis extends and generalizes the one first proposed in Muscettola & Smith (1987). The logic behind the method is quite simple. Although it is difficult to complete an intermediate problem solving state into a consistent schedule because of unresolved disjunctive capacity constraints, it is easy to generate total time assignments that satisfy the temporal constraints already in the network. This can be done by also taking into account additional preference criteria (e.g., select times as soon as possible). For each such assignment, we can identify violations of the still implicit capacity constraints (i.e., times where more than one token uses the same resource). If we generate a sample of N different total time assignments, we can evaluate the following statistical measures of contention and preference:

- **Token demand**: For each token τ and for each time $EST(\tau) \le t_i < LFT(\tau)$, token demand $\Delta(\tau, t_i)$ is equal to n_{t_i}/N, where n_{t_i} is the number of elements in the sample for which the token's interval of occurrence overlaps t_i.
- **Resource contention**: For each resource $\rho \in R$ and for each time t_j within the scheduling horizon H, resource contention $X(\rho, t_j)$ is equal to n_{t_j}/N, where n_{t_j}

is the number of elements of the sample for which ρ is requested by more than one token at time t_j.

Token demand and resource contention represent two different aspects of the current problem solving state. Token demand measures how much the current constraints and preferences bias an activity toward being executed at a given time. Resource contention instead measures how likely it is that the current constraints and preferences will generate congestion of capacity requests (and therefore potential inconsistency) at a given time.

A sample of N total time assignments is given from running the following **stochastic simulation** process N times. Given the time point network $\langle V_t, C_t \rangle$, the following steps are repeated until all variables in V_t have a value:

1. Select a variable $v_t \in V_t$ according to a predefined **variable selection strategy**.
2. Select a value for v_t within its current time bound according to a **stochastic value selection rule**.
3. Assign the value to v_t and propagate the consequences throughout the time point network; this results in new time bound assignments for the variables in V_t.
4. Delete v_t from V_t.

At the end of a stochastic simulation, all tokens in T have a definite start and end time. For each token, we record the interval of occurrence. For each resource at each instant of time within the scheduling horizon, we record if the number of tokens that require the use of the resource exceeds its available capacity. The stochastic simulation is parametric with respect to both variable selection strategy and value selection rule.

A micro-opportunistic search scheduling approach (Sadeh, 1991) has demonstrated the effectiveness of similar token demand and resource contention metrics. However, there the two metrics are computed independently and according to different, sometimes stronger relaxation assumptions. In particular, several precedence constraints present in the time point network are disregarded when computing resource contention. Dropping constraints during capacity analysis allows fast computability of the metrics, but these computational savings might be offset by a decrease in the predictive power of the metrics. This decrease can cause an increase in the number of scheduling cycles needed to reach a solution (Muscettola, 1993a).

Relying on the search space metrics, the scheduler focuses by first identifying the portion of the token network with the highest likelihood of capacity conflicts (**Bottleneck Detection**) and then by determining a set of potentially conflicting tokens within this subnetwork (**Conflict Identification**). A **bottleneck** is formally defined as follows:

- **Bottleneck:** Given the resource contention $\{X(\rho, t)\}$ with $\rho \in R$ and $t \in H$, we call bottleneck a pair $\langle \rho_b, t_b \rangle$ such that

$$X(\rho_b, t_b) = \max\{X(\rho, t)\}$$

for any $\rho \in R$ and $t \in H$ such that $\{X(\rho, t) > 0\}$.

The conflict set is a set of tokens that request ρ_b, have time bounds that contain t_b, and are not necessarily sequential (i.e., no two tokens in the conflict set are forced to follow each other according to the token network). If multiple conflict sets are possible, CPS prefers tokens whose demand profiles cluster around t_b (Muscettola, 1992).

Conflict Arbitration introduces precedence constraints among the capacity requests within the conflict set in order to decrease the likelihood of inconsistency in the token network. CPS allows the use of several types of arbitration rules. At one extreme, there are minimal approaches, similar in spirit to micro-opportunistic scheduling (Sadeh, 1991). These operate by introducing a single precedence constraint between a pair of tokens extracted from the conflict set. At the other extreme, there are approaches similar in spirit to macro-opportunistic scheduling Adams, Balas, & Zawack, 1988; Smith et al., 1990. These generate a total ordering of all tokens in the conflict set. When designing a Conflict Arbitration procedure within these two extremes, we need to balance the trade-off between minimization of change in the topology of the token network and minimization of the number of problem solving cycles. In fact, posting too many constraints without appropriate guidance from problem space metrics could introduce inconsistencies and require backtracking, but posting too few constraints at each cycle requires a higher number of costly Capacity Analysis steps. The Conflict Arbitration strategy currently used in CPS adopts an intermediate approach; it partitions the conflict set into two subsets, T_{before} and T_{after}, and constrains every token in T_{before} to occur before any token in T_{after}. The choice of the partition relies on the analysis of the token demand profiles, where tokens are assigned to subsets according to clustering of their demand profiles (Muscettola, 1992).

Figures 6-11, 6-12, 6-13, and 6-14 graphically illustrate the consequences of a CPS scheduling cycle.[2] Figure 6-11 shows the initial problem network consisting of 10 jobs of 5 sequential activities. Highlighted tokens indicate capacity requests on the same resource. Each of the highlighted tokens occupies the same position in each job. In this example, the identical position, together with the similarity of

---

[2] The figures were generated using SAGE, a system for the automation of data presentation (Roth & Mattis, 1991).

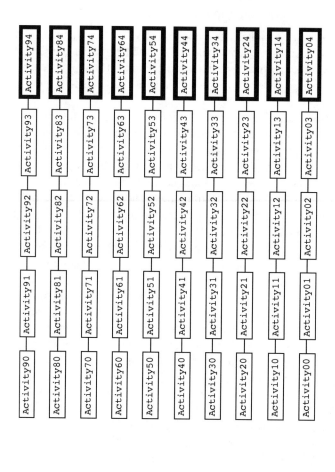

Links: Successor Network-Scheduler/It-0/T--2
Outlined nodes: In-Cycle Network-Scheduler/It-0/T--2

| A | A: ACTIVITY |

Figure 6-11: Initial activity network.

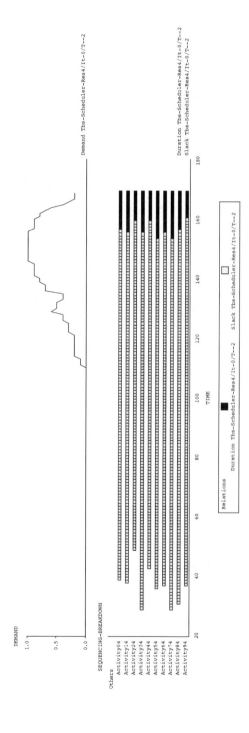

Figure 6-12: Bottleneck resource status before scheduling cycle.

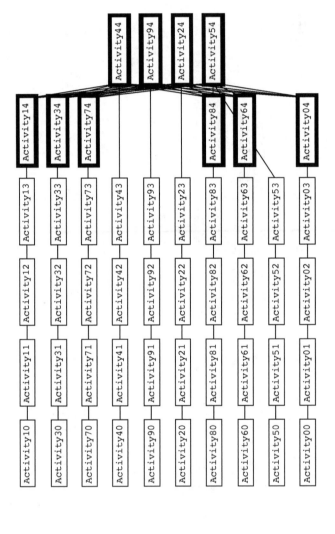

Links: Successor Network-Scheduler/It-1/T--2
Outlined nodes: In-Cycle Network-Scheduler/It-1/T--2

A   A: ACTIVITY

Figure 6-13:   Activity network after Conflict Arbitration.

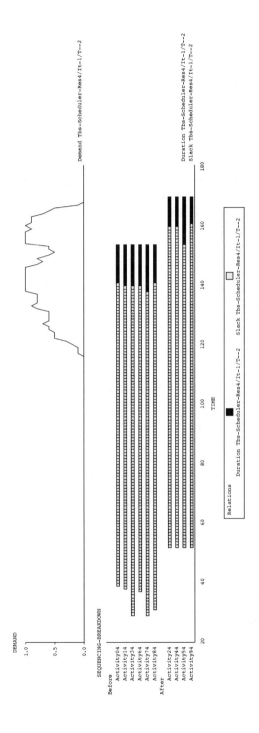

Figure 6-14: New bottleneck resource status.

release and due dates across jobs, causes a high likelihood of conflict on that resource. The contention profile for the resource (top graph of Figure 6-12) shows, in fact, a maximum level of contention; this identifies the current bottleneck. All tokens requesting the resource belong to the conflict set because all their time bounds overlap the bottleneck time (as shown in the bottom part of Figure 6-12). The solid black segment at the far right of each time bound represents the token's duration. Figure 6-13 shows the new topology of the token network after Conflict Arbitration. The initial conflict set is now partitioned into two subsets of lower criticality, with potentially less operations in conflict in each set. As a consequence, the resource contention for the bottleneck resource now has two peaks. Also, the new token clustering is clearly identifiable among the time bounds (Figure 6-14). Notice that partitioning has only slightly reduced the slack associated with each time bound.

6.8.2 Experimental Evaluation

To evaluate the effectiveness of CPS, we compared its performance to two other heuristic scheduling methods over a standard scheduling benchmark. The two competing methods rely on the value commitment approach; they are *micro-opportunistic search* (Sadeh, 1991) and *min-conflict iterative repair* (Minton et al., 1992). Performance was measured according to the number of problem solved and the CPU time required.

6.8.2.1 Experimental Design

Our experimental analysis was conducted on the Constraint Satisfaction Scheduling benchmark proposed in Sadeh (1991). The benchmark consists of 6 groups of 10 problems, each problem including 10 jobs and 5 resources. Each job is a linear sequence of five activities, each requiring a different resource; in each job, the first activity has a release date and the last a due date. Two features characterize the expected difficulty of each problem group. The first is the spread of release and due dates among jobs; this can be (in order of increasing expected difficulty) wide (w), narrow (n), and null (0). The second is the number of a priority bottlenecks; this can be either 1 or 2.[3]

We ran two different configurations of CPS. Backtracking was allowed up to a maximum of 10 times, after which the problem was declared not solved. Each Capacity Analysis step used a total value assignment sample size of $N = 20$. In both cases, the stochastic simulation used forward temporal dispatching as the variable selection strategy; only the value selection rule was different in the two configura-

---

[3] For a more detailed description of the benchmark, see Sadeh (1991).

tions. The *(20, ASAP)* configuration used a linearly biased value selection rule with highest preference to the earliest time and lowest, 0, to the latest time; the *(20, UNIF)* configuration used a uniform value selection rule.

We implemented a scheduler, MIN CONF, that follows the min-conflict approach. The goal was to evaluate the performance of a scheduler relying almost exclusively on the iterative repair process. For this reason, MIN CONF displays several differences with respect to the configuration of the Spike scheduling system that was also applied to this benchmark (Johnston & Minton, 1994). Both MIN CONF and Spike use a basic cycle that generates an initial total value assignment and applies a process of iterative repair to it. In both cases, if a solution is not found after a fixed number of repairs, the cycle is repeated. MIN CONF and Spike differ greatly with respect to the creation of the initial value assignment. MIN CONF does not make any attempt to generate a "good" initial guess. It generates a total time assignment by executing CPS's stochastic simulation once. The simulation is configured as forward temporal dispatching with uniform value selection rule. This guarantees satisfaction of job precedences and of release and due dates but not of capacity constraints. Moreover, the use of a uniform rule biases each operation to occur late in its time bound. Instead, Spike uses a much more informed initialization method that applies a min-conflict approach. It iteratively selects a variable by using "most-constrained first" and by breaking ties randomly; the variable is then bound to the earliest value among those with the minimum number of conflicts. Both MIN CONF and Spike use similar min-conflict iterative repair cycles. The repair variable is chosen randomly among those currently in conflict. Both methods count capacity conflicts in the same way, but there is a difference in the way job precedence conflicts are counted. MIN CONF counts a single conflict for an activity that violates job precedence constraints with any number of activities. On the other hand, Spike counts one conflict for each job precedence that is violated.

Because the iterative repair phase could cycle indefinitely, MIN CONF limits the number of repairs to 25,000; after this threshold, the scheduler declares a failure. To evaluate the effect of the length of the repair process, we ran MIN CONF in two configurations. In the first, MIN CONF *(50, 500)*, the initialization occurs every 500 unsuccessful repairs; in the second, MIN CONF *(5, 5000)*, the limit for each repair phase is 5000 cycles. In both configurations, the initialization effort is negligible compared to the time spent repairing. This bias is consistent with our interest toward isolating the effects of the repair process as much as possible.

The performance of micro-opportunistic search scheduling (MICRO OPP) comes directly from the literature (Sadeh, 1991; Sadeh, Sycara, & Xiong, 1993). Micro opportunistic search uses variable and value ordering heuristics based on capacity analysis metrics similar to those of CPS. The performance results refer to two configurations differing on the strategy used to recover from dead ends. The first configuration, MICOR OPP *CHRON BKTRK*, uses chronological backtracking (Sadeh, 1991). The second, MICRO OPP *INTEL BKTRK*, uses a series of intelligent dead end recovery techniques (Xiong, Sadeh, & Sycara, 1992).

6.8.2.2 Experimental Results

Tables 6-2 and 6-3 report the comparative performance results. The rows refer to each problem group in the benchmark; for example, row w/2 refers to problems with wide spread and two a priori bottlenecks. The last row reports a summary of the performance over the whole benchmark. Because both CPS and MIN CONF have a randomized nature, we estimated their average performance over five independent runs. This is not necessary for MICRO OPP because as we already mentioned in Section 6.8.1, its heuristics are deterministic, although based on probabilistic assumptions.

Table 6-2: Comparative results: Number of problems solved.

	CPS		MIN CONF		MICRO OFF	
	(20, ASAP)	*(20, UNIF)*	*(50, 500)*	*(5, 5000)*	*CHRON BKTRK*	*INTEL BKTRK*
w/1	10	10	9.8	9.2	10	10
w/2	10	10	2.2	3.2	10	10
n/1	10	10	7.4	6.6	8	10
n/2	10	9.4	1	1.2	9	10
0/1	10	9.4	4.2	3.4	7	10
0/2	10	9	0	0.4	8	10
TOT	60	57.8	24.6	24.0	52	60

Table 6-3: Comparative results: CPU time.

	CPS		MIN CONF		MICRO OFF	
	(20, ASAP)	*(20, UNIF)*	*(50, 500)*	*(5, 5000)*	*CHRON BKTRK*	*INTEL BKTRK*
w/1	68.08	66.09	95.49	152.40	78.00	90.66
w/2	70.67	77.62	383.34	336.17	82.75	94.95
n/1	69.43	71.64	159.92	235.08	359.25	106.22
n/2	72.16	106.17	418.53	408.83	151.00	119.53
0/1	80.20	91.82	297.41	333.13	462.25	134.75
0/2	110.04	142.54	435.83	425.10	275.00	226.56
AVG	78.43	92.64	298.42	315.12	234.71	128.78

Table 6-2 reports the number of problems solved. The results show that CPS *(20, ASAP)* and MICRO OPP *INTEL BKTRK* are the only two techniques that consistently solved all the problems. The performance differences across the two CPS configurations indicate the importance of the stochastic simulation strategy. For example, the choice of different value selection rules impacts the region of the search space from which sample elements are more likely to be generated. In our case, it can be demonstrated that the sample base obtained with a *UNIF* rule is, in fact, narrower than the one obtained with an *ASAP* rule. The evaluation of the effect of different sampling strategies on the performance of the scheduler is an important open problem.

Both configurations of MIN CONF performed significantly worse than both CPS and MICRO OPP.[4] At first glance, this result might seem at odds with the excellent performances displayed on this benchmark by Spike (Johnston & Minton, 1994). However, the balance between initialization and repair efforts is very different in the two schedulers. As we mentioned before, because MIN CONF was mainly intended to evaluate the repair process, initialization effort is negligible with respect to repair. Considering the number of time value assignments in each phase, MIN CONF *(50, 500)* has a 1 to 10 ratio, and MIN CONF *(5, 5000)* has a 1 to 100 ratio. Because each initialization assignment is not as "informed" as an assignment during repair, the ratio is even more biased toward repair. Conversely, in Spike, initialization and repair efforts are balanced because the same number of value assignments to variables is executed in both phases. Moreover, initialization and repair assignments use the same kind of heuristics. An important consequence of this is that when Spike succeeds, most of the time it does not repair. The dependency of the convergence of the repair process from the choice of a "good" initial solution is still an open problem.

The performance of MIN CONF across problem subsets is worst on the problems with two a priori bottlenecks. When a problem presents several bottlenecks, scheduling algorithms are known to have difficulty in dealing with the complex interactions. These results suggest that the local nature of the conflict measure used in MIN CONF is unable to detect such interactions.

Table 6-3 reports average CPU times for a problem run in each subset. The times were obtained by summing up all the processing times for all the problem instances (successful and unsuccessful), dividing by the number of problems, and then averaging over the five independent runs. The last row contains average CPU time over the entire benchmark. All the run times refer to implementations in Common Lisp, using CRL as an underlying knowledge representation language.

---

[4] In fact, they also are inferior to a number of other heuristic search methods (Sadeh, 1991).

The run times of CPS and MICRO OPP were obtained on a DEC 5000/200 workstation.[5]

To ensure a fair comparison, we reduced the actual CPU times for MIN CONF by a factor, taking into account the inefficiency of our current implementation. This was done by assuming that the maximum CPU time of any CPS run was equivalent to the time taken to execute the 25,000 repairs of a maximum length MIN CONF run; we do not consider the time spent during initialization. These times would require a speed-up of 20 times over our current, inefficient MIN CONF implementation, a factor that we think can easily be achieved by just using more efficient data structures.

A comparison of CPU times serves two main purposes. In the first place, the compared techniques are extremely different with respect to several factors. These include the underlying search method, the computational effort needed to evaluate heuristics, and the balance between the time spent in evaluating heuristics and the time spent expanding alternatives. CPU times are the only reasonable way to ensure that each technique is given a comparable "computational allowance" before declaring a failure. In the second place, CPU time indeed depends on the implementation. Implementations are likely to improve with time, and the degree of improvement might differ across techniques. However, if we assume some basic factors as constant, such as hardware and programming languages, CPU times are a fair description of the current state of the art of the different techniques.

The comparison of the CPU times shows that CPS is consistently faster than all the other techniques. In particular, comparing the only two techniques that can solve all the problems in the benchmark, CPS *(20, ASAP)* is about 64% faster on average than MICRO OPP *INTEL BKTRK*. The experimental results clearly show that CPS outperforms both MIN CONF and MICRO OPP on this benchmark.

6.9 CONCLUSIONS

The effectiveness of HSTS has been demonstrated by modeling and solving complex planning and scheduling problems. The principal advantages are the intrinsic modularity of the representation framework, its independence from the problem solving methodology, and the flexibility of the constraint posting and propagation mechanisms. Integrated planner/schedulers have been implemented in domains such as space mission scheduling and transportation planning. Although simplified, they have demonstrated the ability to deal effectively with all the important domain constraints. For more classical job-shop constraint satisfaction

---

[5]The run times from MICRO OPP *CHRON BKTRK* have been obtained from those reported in Sadeh (1991) by assuming the maximum speed-up factor of 2 for moving from a DEC 3100 workstation to a DEC 5000/200.

scheduling problems, the combination of flexibility of the temporal database and of statistical measures of the search space has yielded promising results. Future research will further address the issue of scalability of the domain models and problem solvers, the extension of constraint language and propagation mechanisms, the development and evaluation of alternative methodologies for capacity analysis, the extension of the statistical search space metrics to integrated planning/scheduling domains, and the assessment of the effectiveness of flexible plan/schedule representations during reactive plan execution.

ACKNOWLEDGMENTS

Since the beginning of the project, Stephen Smith has always given valuable support and contributions. Other contributors are Gilad Amiri, Amedeo Cesta, Daniela D'Aloisi, Robert Frederking, and Dhiraj Pathak. Dina Berkowitz, Gregg Podnar, and David Greene helped review a previous draft of this chapter. This work was carried out when the author was at the Center for Integrated Manufacturing and Decision Systems, The Robotics Institute, Carnegie Mellon University.

This work was sponsored in part by the National Aeronautics and Space Administration under contract #NCC 2-707, the Defense Advanced Research Projects Agency under contract #F30602-91-F-0016, and the Robotics Institute.

References

Adams, J., E. Balas, and D. Zawack. 1988. "The Shifting Bottleneck Procedure for Job Shop Scheduling," *Management Science,* 34, pp. 391–401.

Allen, J.F. 1983. "Maintaining Knowledge about Temporal Intervals," *Communications of the ACM,* 26, 11, 832–843.

Allen, J., and J.A. Koomen. 1983. "Planning Using a Temporal World Model," *Proceedings of the 8th International Joint Conference on Artificial Intelligence.* AAAI Press, Menlo Park, Calif., pp. 741–747.

Armed Forces Staff College. 1988. "The Joint Staff Officer's Guide," Publication 1, Armed Forces Staff College, Hanes, S.H. ed., U.S. Government Printing Office, Washington, D.C.

Baker, K.R. 1974. *Introduction to Sequencing and Scheduling,* John Wiley and Sons, New York.

Biefeld, E., and L. Cooper. 1991. "Bottleneck Identification Using Process Chronologies," *Proceedings of the 12th International Joint Conference on Artificial Intelligence,* AAAI Press, Menlo Park, Calif., pp. 218–224.

Currie, K., and A. Tate. 1991. "O-plan: The Open Planning Architecture," *Artificial Intelligence,* 52, 1, 49–86.

Dean, T.L., and D.V. McDermott. 1987. "Temporal Data Base Management," *Artificial Intelligence,* 32, 1–55.

Dean, T., and M. Wellman. 1991. *Planning and Control,* Morgan Kaufmann, San Francisco, Calif.

Dean, T., R.J. Firby, and D. Miller. 1988. "Hierarchical Planning Involving Deadlines, Travel Time, and Resources," *Computational Intelligence,* 4, 381–398.

Dechter, R., I. Meiri, and J. Pearl. 1991. "Temporal Constraint Networks," *Artificial Intelligence,* 49, 61–95.

Fikes, R.E., P.E., Hart, N.J. Nilsson. 1972. "Learning and Executing Generalized Robot Plans," *Artificial Intelligence,* 3, 251–288.

Forbus, K.D. 1989. "Introducing Actions into Qualitative Simulation," *Proceedings of the Eleventh International Joint Conference on Artificial Intelligence.* AAAI Press, Menlo Park, Calif., pp. 1273–1278.

Fox, M.S., and S.F. Smith. 1984. "ISIS: A Knowledge-Based System for Factory Scheduling," *Expert Systems,* 1, 1, 25–49.

Frederking, R.E., and N. Muscettola. 1992. "Temporal Planning for Transportation Planning and Scheduling," *Proceedings of 1992 IEEE International Conference on Robotics and Automation,* IEEE Computer Society Press, Los Alamitos, Calif., pp. 1225–1230.

Haralick, R.M., and G.L. Elliot. 1980. "Increasing Tree Search Efficiency for Constraint Satisfaction Problems," *Artificial Intelligence,* 14, 3, 263–313.

Johnston, M.J., and S. Minton. 1994. "Analyzing a Heuristic Strategy for Constraint Satisfaction and Scheduling," *Intelligent Scheduling,* Fox, M.S. and Zweben, M., eds., Morgan Kaufmann, San Francisco, Calif.

Kalman, R.E., P.L. Falb, and M.A. Arbib. 1969. *Topics in Mathematical System Theory,* McGraw-Hill, New York.

Knoblock, C.A. 1991. "Automatically Generating Abstractions for Problem Solving," School of Computer Science, Carnegie Mellon University.

Lansky, A. 1988. "Localized Event-based Reasoning for Multiagent Domains," *Computational Intelligence,* 4, 319–340.

Manna, Z., and A. Pnueli. 1991. *The Temporal Logic of Reactive and Concurrent Systems,* Springer-Verlag, New York.

Minton, S., M.D. Johnston, A.B. Philips, and P. Laird. 1992. "Minimizing Conflicts: A Heuristic Repair Method for Constraint Satisfaction and Scheduling Problems," *Artificial Intelligence,* 58, 161–205.

Muscettola, N. 1993. "An Experimental Analysis of Bottleneck-centered Opportunistic Scheduling," #CMU-RI-TR-93-06, The Robotics Institute, Carnegie Mellon University.

Muscettola, N. 1993b. "Scheduling by Iterative Partition of Bottleneck Conflicts," *Proceedings of the 9th Conference on Artificial Intelligence for Applications,* IEEE Computer Society Press, Los Alamitos, Calif., pp. 49–55.

Muscettola, N. 1992. "Scheduling by Iterative Partition of Bottleneck Conflicts," #CMU-RI-TR-92-05, The Robotics Institute, Carnegie Mellon University.

Muscettola, N. 1990. "Planning the Behavior of Dynamical Systems," #CMU-RI-TR-90-10, The Robotics Institute, Carnegie Mellon University.

Muscettola, N., and S.F. Smith. 1990. "Integrating Planning and Scheduling to Solve Space Mission Scheduling Problems," *Proceedings of the DARPA Workshop on Planning,* Morgan Kaufmann, San Francisco, Calif., pp. 220–230.

Muscettola, N., and S.F. Smith. 1987. "A Probabilistic Framework for Resource-Constrained Multi-Agent Planning," *Proceedings of the 10th International Joint Conference on Artificial Intelligence,* AAAI Press, Menlo Park, Calif., pp. 1063–1066.

Muscettola, N., S.F. Smith, A. Cesta, and D. D'Aloisi. 1992. "Coordinating Space Telescope Operations in an Integrated Planning and Scheduling Architecture," *IEEE Control Systems Magazine,* 12, 2, pp. 28–37.

Ow, P.S., and S.F. Smith. 1988. "Viewing Scheduling as an Opportunistic Problem Solving Process," R.G. Jeroslow, ed., Basel, Switzerland, Baltzer Scientific Publishing Co., *Annals of Operations Research,* 12, 85–108.

Panwalker, S.S., and W. Iskander. 1977. "A Survey of Scheduling Rules," *Operations Research,* 25, 45–61.

Roth, S.F., and J. Mattis. 1991. "Automating the Presentation of Information," *Proceedings of the Conference on Artificial Intelligence Applications,* IEEE Computer Society, Los Alamitos, Calif., pp. 90–97.

Sadeh, N. 1991. "Look-Ahead Techniques for Micro-Opportunistic Job Shop Scheduling," #CMU-CS-91-102, School of Computer Science, Carnegie Mellon University.

Sadeh, N., K. Sycara, and Y. Xiong. 1993. "A Comparative Study of Backtracking Techniques for Hard Scheduling Problems," The Robotics Institute, Carnegie Mellon University.

Schrag, R.. M. Boddy, and J. Carciofini. 1992. "Managing Disjunction for Practical Temporal Reasoning," *Proceedings of the Third International Conference on Principles of Knowledge Representation and Reasoning,* Morgan Kaufmann, Cambridge, MA, pp. 36–46.

Smith, S.F and D.K. Pathak. 1992. "Balancing Antagonistic Time and Resource Utilization Constraints in Over-Subscribed Scheduling Problems," *Proceedings of the 8th IEEE Conference on AI Applications.* IEEE Computer Society Press, Los Alamitos, Calif., pp. 115–119.

Smith, S.F., P.S. Ow, J.Y. Potvin., N. Muscettola, and D. Matthys. 1990. "An Integrated Framework for Generating and Revising Factory Schedules," *Journal of the Operational Research Society,* 41, 6, 539–552.

Space Telescope Science Institute. 1986. *Proposal Instructions for the Hubble Space Telescope,* Space Telescope Science Institute, John Hopkins University, Baltimore, MD.

Vere, S. 1983. "Planning in Time: Windows and Durations for Activities and Goals," *IEEE Transactions on Pattern Analysis and Machine Intelligence,* PAMI-5, 246–267.

Vilain, M., H. Kautz, and P. van Beek. 1990. "Constraint Propagation Algorithms for Temporal Reasoning: A Revised Report," *Qualitative Reasoning about Physical Systems,* Morgan Kaufmann, San Francisco, Calif., pp. 373–381.

Wilkins, D.E. 1988. *Practical Planning*, Morgan Kaufmann, San Francisco, Calif.

Xiong, Y., N. Sadeh, and K. Sycara. 1992. "Intelligent Backtracking Techniques for Job Shop Scheduling," *Proceedings of the Third International Conference on Principles of Knowledge Representation and Reasoning*, Morgan Kaufmann, San Francisco, Calif., pp. 14–23

Zweben, M., M. Deale, and R. Gargan. 1990. "Anytime Rescheduling," *Proceedings of the DARPA Workshop on Innovative Approaches to Planning, Scheduling and Control*, Morgan Kaufmann, San Francisco, Calif., pp. 251–259.

7

O-Plan2:

An Open Architecture for Command, Planning, and Control

Austin Tate
Brian Drabble
Richard Kirby
(Artificial Intelligence Applications Institute,
University of Edinburgh)

7.1 INTRODUCTION

O-Plan2 (the Open Planning Architecture) provides a generic domain-independent computational architecture suitable for command, planning, and execution applications. The main contribution of the O-Plan2 research has been a complete vision of a modular and flexible planning and control system incorporating artificial intelligence methods.

This chapter describes the O-Plan2 agent oriented architecture and describes the communication that takes place between planning and execution monitoring agents built upon the architecture. Separate modules of such a system are identified along with internal and external interface specifications that form a part of the design.

Time constraints, resource usage, object selection, and condition/effect causal constraints are handled as an integral part of the overall system structure by treating specialized constraint management as supporting the core decision making components in the architecture. A close coupling of planning and time or resource scheduling is therefore possible within a system employing an activity based plan representation.

7.2 HISTORY AND TECHNICAL INFLUENCES

O-Plan grew out of the experiences of other research into AI planning, particularly with Nonlin (Tate, 1977) and "blackboard" systems (Nii, 1986). The *Readings in Planning* volume (Allen, Hendler, & Tate, 1990) includes a taxonomy of earlier planning systems that places O-Plan in relation to the influences on its design. It is assumed that the reader is familiar with these works because the references do not include them all. The same volume (Allen, Hendler, & Tate, 1990) includes an introduction to the literature of AI planning.

The main AI planning techniques that have been used or extended in O-Plan are as follows:

- It is a hierarchical planning system that can produce plans as partial orders on actions (as suggested by Sacerdoti [1977]), although O-Plan is flexible concerning the order in which parts of the plan at different levels are expanded.
- It is an agenda-based control architecture in which each control cycle can post pending tasks during plan generation. These pending tasks are then picked up from the agenda and processed by appropriate handlers (HEARSAY-II [Lesser & Erman, 1977] and OPM [Hayes-Roth & Hayes-Roth, 1979] use the term *Knowledge Source* for these handlers).
- O-Plan uses the notion of a "plan state," which is the data structure containing the emerging plan, the "flaws" remaining in it, and the information used in building the plan. This is similar to the work of McDermott (1978).
- Constraint posting and least commitment on object variables are used, as seen in MOLGEN (Stefik, 1981).
- Temporal and resource constraint handling, shown to be valuable in realistic domains by Deviser (Vere, 1981), has been extended to provide a powerful search space pruning method. The algorithms for this are incremental versions of Operational Research (OR) methods. O-Plan has integrated ideas from OR and AI in a coherent and constructive manner.
- O-Plan is derived from the earlier Nonlin planner (Tate, 1977) from which we have taken and extended the ideas of Goal Structure, Question Answering (QA), and typed preconditions.
- We have maintained Nonlin's style of domain and task description language (Task Formalism or TF) and extended it for O-Plan2.

7.2.1 O-Plan1

The main effort on the first O-Plan project (now referred to as O-Plan1) was concentrated in the area of plan generation. The work on O-Plan1 is documented in an article in *Artificial Intelligence* (Currie & Tate, 1991). One theme of the O-Plan1 research was search domain knowledge-based space control in an AI planner. The output of that work gave a better understanding of the requirements of planning methods, improved heuristics and techniques for search space control, and a demonstration system embodying the results in an appropriate framework and representational scheme.

O-Plan1 sought to build an open architecture for an AI planning system. It was our aim to build a system in which it was possible to experiment with and integrate developing ideas. Further, the system was to able to be tailored to suit particular applications. Time and resource constraints were handled to restrict search and still work within an activity based plan representation.

7.2.2 O-Plan2

The O-Plan2 project began in 1989 and had the following new objectives:

- to consider a simple "three agent" view (the three agents being the task assignment agent, the planning agent, and the execution agent) of the environment for the research to clarify thinking on the roles of the user(s), architecture, and system

- to explore the thesis that communication of capabilities and information between the three agents could be in the form of *plan patches*, which, in their turn, are in the same form as the domain information descriptions, the task description, and the plan representation used within the planner and the other two agents

- to investigate a single architecture that could support all three agent types and that could support different plan representations and agent capability descriptions to allow for work in activity planning or resource scheduling

- to clarify the functions of components of a planning and control architecture

- to draw on the earlier Edinburgh planning experience in O-Plan1 (Currie & Tate, 1991) and to improve on it, especially with respect to flow of control (Tate, 1990)

- to provide an improved version of the O-Plan1 system suitable for use outside of Edinburgh within Common Lisp, X-Windows, and UNIX

- to provide a design suited to use on parallel processing systems in future

This chapter gives an overview of the O-Plan2 architecture and its use in a prototype planning system. Further details of the system are available in Tate, Drabble, & Kirby (1992).

7.3 CHARACTERIZATION OF O-Plan2

The O-Plan2 approach to command, planning, scheduling, and control can be characterized as follows:

- successive refinement/repair of a complete but flawed plan or schedule
- least commitment approach
- opportunistic selection of the focus of attention on each problem solving cycle
- information built incrementally in "constraint managers":
  - effect/condition manager
  - resource utilization manager
  - time point network manager
  - object/variable manager
- localized search to explore alternatives where advisable
- global alternative re-orientation where necessary

O-Plan2 is aimed to be relevant to the following types of problems:

- project management for product introduction, systems engineering, construction, process flow for assembly, integration and verification, etc.
- planning and control of supply and distribution logistics
- mission sequencing and control of space probes such as Voyager, and ERS-1

These applications fit midway between the large scale manufacturing scheduling problems found in some industries (where there are often few inter-operation constraints) and the complex *puzzles* dealt with by very flexible logic based tools. However, the problems of the target type represent an important class of industrial, scientific, and engineering relevance.

7.4 COMMUNICATION IN COMMAND, PLANNING, AND CONTROL

7.4.1 The Scenario

The scenario we are investigating is as follows:

- A user specifies a task that is to be performed through some suitable interface. We call this process *task assignment.*
- A *planner* plans and (if requested) arranges to execute the plan to perform the task specified. The planner has knowledge of the general capabilities of a semi-autonomous execution system but does not need to know about the actual activities that execute the actions required to carry out the desired task.
- The *execution system* seeks to carry out the detailed tasks specified by the planner and works with a more detailed model of the execution environment than is available to the task assigner and to the planner.

The central planner, therefore, communicates a general plan to achieve a particular task and responds to failures fed back from the execution agent that are in the form of flaws in the plan. Such failures might be the result of the inappropriateness of a particular activity or because the desired effect of an activity was not achieved because of an unforeseen event. The reason for the failure dictates whether the same activity should be re-applied, or replaced with other activities or whether re-planning should take place.

We have deliberately simplified our consideration to three agents with these different roles and with possible differences of requirements for user availability, processing capacity, and real-time reaction to clarify the research objectives in our work.

7.4.2 A Common Representation for Communication between Agents

We have been exploring a common representation to support the communication between a user requesting the plan and the real world in which the plan is being executed. Such communication can take place either directly through a planner or indirectly via a central planner and a dumb or semi-autonomous execution agent.

The common representation includes knowledge about the capabilities of the planner and execution agent, the requirements of the plan, and the plan itself either with or without flaws (see Figure 7-1). Thus, a planner will respond to the requirements of a user. Based on the knowledge of its own capabilities and that of the execution environment, it will generate a plan. This plan can then be executed directly in the real world or indirectly via an execution agent. The execution agent executes this plan in the real world and monitors the execution, responding to failures in one of two ways. If it does not have knowledge of its own capabilities, it simply returns knowledge of the failure to the central planner and awaits a revised plan to be sent. In this case, the execution agent is dumb. If it does have knowledge of its own capabilities, it might attempt to repair the plan and then continue with execution. On the other hand, if a repair is beyond the capabilities of the execution

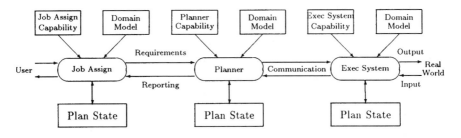

Figure 7-1: Communication between central planner and execution agent

agent, then this knowledge is fed back to the central planner, and again, a revised plan is expected. In this case, the execution agent is semi-autonomous. When failures during the application of the plan are fed back to the planner, these might be acted upon by it and a repair of the plan made or total re-planning instigated. This can, in turn, involve the user in reformulating the task requirement. A revised or new plan is then executed. Finally, success of the execution or partial execution of the plan is fed back to the user.

The communication of task, plan and execution information between agents is in the form of *plan patches* because it is assumed that each agent is operating asynchronously with its own plan state and model of the environment. Further details are given in Tate (1989).

7.5 O-Plan2 ARCHITECTURE

This section describes the O-Plan2 architecture and describes the major modules that make up the system. An agenda based architecture has been used as the central feature of the system and the design approach. Within this framework, there has been consideration of choice enumeration, choice ordering, choice making, and choice processing. This is important because it allows us to begin to justifiably isolate functionality that can be described in terms of

- triggering mechanisms, *i.e.*, what causes the mechanism to be activated
- decision making roles—precisely what type of decision can be made
- implications for search—whether the search space been pruned, restricted, or further constrained as far as possible
- decision ordering—the order in what we should choose between the alternative decisions possible
- choice ordering—for a decision to be made, the open choices that we should adopt

The main components of an O-Plan2 agent are

- domain information—the information that describes an application and the tasks in that domain to the agent
- Plan state—the emerging plan to carry out identified tasks
- Knowledge sources—the processing capabilities of the agent (*plan modification operators*)
- Support modules—functions that support the processing capabilities of the agent and its components
- Controller—the decision maker on the *order* in which processing is done

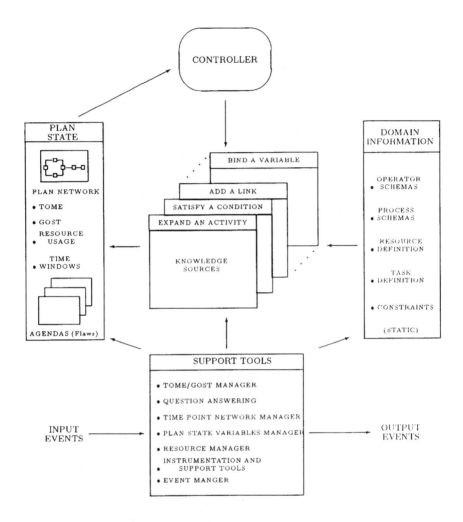

Figure 7-2: O-Plan2 architecture.

A generalized picture of the architecture, illustrated with the components to specialize the architecture to be a planning agent, is shown in Figure 7-2. Further details of each component follow in subsequent sections. In these sections, illustrations of the contents of the main components are made by referring to the parts of a planning agent.

7.5.1 Domain Information

Domain descriptions are supplied to O-Plan2 in a language called Task Formalism (TF). This is compiled into the internal data structures to be used during planning. A TF description includes details of

1. activities and events that can be performed or occur in the domain
2. information about the environment and the objects in it
3. task descriptions that describe the planning requirements

TF is the means through which a domain writer or domain expert can supply the domain specific information to the O-Plan2 system, which itself is domain *independent*. O-Plan2 embodies search space pruning mechanisms using this domain information (strong search methods) and will fall back on other weak methods if these fail. TF is the mechanism that enables the user of the system to supply domain dependent knowledge to assist the system in its search.

7.5.2 Plan State

In contrast to the relatively static information outlined above, the plan state (on the left of Figure 7-2) is the dynamic data structure used during planning and houses the emerging plan. There are a number of components to this structure; the principal ones are as follows:

- The plan network itself: This is based on a partial order of activities, as originally suggested in the NOAH planner (Sacerdoti, 1977). In O-Plan2, the plan information is concentrated in the "Associated Data Structure" (ADS). The ADS contains node and link structures, noting temporal and resource information, plan information, etc.

- The plan rationale: As in Nonlin and O-Plan1, the system keeps explicit information to "explain" why the plan is built the way it is. This rationale is called the Goal Structure (GOST) and, along with the Table of Multiple Effects (TOME), provides an efficient data structure for the condition achievement support module used in O-Plan2 (Question Answerer—QA—*c.f.* Chapman's Modal Truth Criteria [Chapman, 1987]).

- The agenda: O-Plan2 starts with a complete plan but one that is "flawed," hence preventing the plan from being capable of execution. The nature of the flaws present will be varied, from actions that are at a higher level than that which the executing agent can operate to linkages necessary in the plan to resolve conflict. Some agenda entries can represent potentially beneficial but not yet processed information. The agenda is the repository for this "pending" information, which must be processed in order to attain an executable plan.

The plan state is a self-contained snapshot of the state of the planning system at a particular point in time in the plan generation process. It contains all the state of the system; hence, the generation process can be suspended and this single structure rolled back at a later point in time to allow resumption of the search.[1]

7.5.3 Knowledge Sources

These are the computational capabilities associated with the processing of the flaws contained in the plan, and they embody the planning knowledge of the system. There are as many Knowledge Sources (KS) as there are flaw types, including the interface to the user wishing to exert an influence on the plan generation process. A KS can draw on domain information (*e.g.*, the use of an action schema for purposes of expansion) to process a flaw, and in turn, they can add structure to any part of the plan state (*e.g.*, adding ordering links to the plan, inserting new effects, or further populating the agenda with flaws).

7.5.4 Support Modules

In order to efficiently support the main planning functionality in O-Plan2, there are a number of support modules separated out from the core of the planner. These modules have carefully designed functional interfaces in order that we can both build the planner in a piecewise fashion and, in particular, that we can experiment with and easily integrate new implementations of the modules. The modularity is possible only through the experience gained in earlier planning projects where support function requirements were carefully separated out from the general problem solving and decision making demands of the system.

Support modules are intended to provide efficient support to the higher level Knowledge Sources where decisions are taken. They should not take any decision themselves. They are intended to provide complete information about the questions asked of them to the decision making level itself. Some support modules act as *constraint managers* for a sub-set of the plan state information.

The support modules include the following:

- Question-Answerer (QA) is the process at the heart of O-Plan2's condition satisfaction procedure. It can establish whether a proposition is true or not at a particular point in the plan. The answer it returns might be (1) a categorical "yes"; (2) a categorical "no"; or (3) a "maybe," in which case QA will supply an alternative set (structured as an and/or tree) of strategies that a Knowledge Source can choose from in order to ensure the truth of the proposition. The

---

[1]This is assuming that the Task Formalism and the Knowledge Sources used on re-start are the same "static" information used previously.

QA procedure makes use of the information managed by the time point network and condition/effect constraint management components (see below) to filter the answers provided to the decision making level above.

- Time Point Network Manager (TPN) manages metric and relative time constraints in a plan.
- TOME and GOST Manager (TGM) manages the causal structure (conditions and effects that satisfy them) in a plan.
- Plan State Variable Manager manages partially bound objects in the plan.
- Resource Utilization Manager monitors and manages the use of resources in a plan.
- Instrumentation and Diagnostics routines allow the developer to set and alter levels of diagnostic reporting within the system. These can range from full trace information to fatal errors only. The instrumentation routines allow performance characteristics to be gathered while the system is running. Information such as how often a routine is accessed and what time it takes to process an agenda entry can be gathered.

7.5.5 Controller

Holding this loosely coupled framework together is the Controller acting on the agenda. Items on the agenda (the flaws) have a context dependent priority that the Controller can re-compute and that allows for the opportunism required to drive plan generation. Agenda entries can be triggered by specific plan state changes or other events, such as the binding of a variable, the satisfaction of a condition, the occurrence of an external event, and a reminder from an internal agent diary.

The controller also provides the framework to activate Knowledge Sources on Knowledge Source Platforms and to give them appropriate access to domain and plan information. Further details of the choice ordering mechanisms in O-Plan2 are given in Tate (1990).

The controller provides facilities for managing alternative plan states for internal search within an O-Plan2 agent where this is feasible.

7.6 PROCESS STRUCTURE OF THE O-Plan2 IMPLEMENTATION

The current O-Plan2 prototype system is able to operate both as a planner and a simple execution agent. The task assignment function is provided by a separate process that has a simple menu interface.

The abstract architecture described in Figure 7-2 can be mapped to the system and process architecture detailed in Figure 7-3, which shows the specialization of the architecture to the O-Plan2 planner agent. Communication between the various

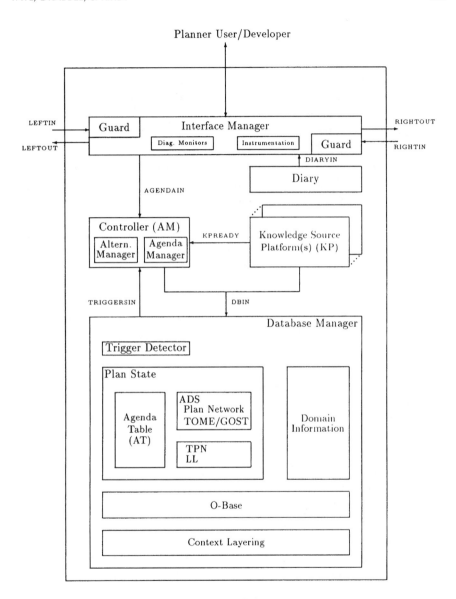

Figure 7-3: Internal structure of the current O-Plan2 planner.

processes and managers in the system is shown. Each entry within the figure is explained later in this section.

The basic processing cycle of O-Plan2 (as illustrated by the planner agent) is as follows:

1. An event is received by the Event Manager, which resides within the Interface Manager (IM) process. The IM is in direct contact with all other processes of the architecture through the Module Communication Channel (MCC).[2] Support modules allow the developer to change levels of diagnostics and to set up instrumentation checks on the planner. The Event Manager has two Guards, one on the left input channel (from the task assigner) and one on the right input channel (from the execution system). The input channels themselves are separated into priority levels.

   The guards verify and, if necessary, reject events that are not relevant to the system. The guards use knowledge of the system's capabilities derived from the Knowledge Sources and domain model (TF) currently loaded into the system.

2. If the event is approved by the guard, then it is passed to the Controller/Agenda Manager (AM), which assigns it the necessary triggers and Knowledge Source activation entry. The entry (now referred to as an Agenda Entry) is then passed to the Database Manager (DM) to await triggering. The entry is placed in the Agenda Table (AT) monitored by the Trigger Detector (TD).

3. When triggered, the Trigger Detector informs the Agenda Manager and can *cache* a copy of the triggered agenda entry in the Agenda Manager. The order of entries on the triggered agenda is constantly updated as new agenda entries are added or as triggers on waiting agenda entries become invalid. A trigger can become invalid because its triggering condition ceases to hold.

   Knowledge Sources can use the Diary Manager functions to assist them to perform their task. The Diary Manager (DIARY) is responsible for handling triggers associated with a given time. For example, send an action for execution at a specific time, or trigger a regular event.

   Eventually, the agenda entry is selected for processing by the Controller/Agenda Manager.

4. The Controller/Agenda Manager assigns an available Knowledge Source Platform (KP) that can run the pre-nominated Knowledge Source on the triggered agenda entry.

5. When a Knowledge Source Platform has been allocated, if it does not already contain the nominated Knowledge Source, the Platform can request the body of the Knowledge Source from the Database Manager in order to process the agenda entry. Knowledge Sources can be preloaded on the Platform, so this request is not necessary in all cases. Some Platforms might be best suited to run particular Knowledge Sources; hence, the system will not store all

---

[2] The MCC is not shown in Figure 7-3 to simplify the diagram.

Knowledge Sources at all Platforms. The Knowledge Source Platforms will eventually have their own local libraries of Knowledge Sources. Locking down of a specific real time Knowledge Source to a dedicated Platform is allowed for in the design.

6. A protocol (called the Knowledge Source Protocol) and an access key are used to control communication between the Controller/Agenda Manager and a Knowledge Source running on a Platform. This controls the processing that the Knowledge Source can do and the access it has to the current plan state via the Database Manager (DM).

A Knowledge Source can terminate with none, one, or multiple alternative results through interaction with the Controller via the protocol. The Controller uses an Alternatives Manager Support Module to actually manage any alternatives it is provided with and to seek alternatives when no results are returned by a Knowledge Source. A Knowledge Source can also be asked to terminate at suitable internal "stage" boundaries by the Controller.[3]

The internal details of the Database Manager (DM) will depend upon the particular representation chosen for the Plan State. In Figure 7-3, the internal details of the Database Manager relate to the O-Plan2 planner. Here there is a separation of the Associated Data Structure (ADS) level that describes the plan network, the Table of Multiple Effects (TOME), and the Goal Structure (GOST) from the lower level time constraint management done via the Time Point Network (TPN) and its associated metric time point list called the Landmark Line (LL) and the underlying resource constraint management (done via a Resource Utilization Manager).

7.7 O-Plan2 PLANNER

The O-Plan2 planner agent has been the main focus of our work to date. The following sections describe the ways in which the generic O-Plan2 architecture has been specialized for this planner.

7.7.1 Plan State

The planning agent plan state holds information about decisions taken during planning and information about decisions that are still to be made (in the form of an agenda).

---

[3] O-Plan2 Knowledge Sources can comprise a number of separate stages where suspension of processing can occur at any stage boundary.

7.7.1.1 Plan Network

The Associated Data Structure (ADS) provides the *plan entities* that define the plan as a set of activity and event nodes, with ordering information in the form of links as necessary to define the partial order relationships between these elements. The end points of these plan entities are associated with a lower level Time Point Network (TPN). Effects, conditions, time windows, and resource utilization information is also attached to the nodes at the ADS level.

Time windows play an important part in O-Plan2 in two ways: first, as a means of recording time limits on the start and finish of an action and on its duration and delays between actions, and second, during the planning phase itself as a means of pruning the potential search space if temporal validity is threatened.

Time windows in O-Plan2 are maintained as **min/max** pairs, specifying the upper and lower bounds known at the time. Such bounds can be symbolically defined, but O-Plan2 maintains a numerical pair of bounds for all such numerical values. In fact, a third entry is associated with such numerical bounds.[4] This third entry is a *projected* value (which could be a simple number or a more complex function, data structure, etc.) used by the planner for heuristic estimation, search control, and other purposes. The numerical outer bounds on time windows that are maintained by the Time Point Network Manager are used in the QA process at the heart of the planner, and if there are tight time constraints on a plan, they can effectively prune valid responses for ways to satisfy conditions or correct for interactions between conditions and effects.

7.7.1.2 TOME and GOST

The Table of Multiple Effects (TOME) holds statements of the following form:

```
fn(arg1 arg2 ...) = value at time-point
```

The Goal Structure (GOST) holds statements of the following form:

```
<condition-type> fn(arg1 arg2 ...)   = <value> at <time-point>
                                       from <contributor-list>
where <contributor-list> is a set of pairs of format:
(<time-point> . <method-of-satisfaction-of-condition>)
```

In the current implementation, effects and conditions are kept in a simple pattern-directed lookup table as in Nonlin (Tate, 1977). The O-Plan1 *Clouds* mechanism (Tate, 1986) for efficiently manipulating large numbers of effects and their relationship to supporting conditions will be used in O-Plan2 in due course.

---

[4] All numerical values in O-Plan2 are held as triples: minimum, maximum, and projected values.

7.7.1.3 Plan State Objects and Variables

O-Plan2 can keep restrictions on plan state objects without necessarily insisting that a definite binding is chosen as soon as the object is introduced to the Plan State. Plan State Variables can be used in effects, conditions, etc.

7.7.1.4 Resource Utilization Table

The Resource Utilization Table holds statements of the following form:

```
set/+/- resource(<resource-name> <qualifier> ...) = <value>
                                        at <time-point>
```

The statement declares that the particular resource is set to a specific value or changed by being incremented or decremented by the given value at the indicated time point. There can be uncertainty in one or both of the value and the time point, which are held as **min/max** pairs.

Task Formalism resource usage specifications on actions are used to ensure that resource usage in a plan stays within the bounds indicated. There are two types of resource usage statements in TF. One gives a *specification* of the **overall** limitation on resource usage for an activity (over the total time that the activity and any expansion of it can span). The other type describes actual resource *utilization* **at** points in the expansion of an action. It must be possible (within the min/max flexibility in the actual resource usage statements) for a point in the min/max range of the sum of the resource usage statements to be within the overall specification given. The Resource Utilization Table is used to manage the actual resource utilization **at** points in the plan.

7.7.2 Planning Knowledge Sources

The O-Plan2 architecture is specialized into a planning agent by including a number of Knowledge Sources that can alter the Plan State in various ways. The planning Knowledge Sources provide a collection of *plan modification operators* that define the functionality of the planning agent beyond its default O-Plan2 architecture properties (essentially limited to initialization and communication capabilities by default).

The planning Knowledge Sources in the current version of the O-Plan2 planner includes

- KS_SET_TASK, a Knowledge Source to set up an initial plan state corresponding to the task request from the task assignment agent
- KS_EXPAND, a Knowledge Source to expand a high level activity to lower levels of detail

- KS_CONDITION, a Knowledge Source to ensure that certain types of condition are satisfied (this is normally posted by a higher level KS_EXPAND)
- KS_ACHIEVE, a Knowledge Source initiated by KS_EXPAND to achieve conditions possibly by inserting new activities into the plan
- KS_OR, a Knowledge Source to select one of a set of possible alternative linkings and plan state variable bindings (the set of alternative linkings and bindings will have been created by other Knowledge Sources [such as KS_CONDITION] earlier—normally as a result of a Question Answerer [QA] call)
- KS_BIND, a Knowledge Source used to select a binding for a plan state variable in circumstances where alternative possible bindings remain possible
- KS_USER, a Knowledge Source activated at the request of the user acting in the role of supporting the planning process (this is used at present to provide a menu to browse on the plan state and potentially to alter the priority of some choices)
- KS_POISON_STATE, a Knowledge Source used to deal with a statement by another Knowledge Source that the plan state is inconsistent in some way or cannot lead to a valid plan (as far as that Knowledge Source is aware)

In addition, the default Knowledge Sources available in any O-Plan2 agent are present and are as follows:

- KS_INIT initializes the agent.
- KS_COMPILE alters the Knowledge Source (*agent capability*) Library of an O-Plan2 agent by providing new or amended Knowledge Sources (described in a *Knowledge Source Framework* language). In the current implementation of O-Plan2, this cannot be done dynamically.
- KS_DOMAIN calls the Domain Information (normally TF) compiler to alter the Domain Information available to the agent.
- KS_EXTRACT_RIGHT extracts a plan patch for passing to the subordinate agent to the 'right' of this agent, i.e., the execution agent.
- KS_EXTRACT_LEFT extracts a plan patch for passing to the superior agent to the 'left' of this agent, i.e., the task assignment agent.
- KS_PATCH merges a plan patch from an input event channel into the current plan state.

7.7.3 Use of Constraint Managers to Maintain Plan Information

The O-Plan2 planner uses a number of *constraint managers* to maintain information about a plan while it is being generated. The information can then be utilized to prune the search (where plans are found to be invalid as a result of propagating the constraints managed by these managers), to restrict the range of valid answers provided by the Question Answerer (QA) procedure in the planner, or to order search alternatives according to some heuristic priority. The constraint managers are provided as a collection of *support modules* that can be called by Knowledge Sources to maintain specialized aspects of the information in a plan or to answer queries based upon this information.

7.7.3.1 Time Point Network Manager (TPNM)

O-Plan2 uses a point based temporal representation with range constraints between time points and with the possibility of specifying range constraints relative to a fixed time point (time zero). This provides the capability of specifying relative and metric time constraints on time points. The functional interface to the Time Point Network (TPN), as seen by the Associated Data Structure (ADS), has no dependence on a particular representation of the plan state. Further details are given in Drabble & Kirby (1991).

The points held in the TPN can indirectly be associated with actions, links, and events, with the association being made at the Associated Data Structure level. The points are numbered to give an index with a constant retrieval time for any number of points. This structure allows points to be retrieved and compared through a suitable module interface and with a minimum of overhead. The interface reflects the *functionality* required of the TPN and hides the detail. This ensures that we have no absolute reliance on points as a necessary underlying representation. Time points whose upper and lower values have converged to a single value are inserted into a time ordered Landmark Line (LL). This allows the planner to quickly check the order of certain points within the plan. The TPN and LL are maintained by the Time Point Network Manager (TPNM). As well as its use in the O-Plan2 activity orientated planner, the current TPNM has also been applied to large resource allocation scheduling problems in the TOSCA scheduler (Beck et al., 1992), where the number of time points was in excess of 5000, and the number of temporal constraints exceeded 3000.

7.7.3.2 TOME/GOST Manager (TGM)

The conflict free addition of effects and conditions into the plan is achieved through the TGM, which relies in turn on support from the Question Answerer (QA) module, which suggests resolutions for potential conflicts. The resolutions proposed are sensitive to metric time constraints as managed by the Time Point Network Manager.

7.7.3.3 Resource Utilization Management (RUM)

O-Plan2 uses a Resource Utilization Manager to monitor resource levels and utilization. Resources are divided into different types such as

1. consumable, i.e., resources that are "consumed" by actions within the plan, for example, bricks, fuel, and money
2. re-usable, i.e., resources that are used and then returned to a common "pool," for example, robots, workmen, and lorries

Consumable resources can be subcategorized as *strictly consumed* or can be *producible* in some way. Substitutability of resources one for the other is also possible. Some can have a single way mapping, such as money for fuel, and some can be two-way mappings, such as money for travellers' cheques. Producible and substitutable resources are difficult to deal with because they *increase* the amount of choice available within a plan and, thus, *open up* the search space.

The current O-Plan2 Resource Utilization Manager uses the same scheme for strictly consumable resources, as in the original O-Plan1. However, a new scheme based on the maintenance of optimistic and pessimistic resource profiles, with resource usage events and activities tied to changes in the profiles, is now under study.

7.7.3.4 Plan State Variables Manager (PSVM)

The Plan State Variable Manager is responsible for maintaining the consistency of restrictions on plan objects during plan generation. O-Plan2 adopts a least commitment approach to object handling in that variables are only bound as and when necessary. The Plan State Variables Manager within the Database Manager (DM) maintains an explicit "model" of the current set of plan object restrictions and seeks to ensure that a possible instantiation of the object is possible at all times.

When a Plan State Variable (PSV) is created by the planner, the Plan State Variables Manager creates a plan state variable name (PSVN), a plan state variable body (PSVB), and a range list from which a value must be found. For example, the variable could be the color of a spacecraft's camera filter, which could be taken from the range (**red green blue yellow opaque**). A plan state variable must have an enumerable type and, thus, cannot be, for example, a real number. The PSVB holds the **not-sames** and **constraint-lists** and can be pointed to by one or more PSVNs. This allows easier updating as new constraints are added, and PSVBs are made the same. Two or more PSVBs can be collapsed into a single PSVB if all the constraints are compatible, i.e., the **not-sames** and **constraints-list**. A PSVN pointing to a collapsed PSVB is then redirected to point at the remaining PSVB. This scheme allows triggers to be placed on the binding of PSVs (e.g., do not bind until the choice set is less than 3) and allows variables that are creating bottlenecks to be identified and, if necessary, further restricted or bound.

7.7.4 Other Support Modules in O-Plan2

As well as the managers referred to above, a number of other support routines are available for call by the Knowledge Sources of O-Plan2. The main such support mechanisms that have been built into the current O-Plan2 Planner include:

- **Question Answerer** (QA)
  The Question-Answering module is the core of the planner and must be both efficient and able to account for both metric and relative time constraints. QA supports the planner to satisfy and maintain conditions in the plan in a conflict free fashion, suggesting remedies where possible for any interactions detected. The QA procedure makes use of the constraint managers to reduce the number of legal answers it provides.

- **Graph Operations Processor** (GOP)
  The GOP provides efficient answers to ordering related questions within the main plan (represented by a graph). GOP works with metric time ordered and relative or partially ordered activities in the graph.

- **Contexts**
  All data within the O-Plan2 plan state can be "context layered" to provide support for alternatives management and context based reasoning. An efficient, structure sharing support module provides the ability to context layer any data structure access and update function in Lisp. This is particularly useful for the underlying content addressable database in the system: O-Base.

- **O-Base**
  This database support module supports storage and retrieval of entity/relationship data with value *in context*. This model allows for retrieval of partially specified items in the database.

In addition, there are support modules providing support for the User Interface, Diagnostics, Instrumentation, etc.

7.7.5 Alternatives Manager

There is an additional support module capability in O-Plan2 that is utilized by the Controller. This provides handling of alternative plan states within an O-Plan2 agent.

If a Knowledge Source finds that it has alternative ways to achieve its task, and it finds that it cannot represent all those alternatives in some way within a single plan state, then the Controller provides support to allow the alternatives that are generated to be managed. This is done by the Knowledge Source telling the

Controller about all alternatives but one favored one and asking for permission to continue to process this. This reflects the O-Plan2 search strategy of *local best, then global best*. A support routine is provided to allow a Knowledge Source to inform the Controller of all alternatives but the selected one.

A Knowledge Source that cannot achieve its task or that decides that the current plan state is illegal and cannot be used to generate a valid plan can terminate and tell the Controller to poison the plan state. In the current version of O-Plan2, this will normally initiate consideration of alternative plan states in a dialogue between the Controller and the alternatives manager. A new current plan state will be selected and become visible to new Knowledge Source activations. Concurrently running Knowledge Sources working on the old (poisoned) plan state will be terminated as soon as possible because their efforts will be wasted.

As well as having the existing system's option to explore alternative plan states, future versions of O-Plan2 will consider ways to *unpoison* a plan state by running a nominated *poison handler* associated with the Knowledge Source that poisoned the plan state or with the *reason* for the plan state poison. This is important because we envisage O-Plan2 being used in continuous environments where alternative plan states will become invalid.

7.7.6 Implementation as Separate Processes

In the current UNIX and Common Lisp-based implementation of O-Plan2, the main managers and Knowledge Source Platforms are implemented as separate processes. One advantage to this approach is that Knowledge Sources can be run in parallel with one another and that external events can be processed by the Interface Manager (the manager in charge of all interaction, diagnostic handling, and instrumentation) as they occur. The agent latency or reaction time performance of the system is measured by the time taken to move an incoming event through the agenda triggering mechanism to a waiting Knowledge Source Platform. The cycle time performance of the system is measured by the time taken to move an agenda entry posted by one Knowledge Source through the triggering mechanism to run on a waiting Knowledge Source Platform.

7.8 O-Plan2 USER INTERFACE

7.8.1 Planner User Interface

AI planning systems are now being used in realistic applications by users who need to have a high level of graphical support for the planning operations they are being aided with. In the past, our AI planners have provided custom built graphical interfaces embedded in the specialist programming environments in which the planners have been implemented. It is now important to provide interfaces to AI planners that are more easily used and understood by a broader range of users. We have characterized the user interface to O-Plan2 as being based on two *views* supported for the user. The first is a *Plan View*, which is used for interaction with a user in planning entity terms (such as the use of PERT-charts, Gantt charts, resource profiles, etc). The second is the *World View*, which presents a domain oriented view or simulation of what could happen or is happening in terms of world state.

Computer Aided Design (CAD) packages available on a wide range of micro-computers and engineering workstations are in widespread use and will probably be known to potential planning system users already or will be in use somewhere in their organizations. There could be benefits to providing an interface to an AI planner through widely available CAD packages, so that the time to learn an interface is reduced, and a range of additional facilities can be provided without additional effort by those implementing AI planners.

We have built an interface to the Edinburgh AI planning systems that is based on AutoCAD (Smith & Gesner, 1989). A complete example of the use of the interface has been built for a space platform building application. O-Plan2 Task Formalism has been written to allow the generation of plans to build various types of space platform, with connectivity constraints on the modules and components. A domain context display facility has been provided through the use of AutoLISP. This allows the state of the world following the execution of any action to be visualized through AutoCAD. Means to record and replay visual simulation sequences for plan execution are provided.

A sample screen image is included in Figure 7-4. There are three main windows. The planner is accessible through the Task Assignment window at the top left hand corner that is showing the main user menu. The planner is being used on a space station assembly task and has just been used to get a resulting plan network. In the *Plan View* supported by O-Plan2, this has been displayed in the large AutoCAD window along the bottom of the screen. Via interaction with the menu in the AutoCAD window, the planner has been informed that the user is interested in the world context at a particular point in the plan—the selected node is highlighted in the main plan display. In the *World View* supported by O-Plan2, the planner has then provided output that can be visualized by a suitable domain specific interpreter. This is shown in the window at the top right hand corner of the screen where plan, elevation, and perspective images of the space station are simultaneously displayed.

The O-Plan2 Plan View and World View support mechanisms are designed to retain independence of the actual implementations for the viewers themselves. This allows widely available tools such as AutoCAD to be employed where appropriate but also allows text based or domain specific viewers to be interfaced without change to O-Plan2 itself. The specific viewers to be used for a domain and the

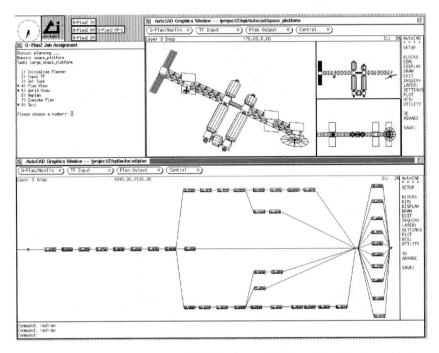

Figure 7-4:   Example output of the PlanWorld Viewer AutoCAD-based user interface.

level of interface they can support for O-Plan2 use is described to O-Plan2 via the domain Task Formalism (TF). A small number of *viewer characteristics* can be stated. These are supported by O-Plan2, and a communications language is provided such that plan and world viewers can input to O-Plan2 and take output from it.

7.8.2 System Developer Interface

When O-Plan2 is being used by a developer, it is typical to have a number of windows active to show the processing going on in the major components of the planner. There is a small window acting as the task assignment agent with its main O-Plan2 menu. There are then separate windows for the Interface Manager (IM)—through which the user can communicate with other processes and through which diagnostic and instrumentation levels can be changed. The Agenda Manager/Controller (AM), the Database Manager (DM), and the Knowledge Source Platform(s) (KP) then have their own windows. Further pop-up windows are provided when viewing the plan state graphically or when getting detail of parts of the plan, etc.

A sample developer screen image is shown in Figure 7-5.

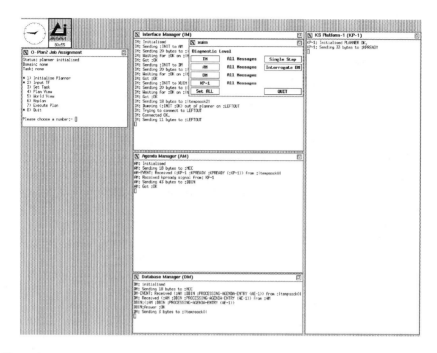

Figure 7-5:   Example developer interface for the O-Plan2 planning agent.

7.9 APPLICATIONS

The O-Plan2 prototype has been tested on a number of simple but realistic domains as well as on puzzles intended to test specific features.

Block Stacking. This involves a set of *puzzle* problems used to test effect/condition interaction and goal handling in O-Plan2.

House Building. This is a "standard" domain for tests of the Edinburgh planners, with a number of variants to test specific features. The aim is to construct a project plan to build a house with certain requirements.

Space Station Assembly. This application shows the development of a plan for the construction of one of a number of different Space Platforms. Platforms are constructed from a series of joints, trusses, pressurized modules, solar panels, radiators, and antennas. This example has been included to demonstrate the AutoCAD user interface that has been constructed for O-Plan2.

Satellite Control. This application shows the development of a plan for the control of a simple satellite we have called EUSAT (Edinburgh University Satellite), which is based on the University of Surrey's successful UOSAT-II.

The O-Plan2 planning agent was demonstrated generating a plan for operation of the spacecraft for one day by generating the actual on-board computer Diary commands and was able to pass it to an O-Plan2-based execution agent for simulated dispatch and monitoring to take place.

7.10 RELATED PROJECTS

O-Plan2 is one of several projects at Edinburgh grouped under the title of EUROPA (Edinburgh University Research into Open Planning Architectures). The combined research of these projects covers issues in Knowledge-Based Planning and Scheduling and is anchored around the two main, long-term research projects of O-Plan2 and TOSCA (The Open SCheduling Architecture [Beck et al., 1993]). O-Plan2 has concentrated on an activity based plan state with good time and resource constraint handling for this base. TOSCA is a variant of the same ideas applied to the area of operations management in the factory (job shop) environment. TOSCA employs appropriate Knowledge Sources for its domain of application (e.g., resource assignment, bottleneck analysis) that operate on an emerging schedule state, similar to the notion of the plan state mentioned above. There is a good measure of overlap between the techniques used on these projects, particularly with respect to time and resource handling. Our aim is to develop designs and architectures suited to both activity planning and scheduling problems and to develop as much common ground as is possible. O-Plan2 plays a key role in this plan.

ACKNOWLEDGMENTS

The O-Plan2 project has been supported by the US Air Force Rome Laboratory through the Air Force Office of Scientific Research (AFOSR) and their European Office of Aerospace Research and Development under contract number F49620-89-C0081 (EOARD/88-0044) monitored by Dr. Northrup Fowler III at the USAF Rome Laboratory. Additional resources for the O-Plan work have been provided by the Artificial Intelligence Applications Institute through the EUROPA (Edinburgh University Research on Planning Architectures) Institute development project.

References

Allen, J., J. Hendler, & A. Tate. 1990. *Readings in Planning*. Morgan Kaufmann, San Francisco, Calif.

Beck, H. "TOSCA: A Novel Approach to the Management of Job-Shop Scheduling Constraints," *Realising CIM's Industrial Potential: Proceedings of the Ninth CIM-Europe Annual Conference*, (eds. C Kooij, P.A. MacConall, and J. Bastos) 12–14 May 1993, Amsterdam, Holland, pp. 138–149.

Chapman, D. 1987. Planning for Conjunctive Goals. *Artificial Intelligence* Vol. 32, pp. 333–377.

Currie, K.W., & A. Tate. 1985. "O-Plan: Control in the Open Planning Architecture," Presented at the BCS Expert Systems 85 Conference, 17–19 December, 1985, Warwick, UK, Cambridge University Press.

Currie, K.W., & A. Tate. 1991. O-Plan: The Open Planning Architecture, *Artificial Intelligence* Vol 51, No. 1.

Daniel, L. 1983. "Planning and Operations Research," *Artificial Intelligence: Tools, Techniques and Applications* (eds. T. O'Shea and M. Eisenstadt), pp. 423–452, Harper and Row, New York.

Drabble, B. 1992. "Planning and Reasoning with Processes," Presented at the 8th Workshop of the Alvey Planning SIG, 17–18 November, 1988, The Institute of Electrical Engineers.

Drabble, B. "EXCALIBUR: A Program for Planning and Reasoning with Processes," *Artificial Intelligence Journal*, Vol 62, No. 1, October, 1993, pp. 1–40.

Drabble, B., & R.B. Kirby. 1991. "Associating AI Planner Entities with an Underlying Time Point Network," *Proceedings of the European Workshop on Planning, Lecture Notes in AI* No. 522, pp. 27–38, Springer-Verlag, New York.

Drabble, B., & A. Tate. 1991. "Using a CAD System as an Interface to an AI Planner," presented at the Artificial Intelligence and Knowledge Based Systems for Space Conference, 22–24 May, 1992, European Space Agency, Noordwijk, Holland.

Drummond, M., & K. Currie. 1989. "Exploiting Temporal Coherence in Nonlinear Plan Construction," Proceedings of IJCAI-89, pp. 960–963, AAAI Press, Menlo Park, Calif.

Drummond, M.E., K.W. Currie, & A. Tate. 1988. "O-Plan Meets T-SAT: First Results from the Application of an AI Planner to Spacecraft Mission Sequencing," AIAI-PR-27, AIAI, University of Edinburgh.

Fikes, R.E., P.E. Hart, & N.J. Nilsson. 1972. "Learning and Executing Generalized Robot Plans," *Artificial Intelligence*, Vol. 3, pp. 251–288.

Georgeff, M. P., & A. L. Lansky. 1986. "Procedural Knowledge," Proceedings of the IEEE, Special Issue on Knowledge Representation, Vol. 74, pp. 1383–1398, IEEE Computer Society Press, Los Alamitos, Calif.

Hayes, P.J. 1975. "A Representation for Robot Plans," Proceedings of the International Joint Conference on Artificial Intelligence (IJCAI-75), pp. 181–188, AAAI Press, Menlo Park, Calif.

Hayes-Roth, B., & F. Hayes-Roth. 1979. "A Cognitive Model of Planning," *Cognitive Science*, Vol. 3, pp. 275–310.

Lesser, V., & L. Erman. 1977. "A Retrospective View of the Hearsay-II Architecture," Proceedings of the International Joint Conference on Artificial Intelligence (IJCAI-77), pp. 27–35, AAAI Press, Menlo Park, Calif.

Liu, B. 1988. *Knowledge Based Scheduling*, Ph.D. Thesis, Edinburgh University.

McDermott, D.V. 1978. "A Temporal Logic for Reasoning about Processes and Plans," *Cognitive Science*, 6, pp. 101–155.

Malcolm, C., & T. Smithers. 1988. "Programming Assembly Robots in Terms of Task Achieving Behavioural Modules: First Experimental Results," Presented at the Second Workshop on Manipulators, Sensors, and Steps towards Mobility as Part of the International Advanced Robotics Programme, Salford, UK.

Nii, P. 1986. "The Blackboard Model of Problem Solving," *AI Magazine*, Vol. 7, Nos. 2 & 3, pp. 38–53.

Nilsson, N.J. 1988. "Action Networks," Presented at the Rochester Planning Workshop, 27–29 October.

Rosenschein, S.J., & L.P. Kaelbling. 1987. *The Synthesis of Digital Machines with Provable Epistemic Properties*, AI Center Technical Note 412, SRI International, Menlo Park, Calif.

Sacerdoti, E. 1977. *A Structure for Plans and Behaviours*, Artificial Intelligence Series, North Holland.

Sadeh, N., & M.S. Fox. 1988. "Preference Propagation in Temporal/Capacity Constraint Graphs," Technical Report CMU-CS-88-193, Computer Science Dept, Carnegie Mellon University.

Smith, J., & R. Gesner. 1989. *Inside AutoCAD*, New Riders Publishing Co., Thousand Oaks, Calif.

Smith, S., M. Fox, & P.S. Ow. 1986. "Constructing and Maintaining Detailed Production Plans: Investigations into the Development of Knowledge Based Factory Scheduling Systems," *AI Magazine*, Vol. 7, No.4, pp. 45–61.

Tate, A. 1977. "Generating Project Networks," Proceedings of IJCAI-77, pp. 888–893, AAAI Press, Menlo Park, Calif.

Tate, A. 1984. "Planning and Condition Monitoring in a FMS," Proceedings of the International Conference on Flexible Automation Systems, Institute of Electrical Engineers, 10–12 July, 1984, London, UK.

Tate, A. 1986. "Goal Structure, Holding Periods and 'Clouds'," Proceedings of the Reasoning about Actions and Plans Workshop, Timberline Lodge, Oregon, USA, pp. 267–278, (eds. M.P. Georgeff, & A. Lansky), Morgan Kaufmann, San Francisco, Calif.

Tate, A. 1989. "Coordinating the Activities of a Planner and an Execution Agent," Proceedings of the Second NASA Conference on Space Telerobotics (eds. G. Rodriguez & H.Seraji), JPL Publication 89-7, Vol. 1, pp. 385–393, Jet Propulsion Laboratory.

Tate, A. 1990. "O-Plan2: Choice Ordering Mechanisms in an AI Planning Architecture," Proceedings of the 1990 DARPA Workshop on Innovative Approaches to Planning, Scheduling, and Control, San Diego, California, USA, on 5-8 November 1990, pp. 192–196, Morgan Kaufmann, San Francisco, Calif. Also updated with B. Drabble as AIAI-TR-86, AIAI, University of Edinburgh.

Tate, A., B. Drabble, & R.B. Kirby. 1992. "Spacecraft Command and Control using AI Planning Techniques—The O-Plan2 Project—Final Report," USAF/AFOSR contract no. F49620-89-C0081, Technical Report, Rome Laboratory, Griffiss AFB, N.Y. Also available as AIAI-TR-109, AIAI, University of Edinburgh.

Teknowledge. 1988. "S.1 Product Description," Teknowledge Inc., Palo Alto, Calif.

Stefik, M. 1981. "Planning with Constraints," *Artificial Intelligence*, Vol. 16, pp. 111–140.

Vere, S. 1983. "Planning in Time: Windows and Durations for Activities and Goals," *IEEE Transactions on Pattern Analysis and Machine Intelligence*, Vol. 5, pp. 246–267.

Wilkins, D.E. 1985. "Recovering from Execution Errors in SIPE," *Computational Intelligence*, Vol. 1, pp. 33–45.

Wilkins, D.E. 1988. *Practical Planning*, Morgan Kaufmann, San Francisco, Calif.

8

SCHEDULING AND RESCHEDULING
WITH ITERATIVE REPAIR

Monte Zweben
(NASA Ames Research Center)

Brian Daun
Eugene Davis
(Recom Technologies)

Michael Deale
(Lockheed Space Operations Company)

8.1 INTRODUCTION

GERRY uses constraint-based iterative repair to schedule and reschedule the tasks of a plan according to temporal constraints, milestones, resource constraints, and state constraints. *Iterative repair* methods such as those of Lin & Kernighan (1973), Glover (1989), Kurtzman & Aiken (1989), Johnson et al. (1990), Minton et al. (1990), Morris (1990), Zweben, Deale, & Gargan (1990), Biefeld & Cooper (1991) differ from *constructive* scheduling methods in that they begin with a complete but possibly flawed set of assignments and then iteratively modify or repair those assignments to improve the overall schedule. Constructive scheduling methods (Fox, 1987; Sadeh & Fox, 1989) incrementally extend valid, partial schedules until a complete schedule is synthesized or until backtracking is required.

In 1990, we initiated a new application project with the goal of applying GERRY to the Space Shuttle Ground Operations problem. This is the problem of scheduling the repair and refurbishment of Space Shuttles between flights. Details of this application are presented in Chapter 15 in this volume.

The original version of GERRY employed constructive search with dependency-directed backtracking to produce schedules subject to temporal, milestone, and resource constraints (Zweben & Eskey, 1989). This version, however, was not powerful enough to be useful to Space Shuttle Ground Processing schedulers because state constraints, preemption, and rescheduling capabilities were deemed essential for the NASA application. GERRY thus evolved into a repair-based framework that also supported the representation and reasoning of state constraints and preemptive tasks.

8.2 MODELING ISSUES IN GERRY

This section presents the GERRY modeling language. We first describe each constraint type and then describe how GERRY manages preemption.

8.2.1 Temporal and Milestone Constraints

Temporal constraints order tasks with respect to each other. Specifically, they order the start-times and end-times of tasks. GERRY supports finish-to-start, start-to-start, finish-to-finish, start-to-finish orderings, along with positive and negative delays on these orderings. An example of a temporal constraint is *end-time(Task1) ≤ start-time(Task2)*.

GERRY preserves temporal constraints in all its problem solving operations. In other words, although the system is referred to as repair-based in general, none of the temporal constraints will ever require repair. GERRY uses the Waltz constraint propagation algorithm (Waltz, 1975) to accomplish temporal consistency by recursively enforcing temporal constraints until there are no outstanding temporal violations. This maintains a form of arc-consistency (Mackworth, 1977; Freuder, 1982) in the schedule at all times. When rescheduling a task causes other temporal constraints to be violated, GERRY moves other tasks using the Waltz algorithm until the temporal constraints are satisfied. If there is no way to re-establish temporal consistency via the Waltz algorithm, the system rejects the original rescheduling move.

Milestone constraints relate tasks to fixed metric times. This prevents tasks from moving beyond a certain date. An example of a milestone constraint is *end-time(Task1) ≤ 11/23/92 12:00:00*.

8.2.2 Resource Constraints

The GERRY representation language models resources with *classes* and *pools*. A *class* represents a type of resource consisting of a set of resource pools. A *pool* represents a collection of indistinguishable resources. Each pool's initial capacity designates the maximum amount of the resource that is initially available. GERRY maintains a *history* (Williams, 1986) for each pool that tracks the availability of the pool over time. An example from the Space Shuttle domain is the resource class HEAVY-EQUIPMENT, which contains the pools CRANE CREW and HIGH CREW.

Each task in the GERRY modeling language has a set of resource requirements that designate the amount of resources required by the task. Each resource requirement consists of a type and quantity. The type specification defines the resource class that will satisfy the requirement. The quantity is the amount of the resource that will be decremented from a specific resource pool's availability. A resource requirement always extends from the start-time to the end-time of a task. An example of a resource requirement is *Task1 requires 4 technicians from the start-time of Task1 to the end-time of Task1.*

GERRY automatically declares a *capacity constraint* for each resource requirement. A capacity constraint states that the resource must not be overallocated during the duration of the resource requirement.

8.2.3 State Constraints

GERRY can also model arbitrary domain *attributes* that change over time. Each attribute can have several possible values or states. Examples from the Space Shuttle domain are the attributes POWER and LEFT-PAYLOAD-BAY-DOOR. POWER models the electrical power for the on-board orbiter systems and has POWER-UP and POWER-DOWN as possible values. LEFT-PAYLOAD-BAY-DOOR has CLOSED, OPEN-145-DEGREES, and OPEN-175-DEGREES as possible states.

Each task has a set of *state effects* that represent the changes it imposes upon attributes. An effect simply sets the value of an attribute during the interval of time specified by the effect. This interval can be open-ended, designating that the value should persist indefinitely. For example, a task can have an effect that changes the value of attribute POWER to be POWER-UP from its start-time to its end-time, or the effect could extend to positive-infinity, which would leave the state as POWER-UP until some other task specifies otherwise.

Although task effects designate the changes in attribute values, *state requirements* designate the *state constraints* that attributes impose on tasks. An example of a state requirement would be *Task1 requires the value of* POWER *to be* POWER-UP *from the start-time of Task1 to the end-time of Task1.* Another example is the requirement of the attribute BAY-ACCESS to have the value BAY-OPEN. BAY-ACCESS models whether the Orbiter Processing Facility is inaccesible because of hazardous operations (i.e., BAY-CLEARED) or whether it is open for work (i.e., BAY-OPEN). Hazardous tasks have an effect that causes the attribute BAY-ACCESS to have the value of BAY-CLEARED during the duration of the tasks.

Each attribute maintains a history analogous to the histories of resource pools. Histories track the value of attributes over intervals of time. Along with storing the current value, a history maintains the *changers* and *users* of an attribute during an interval of time. A changer of an attribute is a task whose effect changes the value of the attribute. A user of an attribute is a task that has a state requirement for the attribute. A task that has an effect on an attribute during the interval $(x \cdot y)$ will be a changer in the history of that attribute during $(x . y)$. Likewise, a task that has a requirement for a value of an attribute during $(x . y)$ will be a user in the history of that attribute during $(x . y)$. This forms a dependency network similar in nature to truth maintenance systems and to the depedency information stored by the PRIAR planning system (Kambhampati, 1990).

GERRY determines the value of an attribute during specific time intervals by calculating the *latest-changer* of the attribute for that time interval. The latest-changer at a specific time is the changer that last affected the value of the attribute. Notice that the Modal Truth Criterion is bypassed because the metric time assignments to the start and end times of tasks impose a total ordering on the network of tasks. This makes it efficient to determine how a task affects the state of the world. An example of this calculation is as follows:

For this example the form

$(((x . y)$ *value users changers latest-changer)...)* will be used to represent a history.

For the attribute POWER, assume that time is represented from 12:00 noon to 12:00 midnight, and no effects or requirements have been added.

The initial POWER history is

((((12:00noon . 12:00midnight) POWER-DOWN nil nil nil))

This states that from 12:00 noon to 12:00 midnight, the value of attribute POWER is POWER-DOWN. There are no users or changers in the history.
(Because there are no changers, a latest-changer does not exist).

Task1 has an effect on the attribute POWER to be POWER-UP from 1:00 pm to 2:00 pm. Because there are no other changers during this time, Task1 is the latest-changer from 1:00 pm to 2:00 pm, changing the value of attribute POWER to be POWER-UP.

The resulting POWER history is

((((12:00noon . 1:00pm) POWER-DOWN nil nil nil)

((1:00pm . 2:00pm) POWER-UP nil (Task1) Task1)

((2:00pm . 12:00midnight) POWER-DOWN nil nil nil))

Task2 has an effect on attribute POWER to be POWER-DOWN from 1:30 pm to 2:30 pm. Task2 is the latest-changer from 1:30 pm to 2:30 pm, changing the value of attribute POWER to POWER-DOWN. Task1 would still be the latest-changer from 1:00 pm to 1:30 pm, having its effect superseded by Task2 at 1:30 pm.

The resulting POWER history is

((((12:00noon . 1:00pm) POWER-DOWN nil nil nil)

((1:00pm . 1:30pm) POWER-UP nil (Task1) Task1)

((1:30pm . 2:00pm) POWER-DOWN nil (Task1 Task2) Task2)

((2:00pm . 2:30pm) POWER-DOWN nil (Task2) Task2)

((2:30pm . 12:00midnight) POWER-DOWN nil nil nil))

If the persistence of the effect from Task1 is changed from 2:00 pm to positive-infinity, then Task1 is the latest-changer again at 2:30 pm (when the effect of Task2 ends).

The resulting POWER history is

(((12:00noon . 1:00pm) POWER-DOWN nil nil nil)

((1:00pm . 1:30pm) POWER-UP nil (Task1) Task1)

((1:30pm . 2:30pm) POWER-DOWN nil (Task1 Task2) Task2)

((2:30pm . 12:00midnight) POWER-UP nil (Task1) Task1))

Because metric times are used to determine the latest-changer, it is possible for two or more changers to "tie" in their attempts to become the latest-changer. When a tie for the latest-changer occurs, the tie is broken by one of the following methods:

1. If the changers are asserting the same attribute value, the latest-changer is chosen by comparing the names of the changers alphabetically.

2. If the changers are not asserting the same attribute value, the latest-changer is choosen by comparing the priorities of the distinct attribute values. The priority of an attribute value is an arbitrary number assigned when the attribute is created.

Because a tie should never naturally occur, the main concern is to make the tie breaking procedure deterministic.

Because of the large number of effects and requirements on tasks in the Space Shuttle domain, updating and accessing histories has proven to be a bottleneck in the GERRY scheduling system. In fact, much of the computation time spent in the rescheduling process involves updating histories. For this reason, all histories are indexed to improve efficiency. The indices point to interspersed locations within the history. Instead of starting at the beginning of the history to find a value at a specific time, the nearest index prior to the time requiring reference is selected, and a linear search for the desired time begins. Without this index, the history mechanism would be too slow for the Space Shuttle application.

8.2.4 Fixed Preemptive Scheduling

Preemption is an additional complicating factor introduced by the Space Shuttle domain. In preemptive scheduling, each task is associated with a calendar of legal work periods that determine when the task can be performed. For example, suppose a task has a duration of 16 hours and a calendar indicating that only the first shift of each non-weekend day is legal. Given that the first shift of the day extends from 8:00 am to 4:00 pm, if the task is started on Monday at 8:00 am, then it will be suspended at the end of the shift (at 4:00 pm). It would restart on Tuesday at 8:00 am and would complete the same day at 4:00 pm. However, if the same task had been started on Friday, then it would not complete until the following Monday at 4:00 pm because the task could not be scheduled on a weekend day. Preemptive scheduling requires additional computational overhead because for each task-time assignment, the preemption times must be computed, and the appropriate constraint manipulation must be performed.

Preemption splits a task into a set of subtasks. Resource and state constraints can be enforced during each individual subtask or during the time interval spanning from the earliest subtask to the latest subtask. If the constraints are enforced on the subtasks, then the constraints are ignored during the suspended periods between the individual subtasks, but if the constraints are enforced between the earliest and latest subtasks, then the entire length of the task must satisfy the resource and state constraints. For example, labor is a resource type that is not usually required during the suspended periods. In contrast, heavy machinery is difficult to relocate and might remain allocated (and, thus, unavailable for use by other tasks) during the suspended periods of a task.

8.3 SEARCH USING ITERATIVE REPAIR

There are several reasons why iterative repair was chosen as the scheduling engine for GERRY instead of constructive methods. To begin with, Space Shuttle Ground Processing is predominately a rescheduling problem. Constructive methods (Zweben & Eskey, 1989; Eskey & Zweben, 1990) are difficult if not impossible to adapt to the Space Shuttle rescheduling problem. To reschedule with a constructive method, the system must remove some tasks from the schedule and then restart the scheduling process. Unfortunately, determining which tasks to *unschedule* is not straightforward. The repair method solves this problem by never unscheduling a task. Task assignments are changed but never removed from the schedule.

Further, even though a task is unaffected by an exogenous event (i.e., the task does not explicitly require a "repair" per se), it might be possible to create a better schedule by altering its current assignments. For example, placing an unaffected task much later in the schedule might cause little perturbation and allow many tasks (which are affected by the exogenous events) to fit in its place. This opportunity is missed if the unaffected tasks are not considered in the rescheduling process.

Another reason for choosing iterative repair is that the schedules for the Space Shuttle domain are over-constrained. If a problem is over-constrained, a constructive method must exhaust all possibilities before it can infer that constraints must be relaxed. Repair-based methods attempt to iteratively improve solutions regardless of whether the problem is over-constrained. They terminate with a set of assignments that is as close to a solution as could be derived in the time allotted. At KSC, milestones can be overly ambitious and impossible to meet when considering all resource and state constraints. Also, the resource and state constraints can be too conservative. For example, suppose there are two tasks, each requiring a quality assurance officer. If these two tasks are physically proximate, one of the officers might be able to handle both jobs.

Global and optimization constraints provide yet another reason for choosing iterative repair. Because repair methods search through a space of complete schedules, "global" constraints and optimization criteria can be evaluated cheaply. With a partial schedule, the evaluation of global criteria can only be approximated. For example, suppose that in a particular domain, it is desirable to minimize the use of labor resources on the weekends (which is a global optimization criterion) or that a particular machine is not allowed to change configuration more than a certain number of times per month (which is a global constraint). The evaluation of this criterion and constraint is easily calculated with a complete schedule but can only be estimated (based on the remaining tasks and possible times) with a partial schedule.

Although repair methods are efficient for large problems such as Space Shuttle scheduling, they also have their shortcomings. One problem is that repair methods could suffer from local minima in the sense that they can cycle indefinitely through a set of unsatisfactory solutions. Another problem is that repair methods are usually not complete and, therefore, not guaranteed to encounter the best possible solutions. GERRY employs techniques to counteract these drawbacks (discussed below), but nonetheless, problems can still occur.

The following is a description of the iterative repair framework in GERRY. For this chapter, only the repairs for resource and state constraints are described. We have also experimented with a number of other optimization constraints. In Zweben et al. (1992), we demonstrate the ability to reduce perturbation in rescheduling problems. We have also demonstrated the ability to reduce weekend work in a schedule, resulting in lower overtime labor costs.

Constraint-based iterative repair begins with a complete schedule of unacceptable quality and iteratively modifies it until its quality is found to be satisfactory or until a designated time bound is reached. The quality of a schedule is measured by the *cost* function;

$$cost(s) = \sum_{c \in constraints} penalty_{c_i}(s) * weight_{c_i}(s),$$

which is a weighted sum of constraint violations. The *penalty* function of a constraint returns a non-negative number reflecting the degree to which the constraint is violated. The *weight* function of a constraint returns a non-negative number representing the importance or utility of a constraint.

The GERRY system resolves violated constraints through local repairs invoked during each iteration of the iterative repair loop. N violations of each constraint type are repaired in succession, allowing the repairs to "focus" upon a particular constraint type.

A different constraint repair exists for each constraint type. Each repair tries to satisfy a constraint violation without concern for how the repair will interact with other constraints. Local repairs do occasionally produce globally undesirable states. However, the undesirable states, if accepted, are generally improved upon after several iterations. Repairing a constraint violation generally involves rescheduling one task. As necessary, predecessors or successors of a task will also be moved to maintain temporal constraints. The repair process is described later in more detail.

At the end of each iteration, the system re-evaluates the cost function to determine whether the new schedule resulting from the repairs is better (i.e., has lower cost) than the existing schedule. If the new schedule is an improvement, it becomes the current schedule for the next iteration. If the new schedule is also better than any previous solution, it is cached as the best solution so far. If it is not an improvement, the new schedule is either accepted anyway with some probability (see below), or it is rejected, and the changes are not kept. When the changes are not kept, it is hoped that repairs in the next iteration will select a different set of tasks to move, and the cost of the schedule will improve.

The system sometimes accepts a new solution that is worse than the current solution in order to escape local minima and cycles. This stochastic technique is referred to as simulated annealing (Kirkpatrick, Gelatt, & Vecchi, 1983). The escape function for accepting an inferior solution is $Escape(s,s',T) = e^{-|Cost(s) - Cost(s')| /T}$, where T is a "temperature" parameter that is gradually reduced (i.e., *cooled* during the search process). When a random number between 0 and 1 exceeds the value of the escape function, the system accepts the worse solution. Note that escape becomes less probable as the temperature is lowered.

8.3.2 Repairing Resource Constraints

The penalty of a resource capacity constraint is 1 if the resource is overallocated. If K simultaneous tasks overallocate the resource, then all K tasks are considered violated. One of these tasks will be selected in an attempt to repair as many of the K violations as possible. The heuristic used to select this task considers the following information.

Fitness: *Move the task whose resource requirement most closely matches the amount of overallocation.* A task using a significantly smaller amount is not likely to have a large enough impact on the current violation being repaired. A task using a far greater amount is more likely to be in violation wherever it is moved.

Temporal Dependents: *Move the task with the fewest number of temporal dependents.* Moving a task with many dependents is likely to cause temporal constraint violations and result in many tasks being moved.

Distance of Move: *Move the task that does not need to be shifted significantly from its current time.* A task that is moved a greater distance is more likely to cause other tasks to move as well, increasing perturbation and potentially causing more constraint violations.

For each of the K tasks contributing to the violation, the system considers moving the task to the *next earlier* and *next later* times where the resource is available. Each candidate move is scored using a linear combination of the *fitness*, *temporal dependents*, and *distance to move* heuristic values. The repair then converts each score into a probability, and a task move is selected based on the probabilities.

In summary, the resource repair considers two possible moves for tasks participating in a violation: one earlier and one later. The evaluation criterion used to select a repair is based upon three computationally inexpensive heuristic criteria: degree of fitness, number of temporal dependents, and distance to move.

8.3.2 Repairing State Constraints

When a required attribute value conflicts with the existing attribute value, the associated state constraint is violated and returns a penalty of 1. To repair a state requirement, either the task with the violated state requirement is reassigned to a time when the current attribute value is set to the required attribute value, or a new task that achieves the required attribute value is added to the schedule. The addition of new tasks is analogous to the operations performed by traditional planning systems (Fikes, Hart, & Nilsson, 1972; Wilkins, 1984; Chapman, 1987). In GERRY, these new tasks are called *achievers*. For now, achievers cannot be added to a schedule during the repair process if they violate existing state requirements.

To repair a violated state requirement, the system selects one of the following methods:

1. Insert an achiever that sets the needed attribute value from the start-time to the end-time of the violated task. The addition of an achiever will be prevented if it produces other state violations in the schedule.

2. Move the violated task forward to a time where the required attribute value exists.

3. Move the violated task backward to a time where the required attribute value exists.

4. Move the violated task forward to a time where the attribute value can be changed (by an achiever) without causing additional state violations. Then

insert an achiever to change the attribute value for at least the duration of the violated task.[1]

5. Move the violated task backward to a time where the attribute value can be changed (by an achiever) without causing additional state violations. Then insert an achiever to change the attribute value for the needed duration.

The first method is always considered before the others. If it is successful, the other methods are ignored. This prevents unneccessary task rescheduling. If the first method is not successful, then one of the other methods is selected. To choose between the methods, each method is given a score based on what the distance is that the task must be moved to fix the violation and whether any temporal dependents would have to be moved as well. Then the system selects one of the repairs stochastically with respect to the scores.

In summary, the state repair strategy chooses between five possible repairs. Several repairs involve adding new tasks called *achievers* to the schedule. The achievers can set the needed attribute value only if other state violations are not produced.

8.4 EXPERIMENTS

To demonstrate the effectiveness of GERRY, we performed scheduling and rescheduling experiments. Our rescheduling experiments were performed on actual Space Shuttle data, and our scheduling experiments were performed on randomly generated problems. We ran all experiments on a Sun SPARCstation 2 with 32MB of memory. Each experiment ran until there were no outstanding violations or until a 30-minute CPU time bound was reached. The results of the experiments measure the average time for the system to converge to zero cost. For the problems that timed-out before reaching a zero cost, the average cost at time-out is presented.

The rescheduling experiments used the STS55 mission data, which contained over 1400 tasks that were split into more than 7000 subtasks and contained over 8000 state constraints. This data set did not have resource constraints. Each experiment started with an STS55 schedule that was free of state conflicts and had the end-of-schedule milestone fixed.

A rescheduling experiment was initiated by moving N random tasks to produce state violations. There were four sets of rescheduling experiments of increasing difficulty. In the first set, one task was moved to create conflicts. Then in the

---

[1] The persistence of the effect is a function of the attribute in question. For example, when the power onboard the orbiter is turned ON, it remains ON for an entire 8-hour shift because it is costly to repeatedly cycle the power.

Table 8-1: Results of iterative repair after randomly rescheduling 1, 10, 50, and 100 tasks.

Number of Tasks Moved	Average Initial Cost	Average Time to Solution (min)	Percent Timeouts	Average Cost at Timeouts
1	5.37	0.25	0	—
10	11.20	1.83	0	—
50	37.17	1.69	0	—
100	61.27	4.72	13	8.25

second, 10 were moved, 50 in the third, and 100 in the fourth. There were 30 different trials for each experiment set.

Table 8-1 presents the results of rescheduling tasks in the STS55 data set. In all data sets except the most difficult, all problems converged to a solution. When a solution was not found (13% of the time for the largest problem set), the final cost was less than 9, with an average initial cost of 61. This performance is quite good for such a large problem set.

For the scheduling experiments, four randomly generated problems were used. The number of tasks in each problem were 20, 80, 160, and 320. Because tasks are preempted, the problems had at least five times as many subtasks as tasks and contained both resource and state constraints. The end-of-schedule milestone was set at two times the distance of shortest possible schedule when considering only temporal constraints for each problem. The initial schedule for these problems was determined by the well known critical path method (CPM). For each problem size, 30 different trials were performed.

Table 8-2 presents the results of scheduling randomly generated data sets. In the largest data set, the system converged 50% of the time. When a solution was not found, there were 10 violations on average. Because the average time to solution was almost 24 minutes, a longer time limit would probably have allowed GERRY to find more solutions. Interestingly, the 80-task problem was more difficult on average than the 160-task problem. Because problems were randomly generated, it appears that the smaller 80-task problem was more constrained than the 160-task

Table 8-2: Results of scheduling randomly generated datasets with task sizes of 20, 80, 160, and 320.

Number of Tasks	Initial Cost	Average Time to Solution (min)	Percent Timeouts	Average Cost at Timeouts
20	47.00	0.36	0	—
80	312.00	7.96	10	8.00
160	694.00	8.15	7	4.00
320	1119.00	23.88	50	10.00

problem. One intriguing result is that when the 80-task problem converged, it did so in 8 minutes on average. However, 10% of the time, the system timed-out. This demonstrates a negative aspect of stochastic decision-making with an incomplete search method—sometimes the dice are not very friendly. Overall, the system performs effectively.

8.5 RELATED WORK

Our work was heavily influenced by previous constraint-based scheduling (Fox & Smith, 1984; Fox, 1987; Sadeh & Fox, 1989) and rescheduling efforts (Ow, Smith, & Thiriez, 1988).

ISIS (Fox, 1987) and GERRY both have metrics of constraint violation (the *penalty* function in GERRY) and constraint importance (the *weight* function in GERRY). In contrast with our repair-based method, ISIS uses an incremental beam search through a space of partial schedules and reschedules by restarting the beam search from an intermediate state.

OPIS (Fox & Smith, 1984; Ow, Smith, & Thiriez, 1988), which is the successor of ISIS, opportunistically selects a rescheduling method. It chooses between the ISIS beam search, a resource-based *dispatch* method, or a repair-based approach. The *dispatch* method concentrates on a bottleneck resource and assigns tasks to it according to its dispatch rule. The *repair* method shifts tasks until they are conflict-free. These "greedy" assignments could yield globally poor schedules if used incorrectly. Consequently, OPIS only uses the dispatch rule when there is strong evidence of a bottleneck and only uses the repair method if the duration of the conflict is short. In contrast, GERRY uses the simulated annealing search to perform multiple iterations of repairs, possibly retracting "greedy" repairs when they yield prohibitive costs.

Our use of simulated annealing was influenced by the experiments performed in Johnson et al. (1990b; 1990c). In contrast with our constraint-based repair, their repairs were generally uninformed.

The repair-based scheduling methods considered here are related to the repair-based methods that have previously been used in AI planning systems, such as the "fixes" used in Hacker (Sussman, 1973) and, more recently, the repair strategies used in the GORDIUS (Simmons, 1988) generate-test-debug system, in the PRIAR plan modification system (Kambhampati, 1990), and the CHEF cased-based planner (Hammond, 1986).

In Minton et al. (1990), it is shown that the MIN-CONFLICTS heuristic is an extremely powerful repair-based method. For any violated constraint, the MIN-CONFLICTS heuristic chooses the repair that minimizes the number of remaining conflicts resulting from a one-step lookahead. However, in Zweben, Davis, & Deale

(1993), we show that in certain circumstances, this lookahead could be computationally prohibitive.

Our technique is also closely related to the Jet Propulsion Laboratory's OMP scheduling system (Biefeld & Cooper, 1991). OMP uses procedurally encoded patches in an iterative improvement framework. It stores small snapshots of the scheduling process (called *chronologies*) that allow it to escape cycles and local minima.

Miller et al. (1988), Currie & Tate (1991), and Drummond & Bresina (1990) describe other efforts that deal with resource and deadline constraints.

8.6 CONCLUSION

Our experiments demonstrate that GERRY performs well on scheduling and rescheduling problems and that the system performs admirably as problem size increases. The ability of GERRY to find quick solutions is very useful for real-world problems such as the Space Shuttle domain where deadlines and scheduling meetings are frequent. We believe that the GERRY architecture is a powerful domain-independent scheduler. To incorporate a new constraint, the user defines a penalty function, a weight function, and a repair function. No other code is necessary, but the user could also add focusing heuristics that order the selection of constraints for repair. We have tested the system on a host of different problems of varying complexity and scale.

References

Biefeld, E., and L. Cooper. 1991. "Bottleneck Identification Using Process Chronologies," *Proceedings of IJCAI-91*, Sydney, Australia.

Chapman, D. 1987. "Planning for Conjunctive Goals," *Artificial Intelligence*, Vol. 32, #4.

Currie, K., and A. Tate. 1991. "O-Plan: The Open Planning Architecture," *Artificial Intelligence*, Vol. 52, #1.

Davis, E. 1987. "Constraint Propagation with Interval Labels," *Artificial Intelligence*, Vol. 32, #3.

Drummond, M., and J. Bresina, J. 1990. "Anytime Synthetic Projection: Maximizing the Probability of Goal Satisfaction," *Proceedings of AAAI-90* .

Eskey, M., and M. Zweben. 1990. "Learning Search Control for a Constraint-Based Scheduling System," *Proceedings of AAAI-90*, Boston, MA.

Fikes, R.E., P.E. Hart, and N.J. Nilsson. 1972. "Learning and Executing Generalized Robot Plans," *Artificial Intelligence*, Vol. 3.

Fox, M. 1987. "Constraint-Directed Search: A Case Study of Job Shop Scheduling," Morgan Kaufmann, San Francisco, CA.

Fox, M., and S. Smith. 1984. "A Knowledge Based System for Factory Scheduling," *Expert System*, Vol. 1, #1.

Freuder, E.C. 1982. "A Sufficient Condition for Backtrack-Free Search," *J. ACM*, Vol. 29, #1.

Glover, F. 1989. "Tabu Search: Part I," *ORSA Journal on Computing*, Vol. 1, #3.

Hammond, K. J. 1986. "CHEF: A Model of Case-Based Planning," *Proceedings of AAAI-86*.

Johnson, D.S., C.R. Aragon, L.A. McGeoch, and C. Schevon. 1990a. "Optimization By Simulated Annealing: An Experimental Evaluation, Part I (Graph Partioning)," *Operations Research*.

Johnson, D.S., C.R. Aragon, L.A. McGeoch, and C. Schevon. 1990b. "Optimization By Simulated Annealing: An Experimental Evaluation, Part II (Graph Coloring and Number Partioning)," *Operations Research*.

Kambhampati, S. 1990. "A Theory of Plan Modification," *Proceedings of AAAI-90* .

Kirkpatrick, S., C.D. Gelatt, and M.P. Vecchi. 1983. "Optimization by Simulated Annealing," *Science*, Vol. 220, #4598.

Kurtzman, C.R., and D.L. Aiken. 1989. "The Mfive Space Station Crew Activity Scheduler and Stowage Logistics Clerk," *Proceedings the AIAA Computers in Aerospace VII Conference*, Monterey, CA.

Lin, S., and B. Kernighan. 1973. "An Effective Heuristic for the Travelling Salesman Problem," *Operations Research*, Vol. 21.

Mackworth, A.K. 1977. "Consistency in Networks of Relations," *Artificial Intelligence*, Vol. 8, #1.

Miller, D., R.J. Firby, and T. Dean. 1988. "Deadlines, Travel Time, and Robot Problem Solving," *Proceedings of AAAI-88*, St. Paul, MN.

Minton, S., A. Phillips, M. Johnston, and P. Laird. 1990. "Solving Large Scale CSP and Scheduling Problems with a Heuristic Repair Method, *Proceedings of AAAI-90*.

Morris, P. 1990. "Solutions Without Exhaustive Search: An Iterative Descent Method for Binary Constraint Satisfaction Problems," *Proceedings the AAAI-90 Workshop on Constraint-Directed Reasoning*, Boston, MA.

Ow, P., S. Smith, and A. Thiriez. 1988. "Reactive Plan Revision," *Proceedings AAAI-88*.

Sadeh, N., and M.S. Fox. 1989. "Preference Propagation in Temporal/Capacity Constraint Graphs," The Robotics Institute, Carnegie Mellon University.

Simmons, R.G. 1988. *Combining Associational and Causal Reasoning to Solve Interpretation and Planning Problems,* MIT Artificial Intelligence Laboratory.

Sussman, G.J. 1973. "A Computational Model of Skill Acquisition," AI Laboratory, MIT.

Waltz, D. 1975. "Understanding Line Drawings of Scenes with Shadows," *The Psychology of Computer Vision*, P. Winston, ed., McGraw-Hill.

Wilkins, D.E. 1984. "Domain Independent Planning: Representation and Plan Generation," *Artificial Intelligence*, Vol. 22.

Williams, B.C. 1986. "Doing Time: Putting Qualitative Reasoning on Firmer Ground," *Proceedings of AAAI-86* .

Zweben, M., and M. Eskey. 1989. "Constraint Satisfaction with Delayed Evaluation," *Proceedings of the Eleventh International Joint Conference on Artificial Intelligence*, Detroit, MI.

Zweben, M., E. Davis, and M. Deale. 1993. "Iterative Repair for Scheduling and Rescheduling," *IEEE Systems, Man, and Cybernetics*, Special Issue on Planning, Scheduling, and Control.

Zweben, M., E. Davis, B. Daun, and M. Deale. 1992. "Rescheduling with Iterative Repair," *Proceedings of the AAAI 1992 Spring Symposium on Practical Approaches to Scheduling and Planning*, Stanford University.

Zweben, M., E. Davis, B. Daun, E. Drascher, M. Deale, and M. Eskey. 1992. "Learning To Improve Constraint-Based Scheduling," *Artificial Intelligence*, Vol. 58, #1-3.

9

ANALYZING A HEURISTIC STRATEGY FOR CONSTRAINT-SATISFACTION AND SCHEDULING

Mark D. Johnston
(Space Telescope Science Institute, Baltimore, MD)

Steven Minton
(NASA Ames Research Center, Moffett Field)

9.1 INTRODUCTION

One of the most promising general approaches for solving combinatorial search problems is to generate an initial, suboptimal solution and then to apply local *repair* heuristics (Kurtzman & Aiken, 1989; Johnson *et al.*, 1990; Minton *et al.*, 1990; Sosic & Gu, 1990; Zweben, 1990; Morris, 1991). Techniques based on this approach have met with empirical success on many combinatorial problems, including the traveling salesman and graph partitioning problems (Johnson, Papadimitrou, & Yannakakis, 1988). Such techniques also have a long tradition in AI, most notably in problem-solving systems that operate by debugging initial solutions (Sussman, 1975; Simmons, 1988). In this chapter, we describe how this idea can be extended to constraint satisfaction problems (CSPs) in a natural manner.

Most of the previous work on CSP algorithms has assumed a "constructive" backtracking approach in which a partial assignment to the variables is incrementally extended. In contrast, our method creates a complete but inconsistent assignment and then repairs constraint violations until a consistent assignment is achieved. The method is guided by a simple ordering heuristic for repairing constraint violations: identify a variable that is currently in conflict, and select a new value that minimizes the number of outstanding constraint violations.

On some standard CSP problems, such as the well-known N-queens problem, our *min-conflicts* approach has been shown to be considerably more efficient than traditional constructive backtracking methods. We argue here that the reason that repair-based methods can outperform constructive methods is because a complete assignment can be more informative in guiding search than a partial assignment. To help clarify the nature of this potential advantage, we present a theoretical analysis that describes how various problem characteristics might affect the performance of the min-conflicts approach. This analysis shows, for example, how the "distance" between the current assignment and solution (in terms of the minimum number of repairs that are required) affects the expected utility of the heuristic.

The work described in this chapter was inspired by a neural network originally developed (Johnston & Adorf, 1989, 1992; Adorf & Johnston, 1990) for use in SPIKE (Johnston & Miller, Chapter 14 [this book]), a system for scheduling astronomical observations on the Hubble Space Telescope. The min-conflicts heuristic was distilled from an analysis of the network, as described in Minton *et al.* (1990, 1991, 1992). The heuristic has now replaced the neural network in the SPIKE system because it can be implemented in a very simple and efficient fashion.

We begin the chapter with a description of the min-conflicts approach. Following this, we describe empirical results in several domains, including the Hubble Space Telescope scheduling application. Finally, we consider a theoretical model identifying general problem characteristics that influence the performance of the method.

9.1.1 The Min-Conflicts Heuristic

A constraint-satisfaction problem (CSP) consists of a set of variables and a set of constraints. The constraints indicate the allowable combinations of values that can be assigned to the variables. A solution is an assignment specifying a value for each variable, such that all the constraints are satisfied.

A repair-based constraint-satisfaction method takes the variables and the constraints and begins by generating an initial assignment for the variables. The initial assignment is then repeatedly "repaired" until a solution is found. Unfortunately, there is no guarantee that a solution will be found quickly or even that a solution will be found at all. In previous work, we proposed that one can guide the search by attempting to minimize the number of conflicts in an assignment. The min-conflicts heuristic method can be characterized by the following procedure for selecting a value for a variable:

Min-Conflicts Heuristic:

Given: There is a set of variables, a set of binary constraints, and an assignment specifying a value for each variable. Two variables *conflict* if their values violate a constraint.

Procedure: Select a variable that is in conflict, and assign it a value that mini-mizes the number of conflicts.[1] (Break ties randomly.)

This procedure results in a hill-climbing search. The system starts with an initial assignment generated in a preprocessing phase. At each choice point, the heuristic chooses a variable that is currently in conflict and reassigns its value until a solution is found. The system thus searches the space of possible assignments, favoring assignments with fewer total conflicts. The hill-climbing search can still become "stuck" in a local maximum, but the search tends to be much more focused than if no heuristic is used.

There are two aspects of the min-conflicts hill-climbing method that distin-guish it from standard CSP algorithms. First, instead of incrementally constructing a consistent partial assignment, the min-conflicts method *repairs* a complete but inconsistent assignment by reducing inconsistencies. Thus, it uses information about the current assignment which is not available to a standard backtracking algo-rithm to guide its search. Second, the use of a hill-climbing strategy, rather than a backtracking strategy, produces a different style of search.

There are also several variations of the min-conflicts hill-climbing method that we have experimented with. For example, we have considered a variation that uses "max-conflicts" as a variable ordering heuristic in conjunction with the min-conflicts value ordering heuristic. Instead of picking a variable randomly from the set of variables in conflict, the "max-conflicts" variation will randomly choose from among the variables with the most-conflicts. The min-conflicts heuristic then selects the value with the fewest conflicts.

The min-conflicts heuristic can also be used with other search strategies in addition to simple hill climbing. For example, rather than hill-climbing, we can backtrack through the space of possible repairs. In this variation, as shown in Figure 9-1, all the variables are initially on a list, VARS-LEFT, and as they are repaired, they are pushed onto a different list VARS-DONE. The algorithm attempts to find a sequence of repairs such that no variable is repaired more than once. If there is no way to repair a variable in VARS-LEFT without violating a previously repaired variable (a variable in VARS-DONE), the algorithm backtracks.

Notice that this algorithm is simply a standard backtracking algorithm aug-mented with the min-conflicts heuristic to order its choice of which variable and value to attend to. This illustrates an important point. The backtracking repair algo-

---

[1] In general, the heuristic attempts to minimize the number of other variables that will need to be repaired. For binary CSPs, this corresponds to minimizing the number of conflicting variables. For general CSPs, where a single constraint can involve several variables, the exact method of counting the number of variables that will need to be repaired depends on the particular constraint. The space telescope scheduling problem is a general CSP, whereas the other tasks described in this chapter are binary CSPs.

```
Procedure INFORMED-BACKTRACK (VARS-LEFT VARS-DONE)
  If all variables are consistent, then solution found, STOP.
  Let VAR = a variable in VARS-LEFT that is in conflict.
  Remove VAR from VARS-LEFT.
  Push VAR onto VARS-DONE.
  Let VALUES = list of possible values for VAR ordered in
                ascending order according to number of conflicts
                with variables in VARS-LEFT.
For each VALUE in VALUES, until solution found:
  If VALUE does not conflict with any variable that is in
  VARS-DONE,
    then Assign VALUE to VAR.
        Call INFORMED-BACKTRACK(VARS-LEFT VARS-DONE)
  end if
  end for
end procedure

Begin program
  Let VARS-LEFT = list of all variables, each assigned an initial
  value.
  Let VARS-DONE = nil
  Call INFORMED-BACKTRACK(VARS-LEFT VARS-DONE)
End program
```

Figure 9-1: Informed backtracking using the min-conflicts heuristic.

rithm incrementally extends a consistent partial assignment (i.e., VARS-DONE), as does a constructive backtracking program, but in addition, it uses information from the initial assignment (i.e., VARS-LEFT) to bias its search. Thus, it is a type of *informed backtracking*. We still characterize it as a repair-based method because its search is guided by a complete, inconsistent assignment.

9.2 EXPERIMENTAL RESULTS

In this section, we summarize our experiments with the min-conflicts approach on some standard problems. These experiments identify problems on which min-conflicts performs well as well as problems on which it performs poorly. For brevity, we restrict our discussion to the hill-climbing search strategy described in the previous section.

9.2.1 The N-Queens Problem

The *n*-queens problem, originally posed in the nineteenth century, has become a standard benchmark for testing CSP algorithms. In a sense, the problem of finding a single solution has been solved because there are a number of analytic methods that yield a solution in linear time (Abramson & Yung, 1989). For example, there are certain well-known patterns that can be used to produce a solution to any instance of the n-queens problem. Nevertheless, the problem has been perceived as relatively "hard" for heuristic search methods. Several studies of the n-queens problem (Haralick & Elliot, 1980; Stone & Stone, 1987; Keng & Yun, 1989) have compared heuristic backtracking methods such as search rearrangement backtracking (e.g., most-constrained first), forward checking, and dependency-directed backtracking.

To solve the n-queens problem, we constructed a hill-climbing program that operates as follows. A preprocessing phase creates an initial assignment using a greedy algorithm that iterates through the rows, placing each queen on the column where it conflicts with the fewest previously placed queens (breaking ties randomly). In the subsequent repair phase, the program keeps repairing the assignment until a solution is found. To make a repair, the program selects a queen that is in conflict and moves it to the column (within the same row) where it conflicts with the fewest other queens (breaking ties randomly). A repair can be accomplished in $O(n)$ time by maintaining a list of the queens currently in conflict and an array of counters indicating the number of conflicts in each column and diagonal.

The average run time for the hill-climbing program is very close to linear. In terms of real-time performance, this program solves the million queens problem in less than four minutes on a SPARCstation1. As discussed in Minton *et al.* (1990), these results are substantially better than those of traditional AI search methods, which have trouble solving even the thousand queens problem in a reasonable time.

An examination of the behavior of our algorithm shows that the number of repairs required to solve the problem remains close to constant (about 50 repairs) regardless of the size of the problem! However, the time to accomplish a repair grows with the size of the problem; we note that each repair requires approximately $O(n)$ time in the worst case. In fact, this cost is reflected in the program's run-time behavior, which, as noted above, is approximately linear.

The cost of making a repair can be optimized for large problems; in which case, the average solution time for the million-queens problem was reduced to less than a minute and a half. The program maintains a list of queens that are in conflict as well as three arrays of counters indicating the number of queens in each column, row, and diagonal. Rather than scanning a row for the position with the fewest conflicts, the optimized program maintains a list of empty columns (which tends to be quite small); it first checks for a zero-conflict position by looking for an empty column with no conflicts along the diagonals. If there is no zero-conflict position, the program repeatedly looks for a position with one conflict by randomly selecting a position and checking the number of conflicts in that position. Because there tend to be many positions with one conflict, this technique tends to succeed after just a few tries; so, the total number of positions examined is generally very low.

One obvious conclusion from these results is that n-queens is actually a very easy problem given the right method. Interesting, two other heuristic methods that can quickly solve n-queens problems have also recently been invented. (By coincidence, these two other methods and our method were all developed and published independently.) Although both methods are specific to n-queens, one method is a repair-based method that is similar to ours in spirit (Sosic & Gu, 1990), whereas the other employs a constructive backtracking approach (Kale, 1990). This latter method uses a combination of variable and value-ordering heuristics that take advantage of the particular structure inherent in n-queens. This shows that one *can* solve n-queens problems quickly with a traditional, constructive backtracking method. Nevertheless, given the comparative simplicity of our method, it would seem that n-queens is more naturally solved using a repair-based approach.

9.2.2 Scheduling Applications

Whereas the n-queens problem is only of theoretical interest, scheduling algorithms have many practical applications. A scheduling problem involves placing a set of tasks on a time line, subject to temporal constraints, resource constraints, preferences, etc. One such problem, that of scheduling Hubble Space Telescope, has already been noted as the original motivation for this work. We have also applied the technique to a sample of job-shop scheduling problems in order to obtain some comparison with other approaches. Both of these areas are discussed in this section.

Hubble Space Telescope.   The Hubble Space Telescope scheduling problem can be considered a constrained optimization problem (Fox, 1987; Freuder, 1989) where we must maximize both the number and the importance of the constraints that are satisfied. As noted in Minton *et al.* (1990, 1992), the initial scheduling system developed for this application had difficulty producing schedules efficiently. The constraint-based system, SPIKE, that was developed to augment (and partially replace) the initial system has performed quite well using a relatively simple approach.

In part, the HST scheduling problem was made more tractable by dividing it into two parts; a long-term scheduling problem and a short-term scheduling problem. Currently, SPIKE is used only on the long-term problem. The long-term problem involves assigning approximately one year's worth of exposures to a set of "bins" or time segments of several days length. (The short-term problem involves deriving a detailed series of commands for the telescope and is addressed using different techniques [Muscettola *et al.*, 1989].) The input to SPIKE is a set of detailed specifications for exposures that are to be scheduled on the telescope. The constraints relevant to the long term problem are primarily temporal constraints. As outlined in Johnston (1987), some exposures are designed as calibrations or target acquisitions for others and so must proceed them. Some must be executed at specific times or at specific phases in the case of periodic phenomena. Some observations must be made at regular intervals or grouped within a specified time span. The constraints vary in their importance; they range from "hard" constraints that cannot be violated under any circumstances to "soft" constraints that represent good operating practices and scheduling goals.

SPIKE operates by taking the exposure specifications prepared by astronomers and compiling them into a set of tasks to be scheduled and a set of constraints on those tasks. Among other things, the compilation process takes the transitive closure of temporal constraints and explicitly represents each inferred constraint. For example, if TaskA must be before TaskB, and TaskB must be before TaskC, then the system will explicitly represent the fact that TaskA must be before TaskC as well. This explicit representation enables the scheduler to obtain a more accurate assessment of the number of conflicts in a given schedule.

One of the original and most effective SPIKE search strategies was based on a neural network model designated "guarded discrete stochatic," or GDS (Johnston & Adorf, 1992). In searching for a schedule, the GDS network effectively employed the same constraint satisfaction approach used by our min-conflicts method. In effect, if a task was in conflict, then it was removed from the schedule, and if a task was unscheduled, then the network scheduled it for the time segment that had the fewest constraint violations. However, the network used only the hard constraints in determining the time segment with the fewest violations. Soft constraints were consulted when there were two or more "least conflicted" places to move a task.

The min-conflicts hill-climbing method has been shown to be as effective as the GDS network on representative data sets used for testing SPIKE, and it has now been incorporated fully into the SPIKE system. One advantage in using the min-conflicts method, as opposed to the GDS network, is that much of the overhead of using the network can be eliminated (particularly the space overhead). Moreover, because the min-conflicts heuristic is so simple, the min-conflicts scheduler was quickly coded and is extremely efficient. (The C version of the min-conflicts scheduler runs about an order of magnitude faster than the network, although some of the improvement is the result of factors such as programming language differences, making a precise comparison difficult.) Although this might be regarded as just an implementation issue, we believe that the clear and simple formulation of the method was a significant enabling factor. In addition, the simplicity of the method makes it easy to experiment with various modifications to the heuristic and the search strategy. This has significant practical import because SPIKE is currently being used on other types of telescope scheduling problems where a certain amount of modification and tuning is required.

Job Shop Scheduling. One of the simplest non-trivial types of scheduling problem is the job-shop problem, for which a large literature exists. In this problem, we have to schedule n jobs on m machines, where each job requires processing on each machine in a particular order (which differs from one job to another). Although a variety of optimization criteria can be defined for this problem, we consider here the *decision problem* of whether a schedule can be found that processes all jobs between their specified release and due dates and meet all processing order constraints. This can easily be cast as a constraint satisfaction problem with binary temporal constraints among nm tasks. A set of 60 such problems was defined by Sadeh (1991) and used in a comparison of his "micro-opportunistic" scheduler with other techniques, including some of the major current approaches from the operations research community. These same problems were also used by Muscettola (1992) to evaluate his "conflict partition scheduling" approach. We have applied SPIKE to these problems, using the current SPIKE version of the min-conflicts algorithm that has superseded the GDS network.

The 60 job-shop constraint satisfaction problems each consist of 10 orders and 5 activities per order, for a total of 50 tasks per problem. There are 10 problem instances for each of 6 different sets of parameters, covering a range of release and due dates and a number of bottleneck resources. In the results reported by Sadeh (1991), runs were constrained to expand no more than 1000 search states in order to provide a reasonable basis for comparing different methods. In the SPIKE runs on these problems, the 1000-state limit was imposed by allowing as many as 10 initial-guess/repair cycles for each run, where the limit on the number of repairs was 50. Thus, if no solutions were found, 10 sets of 50 initial guess assignments plus 50 repairs would have been made, for a total of 1000 assignments. Although several initial guess methods were tried, the most effective was a variant of "most-constrained first," which effectively focused on one job at a time.

The results are shown in Table 9-1, which lists the number of problems of each type that were solved by each of a variety of methods. The SPIKE results are in column 1: SPIKE was the only method to solve all 60 problems. In columns 2 and 3 are the results for CPS = Conflict Partition Scheduling and "MIN-CONF," a variant of min-conflicts reported by Muscettola (1992). This min-conflicts technique differs from the one used by SPIKE in the initial guess technique, the number of repair cycles permitted, and the method of counting constraint conflicts (SPIKE uses an arc- and path-consistent form of the temporal constraints and counts conflicts for inferred, as well as explicit, constraints). Columns 5 through 8 are the results from Sadeh (1991), which includes detailed references to the various algorithms, where DSR = dynamic search rearrangement, ABT = advised backtracking, ORR = opera-

Table 9-1:   Comparison of SPIKE min-conflicts with other approaches on the set of 60 job-shop
scheduling constraint satisfaction problems defined by Sadeh: the table lists the number
of problems of each type solved by each method. The problem instances are designated
by the values of the parameters for due and release date range (RG) and by the number
of bottleneck resources (BK). Only SPIKE (column 1) found solutions to all 60 problem
instances.

CASE	(1)	(2)	(3)	(4)	(5)	(6)	(7)	(8)
	SPIKE	CPS	"MIN CONF"	ORR & FSS	SMU	ORR & ABT	DSR & FSS	DSR & ABT
RG=0.2, BK=1	10	10	10	10	10	10	8	8
RG=0.2, BK=2	10	9	3	10	8	6	7	7
RG=0.1, BK=1	10	10	5	8	6	9	8	8
RG=0.1, BK=2	10	10	1	9	7	6	4	3
RG=0, BK=1	10	10	4	7	4	7	3	2
RG=0, BK=2	10	9	0	8	8	5	3	3
TOTAL	60	58	23	52	43	43	33	31

tions resource reliance, FSS = filtered survivable schedules, and SMU = Southern
Methodist University heuristics.

Although it is not possible to compare run-time performance in any detailed
way, it is interesting to note that the median times required for SPIKE to find solutions to these problems were only a few seconds each (on a Sparcstation 2, running
Allegro Common Lisp)—much faster than the characteristic times of minutes
reported in Sadeh (1991). It is also interesting to note that the initial guess method
appears to play a very important role here: most of the solutions found by SPIKE to
these problems did not require very much repair, a fact that also helps explain the
difference in success rate between SPIKE and "MIN-CONF" (columns 1 and 3).
This is in contrast to the results for n-queens and certain graph colorability problems where the initial guess appears to matter much less. This issue is taken up
below in Section 9.3 when we discuss the statistical model for the behavior of the
min-conflicts heuristic.

Repair-Based Methods and Scheduling.   In general, scheduling appears to be an
excellent application area for repair-based methods. Supporting evidence comes
from previous work on other real-world scheduling applications by Zweben *et al.*
(1990), Biefeld and Cooper (1991), and Kurtzmann (1988). Each of these projects
uses iterative improvement methods that can be characterized as repair-based.
There are several reasons why repair-based methods are well-suited to scheduling
applications. First, as Zweben, Deale, & Gargan (1990) have pointed out, unexpected events can require schedule revision; in which case, dynamic rescheduling
is an important issue. Repair-based methods can be used for rescheduling in a

natural manner. Second, most scheduling applications involve optimization, at least to some degree, and repair-based methods are also naturally extended to deal with such issues. For example, in scheduling the Hubble Space Telescope, the goal is to maximize the amount of observing time and the priority of the chosen observations. The telescope is expected to remain highly over-subscribed in that many more proposals will be submitted than can be accommodated by any schedule. On such problems, repair-based methods offer an alternative to traditional branch-and-bound techniques. Finally, as Biefeld and Cooper (1991) have pointed out, there are real-world scheduling problems where humans find repair-based methods very natural. For example, human schedulers at JPL employ repair-based methods when constructing mission schedules for robotic spacecraft. For such problems, it can be relatively easy for people using a repair-based system to understand the system's solution and the way in which it was determined.

9.2.3 Graph Coloring

In addition to n-queens problem and HST scheduling, we have also tested the min-conflicts hill-climbing method on graph 3-colorability problems. A graph 3-colorability problem consists of an undirected graph with n vertices. Each vertex must be assigned one of three colors subject to the constraint that no neighboring vertex is assigned the same color. Graph 3-colorability is a well-studied NP-complete problem that is used to model certain types of scheduling and resource allocation problems, such as examination scheduling and register allocation.

In our experiments, we used the following procedure for randomly generating solvable graph 3-colorability problems with n nodes and m arcs:

1. Create three groups of nodes, each with $n/3$ nodes.
2. Randomly create m arcs between nodes in different groups.
3. Accept the graph if it has no unconnected components.

We experimented with two classes of problem instances: one set with $m = 2n$ (i.e., average vertex degree of 4) and another with $m = n(n - 1)/4$. We will refer to the former as the sparsely connected graphs and the latter as the densely connected graphs.

Unfortunately, we found that the min-conflicts hill-climbing method performed relatively poorly when compared against a more traditional search algorithm. Specifically, we compared the min-conflicts method to a simple constructive backtracking algorithm that is known to perform well on graph-coloring problems. The algorithm, originally proposed by Brelaz (1979) and Turner (1988), can be described as the repeated application of the following rule for choosing a node to color:

Find the uncolored node that has the fewest consistent colorings with its neighbors. If there is more than one, then choose one that has the maximum degree in the uncolored subgraph. Break ties randomly.

Essentially, this is a variable ordering rule consisting of two criteria. The first criterion is a preference for the "most-constrained" variable. The tie-breaking criterion is a preference for the "most-constraining" variable. Thus, this rule is composed of two generic variable-ordering heuristics. No value-ordering heuristic is required.

Although the min-conflicts method performed poorly compared to the Brelaz algorithm, our experiments yielded some interesting insights. Most importantly, the experiments illustrated that the performance of the min-conflicts method depends greatly on the connectivity of the graph. On densely connected graphs, the search converged rapidly to a solution, but on sparsely connected graphs, min-conflicts performed much more poorly. (These results were not surprising, however, because earlier work by Johnston and Adorf suggested this would be the case.) Intuitively, the reason that dense graphs are easy to color is that they are overconstrained. In other words, a mistake is easily corrected because the choice of color at a vertex is greatly influenced by the colors of all its neighbors. The sparsely colored graphs were significantly more difficult because there is less information conveyed by a node's neighbors regarding the correct choice of color.

In a related study, Cheeseman, Kanefsky, & Taylor (1991) have shown that as the average connectivity of a (connected) graph increases, a "phase transition" occurs, and it is at this point that most of the hard graph colorability problems are found. In other words, because a constraint satisfaction problem is easy if it is either underconstrained or overconstrained, hard problems can be expected to lie within the boundary between overconstrained and underconstrained problems. Our sparsely connected graphs lie within this boundary area.

Figure 9-2 illustrates how the difficulty of sparsely-connected connected graphs manifests itself for min-conflicts. The group of nodes on the left of the graph represents one consistent coloring, and the group on the right represents a different consistent coloring. However, the two colorings are inconsistent with each other. This situation frequently arises as a result of the initialization process. On the surface, the assignment appears to be a good one because there are at most three pairs of nodes in conflict. However, to achieve a solution, the boundary between the consistent colorings must be "pushed" completely to the left or right during the repair phase. Unfortunately, in this situation, there is not enough information locally available to direct min-conflicts. We have observed in animations of the hill-climbing program that the boundary tends to vacillate back and forth, with little overall progress being made.

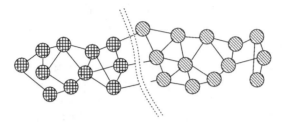

Figure 9-2:   An unlucky initialization.

9.2.4 Summary of Experimental Results

In this section, we have identified two tasks—n-queens and HST scheduling—that appear more amenable to our repair-based method than traditional constructive approaches. This is not to say that a repair-based approach will do better than *any* constructive approach on these two tasks, but merely that our simple, repair-based approach has done relatively well in comparison to the obvious constructive strategies we tried. On the other hand, our graph-coloring results indicate that our repair-based approach is not ideal for all domains.

In addition, we have found that the method has two other advantages. First, it is very simple and, thus, can be programmed extremely efficiently, especially if done in a task-specific manner. Second, the heuristic we have identified, that is, choosing the repair that minimizes the number of conflicts, is very general. It can be used in combination with different search strategies and task-specific heuristics, an important factor for most practical applications. Finally, we also note that repair-based methods have a special advantage for scheduling tasks because they can be used for overconstrained problems and for rescheduling problems in a natural manner. Thus, it seems likely that there are other applications for which our approach will prove useful.

9.3 ANALYSIS

The previous section showed that compared to traditional approaches, the min-conflicts approach is extremely effective on some tasks, such as placing queens on a chessboard, and less effective on other tasks, such as coloring sparsely connected graphs. We claimed that the min-conflicts heuristic takes advantage of information in the complete assignment to guide its search; this information is not available to a traditional backtracking algorithm that incrementally extends its search. Thus, the advantage of the min-conflicts heuristic over traditional approaches depends on how "useful" this information is. In this section, we formalize this intuition. Specifically, we investigate how the use of a complete assignment informs the choice of which value to pick. The analysis reveals how the effectiveness of the min-conflicts heuristic is influenced by various characteristics of a task domain. The analysis is independent of any particular search strategy, such as hill-climbing or backtracking.

9.3.1 Modeling the Min-Conflicts Heuristic

Consider a constraint satisfaction problem with n variables, where each variable has k possible values. We restrict our consideration to a simplified model where every variable is subject to exactly c binary constraints, and we assume that there is only a single solution to the problem, that is, exactly one satisfying assignment. We address the following question: What is the probability that the min-conflicts heuristic will make a mistake when it assigns a value to a variable that is in conflict? We define a mistake as choosing an incorrect value that will have to be changed before the solution is found. We note that for our informed backtracking program, a mistake of this sort can prove quite costly because an entire subtree must be explored before another value can be assigned.

For any assignment of values to the variables, there will be a minimum set of d variables whose values will have to be changed to convert the assignment into the solution (Figure 9-3). We can regard d as a measure of distance to the solution. The key to our analysis is the following observation: Given a variable V to be repaired, only one of its k possible values will be correct,[2] and the other $k-1$ values will be incorrect (i.e., mistakes). Whereas the correct value can conflict with at most d other variables in the assignment, an incorrect value can conflict with as many as c other variables. Thus, as d shrinks, the min-conflicts heuristic should be less likely to make a mistake when it repairs V. In fact, if each of the $k-1$ incorrect values has more than d conflicts, then the min-conflicts heuristic cannot make a mistake—it will select the correct value when it repairs this variable because the correct value will have fewer conflicts than any incorrect value.

We can use this idea to bound the probability that the min-conflicts heuristic will make a mistake when repairing variable V. Let V' be a variable related to V by a constraint. We assume that an incorrect value for V conflicts with an arbitrary value for V' with probability p, independent of the variables V and V'. Consider an arbitrary incorrect value for V. Let N_b be the total the number of conflicts between this incorrect value and the assigned values for the other variables. Given the above assumptions, the expected value of N_b is pc because there are exactly c variables that share a constraint with V, and the probability of a conflict is p. As mentioned above, the min-conflicts will not make a mistake if the number of conflicts N_b for

---

[2] Although a variable is in conflict, its current value can actually be the correct value. This can happen when the variable with which it conflicts has an incorrect value. In this chapter, we have defined the min-conflicts heuristic so that it can choose *any* possible value for the variable, including its initial value.

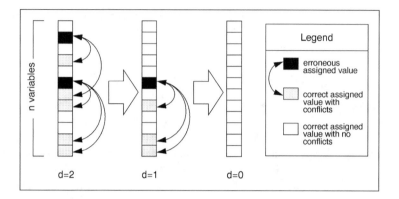

Figure   9-3:   A schematic illustration of the min-conflicts model and terminology. The state of the constraint satisfaction problem is illustrated by a vertical column of n variables. The distance d (at the bottom of each column) is the minimum number of variables whose values have to be changed to reach the solution. In the initial $d = 2$ state, there are two variables with incorrect assigned values (shown as solid black), each of which induces conflicts with variables that have correct assignments (shown as gray). The arcs indicate the presence of constraints on variables with incorrect assigned values. In the $d = 1$ state, one of the incorrect assigned values has been changed to the correct one, and in the final $d = 0$ solution state, all variables have correct assigned values.

each incorrect value is greater than d. We can, therefore, bound the probability of making a mistake by bounding the probability that N_b is less than or equal to d.

To bound N_b, we use Hoeffding's inequality, which states that the sum N of n independent, identically distributed random variables is less than the expected value $\overline{N}$ by more than sn only with probability at most $e^{-2s^2 n}$. In our model, N_b is the sum of c potential conflicts, each of which is either 1 or 0 depending on whether there is a conflict. The expected value of N_b is pc, thus

$$\Pr(N_b \leq pc - sc) \leq e^{-2s^2 c}$$

Because we are interested in the behavior of the min-conflicts heuristic as d shrinks, let us suppose that d is less than pc. Then, if we let $s = (pc - d)/c$, we obtain

$$\Pr(N_b \leq d) \leq e^{-2(pc - d)^2/c}$$

To account for the fact that a mistake can occur if *any* of the $k - 1$ incorrect values has d or fewer conflicts, we bound the probability of making a mistake on any of them by multiplying by $k - 1$:

$$\Pr(\textit{mistake}) \leq (k - 1)e^{-2(pc - d)^2/c}$$

Note that as c (the number of constraints per variable) becomes large, the probability of a mistake approaches zero if all other parameters remain fixed. This analysis thus offers an explanation as to why 3-coloring densely connected graphs is relatively easy. We also see that as d becomes small, a mistake is also less likely, explaining our empirical observation that having a "good" initial assignment can be important. (Of course, an assignment with few conflicts does not necessarily imply small d, as was illustrated by the 3-colorability problem in Figure 9-2.) Finally, we note that the probability of a mistake also depends on p, the probability that an incorrect value conflicts with another variable's value, and k, the number of values per variable. The probability of a mistake shrinks as p increases or k decreases.

9.3.2 A Statistical Model for CSP Repair

The simple model presented in the previous section shows, in a qualitative way, how various problem characteristics influence the effectiveness of the min-conflicts heuristic. Augmenting the model with statistical assumptions about the task domain provides the basis for a quantitative analysis. The augmented model assumes that conflicts between variables can be characterized by probability distribution functions, as illustrated in Figure 9-4. Also, as in the original model, a single solution is assumed. Although these assumptions might not precisely be met in practice on any particular CSP, the augmented model turns out to be a surprisingly accurate predictor of the performance of several heuristics, including min-conflicts, on some interesting classes of problems.

We continue to assume a binary CSP with n variables and k possible values per variable. For a given assignment, the distance d is the *minimum* number of variables that must be corrected to obtain a solution. As a measure of heuristic performance, we use the probability that after a particular repair step, *the distance d is decreased*. This only occurs when the heuristic selects a variable that is assigned an incorrect (non-solution) value and changes it to the unique correct (solution) value. This probability is given by

$$P_{d \to d-1} = P_{\bar{s}} P_{c|\bar{s}}$$

where $P_{\bar{s}}$ is the probability that the variable selection heuristic chooses a variable currently assigned an incorrect (non-solution) value, and $P_{c|\bar{s}}$ is the probability that the value selection heuristic chooses the correct value given that the selected variable has an incorrect value currently assigned. (Subscripts s and $\bar{s}$ indicate variables assigned solution and non-solution values, respectively. For a given variable, the subscripts c and $\bar{c}$ refer to correct and incorrect values, respectively.)

Similarly, the probability of *increasing* the distance from the solution is

$$P_{d \to d+1} = P_s(1 - P_{c|s})$$

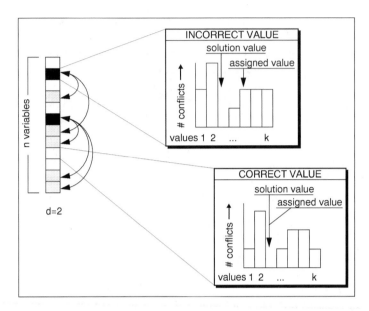

Figure 9-4:   A more detailed look at the state of the illustrative constraint satisfaction problem. The blown-up boxes show a histogram of the number of conflicts on each of the k values that a variable can assume. In the upper box, a variable has an erroneous assigned value that has conflicts. In the lower box, a variable is assigned the correct (solution) value, and there happen to be no conflicts on that value in this state. The probability distributions that describe these and related situations are derived from the detailed statistical model.

where $P_s = 1 - P_{\bar{s}}$ is that probability that the variable selection heuristic will choose a variable currently assigned a correct value, and $P_{c\,|\,s}$ is the probability that the value selection heuristic will choose the correct value given that the chosen variable already has the correct value assigned. The third possibility, that d will remain unchanged, has probability $P_{d \to d} = 1 - P_{d \to d-1} - P_{d \to d+1}$. The quantity $P_{d \to d-1} / P_{d \to d+1}$ is of particular interest because as long as it is > 1, a heuristic is more likely to move *toward* the solution than *away* from it.

In the remainder of Section 9.3.2, we develop a model that permits the calculation of these probabilities and their comparison with empirical results for a certain class of CSPs. There are three basic components to the model, as illustrated in Figure 9-5:

- definition of expressions for the *conflict probability distributions* $\theta(v)$ for the probability of v conflicts on potential value assignments (Section 9.3.2.1)

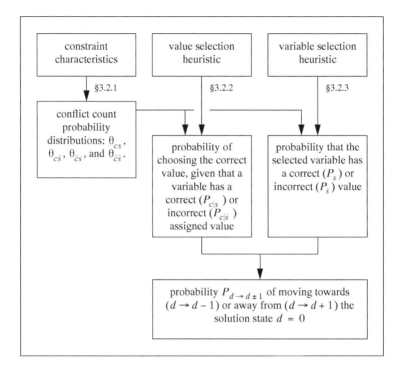

Figure 9-5:   The major elements of the statistical model and how they are related.

- derivation of expressions for the probability of choosing *solution or non-solution values* when different value selection heuristics are employed (Section 9.3.2.2)
- similar derivations for the probability of choosing *variables with incorrect assigned values for repair* (Section 9.3.2.3)

The resulting expressions are used to evaluate the performance measures $P_{d \to d, d \pm 1}$ for some specific CSP types in Section 9.3.2.4. These are compared with empirical data for specific problem instances to provide confidence in the model assumptions for these cases. The results also illustrate how much can be gained by basing value selection on a heuristic that considers the *number* of conflicts rather than just *whether* there are conflicts. In some limiting cases, analytic expressions can be derived that permit some general conclusions to be drawn about performance for large n (Section 9.3.2.5). Finally, Section 9.3.2.6 summarizes the main conclusions we have drawn from the statistical model and suggests some directions for further research.

		current assigned value is:	
		correct (s)	incorrect ($\bar{s}$)
probability of v conflicts on:	correct value (c)	$\theta_{cs}(v),$ $0 \le v \le d$	$\theta_{c\bar{s}}(v),$ $0 \le v \le d - 1$
	incorrect value ($\bar{c}$)	$\theta_{\bar{c}s}(v),$ $0 \le v \le n - 1$	$\theta_{\bar{c}\bar{s}}(v),$ $0 \le v \le n - 1$

Figure 9-6:   The definitions of the four underlying conflict probability distributions $\theta(v)$ that are used in the definition of the statistical model.

9.3.2.1 Conflict Probability Distributions

Definitions.   The first step in developing expressions for the performance measures $P_{d \to d, d \pm 1}$ requires the probability distributions for conflicts. Four such distributions are required (see Figure 9-4) to describe the conflict count distributions for solution and non-solution values for variables with and without correct assigned values. The terminology we use is summarized in Figure 9-6. For the cumulative distributions, we use the following notation:

$$\theta_{\bar{c}s}(> v) \equiv \sum_{w > v} \theta_{\bar{c}s}(w)$$

In the remainder of this section, we discuss the derivation of these conflict probability distributions θ for the class of CSPs with random independent constraints.

Random CSPs.   These can be characterized by two probabilities, as follows:

- $p_{c \Rightarrow \bar{c}} \equiv p_{\bar{c} \Rightarrow c}$ is the probability that a *correct* value for variable V conflicts with an *incorrect* value for variable V'.

- $p_{\bar{c} \Rightarrow \bar{c}}$ is the probability that an *incorrect* value for variable V conflicts with an *incorrect* value for variable V'.

Note that by definition, $p_{c \Rightarrow c} = 0$ (there can be no conflicts between correct values).
    Consider a state in which there are d variables assigned incorrect values. If a variable is assigned the correct value, then it can conflict with at most the d variables assigned incorrect values. Assuming that *the probability of each conflict is independent*, the total number of conflicts follows a binomial distribution:

$$B(x, p, N) = \binom{N}{x} p^x (1 - p)^{N - x}$$

where x is the number of "successes," p is the probability of success in a single "trial," and N is the number of trials; thus,

$$\theta_{cs}(v) = B(v, p_{\bar{c} \Rightarrow c}, d)$$

Incorrect values can conflict with the d incorrectly assigned variables, each with probability $p_{\bar{c} \Rightarrow \bar{c}}$, and with the other $n - d - 1$ correctly assigned variables, each with probability $p_{c \Rightarrow \bar{c}}$. The distribution is

$$\theta_{\bar{c}s}(v) = \sum_{k=0}^{v} B(k, p_{\bar{c} \Rightarrow \bar{c}}, d)B(v - k, p_{c \Rightarrow \bar{c}}, n - d - 1)$$

This is the distribution for the sum of two binomially distributed variables with different values for N and p. In the case where $p_{\bar{c} \Rightarrow \bar{c}} = p_{c \Rightarrow \bar{c}} = p_c$, this reduces to $\theta_{\bar{c}s}(v) = B(v, p_c, n - 1)$.

For variables currently assigned incorrect values, the correct value can conflict with at most the $d - 1$ other variables assigned incorrect values, each with probability $p_{c \Rightarrow \bar{c}}$:

$$\theta_{c\bar{s}}(v) = B(v, p_{c \Rightarrow \bar{c}}, d - 1)$$

Incorrect values can conflict with the other $d - 1$ incorrect variables, each with probability $p_{\bar{c} \Rightarrow \bar{c}}$, and by the $n - d$ correct variables, each with probability $p_{c \Rightarrow \bar{c}}$. The distribution function is

$$\theta_{\bar{c}\bar{s}}(v) = \sum_{k=0}^{v} B(k, p_{\bar{c} \Rightarrow \bar{c}}, d - 1)B(v - k, p_{c \Rightarrow \bar{c}}, n - d)$$

In the case where $p_{\bar{c} \Rightarrow \bar{c}} = p_{c \Rightarrow \bar{c}} = p_c$, this reduces to $\theta_{\bar{c}\bar{s}}(v) = B(v, p_c, n - 1) = \theta_{\bar{c}s}(v)$.

To calculate $p_{\bar{c} \Rightarrow \bar{c}}$ and $p_{c \Rightarrow \bar{c}}$, suppose that each variable constrains on average c other variables and, if there is a constraint between any two variables V and V', that each value for V conflicts with an average k' values for V'. Then, the probability that V constrains V' is $c/(n - 1)$, and the probability that the correct value for V conflicts with an incorrect value for V' is $k'/(k - 1)$, where k is the domain size. Thus, we have

$$p_{c \Rightarrow \bar{c}} = \frac{c}{n - 1} \frac{k'}{k - 1}$$

A similar argument for incorrect values yields

$$p_{\bar{c} \Rightarrow \bar{c}} = \frac{c}{n - 1} \frac{k'}{k - 1} \frac{k - 2}{k - 1} = \frac{k - 2}{k - 1} p_{c \Rightarrow \bar{c}}$$

Table 9-2: Probabilities of conflicts between solution and non-solution values $p_{c \Rightarrow \bar{c}}$ and between non-solution and non-solution values $p_{\bar{c} \Rightarrow \bar{c}}$, for some CSPs that can be treated as "random." For graph 3-colorability problems, the mean vertex degree (VD) of the problem graph is indicated. The Dechter-Pearl problem, shown for comparison, has probability p_1 of a constraint between variables, and p_2 that a constraint permits any specific pair of values. c is the mean number of variables constrained by any variable, k' is the mean number of values prohibited by a constraint between two variables, and k is the domain size.

Problem	c	k'	k	$p_{c \Rightarrow \bar{c}}$	$p_{\bar{c} \Rightarrow \bar{c}}$
Sparse Graph 3-Colorability VD = 4	4	1	3	$\dfrac{2}{n-1}$	$\dfrac{1}{n-1}$
Dense Graph 3-Colorability VD = $2n/3$	$\dfrac{2n}{3}$	1	3	$\dfrac{1}{3}\dfrac{n}{n-1}$	$\dfrac{1}{6}\dfrac{n}{n-1}$
Dechter-Pearl General Case	$p_1 n$	$(1-p_2)k$	k	$\dfrac{p_1(1-p_2)kn}{(k-1)(n-1)}$	$\dfrac{p_1(1-p_2)k(k-2)n}{(k-1)^2(n-1)}$
Dechter-Pearl $k=5$ $p_1=0.5, p_2=0.6$	$\dfrac{n}{2}$	2	5	$\dfrac{1}{4}\dfrac{n}{n-1}$	$\dfrac{3}{16}\dfrac{n}{n-1}$

Values for $p_{c \Rightarrow \bar{c}}$ and $p_{\bar{c} \Rightarrow \bar{c}}$ are given in Table 9-2 for some illustrative problem types, including sparse and dense graph 3-colorability problems. For comparison, the table also shows the corresponding values for the random problem described by Dechter & Pearl (1988).

9.3.2.2 Value Selection Heuristics

The second step in realizing the model is to obtain expressions for the probability of choosing a correct value ($P_{c|s}$ and $P_{c|\bar{s}}$) based on the conflict probability distributions defined in Section 9.3.2.1. It is important to note that the derived probabilities depend only on the existence of the θ distributions and not on their specific form. For brevity, derivations are omitted here: they follow the same lines as Minton *et al.* (1992). Here, we simply state the expressions for $P_{c|s}$ and $P_{c|\bar{s}}$ for three different value selection methods.

Min-Conflicts Value Selection. The min-conflicts value selection heuristic can be stated as

Choose a value that has the *minimum* number of conflicts with the assigned values for the other variables. If there is more than one such value, select one at random.

Note that with this rule, there need be no change in the assignment.

For a variable with a correct value assigned, the probability that this heuristic will leave the assignment unchanged is

$$P_{c|s} = \sum_{v=1}^{d} \frac{\theta_{cs}(v)}{1 - \theta_{cs}(0)} P^{sol}(v),$$

where

$$P^{sol}(v) = \sum_{m=0}^{k-1} \binom{k-1}{m} \theta_{\bar{c}s}(v)^m \theta_{cs}(> v)^{k-1-m} \frac{1}{m+1}$$

For a variable with an incorrect value assigned, the probability that the heuristic will choose the correct value is

$$P_{c|\bar{s}} = \sum_{w=1}^{n-1} \sum_{v=0}^{d-1} \theta_{c\bar{s}}(v) \frac{\theta_{\bar{c}\bar{s}}(w)}{1 - \theta_{\bar{c}\bar{s}}(0)} P^{sol}(v,w)$$

where

$$P^{sol}(v,w)|_{v=w} \equiv R^{v=w}(v) = \sum_{m=0}^{k-2} \binom{k-2}{m} \theta_{\bar{c}\bar{s}}(v)^m \theta_{\bar{c}\bar{s}}(> v)^{k-2-m} \frac{1}{m+2}$$

and

$$P^{sol}(v,w)|_{v<w} \equiv R^{v<w}(v) = \sum_{m=0}^{k-2} \binom{k-2}{m} \theta_{\bar{c}\bar{s}}(v)^m \theta_{\bar{c}\bar{s}}(> v)^{k-2-m} \frac{1}{m+1}$$

Random-Conflicts Value Selection. The min-conflicts heuristic examines the *number* of conflicts on each value to determine which to assign. A less informed heuristic could simply check *whether* there are any conflicts on values. This approach is captured by the "random-conflicts" rule:

If one or more values has *no* conflicts, select one of these values (at random).

If *all* values have conflicts, select one at random.

The assignment is not required to change (although it must change if at least one value has zero conflicts).

The quantities $P_{c|s}$ and $P_{c|\bar{s}}$ are given by

$$P_{c|s} = \theta_{cs}(> 0)^{k-1} \frac{1}{k}$$

and

$$P_{c|\bar{s}} = \theta_{c\bar{s}}(0) P^{sol}(v,w)|_{v=0} + [1 - \theta_{c\bar{s}}(0)] P^{sol}(v,w)|_{v>0}$$

where

$$P^{sol}(v,w)|_{v=0} = \sum_{m=0}^{k-2} \binom{k-2}{m} \theta_{c\bar{s}}(0)^m \theta_{c\bar{s}}(>0)^{k-2-m} \frac{1}{m+1}$$

$$P^{sol}(v,w)|_{v>0} = \theta_{c\bar{s}}(>0)^{k-2} \frac{1}{k}$$

$P^{sol}(v,w)$ is the probability of choosing the correct value for a variable with v conflicts on the correct value and $w > 0$ conflicts on an incorrect value.

Random Value Selection. This is the "least-possible-informed" value selection rule:

Select a value at random, regardless of conflicts.

With this rule, the probability of choosing the correct value is independent of the variable's current assignment:

$$P_{c|s} = P_{c|\bar{s}} = 1/k$$

9.3.2.3 Variable Selection

The final step in realizing the model is to obtain expressions for the probability that a variable selected for repair has a correct (P_s) or incorrect ($P_{\bar{s}}$) value. Here we consider only the following simple variable selection rule:

Select for repair a variable at random from the set of all variables that are currently in conflict.

Consider first a variable that is assigned an incorrect value. The probability that there are one or more conflicts on its assigned value is $1 - \theta_{c\bar{s}}(0)$. Because there are a total of d such variables, the expected number with conflicts is

$$N_{\bar{s}, \text{conf}} = d[1 - \theta_{c\bar{s}}(0)]$$

Now consider a variable that is assigned a correct value. The probability that there are one or more conflicts on its assigned value is $1 - \theta_{cs}(0)$. Because there are a total of $n - d$ such variables, the expected number with conflicts is

$$N_{s, \text{conf}} = (n - d)[1 - \theta_{cs}(0)]$$

Thus, for a variable with conflicts that is picked at random, the probability that it is currently assigned a correct value is

$$P_s = \frac{N_{s, \text{conf}}}{N_{\bar{s}, \text{conf}} + N_{s, \text{conf}}}$$

but the probability that it is currently assigned an incorrect value is

$$P_{\bar{s}} = 1 - P_s = \frac{N_{\bar{s}, \text{conf}}}{N_{\bar{s}, \text{conf}} + N_{s, \text{conf}}}$$

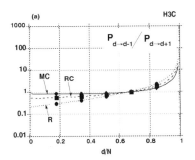 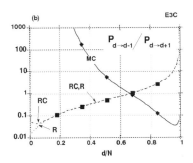

Figure 9-7: $P_{d \to d-1}/P_{d \to d+1}$ for the three value selection heuristics.

9.3.2.4 Evaluation of the Statistical Model

We have numerically evaluated the expressions above for $P_{d \to d,d \pm 1}$, $P_{c|\bar{s}}$, $P_{c|s}$, etc., on two random CSP problem types in order to compare the predicted performance of the three value selection heuristics discussed above. We have also generated sample problems and computed the probabilities empirically for comparison with the model. These results are described in this section.

Random CSPs. We have taken two graph 3-colorability problems for comparison of the heuristics:

- **H3C** is a "hard" 3-colorability, random sparsely connected graph, with mean vertex degree = 4. In the solution state, the expected number of conflicts on incorrect values is 2, approximately independent of problem size n.

- **E3C** is an "easy" 3-colorability, random densely connected graph, with mean vertex degree = $2n/3$. In the solution state, the expected number of conflicts on incorrect values is $n/3$, i.e., increasing linearly with problem size.

The relevant conflict probabilities for these two problems are given in Table 9-2. Probabilities were calculated for both problem types for $n = 90$. Value selection heuristics (Section 9.3.2.2) are labelled as follows in the figures: **MC**, min-conflicts; **RC**, random-conflicts; and **R**, random.

Combined Variable and Value Selection. The ratio $P_{d \to d-1}/P_{d \to d+1}$ provides a useful comparison of combined variable and value selection performance: it is greater than unity when a heuristic is more likely to improve the state than to worsen it. Figure 9-7 plots this ratio on a logarithmic scale vs. d/n for each of the three value selection methods. For H3C (Figure 9-7a), MC is best (for $d \ll n$), followed by RC and R, but in all cases, the ratio is < 1. For E3C (Figure 9-7b), the

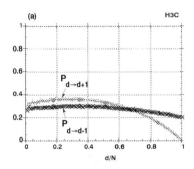 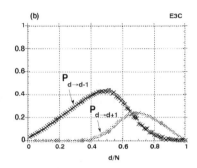

Figure 9-8:   Comparison of predicted results with empirical results for min-conflicts value selection
for (a) H3C and (b) E3C.

results are very different: MC shows a much higher chance of improving the state,
but both RC and R worsen it. RC is significantly better than R only for very small
d/n.

Comparison with Empirical Results.   To see how well the model captures features
of the heuristics when applied to actual problems, we have generated random problem instances with known solutions,[3] then assigned incorrect values to some of the
variables and calculated empirically the same probabilities that are predicted by the
statistical model. Figure 9-8 shows the comparison for MC value selection: the
empirical data points, indicated by the + and × symbols, show the results of averaging 200 states for each value of d. The agreement with the model probability
calculations is excellent.

9.3.2.5 Limiting Behavior for Random CSPs

There are two interesting limiting cases of the model for random CSPs, corresponding to limiting forms of the conflict probability distribution functions θ (see
Section 9.3.2.4). These limits are discussed in this section.

Poisson Limit.   In the case $n \to \infty$, $p_{\bar{c} \Rightarrow \bar{c}} \to p_{c \Rightarrow \bar{c}} = p_c$, and $np_c \to$ constant, the conflict distribution functions approach the Poisson distribution: $\theta_{cs}(v) \approx \theta_{\bar{c}s}(v) \approx$
$P_{\text{poisson}}(v, dp_c)$ and $\theta_{\bar{c}s}(v) \approx \theta_{\bar{c}\,\bar{s}}(v) \approx P_{\text{poisson}}(v, np_c)$, where $P_{\text{poisson}}(v, \mu) = e^{-\mu}\mu^v/v!$ If we
let $d = fn$—i.e., f is the fraction of variables assigned incorrect values—we can
write the distributions for $\theta_{cs}(v)$ and $\theta_{\bar{c}s}(v)$ as

---

[3]The random problem instances were not guaranteed to have unique solutions; simple relabelling of
colors will yield several.

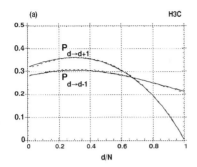
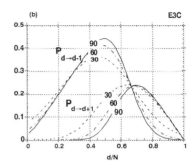

Figure 9-9:   Scaling behavior with n, illustrating the Poisson and Gaussian limits of the model for $n=30$, 60, and 90 for the two problem types (a) H3C and (b) E3C.

$$\theta_{cs}(v) \approx \theta_{c\bar{s}}(v) \approx \frac{(e^{-\mu})^f (f\mu)^v}{v!}$$

where $\mu = np_c$. The result is independent of n, and thus we have the important conclusion that *the performance of value selection heuristics depends only on d/n in the Poisson limit $p_c \propto 1/n$ for small np_c.* This is also true of the variable selection method used in the model (which depends only on $\theta_{c\bar{s}}(0)$ and $\theta_{cs}(0)$). Figure 9-9a illustrates this dependence on d/n for the H3C problem for $n = 30$, 60, and 90: the differences are already nearly indistinguishable.

Gaussian Limit.   At the other extreme, consider the case when the mean number of conflicts *increases* with n, e.g., when $p_{c \Rightarrow \bar{c}}$ is approximately constant, and $np_{c \Rightarrow \bar{c}}$, the expected number of conflicts for an incorrect value for a variable when in the solution state, increases linearly with n. In this case, for sufficiently large n, the distributions can be approximated by Gaussian distributions with mean $np_{c \Rightarrow \bar{c}}$ and variance $\sigma^2 = np_{c \Rightarrow \bar{c}}(1 - p_{c \Rightarrow \bar{c}})$. We can derive the dominant behavior of min-conflicts value selection in the limit $n \gg d \gg 1$ by approximating the sums in the expressions for $P_{c|\bar{s}}$ and $P_{c|s}$ by integrals over the Gaussian distribution. Only values near the peak of the Gaussian make significant contributions and in the limit $P_{c|\bar{s}} \approx P_{c|s} \approx 1$. The probability of choosing a variable with an incorrect value becomes $P_{\bar{s}} \approx d/n$ because $N_{\bar{s}, \text{conf}} \approx d$ and $N_{s, \text{conf}} \approx n - d$. From this, it follows that $P_{d \to d-1} \approx d/n$ and $P_{d \to d+1} \approx 0$. This linear dependence of $P_{d \to d-1}$ on d for large n is evident in Figure 9-9b, which shows $P_{d \to d-1}$ and $P_{d \to d+1}$ for $n = 30$, 60, and 90.

Global Performance of Min-Conflicts Hillclimbing Repair.   The   simple   limiting forms above permit some general statements to be made about the behavior of hillclimbing repair methods based on min-conflicts value selection. Hillclimbing repair can be modelled as a random (Markovian) walk described by the probabilities $P_{d \to d, d \pm 1}$ of moving toward or away from an "absorbing barrier" at $d = 0$.

In the Gaussian limit where $P_{d \to d+1} \approx 0$, $P_{d \to d-1} \approx d/n$, the expected number of hillclimbing steps to transition from d to $d-1$ is $1/P_{d \to d-1} = n/d$. From an initial distance d_0, the expected number of steps t to reach $d = 0$ is thus

$$t_{d_0 \to 0} = \sum_{i=1}^{d_0} \frac{n}{i} \approx n \left[\gamma + \ln d_0 + O(\frac{1}{d_0^2}) \right]$$

where $\gamma = 0.577 \cdots$ is Euler's constant. Thus, *the expected number of steps to reach the solution is linear in the problem size n and depends only logarithmically on how far away the initial guess is from the solution.*

In the Poisson limit where $P_{d \to d+1} > P_{d \to d-1}$ but both are nearly constant (cf. Figure 9-9a), the distance from the solution after t steps can be written as $d(t) = d_0 + \sum_{i=1}^{t} \xi_i$, where ξ_i is a random variable representing the change in d with each step. The probability distribution for ξ has mean $\mu = P_{d \to d+1} - P_{d \to d-1}$ and variance $\sigma^2 = P_{d \to d+1} + P_{d \to d-1} - (P_{d \to d+1} - P_{d \to d-1})^2$. After a sufficiently large number of steps, the distribution for $d(t)$ is approximately Gaussian with mean $\mu_d = d_0 + t\mu$ and variance $\sigma_d^2 = t\sigma^2$. The mean μ_d represents a drift of the expected value of $d(t)$ *away* from the solution $d = 0$. The probability of reaching the solution after t steps is approximately given by the tail of the Gaussian distribution for $d \leq 0$, which approaches

$$\frac{\sigma}{\mu \sqrt{2\pi t}} \exp\left(-\frac{\mu^2 t}{2\sigma^2} \right)$$

for large t. The important point is the predicted *exponential decline in the probability of reaching the solution as the number of hillclimbing steps increases.* This result provides an explanation for the observed behavior of the GDS network and of min-conflicts hillclimbing on sparse 3-colorable graphs, as described above in Section 9.2.3: when the number of steps is limited to $t \propto n$, there is an exponential decline with problem size n of the probability of finding the solution.

9.3.2.6 Summary and Caveats

The statistical model of CSP repair described here is a surprisingly good predictor of "conflict-informed" value selection performance for random CSPs. The model has both theoretical and practical benefits. It permits average-case comparisons of different variable and value selection heuristics, from which can be drawn general conclusions about their relative effectiveness. For particular problem types, limiting behavior for large n can be derived, including general statements as to whether heuristics will show better or worse performance as problem size increases. For random CSPs discussed in detail above, these conclusions include

- min-conflicts is the most effective value selection method among those considered.
- min-conflicts performs relatively better as n increases, particularly when $p_{c \Rightarrow \bar{c}}$ increases with n or remains constant.
- If the Gaussian limit applies, then hillclimbing with min-conflicts is an effective repair strategy, showing only weak dependence on the initial guess and $O(n)$ dependence on problem size n.
- If the Poisson limit applies, then the probability of reaching the solution declines exponentially with the number of hillclimbing steps.

Application of the model to other problem types is the subject of future research.

There are, however, several factors that limit the applicability of the model. The most important are that conflicts are assumed to be independent and that a single solution state is assumed. The presence of multiple solutions might not be a serious limitation as long as the model is applied in the vicinity of a solution, and solutions are not so dense as to render this meaningless. Conflict independence is more significant because highly structured problems that occur in practice can violate this assumption, and even "random" problems possess fine struture that is ignored by the model. This fine structure leads to the possibility of pathological configurations, e.g., manifested in hill-climbing techniques as "cycles" where the same variables are repaired again and again, but no progress is made toward the solution. To model the performance of the min-conflicts heuristic in conjunction with a particular search strategy, such as hill-climbing, a more detailed analysis might be required. Nevertheless, to the extent that the statistical properties of classes of problems can be established, it might still be possible to use the model to perform average-case analysis of heuristics.

9.4 RELATED WORK

The heuristic hill-climbing method described in this chapter can be characterized as a *local search* method (Johnson, Papadimitrou, & Yannakakis, 1988) in that each repair minimizes the number of conflicts for an individual variable. Local search methods have been applied to a variety of important problems, often with impressive results. For example, the Kernighan-Lin method, perhaps the most successful algorithm for solving graph-partitioning problems, repeatedly improves a partitioning by swapping the two vertices that yield the greatest cost differential. The much-publicized simulated annealing method can also be characterized as a form of local search (Johnson *et al.*, 1990).

The min-conflicts approach is also closely related to previous work in AI. In particular, there is a long history of AI programs that use repair or debugging strategies to solve problems, primarily in the areas of planning and design (Sussman, 1975; Simmons, 1988). This approach has recently had a renaissance with the emergence of case-based (Kolodner, Simpson, & Sycosa-Cyranski, 1985; Hammond, 1986) and analogical (Hickman & Lovett, 1991; Kambhampati, 1992; Veloso & Carbonell, 1992) problem solving. To solve a problem, a case-based system will retrieve the solution from a previous, similar problem and repair the old solution so that it solves the new problem.

There has also been related work in AI on sophisticated methods for measuring the *contention* between resources in scheduling problems. This information can then be used in heuristic search (Fox, Sadeh, & Baykan, 1989; Sadeh, 1991; Muscettola, 1992). The use of "conflict counts" can be viewed as a simple measure of resource contention.

The fact that the min-conflicts approach performs well on n-queens, a well-studied, "standard" constraint-satisfaction problem, suggests that AI repair-based approaches might be more generally useful than previously thought. Additional evidence also comes from some recent flurry of related studies. For instance, Selman, Levesque, & Mitchell (1992) showed that GSAT, a repair-based algorithm that uses a form of min-conflicts for satisfiability problems, outperforms traditional satisfiability algorithms. Specifically, they demonstrated that GSAT is superior to the well-known Davis-Putnam satisfiability algorithm on "hard" satisifiability problems. Selman, Levesque, & Mitchell (1992) also claim that GSAT performs relatively well on graph-coloring problems; because GSAT is essentially the same as our min-conflicts hill-climbing method, this implies that min-conflicts should perform well on graph-colorability problems if a similar problem encoding is used (i.e., representing coloring problems as satisfiability problems). Another notable, recent study with repair-based algorithms was conducted by Zweben and his collegues on scheduling problems (Zweben, 1990; Zweben *et al.*, 1992), where a system that employs a similar heuristic approach is being used to schedule ground maintenance for the space shuttle. Other encouraging studies on repair-based algorithms include Sosic and Gu's work with N-queens (Sosic & Gu, 1990); Morris's work on constraint-satisfaction problems (Morris, 1990, 1991, 1992); and a variety of studies on Tabu Search (e.g., Hertz & de Werra [1987] and Glover & Laguna [1992]), a hill-climbing, local search technique that maintains a list of forbidden moves in order to avoid cycles.

9.5 FUTURE WORK

The min-conflicts method outlined in this chapter, and repair-based methods in general appear to offer exciting new possibilities for scheduling. There are many possible extensions to the work reported here, but several are particularly worth mentioning.

First, we expect that there are interesting ways in which the min-conflicts heuristic could be combined with other heuristics. For example, as mentioned earlier, when a "most-conflicted" variable ordering strategy is used together with min-conflicts, the resulting program outperforms min-conflicts alone on graph 3-colorability problems. Another, interesting possibility is combining the min-conflicts heuristic with other search techniques. In this chapter, we only considered two very basic methods: hill climbing and backtracking. However, more sophisticated techniques such as best-first search are obvious candidates for investigation because the number of conflicts in an assignment can serve as a heuristic evaluation function.

Finally, we close by noting that the theoretical analysis we presented can be extended. Our work and other recent work on analyzing repair-based search methods (Musick & Russell, 1992) identifies some of the important factors that determine the relative performance of the method. In the future, we would like to extend our analysis to repair methods for other tasks, such as case-based planning methods. We conjecture that for each of the factors affecting the performance of min-conflicts, such as the expected "distance" from the initial assignment to the solution and the degree that each variable is constrained, there are analogous factors for other tasks. Furthermore, we note that our analysis only begins to explain why the method works well. In the ideal case, we would like to be able to predict when the method will work better than constructive approaches. This would be of considerable utility but would require signficant advances in our theory.

ACKNOWLEDGMENTS

Andy Philips and Philip Laird contributed significantly to the development of the min-conflicts method and its analysis. Parts of this chapter are based on previous papers that Philips and Laird co-authored. We also thank the editors for their helpful comments. The Space Telescope Science Institute is operated by the Association of Universities for Research in Astronomy for NASA.

References

Abramson, B., and M. Yung. 1989. "Divide and Conquer under Global Constraints: A Solution to the N-Queens Problem," *Journal of Parallel and Distributed Computing*, Vol. 61, pp. 649–662.

Adorf, H.M., and M.D. Johnston. 1990. "A Discrete Stochastic Neural Network Algorithm for Constraint Satisfaction Problems," *Proceedings of the International Joint Conference on Neural Networks*. IEEE Press, Piscataway, NJ, Vol. III, pp. 917–924.

Akiyama, Y., A. Yamashita, M. Kajiura, Y. Anzai, and H. Aiso. 1989. "Gaussian Machines: A Stochastic Neural Network Model for Solving Assignment Problems," *Proceedings of the ACM SIGART*

5th Annual Aerospace Applications of AI Conference, Association of Computing Machinery, New York.

Biefeld, E., and L. Cooper. 1991. "Bottleneck Identification Using Process Chronologies," *Proceedings IJCAI-91*, AAAI Press, Menlo Park, Calif.

Bitner, J., and E.M. Reingold. 1975. "Backtrack Programming Techniques," *Communications of the ACM*, Vol. 18, pp. 651–655.

Brassard, G., and P. Bratley. 1988. *Algorithmics—Theory and Practice*, Prentice Hall, Englewood Cliffs, NJ.

Brelaz, D. 1979. "New Methods to Color the Vertices of a Graph," *Communications of the ACM*, Vol. 22, pp. 251–256.

Cheeseman, P., B. Kanefsky, and W.M. Taylor. 1991. "Where the *Really* Hard Problems Are," *Proceedings IJCAI-91*, AAAI Press, Menlo Park, Calif.

Cowen, R. 1990. "Space Telescope: A Series of Setbacks," *Science News*, Vol. 37.

Dechter, R. 1986. "Learning While Searching in Constraint Satisfaction Problems," AAAI Proceedings, AAAI Press, Menlo Park, Calif., pp. 490–495.

Dechter, R., and I. Meiri. 1989. "Experimental Evaluation of Preprocessing Techniques in Constraint Satisfaction Problems," *Proceedings IJCAI-89*, AAAI Press, Menlo Park, Calif., pp. 271–277.

Dechter, R., and J. Pearl. 1988. "Network-Based Heuristics for Constraint Satisfaction Problems," *Artificial Intelligence*, Vol. 34, pp. 1–38.

Eskey, M., and M. Zweben. 1990. "Learning Search Control for Constraint-Based Scheduling," AAAI *Proceedings*, AAAI Press, Menlo Park, Calif., pp. 908–915.

Fox, M.S. 1987. *Constraint-Directed Search: A Case Study of Job-Shop Scheduling*, Morgan Kaufmann, San Francisco, Calif.

Fox, M.S., N. Sadeh, and C. Baykan. 1989. "Constrained Heuristic Search," *Proceedings IJCAI-89*, AAAI Press, Menlo Park, Calif., pp. 309–315.

Freuder, E.C. 1989. "Partial Constraint Satisfaction," *Proceedings IJCAI-89*, AAAI Press, Menlo Park, Calif.

Freuder, E.C. 1982. "A Sufficient Condition for Backtrack-Free Search," *Jounal of the ACM*, Vol. 29, pp. 24–32.

Garey, M.R., and D.S. Johnson. 1979. *Computers and Intractability: A Guide to the Theory of NP-Completeness*, W.H. Freeman and Co., San Francisco, Calif.

Ginsberg, M.L., and W.D. Harvey. 1990. "Iterative Broadening," *AAAI Proceedings*. AAAI Press, Menlo Park, Calif.

Glover, F., and M. Laguna. 1992. "Tabu Search," *Modern Heuristic Techniques for Combinatorial Problems,* Blackwell Scientific Publishers.

Hammond, K.J. 1986. "Case-Based Planning: An Integrated Theory of Planning, Learning, and Memory," Department of Computer Science, Yale University.

Haralick, R.M., and G.L. Elliot. 1980. "Increasing Tree Search Efficiency for Constraint Satisfaction Problems," *Artificial Intelligence*, Vol. 14, pp. 263–313.

Hertz, A., and D. de Werra. 1987. "Using Tabu Search Techniques for Graph Coloring," *Computing*, Vol. 39, pp. 345–351.

Hickman, A.K., and M.C. Lovett. 1991. "Partial Match and Search Control via Internal Analogy," *Proceedings of the Thirteenth Annual Conference of the Cognitive Science Society*.

Hopfield, J.J. 1982. "Neural Networks and Physical Systems with Emergent Collective Computational Abilities," *Proceedings of the National Academy of Sciences*, Vol. 79, pp. 2554–2558.

Johnson, D.S., C.H. Papadimitrou, and M. Yannakakis. 1988. "How Easy Is Local Search?" *Journal of Computer and System Sciences*, Vol. 37, pp. 79–100.

Johnson, D.S., C.R. Aragon, L.A. McGeoch, and C. Schevon. 1990. "Optimization by Simulated Annealing: An Experimental Evaluation, Part II," *Journal of Operations Research*.

Johnston, M.D. 1987. "Automated Telescope Scheduling," *Proceedings of the Symposium on Coordination of Observational Projects*. Cambridge University Press, Cambridge, England, pp. 219–226.

Johnston, M.D., and H.M. Adorf. 1992. "Scheduling with Neural Networks—The Case of the Hubble Space Telescope," *Computers and Operations Research*, Vol. 19, pp. 209–240.

Johnston, M.D., and H.M. Adorf. 1989. "Learning in Stochastic Neural Networks for Constraint Satisfaction Problems," *Proceedings of NASA Conference on Space Telerobotics*, NASA Jet Propulsion Laboratory, Pasadena, Calif., pp. 367–376.

Kale, L.V. 1990. "An Almost Perfect Heuristic for the N Nonattacking Queens Problem," *Information Processing Letters*, Vol. 34, pp. 173–178.

Kambhampati, S. 1992. "Supporting Flexible Plan Reuse," *Machine Learning Methods for Planning and Scheduling*, Morgan Kaufmann, San Francisco, Calif.

Keng, N., and D.Y.Y. Yun. 1989. "A Planning/Scheduling Methodology for the Constrained Resource Problem," *Proceedings IJCAI-89*, AAAI Press, Menlo Park, Calif.

Knoblock, C.A. 1989. "Learning Hierarchies of Abstraction Spaces," *Proceedings of the Sixth International Conference on Machine Learning*.

Kolodner, J.L., R.L. Simpson, Jr., and K. Sycara-Cyranski. 1985. "A Process Model of Case-Based Reasoning in Problem Solving," *Proceedings IJCAI-85*, AAAI Press, Menlo Park, Calif.

Kurtzman, C.R. 1988. "Time and Resource Constrained Scheduling, with Applications to Space Station Planning," Dept. of Aeronautics and Astronautics, Massachusetts Institute of Technology.

Kurtzman, C.R., and D.L. Aiken. 1989. "The Mfive Space Station Crew Activity Scheduler and Stowage Logistics Clerk," *Proceedings the AIAA Computers in Aerospace VII Conference*, American Institute of Aeronautics and Astronautics, Washington, D.C.

Langley, P. 1992. "Systematic and Nonsystematic Search Strategies," *AAAI Proceedings*, AAAI Press, Menlo Park, Calif., pp. 223–228.

Mackworth, A.K. 1977. "Consistency in Networks of Relations," *Artificial Intelligence*, Vol. 8, pp. 98–118.

Minton, S. 1988. "Empirical Results Concerning the Utility of Explanation-Based Learning," *AAAI Proceedings*, pp. 564–569.

Minton, S., J.G. Carbonell, C.A. Knoblock, D.R. Kuokka, O. Etzioni, and Y. Gil, Y. 1989. "Explanation-Based Learning: A Problem Solving Perspective," *Artificial Intelligence*, Vol. 40, pp. 63–118.

Minton, S., M. Johnston, A.B. Philips, and P. Laird. 1990. "Solving Large Scale Constraint Satisfaction and Scheduling Problems Using a Heuristic Repair Method," *AAAI Proceedings*, AAAI Press, Menlo Park, Calif.

Minton, S., M. Johnston, A.B. Philips, and P. Laird. 1992. "Minimizing Conflicts: A Heuristic Repair Method for Constraint Satisfaction and Scheduling Problems," *Artificial Intelligence*, Vol. 58, pp. 161–205.

Minton, S., A.B. Philips, M. Johnston, and P. Laird. 1991. "The Min-Conflicts Heuristic: Experimental and Theoretical Results," #FIA-91-25, Artificial Intelligence Research Branch, NASA Ames.

Morris, P. 1992. "On the Density of Solutions in Equilibrium Points for the Queens Problem," *AAAI Proceedings*, pp. 428–433, AAAI Press, Menlo Park, Calif..

Morris, P. 1991. *An Iterative Improvement Algorithm with Guaranteed Convergence,* #TR-M-91-1, Technical Note, Intellicorp, Mountain View, Calif.

Morris, P. 1990. "Solutions without Exhaustive Search: An Iterative Descent Method for Binary Constraint Satisfaction Problems," *Proceedings the AAAI-90 Workshop on Constraint-Directed Reasoning*, AAAI Press, Menlo Park, Calif.

Muscettola, N. 1992. "Scheduling by Iterative Partition of Bottleneck Conflicts," #CMU-RI-TR-92-05, Robotics Institute, Carnegie Mellon University.

Muscettola, N., S.F. Smith, G. Amiri, and D. Pathak. 1989. "Generating Space Telescope Observation Schedules," #CMU-RI-TR-89-28, Robotics Institute, Carnegie Mellon University.

Musick, R., and S. Russell. 1992. "How Long Will It Take?" *AAAI Proceedings*, pp. 466–471, AAAI Press, Menlo Park, Calif.

Pearl, J. 1984. *Heuristics*, Addison-Wesley, Reading, Mass.

Sadeh, N. 1991. "Look-Ahead Techniques for Micro-Opportunistic Job Shop Scheduling," School of Computer Science, Carnegie Mellon University.

Selman, B., H. Levesque, and D. Mitchell. 1992. "A New Method for Solving Hard Satisfiability Problems," *AAAI Proceedings*, pp. 440–446, AAAI Press, Menlo Park, Calif.

Simmons, R.G. 1988. "A Theory of Debugging Plans and Interpretations," *AAAI Proceedings*, AAAI Press, Menlo Park, Calif.

Sosic, R., and J. Gu. 1990. "A Polynomial Time Algorithm for the N-Queens Problem," *SIGART*, Vol. 1, #3.

Stone, H.S., and J.M. Stone. 1987. "Efficient Search Techniques—An Empirical Study of the N-Queens Problem," *IBM Journal of Research and Development*, Vol. 31, pp. 464–474.

Sussman, G.J. 1975. *A Computer Model of Skill Acquisition*, American Elsevier, New York.

Turner, J.S. 1988. "Almost All K-Colorable Graphs Are Easy to Color," *Journal of Algorithms*, Vol. 9, pp. 63–82.

Veloso, M.M., and J.G. Carbonell. 1992. "Towards Scaling Up Machine Learning: A Case Study with Derivation Analogy in Prodigy," *Machine Learning Methods for Planning and Scheduling,* Morgan Kaufmann, San Francisco, Calif.

Waldrop, M. 1989. "Will the Hubble Space Telescope Compute?" *Science*, Vol. 243, pp. 1437–1439.

Yaglom, A.M., and I.M. Yaglom. 1964. *Challenging Mathematical Problems with Elementary Solutions*, Holden Day, San Francisco, Calif.

Zweben, M. 1990. "A Framework for Iterative Improvement Search Algorithms Suited for Constraint Satisfaction Problems," #RIA-90-05-03-1, AI Research Branch, NASA Ames Research Center, Moffett Field, Calif.

Zweben, M., M. Deale, and R. Gargan. 1990. "Anytime Rescheduling," *Proceeedings of the Workshop on Innovative Approaches to Planning, Scheduling, and Control,* Morgan Kaufmann, San Francisco, Calif.

Zweben, M., E. Davis, B. Daun, E. Drascher, M. Deale, and M. Eskey. 1992. "Learning to Improve Constraint-Based Scheduling," *Artificial Intelligence*, Vol. 58, pp. 271–296.

Zweben, M., and M. Eskey. 1989. "Constraint Satisfaction with Delayed Evaluation," *Proceedings IJCAI-89*, AAAI Press, Menlo Park, Calif., pp. 875–880.

10

ADAPTIVE CASE-BASED CONTROL
OF SCHEDULE REVISION

Kazuo Miyashita
Katia Sycara
(Carnegie Mellon University)

10.1 INTRODUCTION

Job shop scheduling deals with allocating a limited set of resources to a number of activities (operations) associated with a set of orders (jobs). Job shop scheduling is a well-known NP-complete problem (French, 1982). Constraint-based approaches have been applied to the scheduling problem with very good results (Fox, 1983; Smith et al., 1986; Sadeh, 1991). The dominant constraints in job shop scheduling are *temporal activity precedence* and *resource capacity* constraints. The activity precedence constraints, along with a job's release date and due date, restrict the set of acceptable start times for each activity. The capacity constraints restrict the number of activities that can use a resource at any particular point in time and create conflicts among activities that are competing for the use of the same resource at overlapping time intervals. The goal of a scheduling system is to produce schedules that respect temporal relations and resource capacity constraints and optimize a set of objectives, such as minimize tardiness, minimize work in process inventory (WIP), maximize resource utilization, and minimize cycle time. In contrast to approaches (Fox, 1983; Sadeh, 1991) that utilize incremental construction of partial schedules to produce a complete schedule, our approach *incrementally revises a complete but suboptimal schedule* to produce a better schedule according to a set of optimization criteria.

In this chapter, we present a methodology, implemented in the CABINS system, for learning a control level model for selection of heuristic repair actions (tactics) based on experience. The general approach interactively learns patterns of search space features that are predictive of high quality repair actions and reuses them to guide selection in future similar situations. The procedure operates by iterative repair in the space of complete schedules. The application of a selected repair action results in adapting the search procedure by selectively biasing contention metrics in the search space. Experimental results show that the approach greatly increased schedule quality without undue degradation in efficiency compared with (1) a constraint-based scheduler that operates with a static model of focusing the search procedure and (2) a number of well regarded dispatch heuristics.

Our approach to incremental schedule repair uses an integration of Case-based Reasoning (CBR) (Kolodner, Simpson, & Sycara, 1985) and fine granularity constraint-directed scheduling mechanisms based on Sadeh & Fox (1990). CBR is used for the acquisition and flexible reuse of scheduling preferences and selection of repair actions. Constraint-based mechanisms are used to propagate the consequences of the case-based schedule modifications and apply the selected repair actions. The case base incorporates a distribution of examples that collectively capture performance trade-offs under diverse problem solving circumstances and are used to map aspects of the current problem solving state to appropriate parameterizations of the search procedure.

Integrating CBR with constraint-based scheduling stems from a variety of motivations. Because a case describes a particular specific experience, the factors that were deemed relevant to this experience can be recorded in the case. This description captures the dependencies among scheduling features, the repair context, and a suitable repair action. CBR allows capture and reuse of this dependency knowledge to dynamically adapt the search procedure and differentially bias scheduling decisions in future similar situations. On the other hand, because of the tightly coupled nature of scheduling decisions, a revision in one part of the schedule might cause constraint violations in other parts. It is, in general, impossible to predict in advance either the extent of the constraint violations resulting from a repair action or the nature of the conflicts. Therefore, constraint propagation techniques are necessary to determine the "ripple effects" that spread conflicts to other parts of the schedule as case-based repair actions are applied, and specific schedule revisions are made. Moreover, it is impossible to judge a priori the effects of a repair action on the optimization objectives. Therefore, the repair action must be applied, and the repair outcome must be evaluated in terms of the resulting effects on scheduling objectives. The evaluation criteria for judging the acceptability of the outcome of a repair action are often context dependent and reflect user judgment of trade-offs. For example, WIP and weighted tardiness are not always compatible with each other. There are situations where WIP is reduced, but weighted tardiness increases. In general, when a user wants to optimize a schedule according to multiple objectives (as is usually the case), trade-offs among the objectives must be taken into consideration. Trade-offs are context-dependent and, therefore, difficult to describe in a simple manner. CABINS induces the trade-offs from the cases that store the user's evaluation of schedule repair results. User feedback is used to incrementally acquire context dependent schedule evaluations and their justifications. These are recorded in the case base and can be reused to evaluate future repair outcomes. Hence, user preferences are reflected in the case base in two ways: as *preferences for selecting a repair tactic* depending on the features of the repair context and as *evaluation preferences* for the repair outcome that resulted from selection and application of a specific repair tactic.

10.1.1 Schedule Revision

The need for schedule revision arises in several circumstances: first, to fix a complete but flawed (i.e., containing constraint violations) schedule, as in Zweben, Deale, & Gargan (1990) and Minton et al. (1990) and, second, when the environment changes during execution, and parts of the schedule become invalidated, as in Ow, Smith, & Thiriez (1988) and Zweben et al. (1992a). Third, it can occur in response to the need to incorporate context-dependent user preferences and additional constraints that have not been represented in the scheduling model. CABINS provides a unified framework for schedule improvement and reactive schedule management in response to unforeseen events during schedule execution. In addition, the approach allows interactive capture of user context-dependent preferences and constraints and re-use of the learned knowledge to differentially select repair actions. The approach has been evaluated experimentally in the context of improving the quality of an initially conflict-free but suboptimal schedule and also in the context of execution time revision (Sycara, 1993). In this chapter, we report results in improvement of schedule quality.

It has been observed (Zweben et al., 1992b) that iterative repair is a very suitable method for complex scheduling problems that might require extensive rescheduling. Iterative repair is a general search procedure that constructs an initial suboptimal and, possibly, flawed schedule, the *seed* schedule, and then modifies it so that its quality improves. In other iterative repair approaches (e.g., Zweben et al. [1993]; Biefeld & Cooper [1991]), schedule quality is measured in terms of minimization of number of remaining conflicts. In CABINS, the repair method guarantees a conflict free schedule at the end of each repair iteration, thus exhibiting *anytime executable behavior* (Dean & Boddy, 1988). In addition, the resulting schedule is of high quality along a variety of criteria, such as minimizing disruption and minimizing WIP and weighted tardiness. In CABINS, generation of the seed schedule can be done using any scheduling method. This property enhances applicability of the approach in real manufacturing environments. In Sycara (1993), we report experimental results of repair based improvement, where the seed schedule was generated using a variety of dispatch heuristics and a constraint-based scheduling approach. The experimental results showed that (1) schedule repair always improved schedule quality irrespective of method of seed schedule generation and (2) the better the quality of the seed schedule, the better the quality of the repaired schedule.

In Ow, Smith, & Thiriez (1988), three criteria were stated for evaluating the utility of various revisions to a schedule: (1) attendance to scheduling objective: what is the quality of the revision with respect to the desired optimization criteria? (2) amount of disruption: how many changes to the original schedule are made? (3) efficiency of revision: how quick is the revision process? These criteria must be balanced and are usually inversely related. In general, either schedule quality is sacrificed to reduce response time and disruption, or when the emphasis is on schedule quality, efficiency concerns are not addressed. In Zweben et al. (1993), these trade-offs have been investigated experimentally within the context of an iterative repair methodology based on simulated annealing. Our approach minimizes disruption of the existing schedule by only modifying activities that are involved in constraint violations. More importantly, our experimental results show that our approach outperformed other approaches (a variety of dispatch heuristics and a constraint-based method) in increasing schedule quality and decreasing schedule disruption without unduly sacrificing efficiency.

CABINS can operate in different modes that exhibit various levels of autonomy. First is *user-directed* mode, where the user selects a repair tactic and evaluates the results of its application. Second is *interactive assistance* mode, where CABINS suggests repair tactics and evaluations of repair tactic application, but the user can override the suggestions and make new selections. Both the user-directed and interactive assistance modes are used for acquisition of the case base. Third is *autonomous* mode, where without user intervention, CABINS uses the case base that was acquired in the training phase for repair selection and evaluation of repair results. In the reported experiments, CABINS operated autonomously.

The overall repair process in autonomous operating mode is as follows (for a detailed presentation of the procedure, see Section 10.3):

- Suboptimal jobs in the seed schedule are identified, sorted according to degree of suboptimality, and repaired according to this sorting (e.g., if the optimization criterion is minimization of tardiness, the most tardy job is repaired first). Within a job, repair is iterative focusing on one activity at a time. The job under current repair consideration is called the *focal_job*, and the activity under current repair consideration is called the *focal_activity*.

- CBR is used to retrieve a repair action/tactic and apply it to the current schedule.

- The result of repair tactic application is evaluated in the context of the current repair model encoded in the case base. If the result is deemed a success, CBR is invoked to select a repair tactic for the next focal_activity. If the result is deemed a failure, CBR is invoked to select another tactic for the current focal_activity. The process terminates when there are no more activities that could be repaired.

In contrast to approaches that utilize a single repair heuristic (e.g., Minton [1990]) or use a statically predetermined model for selection of repair actions (e.g.,

Ow, Smith, & Thiriez [1988]), our approach utilizes a repair model that is incrementally learned and encoded in the case base. Learning allows dynamic switching of repair heuristics, depending on the repair context. In addition, as the case base is enriched with new repair experiences, the model can adapt to changing circumstances. The approach is powerful because (1) it relies on a dynamic case-based repair model for selection and evaluation of different repair actions and (2) it uses the model to tune the search procedure.

The rest of the chapter is organized as follows: Section 10.2 presents the constraint-based mechanisms incorporated in CABINS. Section 10.3 presents the case representation and the processes of case acquisition and case-based repair. Section 10.4 presents experimental evaluation of the approach, Section 10.5 presents related work, and Section 10.6 gives concluding remarks.

10.2 CONSTRAINT-BASED SCHEDULING MECHANISMS

The constraint-based scheduling component of CABINS is based on Sadeh & Fox (1990) and views each activity as a *variable*. A variable's *value* corresponds to a reservation for an activity. A reservation consists of a start time and the set of resources needed by the activity. A schedule is built by opportunistically selecting an activity to be scheduled and a reservation for that activity. Each time a new activity is scheduled, new constraints that reflect the new activity reservation are added to the initial scheduling constraints. These new constraints are then propagated (consistency checking). If an inconsistency (i.e., a constraint violation) is detected during propagation, the system backtracks. Otherwise, the scheduler moves on and looks for a new activity to schedule and selects its corresponding reservation. The process goes on until all activities have been scheduled successfully. Because scheduling is NP-hard, it is important to focus search in ways that reduce backtracking. This is accomplished by utilizing good *variable* (i.e., activity) and *value* (i.e., reservation) ordering heuristics.

A variable ordering determines which activity is going to be scheduled next, and value ordering determines which reservation should be assigned to the selected activity. The variable ordering heuristic utilized in the system is called Activity Resource Reliance (ARR) and selects the *most critical activity first*, i.e., the activity with the highest probability of being involved in a capacity constraint violation over particular time intervals.

Once the activity to be scheduled next has been selected, the value ordering heuristic determines which reservation to assign to the activity. The two value ordering heuristics relevant to this chapter are Least Constraining Value (LCV) Ordering and Greedy Value (GV) Ordering. The heuristic LCV selects the reservation that is the *least likely to prevent other activities from being scheduled*. LCV is characterized by the use of an *unbiased utility function* (see Figure 10-1) for each activity; i.e., there is no preference for a particular start time out of the activity's

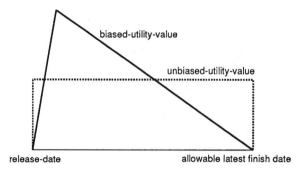

Figure 10-1:   Utility functions

available start times. The heuristic GV selects *the best reservation based on local preferences* that are expressed via a *static* piece-wise linear *biased utility function* associated with each activity (see Figure 10-1). This biases value ordering to prefer activity start times with high utility values. For scheduling problems with substitutable resources, static utilities that express differential resource preferences are used in the selection of an activity's reservation.

Experiments in Sadeh & Fox (1990) indicate that the ARR variable ordering with LCV value ordering produces suboptimal schedules with minimal backtracking; ARR variable ordering with GV value ordering with statically predetermined utility functions, henceforth referred to as constraint-based scheduling (CBS), has been shown to produce high quality schedules. In the set of experiments reported in Section 10.4, CABINS uses ARR variable ordering with LCV value ordering to produce a seed schedule that is subsequently repaired. The set of activities that get involved in constraint violations as a result of repairing a focal_activity is the *conflict set* of the focal_activity. The repair process selectively modifies the bias of the utility functions associated with the members of the current focal_activity's conflict set (see Section 10.3.4). This bias reflects the effects of learning context-dependent user preferences and evaluations of repair outcomes that have been stored in the case base. Dynamic bias modification tunes the search to the characteristics of the problem at hand. Our experimental results show that repair-based scheduling outperformed CBS with respect to schedule quality without compromising schedule efficiency. The repair-based procedure also outperformed in schedule quality a number of widely used dispatch heuristics (Section 10.4).

10.3 ITERATIVE SCHEDULE REPAIR

CABINS uses two levels of repairs: *repair strategies* and *repair tactics*. A repair strategy is associated with a particular high level description of classes of defects. Each repair strategy has a variety of repair tactics associated with it. The repair tactics are appropriate for particular specializations of the defect classes. We have identified two general types of repair strategies: *local patching* and *model modification*. Local patching is generally less costly and less disruptive to factory operation. For example, if the repair goal is to reduce order tardiness, specific local patching strategies include "reduce the slack between activities in the tardy order" and "reduce the idle-time of resources needed by activities in the tardy order." Specific model modification strategies include "change the due date constraint of the tardy order (so it is no longer considered tardy—a trivial repair)," "change the release-date constraint of orders (the tardy order or interfering orders)," "reduce the shop load," "increase number of shifts," and "increase resource capacity." Model modification strategies amount to relaxation of temporal and capacity constraints. To execute a model modification strategy, the user would have to incur extra cost (e.g., buy new equipment in order to increase resource capacity, or pay overtime to increase number of shifts). The default CABINS strategy is local patching, a computationally more challenging task because the system must improve the schedule without relaxing the already imposed constraints. If no local patching heuristic can be successfully applied to fulfill the repair goal, the repair episode is considered a failure. Our experiments were run within these more stringent assumptions.

10.3.1 Case Representation

Each case is indexed in terms of surface features relating to the flexibility of temporal and capacity constraints surrounding the focal_activity, the repair tactic used, repair effects, and the repair outcome. Each feature has a numerical *value* and a numerical *salience* (weight). Our experimental results indicate that these features are predictive of the impact of local decisions on schedule quality, and in addition, they enable transfer across problems. Figure 10-2 shows the information content of a case. The global features give an abstract characterization of potential repair flexibility for the whole schedule. High resource utilization, for example, often indicates a tight schedule without much repair flexibility. High standard deviation of resource utilization indicates the presence of highly contended-for resources, which in turn indicates low repair flexibility.

The repair history records the sequence of applications of successive repair actions, the effects, the repair outcome, and its evaluation as well as failure explanations. Repair effects describe the impact of the application of a repair action on scheduling objectives (e.g., weighted tardiness, WIP). Typically, these effects reflect trade-offs among different objectives. A repair outcome is the evaluation assigned to the set of effects of a repair action and takes values in the set {"acceptable," "unacceptable"}. This judgment is made by the user in the training phase and gets recorded in the case base to guide future evaluations (Section 10.3.3). An outcome is "acceptable" if the user accepts the trade-offs involved in the set of effects for the current application of a repair action. Otherwise, the outcome is

CASE

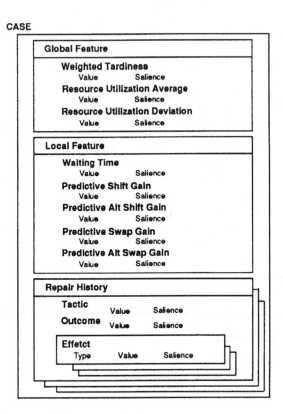

Figure 10-2:   Case representation

"unacceptable." The *repair time horizon* is an interval that temporally spans the focal_activity and is used to place temporal bounds on the repair analysis. Because of the tight coupling among precedence and capacity constraints in job shop scheduling problems, the repair time horizon must be selected judiciously to avoid causing extended ripple effects of constraint violations. Let ACT_n^l be the current focal_activity (the nth activity of order l). The repair time horizon of ACT_n^l is the time interval between the end of activity ACT_{n-1}^l (the activity that precedes the focal_activity in the same order) and the end-time of the focal_activity (see Figure 10-3).

Associated with the repair time horizon are local features that are predictive of the effectiveness of applying a particular repair tactic. These features (Figure 10-2) are in the same spirit as those utilized in Ow, Smith, & Thiriez (1988). The *waiting time* of a focal_activity ACT_n^l is the time interval between the end of activity ACT_{n-1}^l (the activity that precedes the focal_activity in the same order) and the start-time of the focal_activity (see Figure 10-3). *Predictive shift gain* predicts how much overall gain will be achieved by moving the current focal_activity earlier on

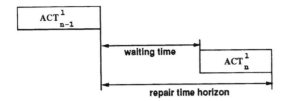

Figure 10-3:   Repair time horizon of focal_activity ACT_n^l

its time horizon. In particular, it predicts the likely reduction of the focal_activity's waiting time when moved to the left on the same resource within the repair time horizon. *Predictive alt shift gain* predicts the likely reduction of the focal_activity's waiting time when moved to the left on a substitutable resource within the repair time horizon. *Predictive swap gain* predicts the amount of likely difference between the reduction of the focal_activity's waiting time and the increase of a swapped activity's waiting time when the focal_activity is swapped within the repair time horizon on the focal_activity's resource. *Predictive alt swap gain* predicts the corresponding likely difference when the focal_activity is swapped within the repair time horizon on the focal_activity's substitutable resources.

When invoked, the case-based reasoner in CABINS retrieves from the case base the case that is most similar to the current problem. The similarity between the ith case and the current problem is calculated as follows:

$$Similarity(i) = \frac{\sum_{j=1}^{N} \left((1.0 + \alpha \times Salience_j^i) \times \exp\left(\left| \frac{ProblemFeature_j - CaseFeature_j^i}{Deviation_j} \right| \right) \right)}{\sum_{j=1}^{N} (1.0 + \alpha \times Salience_j^i)}$$

where $ProblemFeature_j$ is a value of the jth feature in the current problem, $CaseFeature_j^i$ is a value of the jth feature in the ith case, $Salience_j^i$ is the weight of jth feature in the ith case, and $Deviation_j$ is the standard deviation of the jth feature value in the case-base. α is a parameter to control the feature matching. In Cain, Pazzani, & Silverstein (1991), it was demonstrated that such a metric performed well in predicting the outcome in a CBR system with a weak domain theory of foreign trade negotiations. In scheduling, as in foreign trade negotiations, the lack of a strong domain theory implies lack of an a priori known set of features (relevant features) or feature values whose presence can predict the acceptability of a repair outcome. The user's judgment as to feature salience, recorded in the case base, can be viewed as the domain theory. In domains with a strong theory, the number of matches of the current case to previous cases can be used to determine case similarity. CABINS's similarity metric balances concerns of salience and number of feature matches. For example, it trades off retrieval of cases with a large number of matching features with low salience for retrieval of cases with a small number of matches of features with high salience.

10.3.2 Case Acquisition

In CABINS, the session starts with an empty case-base. A set of training cases is presented to the user who interacts with CABINS to repair schedules. After determination of a current focal_activity, the user selects a repair tactic to be applied.

The tactics currently available in CABINS are

- left_shift: Try to move the focal_activity on the same resource as much to the left on the timeline as possible within the repair time horizon to minimize the amount of capacity overallocation created by the move.
- left_shift_into_alt: Try to move the focal_activity on a substitutable resource as much to the left on the timeline as possible within the repair time horizon to minimize the amount of capacity overallocation created by the move.
- swap: Swap the focal_activity with the activity on the same resource within the repair time horizon that causes the least amount of precedence constraint violations.
- swap_into_alt: Swap the focal_activity with the activity on a substitutable resource within the repair time horizon that causes the least amount of precedence constraint violations.

After the user selects a tactic, it is applied to the current schedule (see Section 10.3.4), and the repair effects are calculated and shown to the user who is asked to evaluate the outcome of the repair. For example, repair of the current focal_activity might decrease WIP by 200 units and decrease weighted tardiness of the focal_order by 180 units and at the same time increase weighted tardiness of another order by 130 units and increase WIP by 300 units. If the user evaluates the repair outcome as "acceptable," CABINS proceeds to repair another focal_activity, and the process is repeated. If the user evaluates the repair outcome as "unacceptable," s/he is asked to supply an explanation in terms of rating the salience/importance of each of the effects. The repair is undone, and the user is asked to select another repair tactic for the same focal_activity. The process continues until an acceptable outcome for the current focal_activity is reached, or failure is declared. Failure is declared when there are no more tactics to be applied to repair the current focal_activity. The sequence of applications of successive repair actions, the effects, the repair outcome, and the user's explanation for failed application of a repair tactic are recorded in the repair history of the case. In this way, a number of cases are accumulated in the case base. Currently, CABINS has acquired in the training phase more than 4,000 cases.

10.3.3 Case-Based Schedule Repair

Once the case base has been acquired, CABINS can operate autonomously without any further user interaction. At different stages of the autonomous repair process, CABINS uses different sets of the case features as indices for case retrieval. The overall revision process in CABINS has the following steps:

1. CABINS identifies the orders that are suboptimal in the initial schedule, sorts them according to degree of suboptimality, and repairs them according to this sorting. Activities in a focal_order are repaired in a forward fashion, starting with the earliest activity of that order that has slack above a heuristically determined threshold. This mechanism focuses attention on activities that have enough slack so they can be moved, thus (1) avoiding unnecessary computations and (2) limiting the amount of ripple effects that could be caused by moving activities that are too tightly scheduled and whose move would cause many constraint violations.

2. Each focal_activity is repaired through CBR. The CBR repair process is iterative and has been adapted from our earlier work on negotiation (Sycara, 1990). The set of global and local case features are used as indices to retrieve past repair episodes. Each invocation of CBR suggests a (not necessarily different) repair tactic to be applied. The process of applying a repair tactic is described in Section 10.3.4.

3. To evaluate the repair result after repair tactic application, the conjunction of effect type, effect value, and effect salience are used as new indices. CBR is invoked and returns an outcome value in the set: {acceptable, unacceptable}. If the returned outcome is "unacceptable," CABINS performs another CBR invocation, using as indices the conjunction of the current outcome (unacceptable), the failed heuristic, and the case global and local features to find another possibly applicable repair heuristic. Invoking CBR with these indices retrieves cases that have failed in the past in a similar manner as the current repair. This use of CBR in the space of failures is a domain independent method of failure recovery (Sycara, 1987), and allows the problem solver to access past solutions to the failure. If the result is "acceptable," CABINS proceeds to repair another activity.

10.3.4 Application of a Selected Repair Tactic

Repair of the current focal_activity is performed by applying the repair tactic that is selected by CBR within the repair time horizon of the focal_activity.

The process of applying a repair tactic has the following steps:

1. Determine the *predictive* start time of the focal_activity. The predictive start time of an activity is an estimated temporary start time that is used to calcu-

late the expected ripple effects of the repair. The ripple effects of a repair are a set consisting of all the activities that might need to be re-scheduled because of constraint violations arising from the repair of the focal_activity. Note that this predictive start time might *not* be exactly the same as the start time that will result from execution of the repair (step 5 below). The calculation of the predictive start time is done as follows:

o If left_shift (or left_shift_into_alt) is the tactic being applied, then the predictive start time is the start time that minimizes capacity overallocation as a result of moving the focal_activity on the same (or substitutable) resource within the focal_activity's repair time horizon.

o If swap (or swap_into_alt) is the tactic being applied, then the predictive start time is the start time that causes the least amount of precedence constraint violations on the same (or substitutable) resource within the focal_ activity's repair time horizon.

2. Project the effects of moving the focal_activity to the predictive start time and designated resource. This is done by performing constraint propagation to identify constraint violations.

3. Adjust the reservations of all the activities that are involved in constraint violations (the focal_activity's conflict set, Section 10.2) by simple right-shifting or left-shifting so that all conflicts are resolved.

4. Change the bias of the start time utility functions of all the members of the conflict set in favor of start times calculated in step 3. If the tactic being applied involves a substitutable resource, change the resource utility function so that the substitutable resource has utility higher than the resource on which the focal_activity is currently scheduled. Changing the utility functions biases selection of start times by the value ordering heuristic (Section 10.2) in favor of those with higher utility values, thus reflecting the preferences encoded in the case base.

5. Unschedule the focal_activity and all members of its conflict set and reschedule them using the opportunistic constraint-directed scheduler with ARR variable ordering, GV value ordering, and the utility functions defined in step 4.

The above process results in a conflict free revised schedule. The effects of the revision are calculated. CBR is invoked with the effects as the relevant indices to evaluate the repair outcome.

10.4 EVALUATION OF THE APPROACH

We conducted a set of experiments to test the following hypotheses: (1) our CBR-based incremental modification and re-use methodology could be effective in capturing user preferences and (2) the methodology would improve schedule quality along a variety of optimization objectives without incurring unduly high performance degradation. To investigate our experimental hypotheses, we compared CABINS with a set of well regarded dispatch heuristics, widely used in practical job shop scheduling problems. The dispatch rules selected for the comparison are the Earliest Due Date (EDD) rule, the Weighted Shortest Processing Time (WSPT) rule, and the WSPT with job time urgency factor (R & M) rule. These rules have been reported to be particularly good at reducing tardiness under different scheduling conditions (Morton & Rachamadugu, 1984). We also evaluated the effects of selectively biasing value ordering in constraint based search. We compared the performance of CABINS against CBS (Section 10.2) with static biased start time utility functions. These results show directly the improvement in schedule quality because of learning appropriate adaptations to the value ordering heuristic.

To cover different scheduling conditions, a set of 60 problems was randomly generated. Each problem has 5 resources and 10 jobs of 5 operations each. Each job has a process routing specifying a sequence where each job must visit bottleneck resources after a fixed number of activities to increase resource contention and make the problem tighter. We also varied job due dates and release dates as well as the number of bottleneck resources (1 and 2). Six groups of 10 problems each were randomly generated by considering 3 different values of the range parameter (static, moderate, dynamic) and 2 values of the bottleneck configuration (1 and 2 bottleneck problems). The slack was adjusted as a function of the range and bottleneck parameters to keep demand for bottleneck resources close to 100% over the major part of each problem. Durations for activities in each job were also randomly generated. These problems are variations of the problems originally reported in Sadeh (1991). Our problem sets are different in two respects: (1) we allow substitutable resources for non-bottleneck resources and (2) the due dates of jobs in our problems are tighter by 20%.

To make an accurate determination of CABINS' capabilities, we applied a twofold cross-validation method. Each problem set in each class was divided in half. One half was solved using constraint-based scheduling as the seed method (Section 10.2) and then repaired heuristically to gather cases. These cases were used to iteratively repair the other half of the problem set. We repeated the above process interchanging the sample set and the test set. Our results are the average of the two sets of results using case-based repair. The results in Figures 10-4, 10-5, and 10-6 show that CABINS outperformed all other methods across both 1 and 2 bottleneck problems in all experiments.

10.5 RELATED WORK

Our approach is rooted is concepts and mechanisms of a long line of research in constraint-directed scheduling (Fox, 1983; Smith et al., 1986; Sadeh, 1991). In

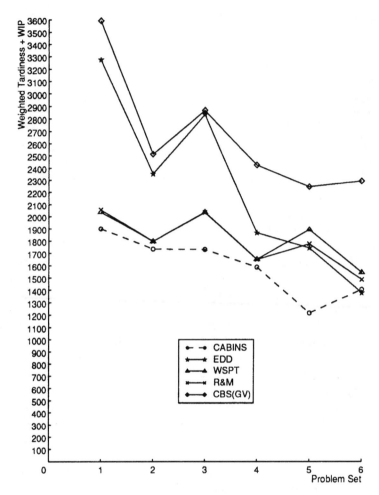

Figure 10-4:   Results on weighted tardiness and WIP

that work, schedules are generated by incrementally constructing and merging partial schedules. That work has extensively investigated various properties and aspects of this scheduling methodology and has proposed sophisticated procedures and techniques for constraint-directed scheduling. Although this research tradition has come to view scheduling as an opportunistic repair process, it has operated under static design assumptions (e.g., deterministic application of variable and value ordering heuristics in Sadeh [1991] or statically determined control level model for application of repair actions [Ow, Smith, & Thiriez, 1988]). Our approach advances the state of the art by learning to dynamically adapt the focus-

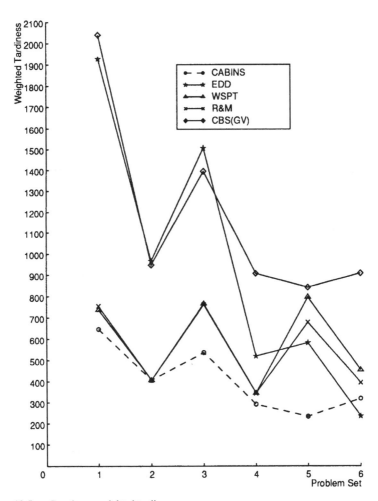

Figure 10-5: Results on weighted tardiness

ing mechanism of the search procedure and by adapting the repair model according to current problem solving circumstances and user preferences and trade-offs.

Our approach generates schedules by repair based scheduling in the space of complete schedules. In this respect, it is similar to Zweben, Deale, & Gargan (1990); Minton et al. (1990); Biefeld & Cooper (1991); and Zweben (1993). In Zweben, Deale, & Gargan (1990) and Zweben (1993), simulated annealing has been used to perform iterative repair. Knowledge in the form of constraint types and evaluation criteria has been added to the basic simulated annealing framework

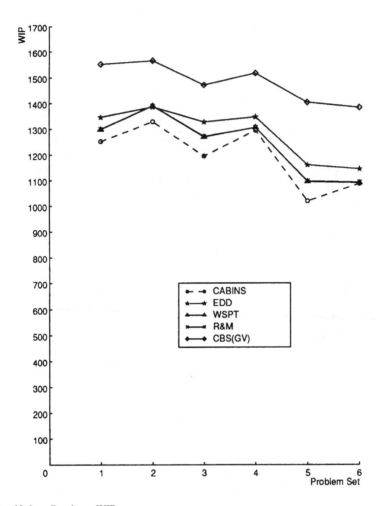

Figure 10-6:   Results on WIP

and has been shown to improve convergence speed (Zweben, 1993). (Zweben, 1992a) has studied the trade-off of minimizing perturbations vs. speed of convergence to a conflict free schedule and vs. schedule quality measured in terms of number of violated resource constraints. In Minton (1990), the min-conflict heuristic, a repair heuristic that chooses the repair that minimizes the number of conflicts that result from a one-step lookahead, has been investigated. Although the heuristic has been shown to be powerful for solving the N-queens problem, it has been shown inadequate for some types of job shop scheduling problems (Muscettola, 1993). In Biefeld & Cooper (1991), schedule modifications are procedurally encoded. Small snapshots of the scheduling process, called chronologies, are used to focus the search by using information gained incrementally during the scheduling process to locate, classify, and resolve bottlenecks.

In Zweben (1992), plausible explanation based learning (PEBL) has been applied to learn search control rules to increase search efficiency in scheduling tasks for NASA Space Shuttle payload and ground processing. PEBL enables a system to generalize a target concept (e.g., chronic resource contention) over a distribution of examples. The cost function is to minimize the number of remaining conflicts in the schedule. CABINS repair heuristics are similar in spirit to the fitness and temporal dependents utilized in (Zweben et al., 1992b).

The repair-based scheduling methods considered here are related to the repair-based methods that have previously been used in AI planning systems. (e.g., Simmons [1988], Kambhampati [1990], and Hammond [1987]).

10.6 CONCLUDING REMARKS

In this chapter, we have advocated an incremental modification and reuse approach for schedule improvement. The approach utilizes CBR-based mechanisms to record user preferences, repair tactics and explanations, and constraint-based scheduling for application of the selected repair tactics. The knowledge recorded in the case base is used to dynamically adapt the search procedure during constraint based scheduling. Initial experimental results show that the approach (1) outperformed a set of well regarded dispatch heuristics, (2) outperformed constraint-based scheduling with static search procedure, and (3) was effective in capturing and utilizing user scheduling preferences that were not present in the scheduling model.

References

Biefeld, E., and L. Cooper. 1991. Bottleneck Identification Using Process Chronologies. *Proceedings of the Twelveth International Joint Conference on Artificial Intelligence (IJCAI-91)*, AAAI Press, Menlo Park, Calif., pp. 218–224.

Cain, T., M. Pazzani, and G. Silverstein. 1991. Using Domain Knowledge to Influence Similarity Judgments. *Proceedings of the 1991 Case-Based Reasoning Workshop*, pp. 191–199.

Dean, T., and M. Boddy. 1988. An Analysis of Time Dependent Planning. In *Proceedings of the Sixth National Conference on Artificial Intelligence*, AAAI Press, Menlo Park, Calif., pp. 49–54.

Fox, M. 1983. Constraint-Directed Search: A Case Study in Job Shop Scheduling. Ph.D. Thesis, Department of Computer Science, Carnegie Mellon University.

French, S. 1982. *Sequencing and Scheduling: An Introduction to the Mathematics of the Job-Shop*. Ellis Horwood, New York.

Hammond, K. 1987. Explaining and Repairing Plans That Fail. *Proceedings of the Tenth International Joint Conference on Artificial Intelligence*, AAAI Press, Menlo Park, Calif., pp. 109–114.

Kambhampati, S. 1990. A Theory of Plan Modification. In *Proceedings of the Eighth National Conference on Artificial Intelligence*, AAAI Press, Menlo Park, Calif.

Kolodner, J., R. Simpson, and K. Sycara. 1985. A Process of Case-Based Reasoning in Problem Solving. *Proceedings of the Ninth International Joint Conference on Artificial Intelligence*, AAAI Press, Menlo Park, Calif., pp. 284–290.

Minton, S., M. Johnson, A. Philips, and P. Laird. 1990. Solving Large-Scale Constraint Satisfaction and Scheduling Problems Using a Heuristic Repair Method. *Proceedings of the Eighth National Conference on Artificial Intelligence*, AAAI Press, Menlo Park, Calif., pp. 17–24.

Morton, T.E., R.M. Rachamadugu, and A. Vepsaleinen. 1984. Accurate Myopic Heuristics for Tardiness Scheduling. Technical Report 36083-84, Graduate School of Industrial Automation, Carnegie Mellon University.

Muscettola, N. 1993. Scheduling by Iterative Partition of Bottleneck Conflicts. *Proceedings of the Ninth Conference on AI Applications*, IEEE Computer Press, Los Alamitos, Calif., pp. 49–55.

Ow, P.S., S.F. Smith, and A. Thiriez. 1988. Reactive Plan Revision. *Proceedings of the Seventh National Conference on Artificial Intelligence*, AAAI Press, Menlo Park, Calif., pp. 77–82.

Sadeh, N. 1991. Look-Ahead Techniques for Micro-Opportunistic Job Shop Scheduling. Ph.D. Thesis, School of Computer Science, Carnegie Mellon University.

Sadeh, N., and M.S. Fox. 1990. Variable and Value Ordering Heuristics for Activity-Based Job-Shop. *Proceedings of the Fourth International Conference on Expert Systems in Production and Operations Management*, Institute of Information Management, Technology, and Policy, University of South Carolina., pp. 134–144.

Simmons, R. 1988. A Theory of Debugging Plans and Interpretations. In *Proceedings of the Seventh National Conference on Artificial Intelligence*, pp. 94–99. AAAI Press, Menlo Park, Calif.

Smith, S.F., P.S. Ow, C. LePape, B. McLaren, and N. Muscettola. 1986. Integrating Multiple Scheduling Perspectives to Generate Detailed Production Plans. *Proceedings of SME Conference on AI in Manufacturing*. Society of Manufacturing Engineers, New York.

Sycara, K. 1987. Resolving Adversarial Conflicts: An Approach Integrating Case-Based and Analytic Methods. Ph.D. Thesis, School of Information and Computer Science, Georgia Institute of Technology.

Sycara, K. 1990. Negotiation Planning: An AI Approach. *European Journal of Operational Research* 46:216–234.

Sycara, K., and K. Miyashita. 1993. Schedule Repair through Case-based Reasoning. Technical Report, The Robotics Institute, Carnegie Mellon University.

Zweben, M., M. Deale, and M. Gargan. 1990. Anytime Rescheduling. *Proceedings of the DARPA Workshop on Innovative Approaches to Planning, Scheduling, and Control*, Morgan Kaufmann, San Francisco, Calif., pp. 251–259.

Zweben, M., E. Davis, B. Daun, and M. Deale. 1992a. Rescheduling with Iterative Repair. *Proceedings of AAAI-92 Workshop on Production Planning, Scheduling, and Control*, AAAI Press, Menlo Park, Calif.

Zweben, M., E. Davis, D. Brian, E. Drascher, M. Deale, and M. Eskey. 1992b. Learning to Improve Constraint-based Scheduling. *Artificial Intelligence* 58(1–3):271–296.

Zweben, M., E. Davis, B. Daun, and M. Deale. 1993. Iterative Repair for Scheduling and Rescheduling. *IEEE Transactions on System, Man, and Cybernetics*, Vol. 23, No. 8, pp. 1588–1596.

11

THE DISTRIBUTED
ASYNCHRONOUS SCHEDULER

Peter Burke
Patrick Prosser
(University of Strathclyde)

11.1 INTRODUCTION

Scheduling can be described as the problem of deciding *What* happens *Where* and *When* (Parunak, 1987). This is in itself a difficult problem, but it is made even more so when it takes place in an open, stochastic world. Rarely do things go as expected. The set of things to do *(What)* is generally dynamic. We might be asked to do additional tasks that we did not anticipate, and sometimes we are allowed to omit certain tasks. The resources available to perform tasks *(Where)* are also subject to change. Resources can become unavailable, and additional resources can be provided. How long a task takes to perform and when it can be performed *(When)* are also subject to variations. A task can take more time than anticipated or less time than anticipated, and tasks can arrive early or late. World dynamics offer up both opportunities and conflicts.

There is a problem in defining the goals of a scheduling system. The clearest statement might be, produce a schedule that maximizes this enterprise's profit. Although this might be considered a clear goal, it can be difficult to accurately define. Any definition of this goal will itself be subject to change, induced by market forces. There can be instances when it is prudent to sacrifice short term profit for long term profit. The definition of this goal can change at the same pace as market changes unfold but can change momentarily on an order by order basis. Even if the scheduling goal could accurately be defined, the stochastic elements described above might drive the system into a chaotic state. Therefore, it might be good enough to produce a scheduling system that is both "satisficing" (rather than optimizing) and "reactive" (rather than purely predictive). Such a system should be able to maintain a satisfactory schedule in an open, dynamic world.

Generally, any non-trivial enterprise is distributed. Distribution can be geographical, logical, temporal, or spatial. In a manufacturing domain, it is not uncommon for production to be distributed geographically, sometimes on a continental scale (the automobile industry is a prime example). An enterprise can logically be distributed, reflecting its organizational structure. Organizational structuring can be a necessity in order to decompose the enterprise's problems into manageable chunks and to better exploit available expertise. Whenever distribution takes place, communication must follow as a necessity.

The scheduling system can be distributed. This distribution can reflect the structure of the enterprise to be scheduled or can be a design decision justified by the bounded rationality of the agents within the system (Simon, 1962). The problem can be considered to be too difficult to address within a centralized architecture but easier to address when decomposed and distributed. The costs of coordination and communication within a distributed scheduling system might then be considered economical.

In the distributed asynchronous scheduler (DAS) (Burke and Prosser, 1990, 1991), the scheduling problem is decomposed and distributed across a hierarchy of intelligent agents. DAS is organized as a three tier hierarchy. Attached to each node in the hierarchy is an intelligent autonomous agent. The position of an agent within this hierarchy defines its role and communication paths. The agent attached to the top, "strategic" level of the hierarchy is responsible for the introduction of work into the system *(What)* and the resolution of conflicts between subordinate agents. The strategic agent (S-agent) is analogous to the highest level of authority. Agents attached to the middle, "tactical" level are responsible for the delegation of tasks to individual resources *(Where)*. A tactical agent (T-agent) is analogous to a group controller within a factory, responsible for a work area made up of a number of similar resources. Agents attached to the lowest, "operational" level are responsible for the execution of tasks on individual resources *(When)*. An operational agent (O-agent) is akin to a shift leader or foreman responsible for an individual machine or resource. A traversal down the hierarchy corresponds to an increase in specialization and a decrease in problem solving discretion.

The architecture of DAS can be considered "loosely coupled" in that it is expected that for each agent within the system, the ratio of communication to processing is low (Lesser and Corkill, 1981). Paradoxically, the scheduling problem is "tightly coupled"; that is, state changes in one task immediately affect the state of another task (Fox, 1981a). In order for the architecture to function effectively, agents must have a reactive capability. There are two reasons for this: (1) the problem is tightly coupled and (2) agents must operate on incomplete and sometimes inconsistent data. Given that the agents within the architecture exhibit this reactive property, the system can be applied to an open world that is both dynamic and stochastic. The external world can be treated as yet another agent within the architecture but one with a special property. Its decisions are non-negotiable.

11.2 AN ARCHITECTURAL OVERVIEW OF DAS

When a job is introduced to the system, the S-agent is notified, and the S-agent then delegates each operation in the process plan of the job to individual T-agents. Each T-agent then delegates its operation to a resource. This action of delegation generates a message sent to the relevant O-agent. The O-agent then attempts to introduce this new operation into its local schedule. If it succeeds, it writes out a start time for that operation, initiating constraint propagation through the job's process plan with resultant messages sent to the agents (be they tactical, operational, or strategic) holding the remaining operations in that plan. These messages are prioritized, such that problem solving effort can be focussed on individual decisions made by O-agents (and this is described later on in detail). At this point, there is no decision ordering through the process plan, and decisions can be made asynchronously. If an O-agent cannot produce a consistent schedule, it delivers a conflict set (a set of operations that the O-agent believes cannot be scheduled consistently on its resource) to its superior T-agent. The superior T-agent then informs its T-assistant[1] of this conflict set. The T-agent then asks its T-assistant for advice, that is, what load balancing options remain. The T-agent then load balances, retracting operations from resources and delegating operations to resources. If there are no load balancing options available,[2] then the T-agent concludes that its problem is over-constrained, and it delivers a conflict set to the superior S-agent, where that conflict set involves operations on a number of resources. The S-agent will analyze conflict sets received from its subordinate T-agents and decide upon a course of action, a combination of *inter-agent* backtracking and "constraint relaxation" (again, described in detail further on).

The above events will have generated new knowledge about the problem at the operational, tactical, and strategic levels. As DAS is forced to backtrack, at the operational, tactical, or strategic levels, it is presented with information in the form of deadends. DAS views these situations as opportunities to learn about the problem and records this knowledge. To support this approach, each agent (be it operational, tactical, or strategic) must have a reactive capability, the capability to do dependency directed backtracking, and some degree of learning. The learning capa-

---

[1] The T-assistant is described later on but is best thought of as a T-agent's personal assistant and plays a clerical role. The T-assistant keeps a record of the decisions that have been made by its "master" (the T-agent) and gives the T-agent advice. The T-agent then makes decisions based on this advice.

[2] It is the T-assistant's responsibility to detect that there are no options remaining.

bility allows the system to retain knowledge of the search space. The representations used for resources and operations allow the system to represent all opportunities remaining within the schedule. Just as change can be imposed on one agent by another, change can also be imposed on the system from the outside world. DAS does not differentiate between internally induced change and externally induced change, nor does it differentiate between predictive and reactive scheduling. Reaction is treated as a continuation of search.

11.3 STRUCTURAL REPRESENTATION

DAS employs frame-based knowledge representation techniques supported by KEE, the software development environment within which DAS was constructed. The frame-based representation facility provided by KEE also supports procedural attachment and object oriented programming. Both these features have been used extensively to deal with the representational issues present in DAS. This section describes the major objects represented within DAS, namely, resources, operations, and plans.

11.3.1 Resources

The resources that DAS is primarily concerned with are shop floor resources and machine centers in particular. Resources are modelled at two levels of abstraction: an individual resource level and an aggregate resource level. Each individual resource has an associated frame that contains slots indicating scheduling preferences, facilitates a dual representation for agents, and gives details of the local scheduling problem. The scheduling preference information concerns choices, such as how to select the next operation to schedule and how to select a start time for an operation. For example, on a particular machine, it might be best to schedule operations using a JIT strategy, whereas on others, it might be better to adopt an earliest dispatch (ED) strategy.

Each agent in the system exists as a unique software process operating asynchronously with respect to other agents in the system. O-agents are attached to specific resources via the resource's *process* slot. The value in slot *process* of a particular resource corresponds directly to the software process being used to implement its associated O-agent. O-agents have their own internal view of the world held within the *internal.representation* slot of a resource. The *message.buffer* slot of a resource is crucial to the maintenance of this internal representation. It is through messages sent to this buffer that an agent can update its internal representation. The *each.tick* slot on a resource allows the granularity of time considered at a resource to be varied in accordance with the typical duration of the operations processed there. For example, it might not be appropriate to schedule an operation

UNIT: saw.20.foot	
MEMBER OF: operational.resources	
SLOT NAME	VALUE
CONSTRAINT:	single.server
EACH.TICK:	180
INTERNAL.REPRESENTATION:	#<*resource* 374055175>
MESSAGE.BUFFER:	unknown
PROCESS:	#<process SAW.20.FOOT 15442365>
QUANTUM:	2000
SCHEDULED.OPS:	L1258.saw, L2541.saw, L2441.saw
SELECT.OP:	most.constrained
SELECT.VALUE:	jit
REST:	5
UNSCHEDULED.OPS:	L8412.saw

Figure 11-1:   An operational resource

of twenty four hours duration to an accuracy of one second. The value held in the *each.tick* slot identifies the smallest unit of time considered to be significant at a resource. An O-agent can therefore reduce the size of an operation's domain by a factor of *each.tick*, thus reducing the scale of the scheduling problem at an operational resource.

Each specific resource has both a *scheduled.ops* slot and an *unscheduled.ops* slot. The *scheduled.ops* slot contains a list of operations that have been given start times on that resource. The *unscheduled.ops* slot contains a list of operations that have been allocated to this resource but as yet have not been given start times. Together, the *scheduled.ops* and *unscheduled.ops* slots partially define the scheduling problem at a resource. The frame representing an operational resource also contains non-negotiable technological constraints. These include physical dimension constraints, weight constraints, and the range of processes that can be performed on the resource. Machine setup times required between different types of work or different processes are also held here. Figure 11-1 shows the more relevant slots present in a frame that is used to represent operational resources.

An aggregate resource is a collection of similar resources. For example, if there are three annealing furnaces in the factory, there will be a single frame representing this aggregation. The information held here is a combination of scheduling preferences, an internal representation of the agent's problem, and a partial definition of the local schedule. Each aggregate resource has an associated temporal horizon, defined in slot *look.a.head*, and a preferred method for selecting the next operation to delegate, held in the *select.strategy* slot.

T-agents are attached to aggregate resources via the *process* slot of the appropriate aggregate resource. In exactly the same way as for operational resources, the

UNIT: saws	
MEMBER OF: aggregate.resources	
SLOT NAME	VALUE
INTERNAL.REPRESENTATION:	#<*tactical-resource* 25633113
LOOK.AHEAD:	30
MESSAGE.BUFFER:	(saw.wessex complete),(add L1412.saw)
OP.STORE:	L1412.saw, L8331.saw
PROCESS:	#<process saws 15442505>
REST:	10
SELECT.STRATEGY:	latest

Figure 11-2:   An aggregate resource

value held in slot *process* of an aggregate resource corresponds directly to the software process being used to implement its associated T-agent. T-agents also have their own internal view of the world held within the *internal.representation* slot of an aggregate resource. The *message.buffer* slot of an aggregate resource is again essential to the maintenance of this internal representation.

The scheduling problem at an aggregate resource is partially defined by the list of operations held in the *op.store* slot. For any particular aggregate resource, this slot holds a list of all the operations that must be processed by one of its subordinate resources but that have not yet been delegated to a specific resource. Figure 11-2 shows the more relevant slots present in a frame used to represent aggregate resources.

The *strategic.unit* is the root of the hierarchy and is concerned with the scheduling problem as a whole. The scheduling problem at the strategic level deals with process plans rather than operations. The *strategic.unit* has a *plan.store* slot containing a list of plans that have not yet been delegated to the tactical level and a *started.plans* slot containing a list of plans that have either partially or wholly been delegated to the tactical level. (See Figure 11.3.) The scheduling preference information held at the *strategic.unit* concerns the selection strategy used when deciding which plan to delegate to the tactical level next. The default value *first* is shown; that is, the S-agent selects the first process plan.

Supporting or secondary resources, with the exception of labor, are not provided for in the current version. To include such a feature requires an extension to, rather than a re-design of, DAS. Within the demonstrator site, secondary resources such as loading cranes and transportation pallets do exist. However, because they do not represent a limiting resource in terms of scheduling, it was considered reasonable to treat them as infinite resources. For all the resources that are to be scheduled, labor is assumed to be a necessary secondary resource.

UNIT: strategic.unit MEMBER OF: entities	
SLOT NAME	VALUE
INTERNAL.REPRESENTATION:	#<*strategic.level* 40045041>
MESSAGE.BUFFER:	unknown
PLAN.STORE:	P1419, P1347
PROCESS:	#<process strategic.unit 15442567>
REST:	20
SELECT.STRATEGY:	first
STARTED.PLANS:	P1258, P2541, P2411, P1412, P8331

Figure 11-3:   The strategic unit

11.3.2 Operations

An operation represents a particular process that must be performed during the manufacturing of a specific work item. Each operation is represented by a frame that has slots containing technological and temporal constraints. The major temporal constraints imposed on an operation are its duration, its release date, and due date of the job it represents. The duration of an operation can vary according to whichever specific resource it is assigned to. Therefore, this variation in temporal constraints must also be represented.

The slot *possible.resources* contains a list of resources capable of performing the operation and effectively represents the technological constraints acting on the operation. Each entry in the list is a pair of the form (*Resource Duration*), the second element being the anticipated duration of the operation on that particular resource.

The slots *start.time* and *resource* on an operation implicitly define the current schedule. If every operation in the system has been allocated to a resource and has been given a start time, the schedule is complete. The *legal.starts* slot of an operation contains an ordered list of intervals indicating when it is possible to schedule this operation and remain consistent with all intra-plan scheduling decisions. The value held in the *legal.starts* slot is maintained by a constraint propagation mechanism discussed in the following section.

The *priority* of an operation is taken as a measure of difficulty associated with the scheduling of the operation. This should not be confused with a user defined metric such as customer importance. The value held in this slot is maintained by the appropriate T-agent and O-agent and is discussed further in later sections. Figure 11-4 shows the more important slots present in a frame used to represent an operation.

UNIT: L2541	
MEMBER OF: operations	
SLOT NAME	VALUE
AFTER:	L2541.packing
BEFORE:	L2541.stretch
CONFLICT.HISTORY:	unknown
DUE.DATE:	unknown
DURATION:	3960 ˙
END.GUESS:	2832520319
EXTERNAL.LEGAL.STARTS:	((2832516360 2832516360))
LEGAL.STARTS:	((L2541.packing start) (0 2832516360)),
	((L2541.stretch start) (2832516360 ∞)),
	((L2541.anneal start) (2832516360 ∞)),
	((L2541.packing due) (0 2956996798)),
	((L2541.anneal guess) (2832514737 ∞))
NOT.DURING:	unknown
OP.TYPE:	simple
PLAN:	P2541
POSSIBLE.RESOURCES:	(saw.20.foot 3960),
	(saw.ty.sa.man.1 2700),
	(saw.wessex 3600)
PRIORITY:	0
PROCESS:	saws
RESOURCE:	saw.20.foot
SELECT.VALUE:	jit
START.TIME:	2832516360
TYPE:	work

Figure 11-4: An operation

Within DAS, resources are assumed to be "up" (that is, the resource can be used when it is free). Three situations that invalidate this assumption are provided for. A resource can be "down" because of a lack of labor, for preventive maintenance, or as a result of machine failure. All three are represented as a special type of operation, thus retaining a consistent model of the scheduling task. A lack of labor is represented by a *no.shift* operation, which has a single value in both its *possible.resources* and *legal.starts* slot. Preventive maintenance tasks are represented by a *maintenance* operation, which has a single value in its *possible.resources* slot but can have a range of values in its *legal.starts* slot. A machine failure is represented by a *repair* operation, which has a single value in its *possible.resources* slot; a single value indicating the time of machine failure in its *legal.starts* slot; and a *duration*, which is the expected time to repair. All three of these operations are identical to the operations that represent work items, with the exception of the values held in slot *type*. Slot *type* is used to specify the class of operation from a range of *work*, *no.shift*, *maintenance*, or *repair*. It is possible to

UNIT: P2541	
MEMBER OF: plans	
SLOT NAME	VALUE
DECISION.ORDER:	(L2541.saw L2541.packing)
OPERATION:	L2541.stretch, L2541.anneal,
	L2541.packing, L2541.saw

Figure 11-5:   A process plan.

schedule these non-work operations in exactly the same manner as *work* operations because the technological and temporal constraints attached to these operations ensure that they are scheduled appropriately.

11.3.3 Plans

Although the temporal relations used within plans are based on Allen's theory of action and time (Allen, 1984), only a subset of these relations is currently employed. Because of the granularity of representation (no secondary resources) and limited opportunism within the current problem domain, the *before* relation and its inverse *after* are sufficient to represent the temporal relationships within process plan. However, we allow a process plan to be a partial order, such that some operations can be performed in any order. This partial ordering is represented via the *not.during* relation. The relation A *not.during* B is defined to mean that A can be executed either *before* B or *after* B, but the execution of A and B must not *overlap*. Therefore, the process plans within DAS represent the implicit opportunism of Fox & Kempf (1985a, 1985b).

The operations graph of a job is explicitly represented by the operations within the plan, where the slots *before*, *after*, and *not.during* represent the arcs of the graph. The slot *operations* of the plan represents the set of nodes of the operations graph. The plan unit allows a decision ordering to be imposed on an operations graph. The slot *decision.order* dictates a sequence for the release of operations into the scheduling system. (See Figure 11.5.)

11.4 THE CONSTRAINT MAINTENANCE SYSTEM (CMS)

The form of propagation that the CMS performs has been classified as label inferencing (Davis, 1987) and is implemented using a combination of object and access oriented programming techniques. The constraint networks to be propagated over contain both unary and binary constraints. Binary constraints represent the precedence relations between operations, and unary constraints (e.g., start time, resource, release date) represent the temporal constraints acting on an operation. The unary and binary constraints combine to give the temporal domain of an operation, namely, its *legal.starts* slot. Change is introduced into a network via a unary constraint. A change in the value of a unary constraint results in a modification to the domain of the affected operation, thus initiating propagation between operations over binary constraints. The CMS therefore performs two primary roles within DAS. First, it maintains the temporal domain of each operation within the scheduling problem. Second, it informs the agents of change that has taken place within their local scheduling problems.

11.4.1 Propagation and Messages

An agent maintains its view of the world by receiving messages and imposes change into the world by generating messages. Many of the events that cause the CMS to initiate propagation also require an agent to update its world view. To cater to this, the CMS generates messages in accordance with the various sources of constraint propagation. Communication via message passing operates on the basis of addressed messaging rather than broadcast; i.e., messages are only sent to agents that have an interest in the message. Therefore, the CMS should be considered as the primary medium for communication.

The most common message generated by the CMS is the $<$modify op_i priority$>$ message. It is sent to an agent whenever one of the operations in its problem has a modification to the value in its *legal.starts* slot. The CMS sends the message to the agent identified by the value held in the *resource* slot of the affected operation. The value of the priority field of a $<$modify op_i priority$>$ message is determined by the source of the modification. A message sent as a result of a non-negotiable event, such as the late completion of an operation, is given a priority of -1. This is interpreted by the receiving agent as a message that cannot be ignored. A more interesting use of the priority field occurs when the message is sent as a result of a negotiable event, such as an operational level scheduling decision. The messages generated as a result of an operation being given a start time take on a priority equal to that of the operation that has just been scheduled.

An $<$add $op_i>$ message is sent to an agent to inform it that op_i has been introduced to its problem. Similarly, a $<$delete op_i $>$ message is sent to an agent to inform it that op_i is no longer part of its problem. The CMS sends these messages in response to a change in value to the *resource* slot of an operation. It sends a $<$delete op_i $>$ to the agent identified by the old value in the *resource* slot and an $<$add op_i $>$ to the agent identified by the new value in the *resource* slot.

As will be discussed later, one of the conflict resolution mechanisms available to the S-agent is the synchronization of decision-making through process plans. To facilitate this, the CMS sends $<$dec-made $op_i>$ messages to the S-agent when a decision order is imposed on op_i. A $<$dec-made $op_i>$ message is sent in response to op_i being given a start time. This informs the S-agent that a scheduling decision has been made on op_i, possibly triggering the release of an operation in the process plan into the system.

11.4.2 Constraint Propagation

Constraint retraction is a common event within DAS because of the asynchronous nature of problem-solving and world dynamics. The degree to which constraint retraction occurs makes the efficiency of this activity a major concern. Consequently, the CMS has been designed to deal with constraint retraction in an incremental manner. Most existing algorithms, such as those analyzed in Mackworth & Freuder (1985), deal with constraint retraction by recomputing the network "from scratch." When incremental constraint retraction is necessary, some apparently redundant propagation might therefore be performed to ensure that constraints and their propagated effects are retracted correctly. The DAS constraint propagation algorithm differs from traditional algorithms in that it performs apparently redundant propagation in order to allow incremental constraint retraction. The algorithm used in the implementation of the CMS propagates throughout the complete plan, regardless of its current implications. The fact that it does so causes some concern about its applicability to large constraint networks. Within the exemplar site for DAS, the size of the constraint networks being propagated over is sufficiently small for this not to be a major concern. A potentially more efficient version of this algorithm can be encoded in which propagation halts after the first unaffected node is reached and is re-started when constraint retraction occurs.[3] Although this is likely to reduce the number of constraint propagations performed, it is not necessarily more efficient. It introduces two additional sources of computation. First, it is now necessary to test the effect of a propagation at each stage in the process to determine if it can be terminated. Second, in the event of a constraint retraction, it is now necessary to determine if there are any propagation processes that halted and must now be re-started. When choosing between the two algorithms, it is necessary to consider the size of the constraint network, the cost of testing versus the expected number of redundant propagations, and the expected number of constraint retractions.

11.4.3 Representation of Temporal Constraints

As suggested in Rit (1986), the CMS of DAS deals with partially ordered process plans by representing temporal constraints as generalized windows, by enumerating disjunctive relations, and by employing an arc consistency algorithm (Mackworth, 1977). The CMS of DAS uses a dual representation of constraints. Externally, temporal constraints are represented as an ordered set of integer pairs, where each integer pair represents a closed contiguous interval. Internally, a tempo-

---

[3] In fact, our most recent work adopts such a strategy within a distributed constraint graph (Prosser et al., 1992a, 1992b).

ral constraint is represented as a collection of component constraints that are combined to generate the external representation.

A component constraint is of the form (*Source* (*S E*)) in which *Source* identifies the source of the component constraint, and (*S E*) indicates the interval of time allowed by the constraint, where *S* is the start of the interval, and *E* is the end of the interval. The allowed intervals are then computed as the intersection of the intervals allowed by all component constraints. When a decision is undone, the component constraint to be retracted can then be identified by matching its *Source* against the decision that is to be undone. The internal representation of a temporal constraint also assists in conflict resolution by allowing an identification of the various unary constraints that play a part in a conflict. This feature is exploited by the S-agent.

11.5 THE OPERATIONAL AGENT

The O-agent's goal is to maintain a satisfactory schedule on a resource in a dynamic/open world and, when it fails to do so, to deliver to its superior T-agent a reasonable explanation of why it has failed (such that its problem might be relaxed). It is possible that the O-agent might be posed a problem that has a near infinite search space (for practical purposes) and is therefore unsatisfiable within a reasonable amount of time. To mitigate against this situation, the O-agent is given a quantum, a limit on the amount of effort it is allowed to expend before it must communicate with its superior agent. When the O-agent exceeds its quantum, it must give up search and attempt to give a reasonable explanation. This explanation must be considered as an educated guess based on incomplete/uncertain knowledge.

The O-agent has a limited contract. The O-agent is only allowed to read messages from its own message buffer, read the *legal.starts* slot of operations on its resource, send messages to its superior T-agent, and write into the *start.time* slot of operations on its resource. The act of writing out start times for operations generates messages, courtesy of the CMS. The O-agent is allowed to impose a schedule on the world only if that schedule is satisfactory (all operations have been given start times, and no conflicts exist within that schedule), and the O-agent has no outstanding messages to process. This corresponds to the "locally complete" communication policy of Durfee, Lesser, & Corkill (1987). It is assumed that at all times, the O-agent is dealing with incomplete/uncertain knowledge. This is because of the asynchronous nature of DAS and world dynamics.

11.5.1 Representation

The O-agent views the scheduling of operations on a resource as an instance of the constraint satisfaction problem (CSP) and, in particular, as an instance of the "dynamic" constraint satisfaction problem. The O-agent represents the scheduling problem as a constraint graph G. The nodes in G, V(G), represent individual operations. A domain D_i is a set of temporal intervals, the set of legal start times for operation op_i. The arcs of the graph, A(G), correspond to binary constraints acting between pairs of operations on that resource, where constraints are represented as binary relations.

The O-agent must address the "executional uncertainty" within the scheduling problem and does so by accepting that the topology of G is unstable. Because of the architecture as a whole, changes to an O-agent's schedule can arise in the normal course of problem solving. Because of the tightly coupled nature of the scheduling problem, when a local decision is made, its consequences must be propagated throughout the system, possibly affecting the domains of operations in other constraint graphs. This has the same local effect as variations in processing time and variations in anticipated arrival. Similarly, if a local schedule is over-constrained, the problem can be relaxed, either by enlarging the domain of an operation or by removing an operation. Relaxation as a result of the removal of an operation has the same local effect as the deletion of work either as a result of the cancellation of orders or the scrapping of a job. That is, problem dynamics experienced by an O-agent can be the result of both exogenous effects (executional uncertainty) and endogenous effects (distributed problem solving), but the O-agent is not concerned as to the source of these dynamics.

11.5.2 The O-Agent Algorithm

The O-agent is at heart a hybrid algorithm (Prosser, 1989, 1991) of forward checking (Haralick & Elliott, 1980), shallow learning (Dechter, 1990), and dependency-directed backtracking (Stallman & Sussman, 1977). This algorithm is augmented such that it can react to changes imposed upon the agent.

A forward move through the search space involve: (1) the selection of an unscheduled operation op_i, (2) the assignment of a start time to op_i from its domain D_i, and (3) the application of forward checking from op_i to each operation that is uninstantiated and adjacent to op_i in the constraint graph. Forward checking from op_i to op_j involves the removal of values in the domain of op_j that are inconsistent with the instantiation of op_i. When inconsistent values are removed from the domain D_j, these inconsistent values are represented explicitly along with their justification (namely, the instantiation of op_i).

If as a result of forward checking from op_i to op_j, the domain of op_j is made empty (annihilated), then learning and backtracking take place. The domain D_j will have been annihilated because there is no value in D_j that is consistent with the instantiations of the operations forward checking against op_j. Because this information is explicitly recorded, there is an opportunity to gain knowledge about the search space immediately before backtracking takes place. The set of operations forward checking against op_j and the operation op_j itself constitute a "conflict set" (Dechter, 1990). The O-agent analyzes the conflict set and derives knowledge of the search space. This knowledge is then exploited in a number of ways. First, it is used to direct backtracking. Second, it allows a pruning of the search space. Third, it allows the O-agent to determine the effects of change to its problem with respect to the search space explored. Finally, in the event that the O-agent's problem is over-constrained, this knowledge allows an explanation of how the problem might be relaxed.

11.6 THE TACTICAL AGENT

The tactical agent (T-agent) is responsible for the delegation of operations to subordinate O-agents and the resolution of conflicts between subordinate O-agents. When a T-agent recognizes that its problem is over-constrained, it delivers an explanation to its superior, the S-agent, as to why it believes its problem to be over-constrained. It then expects the S-agent to relax its problem based on this explanation.

The tactical agent attempts to satisfy the technological constraints on operations by binding operations to resources. Operations can be thought of as variables and the *possible.resources* slot of operations as discrete domains. The delegation of an operation to a resource corresponds to the assignment of a value to a variable, and the consequence of that delegation is the response received from the O-agent responsible for scheduling that resource. Because the T-agent is analogous to a manager, it has an assistant, namely, a T-assistant. The T-agent informs the T-assistant of the decisions it has made (delegations and retractions) and the consequences of these decisions (O-agent response). The T-assistant is then put in a position such that is can advise the T-agent as to what actions are available. That is, the T-assistant is put in an advisory role, whereas the T-agent is in a decision-making role. As will be described below, the T-assistant is implemented as an assumption based truth maintenance system (ATMS), customized for this application.

11.6.1 Delegation

The selection of an operation for delegation is constrained by the *look.ahead* attribute of the aggregate resource. *Look.ahead* acts as a filter, removing all operations with temporal constraints that preclude them from being scheduled within the required temporal horizon. The operations that successfully pass through the temporal filter can then be selected from, using the function specified in the *select.strategy* slot of the aggregate resource. Having selected the next operation op_i for delegation, the T-agent selects a subordinate resource to delegate to. The T-agent consults with its T-assistant. The T-assistant returns a set of resources that it believes the operation op_i can be delegated to without generating an operational conflict. The returned set will be a subset of the resources in the *possible.resources* slot of the operation. Having selected an operation op_i and a resource R_i, the T-agent makes its delegation and informs its T-assistant as to its decision. The T-agent binds op_i to R_i, which results in the CMS sending a message to the O-agent on resource R_i. Eventually, the O-agent on resource R_i sends a message back to the T-agent, informing it as to the success or failure of scheduling operation op_i. The T-agent then passes this information on to the T-assistant as a consequence of the decision that has been made.

11.6.2 Retraction

If an O-agent has an over-constrained scheduling problem, it reports to its superior T-agent with an explanation in the form of a conflict set. This conflict set is the set of operations that the O-agent believes cannot consistently be scheduled on its resource. The T-agent treats this information as the consequence of a decision and passes the conflict set to its T-assistant. The T-agent then asks its T-assistant for advice on how to resolve this conflict. The T-assistant responds with an explanation in disjunctive normal form, where each conjunction is a set of operations to be retracted. The T-agent then selects a conjunction and retracts the operations in that conjunction (removes them from their subordinate resources). In the event that the tactical problem is over-constrained, each conjunction in the T-assistant's advice will involve at least one operation that must be removed from the scheduling problem. The T-agent then reports to the S-agent with a set of options in disjunctive normal form, where each conjunction is a set of operations that, if temporally relaxed (i.e., if we can in some way enlarge their *legal.starts* slot), will resolve the conflict between subordinate resources.

11.6.3 The Tactical Assistant

The T-assistant is essentially an assumption based truth maintenance system (ATMS) (de Kleer, 1986) customized for the dynamic tactical scheduling problem. The T-assistant represents each operation that the T-agent is responsible for as a variable. When a T-agent delegates an operation to a resource, it informs its T-assistant, and the T-assistant represents this decision as an assignment of a value to a variable and, further, as an assumption that is *IN*. When the T-agent is notified of an operational scheduling conflict, it passes the conflict set to its T-assistant. The T-assistant treats the conflict set as a conjunction of assumptions that is illegal; that is, it treats the conflict set as a nogood. By performing negative hyperresolution (Chang and Lee, 1973) on nogoods, the T-assistant is then able to derive conflict sets across subordinate resources. The advice delivered by the T-assistant is then a set of conjunctions of assumptions, such that if all assumptions from any one conjunction are forced *OUT*, all conflicts will be resolved.

11.6.4 Avoiding Ignorance

If we have an operational resource R reporting to two superiors, $T-agent_i$ and $T-agent_j$, it is guaranteed that both tactical agents will suffer ignorance. $T-agent_i$ is ignorant of all delegations performed by $T-agent_j$ and vice versa. When a conflict set occurs on resource R, the O-agent can message both $T-agent_i$ and $T-agent_j$. If the conflict set consists only of operations delegated by one of the T-agents, then the other T-agent will be in complete ignorance because its T-assistant will have no corresponding assumptions regarding the operations within that conflict set. If the conflict set contains operations delegated by both $T-agent_i$ and $T-agent_j$, then both $T-agent_i$ and $T-agent_j$ will be in partial ignorance. This is because both T-assistants have only some but not all of the assumptions that correspond to the operations within the conflict set. In the situation of complete ignorance, one of the T-agents will be unable to take any action, and in the situation of partial ignorance, both T-agents' assistants will deliver bad advice. Therefore, the relationship between T-agent and O-agents can only be a tree, not a lattice. Put another way, matrix management cannot be supported within DAS.[4]

11.7 THE STRATEGIC AGENT

The strategic agent (S-agent) is responsible for accepting new work into the system and delegating it to the lower levels and the resolution of scheduling conflicts between subordinate agents. The S-agent is attached to the strategic unit, the root node of the hierarchy, and dominates its subordinate T-agents. The S-agent is the highest level of authority within the DAS hierarchy.

11.7.1 Delegation

There are two forms of delegation: (1) the delegation of an entire plan and (2) the delegation of an operation from a plan that has an enforced decision-making sequence. The delegation of an entire plan involves the selection of a plan and the delegation of the operations in that plan to the tactical level. Selection is performed by applying a domain specific function to the set of plans that have not yet been delegated. The delegation of the selected plan then involves the binding of the operations in that plan to aggregate resources, identified by the operations' *process* attribute. This, in turn, messages the respective T-agents via the CMS.

---

[4] This observation is based on experience. Before the T-assistant was implemented, DAS was structured as a lattice, such that an operational resource could be subordinate to many aggregate resources. The above scenario was predicted and did occur. The structure of DAS was then changed accordingly, without affecting its function.

When decision-making within a plan is sequenced, the delegation of operations is triggered by operational level scheduling decisions. For example, if a decision ordering has been imposed on $plan_i$, $op_{i1} \rightarrow op_{i2} \rightarrow op_{i3}$ (where $\rightarrow$ is interpreted as "is to be decided before," and op_{ij} is the jth operation in the process plan $plan_i$), when a scheduling decision is made by an O-agent on op_{i1}, the S-agent receives a $<dec\text{-}made\ op_{i1}>$ message. On processing this message, the S-agent examines the process plan, $plan_i$, and delegates the next operation in decision order, namely, op_{i2}. The *process* attribute of op_{i2} then defines the aggregate resource to bind to the operation.

11.7.2 Conflict Resolution

The S-agent receives from its subordinate T-agents' explanations of their conflicts in disjunctive normal form. For example the S-agent can receive the following explanation E_i from a tactical agent $T\text{-}agent_i$: $E_i = ((op_{ai}\ op_{bi}),(op_{bi}\ op_{ci}))$. This can be interpreted as follows: to resolve the conflict on $T\text{-}agent_i$, the operations op_{ai} and op_{bi} must be relaxed, or the operations op_{bi} and op_{ci} must be relaxed. The S-agent might need to resolve conflicts involving more that one T-agent. For example, the S-agent can receive the following conflict explanations from tactical agents $T\text{-}agent_i$ and $T\text{-}agent_j$: $E_i = ((op_{ai}op_{bi}),(op_{bi}op_{ci}))$ and $E_j = ((op_{aj}op_{xj}),(op_{bj}op_{yj}))$. The S-agent attempts to devise a plan of action to resolve these conflicts that is both minimal and complete. It must relax the temporal constraints (using either inter-agent backtracking or due date relaxation, as is discussed shortly) of the operations in one of the conjunctions of E_i and the temporal constraints of the operations in one of the conjunctions of E_j. It is possible that there exist operations in E_i and E_j that share the same process plan. When this occurs, the S-agent can decide to relax a plan rather than relax an operation within a plan. The minimal cross product of E_i and E_j defines a set of minimal actions,[5] where any one of these actions is believed to move the system into a consistent state, for example:

$$actions = ((plan_a\ op_{bi}\ op_{xj}),(op_{ai}\ plan_b\ op_{yj}),(op_{aj}\ op_{bi}\ op_{ci}\ op_{xj}),$$
$$(plan_b\ op_{ci}\ op_{yj}))$$

The first conjunction of *actions* above, namely, $(plan_a\ op_{bi}\ op_{xj})$, is described as follows: The conflict can be resolved by relaxing the process plan $plan_a$ (because a relaxation of op_{ai} and op_{aj} will address part of E_i and E_j) and by relaxing the operations op_{bi} and op_{xj}.

The S-agent then selects an action (conjunction) from the set *actions*. Given a choice, the S-agent selects a course of action in which it can achieve all necessary

---

[5] The minimal cross product of a set of sets is defined to be the set of n-tuples, the elements of which are respectively members of any of the given sets, such that any n-tuple that subsumes another is removed from the result.

temporal relaxations by inter-agent backtracking rather than by due date relaxation. This is consistent with the view that conflicts should be contained as locally as possible. If the S-agent is left with no inter-agent backtracking options, it must modify the problem specification via due date relaxation.

11.7.3 Inter-Agent Backtracking

Inter-agent backtracking can be thought of as dependency-directed backtracking between T-agents. If it is discovered that a T-agent's scheduling problem is over-constrained because of a specific operation, op_{ij}, inter-agent backtracking attempts to find some scheduling decision in the plan, $plan_i$, to undo, thus enlarging the temporal domain of op_{ij}. Whenever a scheduling decision on an operation is undone during inter-agent backtracking, the operation in question has its start time removed and is retracted to the strategic level until the relaxed operation is actually scheduled. The S-agent must consider two factors when deciding whether to invoke inter-agent backtracking. First, it must consider the relative difficulty experienced in making each decision in the process plan, and second, it must consider the temporal constraints acting throughout the plan.

The cost of each scheduling decision in a process plan can be determined from its associated priority. Therefore, only decisions on operations of a lower priority than the one requiring temporal relaxation should be considered as candidates for being undone. Having removed candidate operations that are of a higher priority than the operation to be relaxed, the S-agent next considers the impact of each remaining candidate on the temporal domain of the operation in conflict. This is made possible by the maintenance of a dual representation of the temporal constraint acting on an operation, as described earlier. The S-agent elects to undo the decision that will result in the greatest relaxation of the temporal domain of the restricted operation.

Inter-agent backtracking effectively imposes an ordering on decision-making through part of a process plan by allowing a decision to be made on one operation and its effects propagated before a decision on another. There is a danger of entering into an infinite loop in which the S-agent undoes a decision on one operation to benefit another, only later to repeat the process in the opposite direction. In order to inhibit looping, the S-agent must record the implicit decision-making sequencing that results from explicit inter-agent backtracking. This explicit representation of previously enforced decision-making sequences is inspected by the S-agent when considering inter-agent backtracking to ensure that it does not repeat a decision that was enforced earlier and has apparently failed. If at any point in the process of eliminating candidates for inter-agent backtracking it is discovered that there are no remaining candidates, the S-agent concludes that the process plan in conflict cannot benefit from inter-agent backtracking, and the S-agent resorts to due date relaxation.

11.7.4 Due Date Relaxation

Due date relaxation is the S-agent's final resort in resolving a conflict. It guarantees that DAS will find a solution, if not to the precise scheduling problem it was presented with then at least to a closely related problem. If due date relaxation is to be an effective conflict resolution mechanism in all situations, it must involve significantly more than a simple extension of the due date on a process plan and the propagation of the effects. Certainly, this would be sufficient in some instances, but the position of an operation in a process plan can inhibit this from being an effective solution.

What is actually required is that all the operations in the process plan be unscheduled and subsequently re-scheduled in a left to right order through the process plan. In the case of partially ordered process plans, a strict decision-making sequence is enforced across these plans. The same decision-making sequencing mechanism used within inter-agent backtracking is employed to guarantee the required left-to-right sequencing.

There is naturally concern over the degree of tardiness of an order that has had its due date relaxed. This is particularly true when the due date constraint in question has effectively been removed from the scheduling problem rather than incrementally extended. This would appear to give O-agents operating a JIT strategy a licence to schedule relaxed operations some time very far into the future. To counter this possibility, the S-agent associates a selection strategy of "earliest dispatch" with each operation in a relaxed process plan. This selection strategy takes precedence over the selection strategy currently active at the resource that an operation is delegated to, thus ensuring that such orders are completed in reasonable time.

11.8 COORDINATING PROBLEM SOLVING EFFORT

In ISIS (Fox, 1983), the scheduling system takes an order based perspective, concentrating problem solving effort on orders that are proving difficult to bind to resources over time. OPIS (Smith, Fox, & Ow, 1986) allows both an order based and a resource based perspective of the scheduling task and has the ability to dynamically shift between perspectives. OPIS can focus effort on a critical resource (a bottleneck) or on a critical job. However, it is rarely the case that one order or one resource can be considered as critical with respect to problem solving effort. Resource criticality generally occurs only over certain intervals of time and job criticality over a subset of the operations within a plan. What is required is the ability to focus effort at a finer level of granularity, that is, on individual operations, at resources, over specific intervals of time. This is similar to the "micro-opportunism" of CORTES (Fox, Sadeh, & Baykan, 1989; Sadeh, 1991). In DAS, this is achieved by a priority mechanism, where priority is a measure of problem solving difficulty associated with individual scheduling decisions.

11.8.1 Operational Priority

Each operation within the system has a "priority" attribute, which is initialized to zero. The priority of an operation is a measure of the difficulty associated with the satisfaction of its temporal and technological constraints. It can be considered as a history of problem solving effort expended in reaching a scheduling decision on an individual operation.

For the sake of example, assume an O-agent on resource R_x has been delegated operations op_{i3}, op_{j3}, and op_{k3} and that the O-agent discovers a conflict set, CS = $(op_{i3}\ op_{k3})$. That is, the O-agent cannot schedule both op_{i3} and op_{k3} on its resource. The conflict set CS is then passed up to the superior T-agent. The T-agent increments the priority of the operations in CS, namely, op_{i3} and op_{k3}. The T-agent can then attempt to resolve the operational conflict CS by retracting op_{k3} from resource R_x and by delegating op_{k3} to some other subordinate resource. Further assume that the O-agent on resource R_x can now schedule operations op_{i3} and op_{j3}. When op_{i3} is allocated a start time, the CMS will update the temporal domains (*legal.starts*) of each operation that shares the process plan of op_{i3}. A series of messages will then be generated: *<modify op_{i1} pri>*, *<modify op_{i2} pri>*, *<modify op_{i4} pri>*, where *pri* is the priority of op_{i3}. These messages will be directed to the agents holding the operations op_{i1}, op_{i2}, and op_{i4}. When an O-agent receives a message *<modify op_{mn} pri>*, it checks the priority of the operation op_{mn} against the priority of the message. If the message priority is greater than or equal to the priority of the operation, then the O-agent must adjust its beliefs in the *legal.starts* slot of operation op_{mn}. If the message priority is less than the priority of the operation, and the modified domain of op_{mn} has been restricted, then the O-agent can ignore the message and continue to believe the more relaxed temporal domain of op_{mn}. This mechanism allows an O-agent to make a dominant decision within a process plan.

As was stated above, initially all operations in a plan have a priority of zero. This can be considered a special case. It is possible to pre-process plans, attaching a non-zero priority to operations before introduction to the scheduling problem. When it is expected that an operation has a demand for a critical resource, the priority of that operation can be made high relative to other operations in the plan. As problem solving progresses, the above mechanism will allow priorities to fluctuate within the plan.

11.8.2 Decision-Making Sequencing

The priority mechanism described above is not a problem solving panacea. When a plan is introduced to the system, there is no decision-making sequence imposed on that plan, and O-agents can make decisions on that plan in any order. It is possible that an O-agent, call it $O-agent_i$, has a relatively under-constrained scheduling problem and can make decisions earlier than some other O-agent, call it $O-agent_j$. $O-agent_i$ can then make a dominant decision within a process plan, although its problem is under-constrained. In order to correct this situation, the system resorts to "inter-agent" backtracking. $O-agent_i$ is forced to undo its decision on a specific operation within its local schedule to allow $O-agent_j$ to make its decision.[6]

Again the initial condition of no decision ordering can be considered a special case. The plan can be pre-processed and a decision-making sequence imposed using a strategy similar to that described in the preceding section. The S-agent then releases operations within a plan into the system in a controlled manner, and the scheduling of an operation triggers the release of the next operation in that process plan into the system in a decision-making sequence. In fact, the pre-processing of priority has the same end effect as pre-processing decision ordering but at a higher problem solving cost. The prioritization of operations can cause O-agents to waste problem solving effort.

11.8.3 Synchronization between Tactical and Operational Levels

The relationship between a T-agent and its subordinate O-agents can be "disciplined" or "undisciplined." In a disciplined regime, the T-agent performs no action until all its subordinate O-agents have reached a terminal state. That is, all subordinates have either solved their problems or have recognized that they are in need of T-agent intervention. If there exists a subordinate that is in need of assistance, the T-agent performs conflict resolution. Only when all subordinates have solved their problems can the T-agent make delegations.

In an undisciplined regime, the T-agent interleaves conflict resolution with delegation. The T-agent is allowed to delegate to any subordinate that it believes has solved its problem and can retract work from any agent that it believes to be in need of assistance. In the undisciplined regime, the T-agent can deny itself opportunities. Having just delegated work to a resource, it will not allow a further delegation to that resource until the O-agent reports back that it has solved its problem. In the gap between delegation and the O-agent reporting back, the T-agent can select another operation for delegation. The T-agent can then be denied a delegation

---

[6] There is an alternative means of preventing this scenario. The O-agent can be given the ability to maintain an internal representation of operational priorities during the search process. For example, priority might then be a count of the number of times the operation has been the current variable or a count of the number of times forward checking has occurred against an operation. In addition, the O-agent can be modified such that it only reads its message buffer when its search process has terminated. It is believed that this would reduce the incidence of inter-agent backtracking. This has not yet been implemented.

opportunity for that operation. Similarly, when performing conflict resolution, the T-agent is working with incomplete information.

In the disciplined regime, the T-agent enjoys the complete information of its subordinates and can therefore make accurate decisions. The cost associated with this complete information is a loss of asynchrony. In an under-constrained environment, this can be an unacceptable cost. The undisciplined regime forces the T-agent to make decisions based on incomplete and unreliable information. Consequently, the T-agent frequently makes poor decisions and denies itself opportunities. It does, however, enjoy a greater degree of asynchrony. In an over-constrained environment, the cost of poor decision making can be unacceptable.

11.8.4 Synchronization between Strategic and Tactical Levels

The relationship between the strategic and tactical levels can similarly be disciplined or undisciplined. In a disciplined regime, the S-agent defers action until all subordinate T-agents are in a terminal state (and if there is discipline between tactical and operational levels, all O-agents will be in a terminal state). The S-agent is then in a position of complete information and can either perform conflict resolution or introduce new work into the system. When it performs conflict resolution, it has sufficient information to implement a plan of action that is commensurate with the global problem.

In an undisciplined regime, the S-agent interleaves delegation with conflict resolution and makes decisions with incomplete information. In the undisciplined regime, the S-agent is allowed to make decisions with incomplete knowledge, possibly resulting in an over-reactive style of management with a loss of strategic information. In the disciplined regime, there is a loss of asynchrony.

11.8.5 From Disorder to Order

In the current implementation of DAS, a mid-ground has been found between the extremes of total discipline and complete lack of discipline. This has been achieved by allowing the S-agent to introduce new work to the system only if all subordinate T-agents have no work to delegate to the O-agents. This does not imply that all T-agents and all O-agents are in a terminal state, nor does it imply that the S-agent works with complete information. It does imply that the S-agent's knowledge is "nearly" complete. A balance is then found between complete information and complete asynchrony.

11.9 CURRENT STATUS

The current instantiation of DAS is deployed at Alcan Plate Ltd. (APL) in Kitts Green, Birmingham, U.K. APL produces high quality aluminium plate for the aerospace and defense market. APL production is divided into three broad areas: "upstream," "midstream," and "downstream." Upstream produces cast aluminium slabs for hot rolling, and midstream takes aluminium slabs and produces hot rolled plates that have been edge cropped and heat treated. The downstream activity is "plate finishing" and is made up of the following processes: stretching (ST), annealing (ANN), precipitation treatment (P/T), ultrasonic testing (US), final sawing (SAW), and inspection and packing (I&P). The processes of annealing and precipitation treatment are performed in batch mode (that is, a number of plates can be put in a furnace together and processed at the same time, so long as they have compatible processing requirements), and all other processes are performed in single server mode.

DAS is applied to the downstream of APL. This involves the modelling of 18 operational resources (3 stretchers, 1 annealing furnace, 3 precipitation furnaces, 2 ultrasonic testing tanks, 6 saws, and 3 inspection and packing stations) and 6 aggregate resources (ST, ANN, P/T, US, SAW, I&P). On average, there are 100 jobs in the downstream at any time, each with a process plan of on average 4 operations (approximately 400 operations). The majority of process plans involve a partial order; there exists an opportunity to permute the processes of precipitation treatment (P/T) and ultrasonic scanning (US). A typical plan is therefore {ST → {P/T *not.during* US} → SAW → I&P}, where → is interpreted as "is done before." Each job represents a lot, where a lot is a number of identical plates, each sharing the same process plan. Lots with identical process plans can have different makespans because of differences in material content or differences in product type. Processing times are typically as follows: stretching takes approximately 15 minutes per plate, annealing takes between 18 and 96 hours per batch of lots depending on product type, precipitation treatment takes similar processing times as annealing and again is dependent on product type, ultrasonic testing takes approximately 2 hours per plate, sawing takes 5 minutes per plate and is dependent on the resource performing the process, and inspection and packing takes approximately 30 minutes per lot. There is a high variation in processing times because of operational uncertainty; in particular, the stretching process is highly unreliable.

11.9.1 Interfaces

There are two interfaces to DAS (Costello, 1988). The first is used for introducing jobs to the system. The external representation of lots must be mapped into the internal representation of plans and operations used by DAS. This function is performed by the "Domain KB." APL already has a process planning system (the Special Metallurgical Practices system (SMP)), which takes orders as input and outputs planned lots. The Domain KB, with its suite of functions, maps a lot into a process plan of operations. The second interface allows DAS to be updated with respect to events that have occurred on the shop floor. APL already has an on-line

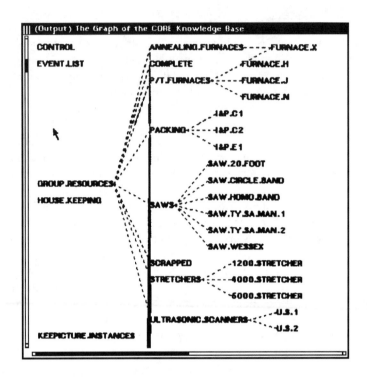

Figure 11-6: The resource hierarchy

Shop Floor Reporting system (SFR). A SFI (shop floor image) KB with associated methods allows the SFR system to notify DAS of the progress of work on the shop floor and of the availability of individual resources and manpower. The SFI KB is also used for interfacing DAS to a simulator.

11.9.2 Implementation

The system runs on a Symbolics 3620 with 8MBytes of RAM and 370MBytes of hard disk. DAS is implemented in Symbolics Common Lisp and uses KEE to represent resources, plans, and operations. Figure 11-6 shows a graph of the hierarchy of resources modelled within the APL site.

Figure 11-7 shows a process plan (Lot L184125381) containing 5 processes (stretching, p/t, us.scanning, final.sawing, and packing). A grey horizontal box shows the intervals of time in which it is acceptable to start the operation without violating temporal constraints within the plan. A solid black bar represents a scheduling decision on an operation, where the length of the box is the duration of the operation, and the position represents its scheduled start time. A white box repre-

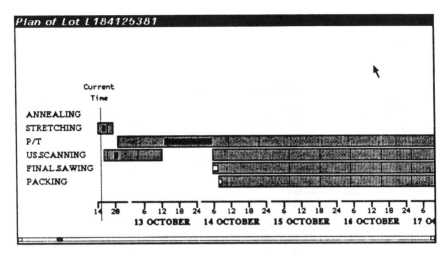

Figure 11-7:   Lot L184125381

sents an unscheduled operation, and the length of the white box corresponds to the expected duration of the operation. The plan shown has a partial ordering because the processes of us.scanning and p/t can be permuted (us.scanning *not.during* p/t).

Figure 11-8 shows a schedule on an individual resource, U.S.2 (ultrasonic tank 2). Again, there is evidence of partial ordering (see operations L234123211. US, L234123210.US, and L204120729.US). The resource U.S.2 is a single server; only one operation can be executed at any one time.

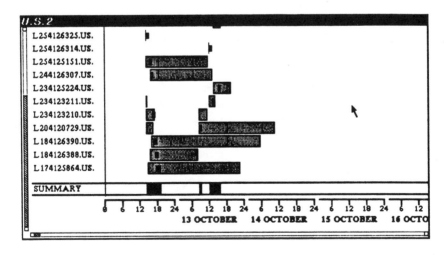

Figure 11-8:   Schedule on ultrasonic tank 2

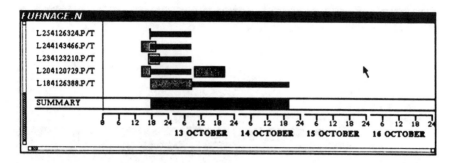

Figure 11-9:   Schedule on furnace N

Figure 11-9 shows a schedule on a resource (FURNACE.N) that allows batching of operations. Operations are allowed to start simultaneously when they have a common point in their temporal domains, are of the same product type, and can have a common duration without violating temporal constraints. Again, there is evidence of partial ordering (operation L204120729.P/T).

11.9.3 Typical Performance

In addition to the particular data set, there are a large number of system parameters that have an impact on how long it takes DAS to generate/maintain a schedule. This section attempts to give only a feel for the typical performance. A description of how various parameters are set is given before a typical performance figure is presented.

In total, there are 18 O-agents, 6 T-agents, and 1 S-agent spawned as concurrent processes (25 total) on the Symbolics. The following selection strategies are used by the O-agents: the stretchers use ED; the precipitation furnaces, ultrasonic tanks, and saws use MID; and inspection and packing uses JIT.[7] All O-agents have a "quantum" of 2000, allowing 2000 applications of forward checking between operations before being forced to give up search and communicate with their superior T-agent. On a quiescent machine, a single O-agent will make 2000 applications of forward checking in approximately 1 second. All agents have a rest interval of 5 seconds. Currently, the T-agents and the S-agent have no domain knowledge. When making a selection, the Lisp function "first" is applied to the set of available

---

[7] These selection strategies should be considered as preference constraints. They describe a strategy for selecting a start time for an operation on a resource. ED is early dispatch and attempts to schedule operations as early as is possible. MID attempts to select a time from the middle of the temporal domain, introducing an element of slack into the schedule. JIT is Just In Time, selecting the latest possible time.

options. No attempt is made to maintain shop stability, and agents are allowed to be totally opportunistic.

T-agents are allowed to delegate work so long as at least one of its subordinate O-agents has produced a satisfactory schedule. This allows the T-agent to interleave conflict resolution with delegation. This can reduce the opportunities available to the T-agent when making a delegation. The S-agent similarly interleaves conflict resolution with delegation. This can allow the S-agent to over-react to conflicts.

For a 90-job scheduling problem (360 operations, 18 resources), a schedule is produced from scratch in less than 60 minutes. On average, a job (lot) can be introduced to the schedule in under 1 minute. A pathological breakdown of a resource, requiring significant reaction, is managed (on a 90-job scheduling problem) in less than 5 minutes. It is expected that significant performance improvements can be gained by introducing domain knowledge to the system, disciplining problem solving strategy between levels, and distributing agents across processors.

11.10 CONCLUSION

The goal of the Distributed Asynchronous Scheduler (DAS) is to maintain a satisfactory schedule in an open world in near-real time. In that respect DAS might be thought of as an *anytime* system, such as those of Fox (1981b); Drummond & Besina (1990); Zweben, Deal, & Gargan (1990); and Zweben et al. (1992). DAS views the scheduling problem as one of satisfaction rather than one of optimization. The satisfaction of temporal constraints is considered a major goal and the relaxation of temporal constraints as a last resort. That is, DAS attempts to meet due dates.[8]

The scheduling problem is distributed across a three tier hierarchy of communicating agents. This reflects the organization within which DAS exists and the structure of the problem that DAS addresses. However, this should be considered as only part of the justification for distributing the scheduling effort. By distributing the problem across a society of agents, we can allow agents to take different perspectives on that problem. For example, we have seen that some agents attempt to minimize inventory (by using a JIT selection strategy), whereas other agents attempt to maximize the utilization of resources (by taking an earliest dispatch [ED] strategy). This is one of the arguments for the distribution of the $REDS^2$ system of Hadavi et al. (1992), and for the adopting of the blackboard in OPIS (Smith, Fox, & Ow, 1986). A third reason for distribution was "technology push." That is, we wanted to see if we could do it. If the scheduling problem could be

---

[8]However, Berry has enhanced DAS such that it addresses the optimization of multiple and conflicting objectives (Berry, 1992a, 1992b).

addressed efficiently by a society of agents, we might then be able to construct systems by plugging scheduling agents together. To do this, agents would have to be truly reactive (and we believe that we have achieved this) and be able to exist within a democratic society (in that respect we have failed).

DAS was developed "bottom up." The first version of DAS was made up only of O-agents, the CMS, and the priority mechanism. We hoped that the system would converge onto a solution via a process similar to that of simulated annealing (Kirkpatrick, Gelatt, & Vecchi, 1983). The system rarely converged into a stable state (and when it did, it was only because of good fortune) but instead diverged into a state of chaos. In order to overcome this, we put in place the hierarchy, the mechanisms of inter-agent backtracking, decision sequencing, and due date relaxation. The system was then guaranteed to converge onto a solution, although it might have to relax the problem to achieve this. In that respect, DAS is not "complete." For example, if we cast the n-queens as a scheduling problem and delegated each row to an O-agent, DAS would find a solution but would probably mutilate the chess board in the process! This lack of completeness shouldn't be thought of as a major limitation. In fact, it might be considered as an inevitable feature of any reactive/anytime system that attempts to address problems that are of a combinatorial nature.

DAS decomposes the scheduling problem and distributes parts of that problem to agents. This appears to be a "natural" distribution, a delegation of tasks to specialists. There is another form of distribution that also appears to be natural. That is, we have a society of agents, and each agent is capable of solving the problem on its own. The agents can use different techniques, can look at the problem in different ways, and can have different goals. During the process of exploration, agents share their findings.[9] This can bring about a super-linear speed-up, or a "combinatorial implosion" (Clearwater, Huberman, & Hogg, 1991). It appears that adopting that style of distribution with stochastic search techniques might be a promising way forward (Muller, Magill, & Smith, 1992; Ghedira & Verfaillie, 1992).

References

Allen, J.F. 1984. "Towards a General Theory of Action and Time." *Artificial Intelligence*, Vol. 23, pp. 123–154.

Berry, P.M. 1992a. "A Predictive Model for Satisfying Conflicting Objectives in Scheduling Problems." *AI Magazine*, 13(1), pp. 13–15.

---

[9] Generally, this is how research is carried out and how science advances.

Berry, P.M. 1992b. "Scheduling: A Problem of Decision Making under Uncertainty." *Proceedings ECAI-92*, John Wiley & Sons, Chicester, U.K., pp. 638–642.

Burke, P., and P. Prosser. 1990. "Distributed Asynchronous Scheduling." *Applications of Artificial Intelligence in Engineering* V, Vol. 2 (ed. G. Rzevski), Springer-Verlag, New York, pp. 503–522.

Burke, P. and P. Prosser. 1991. "A Distributed Asynchronous System for Predictive and Reactive Scheduling." *Artificial Intelligence in Engineering*, Vol. 6, No. 3, pp. 106–124.

Chang, C., and R.C. Lee. 1973. *Symbolic Logic and Mechanical Theorem Proving.* Academic Press, New York.

Clearwater, S.H., B.A. Huberman, and T. Hogg. 1991. "Cooperative Solution of a Constraint Satisfaction Problem. *Science*, Vol. 254, pp. 1181–1183.

Costello, J. 1988. *A Common Knowledge Base for Multiple Applications.* Technical report AISL35, University of Strathclyde.

Davis, E. 1987. "Constraint Propagation with Interval Labels." *Artificial Intelligence*, Vol. 32, pp. 281–331.

Dechter, R. 1990. "Enhancement Schemes for Constraint Processing: Backjumping, Learning, and Cutset Decomposition." *Artificial Intelligence*, Vol. 41 No. 3, pp. 273–277.

de Kleer, J. 1986. "An Assumption-Based TMS." *Artificial Intelligence*, Vol. 28, pp. 127–162.

Drummond, M., and J. Besina. 1990. "Anytime Synthetic Projections: Maximizing the Probability of Goal Satisfaction." *Proceedings AAAI-90*, AAAI Press, Menlo Park, Calif., pp. 138–144.

Durfee, E.H., V.R. Lesser and D.D. Corkill. 1987. "Cooperation through Communication in a Distributed Problem Solving Network." *Distributed Artificial Intelligence 1* (ed. M. Huhns), Morgan Kaufmann, San Francisco, Calif.

Fox, M.S. 1981a. "An Organizational View of Distributed Systems." *IEEE Transactions on Systems, Man, and Cybernetics*, Vol. SMC-11, pp. 70–80.

Fox, M.S. 1981b. "Reasoning with Incomplete Knowledge in a Resource-Limited Environment: Integrating Reasoning and Knowledge Acquisition." *Proceedings IJCAI-81*, AAAI Press, Menlo Park, Calif., pp. 313–318.

Fox, M.S. 1983. *Constraint-Directed Search: A Case Study of Job-Shop Scheduling.* Ph.D. Thesis, Carnegie Mellon University.

Fox, B.R., and K.G. Kempf. 1985a. "A Representation for Opportunistic Scheduling." *Proceedings Third International Symposium of Robotics Research*, MIT Press, Cambridge, Mass., pp. 109–115.

Fox, B.R., and K.G. Kempf. 1985b. "Opportunistic Scheduling of Robot Assembly." *Proceedings IEEE International Conference on Robotics and Automation*, IEEE Computer Society Press, Los Alamitos, Calif., pp 880–889.

Fox, M.S., N. Sadeh, and C. Baykan. 1989. "Constrained Heuristic Search." *Proceedings IJCAI-89*, AAAI Press, Menlo Park, Calif., pp. 309–315.

Ghedira, K., and G. Verfaillie. 1992. "Approche Multi-Agent d'un Probleme de Satisfaction de Contraintes: Optimalite and Reactivite," *Proceedings AVIGNON-92*, EC2, Nanterre, France, pp. 377–390.

Hadavi, K., W.L. Hsu, T. Chen, and C.N. Lee. 1992. "An Architecture for Real-Time Distributed Scheduling." *AI Magazine*, Vol. 13, No. 3, pp. 46–56.

Haralick, R.M., and G.L. Elliott. 1980. "Increasing Tree Search Efficiency for Constraint Satisfaction Problems." *Artificial Intelligence*, Vol. 14, pp. 263–314.

Kirkpatrick, S., C.D. Gelatt, and M.P. Vecchi. "Optimization by Simulated Annealing." *Science*, Vol. 220, No. 4598, pp. 671–679.

Lesser, V.R., and D.D Corkill. 1981. "Functionally Accurate, Cooperative Distributed Systems." *IEEE Transactions on Systems, Man and Cybernetics*, Vol. SMC-11, No. 1, pp. 81–96.

Mackworth, A.K. 1977. "Consistency in Networks of Relations." *Artificial Intelligence*, Vol. 8, pp. 99–118.

Mackworth, A.K., and E.C. Freuder. 1985. "The Complexity of Some Polynomial Network Consistency Algorithms for Constraint Satisfaction Problems." *Artificial Intelligence*, Vol. 25, pp. 65–74.

Muller, C., E.H. Magill, and D.G. Smith. 1992. "Distributed Genetic Algorithms for Resource Allocation." Presented at Workshop W7, Scheduling of Production Processes, pp. 37–45.

Parunak, H.V. 1987. "Why Scheduling Is Hard (And How to Do It Anyway)." Presented at the 1987 Material Handling Focus, Georgia Institute of Technology, September.

Prosser, P. 1989. "A Reactive Scheduling Agent." *Proceedings IJCAI-89*, AAAI Press, Menlo Park, Calif., pp. 1004–1009.

Prosser, P. 1991. *Hybrid Algorithms for the Constraint Satisfaction Problem.* Technical report AISL-46-91, Department of Computer Science, University of Strathclyde.

Prosser, P., C. Conway, and C. Muller. 1992. "A Distributed Constraint Maintenance System." *Proceedings AVIGNON-92*, pp. 221–231.

Prosser, P., C. Conway, and C. Muller. "A Constraint Maintenance System for the Distributed Resource Allocation Problem." *Intelligent Systems Engineering*, Vol. 1, No. 1, pp. 76–83.

Rit, J-F. 1986. 1986. "Propagating Temporal Constraints For Scheduling." *Proceedings AAAI-86*, AAAI Press, Menlo Park, Calif., pp. 383–388.

Sadeh, M. 1991. *Look-Ahead Techniques for Micro-Opportunistic Job Shop Scheduling.* CMU-CS-91-102, Ph.D. Thesis, School of Computer Science, Carnegie Mellon University, Pittsburgh, Penn.

Simon, H.A. 1962. "The Architecture of Complexity." *Proceedings American Phil. Soc.*, Vol. 106, pp. 467–487.

Smith, S.F., M.S. Fox, and P.S. Ow. 1986. "Constructing and Maintaining Detailed Production Plans: Investigations into the Development of Knowledge-Based Factory Scheduling Systems." *AI Magazine*, Vol. 7, No. 4, pp. 45–61.

Stallman, R.M., and G.J. Sussman. 1977. "Forward Reasoning and Dependency Directed Backtracking in a System for Computer-Aided Circuit Analysis." *Artificial Intelligence*, Vol. 9, pp. 138–196.

Zweben, M., M. Deal, and R. Gargan. 1990. "Anytime Rescheduling." *Innovative Approaches to Planning, Scheduling, and Control. Proceedings of the 1990 DARPA Workshop*, Morgan Kaufmann, San Francisco, Calif., pp. 251–259.

Zweben, M., E. Davis, B. Daun, and M. Deal. 1992. *Scheduling and Rescheduling with Iterative Repair.* Technical report FIA-92-16, Artificial Intelligence Research Branch, NASA Ames Research Center.

12

ROBUST SCHEDULING AND EXECUTION FOR AUTOMATIC TELESCOPES

Mark Drummond
Keith Swanson
John Bresina
(NASA Ames Research Center)

12.1 INTRODUCTION

Efficiency of operations has long been an area of special interest to NASA. The current environment within NASA is characterized by the catch-phrase "better, cheaper, faster, with no compromise of safety." This environment is one that nurtures the development of automated scheduling and the efficiencies it offers. A significant part of NASA's business is space science, in which telescopes play an important role. Telescopes are expensive to build and operate; thus, they should be used as efficiently and effectively as possible. Our work involves building automated systems that accomplish this objective.

The work reported in this chapter describes an active research and development project, the goal of which is a fully automated planning, scheduling, and schedule execution system for remotely located automatic telescopes. The work has been carried out at the NASA Ames Research Center, with the active support and encouragement of a number of astronomers located at various universities, companies, and observatories throughout the United States. This work has produced a prototype scheduler, called CERES,[1] that has been tested against a high-fidelity sim-

---

[1] CERES is an acronym for Celestial ERE System, where ERE is, in turn, is an acronym for Entropy Reduction Engine (see Bresina, Drummond, & Kedar, 1993).

ulator built by one of our industry collaborators. Our next step is to test CERES on a real, remotely located automatic telescope.

The overall goals of this chapter are to introduce the general architecture of CERES, to explain how its search space is organized, to empirically map out that search space, and to discuss aspects of a new research topic called "contingent scheduling."

To accomplish these goals, the chapter is structured as follows. Section 12.2 presents the problem, and Section 12.3 defines our approach. Section 12.4 presents the results of an empirical search-space mapping exercise, the goal of which is to compare an existing heuristic dispatcher against a very simple hill-climbing algorithm. Section 12.5 explains how CERES executes schedules; the goal of this section is to show how the system uses heuristic dispatch when necessary but can execute higher-quality schedules whenever they are available. Section 12.6 uses aspects of our automatic telescope scheduling and execution problem to introduce the idea of "contingent scheduling," a technique that promises to improve the robustness of schedule execution. Section 12.7 presents other related work not discussed in previous sections, and Section 12.8 briefly outlines future directions for our work. We conclude with a summary in Section 12.9.

12.2 APT PROBLEM DEFINITION

An Automatic Photoelectric Telescope (APT) is a telescope controlled by a dedicated computer for the purpose of gathering photometric data about objects in the sky. APTs are typically modest aperture telescopes located on remote mountain tops, operated at a distance by academic institutions. An APT is expected to operate without human attention for months at a time, with all local observatory and telescope management carried out by a small control computer. Hall and Genet (1988) give an excellent overview of photometry, and Genet and Hayes (1989) describe automatic photoelectric telescopes in some detail. It is worth noting that although we have only studied the scheduling of photometric observations, our approach should easily extend to other types of optical astronomy such as imaging and spectroscopy.

This section presents information that is needed to understand the basic APT scheduling problem. The following subsections describe the general modus operandi for APTs and the current way of doing telescope scheduling.

12.2.1 Modus Operandi

In aperture photometry, a *group* is the primitive unit to be scheduled and executed. A group is a sequence of telescope and photometer commands defined by an astronomer. Any given astronomer has certain scientific goals, and he or she uses the group as the primary unit of instruction to an APT in order to achieve those goals. The language used to define groups is called ATIS (for Automatic Telescope Instruction Set); ATIS is an ASCII-based language, currently the *de facto* standard.[2]

With ATIS, the communication process between astronomer and APT proceeds as follows. First, an astronomer who wishes to use an APT forms a set of ATIS groups that can gather data relevant to his or her scientific goals. Because telescopes typically vary in terms of instruments, optical characteristics, mechanical characteristics, and location on the earth, groups must be formulated in terms of a specific target telescope.

For any given APT, there is a single person who acts as a central clearinghouse for requests; such a person is known as the APT's *Principal Astronomer*, or PA. Thus, once an astronomer has assembled his or her set of ATIS groups, the groups are sent to the appropriate PA. The PA collects together ATIS files from a number of astronomers, possibly edits the files slightly, and then sends the resulting composite ATIS file to the computer controlling the telescope. Actual communication between PA and APT is typically carried out using personal computers, modems, and phone lines, but the particular technology is not critical for our purposes. The PA can be located anywhere on the planet and need only have electronic access to the telescope.

The PA sends a set of groups to an APT with the intention that these groups should be run on the telescope by the local control computer. Eventually, the PA retrieves the results that have been obtained via the execution of the groups. The elapsed time varies depending on the telescope, the groups, the PA, the astronomers, and a variety of other factors. The entire process is designed to worry the astronomers (and the PA) as little as possible about the picayune details of day-to-day telescope management. Thus, the telescope is often left alone for significant periods of time: days, weeks, sometimes months.

Data are returned from the telescope to the PA as a "results file," the syntax of which is also defined by the ATIS standard. The results file contains a record of the requested groups that were actually executed, relevant observing parameters to help with data reduction, and the raw data obtained from the observations. The PA edits the results file, breaking it into the parts relevant to each astronomer. Each astronomer receives the data generated by his or her requested groups, along with other parameters required for data analysis.

---

[2] At the time of writing, ATIS is undergoing an international standardization effort. Since its first formal introduction, there have been a number of extensions proposed to the basic ATIS standard. In Dublin, Ireland, in early August of 1992, the International Astronomical Union (IAU) sponsored a colloquium on stellar photometry. As part of this effort, the IAU also established a committee to define a detailed standard, in writing, as quickly as possible. A number of extensions to ATIS have been collected by the ATIS-standardization committee, and the new version of the language will be called ATIS-93. The formal definition should be published in the summer of 1993 as a special issue of the *International Amateur-Professional Photoelectric Photometry Association Communications*.

12.2.2 Dispatch at the Telescope

Although there are different implementations of ATIS-interpretation software, we concentrate on the implementation that we are most familiar with: the ATIScope system of the AutoScope Corporation.[3] ATIScope manages the execution of an ATIS file at the telescope. ATIScope runs on the local telescope control computer, using observatory and telescope sensors to determine when to execute the provided groups. ATIScope has a variety of general observatory and telescope management responsibilities, but we only discuss *group selection*, that is, the determination of the order in which the groups should be executed on the telescope. We often refer to ATIScope as a *controller* because its major role is to control the behavior of the telescope under the guidance of the current ATIS file.

Group selection is accomplished by a heuristic process that attempts to find the "locally best" executable group. A group is executable if the logical preconditions specified by its astronomer are met. ATIS provides a way for an astronomer to establish group preconditions that relate to the current date and current time and whether the moon is up or down. The date for a group is specified as a window, that is, as a pair: earliest acceptable day and a latest acceptable day. The time is also specified as a window: earliest acceptable hour and latest acceptable hour. An astronomer can specify a group *priority*, which is used by ATIScope to sort the groups in order of apparent importance. ATIS also allows an astronomer to specify the number of times the group should be executed. See Genet and Hayes (1989, p. 208) for more details.

At the core of ATIScope is a sense-check-execute loop. In sensing, all relevant environmental parameters are determined (date, time, moon status). ATIScope next checks to see which of the groups are enabled according to the match between the current sensor values and the astronomer-provided preconditions. We call the set of groups that pass this matching test the *enabled* groups. The set of enabled groups is winnowed by the application of *group selection rules*. These rules capture heuristic knowledge about which group to execute *next*. In scheduling parlance, this scheme is often called *heuristic dispatch* because at any point in time, some task (here, a group) is "dispatched" for execution, and the selection of a task is determined, purely locally (without look-ahead), by the application of domain-specific heuristics.

12.2.3 The Group Selection Rules

The domain-specific heuristics reduce the set of enabled groups to a single group to be executed next. There are four heuristic group selection rules specified

---

[3] AutoScope Corporation is now located in Fort Collins, Colorado.

in the ATIS standard: priority, number-of-observations-remaining, nearest-to-end-local-sidereal-time,[4] and file-position. The rules are applied in the sequence given. If the result of applying any rule is that there is only one group remaining, that group is selected for execution, and no further rules are applied. Because the final heuristic (file-position) always prefers a unique group, application of the group selection rules deterministically makes a unique selection.

The heuristics look at data provided by the individual astronomers and what has been done so far. The first heuristic, priority, simply says that the highest priority group should be selected. Because there can be multiple groups having equal priority, this heuristic might return a set of groups. Whenever two or more groups remain, the next heuristic, number-of-observations-remaining, is applied. This heuristic prefers groups that have the greatest disparity between how many times they have been observed so far and how many observations have been requested. Again, this can result in a set of groups. The nearest-to-end-LST heuristic next prefers the group that will move out of its observation window first. This heuristic tends to extend the interval of time over which a given group can be observed. Finally, on the rare occasion that the nearest-to-end-LST heuristic fails to produce a unique group, the candidate group closest to the top of the ATIS file is selected.

Following selection, the lucky group is executed, and telescope control is surrendered to the detailed commands of the astronomer who wrote the group. While a group is executing, there are safety checks to ensure that the astronomer's commands do not damage equipment. If the commands are well-behaved (and if the weather cooperates), group execution finishes normally, and ATIScope performs another iteration of its sense-check-execute loop.

12.2.4 The Question of Dispatch Performance

How well does ATIScope perform? It is clear that the ATIS heuristic dispatch rules do provide a reasonable level of performance for some situations. ATIS has been in use for almost seven years, and there is general agreement in the astronomy community that it has enabled certain science that would have otherwise been impossible. However, it should be possible to improve telescope utilization through better group scheduling. With the heuristic dispatch technique, all decisions are *local* in the sense that no temporal look-ahead is performed to evaluate the ramifications of executing a given group. It is worth noting that although the behavior produced by ATIScope might not be optimal, the controller defined by ATIScope is extremely robust. The ATIScope "schedule" breaks only when no group is currently

---

[4] Local sidereal time, or LST, is a commonly used time measurement system in astronomy. The precise details of its definition do not concern us here.

enabled. Section 12.6 discusses the trade-off between schedule *quality* and *robustness* in more detail.

The next section defines the search space used by CERES so that Section 12.4 can precisely answer the question of dispatch performance.

12.3 THE SEARCH SPACE OF SCHEDULES

Any scheduler based on look-ahead must *search*, generating and evaluating alternative schedules. This section explains how the search space of CERES is organized. Our general approach is based on ERE (the Entropy Reduction Engine), an architecture for planning, scheduling, and execution systems. This chapter only explains aspects of the architecture that are relevant to the APT scheduling problem. For more information about the ERE architecture itself, see Bresina & Drummond (1990); Drummond, Bresina, & Kedar (1991); and Bresina, Drummond, & Kedar (1992).

There are many different ways of organizing a scheduler's search space. For convenience, however, we can classify techniques based on a simple distinction: if each "node" in a scheduler's search space contains an entire schedule, we say that the scheduler searches through a *space of schedules*; if, on the other hand, each node in the search space describes a possible state of the world, we say that the scheduler searches through a *space of world states* (see Hendler, Tate, & Drummond [1990] for more on this distinction).

There are a large number of techniques for searching through a space of schedules, many of them based on traditional constraint satisfaction techniques. The OPIS (Smith, *et al.*, 1990) and Cortes (Fox & Sycara, 1990) systems, for instance, search through a space of schedules, as do HSTS (Muscettola, *et al.*, 1989), GPSS (Zweben, Deale, & Gargan, 1991), and Sonia (Collinot, Le Pape, & Pinoteau, 1988). Search in such systems is the process of repeatedly taking one schedule S and transforming it into another schedule S', such that (hopefully) S' is better than S according to the objectives of the scheduling problem. There is a growing body of techniques for performing such schedule transformations, but we do not have space to discuss them here; the interested reader is referred to other chapters in this volume.

The other approach is to search through world states. In this approach, each node in the search space describes a possible world state. This approach draws from the techniques of classical physics, where a "vector of basis variables" is used to characterize the world at each point in time, and a transition function maps one vector at time t into another vector at time $t + \Delta$. Discrete event simulation systems are also based on this idea. The functionality that typically separates a scheduler from a simulator is that the scheduler is able to search, backtracking to previous states as necessary. Simulators typically have a fixed strategy by which actions are

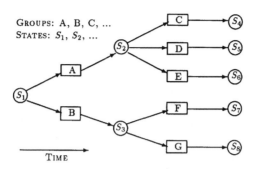

Figure 12-1:   Forward chronological search space for schedules

selected for execution. In fact, a heuristic dispatch scheduler can easily be modeled by such a simulator because search is unnecessary.

CERES searches through a space of world states, forward in time from some given start state. We say that CERES uses *forward chronological search* and call this process *temporal projection*. For a sketch of how this works, see Figure 12-1. In the figure, the search space is shown as a branching tree structure where a circular node represents a world state. For the APT problem, the state of the world is essentially the state of the telescope, observatory, and environment. A rectangular node represents the execution of a group. The tree begins at a point in time early in the evening at the state node labeled S_1. For this example, branching out and forward from S_1 are two possible groups to execute: A or B. The branching indicates an exclusive-or choice—one of the groups must be chosen but not both. The alternative branches out of any given state represent the groups enabled in that state. Recall that a group is enabled in a state if all the group's preconditions are true in the state. In terms of the example given in Figure 12-1, we say that in state S_1, group A can be *applied* to produce state S_2.

CERES is not the first scheduler to search a space of world states. In fact, ISIS (Fox & Smith, 1984) is the first scheduler of which we are aware that did this. There are a number of arguments for and against such a representation, and we will not consider them all here. We have chosen the representation for the fact that it simply and easily supports the idea that the immediate future is more certain, the distant future less so. It is very easy to attach probabilistic information to the states and transitions in a world-state search space and to use this information to support probabilistic reasoning during search. It is possible to do such reasoning with other representations, of course; we have simply chosen one convenient and perspicuous representation. Indeed, there have been a number of approaches presented that can represent the decay of information out into the future (Dean & Kanazawa, 1988; Hanks, 1990). We discuss the use of such information in Section 12.6.

We call the branching temporal structure a *projection graph* or, simply, a *projection*. A projection graph defines a tree of possible telescope schedules, where each trajectory through the projection defines a different possible schedule. The overall theoretical space that includes all possible schedules is called the *implicit* projection, and the sub-graph that is actually enumerated during any given search is called the *explicit* projection.

Schedules that are identical up to a given branching point share a common prefix. A *single* schedule is represented by a sequence of groups contained in a trajectory from the root state of the projection to some state accessible from the root. For example, A followed by C would be a very short schedule. Of course, the size of the implicit projection is exponential in the number of ATIS groups, so it is impractical to exhaustively search it. This is not a surprise because scheduling is known to be a combinatorially explosive problem in general, and there is no reason to expect to be able to avoid this for the APT scheduling problem. Thus, the explicit projection must be kept manageably small.

Because groups are enabled in a state only if their astronomer-defined preconditions are satisfied, a CERES projection defines all technically feasible schedules. A PA-provided objective function can be applied to any given schedule in the projection, giving us an evaluation of how well that schedule meets the PA's goals. In a sense, a projection is defined so that each possible schedule satisfies all the problem's "hard" constraints. A *hard* constraint is one that absolutely must be satisfied in any given solution schedule. In contrast, *soft* constraints are said to be user-preferences, typically relating to cost or performance. Thus, the objective function encodes the PA's soft constraints. Ideally, the output from a scheduler is a schedule that satisfies all hard constraints and that also achieves the best possible score on all the soft constraints. In reality, schedules must satisfy all hard constraints and achieve "reasonably good" performance on the soft constraints. This means that the basic business of CERES is that of selective temporal projection to find schedules that score well under the PA-provided objective function.

12.4 EXPLORING THE SEARCH SPACE

This section "maps" the search space of CERES for a particular problem instance. The purpose of the mapping is to measure three things, each with respect to a given objective function. First, for a given score under the objective function, how many schedules in the search space achieve that score? An answer to this question will help us determine how hard the given problem instance really is (with respect to the given objective function). Second, how well does the ATIS heuristic dispatcher perform? Third, is it possible to outperform the heuristic dispatcher by using the objective function as a heuristic evaluation function in a hill-climbing search algorithm? This section provides answers to these three questions. The

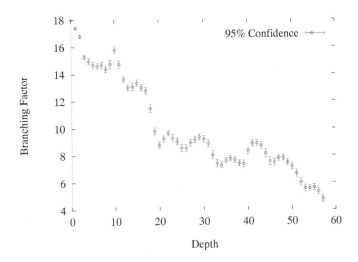

Figure 12-2:   Average branching factor as a function of projection tree depth

results of this section are only illustrative, based on a single but real ATIS input file. This file contains 194 groups that represent the combined observation requests of three users.

12.4.1 Search Space Size

An important determinant of problem difficulty is the size of the implicit projection graph. Although it is not practical to enumerate each schedule of the implicit graph, its size can be estimated using a technique called *iterative sampling* (Knuth, 1975; Chen, 1989; Langley, 1992; Minton *et al.*, 1992). This technique is a type of Monte Carlo method that estimates projection graph size based on a set of randomly selected trajectories. Each trajectory is selected by starting at the initial state and choosing randomly among the groups enabled in that state. The selected group is applied, producing a new projection state, and the process of random selection and application continues until enablement is no longer defined. The size of the projection graph is determined by its depth and branching factor. These two factors are estimated from the set of randomly selected trajectories. To our knowledge, Knuth (1975) was the first person to use this approach to estimate the size of a search space. Chen (1989) refined, extended, and analyzed the technique.

Figure 12-2 shows the results of 100 runs of iterative sampling with error bars representing the 95% confidence interval. The branching factor is history-dependent; that is, the number of enabled groups decreases through the night. The primary reason for this is that as groups are selected for execution, the number of unscheduled groups decreases. These data suggest that the number of schedules in the projection graph is between 10^{56} and 10^{57}. From this, we can easily see that there is no shortage of possible schedules.

12.4.2 Search Space Quality

It is not simply the *size* of the projection graph that determines the difficulty of finding a good schedule; the distribution of high quality schedules is also important. Schedule quality is defined with respect to some objective function. For our experiments, we have constructed a simple but representative objective function based on comments we have received from PAs.

The objective function is a weighted combination of four components: (1) priority, (2) fairness, (3) airmass, and (4) duration. For a given schedule, the first component is computed as the average group priority. In ATIS, a higher priority is indicated by a lower number; hence, a lower average is better. The second component attempts to measure how fair the schedule is in terms of the time allocated to each user. Because each user can request a different amount of observation time, the fairness measure is computed as the sum of the differences between the amount of time requested in the ATIS file and that allocated in a given schedule. Hence, smaller fairness scores are better. The third component attempts to improve the quality of observations by reducing the amount of atmosphere (airmass) through which observations are made. For an object of a given declination, airmass is minimal when the telescope is pointing on the meridian. We approximate the airmass measure as the average deviation from the meridian (in local hour angle units).[5] The duration measure is computed as the amount of time spent executing groups. Unlike the other components, a high score for duration is better; hence, this component is inverted before it is combined with the others. The four component measures are combined linearly to yield an overall objective function score. Under this objective function, better schedules achieve lower scores. In the experiments reported here, the weights have been set in an attempt to give equal importance to each component.

We would like to determine the difficulty of finding schedules of a given quality, and iterative sampling can be used to provide an estimate. Evaluating the schedules found via iterative sampling yields a distribution of expected scores. In our experiments, we performed 1000 iterative samples and computed the composite objective function score as well as the component scores for priority, fairness, and airmass. We also evaluated the schedule produced by the ATIScope heuristic dispatcher as a point of comparison. In addition, we used the objective function as a heuristic for a traditional hill-climbing algorithm. This algorithm implements a

---

[5] Our measure is only an approximation of the true value because airmass is non-linearly related to local hour angle. Airmass is, in fact, linearly related to the secant of the local hour angle.

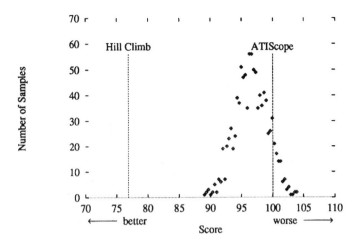

Figure 12-3:   Objective function—random *vs.* ATIScope and hill climbing

"greedy" search as follows: at each choice point, the group that produces the best scoring state is added to the schedule.

Figure 12-3 shows the composite objective function scores obtained by the three search techniques. The scores from iterative sampling are grouped into 50 "score buckets" (or "bins") of equal size. For each point, the *x*-coordinate is the mid-point of a score bucket, and the *y*-coordinate is the number of samples that obtained a score in that bucket. For comparison, the single score obtained by hill climbing and the single score obtained by the ATIScope dispatcher are also shown in the figure. For example, Figure 12-3 shows that hill climbing obtained a score of approximately 76.9, and this is indicated in the graph as a single vertical line (the height of the line is not significant). ATIScope obtained a score of 100, and this is shown by another single vertical line.

It is interesting that the majority of objective function scores obtained by iterative sampling are actually better than the score obtained by ATIScope. In contrast, the score obtained by hill climbing is much better than both the majority of scores obtained by iterative sampling and the single score obtained by ATIScope (recall that lower scores are better). Figures 12-4, 12-5, and 12-6 show a comparison of the three search techniques for the individual component scores of priority, fairness, and airmass, respectively. Notice that ATIScope obtains the best score for priority (Figure 12-4), as might be expected.[6] In each figure, the scores produced

---

[6] This is a natural result of the fact that ATIScope applies a priority-oriented group selection rule first. In essence, this induces a priority-sort on the groups, and all subsequent dispatch rules operate within this sort.

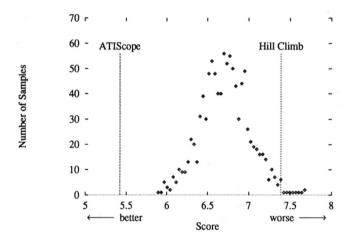

Figure 12-4:   The priority component of the objective function

by iterative sampling provide a feeling for the expected distribution of possible scores in the projection graph.

We note that the specific results obtained in this experiment are extremely sensitive to the particular components and weights used in the objective function. There are many attributes of good schedules that this objective ignores, and we plan on refining and extending it over time. Additionally, although these results suggest that hill climbing finds good schedules, we have defined other search strategies that seem to outperform hill climbing. Our initial experiments only suggest

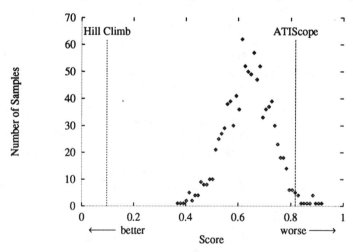

Figure 12-5:   The fairness component of the objective function

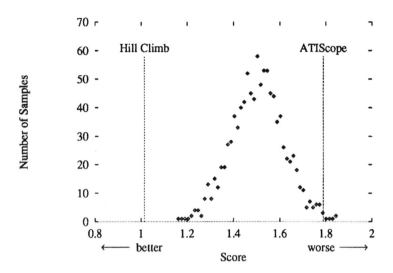

Figure 12-6: The airmass component of the objective function

that there is significant expected gain associated with heuristic search techniques in general. Future work will explore and report on other search techniques that perform well for the APT group scheduling problem.

The goal of this section has been to map the search space and to measure the performance of the ATIS heuristic dispatcher. We wanted to see if heuristic hill climbing could outperform the dispatcher, and the answer is *yes*, it can, on this problem instance, for this particular objective function. However, one must be careful not to infer from these data that the APT observation scheduling problem is easy! The ATIS file we used had already, to some extent, been edited by a PA, so it does not represent a simple union of raw ATIS from three users. To make more general conclusions, one would have to map the search space for a number of ATIS files and a variety of objective functions.

12.5 EXECUTION OF A SCHEDULE

Finding a high-quality schedule is all very well, but once found, it must be effectively translated into action; that is, once found, a schedule must be *executed*. This section explains our approach to schedule execution, where the key result is as follows: the telescope controller uses a schedule found by CERES if one appropriate to the current situation exists; otherwise, rather than sit idle, it "falls back" on the ATIS heuristic dispatcher in order to keep the telescope usefully occupied.

12.5.1 Policies and SCRs

CERES compiles any given schedule for the telescope into a policy for controlling the telescope's behavior. A *policy* is a partial function that maps from states into control actions. For the APT domain, the states describe the status of the telescope and other relevant conditions, including the local sidereal time, and each control action recommended by a policy is a group. Thus, for the APT problem, a policy defines what group the telescope should execute for a given set of states. It is important to note that a policy is a *partial* function, in the sense that it will typically not be defined for the entire state space of the system; in fact, a policy is typically defined only for a small subset of all possible states. If a policy is undefined for a given state, it simply provides no advice about what group to execute in that state. If the policy is undefined for the current world state, we say that the schedule (represented by the policy compiled from that schedule) is *broken*.

We represent a policy as a set of *situated control rules*, or SCRs (Drummond, 1989). Each SCR is a rule of the form

$$N: S \to A \{N', N'', \ldots\}$$

where each N is an integer identifier, S is a conjunctive set of state conditions, and A is a recommended group. The identifier N is simply a numeric label for the rule. The final component of the SCR, $\{N', N'', \ldots\}$, indicates a set of possible successors. The interpretation of such an SCR is this: "if the current state satisfies conditions S, then take action A, and consider any one of SCRs $\{N', N'', \ldots\}$ next." For a simple example, consider the following:

$$1: (1400 \leq \text{LST} \leq 1700) \to \text{G42} \{2\}.$$

This SCR, labeled "1," says that if the local sidereal time (LST) is between 1400 and 1700, then group G42 should be executed, and the SCR labeled "2" should be preferentially considered next.

These SCRs differ in one significant way from those originally defined by Drummond (1989). In our previous work, each SCR was a simple if-then rule of the form "$S \to A$." Following the advice of Kabanza (1992), we have added SCR labels and sequencing. The benefit is that the SCR interpretation process no longer needs to search the entire set of SCRs; instead, it is biased by the recommendation from the previously executed SCR. Basically, this sequencing approach preserves group ordering information that is explicitly represented in the projection.

Currently, we take a relatively simple approach to compiling a given schedule into a set of SCRs. For each projection state on the path that defines the schedule, we form an SCR as follows. The preconditions of the SCR are formed from the relevant conditions in the state, including the local sidereal time. To increase the applicability of the SCR, we form a fixed-width LST window centered around the state's LST. Although we have done some work in the past on how to select and generalize relevant state conditions (Bresina, Drummond, & Kedar, 1993), there are still open research issues regarding how this work can be applied to the telescope scheduling problem. The group recommended by the SCR is simply the group whose application to the current state generates the next state in the path. Each SCR compiled from a projection path "points to" the next SCR in the sequence.

12.5.2 Group Selection and SCRs

We modified the existing ATIScope system to accept a schedule represented as a set of SCRs. The new version of the telescope controller is called SCRscope, and it interprets a set of SCRs as follows. To begin with, the SCR with a label of 1 is tested to see if its preconditions are met. If so, the group recommended by the SCR is executed, and the current rule's next-SCR becomes the recommended SCR to consider first on the next cycle. If each recommended SCR is in fact applicable, then the behavior of SCRscope is simply to execute the groups exactly as specified in the schedule. Otherwise, any currently applicable SCR can be used, and one is chosen at random. This means that schedule execution is not as rigid as is the case for an execution system that follows a schedule by strict sequencing constraints (see Fikes & Nilsson [1972], for a discussion of this idea in a traditional plan execution framework).

If the preconditions of a recommended SCR are false, then the schedule is not executing as predicted. For instance, if the weather turns bad, a group might abort because of a star acquisition failure. If this happens, the group will take less time than predicted, and the next SCR might not be applicable. In such a situation, SCRscope attempts to find *any* SCR whose preconditions are true in the current state. If such an SCR is found, then the system recovers back onto an alternative schedule. If no applicable SCRs are found, then SCRscope does exactly what ATIScope itself would do: it selects a group via heuristic dispatch. This interpretation of the SCRs by SCRscope means that a desired schedule is followed as long as possible, but if the schedule breaks, the entire system does not grind to a halt. Instead, *some* appropriate group is selected through heuristic dispatch, and the telescope remains busy.

This approach is an example of what we call the "principle of independent competence" (Bresina & Drummond, 1990). In the context of the APT problem, the principle of independent competence requires that CERES not degrade the baseline performance of the telescope controller. Thus, if CERES has a schedule that can improve the telescope controller's operation, it should be used. However, in the absence of a workable schedule, the default group selection rules define a behavior that is better than doing nothing. The assumption underlying this principle is that the opportunity cost of a round of heuristic dispatch is less than the opportunity cost of doing nothing at all. Said another way, heuristic dispatch is unlikely to take an action that, in the long run, is actually worse than taking no action at all.

12.5.3 Scheduler and Controller Interaction

We have implemented the scheduler/controller interface based on the idea of loosely synchronized communication. CERES tracks the controller's progress by reading reports issued as groups are executed; the controller accepts new sets of SCRs as it runs, providing the ability to dynamically reschedule on-line. CERES, written in Lisp, running on a Sparc II, communicates with the SCRscope controller, written in Pascal and running on an IBM-compatible PC (currently, a 386-based machine).

The basic scheduler/controller interaction is as follows. First, CERES builds a temporal projection to find a specific schedule. Once found, the schedule is compiled into SCRs, which are sent to SCRscope. CERES accepts status reports from SCRscope and uses these to determine whether or not the schedule is being followed. Essentially, each status report indicates the group that has been chosen for execution *next*. If the indicated group is on the schedule, then CERES throws away those components of the projection that are inconsistent with the history. If the indicated group is not on the schedule, then something has gone wrong, and the current schedule has broken. When this happens, CERES reschedules.

The interaction from the SCRscope (controller) side is straightforward. At the start of a night, it reads the ATIS file and initializes all required telescope and observatory parameters (this functionality is provided by the original ATIScope code). It then goes into its sense-check-execute loop, preferentially using SCRs in the manner described above. Just before each group execution, the controller issues a report that indicates the next group to be executed, and this is used by CERES as described. On each pass through the loop, the controller also checks if there are any new SCRs: if so, these new SCRs are read, and the old ones are discarded. Thus, once a new schedule has been produced by CERES, it is accepted by SCRscope and used immediately.

This architecture has an interesting feature: as long as a schedule is executing as expected, the scheduler has some free reasoning time. The execution of a group typically takes about 10 minutes, and this gives the scheduler plenty of time to do other things. For instance, the scheduler might look for better alternative schedules, or it might reason about how to make the existing schedule more robust (more on this in the next section). CERES can find a possible schedule in a matter of seconds, so it can consider a large number of alternative schedules in the time required to execute a group. Whenever CERES finds a better schedule, it is compiled into SCRs and transmitted to the controller.

It is useful to view SCRs as dispatch rules automatically formulated specifically for a given problem. The execution of these dispatch rules produces a behavior that achieves the desired objective function score. The policy defined by the automatically produced rules is *extremely* specific to the given problem, and our approach makes little effort to generalize the policy; thus, these automatically produced policies tend to be rather brittle. However, the group selection rules also define a policy, and this policy is extremely general and robust. The problem, of course, is that the behaviors produced by the heuristic dispatch policy are typically of lower quality than those discovered by temporal projection. The management of this trade-off between quality and robustness is the topic of the next section.

The system of communication described above has been implemented and extensively tested on a simulator provided by AutoScope Corporation.[7] As a result of this work, SCRs will be included in the next definition of the ATIS language, ATIS-93. There is a new instruction in ATIS-93 patterned after our SCRs, with some refinements suggested by Lou Boyd of Fairborn Observatory. We are now in the process of modifying CERES and SCRscope so that the communication described above adheres to the ATIS-93 standard. Until now, all communication has occurred over a special-purpose connection on the network file system of our local area network.

12.6 CONTINGENT SCHEDULING

There is a recurrent tension between schedule quality and schedule robustness. The robustness of a schedule relates to the ability of that schedule to withstand environmental perturbations. Schedules that are of high quality tend to be rather brittle. For instance, if an objective function seeks to maximize the number of observations in a given night, then the resulting schedules will tend to be packed tightly with groups. If only one of these groups takes longer than projected, then the entire schedule might fail. In contrast, the heuristic dispatch technique is extremely robust with respect to environmental perturbations. The dispatch approach forms no expectations about the future, so it can hardly be disappointed when any given observation takes longer than it might otherwise. Indeed, the entire notion of *failure* is defined with respect to a specific prediction, so heuristic dispatch can never fail, at least in this technical sense. The problem with using pure dispatch, of course, is that it is hard to ensure that the behaviors produced are of high quality.

To better manage the robustness/quality trade-off, we have begun to study a class of techniques that explicitly consider the way in which actions might fail and how such failures can impact the desired schedule. These techniques require a model of the way in which scheduled actions can fail in order to form schedules, in advance, for the situations that can arise under the possible failures. These techniques do not assume that all contingencies can be mapped out in advance; hence, rescheduling is still a basic part of our architecture (as outlined in the previous

[7] Development of the simulator was funded by a 1991 NASA Ames Director's Discretionary Fund.

section). We are studying these proactive error management techniques in order to better understand when and where they might be appropriate.

This section motivates and defines these proactive error management techniques and discusses some of the important issues they raise.

12.6.1 Reasoning about Disjunction

There are many sorts of disjunction one might consider, but we restrict our discussion to the sort caused by the presence of "stochastic" actions. A *stochastic* action is one that does not have a single uniquely predictable outcome. For example, when you choose to drop a glass on the floor, *you* have control over the execution of that action (you can choose to release the glass or not), but you do not have direct control over the action's outcome: the glass might break, or it might not. The outcome is certainly conditioned on the state of the world when the action is executed. Is there a rug on the floor? How high is your hand when the glass is released? The best we can do from a modeling perspective is to probabilistically characterize relative outcome frequency.

In the APT problem, each group is best viewed as a stochastic action. The primary effect of each group is to occupy the telescope for a certain amount of time. The termination time for a group is a function of when the group starts and the group's predicted duration. One might simply associate a nominal duration with each group based on how long it takes to execute when nothing goes wrong. However, this misses critical information that can be of value: what happens if the group aborts only seconds into its execution? This might happen if the very first star acquisition command fails because of cloud cover, for instance. We can instead characterize each group as a stochastic action, where the various effects model the different possible group durations. Estimating the various durations is reasonably easy.

It is straightforward to include stochastic actions in our temporal projections. See Figure 12-7 for a simple example. A projection is now a bipartite graph, where the interpretation is that actions are disjunctively enabled in states, and the application of an action to a state gives rise to a disjunctive set of possible successor states.[8] For example, the figure shows that in state S_1, there are two enabled groups: G_1 and G_2. The split out of S_1 represents a choice between the two groups; it is important to note, however, that this is a choice that will be made by the scheduler (between G_1 or G_2). In contrast, the figure shows that the execution of group G_1 can stochastically give rise to any one of three possible successor states: S_2, S_3, or S_4. This split is *not* under the system's control and is determined by exogenous factors

---

[8] Such a representation is functionally equivalent to a decision tree, and the contingent reasoning we will shortly outline approximates that of true decision theory.

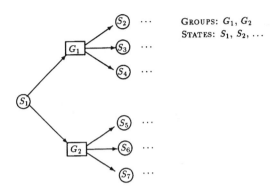

Figure 12-7:   A projection with stochastic actions

such as cloud cover. The states that G_1 can produce are differentiated by the local sidereal time at which they can occur. Thus, each of these states models the termination of group G_1 after a certain amount of time has passed.

Formally, we characterize the probability of a given state in terms of the probability of getting to that state via a given trajectory in the projection. For the projection fragment in Figure 12-7, the probability of the system arriving in state S_2, notated $pr\,(S_2)$, is given by $pr\,(S_1) * pr\,(S_2 \mid G_1)$. That is, the probability of being in S_2 is the probability of being in S_1 multiplied by the probability of outcome S_2 given the choice of executing group G_1. Given transition probabilities for each of the various possible outcomes, the projection process can easily compute a probability for every state in the graph.

What we are concerned with is the utility of reasoning about the stochastic disjunctions in the projection. All schedulers we know of consider only a single, non-disjunctive schedule during search. That is, at any point during search, a standard scheduler has available only a *single* schedule. Of course, a single schedule might be represented as a partial order; in which case, there are a number of totally ordered schedules consistent with it; however, a partial order cannot represent a true disjunction, where a given group might or might not actually be in the schedule. All a partial order does is avoid commitment with respect to group ordering—each group that is in the partial order *is* in the schedule.

More generally, a schedule might be represented as a set of constraints on possible completions; in which case, one might argue that the scheduler is considering *sets* of schedules during search. This is undoubtedly true, but one must carefully study the constraint language used. The partial order, for instance, is a special case of this idea. The constraints of a partial order, namely, ordering relations

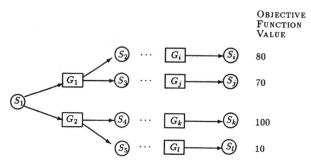

Figure 12-8:   A stochastic projection and evaluation

between actions, do not allow for the representation of contingent actions based on the outcome of action execution. Schrag, Boddy, & Carciofini (1992) discuss this issue and show that their particular partial-order-based system cannot represent true disjunction of action existence.

We are not aware of any scheduler that provides a representation that allows for true action disjunction. The representation of Allen (1984), for instance, allows one to state a disjunction between interval relations but does not allow one to state a disjunction of action existence.[9] To state a true disjunction between actions, one requires a branching temporal logic with a possible worlds semantics (Drummond, 1989). This is precisely the semantics of our temporal projection structure; as a result, our scheduler is able to represent true disjunction of action existence and, thus, can represent and reason over conditional schedules.

We have been studying the situations in which it might be beneficial for a scheduler to reason about conditional schedules. Consider the simple projection sketched in Figure 12-8. There are two groups enabled in state S_1: G_1 and G_2. Each of these groups has two outcomes: G_1 can stochastically give rise to S_2 or S_3, and G_2 can similarly give rise to S_4 or S_5. For simplicity, let us suppose that there are no further stochastic splits in the projection and that after some sequence of intervening groups, each of the possible trajectories terminates in one of the final states (S_i, S_j, S_k, or S_l). The scores of these trajectories under an objective function are shown in the figure; note that in this example, higher scores are better.

Suppose that $pr(S_1) = 1$, $pr(S_2 \mid G_1) = 0.5$, and $pr(S_3 \mid G_1) = 0.5$. The expected value of executing group G_1 in state S_1 is 75, obtained as $0.5 * 80 + 0.5 * 70$. If $pr(S_4 \mid G_2) = 0.5$ and $pr(S_5 \mid G_2) = 0.5$, then the expected value of executing group

----

[9] For instance, if $T1$ and $T2$ are intervals, one can use Allen's (1984) logic to say that $T1$ precedes $T2$ or $T2$ precedes $T1$. Such a disjunction only expresses a lack of commitment to an ordering between the two intervals. $T1$ *and* $T2$ are both necessarily in the schedule.

G_2 in S_2 is only 55. Thus, by explicitly representing the stochastic outcomes of groups G_1 and G_2, a scheduler can make an informed choice between them.

Of course, this example is highly stylized, intended only to make a simple point. Whether or not actual telescope operations follow this pattern is an empirical question and one that we intend to answer. The point is simply that by explicitly considering various action outcomes, it is theoretically *possible* for a scheduler to make better decisions.

If the stochastic outcomes are not represented, what might a scheduler do? When modeling the effects of groups G_1 and G_2, a person would have to make a decision about which particular outcome to include. Presumably, this person would choose the outcome with the highest probability because this describes the group's "nominal" behavior. Under this scheme, for the example given, the choice of which outcome to include would be arbitrary. However, let us assume that the person gives the outcome that he or she feels might give rise to the best possible objective function score. In this case, the person would model only S_2 for G_1 and S_4 for G_2. It is easy to see that a scheduler that is given such an impoverished model will tend to make poorer quality decisions than one that has the stochastic model discussed above.

12.6.2 Executing Disjunctive Schedules

Schedule quality is not the only reason to use disjunctive schedules. An additional aspect of schedule disjunction arises in schedule *execution*. This section argues that there is a significant benefit associated with giving disjunctive schedules to an execution system. The essence of the argument is this: if a scheduler considers execution errors in advance, then the amount of telescope "dead time" can be reduced. We use the term *dead time* to refer to the time that the telescope is not carrying out useful scientific work.

Consider what might happen in a non-disjunctive scheduler. An execution system attempts to execute scheduled actions in sequence, eventually succeeding if each action in the sequence succeeds, failing if any one action fails. Many schedule execution environments are characterized by the possibility of failure, and this is certainly true for the APT problem. Thus, the execution system will typically get part way through a given schedule, and then the schedule will break, forcing the scheduler to respond to a new situation. This is sketched in the top half of Figure 12-9, where interleaved scheduling and execution occurs over time. First, an interval of time from $T0$ until $T1$ is used to find the initial schedule. Next, an interval from $T1$ until $T2$ elapses while that schedule is executed. At $T2$, the schedule breaks, and the system is forced to reschedule from time $T2$ until $T3$. The resulting schedule is given to the execution system, and the cycle continues, with another schedule execution failure at $T4$ and rescheduling occurring from $T4$ to $T5$.

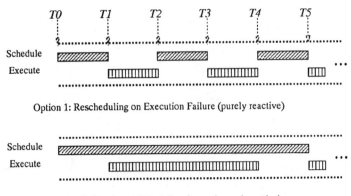

Option 1: Rescheduling on Execution Failure (purely reactive)

Option 2: Contingent Scheduling (proactive and reactive)

Figure 12-9:   Two options for managing schedule failure

If the mean time for rescheduling is S, and if there are F many execution failures, then the expected telescope dead time is $S * F$. For the example given, if the duration of each scheduling interval is 1 and if accounting begins after the initial schedule is found (at $T1$), then the telescope experiences a dead time of two units.

The story for our disjunctive scheduler is sketched in the lower half of Figure 12-9. The disjunctive scheduler can find a single schedule in the same amount of time as the non-disjunctive scheduler. This can be guaranteed, if needed, by simply using the schedule found by a non-disjunctive scheduler as search advice for the disjunctive scheduler. That is, one could run the non-disjunctive scheduler; take the resulting schedule; and use it to create a projection, step-by-step. There is a constant amount of overhead incurred per step because of the inclusion of stochastic group outcomes, and this overhead is incurred once per group in the schedule. Thus, there is an insignificant increase in the cost incurred by the contingent scheduler in finding the first nominal schedule.

However, for this hypothetical example, we are not making an argument about the relative efficiency of the two systems, so let us simply assume that the disjunctive scheduler can find a single schedule in the same amount of time as the non-disjunctive scheduler. Thus, execution of the single schedule begins at time $T1$. However, because our scheduler can reason about alternative possible time lines, it can continue reasoning about errors that might occur during the execution of the initial schedule. This is shown in the figure by extending the scheduling activity bar through time $T1$. By reasoning about possible execution errors in advance, our disjunctive scheduler can create alternative schedules for the execution system. By time $T2$, where the initial schedule would have failed, the contingent scheduler has already found an alternative and given it to the execution system. Thus, instead of failing, the execution system carries on through *T2*, keeping the telescope usefully occupied. To be fair, the figure also shows a situation where a specific execution failure has not been considered by the disjunctive scheduler: at time *T4*, the contingent schedule breaks, and rescheduling is carried out from time *T4* until *T5*, as for the non-disjunctive scheduler.

It is important to understand that the purely *reactive* approach of rescheduling is a special case of the *proactive* approach that we are advocating. We do not assume that the contingent scheduler always considers in advance exactly the schedule breakages that actually occur. Reactive rescheduling upon failure occurrence is explicitly part of our approach. What we are proposing is an additional technique that uses available information to avoid rescheduling *when possible* because time spent rescheduling is time wasted at the telescope.

As for the non-disjunctive scheduler, let the time required to create a single schedule be *S*. Further, assume that *G* is the mean time required to execute a group and that $S < G$; that is, assume that the time required to find a schedule is less than the time required to execute any given step of a schedule (this is certainly true of our current scheduler for the APT problem). If the probability of a prediction failure is *P*, and there are *F* many execution failures of the non-disjunctive schedule, then the expected amount of telescope dead time under the disjunctive scheduler is $P * F * S$. For the example given, let's suppose that the probability of a prediction failure is 0.5 and that the time cost of scheduling is one unit. There are two execution failures experienced by the non-disjunctive scheduler; thus for the disjunctive scheduler, the *expected* telescope dead time is one unit (consistent with the example in Figure 12-9).

Please note that for simplicity, this discussion has ignored the principle of independent competence, introduced in the previous section. Recall that independent competence allows a round of heuristic dispatch while rescheduling. Including this does not change the nature of our argument, but it does complicate the story somewhat. Essentially, if independent competence is used, the telescope does not experience dead time *per se* but, instead, exhibits lower-quality behavior over time because of the increased frequency of dispatch-selected groups.

12.6.3 When to Predict, When to React?

The example given in this section is intended only to illustrate the general point. In reality, the efficiency and value of contingent scheduling depend on a number of factors we can only begin to characterize.

For instance, suppose that the schedule simply *never* breaks. Clearly, reasoning about contingencies is a waste of processor time. However, consider the other extreme, where the schedule breaks on every group: in this case, contingent scheduling might keep the telescope usefully employed for significantly more of the night than the pure rescheduling approach. Additionally, consider the case where the stochastic action model used by the scheduler is 100% correct; that is, the model has perfect fidelity, and all predictions are correct. Clearly, more work done by the contingent scheduler is directly useful to the task at hand. Alternatively, imagine that the stochastic action model is 100% *incorrect*. This means that each prediction that is made is wrong, and all the reasoning about possible errors is likely to be for naught. We list these factors simply to suggest that the reality of contingent *vs.* non-contingent scheduling is more subtle than our simple example might suggest. However, it is clear from the discussion that there *are* cases where contingent scheduling should be of use.

We are developing a technique called *Just-In-Case* scheduling, or JIC for short.[10] The technique is based on the work of Drummond and Bresina (1990), where information regarding stochastic action outcome is used to patch possible errors in advance of their occurrence.

There are a number of factors that determine whether or not JIC (and other proactive error management techniques) will work. Among these are the nature of the stochastic action "splits." We have hypothesized that if the average stochastic branching factor out of each action is low and that if the probability distribution over the stochastic outcomes is non-uniform, then there is a good chance that JIC will perform well when compared to traditional schedule-repair techniques. The intuition is that when there are few possible errors, and some errors are *much* more likely than others, then there is useful information in the stochastic action model, and the reasoning performed by JIC will be of benefit to the system. The jury is still out, however, because there are a number of other factors that might well dominate our hypothesized factors. We are currently defining an experiment designed to elucidate and quantify some of the most important factors.

12.7 RELATED WORK

Our general search technique borrows heavily from the MicroBoss (Sadeh, 1991) and HSTS (Muscettola, 1992) systems. Both these systems use a kind of forward random sampling to build a picture of the local search space. MicroBoss uses *demand profiles* and forward simulation to help find and remove bottleneck regions. HSTS uses a related technique called *conflict partition scheduling* to find likely bottlenecks and iteratively split them into increasingly small intervals of time. Our iterative sampling mapping technique bears some similarity to these previous approaches. Although we do not yet make sophisticated use of sampling

---

[10] This has been motivated by the scheduling term "Just-In-Time", or JIT. The term "*Just-In-Case*" has apparently been used in other contexts to refer to other concepts; we have decided to keep using the term to refer to proactive contingency management and hope that it will not confuse or offend any readers.

information as do these other techniques, we are currently studying such an approach. We feel that there is exceptional potential for the general class of methods that sample to estimate parameters of the search space and then use those parameters to more carefully control subsequent search.

The language that ATIS supplies for specifying group enablement does not allow an astronomer to express preferences over those times at which the group is enabled. The SPIKE system (this volume) introduced the idea of a *suitability function*, which is a mechanism by which a user can define a preference measure for the assignment of a given observation to a given point in time. The function can be used by a scheduler to arrive at a suitable assignment of all observations to the time line. Suitability functions have also been tested in the context of the International Ultraviolet Explorer observatory, and early results were promising (Shrader, 1990). We have not yet implemented suitability functions but plan to do so.

12.8 FUTURE WORK

Our implementation to date has concentrated on using a telescope control system provided by AutoScope Corporation. Although we have integrated our scheduler with their controller successfully (as described in Section 12.5), we have only tested CERES against a simulator because we do not yet have a real telescope. We are, however, in the process of acquiring some time on a real APT and will repeat our tests in the real world. Our goal is to make our system available over the InterNet in such a way that remotely located astronomers can electronically mail us ATIS request files. The first target is to have CERES automatically accept ATIS files, form a preliminary schedule from them, and reactively manage schedule execution at the telescope. Users will receive their requested data via return electronic mail or will be given access to an FTP site where their data can be retrieved.

We hope that our demonstration of fully automatic telescope operations will serve to lay the groundwork for other sorts of astronomy. Of particular interest is the possibility of placing a number of small telescopes on the moon (Genet *et al.*, 1991). A lunar telescope facility would be an excellent test of our approach. We feel that our technology can provide a solid basis for the development of integrated telescope planning, scheduling, and control systems that help to fulfill the goal of "better, cheaper, faster, with no compromise of safety."

Once individual telescopes are routinely used by remotely located astronomers, there are a number of new opportunities that arise. For instance, at this point, it is practical to consider an electronic network of telescopes located around the world. One goal for such a network is responding quickly and efficiently to astronomical targets of opportunity. For instance, if one automatic telescope observes a supernova, it should immediately make this information available to other telescopes on the network. Some form of distributed scheduling (or negotiation) can follow, the result being that other telescopes in the network agree to start tracking the new target. We currently have plans to test our telescope as part of a small three-node network in order to gain some practical network scheduling experience. Once CERES can schedule this small network, we plan to implement the design on a much larger scale.

12.9 SUMMARY

This chapter has described our approach to the scheduling of remotely located, fully automatic telescopes.

The primary focus has been on defining the search space of our scheduler and mapping that space to determine the performance of an existing heuristic dispatcher and of a hill-climbing algorithm. The results from this mapping exercise indicate that heuristic dispatch performs acceptably but that it is relatively easy to do much better using more sophisticated techniques. Our mapping exercise considered only a single ATIS file, and future work must expand this to look at multiple files and better objective functions.

The secondary focus of this chapter has been on the interaction of CERES, the scheduler, and SCRscope, the schedule executor. SCRscope executes a schedule if one exists; otherwise, it falls back on heuristic dispatch. This approach means that even when schedules break, the telescope can be kept busy making useful observations.

The final focus of this chapter has been on a class of techniques for proactive contingency management. We discussed the nature of these techniques and explained how they can be expected to give rise to better system behavior by reasoning about *and* executing disjunctive schedules. Although the jury is still out on the fundamental utility of these techniques, we are actively experimenting with them and hope to discover the conditions under which they function well.

Our scheduling system, CERES, has been implemented and tested on a commercially built telescope simulator; early results are encouraging, and future work will test CERES on a real telescope.

ACKNOWLEDGMENTS

We would like to thank Bill Borucki, Russ Genet, David Genet, Butler Hine, Andy Philips, Phil Laird, and Denise Draper. Butler Hine provided a library of ephemeris routines, and this proved essential in getting started. Andy Philips implemented a C-to-Lisp translation of each ephemeris function that allows CERES to compute group enablement. Dave Genet kindly provided source code for the ATIScope dispatcher, without which we would have been unable to implement our SCRscope schedule execution system. Bill Borucki has wrestled with various versions of CERES, providing excellent feedback at every point, and we thank him for doing so. Thanks are owed to Phil Laird for providing code implementing a simple version of his learning algorithm (Laird, 1992) that allows CERES to decompile raw ATIS into PA-comprehensible group specifications. Denise Draper has had a significant impact on this work: she designed and implemented the CERES execution tracking and rescheduling mechanism and helped us to focus our claims about disjunctive scheduling. Thanks to Denise Draper, Russ Genet, Mark Fox, Othar Hansson, Andrew Mayer, Glenn Miller, Mark Trueblood, and Monte Zweben for useful comments on a previous draft of this chapter.

References

Allen, J.F. 1984. Towards a General Theory of Action and Time. *Artificial Intelligence Journal*, Vol. 23, No. 2. pp. 123–154.

Bresina, J., and M. Drummond. 1990. Integrating Planning and Reaction: A Preliminary Report. *Proceedings of the AAAI Spring Symposium Series* (Session on Planning in Uncertain, Unpredictable, or Changing Environments). AAAI Press, Menlo Park, Calif.

Bresina, J., M. Drummond, and S. Kedar. 1993. Reactive, Integrated Systems Pose New Problems for Machine Learning. *Machine Learning Methods for Planning,* edited by S. Minton. Morgan Kaufmann, San Francisco, Calif.

Chen, P.C. 1989. Heuristic Sampling on Backtrack Trees. Ph.D. Dissertation, Report No. STAN-CS-89-1258, Department of Computer Science, Stanford University.

Collinot, A., C. Le Pape, and G. Pinoteau. 1988. SONIA: A Knowledge-Based Scheduling System. *Artificial Intelligence in Engineering*, Vol. 3., No. 2. pp. 86–94.

Currie, K., and A. Tate. 1991. O-Plan: The Open Planning Architecture. *Artificial Intelligence*, Vol. 52, No. 1, pp. 49–86.

Dean, T., and Kanazawa, K. 1989. A Model for Projection and Action. *Proceedings of IJCAI-89*, AAAI Press, Menlo Park, Calif., pp. 985–990.

Drummond, M. 1989. Situated Control Rules. *Proceedings of Conference on Principles of Knowledge Representation & Reasoning.* Morgan Kaufmann, San Francisco, Calif.

Drummond, M., and J. Bresina. 1990a. Anytime Synthetic Projection: Maximizing the Probability of Goal Satisfaction. *Proceedings of AAAI-90*, AAAI Press, Menlo Park, Calif., pp. 138–144.

Drummond, M., and J. Bresina. 1990b. Planning for Control. *Proceedings of Fifth IEEE International Symposium on Intelligent Control*, IEEE Computer Society Press, Los Alamitos, Calif., pp. 657–662.

Drummond, M., J. Bresina, and S. Kedar. 1991. The Entropy Reduction Engine: Integrating Planning, Scheduling, and Control. *Proceedings of the AAAI Spring Symposium Series* (Session on Integrated Intelligent Architectures), AAAI Press, Menlo Park, Calif., pp. 48–53.

Fox, M.S., and S.F. Smith. 1984. ISIS: A Knowledge-Based System for Factory Scheduling. *Expert Systems*. Vol. 1, No. 1, pp. 25–49.

Fox, M.S., and K.P. Sycara. 1990. The CORTES Project: A Unified Framework for Planning, Scheduling, and Control. *Proceedings of the DARPA Workshop on Innovative Approaches to Planning, Scheduling, and Control*, Morgan Kaufmann, San Francisco, Calif., pp. 412–421.

Genet, R.M, D.R. Genet, D.L. Talent, M. Drummond, B. Hine, L.J. Boyd, and M. Trueblood. 1991. Multi-Use Lunar Telescopes. *Robotic Observatories in the 1990's*, edited by Alexei V. Filippenko, Astronomical Society of the Pacific Conference Series, San Francisco, Calif., pp. 34–50.

Genet, R.M., and D.S. Hayes. 1989. *Robotic Observatories: A Handbook of Remote-Access Personal-Computer Astronomy*. AutoScope Corporation, Mesa, Ariz.

Hall, D.S., and R.M. Genet. 1988. *Photoelectric Photometry of Variable Stars*. Wilmann-Bell, Richmond, Va.

Hanks, S. 1990. Projecting Plans for Uncertain Worlds. YALE/CSD/RR#756, CS Department, Yale University.

Hendler, J., A. Tate, and M. Drummond. 1990. AI Planning: Systems and Techniques. *AI Magazine*, Vol. 11, No. 2, pp. 61–77.

Kabanza, F. 1992. Reactive Planning of Immediate Actions. Doctoral dissertation, University of Liege, Belgium.

Knuth, D.E. 1975. Estimating the Efficiency of Backtrack Programs. *Mathematics of Computation*, 29. pp. 121–136.

Laird, P. 1992. Discrete Sequence Prediction and its Applications. *Proceedings of AAAI-92*. AAAI Press, Menlo Park, Calif., pp. 135–140.

Langley, P. 1992. Systematic and Nonsystematic Search. *Proceedings of AIPS-92*, Morgan Kaufmann, San Francisco, Calif., pp. 145–152.

Minton, S., M. Drummond, J. Bresina, and A.B. Philips. 1992. Total Order *vs.* Partial Order Planning: Factors Influencing Performance. *Proceedings of KR'92*, Morgan Kaufmann, San Francisco, Calif., pp. 83–92.

Muscettola, N., S. Smith, G. Amiri, and D. Pathak. 1989. Generating Space Telescope Observation Schedules, CMU-RI-TR-89-28, Robotics Institute, Carnegie Mellon University.

Muscettola, N. 1992. Scheduling by Iterative Partition of Bottleneck Conflicts, CMU-RI-TR-92-05, Department of Computer Science, Carnegie Mellon University.

Nilsson, N. editor. 1984. Shakey the Robot. Technical Note 323, SRI International, Menlo Park, Calif.

Sadeh, N. 1991. Look-Ahead Techniques for Micro-Opportunistic Job-Shop Scheduling, CMU-CS-91-102, Department of Computer Science, Carnegie Mellon University.

Schrag, R., M. Boddy, and J. Carciofini. 1992. Managing Disjunction for Practical Temporal Reasoning. *Proceedings of KR'92*, Morgan Kaufmann, San Francisco, Calif., pp. 36–46.

Shrader, C. R. 1990. "Knowledge Based Automated Scheduling and Planning Tools for IUE." *Observatories in Earth Orbit and Beyond*, edited by Y. Kondo, Kluwer Academic Publishers, pp. 525–530.

Smith, S.F., P.S. Ow, J.Y. Potvin, N. Muscettola, and D. Matthys. 1990. An Integrated Framework for Generating and Revising Factory Schedules, *Journal of the Operational Research Society*, Vol. 41, No. 6, pp. 539–552.

Zweben, M., M. Deale, and R. Gargan. 1991. Anytime Rescheduling. *Proceedings of the DARPA Workshop on Innovative Approaches to Planning, Scheduling, and Control*, Morgan Kaufmann, San Francisco, Calif., pp. 251–259.

13

DTS:

A Decision-Theoretic Scheduler for Space Telescope Applications

Othar Hansson
Andrew Mayer
*(Heuristicrats Research Inc. and
University of California, Berkeley)*

13.1 DTS PROBLEM DOMAIN AND REPRESENTATION

The Decision-Theoretic Scheduler (DTS) is designed to solve oversubscribed project scheduling problems. Work on DTS has focused on search control, particularly through the combination of multiple heuristic evaluation functions. As discussed below, this makes DTS a promising approach for new domains in which sophisticated domain-specific heuristic functions have not been developed. The decision-theoretic basis of DTS' optimization criteria makes it an attractive approach for problems in which complex trade-offs must be made among competing tasks and expensive real-world and computational resources.

DTS is specifically targeted toward experiment scheduling on orbiting telescopes. The initial application domain is the Extreme Ultraviolet Explorer (EUVE) (Euve, 1992), which makes observations in the wavelength range of 70 to 760 angstroms. The EUVE is operated by the NASA Goddard Space Flight Center and the Center for EUV Astrophysics (CEA) at the University of California, Berkeley. Although the remainder of the chapter is concerned with the methodology underlying the system, we describe the problem briefly here.

The tasks in the EUVE scheduling problem are astronomical observations. Although an initial EUVE total sky survey employed short observations, the subsequent guest observation phase consists of lengthy observations. In practice, however, observations will be broken into approximately 30-minute chunks by a variety of unavoidable and largely unpredictable interruptions.

The resources in this scheduling problem are observational instruments. Although the EUVE has several on-board instruments, our concern is to schedule guest observations that are restricted to the EUV spectrometer instrument. Thus, we can model EUVE scheduling as a single-resource scheduling problem.

The constraints in the problem are determined by the positions of observational targets; the position of the Observer platform; and the positions of obstacles such as planets, the sun, and atmospheric anomalies. There are few explicit inter-task constraints aside from the time required to retarget the instrument between observations.

13.1.1 Problem Representation

We phrase these scheduling problems in the language of constraint-satisfaction. Formally, a constraint-satisfaction processing (CSP) problem consists of a set of variables together with a set of constraints on the legal values of those variables. The CSP problem is solved when the variables have been instantiated to a set of values that satisfy all the constraints. A wide variety of problems can be phrased as CSP problems, including scheduling, graph-coloring, and interpretation of visual scenes. (van Hentenryck [1989] provides a survey).

A large class of scheduling problems can be represented as constraint-satisfaction problems by representing attributes of tasks and resources as variables. Task attributes include the scheduled time period and resource requirements. The primary attribute of resources is availability or accessibility. A schedule is constructed by assigning times and resources to tasks such that the constraints of the problem are obeyed.

Constraints capture logical requirements: a typical resource can be used by only one task at a time. Constraints also express problem requirements: task T_x requires N units of time, must be completed before task T_y, and must be completed before a specified date. Both van Hentenryck (1989) and Zweben, Deale, & Gargan (1990) provide concise illustrative examples of scheduling problems represented as CSP problems. For compatibility and evaluation purposes, the DTS problem representation is based on that of the SPIKE system (Johnston, 1989), which is currently used by NASA to schedule the observations of the Hubble Space Telescope.

The DTS problem representation reflects the current focus of our research, which is on control rather than representation. Currently, DTS uses fixed duration tasks with Allen constraints between them. Metric constraints (time lags, fixed times, etc.) are handled by a preprocessing step. Complex state constraints are currently handled in an *ad hoc* manner.

13.1.2 Optimization Criteria

DTS uses multiattribute utility functions to represent user preferences for both solution quality and computational costs. Multiattribute utility theory (MAUT) is a formal method for quantifying preference relationships among a set of uncertain outcomes. The next section describes the use of utility functions in search control, but at this point, we can make one simple distinction between DTS and traditional scheduling systems. Most scheduling systems have a single vehicle—the heuristic evaluation function—for representing both search control knowledge and user preferences. The conflation of search control and schedule evaluation complicates the task of constructing good heuristic functions.

For example, the ISIS (Fox, 1987) and SPIKE systems (Johnston, 1989) employ suitability functions that state the "preferences" of the user as a function of a task and a time assignment. Consider the optimal schedule for a set of tasks. For the SPIKE and ISIS systems, the suitability function that best satisfies the user's preferences is that which "encodes" this optimal schedule. In other words, if in the optimal schedule, task A_1 is scheduled at time t_1, then the "best" suitability function for the task is uniformly zero except for a peak at t_1.

Suitability functions are intended to represent schedule evaluation information, but they inevitably encode search control information as well, as in the extreme case above. Such non-modular functions are difficult to construct and equally difficult to modify as user preferences change. As the next section explains, DTS separates search control and schedule evaluation by relating them to semantically clear notions of probability and utility. This yields a mathematically principled search algorithm and at the same time simplifies the knowledge-engineering task for the designer of a new scheduling system.

13.2 DTS SYSTEM OVERVIEW

CSP heuristics often measure fundamentally different problem attributes, e.g., the quality of a partial schedule, the likelihood of finding a feasible solution, the cost of searching a subtree. One great complication in CSP problem solving has been the absence of a calculus to *normalize* the output of different heuristic functions. Having no common "unit of exchange" makes it difficult to compare heuristics other than by inserting them into search algorithms and observing the resulting search behavior. It also makes it impossible to combine multiple heuristics in a sound way.

This has forced human problem solvers into an unpleasant choice:

- decide *a priori* to use one particular heuristic and concentrate on a single attribute, which can badly skew the system's performance at the expense of

other domain attributes (this is particularly inappropriate for complex scheduling domains that are typically multiattribute optimization problems, as has
been noted by Sadeh [1989])

- hand-craft a composite heuristic that captures multiple domain attributes in a
  single function (In general, such heuristics are inaccurate because of complex
  variations in the problem space, problem requirements, and precision of the
  individual heuristic functions.)

For this reason, the selection of appropriate heuristics and problem solving techniques for any given CSP domain remains an art.

The Decision-Theoretic Scheduler (DTS) is designed to address this problem.
DTS is derived from previous work on the Bayesian Problem Solver (BPS) (Mayer,
1994). One BPS innovation central to DTS is the *heuristic error model*: a probabilistic semantics for heuristic information based on the concept of conditional probability in statistical decision-theory (Hansson & Mayer, 1990b). Heuristics are interpreted by building probability distributions that correlate their estimates (return
values) to the actual outcomes (e.g., cost, time) of problem solving instances. These
probability distributions are a common language that permit the comparison and
combination of different heuristics.

DTS offers a coherent way to attack the problems described above. Different
heuristics can be judged by comparing the probability that their use will lead to
desirable outcomes. Multiple heuristics can be combined by producing joint probability distributions from sets of individual heuristic error models. We believe that
this will alleviate the human scheduler's dilemma by providing a sound framework
for comparing and combining an arbitrary number of heuristic functions. In addition, DTS uses statistical learning techniques to automatically adapt to the problem
domain. Learning in DTS is both across-trial and within-trial: the updating of the
heuristic error model occurs while a problem is being solved and can affect later
decisions on the same problem, as well as on subsequent problems drawn from the
same domain.

This section describes the technology that forms the core of DTS. In addition
to the traditional tools developed for scheduling systems, the DTS approach relies
heavily on multiattribute utility theory (Keeney & Raiffa, 1976; vonWinterfeldt &
Edwards, 1986), Bayesian probabilistic inference (Cox, 1946; Savage, 1972; de
Finetti, 1974), information-value theory (Raiffa & Schlaifer, 1961; Howard, 1965)
and Bayesian learning (Duda & Hart, 1973; Lee & Mahajan, 1988). More details
on the DTS approach can be found in Hansson (1994).

13.2.1 Decisions in Scheduling

DTS employs decision-theoretic techniques to guide the search for feasible
and efficient schedules. Decision theory and its central maximum expected utility

(MEU) principle prescribe methods for making decisions when the outcomes of those decisions are uncertain.

The theory of expected utility (von Neumann & Morgenstern, 1944) claims that *rational* decision makers attach *utilities* to all possible outcomes and, when faced with a decision under uncertainty, select that outcome with maximum expected utility. Utility is the subjective assignment of value to potential outcomes when the exact outcome is uncertain. An extension of utility theory, which describes the behavior of a decision maker faced with multiple and, possibly, conflicting objectives, is multiattribute utility theory (MAUT) (Keeney & Raiffa, 1976).

Under certain natural restrictions on the consistency of a sequence of decisions (i.e., the axioms of decision theory), the fundamental theorem of decision theory states that a rational decision maker acts as if he were following the dictates of the theory; i.e., a utility function can be constructed to model his preferences and the MEU principle used to reproduce his decisions. A number of artificial intelligence researchers have recently turned to decision-theoretic principles in attempting to engineer rational systems. Recent examples include work in heuristic search (Hansson & Mayer, 1989), planning (Hansson, Mayer, & Russell, 1990), computer vision (Ettinger & Levitt, 1989), medical diagnosis (Horvitz, 1990; Heckerman, 1991), and game playing (Russell & Wefald, 1989).

The DTS scheduling system is designed to be such a decision maker. The decisions it must make include the following:

1. Which portion of the search tree should be explored next?
2. Should search continue, or should the current best solution be output to the user?
3. If an infeasible schedule must be repaired, which set of repairs is best?

Standard backtracking algorithms make these sorts of decisions in an *ad hoc* manner, using heuristic information less effectively than possible. Preliminary results in our study of search control show that DTS can achieve better performance than these traditional approaches.

13.2.2 Heuristic Error Models

The fundamental problem with prior work in heuristic search is that the semantics of heuristic functions are defined only in terms of performance: heuristics are "magic" parameters that determine the speed of search. Not surprisingly, the effort in development of AI systems based on heuristic search—ranging from scheduling systems to chess-playing programs—is often dominated by time spent hand-crafting a high-performance heuristic through parameter adjustment. Because the semantics of heuristics are unclear, even the most sophisticated combination and learning mechanisms are limited in their effectiveness.

DTS takes the approach that the crucial quantities measuring a state in a search tree are the attributes of the utility function (e.g., search cost and solution quality attributes). If those attributes were known, decision making would be straightforward. In DTS, heuristic evaluation functions are *evidence* bearing on the true value of one or more of the utility attributes. We refer to the attributes of a given state as the *outcome* of that state.

Obviously, different heuristics measure different attributes of utility (e.g., search cost, solution quality, solution probability). For example, a CSP heuristic such as "Most Constraining Variable" is a measure of subtree size and search cost: a variable that heavily constrains unassigned variables generates a smaller search tree.

We refer to the association between raw heuristic values and utility attributes as a *heuristic error model* (Hansson & Mayer, 1990b). The heuristic error model provides a simple means of associating immediately visible features of a state with a belief about the outcome of that state. "Features" of the state S_i are indicated by a heuristic function $h(S_i)$, and the association with outcome attributes A_i is provided by the heuristic error model $Pr\{h(S_i)|A_i\}$: this conditional probability gives the likelihood of the heuristic value given the outcome attributes. By the Bayes' rule inversion, it allows the computation of the *posterior* probability distribution over outcome attributes as follows:

$$Pr\{A_i| h(S_i)\} = \frac{Pr\{h(S_i)| A_i\}}{Pr\{h(S_i)\}} Pr\{A_i\}$$

This formula can be viewed as updating the prior probability, $Pr\{A_i\}$, to the posterior $Pr\{A_i| h(S_i)\}$. The denominator $Pr\{h(S_i)\}$ does need to be computed because it serves to simply normalize the distribution (i.e., make $\Sigma_\alpha Pr\{A_i = \alpha| h(S_i)\}$ sum to 1).

Learning Heuristic Error Models. Historically, nearly all heuristic search algorithms have used the face-value principle of heuristic interpretation, behaving as if heuristics were perfect estimators. As a result, most existing heuristic search algorithms violate the axioms of consistency and rationality in decision making.

In contrast, DTS gathers statistics to calibrate the heuristic error model over time as problems are solved. When introducing the system in a new domain, this learning capability will reduce the burden on human experts to produce highly complex heuristics. Their experience can be encoded as a default initial belief, or *prior* probability distribution.

This prior probability distribution will be fine-tuned based on "training exercises" with representative problems. When the heuristic function makes errors, DTS learns a mapping that "corrects" the heuristic (see the description of Figure

13-5). This calibration process will improve DTS performance, tailoring it to the characteristics of real-world problems as they are encountered. We anticipate that a small set of template prior distributions will suffice, making for a speedy elicitation process in comparison to the effort involved in fine-tuning even a simple heuristic.

Combining Heuristics. In our initial experiments in scheduling, a primary advantage of the heuristic error model has been the ability to combine multiple heuristics. Artificial intelligence techniques have never offered powerful methods for combining heuristics. For example, in branch-and-bound algorithms, the most common approach is to take the maximum of different admissible heuristics (admissible heuristics are guaranteed to underestimate the actual solution cost). Another approach, dating back to Samuel's checkers program (Samuel, 1967), constructs a composite heuristic that is a combination of individual features.

By combining multiple heuristics, DTS isolates measurements of the difficulty and promise of completing potential assignments. Hence, DTS can make use of heuristics that previously have led to inconsistent performance: if there are any easily characterized contexts (in terms of other features) in which the heuristic performs well, DTS should recognize that fact. The context-dependency of heuristic functions has long been recognized in other search applications such as game-playing.

13.2.3 Use of Heuristic Error Models

Bayesian probabilistic inference has emerged as a promising technology for reasoning about uncertainty in artificial intelligence application environments. In recent years, probabilistic inference has been used extensively in complex domains such as situation assessment and computer vision and has been formulated and applied to heuristic search systems for problem solving (Hansson & Mayer, 1989), game-playing (Hansson & Mayer, 1990a), and planning (Hansson, Mayer, & Russell, 1990) domains.

The DTS architecture relies on the Bayesian network data structure (Pearl, 1988), the primary artificial intelligence tool for representing and reasoning with probabilistic information. We use Bayesian networks because they directly support the Bayesian subjective definition of probability, a requirement for using the tools of traditional decision theory. Many other uncertainty formalisms (e.g., Fuzzy Logic, Dempster-Shafer Theory) are not geared toward decision making but instead focus on representation and modeling issues (Pearl & Shafer, 1991). Some of these uncertainty frameworks have been applied to represent the uncertainty in stochastic scheduling problems (Fargher & Smith, 1992) or to provide a "fuzzy" mechanism for integrating inexact constraints (Dorn, Slany, & Stary, 1992). In contrast to these applications of uncertainty management to problem representation, DTS is focused on the uncertainty inherent in every search problem: the problem of making search control decisions in the face of incomplete information.

In DTS, the Bayesian network is used to provide information for decisions such as the most promising region of the search tree to expand next and the most promising schedule extension or modification to choose next. As described below, Bayesian networks integrate a variety of information in the service of such decisions, including multiple heuristic evaluation functions and the search graph's topology.

The nodes of a Bayesian network are variables that represent the attributes of the domain. The arcs of the network connect dependent variables, representing relationships among domain attributes. Dependencies can be the result of functional, causal, or correlative relationships among variables and can be encoded in a modular fashion by specifying a conditional probability distribution for each network node conditioned on the values of its parents (immediate predecessors in the directed graph).

The dependency structure and parameters in the Bayesian network enable the efficient computation of the *joint probability* of any instantiation of variables. A fundamental theorem of probability theory indicates that from a joint probability distribution and, thus, from a Bayesian network, any well-formed probabilistic question (i.e., conditional probability) can be answered. Common queries include

- What is the most crucial piece of evidence to gather next? In search domains, this corresponds to the question of which new node to expand in the search tree.

- What is the conditional probability of a variable instantiation given the available evidence? In search domains, such probability distributions can be used, together with a utility function, for maximum-expected-utility decision making, including the choice of task assignments and schedule modifications.

- What is the most likely instantiation of all variables given the available evidence? In search domains, this can be used as a simplified explanation of the heuristic information and the state of the search.

An example search tree (shaded nodes) and corresponding Bayesian network (white nodes) are shown in Figure 13-1. The large white nodes are variables that represent the multiattribute outcomes (e.g., schedule cost, search cost) of legal partial assignments in the CSP problem's state-space. The small white nodes are variables that represent the values of heuristic evaluation functions, the primitive feature recognizers of the domain (e.g., the number of remaining values, the degree of the constraint graph).

The network represents how beliefs about the outcomes of alternative successor states are influenced by information provided by each of two separate heuristic functions. The heuristic functions (F_1 and F_2) provide evidence that places con-

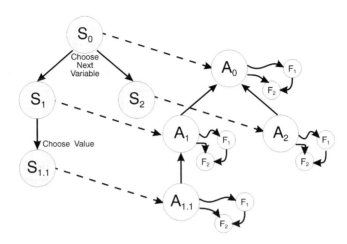

Figure 13-1:   CSP problem search graph and Bayesian network

straints on the probability of different outcomes for their associated states. Although we speak of the heuristics as providing evidence, the evidence is more a result of the correlation between the heuristic value and the outcome of the partial assignment. In addition, the correlation between the two heuristic functions is indicated by an arc between them.

The arcs of the search graph further constrain the set of possible outcomes of states. In this case, the arcs depict functional dependency rather than simple correlation. Consider $A_{1.1}$, which represents the outcome that will result after one of the variables (unconstrained in S_1) is assigned a value. Because $S_{1.1}$ is the only possible continuation of the search space after the state S_1, then A_1 depends entirely on $A_{1.1}$. Hence, there is a directed arc from $A_{1.1}$ to A_1. A similar constraint exists between the current state and its two possible successor states, S_1 and S_2. A particular outcome is possible for the current state only if a corresponding outcome is possible for one of its children. Therefore, an arc points back from each of the successor nodes to the current state. Through these constraints, domain information and heuristic estimates propagate through the Bayesian network, providing a consistent global interpretation of all the heuristic information acquired through search. In particular, the Bayesian network provides the probability distributions for the possible outcomes of each child, e.g., $\Pr\{A_1\}$ and $\Pr\{A_2\}$. Together with a utility function, these distributions allow for a rational choice among the two successors of the current state by choosing the successor with maximum expected utility.

13.2.4 Utility-Directed Selective Search

DTS employs decision-theoretic techniques to direct its search process. Decision theory, together with the probabilistic inference machinery described above, enables DTS to rationally decide on the best portion of the search tree to explore next. By altering the utility function provided as input to the system, DTS might be tailored to trade off increased search time for increases in schedule quality or to produce schedules with different desirable attributes. For reactive scheduling applications, alterations to the existing schedule can be given negative utility, in which case DTS would avoid them where possible.

The essence of decision-theoretic search control is the realization that some pieces of information are more valuable than others. In addition, the acquisition of information has costs: in scheduling search, this cost is increased computation time. If these computations squander time and other resources, the solution might be found too late to be of use. If these computations are neglected, a poor solution might be found. However, if these computations are chosen wisely, the system can provide high quality solutions despite limited computational resources. Decision theory has spawned a subfield known as *information value theory* (Howard, 1965; Raiffa & Schlaifer, 1961), which deals with the issue of deciding what information to acquire in order to make better decisions.

Decision-theoretic search control involves isolating decisions that are made in the course of search and applying the techniques of decision theory to make *rational* decisions at these points. The major decisions made during heuristic search are among possible search tree expansions and possible heuristic evaluations. DTS applies information value theory by using the maximum expected utility criterion to control its information-gathering search. Rather than being a "depth-first" or "breadth-first" search, DTS is a "maximum-expected-utility" search that gathers information most critical to the decisions that must be made.

Because the selective search decisions are based on the global utility function, the system exhibits "real-time" characteristics (depth-first hill-climbing) or "optimizing" (exhaustive, branch-and-bound search) characteristics depending on the preferences expressed in the utility function. For example, optimizing behavior occurs when search time is free. When time considerations are incorporated into selective search, a satisficing search arises (see Hansson & Mayer [1988] for a more thorough exposition of this trade-off). Similarly, memory bounds can be addressed by selectively discarding low-utility portions of the search tree.

An additional benefit of decision-theoretic search control is that heuristic and control information are represented in a declarative manner. DTS can be applied to any search space in which the decision problems can clearly be stated. In the prototype system, the techniques have been applied to search through the space of valid partial schedules.

13.2.5 DTS Version 1.0

The DTS prototype employed a simplified decision-theoretic control mechanism that was grafted onto a conventional backtracking search algorithm: this

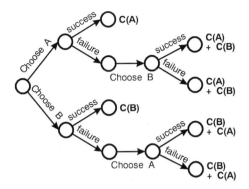

Figure 13-2:   Decision tree for value-ordering problem (values A and B)

allowed for controlled experiments on DTS versus traditional algorithms. In terms of the preceding discussion, the prototype uses a two-level Bayesian network (corresponding to the single level of lookahead used in conventional backtracking) and incorporated only a restricted form of selective search. Despite these simplifications, the application of decision theory to backtracking demonstrates many important ideas.

The only search control decisions made in traditional backtracking systems are the selections of which subtrees of the search graph to explore next. Once a subtree is selected (by selecting the next variable or value), it is explored exhaustively unless a solution is found. Such an ordering problem can be viewed as a decision tree. Figure 13-2 depicts the choice of ordering two subtrees A and B. Following similar work in optimal test sequencing (Mitten, 1960; Simon & Kadane, 1975), a simple theorem (Hansson & Mayer, 1991) shows that the system's expected utility (search time to first solution) is maximized if variables (or values) are ordered by the quantity $P(v)/C(v)$, where $P(v)$ indicates the probability of finding a solution in the subtree, and $C(v)$ indicates the cost of searching the subtree (whether or not a solution is found). $P(v)$ and $C(v)$ are attributes of the payoff mentioned above. The experiments described in the next section indicated that once $P(v)$ and $C(v)$ are learned, this rule outperforms traditional backtracking search algorithms that interpret heuristic estimates at face value. Decision-theoretic search control improved overall system performance. A similar analysis can also be performed for iterative improvement (Hansson & Mayer, 1991).

Although heuristics are often good at rank-ordering nodes based on either $P(v)$ or $C(v)$ individually, the rank-ordering for the combination is typically incorrect. DTS' heuristic error model corrects for this. Figure 13-5 illustrates the value of $P(v)/C(v)$ derived from a simple CSP heuristic.

13.2.6 Prototype Implementation

Although the preceding description has been abstract and technical, the actual prototype DTS algorithm was easily implemented. The estimation of probabilities and search costs in the two-level backtracking decision tree reduces to a small number of hash-table lookups.

The prototype performs a backtracking search using the standard optimizations of forward-checking and dynamic search rearrangement. The search is ordered by the expected utility selection criteria ($P(v)/C(v)$) discussed above. The estimates of $P(v)$ and $C(v)$ are derived from the heuristic error model using traditional CSP heuristics. The heuristic error model is updated during and between trials using a bucketed histogram and interpreted by Laplacian estimation (which estimates probabilities based on histogram counts). For heuristics with a small number of possible values, a histogram bucket was reserved for each value. For those with a larger number of values, the buckets corresponded to ranges of logarithmically increasing size.

Consider a value ordering decision to be made among two values v_1 and v_2. In DTS, heuristic functions are applied to the two subtrees (i.e., partial schedules). These heuristic function values (h_1 and h_2) are used to index a number of histograms and retrieve histogram counts, which are then used to estimate the probability of feasibility $P(v)$ and the expected cost $C(v)$. For example, estimation of $P(v_1)$ is performed by retrieving counts of success and failure from corresponding buckets in the success and failure histograms. The buckets chosen are those whose range includes h_1. This gives the number of times ($N_{success}$ and $N_{failure}$) that similar subtrees (those with heuristic values in a range around h_1) have resulted in success or failure. The Laplacian estimate of the probability of success is $(1 + N_{success}) / (2 + N_{success} + N_{failure})$. The expected cost $C(v)$ is estimated in a similar manner.

13.2.7 Performance

Space limits us to a discussion of only three aspects of the DTS prototype's performance characteristics: combining heuristics, learning heuristic error models, and generalizing learned information.

Combining Heuristics. The primary strength of the DTS prototype is the method for combining information from separate heuristic evaluation functions to improve constraint-satisfaction search control.

Traditionally, CSP algorithms make use of a variable ordering heuristic and a value ordering heuristic. Figure 13-3 shows the performance of a standard CSP algorithm using all possible pairings (A1, A2, B1, B2) of two well-known variable ordering heuristics (Most Constraining Variable (A), Minimum Domain Variable (B)) and two well-known value ordering heuristics (Least Constraining Value (1),

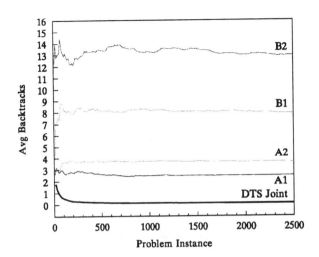

Figure 13-3:   Eight Queens: Combining heuristics vs. heuristics in isolation

Dechter's Value Heuristic (2) [Dechter & Pearl, 1988]). Also shown is the DTS prototype (DTS-Joint), which dominated the competition by using all four heuristics in combination. The horizontal axis plots the number of problem instances solved, and the vertical axis plots the running average of search time over the entire experiment. The plot in Figure 13-3—but not the data on which it is based—begins with the tenth problem instance.

Figure 13-4 shows a corresponding graph for the Bridge-Construction Scheduling problem (van Hentenryck, 1989). The variable ordering heuristic used was Minimum Domain Variable, and the value ordering heuristics were Least Constraining Value (curve A1) and ASAP, "as soon as possible" (curve A2). Also shown are the corresponding individual DTS performance curves (DTS A1, DTS A2) as well as the combined heuristic performance curve (DTS-Joint).

These experiments with the prototype confirm that the combination of heuristic functions can provide more information than any of the heuristics taken individually. To summarize both graphs, the improvement is seen to be nearly 50% on average for Bridge Construction Scheduling and over 95% for the Eight-Queens problem. Note that the sharp downward slope of the DTS-Joint *running average* in Figure 13-4 demonstrates the performance improvement accrued by learning, unattainable using traditional techniques.

Learning Heuristic Error Models.   Figure 13-5 displays an example heuristic error model learned over the course of 2500 Eight-Queens problem instances (for the Minimum Domain heuristic). The horizontal axis plots the heuristic function estimate, and the vertical axis plots the preference for that estimate. In DTS, prefer-

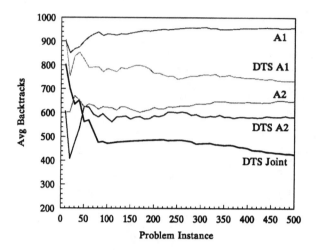

Figure 13-4: Bridge-Construction Scheduling: Combining heuristics vs. heuristics in isolation

ence is based upon the expected utility associated with a heuristic estimate (dashed line). For example, in this case, DTS chooses for instantiation those variables with one value remaining (because expected utility is maximum for $h = 1$) followed by those with six values remaining ($h = 6$). In traditional algorithms, the heuristic is assumed to rank-order alternatives perfectly, and therefore, preference is a monotonic function of the heuristic estimate.

The discrepancy between the heuristic estimates and the actual utilities explains the poor performance of traditional approaches, which assume perfect heuristic estimates. Further, it explains why DTS outperforms these techniques—because it does not make this assumption—and instead learns to correct for the discrepancy.

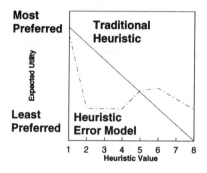

Figure 13-5: Sample heuristic error model

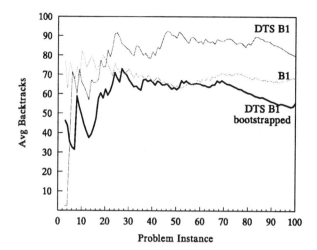

Figure 13-6:   Generalizing data to larger domains

Generalizing Learned Information. An additional benefit of the heuristic error model is the ability to generalize learned data across domains. For example, Figure 13-6 depicts the performance of DTS on the Thirty-two-Queens problem with (1) no prior heuristic error model and (2) a heuristic error model generalized (or "bootstrapped") from the 2500 Eight-Queens examples solved in Figure 13-3. Generalizing data from the simpler domain has reduced search complexity. This is particularly important because the time required to calibrate heuristic error models increases with problem complexity.

13.3 RELATED WORK

The DTS system is based on previous work on the Bayesian Problem Solver (BPS) (Mayer, 1994). BPS has been applied to classic AI problem solving (Hansson & Mayer, 1989), game-playing (Hansson & Mayer, 1990a), and planning (Hansson, Mayer, & Russell, 1990) domains. Similar decision-theoretic approaches are being considered for applications to other complex multiattribute optimization problems.

This work is most closely related, in assumptions and techniques, to the recent work in applying decision theory to problems such as medical diagnosis (Heckerman, 1991) and image interpretation (Ettinger & Levitt, 1989). Others have applied decision theory to heuristic search applications. These researchers have typically limited themselves to grafting decision-theoretic principles onto existing algorithms (Lee & Mahajan, 1988; Russell & Wefald, 1989).

Given its probabilistic basis, this work might be assumed to be related to systems designed for stochastic scheduling problems. Unfortunately, we have not had an opportunity to consider stochastic problems as of yet, although we anticipate that the probabilistic representation and inference mechanisms in DTS will ease the transition to stochastic problems.

13.4 CONCLUSIONS

The use of Bayesian probability theory in DTS underscores that scheduling involves decision making under uncertainty and illustrates how the imperfect information acquired during search can be modeled and exploited. The use of multi-attribute utility theory in DTS underscores that scheduling involves complex trade-offs among user preferences. By addressing these issues, DTS has demonstrated promising performance in preliminary empirical testing. Heuristicrats Research Inc. is developing a commercial version of DTS (available in 1994) that builds upon the approach presented here.

ACKNOWLEDGMENTS

This research was supported by the National Aeronautics and Space Administration under contract NAS2-13340. This research has benefited from comments and suggestions from our thesis advisor, Stuart Russell, and from the research staff of the Artificial Intelligence Research Branch at NASA Ames Research center.

References

Cox, R.T. 1946. "Probability, Frequency, and Reasonable Expectation." *American Journal of Physics*, Vol. 14, No. 1, Jan–Feb 1946, pp. 1–13.

Dechter, R., and J. Pearl. 1988. "Network-Based Heuristics for Constraint-Satisfaction Problems." *Search in Artificial Intelligence*, L. Kanal and V. Kumar, eds., Springer-Verlag, New York, pp. 370–425.

de Finetti, B. 1974. *Theory of Probability*. John Wiley, New York.

Dorn, J., W. Slany, and C. Stary. 1992. "Uncertainty Management by Relaxation of Conflicting Constraints in Production Process Scheduling." *Proceedings of the AAAI Spring Symposium on Practical Approaches to Scheduling and Planning*, AAAI Press, Menlo Park, Calif., pp. 62–66.

Duda, R.O., and P. E. Hart. 1973. *Pattern Classification and Scene Analysis*. John Wiley, New York.

The EUVE Guest Observer Center. 1992. *EUVE Guest Observer Program Handbook*. Appendix G of NASA NRA 92-OSSA-5. Center for EUV Astrophysics, Berkeley, Calif.

Fargher, H.E., and R.A. Smith. 1992. "Planning for the Semiconductor Manufacturer of the Future." *Proceedings of the AAAI Spring Symposium on Practical Approaches to Scheduling and Planning*, AAAI Press, Menlo Park, Calif., pp. 57–61.

Fox, M.S. 1987. *Constraint-Directed Search: A Case Study in Job-Shop Scheduling*. Pitman, London.

Hansson, O. 1994. *Bayesian Problem Solving Applied to Scheduling*. Ph.D. Thesis, University of California, Berkeley.

Hansson, O., and A. Mayer. 1988. "The Optimality of Satisficing Solutions." *Proceedings of the Fourth Workshop on Uncertainty in Artificial Intelligence*, Minneapolis, Minn., August. Assoc. for Uncertainty in AI, Rome, New York., pp. 148–157.

Hansson, O., and A. Mayer. 1989. "Heuristic Search as Evidential Reasoning." *Proceedings of the Fifth Workshop on Uncertainty in Artificial Intelligence*, Windsor, Ontario, Canada, August 18–20. Assoc. for Uncertainty in AI, Rome, New York, pp. 152–161.

Hansson, O., and A. Mayer. 1990a. "A New and Improved Product Rule." Presented at *Eighth International Congress of Cybernetics and Systems*, New York, June.

Hansson, O., and A. Mayer. 1990b. "Probabilistic Heuristic Estimates." *Annals of Mathematics and Artificial Intelligence*, Vol. 2.

Hansson, O., and A. Mayer. 1991. *Decision-Theoretic Control of Artificial Intelligence Scheduling Systems*. Heuristicrats Research, Inc. Technical Report No. 90-1/06.04/5810, Berkeley, Calif.

Hansson, O., A. Mayer, and S. J. Russell. 1990. "Decision-Theoretic Planning in BPS." In *Proceedings of the AAAI Spring Symposium on Planning in Uncertain, Unpredictable, or Changing Environments*, pp. 44–48. AAAI Press, Menlo Park, Calif.

Heckerman, D.E. 1991. *Probabilistic Similarity Networks*. MIT Press, Cambridge, Mass.

Horvitz, E. 1990. *Computation and Action under Bounded Resources*. Ph.D. Thesis, Report KSL-90-76, Knowledge Systems Laboratory, Stanford University.

Howard, R.A. 1965. "Information Value Theory." *IEEE Transactions on Systems, Man, and Cybernetics*, Vol. SSC-2, August, pp. 22–26.

Johnston, M.D. 1989. "Knowledge-Based Telescope Scheduling." *Knowledge-Based Systems in Astronomy*, A. Heck and F. Murtagh, eds., Springer-Verlag, New York, pp. 33–49.

Keeney, R.L., and H. Raiffa. 1976. *Decisions with Multiple Objectives: Preferences and Value Tradeoffs*. John Wiley, New York.

Lee, K.F., and S. Mahajan. 1988. "A Pattern Classification Approach to Evaluation Function Learning." *Artificial Intelligence*, Vol. 36, pp. 1–25.

Levitt, G., J. Ettinger, and T. S. Levitt. 1989. "An Intelligent Tactical Target Screener." In *Proceedings of the 1989 DARPA Image Understanding Workshop*, Morgan Kaufmann, San Francisco, Calif., pp. 283–297.

Mayer, A. 1994. *Rational Search*. Ph.D. Thesis, University of California, Berkeley.

Mitten, L.G. 1960. "An Analytic Solution to the Least Cost Testing Sequence Problem." *Journal of Industrial Engineering*, Vol. 11, p. 17.

Pearl, J. 1988. *Probabilistic Reasoning in Intelligent Systems*. Morgan Kaufmann, San Francisco, Calif.

Pearl, J., and G. Shafer, eds. 1991. *Readings in Uncertain Reasoning.* Morgan Kaufmann, San Francisco, Calif.

Raiffa, H., and R. Schlaifer. 1961. *Applied Statistical Decision Theory.* Harvard University Press, Cambridge, Mass.

Russell, S.J., and E. Wefald. 1989. "Principles of Metareasoning." *Proceedings of the 1st Conference on Principles of Knowledge Representation and Reasoning.* May 15–18. Toronto, Ontario, Canada, Morgan Kaufmann Publishers, San Francisco, Calif., pp. 400–411.

Sadeh, N. 1989. *Lookahead Techniques for Activity-Based Job-Shop Scheduling.* Technical Report TR CMU-RI-TR-89-2, The Robotics Institute, Carnegie Mellon University.

Samuel, A.L. 1967. "Some Studies in Machine Learning Using the Game of Checkers II—Recent Progress." *IBM Journal of Research and Development,* Vol. 11, pp. 601–617.

Savage, L.J. 1972. *The Foundations of Statistics.* Dover, New York.

Simon, H.A., and J. B. Kadane. 1975. "Optimal Problem-Solving Search: All-or-None Solutions." *Artificial Intelligence,* Vol. 6, pp. 235–247.

van Hentenryck, P. 1989. *Constraint-Satisfaction in Logic Programming.* MIT Press, Cambridge, Mass.

von Neumann, J., and O. Morgenstern. 1944. *Theory of Games and Economic Behavior.* Princeton University Press, Princeton, N.J.

von Winterfeldt, D., and W. Edwards. 1986. *Decision Analysis and Behavioral Research.* Cambridge University Press, Cambridge, United Kingdom.

Zweben, M., M. Deale, and R. Gargan. 1990. "Anytime Rescheduling." *Proceedings: Workshop on Innovative Approaches to Planning Scheduling, and Control,* Morgan Kaufmann, San Francisco, Calif., pp. 251–259.

PART
TWO

APPLICATION CASE STUDIES
Space Applications

14

SPIKE:

Intelligent Scheduling of Hubble Space Telescope Observations

Mark D. Johnston
Glenn E. Miller
(Space Telescope Science Institute)[1]

14.1 INTRODUCTION

This chapter describes the SPIKE system, a general framework for scheduling that has been developed by the Space Telescope Science Institute for NASA's Hubble Space Telescope (HST). Efficient use of astronomical observatories is very important to the scientific community: the demand for research-grade telescopes far exceeds the supply. The need for efficient scheduling is especially keen for space-based facilities because of their very high cost, limited numbers, and unique scientific potential. The SPIKE scheduler was developed for Hubble Space Telescope but was designed for generality and flexibility: it has since been adapted for several other astronomical scheduling problems as well as to problems unrelated to astronomy. Although the general approach taken in SPIKE was motivated by the paradigm of scheduling as constraint-directed search (e.g., Smith, Fox, & Ow, 1986; Fox 1987; Fox, Sadeh, & Baykan, 1989), SPIKE incorporates novel approaches to both the quantitative representation and propagation of hard constraints and "soft" preferences and to the use of scheduling search strategies based on multistart stochastic repair.

In the following, we first provide a brief overview of the HST scheduling problem, then we discuss the theoretical and conceptual foundations of SPIKE: Sec-

---

[1]The Space Telescope Science Institute is operated by the Association of Universities for Research in Astronomy for the National Aeronautics and Space Administration.

tion 14.2 describes the SPIKE representation of constraints as "suitability functions," Section 14.3 casts the HST problem as a constraint satisfaction problem (CSP), and Section 14.4 describes the multistart stochastic repair search strategy that is currently the primary scheduling search technique in SPIKE. In Section 14.5, we discuss the HST science ground system as a whole and the role played therein by SPIKE. Section 14.6 describes our operational experience and some of the lessons learned from the past two years of HST operations. Section 14.7 provides a brief overview of the adaptation of SPIKE to other space- and ground-based observatories.

14.1.1 HST Scheduling

Launched in April 1990, the HST has provided important new capabilities for astronomical research because of its unsurpassed combination of wavelength coverage and angular resolution. Despite a manufacturing flaw in the primary mirror, HST is actively engaged in a full research program that has produced a large number of exciting results. HST was serviced by the Space Shuttle in late 1993 to compensate for the mirror's figure and to replace the main camera with a second-generation instrument. These changes have brought the optical quality of the telescope up to original expectations.

The HST scheduling problem ranks among the largest and most complex scheduling problems faced on a continuing basis: some 10,000 to 30,000 observations are scheduled per year, and each is subject to a large number of operational and scientific constraints. Proposers can specify a variety of constraints on exposures in order to express scientific goals: these include relative timing requirements such as precedence, minimum and maximum time separations, ordering, interruptibility, and repetition. Some observations must be executed within a certain absolute time interval. Proposers can constrain the orientation of an instrument's aperture relative to the target or require an observation to be made while the HST is in the earth's shadow. In order to provide flexibility, proposers can mark exposures as "conditional" or "select": "conditional" exposures are contingent upon the results obtained from another exposure in the observing program or, in some cases, upon the results obtained from ground-based observations. These exposures are not scheduled until the proposer has notified the STScI that the condition has been satisfied. The "select" capability allows the proposer to identify alternative sets of exposures from which one or more will be picked for execution. As with "conditional" exposures, exposures contained in "select" sets will be placed on a timeline only after the proposer informs the STScI of a decision.

The HST spacecraft and its associated ground system components introduce a number of scheduling constraints as well. The observatory is in a low earth orbit (590 km), with the result that the earth typically blocks the line of sight to a target for slightly less than half of each 95-minute orbit. Targets within a few degrees of

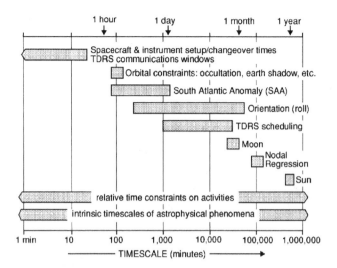

Figure 14-1: The range of timescales for HST scheduling constraints, covering more than six orders of magnitude

the orbital poles are not occulted by the earth and are suitable for uninterrupted observations. Because of the precession of the orbit, the orbital poles move around the sky in a 56-day period, with the result that a target is available for extended observation for no more than about 3 days in each precessional period. When passing over the South Atlantic Ocean, the HST encounters a portion of the earth's radiation belt (called the South Atlantic Anomaly, or SAA) during which instrument operations must be suspended. Sources of bright light such as the sun, moon, and illuminated earth must be avoided. Thermal and power restrictions limit how the telescope can be oriented in order to keep adequate sunlight on the solar panels and off the surfaces that radiate heat.

The primary resource constraint for HST scheduling is the amount of observing time available. Other resources that must not be exceeded include the amount of data that can be processed by the communications and ground systems, onboard tape recorder storage, and onboard command computer storage.

Although the HST operates largely in a preplanned mode (with schedules fixed about two months in advance of execution), disruptions to the schedule occur for a variety of reasons. The most welcome disruptions are so-called "targets of opportunity," which are rare, important astronomical events requiring immediate attention (e.g., a supernova). Other schedule disruptions result from spacecraft anomalies, loss of communications contacts, and changes in observing programs.

Figure 14-1 illustrates schematically the range of constraint timescales for HST. The interaction of so many constraints on varying timescales makes it impossible to identify any one dominant scheduling factor. Many of the constraints are periodic with different periods and phases. As a consequence, there are generally several opportunities during a year to make a particular observation, and a prime goal of HST scheduling is to make an optimal choice among these opportunities for as many observations as possible. This effort is complicated by the fact that the majority of the requested exposures have timing, grouping, repetition, or ordering constraints that couple very strongly with the time-dependent constraints of Figure 14-1. More extensive discussions of the HST scheduling problem can be found in Miller et al. (1987, 1988) and Johnston (1988a, 1989b, 1990).

14.2 REPRESENTATION AND COMBINATION OF CONSTRAINTS AND PREFERENCES

Constraints convey two types of information to the scheduler:

Feasibility constraints specify conditions or times when activities might or might not be scheduled. We interchangeably use the terms *strict* or *hard* constraint for this type because they may not be violated under normal circumstances. A mechanism for relaxing (that is, violating) strict constraints is discussed in Section 14.3. A few examples in the HST scheduling context are

○ Provide a minimum of two months between an observation and a repeat observation on the same target.

○ Never schedule an observation when the sun is within 50° of the target.

○ Don't roll the spacecraft more than 30° from its nominal orientation.

Preference constraints specify quality judgments on scheduling conditions that are preferred but not required. These can be based on objective or subjective factors. In HST scheduling, for example, it is desirable to schedule at times that

○ Minimize scattered light from the bright limb of the earth.

○ Maximize the chance of successfully acquiring guide stars.

○ Place an observation as close to nominal roll as possible.

It is important that both feasibility and preference information be considered simultaneously during schedule construction. Ignoring feasibility constraints can obviously lead to unimplementable schedules, but disregarding preference constraints (in order to simplify the problem) can lead to unacceptably suboptimal schedules. For this reason, the concept of suitability functions (Section 14.2.1) was developed by merging ideas from two well-studied frameworks, namely, constraint satisfaction problems (CSPs) for expressing and manipulating feasibility constraints and evidential reasoning techniques as a means to combine preference constraints.

Consider scheduling some activity A_i given that other activities A_j are already scheduled at times t_j. A human scheduler would assess the opportunities for scheduling A_i at various times by considering the effects of the activities A_j on A_i via the constraints. Constraints can take a variety of forms but can generally be cast into statements of the following type:

Given that activities $A_1, ..., A_{i-1}, A_{i+1}, ..., A_N$ are scheduled at times $t_1, ..., t_{i-1}, t_{i+1}, ..., t_N$, the degree of preference for scheduling activity A_i at time t because of constraint C_α is $W_{i\alpha}(t_1, ..., t_{i-1}, t_i = t, t_{i+1}, ..., t_N) \equiv W_{i\alpha}(t; t_{j \neq i})$.

The degrees of preference can be assigned over some numerical range based on a judgment of the importance of the constraint, with larger values of $W_{i\alpha}$ corresponding to greater preference. $W_{i\alpha}$ can represent both deterministic constraints and intrinsically unpredictable constraints; e.g., $W_{i\alpha}$ can also be formulated in terms of (a function of) the probability that some desirable condition will hold.

14.2.1 Combination of Preferences: Suitability Functions

In general, there will be a number of constraints acting on a task, so it is necessary to combine the degrees of preference $W_{i\alpha}$ from all applicable constraints. This combination process is formally similar to that employed in a number of rule-based expert systems that assess evidence for and against various conclusions (e.g., Shortliffe, 1976; Hart *et al.*, 1978). Although this approach to uncertainty reasoning is known to have its limitations—in particular, the knowledge base should form a tree so that no evidence is counted twice via alternative paths of reasoning (Pearl, 1988)—it is adequate for many scheduling problems and has the advantage of being computationally tractable.

However, the techniques used in rule-based systems for evaluating evidence for or against *discrete* conclusions cannot be applied directly to scheduling because a *continuum* of scheduling conclusions must be considered (e.g., schedule A_i at t_i and A_j at t_j, etc.). What is required instead is a continuum version of uncertainty reasoning, formulated in a way that efficiently expresses the variety of constraints that typically appear in these problems and that retains information about choices that affect schedule optimality. Central to this formulation is a way to combine evidence from two or more independent constraints $\{W_{i\alpha}, W_{i\beta}, ...\}$.

Two conditions for the combination of evidence are reasonable: the combination function for $W_{i\alpha}$ should be a continuous, monotonically increasing function of its arguments, and it should be associative; i.e., it should not matter in what order the evidence is considered. With these assumptions, the preferences $W_{i\alpha}$, together with the combination operator, form an Abelian group isomorphic to the additive group of real numbers on $(-\infty, \infty)$, a result that has independently been discovered by a number of researchers (e.g., Cox, 1946; Good, 1960, 1968; Hájek, 1985; Cheng & Kashyap, 1988). Thus, with no loss of generality, we take the $W_{i\alpha}$ to be real-valued functions that combine simply by addition.

It is common in scheduling problems to have constraints that specify times when an activity is *not* permitted to be scheduled. These are particularly important because they allow the scheduler to eliminate blocks of time from further consideration. In terms of the preferences, these times should have highly unfavorable values, e.g., $W_{i\alpha}(t;t_{j \neq i}) = -w_0$, where $w_0 > 0$ is sufficiently large to indicate *overwhelming* evidence against scheduling activity A_i at time t. We can transform the additive $W_{i\alpha}$ into a multiplicative form $B_{i\alpha}$ by defining

$$B_{i\alpha}(t;t_{j \neq i}) = \exp [W_{i\alpha}(t;t_{j \neq i})] \qquad W_{i\alpha}(t;t_{j \neq i}) > -w_0$$
$$= 0 \qquad\qquad\qquad\qquad W_{i\alpha}(t;t_{j \neq i}) \leq -w_0 \qquad (1)$$

Except where $B_{i\alpha}(t;t_{j \neq i}) = 0$, the use of the exponential function makes the *additive* combination of the weights $W_{i\alpha}$ equivalent to the *multiplicative* combination of $B_{i\alpha}$. When $B_{i\alpha}(t;t_{j \neq i}) = 0$, multiplicative combination provides precisely the desired behavior; i.e., if there is overwhelming evidence against scheduling A_i at t from *any* source, then no amount of evidence from other sources can counteract this. We have found that the multiplicative formulation is particularly convenient for representing practical constraints defined by scheduling experts. In the HST domain, we have further adopted the convention that a value $W_{i\alpha} = 0 \Leftrightarrow B_{i\alpha} = 1$ represents the absence of evidence either for or against a scheduling decision. In practice, the $B_{i\alpha}$ are defined by analysis of the constraints and preferences in consultation with telescope scheduling experts.

It is computationally infeasible to work with the full N-dimensional form of the $B_{i\alpha}(t;t_{j \neq i}) = 0$ in any practical scheduling problem. The approach adopted in SPIKE consists of projecting the $B_{i\alpha}$ into functions of one time variable only:

$$S_{i\alpha}(t) = \max \{B_{i\alpha}(t;t_{j \neq i})| t_{j \neq i}\} \qquad (2)$$

where the maximum operator ranges only over times t_j where activities A_j are permitted to be scheduled (based on the current state of the schedule, i.e., accounting both for times excluded by constraints and for times excluded by decision of the scheduler). $S_{i\alpha}(t)$ is zero only when, solely because of the constraint C_α, *no* possible choices for scheduling activity $A_{j \neq i}$ will permit A_i to be scheduled at time t; otherwise, its value is the best (most preferable) value of $B_{i\alpha}$ that can be obtained by scheduling A_j at t_j given any other possible schedule of the other activities. The former property of $S_{i\alpha}(t)$ ensures that no times are excluded prematurely unless provably in violation of a strict constraint. The latter provides an important indicator of optimal scheduling choices to the scheduling agent by always indicating the *best* that can be achieved, regardless of future scheduling decisions. (It is conceiv-

able that a function other than maximum, e.g., some averaging function or even
minimum, could be useful in some scheduling problems.) We call $S_{i\alpha}(t)$ the *suit-ability function* for activity A_i because of constraint C_α. The *total suitability func-tion* for an activity $S_i(t)$ is the product of the suitability functions from each of its
constraints multiplied by a restriction operator $R_i(t)$ indicating any scheduling deci-sions made so far in constructing the schedule $R_i(t) = 0$ for excluded times, 1 other-wise):

$$S_i(t) = R_i(t) \prod_\alpha S_{i\alpha}(t)$$

(3)

$S_i(t) = 0$ if activity A_i is excluded from being scheduled at time t, either because a
strict constraint would be violated or because of prior scheduling decisions. These
equations implicitly determine the suitability function for an activity and are solved
by an iteration procedure corresponding to the propagation of constraints.

The suitability function concept can be illustrated by a simple example: con-sider a preference constraint of the form

Schedule A_j as soon as possible after the end of A_i but starting no sooner than x
minutes afterwards and ending no later than $x + y$ minutes afterwards.

We can represent this by choosing $B_{j\alpha}(t;t_i) = \varphi(t - t_i)$, where φ is a function
indicating the judgment (objective or subjective) of how much better or worse it is
to delay scheduling A_j after A_i. Given the suitability function $S_i(t)$ of A_i, it is
straightforward to construct $S_{j\alpha}(t)$ because of this constraint, as illustrated in Figure
14-2. Panel a shows what the $B_{j\alpha}(t;t_i)$ could look like for a plausible choice of φ.
Panel b shows what the suitability function $S_i(t)$ might be at some stage in the
scheduling: in this case, there are two disjoint candidate intervals where A_i could be
scheduled. The last panel c shows the resulting suitability $S_{j\alpha}(t)$ for task A_j.

Suitability functions provide a simple but effective framework for capturing
metric-time scheduling constraints, both strict and preference. All the conventional
binary temporal interval relationships (before, after, during, etc.: see Allen [1983])
are easily represented by appropriate suitability functions, along with a large class
of far more general temporal couplings (Shapiro, 1980). Like Rit's (1986) formula-tion of "constrained occurrences" for binary interval constraints, suitability func-tions can represent and propagate disjunctions; more generally, however, they also
handle constraints of higher order than binary and can incorporate preferences as
well. The combination of preferences is analogous to other similar constraint evalu-ation methods (e.g., Fox & Smith, 1984; Smith, Fox, & Ow, 1986) but differs in
that the combination of evidence for or against a scheduling decision is required to
be monotonic and associative. It is also worth noting that although there is a resem-blance between suitability functions and the propagated preferences of Sadeh and
Fox (1988), the latter method is based on a probabilistic model of start time distri-

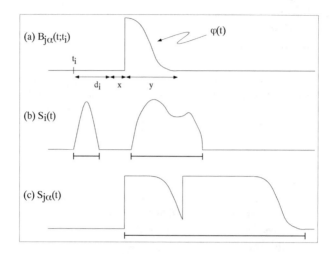

Figure 14-2: Illustration of suitability functions for the case of a binary preference constraint: (a) preference expressing that a task A_j should be scheduled as soon as possible after x minutes from the completion of another task A_i (of duration d_i) and in no case later than $x + y$ minutes; (b) hypothetical suitability of A_i at some stage in the scheduling process; (c) the resulting suitability of A_j. The intervals where each function is non-zero are indicated by bars under the time axes in (b) and (c).

butions. Such a probabilistic characterization of the *results* of scheduling as an input to the scheduling agent differs from the suitability function perspective, which maintains a distinction between the likelihood of different decisions by the scheduler and the characterization of preferences vs. time. However, this does not rule out the use of similar models that attempt to estimate resource demand and contention (e.g., Sadeh, 1991): these can play a useful role as suitability components that reflect resource or capacity limits.

14.2.2 Consistency Methods

Consistency methods have long been known to improve search efficiency for discrete CSPs (see, e.g., Dechter, 1986; Dechter & Pearl, 1988; Dechter & Meiri, 1989; and references therein) and have proven to be useful in SPIKE as well. Consistency techniques make explicit the information that is implicit in the constraints. We have found the following techniques to be useful in speeding scheduling search:

Node-consistency refers to the removal from consideration of domain values that cannot be part of any solution, where this determination is made based on unary constraints. In our formulation, this is explicitly represented in the suitability functions.

Arc-consistency refers to removing values from the domains of variables to satisfy binary constraints. This technique is best illustrated by example: suppose that A_j is constrained to follow A_i with a minimum end-to-start separation of Δt and that both activities have unit durations and are restricted to be scheduled in the interval $[t_A, t_B]$. Then the interval $[t_B - \Delta t - 1, t_B]$ is excluded for A_i, and the interval $[t_A, t_A + \Delta t + 1]$ is excluded for A_j. To introduce arc-consistency into the network, we restrict activities to fall within the overall scheduling interval $[t_A, t_B]$ and then propagate constraints (Equation 3).

Path-consistency refers to the inference of additional (binary) constraints based on those explicitly stated. Again, an example makes the principle obvious. Suppose A_i must precede A_j, which must in turn precede A_k: by explicitly representing the constraint "A_i precedes A_k," we can immediately represent the implication of a decision on scheduling A_i that would otherwise require a further decision about A_j. For simple precedence, the additional constraints inferred by path consistency are just those derived from the transitive closure of the precedence relationship. However, for more general binary constraints that depend on time differences only (e.g., "group $\{A_1A_2A_3\}$ within 24 hours"), it is possible to generalize this calculation and derive much more informative constraints (Johnston & Adorf, 1992).

We have found a substantial benefit in pre-computing and storing for later access the results of node-, arc-, and path-consistency. We have also found that explicit representation of inferred constraints makes the conflict-count repair heuristics (Section 14.4.2) more effective. However, in other scheduling domains, the significant pre-processing computational cost must be traded against the potential speedup during search. To help control this, the constraint propagation code used in SPIKE includes a "time-out" capability that can be used to limit the amount of computation devoted to path-consistency.

14.2.3 Computational Aspects

The implementation of suitability functions on digital hardware requires that continuous suitabilities be discretized, either in time, value, or both. In SPIKE, we have avoided any fundamental discretization in time for two important reasons: (1) it introduces an artificial time granularity into the problem and (2) many important constraints yield suitability functions that have long intervals of constant value and would therefore be represented inefficiently by a large number of identical values for many discrete time points. Instead, we adopted the discretization of suitability function values that allows suitability functions to be represented as *piecewise constant functions* (PCFs). These can conveniently and compactly be expressed as a list of times and values, e.g., $(t_1 \ s_1 \ t_2 \ s_2...t_n \ s_n)$, where the suitability has a value of s_1 from t_1 up to t_2, then a value of s_2, etc. Suitability values are not restricted to a fixed set. Arbitrary values are allowed and are only required to be constant over appropriate intervals (which can be different for different constraints). In this way, the basic constraint representation mechanism places no arbitrary restriction on the timescale or suitability value that can be represented.

The choice of PCFs has other advantages as well. They are closed under all the common operations required for manipulation of suitability functions such as multiplication or maximum (in contrast to other representations such as piecewise linear functions). The cost of storing and combining PCFs is proportional to the number of intervals with distinct values, not the size of the scheduling interval.

Although the PCF representation of suitabilities does not require discretization of suitability values, in practice, this might be useful because small differences in suitability (e.g., a few percent) might not be significant, and "collapsing" these differences in suitability can decrease the storage required for the suitability function and increase the speed of constraint propagation.

14.3 HST SCHEDULING AS A CONSTRAINT SATISFACTION PROBLEM

A constraint satisfaction problem (CSP) consists of a set of variables, each with a domain of discrete values, and a set of constraints that limits the allowed values for each variable based on the assigned values of other variables. The problem is to assign a consistent set of values for all variables such that there are no constraint violations. To cast a scheduling problem into the form of a CSP, we identify each activity to be scheduled with a variable, and we partition the scheduling time range for each activity into intervals that are identified with the domain of the corresponding variable. A CSP, as usually stated, considers only strict constraints and ignores preferences: we place the further condition on the problem that the preferences should be maximized in the solution state. CSPs on discrete domains arise in a variety of applications, and methods for solving them have been studied widely: for a recent survey, see Kumar (1992) and references therein.

SPIKE incorporates a general "toolkit" for representing and manipulating constraint satisfaction problems, which we will briefly describe in this section. This toolkit is used in the SPIKE scheduling search algorithm, which will be discussed in Section 14.4.

14.3.1 The SPIKE CSP Toolkit

The SPIKE CSP toolkit is implemented as a set of object classes and associated methods, the most important of which are the abstract classes for

- **CSP**, representing the collection of variables, constraints, etc., required to represent a particular type of constraint satisfaction problem

- **variable**, representing variables, their assigned values, conflicts, preferences, etc.

These two classes must be specialized for each particular kind of CSP implemented.

The state information maintained by CSP and variable instances can be manipulated with an extensive library of methods. These provide capabilities that have proven extremely useful in a practical scheduling environment. Each variable instance maintains constraint conflicts and preferences data for each of its domain values as well as the variable's current assigned value.

Some of the more important capabilities provided by the CSP toolkit include

- **Inconsistent assignments:** At any point, variables are permitted to have assigned values that are inconsistent with other assigned values. This is important for two reasons: it allows information about constraint linkages among activities to be exploited during scheduling search (Section 14.4), and it allows for search through a relaxed version of the problem. This is an especially important feature when there is no solution to the CSP as originally posed, and the best one can hope for is to solve a relaxed problem where some constraints are violated (cf. Freuder, 1989).

- **Locked and ignored variables:** A variable can be forced to have a specified assigned value, then be ignored thereafter, or can be ignored without an assigned value. This allows the scheduler to partition the activities to schedule into an "active" set and "inactive" set—either with or without assigned values—and, thus, easily control the focus of the search process. Ignored variables are motivated by scheduling problems (like HSTs) where there are *conditional* activities. These start out as ignored until some triggering condition is true, e.g., the commitment of some other observation or notification from the proposer to schedule the observation.

- **Removal and restoration of domain values:** Any domain value for a variable can be excluded from the problem, then restored at any time. This makes it possible to easily search for solutions that contain only high-preference values or to dynamically exclude scheduling times for reasons external to the formal constraint specification.

- **Constraint weights:** Constraints can have any desired weight value, which is the amount the conflict count is incremented for each violation. More important constraints have higher weights. For HST, temporal constraints have higher weight than resource constraints.

- **Constraint caching:** The toolkit provides a mechanism for caching the impacts of the current set of assigned values. This has two major benefits: it allows the system to quickly retract any current assigned value, and it allows for an "explanation" of the conflicts on any particular domain value (because the cache records the conflict source constraint as well as the relevant domain values and conflict weights). The cache mechanism can be turned on or off as appropriate based on the trade-off between time to compute constraint violations and the space to record them.

- **Assignment history and snapshots:** The toolkit provides an assignment history mechanism, with facilities to mark the current state and back up to any marker. There are also facilities for saving the current set of assigned values in various forms, then re-applying them to the problem. The history mechanism can be turned off if desired to improve run-time performance.

- **Capacity constraints:** In addition to temporal constraints between variables, the toolkit implements a general class of capacity (or resource) constraints. The mapping of domain values to capacity "bins" is completely customizable and can be many-to-one or one-to-many.

14.3.2 Time Sampling

As noted above, the scheduling interval for an activity is discretized as part of the translation into the CSP variable domain. It is therefore necessary to consider how to discretize the representation of time (unless there exists some natural time discretization in terms of which the constraints can be defined). As a general rule, the sampling interval must be less than the timescale for significant changes in the scheduling constraints. If this condition is satisfied, then one has to decide upon a suitable *sampling procedure* defining how to treat those strict constraints that would prevent the scheduling of an activity over some but not all of a given interval. The basic choice is whether to exclude the entire interval or not:

- If the entire interval is excluded, then there is a risk that feasible solutions might be missed.

- If the interval is *not* excluded, then the scheduler might find what appears to be a feasible configuration that turns out not to be feasible when the timing is examined in detail.

In HST scheduling, we generally chose the second option for the initial implementation and moved toward the first option for specific constraints as experience was gained with operations. The choice must be determined for each problem type based on the characteristics of the constraints and the difficulty of dealing with the consequences. In some problems, there will be a natural time unit in terms of which constraints are defined, so that no sampling error will occur. A further discussion of sampling and discretization is given in Johnston & Adorf (1992).

14.4 SCHEDULING SEARCH IN SPIKE

SPIKE treats schedule construction as a constrained optimization problem and uses a heuristic repair-based scheduling search technique called *multistart stochastic repair*. This technique consists of the following steps:

1. **Trial assignment:** Make a trial assignment ("initial guess") of activities to times based on heuristics to be discussed further below. Such a schedule will generally have temporal or other constraint violations as well as resource capacity overloads.

2. **Repair:** Apply heuristic repair techniques to try to eliminate constraint violations until either a pre-established level of effort has been expended, or there are no conflicts left.

3. **Deconflict:** Eliminate conflicts by removing any activities with constraint violations or by relaxing constraints until a feasible schedule remains.

The heuristics employed in SPIKE are stochastic, so there is benefit in repeating the three steps above as often as there is time. The general strategy is to select the best of many runs, possibly trying different initial guess and repair heuristics. However, the SPIKE algorithm has desirable "anytime" characteristics (cf. Zweben, Davis, & Gargan, 1990): at any point in the processing after the initial guess has been constructed, a feasible schedule can be produced simply by removing any remaining activities with constraint violations, as described further below.

Two additional factors play a major role in SPIKE's search process:

1. **Optimization:** The trial assignment and repair heuristics pay careful attention to suitability function values and attempt to optimize the total suitability of the resulting schedule.

2. **Oversubscription:** In general, it is known that more HST observations are intended to be in the pool to schedule than can actually fit into the timeline, so there can be no solution with all activities scheduled. Thus, the deconflict step assumes a high degree of importance because it defines the relaxed problem that is being solved.

14.4.1 Trial Assignment Heuristics

The choice of a good trial assignment can be important for repair-based methods, and to this end, we have conducted extensive experiments on different combinations of variable and value selection heuristics to identify the most powerful combinations. Over a thousand combinations of heuristics were tried by making multiple runs on sample scheduling problems. Several heuristics were identified on this basis: one of the most successful selects most-constrained activities to assign first, where the number of min-conflicts times is used as the measure of degree of constraint. Min-conflict times are then assigned, with ties broken by maximum preference derived from suitability functions or by earliest time. Several other heuristics are also employed in some settings, considering, for example, the number of temporally related activities, task priority, maximum suitability (preference), and related tasks and whether they have assigned values. The number of temporally related activities was found to be particularly effective on the 60 CSP scheduling problems defined by Sadeh (1991) and discussed further by Muscettola (1992) and Johnston & Minton (1993). It is worth noting that the SPIKE trial assignment heuristics are quite simple and are based on easy-to-calculate measures of degree of constraint and constraint connectivity. This is in contrast to the much more elaborate analyses that characterize the approaches taken, for example, by Sadeh & Fox (1988), Sadeh (1991), Sycara et al. (1991), and Muscettola (1992). Further research into the cost-effectiveness of lookahead is clearly warranted.

14.4.2 Repair Heuristics

The repair heuristics used by SPIKE are based on a successful neural network architecture developed for SPIKE (Johnston & Adorf, 1989, 1992; Adorf & Johnston, 1990) and later refined into a simple symbolic form (Minton *et al.*, 1990, 1992; Chapter 9 [this book]) that has since superseded the neural network. The SPIKE repair heuristics make highly effective use of *conflict count* information, i.e., the number of constraint violations on scheduled activities or on potential schedule times. Min-conflicts time selection is one such repair heuristic in which activities are moved to times when the number of conflicts is minimized. Both theoretical analysis and numerical experiments have shown that min-conflicts can be very effective in repairing reasonable trial assignments. We have found that further improvement can come from the use of a max-conflicts activity selection heuristic, which selects activities for repair that have the largest number of conflicts on their current assigned time. (This heuristic is also important when constraints have different weights: it then tends to select for repair those activities that violate the most important constraints, i.e., those with the largest weights.)

Both hill climbing and backtracking repair procedures have been tried, but hill climbing has been shown to be the most cost-effective on problems attempted to date. Typically, only a relatively small number of repair steps are allowed, e.g., kN, where N is the number of activities to schedule, and k is usually 2 but is kept in the range 1–5. This helps deal with the problems of "cycles" that can afflict hill-climbing procedures, where the repair process repeatedly attempts to place the same set of activities at mutually inconsistent times. Although cycles are sometimes observed, and there has been some work done to identify and avoid them, they have turned out not to be a significant problem in practice.

14.4.3 Deconflict

SPIKE currently uses a rather simple technique to remove conflicting activities from an oversubscribed schedule: activities to be removed are selected based on lower priority, higher numbers of constraint conflicts, and lower preference time assignments. If there remain gaps when all conflicting activities have been deleted, then a simple best-first pass through the remaining unscheduled activities is used to fill them. This final phase of "schedule deconflicting" has been little studied and is an area that could benefit from further effort.

14.4.4 Schedule Quality Measures

There are several important measures of schedule quality employed, including the number of observations on the schedule, the total observing time scheduled, and the summed degree of preference of the scheduled observations. Although some applications of SPIKE use minimum makespan or related measures, these are not important for HST scheduling: the time boundaries of the schedule are essentially fixed, and the goal is to maximize the quantity and quality of the observations scheduled within them.

One particularly interesting measure plays a role when the activities to be scheduled have durations $d(t)$ that vary as a function of time: in this case, the total *gap* time in the schedule serves as one component of a quality measure because it indicates how much time could potentially be used if there were appropriate activities available. Note that in this case, the total summed activity duration scheduled can be highly misleading—it is possible to construct a very inefficient schedule that rates highly by this measure simply by placing activities at times when they are very inefficient (i.e., $d(t) \gg d_{min}$) but tend to fill up the schedule. Thus, the appropriate quality measure is the non-intuitive sum of total *minimum* activity duration plus the total gap time.

14.4.5 Rescheduling

SPIKE provides support for rescheduling in a variety of ways. Two worth mentioning in particular are provided by the CSP toolkit (Section 14.3): *task locking* and *conflict-cause analysis*. Tasks or sets of tasks can be locked in place on the schedule and will thereafter not be considered during search or repair (unless, of course, the user unlocks them). These tasks represent fixed points on the schedule. Conflict-cause analysis permits the user to force a task onto the schedule, then display what constraints are violated and by which other tasks. The conflicting tasks can be unassigned if desired, either individually or as a group, and returned to the pool of unscheduled tasks. This helps with the most common rescheduling case, where a specific activity (e.g., a target of opportunity) must be placed on the schedule, thereby disrupting at least some tasks that are already scheduled. A limited study of minimal-change rescheduling has been conducted (Sponsler & Johnston, 1990), but much more work remains to be done in this area. Most of the other SPIKE support for rescheduling makes use of facilities provided in the user interface that allow the scheduler to freely manipulate the timeline (Section 14.5.3).

14.5 SPIKE AND HST SCIENCE SCHEDULING

The framework described in the preceding sections has been integrated into an observatory science planning and scheduling system for the Hubble Space Telescope. SPIKE has been used since 1988, first in pre-launch readiness tests and then in science operations since HST launch in 1990. Figure 14-3 shows the high-level scheduling flow for the HST ground system that is described in this section and is covered in more detail in Miller (1989), Adorf (1990), and Miller & Johnston (1991).

- **Proposal preparation:** An astronomer who plans to use HST must create an observing proposal that specifies the observations to be made. This proposal is the primary input to the planning and scheduling process. The Remote Proposal Submission System (RPSS) and Proposal Entry Processor (PEP) handle observing proposals, including electronic submission by astronomers (Section 14.5.1).

- **Planning:** The Transformation (Trans) expert system converts the proposal from a high-level specification into detailed task descriptions for scheduling (Section 14.5.2).

- **Long-term scheduling:** Because the HST scheduling problem covers such a wide range of timescales and tens of thousands of tasks, a two-tiered approach to scheduling was adopted. A long-term plan (Section 14.5.3) spans approximately one year and allocates tasks (as defined by Transformation) to specific weeks or parts of a week. From the long-term plan, week-long segments are extracted for short-term scheduling. Long-range scheduling is done with the SPIKE system, which was developed at the STScI.

- **Short-term scheduling:** Short-term scheduling (Section 14.5.4) with the Science Planning and Scheduling System (SPSS) performs the final sequencing of groups of observations within a week, generates the detailed command list, and transmits the results as the Science Mission Specification (SMS) to the HST Payload Operations Control Center. SPSS was originally developed by TRW and is now maintained by the STScI.

Section 14.5.5 considers some of the implementation issues that were faced during development of the integrated HST ground system.

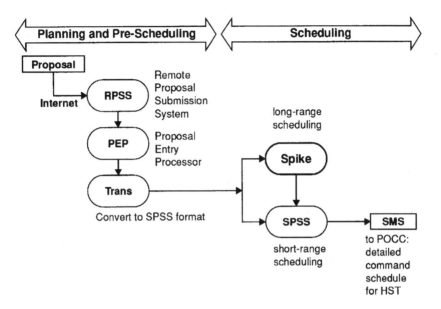

Figure 14-3: The processing flow for HST scheduling. Proposals are received electronically over the Internet and processed through a proposal database. The "Transformation" system converts the astronomer's observing plan into a set of tasks to schedule. SPIKE does the long-range scheduling, then passes off 1-week segments to SPSS for short-term scheduling and instrument command request generation. The main output product, the Science Mission Specification (SMS), is a detailed time-tagged command list for the HST's onboard computers.

14.5.1 Proposal Preparation

The selection of successful proposers for HST is based on a relatively simple ("Phase I") description of the scientific intent of the program and the observatory resources required to accomplish it. Once the observations are approved by a peer review process, each proposer must prepare a detailed ("Phase II") definition of exactly what exposures must be taken. Because the HST and its ground system are very complex, and the astronomer does not have real-time control over the telescope, essentially all observations are scheduled and taken by the staff of the Space Telescope Science Institute (STScI) in Baltimore.

The Phase II proposal contains information on the astronomical objects, individual exposures, instrument parameters, and the relationships (i.e., constraints) among exposures: Table 14-1 lists the kinds of constraints that proposers can specify in the syntax that they actually use. Proposals are submitted electronically in an ASCII file through the Remote Proposal Submission System (RPSS). The RPSS software validates the contents of a proposal file and can detect a wide range of problems, including typographical errors (e.g., a misspelled filter name), values out of range (e.g., a target declination exceeding 90°), and missing or inconsistent information (e.g., an exposure referencing an undefined target). A dedicated RPSS computer is available to the astronomical community over the Internet and the Space Physics Astrophysics Network (SPAN). The RPSS software has been distributed to approximately 100 astronomical institutions around the world and is run by most proposers at their home institutions before they send their proposals to STScI.

Table 14-1: The syntax of constraint specifications used by HST observers to define scheduling constraints on their exposures. Any number of these "special scheduling requirements" can be applied to exposure "lines," referring to their origin on paper forms. Keywords can be abbreviated to the form shown in uppercase letters (e.g., "ACQUISITION" can be abbreviated as "ACQ"). A *line-list* is a list of exposure line numbers, e.g., "1-5, 10, 12, 15-20." Square brackets indicate optional syntactic elements, and the "/line-list" shorthand applies the specific constraint to all listed lines. Most of the phases provide an English-like description of the constraint, all of which must be handled properly by the HST scheduling software.

HST Observing Proposals: Scheduling Constraint Syntax

EARLY ACQuisition FOR *line-list*

ONBOARD ACQuisition FOR *line-list*

INTeractive ACQuisition FOR *line-list*

GUIDing TOLerance angle [*/line-list*]

ORIENTation *angle +/– angle* [*/line-list*]

ORIENTation *angle +/– angle* FROM *line* [*/line-list*]

ORIENTation *angle +/– angle* FROM NOMINAL [*/line-list*]

POSition TARGet *x-val, y-val*[*/line-list*]

SAME ORIENTation FOR *line-list* AS *line*

SAME POSition FOR *line-list* AS *line*

CALIbration FOR *line-list* [NO SLEW]

SPATIAL SCAN [*/line-list*]

TARGet OF OPPortunity [*/line-list*]

CRITical OBServation [*/line-list*]

RealTime ANALYSIS [FOR *line-list*]

REQuires UPLINK [*/line-list*]

AFTER *date\line* [BY *time* [+/– range]]

AT *date +/– range*

BEFORE *date\line* [BY *time* [+/– range]]

DARK TIME [*/line-list*]

DECision TIME *time*

GROUP *line-list* WITHIN *time*

Table 14-1: Continued

HST Observing Proposals: Scheduling Constraint Syntax
GROUP *line-list* NO GAP
GROUP *line-list* NON-INTerruptible
NON-INTerruptible [*/line-list*]
PERIOD *time +/– error*
PHASE *phase +/– range* [OF REF *line*]
REQuires DATA FROM *line-list* [*/line-list*]
REQuires UPDATE [*/line-list*]
SEQuential *line-list*
SEQuential *line-list* NO GAP
SEQuential *line-list* WITHIN *time*
SEQuential *line-list* NON-INT
ZERO-PHASE *date +/– error*
REPEAT *line-list* EVERY *time +/– range* for *number* MORE TIMES
CONDitional [ON *line-list*] IF *condition-text* [*/line-list*]
SELECT *number* OF *line-list* OR *line-list*...

STScI designed RPSS and the HST proposal language with the following goals in mind:

- oriented toward the astronomical community—easy to understand and concise and logical in the amount and sequence of data requested
- able to accommodate both simple and sophisticated observations from novice or experienced HST users
- formulated in declarative terms, i.e., the astronomer can specify what data should be collected without becoming needlessly encumbered by instrument, telescope, and ground system particulars.

RPSS was the first system of its kind for a major scientific installation—it has been in use since February 1986. The ability to locally validate and electronically submit a proposal is an extremely valuable tool, both for proposers and for STScI. Proposers can detect and correct a large class of errors and are assured that typographical errors are not introduced by data entry personnel. The STScI can process proposals more rapidly and avoid the costs of manual data entry. A further discussion of the STScI proposal handling software can be found in Jackson et al. (1988) and Adorf (1990).

14.5.2 Transformation

Given the high-level, astronomically oriented description of the observations found in the Phase II proposal, the next step is essentially one of *planning*. It is the role of the Transformation system to convert the declarative proposal from the astronomer into a set of aggregated exposures and constraints called *scheduling units* (SUs), with all the details required to enable the execution of the exposures on the spacecraft.

Transformation performs several planning tasks, including determining the order to execute observations (when not explicitly specified by the proposer), breaking exposures into pieces to better match target visibility conditions, grouping observations to minimize overhead operations, choosing specific implementation scenarios, and supplying values of instrumental settings that were defaulted by the proposer. Transformation also detects certain errors that might be present in the proposal, including conflicting timing requirements among exposures, loops in precedence constraints, and inconsistencies in instrument parameter settings. Transformation makes use of the suitability function framework (Section 14.2.1) and the SPIKE temporal constraint mechanism to collect and propagate temporal constraints and to achieve path consistency (Section 14.2.2).

The input to Transformation is a file generated from the Proposal Entry Processor (PEP) database that is essentially a parsed version of the astronomer's Phase II proposal. Transformation produces output files that specify the structure of the scheduling units and the nature of any constraints that act on them. These files then become the input to SPIKE and SPSS.

Transformation was initially conceived and implemented as a rule-based expert system implemented in OPS5 (Rosenthal *et al.*, 1986) but was re-implemented in Common Lisp when the complexity of the rule-based system grew too great (Gerb, 1991b). It remains an expert system in that it models a large body of expertise developed by the astronomers who operate the HST scheduling systems.

14.5.3 Long-Term Scheduling

Long-term scheduling begins with a set of observing proposals from Transformation, specified as a set of scheduling units (SUs) and their constraints. An initial pre-processing step calculates absolute time-dependent constraints related to orbit-by-orbit target visibility and the implications of special orientation requirements; the results of these compute-intensive calculations are cached in disk files.

Using SPIKE, SUs can be committed to time intervals either manually or with the automatic (CSP) scheduler (Section 14.4). A graphical user interface (e.g., Figure 14-4) is available to view and manipulate the schedule or to run the automatic scheduler. Scheduling decisions (when final) are recorded in a database, then reported to files and transmitted to SPSS. Once SPSS has completed short-term sequencing, SPIKE software analyzes the calendar to determine what observations were scheduled and what factors could affect the future schedule (e.g., timing, special orientations, or contingent SUs). SPIKE also analyzes a report from the data

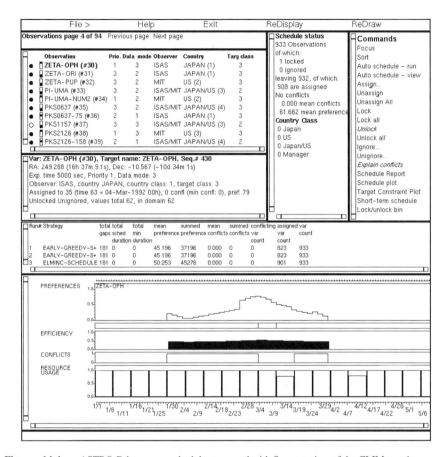

Figure 14-4: ASTRO-D long-term schedule generated with SPIKE: a view of the CLIM user interface on a 6-month schedule. The different panes provide visibility into the list of available observations (upper left) and frequently-used commands (upper right) and provide a graphical view of a single observation, including preferences (i.e., suitability function values), current assigned value, observing efficiency, constraint conflicts, and total resource utilization (lower pane), all displayed here over about a 5-month period. Many of the objects on the screen are CLIM "presentations" and are thus mousable by the user.

archive to verify that the data were received and processed. Observations that are not scheduled by SPSS, which are lost in transmission or which are marked as poor quality, are considered candidates for rescheduling.

SPIKE provides a number of tools to support the scheduling process, including high-resolution PostScript plots of observing constraints and interactive X-window tools for analyzing of complex spacecraft orientation constraints and for viewing the component exposures and constraints from individual proposals. The latter can be analyzed in detail, which is particularly important when it is necessary to examine the effects of individual constraints on potential scheduling decisions. This facility has also proven to be very useful for uncovering and fixing problems with proposals.

SPIKE's central position in the HST scheduling process has led us to develop an integrated tracking system called ASSIST to monitor and report the status of all observations in the scheduling pipeline. Prior to the development of ASSIST, users of the various systems (PEP, Transformation, SPSS, etc.) each maintained separate tracking systems. Because proposals consist of many observations that are executed at different times, finding the status of a proposal required substantial work. ASSIST provides a central repository for data from the various stages of scheduling, including proposal preparation, long-range scheduling, short-range scheduling, and archiving.

Certain combinations of HST instruments can operate in tandem, and for some astronomical targets, such "parallel" observations can yield very interesting data. SPIKE's Parallel Observation Matching System (POMS) analyzes the weekly schedule and finds appropriate matches from a pool of parallel proposals. POMS is an expert system that includes a sophisticated knowledge base and matching strategies for identifying and ranking the quality of matches (Lucks, 1992). Multiple ranked candidate parallel matches are sent to SPSS along with each weekly schedule.

14.5.4 Short-Term Scheduling

Short-term scheduling operates within a week at a time, working from a list of SUs from the long-term plan and generating a week-long sequence of activities called a *calendar*. After the activity sequence is defined, high-level spacecraft instructions are attached to the calendar activities. The output of the process is a Science Mission Specification (SMS) and can be thought of as the "assembly language" that controls the HST. The STScI delivers the SMS to the Payload Operations Control Center (POCC) at NASA's Goddard Spaceflight Center, where it is checked for errors and constraint violations that would affect the health or safety of the HST and its instruments. Based on the SMS, the POCC prepares the binary command loads for the two on-board computers that control the observatory. The POCC also takes requests for Tracking and Data Relay Satellite (TDRS) links from the SMS and passes them on to the TDRS Network Control Center. Some requests will not be granted because of higher priority users (e.g., shuttle or other satellites). The POCC notifies the STScI of this, and the timeline is modified, usually by making use of one of the on-board tape recorders to hold data for later playback but occasionally by rescheduling the observation.

Execution of the observations is monitored by both the STScI and the POCC (by monitoring real-time transmissions or by playback of recorded science and engineering telemetry). The STScI analyzes the data to ensure that scheduled observations were completed successfully. It then calibrates the data and delivers them to the proposer for scientific analysis. Because HST observations are an important astronomical resource, an archive of all HST data is maintained. The proposer is normally granted exclusive access to the data for a proprietary period (usually one year), after which the data become available to the scientific community at large.

14.5.5 Implementation

SPIKE is an operational application of artificial intelligence technology, and in this section, we consider some of the implementation issues. The development of SPIKE started in early 1987 using Texas Instruments Explorer Lisp machines. The SPIKE graphical user interface was implemented in KEE CommonWindows (Intellicorp), but the remainder of the system used only Common Lisp and the Flavors object system. At HST launch, STScI had a complement of eight microExplorers and Explorers used for SPIKE operation, development, and testing.

Since 1987, there has been a great deal of evolution in Lisp hardware and software. We have continued to modify SPIKE to keep pace with these changes. All the Flavors code has been converted to the Common Lisp Object System (CLOS). Between late 1990 and mid-1992, we transitioned from Explorers to Sun SparcStations as the primary operations and development platform: there are currently a total of 22 SparcStation 2s used for Transformation and SPIKE. The Lisp used on the SparcStations is Allegro Common Lisp from Franz, Inc., which supports a version of CommonWindows based on X-windows. Thus, the user interface continued to operate on the SparcStations as it did on the Explorers (and allowed us to operate for some time with a mix of Explorers and SparcStations). After substantial investigation of alternative window systems, we recently reimplemented the user interface tools using the Common Lisp Interface Manager (CLIM). Updating SPIKE for new Lisp language features has not been difficult, and there are currently no plans to convert any of the system to C or C++.

A common feature of PEP, Transformation, and SPIKE development was that each system had to be developed in a short time (about six months for the initial system, with substantial extensions continuing over several years) and with a small staff (two to three people initially). It was also impossible to specify in advance a complete set of requirements for these systems because many important factors were unknown. These considerations led to the use of a rapid prototyping software development methodology instead of a more classical "waterfall" approach (requirements definition, design, implementation, and test). A tool-oriented approach was also encouraged, i.e., the development of general software routines that could be used for other applications later in development.

The most significant advantage of rapid prototyping to the HST was that it allowed PEP, Transformation, and SPIKE to be implemented in time to support testing and operations—in an environment with changing requirements, there is no choice but to use an adaptive software development methodology. Perhaps the most serious complication of this approach is that once the prototype is used operationally, it becomes increasingly difficult to make large changes to it. (In an ideal rapid prototyping situation, a prototype can be discarded after evaluation). Once operational, it is necessary to ensure that each version of the system is upwardly compatible with the previous version. A corollary to this is that pressure on the users to do operational work can prevent them from further participation in the software development process, e.g., critiquing initial requirements and evaluating prototype software. This can lead to a divergence between the needs of the users and the products of the developers, which must carefully be guarded against. We have found two techniques are useful to keep developers in touch with the needs of users. One is for developers to perform *full-scale* end-to-end tests with *real* data to uncover problems and bottlenecks. (This is in advance of any testing that might be performed by a test group affiliated with a software configuration management effort.) The other is to allow developers to apprentice in the user group (typically, for a month or so) in order to gain first-hand knowledge of the operational environment and requirements.

The incorporation of realistic test data proved to be quite important. Because of delays in the launch of HST, we had several hundred observing proposals that were constantly used to test prototype systems and to make development decisions. Had such extensive data not been available, the creation of a substantial body of simulated test data would have been required.

It is interesting to note that some of the most useful software tools were developed as quick-response reactions: a user would informally ask for a tool to handle some problem that was previously unrecognized or thought to be of low priority, and one of the software developers would then provide the tool in a very short time. For example, a number of functions used to fine-tune the long-range plan were developed in this way. One such function identified for a particular week candidate activities scheduled in later weeks that could be moved earlier to compensate for activities that had to be removed from the schedule at the last minute. Also, the ability to store and restore scheduling commitments in files was first implemented informally and was subsequently used to track scheduling decisions until SPIKE's ASSIST database tracking system was completed. A number of useful graphical displays and plots were also developed in this manner, all of which highlights the importance of good communications between developers and users and a certain flexibility in the development schedule to permit timely response to user requests.

Although following a non-classical development methodology, we nonetheless paid careful attention to such classic risk management factors as configuration control and testing. Developers use code management tools (i.e., Unix rcs) to prevent uncoordinated changes. Building, testing, and installing the software are automated with software tools to the greatest extent possible to help detect problems before delivery to the users and to minimize the chance for human errors—indeed, Transformation even incorporates a separate expert system to perform its own testing (Gerb 1991a). Procedures and tools to deliver software changes on a very short timescale (days to hours) are also essential.

14.6 OPERATIONAL EXPERIENCE

HST science operations is divided into "cycles" in which proposals are solicited from the astronomical community, selected, scheduled, and executed. In the long term, cycles will consist of about one year of HST observing. Early HST operations consisted of two special phases: "Orbital Verification" (OV), which assessed the basic capabilities of the telescope and instruments, and "Cycle 0" observations, which contain a mix of Science Verification (SV) and Guaranteed Time Observer (GTO) observations. OV ended in November 1990, and Cycle 0 ended in June 1991. The Cycle 1 observing era mixed GTO observations with the "General Observer" (GO) proposals from the astronomical community at large. Cycle 1 ended in July 1992 and is being followed by the Cycle 2 observations, etc.

The SPIKE system was first used to support HST scheduling for Cycle 0. The timeline for SV observations was established by NASA. The STScI used SPIKE to verify this timeline and to schedule GTO observations during weeks when time was available. Scheduling of these proposals in Cycle 0 used SPIKE in an interactive mode: planners would display individual proposals on timeline displays and choose times of high suitability for observations. Various automatic scheduling tools were sometimes used in conjunction with making manual commitments. Scheduling of early Cycle 1 proposals has also largely been interactive, with little use of the high-level, automated schedulers. The main value of SPIKE in this mode was the identification of problems with proposals and the assignment of observations to feasible but not necessarily optimal weeks.

When used on actual GTO and GO proposals, Transformation and SPIKE reported large numbers of diagnostic messages. Initially, many problems were the result of an incomplete understanding of how to best present complex observations to SPSS. The frequency of problems allowed us to effectively prioritize work in determining requirements and implementing the code. A significant number of problems uncovered by SPIKE and Transformation were the result of an inadvertent specification by the proposer of inconsistent requirements in the proposal. Although the PEP system performs *syntactic* checking on proposal information,

Transformation and SPIKE are the first systems that can detect problems related to planning and scheduling. (In particular, accurate instrument overhead times and orbital viewing conditions are calculated by Transformation, and these can reveal problems with the proposal.) We are currently investigating how to incorporate such checks in PEP and RPSS. Not only will this provide proposers with immediate feedback on certain classes of problems, but it will also reduce the delays in the scheduling process because of late proposal modifications.

We originally anticipated that long term schedules covering 6 to 12 months duration would be maintained beginning with Cycle 0. However, true long-term planning began late in Cycle 1 with schedules of approximately three months duration, and year-long schedules were first generated operationally beginning with Cycle 2. This was not because of any inherent limitation in the software (test schedules of a year duration had been generated well before launch). It was primarily because of a much larger than anticipated rate of change of proposals. Prior to launch, 10% of the proposals were expected to change after submission, whereas the actual rate is nearly 100%. Many proposals have been revised several times. A substantial portion of this can be attributed to the spherical aberration of the HST mirror and other unexpected behaviors of the instruments and spacecraft. Another factor is that the HST and major elements of the ground system are designed for fully pre-planned observations, with little capability to inject changes late in the scheduling process. A change to a proposal can therefore often require a repeat of the entire scheduling process, wasting much, if not all, of the earlier work. Tracking multiple revisions of proposals and their scheduling and execution status also requires substantial effort. Our recommendation to developers of future systems with requirements similar to HST would be to *build in the expectation of change* from the outset and to carefully examine factors in the design that are sensitive to a high rate of change. We realize that such flexibility will increase the initial cost of a system, but it can significantly reduce the life-cycle maintenance and operational costs. A further discussion of the HST experience can be found in Miller & Johnston (1991).

14.7 APPLICATION OF SPIKE TO OTHER ASTRONOMICAL SCHEDULING PROBLEMS

SPIKE has been adapted to schedule a variety of astronomical scheduling problems (see Table 14-2). Of these, two are in flight operations (in addition to HST), and several others are in the prototype or planning phase. The experience of customizing SPIKE for other types of problems has actively been sought during SPIKE development: each case provided feedback on the approach and led to improvements from one version to the next.

Table 14-2: Adaptations of SPIKE to various astronomical scheduling problems.

Mission	Status, Scheduling Mode, and Location
HST	Hubble Space Telescope. SPIKE operational since Oct. '89, HST launch Apr. '90. Used for HST long-term scheduling at Space Telescope Science Institute, Baltimore.
EUVE	Extreme Ultraviolet Explorer. SPIKE operational since Apr. '91, EUVE launch in June '92. Used for one-year scheduling of pointed observations. Run by Center for Extreme Ultraviolet Astrophysics, Univ. Calif., Berkeley.
ASTRO-D	Operational since Nov. '92. Flight operations started following launch in Feb. '93. SPIKE version capable of both long-term and short-term scheduling. Joint Japan/US X-ray telescope mission run from the Institute of Space and Astronautical Sciences in Japan (Isobe *et al.*, 1993)
XTE	X-ray Timing Explorer. Planned for use following launch in 1994. SPIKE would schedule both long-term and short-term. XTE will be run from the GSFC XTE Science Operations Center (Morgan, 1992)
AXAF	Advanced X-ray Astronomy Facility. Prototype developed 1990 as part of a successful science operations center proposal. Under consideration for science scheduling.
ROSAT	Roentgen Satellite. Prototype developed 1992 for feasibility evaluation for operational X-ray satellite. Dual long-term/short-term scheduling mode. German Space Operations Center, Munich.
IUE	International Ultraviolet Explorer. Prototype developed 1988 for evaluation of SPIKE framework. Scheduling mode was 6-months of European half-shifts, optimized for target coverage (Johnston, 1988b).
Ground-based	Prototypes developed in 1988–1992 to demonstrate feasibility. Dual mode: long-term scheduling for night allocation, short-term scheduling for exposure scheduling within a night. Telescopes included ESO (European Southern Observatory) and CFHT (Canada-France-Hawaii Telescope), as well as hypothetical Automatic Photometric Telescope (APT). Feasibility of coordinated ground- and space-based scheduling has also been demonstrated (Johnston, 1988c).

The adaptation of SPIKE for these problems demonstrates the flexibility of the SPIKE scheduling framework. As indicated above, SPIKE was designed so that new tasks and constraints can be defined without changing the basic framework. For ASTRO-D (Isobe *et al.*, 1993) and XTE (Morgan, 1992), SPIKE is operated in a hierarchical manner, with long-term scheduling first allocating observations to weeks much as they are for the HST problem (and with similar types of long-term constraints and preferences). Then, each week is scheduled in detail, subject to the detailed minute-by-minute constraints of low earth orbit operation. The major changes required to implement short-term scheduling were

1. a new type of task that can have variable duration depending on when it is scheduled and that can be interrupted and resumed when targets are occulted by the earth, or the satellite is in the radiation belt (i.e., task preemption)

2. new classes of short-term scheduling constraints that more precisely model target occultation, star tracker occultation, ground station passes, entry into high radiation regions, maneuver and setup times between targets, etc.

3. an interface between different hierarchical levels, by which a long-term schedule constrains times for short-term scheduling and conversely

4. a post-processor that examines short-term schedules for opportunities to extend task durations and, thus, utilize any remaining small gaps in the schedule to increase efficiency

All the general constraint combination and propagation mechanisms (Section 14.2) and the CSP toolkit (Section 14.3) and scheduling search techniques (Section 14.4) apply directly to both long-term and short-term scheduling. Figure 14-4 shows the SPIKE CLIM user interface displaying an ASTRO-D long-term schedule. Figure 14-5 shows a portion of the high-resolution PostScript plot output for a SPIKE short-term schedule for ASTRO-D. Only one day of a seven-day schedule is shown. Note that several observations are broken to fit around earth blockages or radiation belt passages and so are taken in multiple segments.

Most of the effort required to apply SPIKE to the new problems was limited to the specific domain modelling necessary, which typically involves computation related to the geometry of the satellite, sun, target, and earth. These problems can be expected to differ from one satellite to another, and it is not surprising that different models are required. Some of the modelling includes state constraints, although SPIKE does not perform explicit planning (cf. Muscettola *et al.*, 1992).

EUVE is unusual in that it makes long (2–3 days) observations, in contrast to HST and ASTRO-D, which typically make numerous short (15–40 minute) observations. As a consequence, EUVE is schedulable over year-long intervals without breaking the schedule into hierarchical levels. One of the more interesting results from a comparison of search algorithms for scheduling EUVE was that the SPIKE repair-based methods gained an extra *20 days* of observing time in a year compared to the best incremental scheduling approach.

14.8 SUMMARY

The SPIKE scheduling system has supported NASA's Hubble Space Telescope since launch and is integrated with a large and complex spacecraft ground system. The concept of suitability functions used in SPIKE makes it possible to efficiently represent the many factors that are important in real-world scheduling decisions. A powerful multistart stochastic repair technique is used to generate schedules. SPIKE's flexibility has been demonstrated by adapting it for several other spacecraft missions and ground-based observatories and by integrating long- and short-term scheduling at different levels of abstraction in the same constraint representation and search framework.

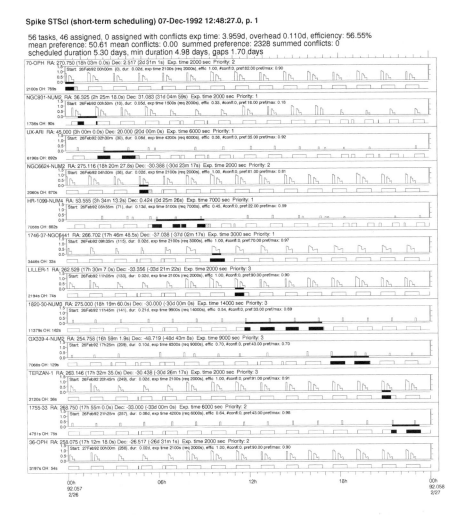

Figure 14-5: An example of SPIKE output on short-term scheduling of astronomical observations. Shown is a 24-hour portion of a 7-day schedule. The start-time suitability for each exposure is plotted as the upper graph, with interruptions due to target blockage by the earth and by satellite passage through high-radiation regions. The available exposure intervals are shown below as open bars, which are filled in to indicate the actual scheduled times. Some of the observations can be fit within one orbit; others must be interrupted and thus span several orbits.

References

Adorf, H.-M. 1990. "The Processing of HST Observing Programs," *Space Telescope European Coordinating Facility Newsletter* 13, 12–15.

Adorf, H.-M., and M. Johnston. 1990. "A Discrete Stochastic 'Neural Network' Algorithm for Constraint Satisfaction Problems," *Proceedings of the International Joint Conference on Neural Networks*, Vol. III, pp. 917–924, IEEE Computer Society Press, Los Alamitos, Calif.

Allen, J.F. 1983. "Maintaining Knowledge About Temporal Intervals." *Communications of the Association of Computing Machin.* 26, 832–843.

Cheng, Y., and R.L. Kashyap. 1988. "An Axiomatic Approach for Combining Evidence from a Variety of Sources," *Journal of Intelligent and Robotic Systems* 1, 17–33.

Cox, R.T. 1946. "Probability, Frequency and Reasonable Expectation." *American J. Phys.* 14, 1–13.

Dechter, R. 1986. "Learning While Searching in Constraint Satisfaction Problems." *Proc. of Fifth National Conf. Artificial Intelligence (AAAI 86)*, pp. 178–183, AAAI Press, Menlo Park, Calif.

Dechter, R., and I. Meiri. 1989. "Experimental Evaluation of Preprocessing Techniques in Constraint Satisfaction Problems," *Proc. of the Eleventh International Joint Conf. on Artificial Intelligence,* pp. 271–277, AAAI Press, Menlo Park, Calif.

Dechter, R., and J. Pearl. 1988. "Network-Based Heuristics for Constraint Satisfaction Problems." *Artificial Intelligence* 34, 1–38.

Fox, M. 1987. *Constraint-Directed Search: A Case Study of Job Shop Scheduling.* Morgan Kaufmann, San Francisco, Calif.

Fox, M., and S. Smith. 1984. "ISIS: A Knowledge-Based System for Factory Scheduling," *Expert Sys.* 1, 45.

Fox, M., N. Sadeh, and C. Baykan. 1989. "Constrained Heuristic Search," *Proc. Eleventh International Joint Conf. on Artificial Intelligence*, pp. 309–315, AAAI Press, Menlo Park, Calif.

Freuder, E. 1989. "Partial Constraint Satisfaction," *Proc. Eleventh International Joint Conf. on Artificial Intelligence*, pp. 278–283, AAAI Press, Menlo Park, Calif.

Gerb, A. 1991a. "The 'Looker': Using an Expert System to Test an Expert System," *Proc. 1991 World Congress on Expert Systems*, pp. 1005–1012, Goddard Space Flight Center, Greenbelt, MD.

Gerb, A. 1991b. "Transformation Reborn: A New Generation Expert System for Planning HST Operations," *Proc. of 1991 Goddard Conference on Space Applications of Artificial Intelligence,* NASA CP 3110, pp. 283–295, Goddard Space Flight Center, Greenbeld, MD.

Good, I.J. 1960. "Weight of Evidence, Corroboration, Explanatory Power, Information, and the Utility of Experiments," *J. Royal Statist. Soc.* 22, 319–331.

Good, I.J. 1968. "Corrigendum: Weight of Evidence, Corroboration, Explanatory Power,...," *J. Royal Statist. Soc.* 30, 203–203.

Hájek, P. 1985. "Combining Functions for Certainty Degrees in Consulting Systems." *Int. J. Man-Machine Studies* 22, 59–76.

Hart, P., P. Duda, and M. Einaudi. 1978. "PROSPECTOR—A Computer-Based Consultation System for Mineral Exploration," *Math. Geol.* 10, 589.

Isobe, T., M.D. Johnston, E. Morgan, and G. Clark. 1993. "The Application of SPIKE to ASTRO-D Mission Planning," *Proc. 2nd Astron. Data Analysis Software and Systems (ADASS)*, pp. 340–344, San Francisco Astronomical Society of the Pacific, Boston, MA.

Jackson, R., M. Johnston, G. Miller, K. Lindenmayer, P. Monger, S. Vick, R. Lerner, and J. Richon. 1988. "The Proposal Entry Processor: Telescience Applications for Hubble Space Telescope Operations," *Proc. of the 1988 Goddard Conference on Space Applications of Artificial Intelligence*, NASA CP 3009, pp. 197–212, Goddard Space Flight Center, Greenbelt, MD.

Johnston, M. 1988a. "Artificial Intelligence Approaches to Spacecraft Scheduling," *Proc. ESA Workshop on Artificial Intelligence Applications for Space Projects*, pp. 5–9, ESTEC, Noordwijk, Holland.

Johnston, M. 1988b. "Automated Observation Scheduling for the VLT," *Proc. ESO Conf. on Very Large Telescopes and Their Instrumentation*, pp. 1273–1282, ESO, Garching, Germany.

Johnston, M. 1988c. "Automated Telescope Scheduling," *Coordination of Observational Projects in Astronomy*, ed. C. Jaschek and C. Sterken, pp. 219–226, Cambridge Univ. Press, Cambridge.

Johnston, M. 1989a. "Knowledge-Based Telescope Scheduling," *Knowledge-Based Systems in Astronomy*, ed. A. Heck and F. Murtagh, pp. 33–49, Springer-Verlag, New York.

Johnston, M. 1989b. "Reasoning with Scheduling Constraints and Preferences," SPIKE Tech. Report 1989-2, Space Telescope Science Institute.

Johnston, M. 1990. "SPIKE: AI Scheduling for NASA's Hubble Space Telescope," *Proc. 6th IEEE Conf. on AI Applications*, pp. 184–190, IEEE Computer Society Press, Los Alamitos, Calif.

Johnston, M.D., and H.-M. Adorf. 1989. "Learning in Stochastic Neural Networks for Constraint Satisfaction Problems," NASA Conf. on Space Telerobotics, 31 Jan–2 Feb 1989, Pasadena, CA.

Johnston, M., and H.-M. Adorf. 1992. "Scheduling with Neural Networks—The Case of Hubble Space Telescope," *Computers and Operations Research* 19, 209–240.

Kumar, V. 1992. "Algorithms for Constraint Satisfaction Problems: A Survey," *Artificial Intelligence* 13, 32–44.

Lucks, M. 1992. "Detecting Opportunities for Parallel Observations on Hubble Space Telescope," *Telematics and Informatics* 9, 331–347.

Miller, G. 1989. "Artificial Intelligence Applications for Hubble Space Telescope Operations," *Knowledge Based Systems in Astronomy*, eds. F. Murtagh and A. Heck, pp. 5–32, Springer Verlag, New York.

Miller, G., and M. Johnston. 1991. "A Case Study of Hubble Space Telescope Proposal Processing, Planning and Long-Range Scheduling," *Proc. of Conf. Computing in Aerospace 8*, pp. 1–13, American Institute of Aeronautics and Astronomics, Washington, D.C.

Miller, G., D. Rosenthal, W. Cohen, and M. Johnston. 1987. "Expert Systems Tools for Hubble Space Telescope Observation Scheduling," *Telematics and Informatics* 4, 301–311.

Miller, G., M. Johnston, S. Vick, J. Sponsler, and K. Lindenmayer. 1988. "Knowledge-Based Tools for Hubble Space Telescope Planning and Scheduling: Constraints and Strategies," *Telematics and Informatics* 5, 197–212.

Minton, S., M. Johnston, A. Philips, and P. Laird. 1992. "Minimizing Conflicts: A Heuristic Repair Method for Constraint Satisfaction and Scheduling," *Artificial Intelligence* 58, 161–205.

Minton, S., M. Johnston, A. Philips, and P. Laird. 1990. "Solving Large-Scale Constraint Satisfaction and Scheduling Problems Using a Heuristic Repair Method," *Proc. of Eighth National Conference on Artificial Intelligence*, pp. 17-24, AAAI Press, Menlo Park, Calif.

Morgan, E. 1992. "Evaluation of SPIKE for XTE," Tech. Report, Center for Space Research, Massachusetts Institute of Technology.

Muscettola, N. 1992. "Scheduling by Iterative Partition of Bottleneck Conflicts," Technical Report, CMU-RI-TR-92-05, Carnegie Mellon University.

Muscettola, N., S.F. Smith, A. Cesta, and D. D'Aloisi. 1992. "Coordinating Space Telescope Operations in an Integrated Planning and Scheduling Architecture," *IEEE Control Systems* 12(2).

Pearl, J. 1988. *Probabilistic Reasoning in Intelligent Systems: Networks of Plausible Inference,* Morgan Kaufmann, San Francisco, Calif.

Rit, J.F. 1986. "Propagating Temporal Constraints for Scheduling," *Proc. of Fifth National Conf. on Artificial Intelligence,* pp. 383–386, AAAI Press, Menlo Park, Calif.

Rosenthal, D., P. Monger, G. Miller, and M. Johnston. 1986. "An Expert System for the Ground Support of Hubble Space Telescope," presented at 1986 Goddard Conf. on Space Applications of Artificial Intelligence, Goddard Space Flight Center, Greenbelt, MD.

Sadeh, N. 1991. "Look-Ahead Techniques for Micro-Opportunistic Job Shop Scheduling," Tech. Report, CMU-CS-91-102, Carnegie Mellon University.

Sadeh, N., and M. Fox. 1988. "Preference Propagation in Temporal/Capacity Constraint Graphs," Tech. Report CMU-RI-TR-89-2, Carnegie Mellon University.

Shapiro, R.D. 1980. "Scheduling Coupled Tasks," *Nav. Res. Logist. Q.*, 27, 489–479.

Shortliffe, E. 1976. *Computer-Based Medical Consultation: MYCIN.* American Elsevier, New York.

Smith, S., M. Fox, and P.S. Ow. 1986. "Constructing and Maintaining Detailed Production Plans: Investigations into the Development of Knowledge-Based Factory Scheduling Systems," *Artificial Intelligence* 7(4), 45–61.

Sponsler, J., and M. Johnston. 1990. "An Approach to Rescheduling Activities Based on Determination of Priority and Disruptivity," *Telematics and Informatics* 7, 243–253.

Sycara, K., S. Roth, N. Sadeh, and M. Fox. 1991. "Resource Allocation in Distributed Factory Scheduling," *IEEE Expert* 6(1), 29–40.

Zweben, M., E. Davis, and R. Gargan. 1990. "Anytime Rescheduling," *Proc. DARPA Workshop on Innovative Approaches to Planning and Scheduling*, Morgan Kaufmann, San Francisco, Calif.

15

THE SPACE SHUTTLE GROUND
PROCESSING SCHEDULING SYSTEM

Michael Deale
Mark Yvanovich
Danielle Schnitzius
Donna Kautz
Michael Carpenter
(Lockheed Space Operations Company)

Monte Zweben
Gene Davis[1]
Brian Daun[1]
(NASA Ames Research Center)

15.1 INTRODUCTION

The Kennedy Space Center (KSC) is responsible for the maintenance and launch of the U.S. Space Shuttle fleet. From the time the shuttle returns to earth to the time it leaves the launch pad, KSC must process the space shuttle components quickly and efficiently. Approximately 40,000 hours of technician labor are spent in the Orbiter Processing Facility (OPF) preparing the orbiter for its next mission. Limited resources, late part deliveries, and orbiter and facility configuration all constrain work in the OPF. The dynamic nature of the OPF orbiter processing environment further complicates scheduling. Approximately 50% of the work in a OPF processing flow is standard and predictable well in advance of the flow. The remaining work is driven by factors such as the payloads on the following mission, the payloads on the previous mission, the testing requirements specific to the age of

---

[1] Affiliated with Recom Software.

the orbiter, new orbiter modifications, diagnosed in-flight anomalies, and unexpected damage caused by the volatile reentry into the atmosphere. Additionally, the OPF is a highly dynamic environment causing frequent rescheduling.

This chapter presents a case study of the Ground Processing Scheduling System (GPSS), a constraint based scheduler using the Gerry scheduling engine developed at NASA Ames Research Center. GPSS is currently used in an operational experiment, scheduling the OPF operations for the orbiters *Columbia, Endeavour,* and *Discovery.* The initial results from the completed OPF flows show great promise for future operational improvements. GPSS has now become the accepted general purpose scheduling tool for OPF operations.

The project is a cooperative effort between the NASA Ames Research Center (ARC), NASA Kennedy Space Center (KSC), the Lockheed Space Operations Company (LSOC), and the Lockheed Artificial Intelligence Center. ARC has been conducting basic artificial intelligence research in scheduling techniques, resulting in the development of the Gerry scheduling engine. LSOC is the prime contractor in the Shuttle Processing Contract (SPC) at KSC and is responsible for scheduling the OPF processing. NASA KSC brought the efforts of NASA ARC and Lockheed together to apply the Gerry scheduling engine to the Space Shuttle program.

15.2 KSC PROCESSING OPERATIONS

A Space Shuttle mission begins when the orbiter component lands at NASA KSC or Edwards AFB in the California desert. The ground processing of the orbiter begins immediately upon landing on the runway: initial ground inspections are performed, hazardous gases are purged, and the orbiter is secured for safe ground operations. If the orbiter lands in California, it is transported to the Space Landing Facility (SLF) at NASA KSC on top of a Boeing 747, and then it is unloaded. The orbiter is then towed to one of three OPF bays where the majority of the maintenance, modification, testing, and repair is conducted. Payloads are removed and installed in the shuttle cargo bay in the OPF, and crew equipment is prepared and checked out. The "average" OPF flow[2] takes approximately 65 days.

When OPF processing is complete, the orbiter is transported to the Vehicle Assembly Building (VAB) where it is mated with the Solid Rocket Boosters (SRBs) and the External Tank (ET), which have all been processed in the VAB prior to the orbiter's arrival. The SRBs, ET, and orbiter are mated on the Mobile Launch Platform (MLP), which is always refurbished between launches. The entire stack is transported to the launch pad by the Crawler/Transporter. VAB processing takes approximately 10 days.

---

[2]An OPF flow is the orbiter processing in the OPF for a single mission. The term *flow* is used to signify the movement of the space shuttle components toward a launch.

Once the orbiter reaches the launch pad, final preparations are made for launch. Some payloads are installed at the pad. Pad processing, which takes approximately four weeks, includes final integrated system checkout, tanking, launch preparations, and the loading of perishable supplies and experiments. The Space Shuttle launches from the pad for missions that last between 7 and 13 days. After completion of a mission, the orbiter conducts a re-entry burn to enter the earth's atmosphere for landing. Upon landing, the orbiter processing cycle repeats.

Given that the VAB and pad processing are relatively static with known scheduling requirements, and the transport time from Dryden to KSC is mostly dependent on weather, the phase in the space shuttle mission where the most significant scheduling improvement can be made is in the OPF.

15.3 OPF PROCESSING

OPF processing has three major phases. The initial phase is making the orbiter safe for processing and gaining access to the orbiter's systems through the installation of access platforms. The largest part of OPF processing is the middle phase where systems are tested and repaired, the orbiter is structurally modified, the replaceable units are serviced, and the thermal protection system of external tiles is repaired.

The middle phase also includes the deservice and reconfiguration of the crew module and the payload bay flight packages. There are many sequences of tasks involved in the middle phase, and many of these sequences can be performed in parallel. The final phase of OPF processing is the closeout and checkout of orbiter systems. This includes complete system integrity and functional checks. Approximately 10,000 shifts of work are scheduled in each OPF flow. Each of these shifts of work must have all the constraints discussed below taken into consideration during the scheduling process.

15.3.1 OPF Scheduling Dynamics

During the months before the orbiter arrives at the OPF, a plan is built for OPF processing. Approximately 50% of the tasks in the plans are performed in every flow. The remaining 50% are either mission specific or generated because of unexpected problems. Payloads are unique to each flow, and many system tests are not performed every flight but at prespecified intervals. Also, many unique modifications are made to the orbiter fleet in the OPF. These mission specific tasks are integrated into the schedule prior to OPF processing. This initial schedule takes into account all the tasks that are generic and unique to a particular flow.

As soon as the orbiter arrives at KSC, the dynamics of OPF scheduling begin. Even the arrival date and the processing on the landing strip are subject to change. Weather plays a major role in the transportation of the orbiter from California to

KSC, and on a number of occasions, the orbiters have been damaged as a result of the weather as they cross the country. As tests are performed in the OPF and some of them fail, new tasks must be added to the schedule to diagnose and fix the problems. Damage to the orbiter can also introduce new tasks. These new tasks can involve small or large amounts of work (hours to weeks) and can require extensive rescheduling. Orbiter modifications are planned in advance, but the exact duration of processing modifications cannot be known in advance. Many modifications take longer than anticipated and require changes to the work steps performed. Even when no new tasks are required, scheduled tasks often deviate from their expected executions, causing substantial schedule perturbation. The result of these different conditions is that the schedule is constantly changing.

15.3.2 OPF Scheduling Constraints

To perform a task in the OPF, a number of separate factors must be coordinated. These factors can be summarized as paper, parts, people, and configuration.

Paper. Every operation on the orbiter must have explicit engineering instructions. These instructions provide a step by step guide for technicians as well as the criteria for considering the work accomplished. This documentation must be reviewed by Rockwell, Lockheed, and NASA engineering before the paper is released to the shop floor. No task can be scheduled before the release date of the engineering paper is identified.

Parts. Parts and supplies are required to perform tasks. Parts include hardware to be installed in the orbiter, supplies used in processing (such as cleaning fluids or bonding agents), tools used on the orbiter, and major equipment used in the OPF bays.

Many parts are supplied to the OPF bay by the KSC logistics organization. Logistics "kits" parts for individual tasks and delivers these kits to the OPF bays directly before they are needed. This minimizes the OPF inventory. The logistics group requires advance notice of the start dates of tasks so that the kitting can be complete and delivered prior to the tasks' starts.

There is a limited amount of Ground Support Equipment (GSE) available for use in processing the orbiters. GSE can range from logic analyzers to mass spectrometers. Some pieces of GSE have only one or two units available for use in all facilities at KSC. The utilization of limited GSE items must be scheduled very carefully because the items can often be connected to the orbiter for extended periods of time.

People. Orbiter technicians assigned to each of the three high bays must be scheduled to work a particular job. Inside an OPF bay, there are a number of different technician organizations that have to be coordinated. Every job requires technicians with specific certifications (electrical technicians, mechanical technicians, TPS technicians), as well as quality technicians to review the work as it is performed. These technicians are with either Lockheed, NASA, or one of the other SPC contractors, depending on the work performed. Testing tasks that require the use of the Launch Processing System (LPS) in the firing room to control, actuate, and observe behavior of orbiter systems require coordination between the technicians on the OPF floor and the orbiter engineers sitting in the firing rooms a few miles away. All these people must be coordinated and available for a given task. There are also certain personnel that are shared between all KSC facilities, such as the crane crews who operate the cranes that lift and maneuver heavy objects in the three OPF bays and other facilities. At any given time, there are zero to two crane crews available on base.

Configuration. Many tasks require the orbiter to be in a particular configuration. Because different tasks require the obiter to be in differing configurations, and it is expensive and time consuming to change some configurations, the efficient scheduling of orbiter configuration is important. An example of orbiter configuration is the state of the payload bay doors (PLBD). These doors have three basic positions. They can be closed, open 145 degrees, or open 175 degrees. The left and right doors can be controlled independently, and the movement of the PLBDs requires that NULL Gravity weights be attached via a strongback to simulate the effects of weightlessness to the PLBD stepper motors. (Strongbacks are steel frames that attach to the PLBDs to reinforce them for manipulation under the effects of the earth's gravity.) The cost of attaching and removing the NULL Gravity weights and the strongbacks (attaching the strongbacks requires the crane crew, a critical capacity resource), and acquiring the personnel to monitor the movement of the bay doors, makes it desirable to minimize the number of position changes that need to be made. Deployment of the KU-Band antenna for servicing requires the PLBDs to be open to 175 degrees. Unfortunately, opening the PLBD to 175 degrees physically restricts access to the external midbody of the orbiter, preventing the performance of other tasks.

15.4 PROBLEM SPECIFICATION

Scheduling in the OPF at KSC can be specified as follows:

Given:
 T, a set of tasks where each element t includes
  ○ work duration required to complete t
  ○ work calendar

    ○ resource requirements

    ○ state requirements

    ○ state effects

    ○ release dates

    ○ due dates

C, a set of temporal constraints relating activities to one another

R, a set of resource objects and the known availability profile of each resource

A, a set of attributes and the initial state of each object

Find: A start and end time for each task such that

- No resource is oversubscribed
- All tasks operate in the required configuration
- All due dates and release dates are met

with additional caveats:

- Schedules must effectively be communicated to the consuming organizations.
- Scheduling data must be available for postmission analysis.
- Schedules must be made available in a timely manner.
- Rescheduling data must be input in a timely manner.
- Schedules should be "optimal" in the current scheduling philosophy.

15.4.1 Tasks

A task is a specification of work that needs to be performed, as shown in Figure 15-1. This task has the unique identifier T1 assigned to it and represents the removal of the #1 main engine from the orbiter. Task T1 is estimated to require 32 hours of work, and the calendar field states it must be scheduled Monday through Friday from 0800 to 1600. These two pieces of information, along with a scheduled start date, define the preemption for the task. For example, if the task were to start at 1200 on Monday, the task would be split, from 1200–1600 Monday, 0800–1600 Tuesday, and so on, until a total of 32 hours of work had been accomplished. Figure 15-2 shows the final splitting of the task T1 that would result.

T1 requires four different resources. These resources are one crane crew, three electrical technicians, and one piece of GSE and reserve space for three people to be inside the aft of the orbiter. The task requires the aft-internals to be accessible and the orbiter to be powered down. It also causes the orbiter aft-internal to be cleared during the task. This aft-internal clear means that the area is considered hazardous, and other tasks that require access to the area cannot be scheduled. The

Name	T1
Description	Space Shuttle Main Engine #1 Required
Work Duration	32 hours
Calendar	MTWRF 0800-1600
Resource List	Crane Crew 1 Electrical Tech 3 GSE Panel S70-0001-0011 1 Aft-Internal-Man-Load 3
Requirements List	Aft-Internal-access: Midbody-Access Orbiter-Power: Powered-Down
Effects List	Aft-Internal-Access: Aft-Internal-Cleared
Due Date	11/2/92 0800
Release Date	10/1/92 1600

Figure 15-1: Task attributes

actual task causing the clear requires access to the area, meaning that another task could not make this same area hazardous at the same time. Finally, this task must be completed by 11/2/92 at 0800 but cannot begin before 10/1/92 at 1600.

15.4.2 Temporal Constraints

Temporal constraints are the set of precedence relations that must hold between tasks in the schedule. The four basic temporal constraints are finish-start, start-start, finish-finish, and start-finish. These represent the relationship between two tasks A and B such that (finish-start A B) represents the constraint that the finish time of A must be before the start time of B. Reading the relation from left to right implies the temporal order of the tasks' end points on a time line. The four basic relations can be augmented by adding a delay interval between the two tasks. The interval can be infinite or finite and can be positive or negative. For example, if task C is the bonding of a thermal protective tile to the skin of the orbiter, and task D is the quality inspection of that tile bond, then the relation (finish-start C D [3 24]) represents the fact that the bond inspection starts between 3 and 24 hours after the tile bond finishes.

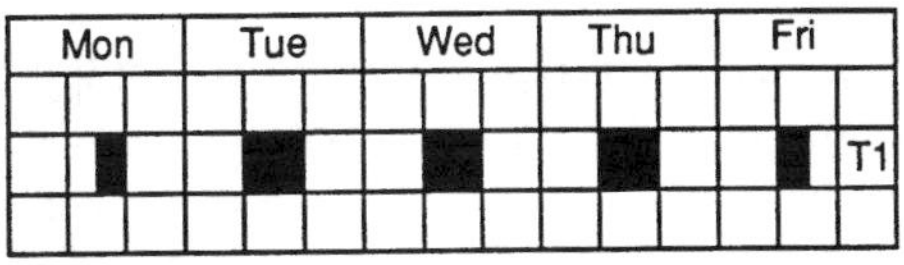

Figure 15-2: Splitting of task T1

15.4.3 Resources

GPSS models the classes and pools of resources available at KSC. Resource pools are collections of a given resource class with a known initial capacity. The amount of resources available at any particular time is the capacity of the resource minus the summation of the quantities allocated to tasks at that time. GPSS models technicians, engineers, inspectors, and equipment as resources. Additionally, physical space is modeled as a resource. The capacity of a resource pool can vary over time; for example, the number of people allowed to work inside the aft end of the orbiter is limited because of space constraints for emergency evacuation. Depending on the number of egress points from the aft, the number of people allowed in the aft changes.

15.4.4 Attributes

Attributes are objects that change state over time. Each attribute has an initial state, and state changes are caused by the specified effects of tasks. The state of an attribute at a particular time is equal to the latest change up to that time. The state of an attribute persists until tasks change them. There are a great number of attributes that are relevant to the OPF scheduling problem. For example, the left and right hand payload bay doors of the orbiter change position during the flow. The payload bay doors are in one of three basic positions: closed, open 145 degrees, or open 175 degrees. Each of these states allows certain work to be performed and precludes other work from being performed. There are two attributes used to represent the state of the left hand PLBD and the right hand PLBD.

15.4.5 Valid Schedule

A valid solution is a schedule where every task in the set T has a start and end time assigned to it and a resource pool assigned for every resource request where all constraints are satisfied. Temporal precedence constraints must be met, and the aggregate demand at all points in time for each resource must not exceed the capacity of that resource pool. Also, the configuration requirements for each task must be met for the specified period of time, and all due dates and release dates must be satisfied. A desirable schedule is one where certain criteria specified by KSC management have been optimized. The minimization of labor costs because of weekend overtime is an example of optimization criteria that is very important to KSC.

Although valid schedules are highly desired and optimal schedules are preferred, there are a number of additional factors that must be included in the scheduling process. Approximately 18,000 employees at KSC are directly or indirectly involved in launch processing. In order for schedules to effectively coordinate work, the schedules produced must be communicated to the work force. This includes electronic access as well as readable and reliable hard copy. The historical execution of the schedule is analyzed after a flow to find troublesome jobs and to improve efficiency. The postflow analysis must reflect the causes and ramifications of schedule perturbations. The timeliness with which schedules are produced is of great importance. There are three shifts of work seven days a week at KSC, and schedules must be produced that accurately reflect the best course of action at all times. This leaves little time for exhaustive rescheduling. The schedules must be turned around in a matter of hours at the most and often in minutes. Finally, the notion of optimal schedules changes over time. At all times, the safety of the work force and the safety of the vehicles are top priority. In the early parts of the flow, emphasis is placed on achieving the rollout milestone (the date the orbiter leaves the OPF bay for the next processing stage) with a minimal amount of cost while trying to maximize contingency. As the flow progresses and the contingency slack in the schedule is consumed, the milestone becomes more urgent. When faced with missing the rollout milestone, the processing philosophy changes. Making the rollout date that has direct impact on the final launch date becomes more important than minimizing cost.

15.5 EXPECTED BENEFITS OF SUCCESSFUL SOLUTION

The processing of the Space Shuttle fleet is an extremely complex and costly process. Many life threatening operations occur during the processing of the orbiter, and millions of dollars are spent in this process. The "average" day of an OPF flow costs approximately $200,000. If schedules can be made 5% more efficient, assuming an average of 65 days per orbiter flow, $650,000.00 can be saved on each flow. With 8 to 9 shuttle launches scheduled a year, an annual savings could reach as high as $5.5 million.

Beyond the cost savings are a number of other advantages that can be achieved by better scheduling. As schedules increase in quality, slips in the manifested launches become less likely, resulting in the possibility of an increased launch rate in future years. This makes the space shuttle an even more attractive launch option and makes maintenance of the Space Station *Freedom* and the transportation of scientific and human resources to and from the station a more viable and reliable operation.

15.6 GROUND PROCESSING SCHEDULING SYSTEM

GPSS takes as its input the sets specified above as **T**, **C**, **R**, and **A**, and either generates an initial schedule using the Critical Path Method or accepts existing scheduling dates from an external source such as the Artemis project management system. From this initial schedule, it generates resource demands and the state of each attribute at all points in time. These resource and attribute histories, combined with the resource requests and state requirements, allow GPSS to derive the set of constraint violations that exist in the current schedule. Although we have a complete schedule (i.e., all tasks have start and end times), we do not necessarily have a valid schedule.

The GPSS general design philosophy is that the human must be involved in schedule development even when the automated optimizer is used. Human schedulers must be able to manipulate the schedule and understand the ramifications of the system's schedule changes. GPSS functionality spans from fully manual scheduling to totally automated scheduling.

15.6.1 Interactive Scheduling

GPSS is an interactive scheduling tool. All scheduling changes made by the user have near instant feedback to show the effects of those changes. These schedule manipulations are made via a friendly interface that has natural and intuitive interactions.

The interface that the user most often interacts with is presented in Figure 15-3. A combination Bar/Resource chart has been opened for manipulation. Direct schedule changes are made on the bar chart by mousing on a task to pop up the task menu containing all options available for that task. These options include rescheduling tasks; entering task status; and adding/deleting a task's resource, configuration, and temporal constraints. The schedule interface is designed to give humans the maximum possible amount of information from the scheduler to make rapid accurate decisions.

The scheduling changes made through this window are submitted to the scheduling engine as transactions. Each transaction is processed, and the changes to the schedule that result from the transaction are immediately updated on the screen. A typical transaction (i.e., moving a task that will cause other tasks to move via temporal constraints) will be completed and updated on screen in a matter of a few seconds—certainly less time than it takes for the human user to look down at the scheduling sheets with handwritten updates to find the next change. More complex operations, such as using the compress option (discussed below) with relevant configuration, will take slightly longer—on the order of 5 to 10 seconds. This is because of the complexity of the rescheduling operation and the quantity of items that are typically changed. The automated search mechanism runs in an unbounded amount of time. Typically, good solutions are found in time measured in minutes to tens of minutes, depending on the complexity of the scheduling problem. When many conflicting optimization criteria are considered by the automated deconflict, the run time to find an optimized solution can be long.

The response time of GPSS to scheduling transactions generally depends on the complexity of the transaction. Simple rescheduling operations respond quickly,

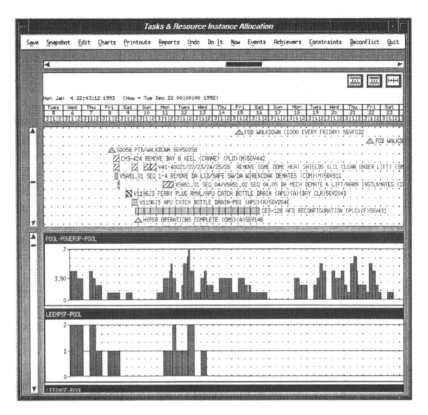

Figure 15-3: Bar/Resource Chart

so that the user feels that the system is responsive. More complex operations take longer and require greater involvement on behalf of the user to review. These longer operations that involve the conflict resolution procedure respond quick enough that human schedulers describe the system as very responsive to their information needs.

15.6.2 Dynamic Rescheduling

As tasks are modified (e.g., moved, changed status, shortened, extended, added, deleted), the scheduling engine dynamically propagates temporal constraints.[3] If necessary, this propagation automatically reschedules the temporal dependents of the tasks that are moved by the human. GPSS dynamically updates

---

[3] See Waltz (1975) for discussion of the Waltz algorithm for propagating constraints.

the resource and attribute histories to reflect the new task times, providing the human scheduler with an exact picture of the current schedule.

15.6.3 Conflict Prediction

Resource requests and state effects associated with each task are continuously used to build resource availability and attribute state histories as scheduling changes are made. Resource over-allocations and unsatisfied state requirements are immediately detected by GPSS. Conflicts can be reported after each scheduling transaction is completed or after a series of scheduling transactions are made. This allows the user to either batch transactions and then examine the ramifications or to receive immediate feedback after each schedule change.

Because GPSS always models an approximation of the real-world, some information is always lost in this abstraction. Sometimes there are violations predicted by the system that might not be valid. To demonstrate how this occurs and why GPSS must deal with the information loss present in modeling, consider the attribute that represents the state of POWER in the orbiter. There are two states that the orbiter POWER can be in: POWERED-UP or POWERED-DOWN. The transition from POWERED-UP to POWERED-DOWN and vice versa is instant for purposes of scheduling tasks and need not be represented. A task that requires the orbiter to be POWERED-DOWN during its execution would be flagged as a conflict if it were scheduled to execute during a time period where the orbiter was POWERED-UP. This conflict might be invalid because the model of orbiter power does not take into account the ability to "safe" particular orbiter systems by performing extra safing work before and after the execution of the task. In concrete terms, suppose there were a task to install a color monitor in the crew module, and it is scheduled during the time the orbiter is powered up. The installation of the color monitor requires the power to be down so the monitor can be wired into the orbiter power system. GPSS will flag a violation for the monitor installation occurring when the orbiter is POWERED-UP. What GPSS does not know is that fuses can be pulled around the monitor's power bus. The decision to pull the fuses must be made by the human. The human scheduler has the ability to inform GPSS that this violation is to be ignored because the safing steps will be performed. The model used is basically correct because the humans do not wish for the scheduling system to automatically decide when to safe the subsystems.

15.6.4 Computer Assisted Conflict Resolution

Conflict resolution is the process of making schedule changes to resolve the conflicts predicted by GPSS. The human schedulers have an array of decision support tools that aid in the manual resolution of conflicts. These decision support tools are designed to resolve individual conflicts given a tight set of assumptions specified by the human.

To pursue these manual conflict resolution goals GPSS has a series of reports that aid the humans in understanding the current conflicts and rescheduling transactions. The reports include graphic/textual violation reports and graphic/textual reports on the attribute/resource histograms. These reports allow the user to understand the violation, make a decision to reschedule the violated task, or find a "work around" to the problem on the shop floor.

A *compress* option exists to move a task (and optional sets of related tasks) earlier without violating any resource or configuration requirements. This move is a complex operation because temporal constraints, calendars, resources, and configurations must all be taken into account when finding a place in the existing schedule for the task to move. When options are invoked to compress a task and its temporal dependents, the compress option is recursively executed on the task and each of its temporal dependents until no further improvements can be made. Although the compress option is useful for manually resolving conflicts, it falls short in that it makes a single attempt to resolve conflicts. It is not capable of making multiple attempts to resolve conflicts, a process that is left to the automated conflict resolution procedure.

15.6.5 Automated Conflict Resolution and Optimization

GPSS can search[4] through the space of all possible schedules looking for schedules that are "better." "Better" is defined by a cost function that uses a set of heuristics supplied by Flow Management. These heuristics are based upon the expertise acquired during the course of 50 space shuttle flows. Automated conflict resolution is invoked after the user enters a series of scheduling changes in order to resolve problems introduced by those scheduling changes. The schedule resulting from the deconflict can be accepted or rejected by the human scheduler and then further changed.

The automated conflict resolution allows the human, in conjunction with GPSS, to produce schedules that are of higher quality in a timely manner. The human scheduler can make a series of scheduling changes, examine the conflicts produced, and have the system automatically resolve these conflicts in a short period of time. Because the deconflict algorithm is an anytime algorithm,[5] the deconflict is an interruptible process where the best solution in the time provided is returned to the user. This places the human in a position of resolving problems and finding ways to work around unresolved problems. It removes them from the role

---

[4] See Zweben (1990, 1993) for a discussion of the search engine used for automated deconflict.

[5] See Drummond & Bresina (1990) and Boddy (1991) for a discussion of anytime algorithms.

of manually examining schedules for conflicts and then manually resolving these conflicts.

The same deconflict algorithm can search for near-optimal schedules with respect to optimization criteria. This is different from finding a valid schedule in that it is now searching for schedules that not only meet all required constraints but also optimize the expected benefit gained from executing the schedule.

In the OPF, there are three primary concerns that determine the benefit of a schedule. The overriding concern is for the safety of the workers and the safety of the orbiter hardware. Second is the cost of executing the schedule, and third is the overall length of the resulting schedule. The relative importance of cost and flow time changes depending on the probability of achieving the rollout date assigned to the flow. The cost of executing the schedule can roughly be approximated by the number of shifts of overtime scheduled. To minimize cost, the deconflict algorithm moves tasks off the weekends and off the third shift. As the flow progresses and problems are encountered, the schedule tends to lengthen, and contingency time shrinks. When the contingency remaining in the schedule approaches zero, the definition of an optimal schedule changes. Slipping the rollout date has direct impact on the launch date for the mission, and this far outweighs the cost of working overtime. This means the importance of maintaining the final rollout date is now more important than avoiding weekends. This serves as the second mode for schedule optimization. GPSS can be configured to automatically optimize with respect to these two different perspectives.

15.6.6 Schedule Publishing

In an operational environment, the publication and distribution of schedules is an important consideration. GPSS has a general schedule publication capability that includes bar charts, resource histograms, configuration histograms, textual output, PERT charts, and other specialized and custom reports.

15.7 GPSS OPERATIONAL ENVIRONMENT

15.7.1 Operations

A number of different types of schedules are used to control OPF processing. The overall Detailed Flow Assessment presents tasks over the entire duration of OPF processing and is used for advanced planning. The Kennedy Integrated Control Schedule (KICS) presents the next 11 days of operations for use by the shop floor personnel to control execution. Certain tasks on the Detailed Assessment and KICS have very complex operations requiring minischedules that contain procedural details. Prior to GPSS, the three different types of schedules were produced and maintained by three independent methods, ranging from manually laying sticky tape on schedule forms to using project management computer scheduling tools. Additionally, these different schedules were reconciled with each other manually.

GPSS integrates all these schedules by using a single database. Customized reports are produced by exploiting a task hierarchy and specialized task sorting fields. Because a single instance of each task exists in the GPSS database, the need for coordinating different schedules is completely eliminated. The job of identifying schedule conflicts is automated through constraint testing in a single automated system.

GPSS is currently used to schedule the OPF flows of *Columbia*, *Discovery*, and *Endeavour*. *Atlantis* is out of service for major modifications. GPSS publishes schedules for these flows after scheduling changes are input and deconflicted. The system is run by the Lockheed In-Process scheduling organization. These schedulers are responsible for the production of the KICS, the Detailed Assessment, and the minischedules. The KICS schedule is used to control the work executed on the shop floor in OPF Bays 1, 2, and 3. The Flow Manager, Vehicle Operations Chief, and the in-process schedulers (collectively known as Flow Management) use the conflicts predicted by GPSS on a daily basis to reschedule tasks that cannot be performed as scheduled. By the end of each flow, there are between 1000 to 2000 tasks that have been scheduled for about 10,000 to 16,000 individual shifts of work. About 100 scheduling changes are made each day to an OPF schedule.

The identification and rescheduling of conflicts in the schedule is starting to save money in the OPF. The flow management teams now rely on the capabilities of GPSS and have confidence in the predictions it provides. As a result, the quality of the GPSS-produced schedules has improved because there are fewer schedule conflicts. Improved confidence in schedules has an enormous impact on the shop floor operations. When a task is scheduled and the confidence in the schedule is high, then the likelihood that all the task's parts, paper, people, and configuration will be ready also increases. This is because no organization wants to be blamed for tasks that do not execute. If these groups believe the schedule as published, then they make an extra effort to support the schedule. Therefore, the efficiency of the OPF is slowly improving.

15.7.2 Cost Savings

During the STS50 flow in mid-1992, a number of scheduling statistics were gathered. This analysis compared the gathered statistics with estimates from previous missions provided by flow management.

The duration of the daily morning scheduling meetings were measured. Every morning a scheduling meeting is held for each orbiter in the OPF Bays. These meetings are attended by representatives from every organization involved in OPF processing. Approximately 100 people attend; an average pre-GPSS duration is about 1 hour. During the STS50 flow, these meetings averaged just over 30 minutes each. The primary reason for the shorter duration is the consistent quality of the schedules published by GPSS. The previous schedules had errors introduced by humans when drawing the schedules. These errors completely disappeared with GPSS. The second scheduling meeting improvement is that GPSS schedules always presented the complete current schedule, and the operations personnel could discuss work for the following week. This means conflicts were addressed and resolved early, before they became a crisis.

The second piece of information collected about the flow was an estimate of the amount of weekend overtime that was spent by the Thermal Protection Systems (TPS) shop. The TPS scheduler indicated that a better job was done on STS50 in scheduling the TPS work around the changing configuration, resulting in a reduction in the amount of weekend overtime spent. Raw time card data were used to determine the actual amount of time spent and compared to a Flow Management estimate of the typical weekend overtime.

These two factors, plus the savings in time to actually produce the schedule, produced a cost savings of roughly $400,000 on the STS50 flow.

15.8 AN EXTENDED EXAMPLE

Here we present an extended example of GPSS as used in the operational setting. The schedule used is the STS56 *Discovery* OPF Flow that began 9 December 1992 and extends to 5 March 1993. The payloads being flown include the *Spartan* probe and the *Astro* observatory. Figure 15-3 shows a fragment of the schedule as it existed on 22 December 1992. On that day, a conflict summary was prepared for the entire STS56 flow, as shown in Figure 15-4. This summary indicates that 86 constraint violations exist in the STS56 schedule, with the violations divided among the 20 relevant configurations.

In this example, only the 4 POWER violations and the 17 BAY-ACCESS violations will be discussed. The POWER attribute has been discussed previously and has the same meaning as earlier. BAY-ACCESS represents the state of hazardous operations in the entire bay. Certain tasks involve hazardous gases that require the high bay to be cleared of all workers not wearing Self-Contained Atmospheric Protective Ensemble (SCAPE) suits. Because all work except SCAPE is shut down during these hazardous operations, they are major factors in developing a schedule.

The Cost Summary screen provides information about the quality of the entire schedule but no information about the individual conflicts in the schedule. The violated constraints screen shown in Figure 15-5 is a window that the user requests that shows a summary of the individual constraint violations in the current schedule. This summary provides information that allows the user to decide if a violation is worth investigating further or ignoring. The four options show for each constraint violation and allow the user to indicate to GPSS how that individual con-

Figure 15-4: Initial cost summary

straint violation is to be handled. The "Perm Del" option deletes the constraint from the schedule permanently and is used when erroneous data are entered on the tasks. The "Temp Del" option indicates that the constraint is no longer to be considered in the cost of a schedule and that the constraint is not to be considered when optimizing and repairing schedules. "Don't Repair" tells GPSS to consider the constraint when calculating the cost of the schedule but not to consider the constraint when running the automatic deconflict. The three constraint violations that are currently visible in the scrolling violations window are all valid constraints violations and, therefore, have the active box marked. The last of the three constraint violations tells the user that the task with Work Authorization Document

◇ Perm Del	◇ Temp Del	◇ Don't Repair ◇ Active	
LH-SWINGS	LH-SWINGS-CLOSED	1/15/1993 8:0:0 1/15/1993 16:0:0	V1180VL1L1 LH/RH OMS POD FUNCTIONAL & C/O 56V047B-3
◇ Perm Del	◇ Temp Del	◇ Don't Repair ◇ Active	
RH-SWINGS	RH-SWINGS-CLOSED	1/15/1993 8:0:0 1/15/1993 16:0:0	V1180VL1L1 LH/RH OMS POD FUNCTIONAL & C/O 56V047B-3
◇ Perm Del	◇ Temp Del	◇ Don't Repair ◇ Active	
BAY-ACCESS	BAY-OPEN	1/20/1993 0:0:0 1/20/1993 8:0:0	V1004L-1 MTU FREQ STABILIZATION (TASK 1) 56V014B-3

Ignore All   Consider All   Done   Cancel

Figure 15-5: Violation Report

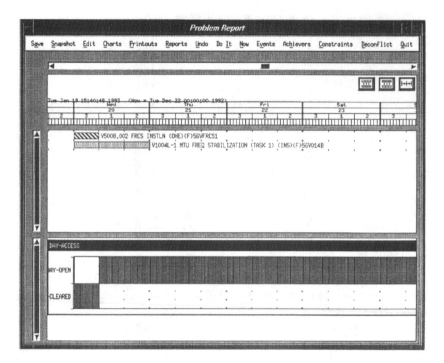

Figure 15-6: Problem Report

V1004L-1, which performs the MTU Frequency Stabilization task, requires the attribute BAY-ACCESS to be BAY-OPEN from 1/20/1993 0000 to 1/20/1993 0800 and that this configuration requirement is not met in the current schedule.

To investigate this constraint violation further, the user moves the mouse over the MTU Frequency Stabilization task item in the Violated Constraints window and presses the right mouse button to get the window shown in Figure 15-6. This Problem Report window provides direct information about the tasks involved in the constraint violation. In this case, the Forward Reaction Control System (FRCS) Installation task is a major hazard task because the FRCS is loaded with highly toxic hypergolic fuels, and the installation of the FRCS requires the bay interior, 200′ outside the bay and 700′ downwind of the bay, to be cleared of all personnel not in SCAPE suits. The BAY-ACCESS histogram shows that the bay is clear during the third shift (0000–0800 hours) on Wednesday, 20 January and before and after that point in time. The histogram indicates that with respect to the BAY-ACCESS requirement, the MTU Frequency Stabilization task can be moved either before or after the FRCS Installation. The FRCS Installation could also be moved, but because of the hazardous nature and the coordination required for SCAPE, it is preferable to leave it as scheduled.

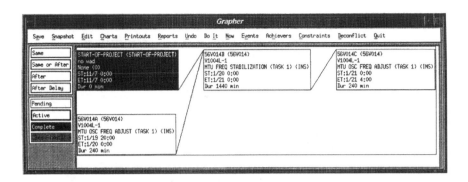

Figure 15-7: Constraint Graph

The user cannot decide yet to move the MTU Frequency Stabilization task earlier or later in time because no information about temporal dependents has been examined. This is done by selecting the constraint grapher option from the MTU Frequency Stabilization task menu. Figure 15-7 shows the constraint grapher window that is produced when a graph is requested for the MTU Frequency Stabilization task. The graph shows only the tasks that are directly related to the MTU Task and the temporal dependencies between them. This chart has a number of simple visual features that make it easy to use. Each box represents a task from the schedule. A line joining a box on the left hand side means the line is indicating a predecessor to the task and on the right hand side indicates a successor to the task. A line joining the top of the box indicates that the constraint is to the start of the task, and the bottom of the box indicates the end time of the task. This chart then tells the user that the MTU Oscillation Frequency Adjustment task's end time must precede the MTU Frequency Stabilization task's start time and that a second MTU Oscillation Frequency Adjustment must come after the Stabilization. This is the traditional finish-to-start temporal constraint found in project management systems. Color is used to indicate the type of constraint. For example, a constraint requiring a delay between the two end-points will be green and will match the color in the key on the left of the screen. Examining the information presented, the user finds that the MTU Frequency Stabilization task has no temporal slack between it and both its predecessor and its successor. Given this, the human scheduler decides to rule out moving this task earlier because it will move an entire series of earlier tasks, disrupting the work planned for return from the Christmas holiday in early January.

The human scheduler has decided to move the MTU Frequency Stabilization task later in time and closes the Constraint Grapher Window, returning to the Problem Report. Before actually making the move, the user decides to check the other resource requests and requirements that exist on the task. By mousing with the left

```
┌─────────────────────────────────────────────────────────────────┐
│        56V014B  (V1004L-1)  MTU FREQ STABILIZATION (TASK 1)       │
├─────────────────────────────────────────────────────────────────┤
│  RESOURCE REQUESTS:                                               │
│  ┌───────────────────────────────────────────────────────────┐▲  │
│  │ 56V014B-3 requests 1.00 LOTORBE from LOTORBE-POOL. (NOT DEDICATED)│   │
│  │ 56V014B-3 requests 1.00 LQQF from LQQF-POOL. (NOT DEDICATED)│   │
│  │ 56V014B-3 requests 1.00 LEEISLF from LEEISLF-POOL. (NOT DEDICATED)│ │
│  │ 56V014B-3 requests 1.00 LEEISL from LEEISL-POOL. (NOT DEDICATED)│ │
│  │ 56V014B-3 requests 1.00 LQQ from LQQ-POOL. (NOT DEDICATED)  │▼  │
│  └───────────────────────────────────────────────────────────┘   │
│  ◁                                                          ▷     │
│  REQUIREMENTS:                                                    │
│  ┌───────────────────────────────────────────────────────────┐▲  │
│  │ 56V014B-3 requires POWER to be POWER-UP. (NOT DEDICATED)    │   │
│  │ 56V014B-3 requires BAY-ACCESS to be BAY-OPEN. (NOT DEDICATED)│  │
│  │ 56V014B-3 requires CREW-MODULE-ACCESS to be CREW-MODULE-OPEN. (NOT DEDICATED)│ │
│  │                                                            │▼  │
│  └───────────────────────────────────────────────────────────┘   │
│  ◁                                                          ▷     │
│  ┌───────────────────────────────────────────────────────────┐   │
│  │                         Close                              │   │
│  └───────────────────────────────────────────────────────────┘   │
└─────────────────────────────────────────────────────────────────┘
```

Figure 15-8: Constraint Report

button on the task, the window shown in Figure 15-8 emerges. This window shows the resource requests, the state requirements, and the state effects (missing in this window, indicating no effects exist for this task) for the MTU Frequency Stabilization task. None of the resources or requirements are a worry at this point, and the scheduler decides to move the MTU Frequency Stabilization task one shift later in time. Using the mouse, the human scheduler points and drags the MTU Frequency Stabilization task. When the mouse is released, the move is submitted as a scheduling transaction to the scheduling engine. This transaction is processed, all temporal constraints are enforced, and the resource and attribute histograms are updated. Within seconds of the transaction submittal, a Comparison Report window is returned, as shown in Figure 15-9, showing all tasks that were changed as a result of the move of the MTU Frequency Stabilization task. Shown are three pairs of

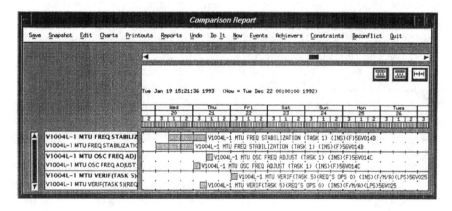

Figure 15-9: Comparison Report

Figure 15-10: Cost Summary

tasks, where the first line of each pair is the final position, and the second line is the starting position for each task. This provides the human scheduler with immediate feedback about the ramifications of the move just made.

Now that the bay access violation has been resolved manually using information provided by the decision support tools of GPSS, the human scheduler looks at the new cost summary shown in Figure 15-10. The total cost of the schedule is unchanged at 86. Examining the POWER and BAY-ACCESS costs, we find that moving the MTU Frequency Stabilization task reduced the BAY-ACCESS violations by 1 and increased the POWER violations by 1. This demonstrates the need for additional support in resolving conflicts. The repair the human scheduler made for the BAY-ACCESS violation unknowingly caused a POWER violation. The human scheduler could be more careful in selecting the move by examining the configuration report in Figure 15-8 and comparing the requirements and resources with histograms brought up in a separate chart. It would be very difficult to manually combine all the information available.

Figure 15-11 shows a problem report for one of the existing POWER violations. The Nose Landing Gear (NLG) Strut Thruster Installation task requires the POWER attribute be POWERED-DOWN. Scheduled in parallel is the Power Up Task that has automatically been generated by GPSS to achieve the POWERED-UP condition. A KSC defined scheduling heuristic states that POWER will be POWERED-UP where it is required, and the POWERED-DOWN requiring tasks will be moved to fit around the POWERED-UP requirements. The POWER attribute histogram in Figure 15-10 shows a number of different places where the POWERED-DOWN state exists for a long enough duration for the NLG Strut Thruster Installation task to fit. The user selects the Compress option from the task menu for the NLG Strut Thruster Installation. This operation moves a task as early

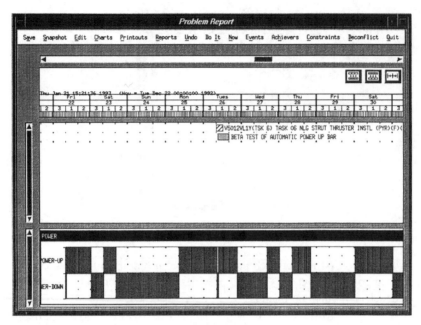

Figure 15-11:   Problem Report for POWER violation

as it can be moved without moving any of its predecessors, such that all configuration requirements and resource requests are met. After this option is selected and submitted to the scheduler, the resulting position of the NLG Strut Thruster Installation task is shown in Figure 15-12. The NLG Strut Thruster Installation task was moved to first shift Saturday the 24th, even though POWERED-DOWN was available before that time. This is because two constraints were not immediately apparent when looking at the schedule. A predecessor task to the NLG Strut Thruster Installation completes the end of first shift Friday the 22nd, preventing the thruster installation from moving before then, and the strut thruster task has a first shift only calendar. These two constraints mean the earliest the task can be scheduled is 0800 on the 24th, as GPSS did. The compress option has many variations that include moving related sets of tasks both earlier and later in time such that configurations and resources are met.

The manual rescheduling of tasks and the compress option help the human scheduler resolve individual constraint violations and understand the direct ramifications of those scheduling changes, but they fall short when the "best" solution to a particular violation might include the introduction and resolution of many different violations. The complex process of making many schedule changes to achieve a schedule that is near-optimal is performed in GPSS by the automated deconflict option. This process uses a set of heuristics to direct GPSS on preferable ways of

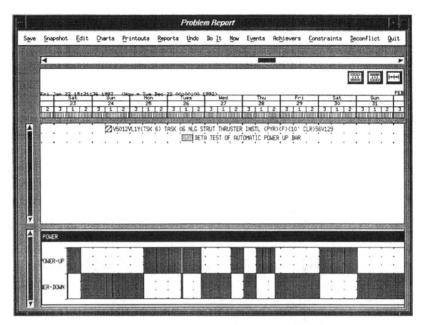

Figure 15-12:   Problem Report for POWER violation after COMPRESS

resolving constraint violations and a heuristic evaluation of the quality of any given schedule. GPSS takes a schedule with violations and transforms that schedule into a new one, where the quality of the new schedule is better, using the user supplied heuristics to develop the new schedule. The deconflict process is described in detail in Zweben, Davis, & Deale (1993).

To examine the deconflict process, GPSS has been told to ignore all configurations except POWER and BAY-ACCESS. The resulting Cost Summary is shown in Figure 15-13. The deconflict process is given a time limit of 10 minutes, or 40 iterations, in which to produce a better schedule. The deconflict is invoked, and GPSS returns after 24 iterations and approximately 5 minutes with a new schedule. All scheduling changes made in the deconflict process are shown in a scrollable window, as shown in Figure 15-14. Like the comparison report in Figure 15-9, the tasks are shown in the final position and the initial position. This allows the human scheduler the ability to see what changed in the deconflict process. The human can accept the new schedule or reject it, as shown in Figure 15-15. Before making that decision, the human examines the current Cost Summary of all resources and attributes to see the quality of the current schedule. That summary, shown in Figure 15-16, shows that the automated deconflict process has improved the schedule from a cost of 86 to a cost of 67, an improvement of 19 fewer violations (remember that deconflict was focused only on the POWER and BAY-ACCESS attributes).

Figure 15-13:   Cost Summary

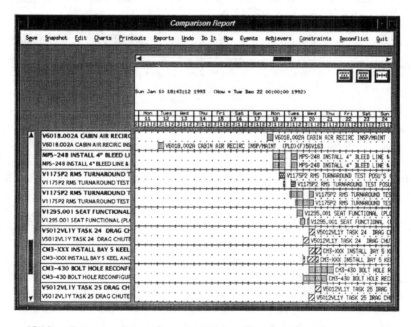

Figure 15-14:   Comparison Report after automated deconflict

The Cost Summary also shows that the deconflict process was unable to resolve one of the BAY-ACCESS conflicts. With additional reporting capabilities, it can quickly be determined that this violation cannot be resolved given the current durations, calendars, and temporal constraints in the GPSS schedule. This violation must be resolved by human intervention.

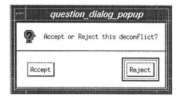

Figure 15-15: Option to reject deconflict

Figure 15-16: Final Cost Summary

15.9 INDUSTRIAL APPLICATIONS OF GPSS

GPSS is a general purpose scheduling tool with customized reporting and charts for the KSC ground processing scheduling problem. Much of the interface and scheduling engine capabilities are generic to scheduling problems that might be encountered beyond the OPF.

A number of other scheduling applications have either been prototyped or discussed using GPSS as the common solution. Scheduling the NASA Ames Wind Tunnel experiments to minimize electrical power costs is an application under way. Scheduling crew activities on an orbital platform to maximize science returned was an application developed several years ago. The scheduling of nuclear power plant maintenance is an application of interest to the electric power industry. Lockheed has investigated the use of GPSS for scheduling the production and maintenance of the Advanced Tactical Fighter. GPSS has already been used on data sets for space shuttle payload processing. GPSS is also applicable to the Space Station *Freedom* program and other NASA missions. Other facilities at KSC, such as the Logistics Service Center, are considering the use of GPSS. Although each of these scheduling problems requires unique heuristic knowledge, the same basic scheduling engine applies.

Given this diverse set of scheduling problems that GPSS can accommodate, what are the features of a scheduling problem that point to GPSS as a solution? First, GPSS handles large scheduling problems. OPF scheduling has approximately 10,000 separately scheduled pieces of work in a single flow. GPSS handles this volume with ease and is capable of handling much larger scheduling problems. The tasks to be scheduled can be related via a complex network of temporal constraints, which is traditionally supported by network-based scheduling tools.

GPSS considers the finite capacity of resources and attempts to reasonably utilize these resources. Although many commercial schedulers can perform resource leveling, this technique is very weak compared to the search mechanism provided in GPSS.

GPSS is also unique in its ability to model attributes. Machine setup configurations and equipment locations are standard elements of scheduling problems that are best represented as attributes. Commercial products cannot support the modeling of attributes.

When the scheduling process is a highly complex one, and many alternative options must be explored to find a "better" schedule, then complex decision support tools are required. GPSS provides a large set of utilities to aid the human scheduler in understanding the complexities of a schedule and the ramifications of the changes made to a schedule.

Scheduling problems where the cost of executing a poor schedule is high and the value of optimized schedules is great require a scheduler that can automatically search for better schedules. GPSS provides this through its automated deconflict mechanism, which considers many options in determining a schedule.

Most importantly, GPSS can keep pace with the dynamics of operations. It can be used on an hourly basis, tracking schedule status and dynamically rescheduling. The philosophy behind GPSS is that optimization is not only important for advanced planning but that it should be considered at all stages during the execution of a schedule. GPSS provides a collection of decision-support tools for the user so that together they can react intelligently to the unmitigated chaos of real-world operations.

References

Boddy, M. 1991. Anytime Problem-Solving Using Dynamic Programming. *Proceedings of AAAI-91*, AAAI Press, Menlo Park, Calif.

Drummond, M., and J. Bresina. 1990. Anytime Synthetic Projection: Maximizing the Probability of Goal Satisfaction. *Proceeding of AAAI-90*, AAAI Press, Menlo Park, Calif.

Waltz, D. 1975. Understanding Line Drawings of Scenes with Shading. *The Psychology of Computer Vision,* P. Winston ed. McGraw-Hill, New York.

Zweben, M., M. Deale, and R. Gargan. 1990. Anytime Rescheduling. *Proceedings of the DARPA Workshop on Innovative Approaches to Planning and Scheduling,* Morgan Kaufmann, San Francisco, Calif.

Zweben, M., E. Davis, and M. Deale. 1993. Iterative Repair for Scheduling and Rescheduling. *IEEE Systems, Man, and Cybernetics.*

16

OPTIMUM-AIV:

A Knowledge-Based Planning and Scheduling System for Spacecraft AIV

M. Aarup
(CRI)

M.M. Arentoft
(CRI [former])

Y. Parrod
(MATRA)

I. Stokes
(Progespace)

H. Vadon
(ESA [former])

J. Stader
(AIAI)

16.1 INTRODUCTION

The size and complexity of the tasks involved in the AIV of spacecraft raise the need for efficient and flexible planning and scheduling tools. An evaluation of the current available and applied commercial tools reveals their inadequacies toward the general problem of AIV.

In 1988, this led ESA to award a contract to a consortium consisting of CRI, MATRA ESPACE, and AIAI whose goal was to assess the applicability of knowledge-based techniques in a prototype AIV planning and scheduling tool. This study resulted in a set of user and software requirements and a demonstration system exploring some of the aspects of AIV planning (Fuchs, 1989).

OPTIMUM-AIV is a follow-up project carried out by CRI, MMS, AIAI, and Progespace. The objectives of the project are three-fold:

- to develop an operational kernel of a planning, scheduling, and plan repair tool consisting of a set of software functionalities for assistance in initial specification of the AIV plan, generation of valid plans and schedules for the various AIV activities, interactive monitoring of the AIV plan execution, and identification of immediate effects and plan repair of problems
- to embed external interfaces that allow integration with alternative scheduling systems and project databases
- to provide facilities that will allow individual projects to customize the kernel to suit their specific needs

The realization of these objectives is explained in the sections to come.

The outline of the chapter is as follows. Section 16.2 outlines the operations domain of spacecraft AIV planning, and the benefits and applicability of OPTIMUM-AIV to this domain are introduced in Section 16.3. Based on this outline, Section 16.4 lists the explicit domain-dependent knowledge to be included in the tool. Before the detailed discussions of the main tool components, Section 16.5 provides an overview of the system process stages. Next, Section 16.6 shows how plan specification permits the user to consult libraries of past and generic plans. Section 16.7 explains how the generation of plans takes into consideration the logical precedence ordering between activities and specifications of the expected outcome and required configuration of the spacecraft equipment being put together and tested. Then, the satisfaction of temporal and resource usage constraints is described. Afterward, the execution monitoring and plan repair are presented in Section 16.8 as plan status updating, progress interpretation, and consistency checking and recovery organized along identified execution problems. Subsequently, Section 16.9 lists the external interfaces to be embedded in the system and explains about their intended use. Finally, the lessons learned with respect to use of AI techniques in the system are discussed in Section 16.10.

16.2 THE SPACECRAFT AIV PLANNING DOMAIN

This section gives a brief outline of the AIV planning process and life cycle and, hence, establishes the function and purpose, environmental considerations, and general constraints of OPTIMUM-AIV.

Spacecraft development projects are typically divided into the following phases:

- **A**, Early feasibility study: The overall mission objectives of the intended program are evaluated, and a feasibility assessment is made based on operational constraints. This serves as a basis for deciding whether the project should be undertaken. The goals of the phase are to derive system requirements, to establish a preliminary model philosophy, and to identify verification aspects and assess their influence on the spacecraft design. An early identification of the required verification tools and a general planning of the program and the AIV are also undertaken.

- **B**, Specification phase: System requirements are extracted in a top-down manner, starting with the total system and ending up with specifications of the various primitive units. The phase is critical to AIV because it must clearly define the AIV approach to be taken in phase C/D. During phase B, the general AIV plan, additional facilities plans, ground support equipment (GSE) requirements, test hardware requirements, and development plans at lower levels are produced. The general AIV plan is part of the overall project management plan.

- **C/D**, Development and integration phase: In this phase, the design is frozen, and manufacturing is undertaken. This is mainly a bottom-up activity where primitive units are put together to form assemblies, assemblies to form subsystems, and subsystems are integrated at the system level. The phase is completed with the integration, verification, and qualification of the spacecraft system. This phase implements the plans generated in phase B and produces detailed AIV plans at different levels. This involves propagation of logical constraints; assignment of dates to activities' logical flow; verification of resource consumptions versus availability; and monitoring of the execution, i.e., updating of each activity's status and handling of failures.

- **E**, Operational phase: This last phase covers the period from the launch until the end of the spacecraft mission. Verification, as such, is completed before this phase. The electrical GSE has served its purpose, and the satellite is instead controlled and operated by the ground segment.

The phases described above define the AIV life cycle:

- Elaboration, Phases A+B: Philosophy and model(s) are selected, e.g., prototype, protoflight, or project specific philosophy and structural, thermal, electrical, protoflight, or flight model. Furthermore, an evaluation of project parameters takes place, for instance, due dates, manpower, GSE, and cost aspects.

- Implementation, Phase C/D: Detailed AIV plans, at different levels and with various time windows, are generated. The required initial configurations and effects of activities are compiled into a sequencing logic, and time and resources are verified and assigned. The resulting schedules are documented in detailed and summary networks.

- Monitoring, Phase C/D: The sequencing logic, temporal and resource usage constraints, and, possibly, AIV objectives are reviewed in case of disturbance. The impacts are analyzed, and critical and degraded activities are identified. New AIV plans are produced, taking into account the current constraints and additional tasks for repair. Phase E is only relevant if there are AIV activities during the operation of the spacecraft, e.g., if a reusable module has to be integrated again.

16.3 SYSTEM OBJECTIVES

This section introduces the benefits and applicability of OPTIMUM-AIV.

The planning tool will assist primarily at the AIV team leader level in the management of day-by-day activities and secondarily at the project management (interface) level.

The tool will cover the phases B and C/D. In phase B, project management will define the high level AIV plans, which must be refined and detailed in phase C/D in order to constitute operational plans. OPTIMUM-AIV will provide a dynamic environment in which the AIV plans can be input and refined using AI based planning and scheduling techniques. Also in phase C/D, the constructed plans are executed. OPTIMUM-AIV will be used to monitor the progress and to assist the users in identifying and solving any unforeseen problems and in producing new plans.

OPTIMUM-AIV shall provide the following facilities:

- definition, from scratch and as extension, of the AIV plan
- derivation and construction of plans and schedules at several levels
- monitoring and assistance in replanning of project execution

Especially on the last point, the planning tool will differ from current planning systems, and assistance in replanning will indeed be the principal objective of OPTIMUM-AIV. The advantage of using knowledge based techniques will be a more flexible system in which planning knowledge is explicitly represented. The knowledge concerning conflict resolution and replanning will be incorporated and used to assist the users in generating feasible plans and solving problems during plan execution.

16.4 SYSTEM KNOWLEDGE

One important aspect of OPTIMUM-AIV and an aspect that makes it different from traditional planning and scheduling tools is the inclusion of explicit domain knowledge. We distinguish entity knowledge from process knowledge as follows:

Entity knowledge	defines and represents the entities that must be manipulated in the domain. For the AIV planning domain, the entity knowledge is the knowledge concerning spacecraft systems and models, generic, past and current projects and plans, AIV activities, resources, and global constraints.
Process knowledge	represents the knowledge stating how the entity knowledge manipulation can be done. For the AIV planning domain, the process knowledge is the general planning and scheduling knowledge plus explicit heuristics and knowledge about the rationale behind the plan structure.

The entity knowledge is represented as user classified objects, in a way similar to the current management of large AIV programmes.

Spacecraft systems and models are decomposed into subsystems and submodels in a part-of hierarchy.

A project consists of a plan of activities, and activities can be decomposed into subplans at any level of detail, so that each subplan can be worked on independently. Whatever constraints apply to an activity also apply to its entire subplan, and whatever resource usages, etc., implied by activities in a subplan will affect the 'parent' activity.

AIV activities have been classified according to their function in the AIV process, e.g., reception, preparation, assembly, integration, functional/performance test, and environmental test. Alternative classification dimensions could be the technological nature of activities or the spacecraft system that is the object of the activity. Indeed, the AIV activity hierarchy can be mapped onto the spacecraft part-of hierarchy through relations expressing that an AIV activity is performed on certain spacecraft subsystems. The use of this type of mapping is to verify the actual AIV plan against rules and policies for subsystems in the spacecraft decomposition.

The description of an activity carries over to the description of a project, or plan, because a plan is simply a description of a parent activity. This parent activity is expanded into a subplan of child activities, which, in turn, can be expanded into more detailed subplans, and so on. Each subplan is independent from other subplans in the sense that it has a unique starting point and a unique completion point, which are exactly equal to the start and completion of the parent activity; i.e., each activity is decomposed into sub-activities independently.

Individual activity descriptions contain information about

- preconditions that must hold for the activity to be appropriate and to be triggered, e.g., house.keeping.module CONNECTED.TO data.handling.subas-
  sembly
- effects (and side effects) of using the activity, e.g., tm-tc-loc INTE-
  GRATED.IN house.keeping.module
- constraints, including target dates and resource requests, e.g., the activity
  requires two electricians for three days
- objectives, documentation, experiences, etc.

An activity is generally regarded as a plan fragment in its own right. Hence, there can be partially ordered activities contained within the description. However, the planning system assumes responsibility for completing the partial order description of the final plan. These descriptions are also generally parameterized, generic descriptions that are instantiated at the time of use. This offers flexibility and assists with a least commitment approach to planning and scheduling.

Resources have been categorized along two dimensions: first, according to predefined resource classes, e.g., GSE, manpower, test facilities, money, etc., second, according to the nature of the resource, i.e., shared or consumable. Resources are shared if their availability must be specified as a function of time, e.g., manpower. Resources are consumable if there is an initial stockpile available that can only be depleted by activities in the plan, e.g., money.

Resource descriptions contain information about

- availability profile, e.g., the resource is present during the third week of May
- alternative and indirect resources
- documentation, experiences, etc.

Activity global constraints can be associated with a plan. They express overall temporal relations between activities in a certain context. The context is defined by a given status of the involved activities and a certain configuration of the spacecraft system. The context can contain arbitrary variables that might be related in general predicates. For instance, we have

```
IF ACTIVITY acoustic.and.vibration.test
    of.Class environment.test
    works.on.System ?s
AND ACTIVITY ?x
    of.Class integration
    works.on.System ?e
AND SYSTEM ?e SUBELEMENT.OF ?s
AND ?x <> power.supply.subsystem.integration
THEN acoustic.and.vibration.test AFTER ?x
```

The process knowledge is represented as rules and tables recording user preferences and decisions.

Heuristics are associated with projects and/or individual activities. Heuristics are different from constraints; they are used to decide on strategies in order to restrict the search space. These strategies are applied when all constraints have been satisfied, and the system is left with degrees of freedom allowing it to follow user preferences. In OPTIMUM-AIV, the user can select various strategies for determining which of several activities should be postponed in case of resource conflicts in the schedule based upon the activities' durations, time margins, etc.

16.5 SYSTEM PROCESS STAGES

An explicit distinction of the different stages of the system processes helps clarify the purpose and rationale of the system functions:

- Knowledge editing and plan specification
  - Definition and input of general domain knowledge: spacecraft system, activity, resource, global constraint classes, and instances
  - Specification of the actual planning problem: project events and strategies, relations between domain object instances
- Plan and schedule generation
  - Planning: finding a logically valid plan in sufficient detail
  - Scheduling: including time and resources in the plan
- Project monitoring and plan repair
  - Monitoring of the execution of the schedule: recording the progress, reminding the user of activities to be started soon
  - Detection of problems and their immediate impacts: deriving local inconsistencies
  - Schedule repair: rescheduling or editing the current schedule locally, e.g., up to the next milestone
  - Plan repair: more serious problems interfering with the plan logic

The first stage requires mostly user input and, thus, editing facilities and some support such as input validation. The latter stages make use of the information gained at this first stage, and they can require additional information from the user. These latter stages are more interactive. In particular, the monitoring and plan repair stage requires an extensive dialogue with the user. The second stage builds the plan and the schedule and records justifications for planning decisions taken by the user in resolving conflicts.

The predictive approach adopted for the second stage is poor with respect to recovery when failure arises. Because the third stage must support rescheduling, we have chosen a more reactive approach for the project monitoring and plan repair stage. It will proceed forward in time only, using dependency recording techniques aimed at enabling repair to be limited to only those components known to be affected by the forced changes.

The different approaches for plan and schedule generation and for execution problem recovery reflect the fact that "there is a trade-off between the predictability of the environment in which the plan is to be executed and the degree of reactivity that is necessary to successfully achieve the goals of the plan" (Swartout, 1987, p. 124). OPTIMUM-AIV uses the predictive approach for plan and schedule generation and offers ease of repair by allowing the user to restrict repairs to a limited time scope.

16.6 PLAN EDITING AND SPECIFICATION

In this initial stage, most of the work relies on the user entering and specifying the AIV activities, their required spacecraft components, resources, links to other activities, as well as their decomposition, which will eventually constitute a plan for the project. This information appears in the AIV plan defined by project management in phases A and B of the spacecraft AIV life cycle. The information is entered through a structured editor environment that has a simple compiler to convert the input to internal form.

The system enables the user to retrieve information from past AIV plans and to browse into the activities of these plans. The past plans are indexed according to their main characteristics: the type of spacecraft system, the types of AIV models used, and the subsystem of the spacecraft for which the plan has been applied. It is thus possible to incorporate heuristics specifying typical scenarios and durations of certain activities and to assist in the assessment of project duration, resource consumption, etc. In this way, previously recorded experience can be used to state the optimistic, expected, and pessimistic estimates for activity attributes, such as duration and resource requirements.

The experience has been recorded during past AIV program executions. The recording is facilitated through a note pad facility and special activity, resource, and global constraint attributes, where the user can record previous results of using the system. Here the user can comment on the actual performance of an activity, and his experience in using a resource or in applying a global constraint. These experience attributes complement the information that can be derived from comparison of estimated versus planned values.

The case-based approach of using past plans is combined with the use of generic plans. Generic plans specify a number of typical activities for a certain (component of a) spacecraft system. The assumption is that general principles of spacecraft AIV can guide the initial plan establishment. The activity attributes could define in which order they must be undertaken. Generic plans, or prototype plans, are thus a collection of imaginary AIV activities that must typically be undertaken to perform the ideal AIV process for a selected ideal system or model. They are generic in the sense that no actual programs will ever be able to use the plans without making modifications to them. Furthermore, they are generic in the sense that all the generic activities and the generic resources must be instantiated to represent the actual world. That is, scheduling information, precise resource specifications, etc., must be added in order to properly instantiate the activities to represent an actual plan, or schedule. OPTIMUM-AIV provides mechanisms that allow the user to search through the various generic plans and to make instantiated versions that can be used as the basis for actual AIV plans.

16.7 PLAN AND SCHEDULE GENERATION

16.7.1 Constraint Satisfaction

During the plan and schedule generation stage, we distinguish five kinds of activity constraints.

1. Precedence:

These predecessor and successor constraints specify explicit user defined orderings on the activities. The constraints are expressed as directed links between activities. They can be used to constrain the temporal specifications of the activity. That is, if any of the predecessors or successors are committed to certain time feasibility windows, then this can reduce the duration of the possible time window of the current activity.

2. Precondition:

These are the more general constraints, which can specify that certain results must have been obtained or some equipment be available before the activity can be undertaken. Preconditions refer to the configuration of the spacecraft at the current position in the plan. This configuration consists of all the effects of the preceding activities in the plan. Most often, the preconditions of an activity will be used to state very basic, almost common sense knowledge of what is required of the spacecraft configuration for the current activity to be performed. The advantage of stating relations between activities this way, instead of by implicit precedence links, is that precedence links do not hold information that explicitly states their purpose in the same way as the precondition does. Generally, the user should specify precedence constraints for explicitly sequencing activities and use preconditions for stating more implicit sequencing constraints based on the spacecraft configuration.

3. Temporal:

Time is one of the major constraining factors in the spacecraft AIV planning domain. Temporal constraints are manifested in a number of ways: first, through the specification of delivery and completion dates that must be satisfied and, second, as a maximum duration within which the activity must be undertaken. These two types are called absolute temporal constraints, but there are a number of relative or second-order temporal constraints that can be deduced. These are deduced on the basis of precedence relations and on the possible temporal limitations on the availability of resources.

4. Resource Usage:

This type of activity constraint specifies which and how much of various resources an activity demands. The constraints are expressed as references to resource instances and a specification of the required consumption profile. The information is used to constrain the time feasibility windows in which the activities can be scheduled.

5. Global Activity Constraints:

Global activity constraints express overall temporal relations that must hold between activities satisfying the 'IF' part of the global constraint.

Verification of precedence and precondition constraints takes place during planning, temporal and resource usage constraints are propagated during scheduling, but global activity constraints can be satisfied at any system process stage. Typically, however, global activity constraints will be checked after scheduling by simple goal processing, or backward chaining, checking each global constraint against the scheduled activities.

16.7.2 Planning

Plan generation entails verification of the plan logic, assistance in conflict resolution, and construction of new precedence relations based on preconditions and effects of activities. The basis is the initially specified AIV plan that must be refined and detailed.

The plan logic verification is divided into the checking of user-defined precedence relations between activities and the validation of preconditions and effects of activities versus actual spacecraft system states.

The checking of precedence relations includes detection and resolution of dangling references to predecessor and successor activities and of cycles specified by the precedence links.

The validation of activity and spacecraft system states checks for interactions between parallel activities and propagates system configurations from the start event to the end event of the project. The propagation ensures that the effects of one activity do not violate the preconditions of a succeeding activity; i.e., the ordering of activities is consistent with the preconditions and effects specified for each activity. There might be two types of conflicts: a precondition of an activity is

1. in conflict with the actual state of the system
2. not found in the actual state of the system

Possible modifications to restore the consistency of the plan logic are

- modification of the preconditions and/or effects of one or many activities
- change in the precedence relations between activities
- addition or deletion of activities to introduce or avoid the configuration in question

None of these modifications are suitable to be performed automatically because they have a high impact on the plan. Instead, the user performs them manually, assisted by the graphical plan editor where the preconditions, effects, and the expected spacecraft configuration are accessible for each activity.

16.7.3 Scheduling

Schedule generation involves not only management of temporal and resource usage constraints but also conflict detection and collection. The relation between an activity and its decomposition is an active relation in the sense that definitions and changes made at one level propagate to the other levels in the plan hierarchy. This applies to time definitions as well as resource assignments.

Time feasibility windows (TFW) for the activities are calculated by a forward and a backward pass of the logical plan. The user can select whether the scheduler shall use the optimistic, expected, or pessimistic estimates for the activity durations when performing this forward and backward propagation.

Within the TFWs, the system places the activities according to the local strategy associated with each activity. If a local strategy is not specified, the project as a whole has defined a global strategy that determines the preferable assignment of actual times to activities. This global strategy defaults to "as soon as possible."

These preferences regarding activity placements can be overruled by violation of resource constraints. The management of shared resources, called resource smoothing, is an inherently intractable problem. We have constructed the following simple heuristics for resource smoothing: calculate the shared resource usage profile; compare this profile with the availability profile; shift activities within their TFWs if necessary; and, if shifting is not sufficient, solve the overconsumption problem in cooperation with the user.

The management of consumable resources is simplified by the fact that the timing of their usage is unimportant. Only the total usage is relevant, and the system must simply guarantee that this does not exceed the initial availability. OPTIMUM-AIV records the consumption of consumable resources by maintaining a consumption profile and checking it against the initial availability. Resources that can be replenished are not handled, although the user can add the replenished amount to the initial availability at any time.

By specifying upper and lower bounds on resource usage, it is a relatively simple and flexible task to track the more detailed specification of actual resource usage as a plan is refined into lower levels of detail, as in hierarchical planning. In fact, the maintenance of bounds makes this a useful checking and pruning mechanism because the expectation should be that lower levels of detail merely provide a more accurate specification of actual use and should not be constrained unnecessarily by complete specifications at higher levels.

16.7.4 Knowledge about Plans and Schedules

OPTIMUM-AIV holds a large amount of information associated with its domain elements, i.e., activities, resources, calendars and constraints. Unlike many other systems serving mainly as bookkeeping systems, OPTIMUM-AIV is able to use this information in an active way in the planning and scheduling process to reason about the plan. This is a necessary requirement for determining immediate impacts of changes to the plan during execution monitoring and for assisting in consistency recovery and plan repair. It is also a useful precondition for detecting and possibly avoiding conflict situations and for explaining and justifying planning decisions.

16.8 PROJECT MONITORING AND PLAN REPAIR

The major use of OPTIMUM-AIV will be during the plan execution phase. This phase covers the period from the time when the AIV plan starts to be executed until the planned process is completed.

In any planning domain, there is a possibility that problems occur when the plan is executed. We distinguish between usual plan failures and plan failures that are specific to the AIV domain: the failure of tests. The usual plan failures are caused by changes in the actual environment in which the plan is executed. They are often caused by unexpected events or organizational issues such as unavailable resources or supplies. When problems occur during plan execution, the original plan becomes, at least partly, invalid, and it has to be revised. This can be done by replanning where the original plan is discarded, and a completely new plan is generated that takes into account the state of execution and the changes of circumstances that led to the plan failure. In domains such as AIV where activities are heavily dependent on external activities or external resources, this approach is not acceptable. Based on the original plan, bookings have been made, and temporal interfaces have been specified. It is important that these interfaces are changed as little as possible, and thus, the original plan must be retained as much as possible.

The failure of tests makes the original plan invalid just like the other problems mentioned above. However, failures are expected as possible outcomes of tests, and in most cases, lines of action are predefined as part of the domain knowledge to deal with test failures. There are various strategies that can be adopted depending on the type of failure. These strategies, or problem scenario subplans, are represented as special cases of generic plans. Some problem scenario plans can be included in the system from scratch, but most will be entered during the actual use of the system in the plan execution phase.

The severity of plan failures varies. Some plan failures have very local effects, and problems can be solved by local schedule repair. It might suffice to move start and finish times of a few activities or to make use of alternative resources or non-nominal availability profiles. However, sometimes this local change of the schedule has effects on other parts of the schedule, e.g., when the alternative resource is scheduled for another activity. In these cases, more global changes are necessary to generate a new valid schedule. Effects of plan failures can become so serious that the logic of the plan is affected. It might be impossible to schedule still outstanding activities using the original plan under the given conditions. Then it becomes necessary to repair the actual plan itself rather than just the schedule in order to retain consistency.

The issue of plan repair and schedule repair is very much a research issue in AI planning, and thus, a fully automated solution to these problems is far beyond the scope here. OPTIMUM-AIV *assists* the user in schedule and plan repair in an interactive way rather than *performs* repair itself.

The possibility of plan failures, whether expected or not, and the need for plan repair require the monitoring of plan execution. In the simplest case, the changes in the current state of execution are given when a plan failure occurs. However, a plan that has not been updated for a long period while work has been undertaken will be more difficult to recover. In the AIV domain where plan failures are frequent and there is need for fast plan repair, it is necessary to monitor plan execution more closely. It is important that the plan is kept up-to-date regularly without much effort. Therefore, the system gives strong facilities for entering the execution progress and for making small and large adjustments to the plan.

The system gathers information about the actual progress to have basis for determining whether the plan has failed. Then it uses that to determine how execution goes, i.e., to detect discrepancies between the proposed schedule and the monitoring information. This, in turn, is used to identify what parts of the schedule are inconsistent with, or affected by, the execution state. The system assists in changing the schedule by displaying relevant information in trying to repair the schedule. The screen dump in Figure 16-1 shows how the user is informed about the immediate impacts of the actual state of the schedule after the daily update of actual versus scheduled execution times. The activities appear in different colors according to

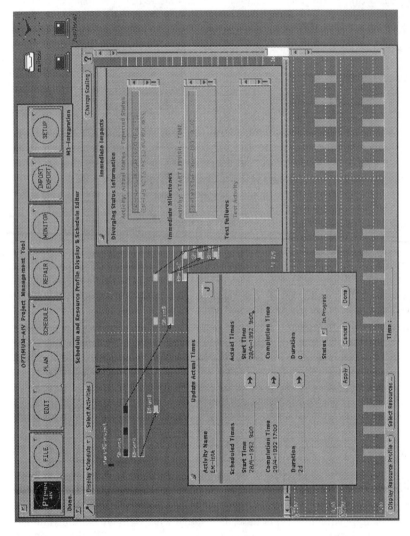

Figure 16-1: OPTIMUM-AIV Gantt Display and Immediate Impacts Window

their status: not started, in progress, completed. The Immediate Impacts window lists the activities having a status that differs from what is expected according to the scheduled times and the current time (visualized as the vertical line marked **CT**). Based on this information, the planner can interactively reorganize activities and re-schedule the plan.

The consistency checking and recovery are organized along execution problem types caused by user changes. We assume that the user is quite capable of solving execution problems him/herself and will use the system to speed up the process to make sure that nothing is forgotten and to explore different solutions and what-if scenarios. For each execution problem type, there are specific standard recovery methods that are most appropriate for solving the problems. To illustrate this, please refer to Figure 16-2. The Resource Conflict Repair window displays information about which resource was insufficient and lists the overconsumption intervals and the activities requesting it. The repair assistance consists of five different actions:

1. Supply more resources: The planner can increase the availability of the insufficient resource.

2. Reduce resource request: The planner can reduce the request for the insufficient resource for one or more of the involved activities.

3. Use another profile: If the availability of the resource in question has non-nominal availability profiles associated with it, they can be activated instead of the nominal availability profile.

4. Use alternative resource: If an alternative to the insufficient resource is defined, the planner can make one or more of the involved activities request the alternative resource instead of the insufficient one.

5. Change plan logic: The last and probably least used possibility is to change the entire plan logic in order to recover from the conflict.

16.9 EXTERNAL INTERFACES

16.9.1 ARTEMIS Interface

The system has a file interface to the widely spread ARTEMIS 7000 (for PCs and workstations) and ARTEMIS 9000 (for mainframes) scheduling tool. The interface is primarily used for

- import of space project data, i.e., network of activities and events, constraints and resources
- export and display of plans

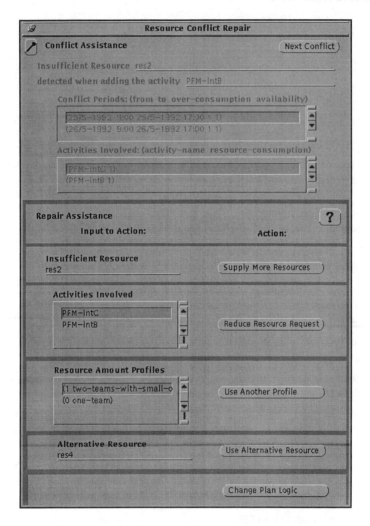

Figure 16-2: OPTIMUM-AIV Conflict Repair Assitance

- report writing and graphics
- aggregation, i.e., summary of numeric data held in network datasets, e.g., resource requirements for all activities

It can also be used for network construction, examination of the network logic, time analysis and updating, resource-limited or time-limited scheduling, and multiple network processing. However, in these latter uses of ARTEMIS, it is not feasible to return the results directly to OPTIMUM-AIV.

16.9.2 Database Interface

During the design phase, OPTIMUM-AIV was prepared to interface to satellite related project databases in a similar way as the ARTEMIS tool. Although not implemented in the current framework, this interface was meant to reduce the work to input data into the system and ensure the coherence between external satellite databases and the OPTIMUM-AIV database.

It allows the loading of all kinds of domain information not explicitly related to the planning/scheduling process (and thus not available in the ARTEMIS tool). This information comprises, e.g., experiences, documentation, objectives, and other domain knowledge, maybe in the form of rules. The management system and the format of those databases might vary, but they are convertible into relational tables. Therefore, the system should provide an SQL interface to fill its internal database.

16.9.3 Programming Interface

The system is designed to allow external documentation programs to be written. It provides an interface that permits any user to develop their own documentation, in particular, any new representation of the plan and schedule. That means that all activities, resources, and constraints and any schedule will be accessible by any external program (written in Lisp, C, Pascal, or Ada).

16.10 APPLIED AI TECHNIQUES

This section describes the AI planning and scheduling techniques integrated in the system. The applied techniques complement existing features of current project management tools such as ARTEMIS.

OPTIMUM-AIV adopts the *non-linear planning* paradigm that enables plan representation to contain causally independent activities that can be executed concurrently. It searches through a space of partial plans, modifying them until a valid plan/schedule is found.

Another important characteristic of the system is *hierarchical planning*. The term hierarchical refers to both the representation of the plan at different levels and also the control of the planning process at progressively more detailed levels.

The scheduling task is considered a *constraint satisfaction* problem solved by constraint-based reasoning. The constraints are propagated throughout the plan, gradually transforming it into a realizable schedule. Invariably, not all the constraints can be met, such that some have to be relaxed.

During plan specification and generation, the system operates on *explicit preconditions and effects of activities* that specify the applicability and purpose of the activity within the plan. With this knowledge, it is possible to check whether the current structure of the plan introduces any conflicts between actual spacecraft system states, computed by the system, and activity preconditions, specified by the user. Such conflicts would arise if one activity deletes the effect of another, thus removing its contribution to the success of a further activity. The facility for checking the consistency of the plan logic, by dependency recording, is not possible within existing project management tools that assume that the user must get this right.

After planning/scheduling has been performed, the system checks the *global activity constraints*. A global activity constraint is an 'IF THEN' formed rule stating a temporal constraint between activities that match the 'IF' form. Global activity constraints can hold variables that are instantiated to objects of the planning domain, i.e., activities and resources.

16.11 CONCLUSION

The current status of the OPTIMUM-AIV project, as of January 1994, is that three OPTIMUM-AIV design documents about the AIV domain, the software requirements, and architectural design have been written (please refer to the literature list in the following section) and approved by ESTEC. The system has been implemented on a Sun Sparc platform running OpenWindows, Lucid Common Lisp, and Common Lisp Object System. OPTIMUM-AIV was delivered to ESA/ESTEC in April 1992 and has been evaluated during a six month warranty period.

The domain analysis has identified areas of AIV expert knowledge that must be incorporated into the system. The SRD has derived a model of the domain and has established the functional and operational requirements that must be satisfied to meet the demands of the AIV experts. The ADD has proposed a design that supports the typical mode of interaction between the user and the system. The AIV experts input the plan specifications and revisions, and the system goes through a series of analyses and identifies, visualizes, and assists the user in case of conflicts. This chapter has discussed in detail the requirements of the AIV experts, the results obtained with regard to knowledge elicitation and requirement formalization, and the results of the design phase in terms of constraint identification and satisfaction and execution problem detection and recovery.

References

Arentoft, M.M., Y. Parrod, and J. Stader. 1990. *OPTIMUM-AIV: Software Requirements Document.* OPT-CRI-SRD-1090, CRI, MATRA, Progespace, AIAI.

Arentoft, M.M., Y. Parrod, J. Stader, and I. Stokes. 1991. *OPTIMUM-AIV: Architectural Design Document.* OPT-CRI-ADD-0291, CRI, MATRA, Progespace, AIAI.

Currie, K.W., and A. Tate. 1991. "O-Plan: The Open Planning Architecture," *Artificial Intelligence* 52, 1, pp. 49–86.

Fuchs, J.J., G.S. Pedersen, and A. Gasquet. 1989. *EPS-AIT: Final Report.* PS-AIT-CRI-FR-0001-89, CRI, MATRA, AIAI.

Parrod, Y., and I. Stokes. 1990. *OPTIMUM-AIV: AIV Knowledge Acquired.* OPT-MATRA-TN1000-0890, CRI, MATRA, Progespace, AIAI.

Swartout, W. 1987. *DARPA Santa Cruz Workshop on Planning*, Santa Cruz, Calif.

Tate, A. 1984. "Goal Structure: Capturing the Intent of Plans." *European Conference on AI,* Pisa, Italy, September.

Wilkins, D.E. 1984. "Domain Independent Planning: Representation and Plan Generation." *Artificial Intelligence*, 22, pp. 269–301.

PART
TWO

APPLICATION CASE STUDIES
Semiconductor Manufacturing

17

LOGISTICS MANAGEMENT SYSTEM (LMS):

Integrating Decision Technologies for Dispatch Scheduling in Semiconductor Manufacturing

Kenneth Fordyce
Gerald (Gary) Sullivan
(International Business Machines Corp.)

17.1 OVERVIEW OF THE ENVIRONMENT

17.1.1 Overview of IBM Burlington

The IBM Burlington Semiconductor development laboratory and manufacturing site develops and manufactures semiconductor memory and logic subsystems for current and future IBM products. Burlington produces some of the world's most complex computer components, which are used throughout the IBM product line. The Burlington Site is located on 720 acres a few miles from Burlington, Vermont, in the towns of Essex Junction and Williston, Vermont. The laboratory and manufacturing plant occupy over 2.7 million square feet and employ over 6,200 people.

The Burlington Advanced Industrial Engineering (AIE) department has the mission to improve Burlington Manufacturing performance by improving manufacturing planning/scheduling or manufacturing logistics (defined shortly). The work done by AIE covers a wide range of decision technologies used across all four decision tiers (defined shortly). This chapter covers the one portion of the work done by AIE, building and deploying the dispatch scheduling system LMS.

17.1.2 Overview of LMS

The Logistics Management System (LMS) is a real-time transaction-based system, combining decision technologies from AI, MS/OR, and DSS, that serves as a dispatcher scheduler, monitoring and controlling the manufacturing flow of IBM's semiconductor facility near Burlington, Vermont. LMS coordinates the actions and decisions of several logically isolated participants in a serially dependent system of activities. Therefore, it balances the requirements of several goals (cycle time, output, on time delivery or serviceability, and inventory management) that compete for the same resource, exploits emerging opportunities on the manufacturing floor, and reduces the distortion from unplanned events. For an excellent review of the costs of rescheduling, see *Economist* (1992).

Support in LMS comes in two flavors (Appendix 1): passive (or decision support) and pro-active (or intervention). In the **decision support mode**, LMS passively waits for the user to make a request for information. In the **intervention mode**, LMS monitors the transaction stream and actively uses its knowledge bases and models to issue alerts and recommend what actions to take next.

This two flavor approach seems useful in other semiconductor fabrication facilities (Kempf, Chee, & Scott, 1988; Kempf, 1989; Morris *et al.*, 1989; Savell, Perez, & Koh, 1989), computer board assembly (Acock & Zelmel, 1986; Ahmadi & Ahmadi, 1990; Thomson, 1990), steel production (Epp, Kalin, & Miller, 1989; Numao & Morishita, 1989), automobile assembly (Jain, Barber, & Osterfeld, 1990), statistical and adaptive process control (Anderson *et al.*, 1989), vehicle routing (Duchessi, Belardo, & Seagle, 1988), medicine (Shortliffe *et al.*, 1987), chess (Byrne, 1989), and as a general approach for some applications (Bobrow, 1991).

Historically, production and operations management has ignored the dispatch decision tier and the concept of incrementally increasing the level of decision support. This has significantly limited our ability to make an impact on the performance of the manufacturing operation.

17.1.3 A Brief Review of Producing Micro-Electronic Chips

The process begins with a pure, thin, and circular (8 inches in diameter) slice or wafer of silicon (which is an insulator). It will eventually become hundreds of chips when the process is complete. Between 200 and 400 complicated operations or steps change the electronic structure of the wafer according to a a very precise plan. Burlington currently produces 13,000 different types of chips. Each has a distinct plan. Each chip on the wafer contains tens of thousands of transistors or other electronic devices wired into monolithic integrated circuits.

The essentials of the circuit or wiring plan for a wafer are a set of masks, one mask for each layer of the chip. The masks are designed by the laboratory. A finished mask consists of chromium patterns deposited on optically pure glass. The patterns represent a negative image of the parts of all the transistors and other components to be built into the silicon wafer.

The process of building circuits into the silicon is as follows (for more details, see Gribbin, 1984; Sequeda, 1985; Dayhoff & Atherton, 1987; IBM, 1988; Sze, 1988; Chen *et al.*, 1988):

Through an oxidation process, a protective covering of oxide is grown on the wafer. Next, it is coated with a light-sensitive material called a photoresist. A mask is precisely registered over the wafer, and ultraviolet light is projected through the mask onto the wafer, causing the photoresist to harden under clear areas of the mask. The image is developed by washing away the unexposed photoresist. Then the wafer is put in an acid bath. The acid passes through the holes in the photoresist and etches similar holes in the oxide layer. Then the remaining photoresist is stripped off.

Controlled amounts of such elements as phosphorus or boron are introduced into the holes in the oxide through diffusion or ion implantation. In diffusion, wafers are placed in high temperature furnaces with the elements to be diffused through the holes in the oxide down into the silicon beneath. The temperature of the furnace controls the depth and concentration of the diffused materials. In ion implantation, dopant atoms are accelerated to a high energy. These atoms strike the wafer and are embedded at various depths, depending on their mass and energy. These "extra atoms" have to squeeze in the best they can with the silicon atoms. Because they typically have one more or one less electron in their "outer shell" than silicon, they squeeze in by giving up an electron (n-type) or taking on an electron and creating a positive hole (p-type).

In the metallization phase, the "wires" connecting the transitory are put in. The process that applies this wiring is evaporation. Pellets of aluminum and copper are place in a chamber with a dome holding the wafers. The air is pumped out of the chamber, and the pellets are heated by an electron beam that causes them to evaporate. The evaporated metal clings to the entire surface of the each wafer. Selective acid etch removes the unwanted metal, leaving only micro miniature wires to connect components.

A wafer is produced in layers. Therefore, the processes of oxidation, photolithography, and diffusion or ion implantation are repeated many times until thousands of circuits are built into each wafer. Metals are done once or twice. There is one set of tools to handle all iterations through a particular process.

17.1.4 Manufacturing Flow as a Folded Serial Line

The primary work unit is a LOT. A lot is group of 25 identical wafers and they always stay together. The batch size (the number of wafers a tool works on at the same time) varies from operation to operation. For example, in photo, the batch size is one; in furnace, it might be 100. After all processing is done, the wafer is cut

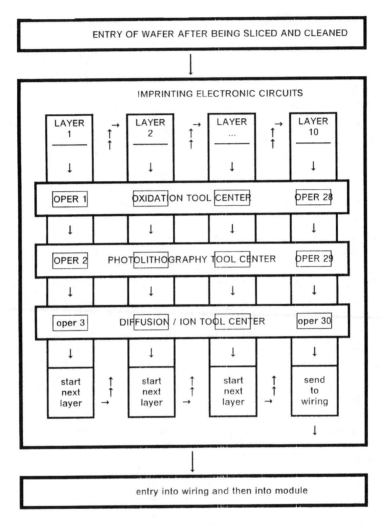

Figure 17-1: Manufacturing Flow as a folded serial line

or diced into chips. The manufacturing flow is best represented by a "folded serial" (Figure 17-1) or re-entrant flow (Graves *et al.*, 1983) line.

Table 17-1 contains a sample OPER fact base that contains key information about the flow through the line for a specific product. It contains information about each operation: the product it belongs to, its sequence position, the tool center it uses, the average raw process time per batch, and batch size.

Table 17-1: Operations table

OPER_TABLE: PRODUCT LION (1)			
Operation ID	Tool Center	Raw Process Time	Batch Size
OPERID	TC	RPT	BS
1	707	30	25
2	724	100	50
3	706	450	100
4	732	35	25
5	713	125	25
6	713	25	25
7	INVEN	0	

Table 17-2 tells us the tools assigned to the tool center. Note the tool centers overlap in a nonexclusive manner. For example, tool centers 707 and 708 have tools common to both (A225 and A226) and tools unique to both (A223 and A224 are only in 707; A227 and A229 are only in 708).

From the wafer's perspective, it is produced by following specific sequence of unique operations without any option for variation ("serial line") except for rework loops. From the tooling center perspective, each wafer makes approximately 10 passes or iterations through one of its tools. Each set of tools handles all the activity across all the iterations for that step. Each tool can handle a variety of tasks and is reconfigured (set up) to handle different wafer types at the specific iterations. For each wafer or part type and iteration step, the raw process time is known within a small tolerance (the values range from 15 milliseconds to 20 minutes). Major tool centers are often viewed as a job shop, with jobs arriving in a random manner.

Table 17-2: Tool center fact base

TOOL CENTER	MEMBER MACHINE					
706	Y323	Y324	Y326			
707	A223	A224	A225	A226		
708			A225	A226	A227	A229
713	W101	W102	W103	W104	W105	W106
724	B111	B112	B113			
725	B111	B112	B113	B114	B115	
732	C821	C822	C833			
733				C824	C825	C836

17.1.5 Scheduling Complexity

Complexity in scheduling semiconductor facilities is the result of (Fowler, 1992) such factors as unreliable equipment, batching, reentrant flows, rework, yield loss, hot lots, combination of production, engineering and R&D lots, and varying product mix and start rates. A few characteristics reduce complexity (Fowler, 1992): (1) Except for rework, most of the flow in a fab is deterministic (instead of probabilistic as in a job shop). (2) The processing time per wafer or per lot or per batch is very nearly deterministic, so that once processing begins, we can get a very good prediction of when the processing will end. (3) The shop floor control systems in place in current wafer fabs provide much of the information we need in order to make good decisions.

17.1.6 Manufacturing Logistics and Decision Tiers

The term *logistics* initially referred to the branch of military science having to do with moving, supplying, and quartering troops. Manufacturing logistics refers to the moving, supplying, and processing of lots as they are transformed from raw materials into finished goods. The technology of manufacturing logistics refers to the study and understanding of this area to develop principles and guidelines that will improve manufacturing performance.

Ongoing goals in manufacturing are to increase product throughput, increase on-time delivery of products, improve quality, and control costs. As the complexity of manufacturing increases, industry has placed additional emphasis on manufacturing logistics and information systems as a key to achieving these goals.

Within the complexity of semiconductor manufacturing, four related decision areas (Kempf, Chee, & Scott, 1988), or tiers, can be distinguished based on the time scale of the decision window. The first decision tier, **strategic scheduling**, concerns a set of problems that are six months to seven years into the future. Here decisions are made about the impact of changes in the product line, in the types of equipment available, in the manufacturing processes, in the availability of workers, and so forth. In the oven example (Figure 17-2 and Appendix 2), decisions are made on whether the ovens are necessary to the production process and, if so, the characteristics needed in the oven.

The second tier, **operational scheduling**, considers the next few months to two years. Here decisions are made concerning changes in demand for existing products, the addition or deletion of products, capital purchases, manpower planning, changes in manufacturing processes, and so forth. In the oven example, decisions are made about how many ovens to buy.

The third tier, **tactical scheduling**, deals with problems the company faces in the next day to six months Here decisions are made about starts into manufacturing line, delivery dates for orders, daily going rates, amount of overtime needed, last

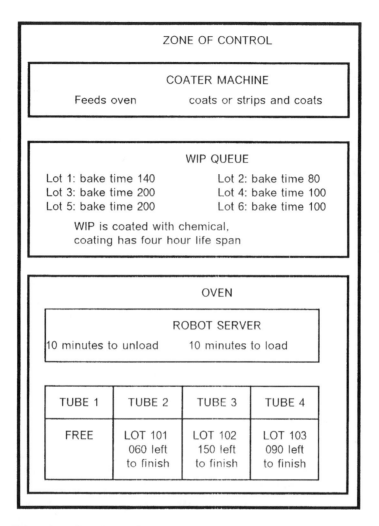

Figure 17-2:   Oven dispatch example

minute capital purchases, operator training, corrections in manufacturing processes, machine dedication, the impact of yield curves, and phase in of the manufacture of new products. In the oven example, decisions would be made on the daily going rate for different products, allocation of resources between operations, the number of operators to assign, and machine dedication. See Leachman & Carmon (1991) for an example of a system that does this type of scheduling.

The fourth tier, **dispatch scheduling or short interval scheduling (SIS)**, addresses the problems of the next hour to a few weeks. Dispatch scheduling decisions concern monitoring and controlling of the actual manufacturing flow or logistics. Here decisions are made concerning trade-offs between running test lots for a change in an existing product or a new product and running regular manufacturing lots, expiring of lots, prioritizing late lots, positioning preventive maintenance downtime, producing similar products to reduce setup time, determining downstream needs, dealing with simultaneous requests on the same piece of equipment and preferred machines for yield considerations, assigning personnel to machines, covering for absences, and reestablishing steady production flow after a machine has been down. In the oven example, the question is which lot (if any) is run next when an oven is free.

Let's look at a two example dispatch decision for the oven scenario described in Figure 17-2 and Appendix 2.

Example 1. Assume that Lot 3 in the oven scenario will expire in 30 minutes; then the opportunity is to run Lot 3 next and avoid the strip and recoat.

Example 2. Assume Lot 3 in the oven scenario will expire in 120 minutes and requires the same setup as Lot 101 in Tube 2. Tube 1 is not presently set up to handle Lot 3. Then we would dispatch another lot to tube 1 and wait to dispatch Lot 101 to Tube 2 to reuse the setup for Lot 101.

Of course, there is overlap and interaction between the four decision tiers, but typically, different groups are responsible for different scheduling decisions. For example, maintenance might decide on training for their personnel, work schedules for their people, preventive maintenance, and the machine to repair next. Finance and each building superintendent might make decisions on capital equipment purchases. Industrial Engineering might have the final say on total manpower, but a building superintendent might do the day-to-day scheduling. Marketing might decide when orders for products can be filled and what schedule commitments to make. For strategic and operational decisions, these groups and their associated decision support tools are loosely coordinated or coupled. Finance only requires an estimate of required new tools from each building to estimate capital purchase. Each building requires an estimate on new tool requirements from the product development people. For dispatch decisions, they must be coupled tightly. Lots only get processed when the appropriate tool, operator, and raw material are available. At dispatch, rough estimates are no longer sufficient. If a machine is down, maintenance must have the appropriately trained individual available to repair the machine. Manufacturing must have the appropriate mix of tools and workers to produce finished goods on a timely basis. At dispatch, the decisions made by various groups must be in sync, or nothing is produced. A manufacturing facility accommodates this tight coupling in only one of two ways: slack (extra tooling and manpower, long lead times, limited product variation, excess inventory and people, differential quality, brand loyalty, and so forth) or strong information systems (Galbraith, 1973) to make effective decisions.

17.1.7 Pre-LMS Decision Support Environment

The Pre-LMS decision support environment for dispatch decisions consisted of the following items:

First is an excellent set of automated, homegrown, and independent data systems (Minnich & Bula, 1985) that reliably (strong data integrity checks, wanding, hardware backup) recorded in real-time all transactions for lots, machines, and orders in manufacturing and provided basic process flow checks and information about the manufacturing process. These systems later serve as the data collectors for LMS.

Some information existed on paper only: process specifications, machine specifications, lot locations, operator abilities, and so on.

An excellent set of reports were generated on a weekly basis describing the performance of the line and the present lot disposition. Limited ad hoc queries could be made on a batch basis. People were just beginning to think out real-time queries.

A number of systems of various levels of quality existed at the decision tier levels 3 and 2 to establish daily plans, priorities, and re-allocate equipment on a monthly or quarterly basis.

In the early 1980s, this combination of decision support for dispatch was state of the art. The requirement for LMS was not generated because the quality of this support structure degraded but was generated because as the size, activity level, and product mix in the facility grew, additional support was required to meet the needs of the business. The Burlington facility remained data rich but was becoming information poor.

17.2 DEVELOPMENT PROCESS

17.2.1 Winning Support for LMS

From 1979 to 1984, the industrial engineering group in Burlington followed a traditional path of doing limited decision tier two and three modeling and studies to improve manufacturing performance and evaluating the latest in end user software.

Three key events events forced a full reassessment of the mission of IE. First, Tom Henry, a building superintendent (within IBM, a building superintendent is responsible for a significant portion of the total product), suggested it would be beneficial if he and his people could be alerted to problems or deviations from plan on the manufacturing floor just as they were unfolding. It would be even better if a solution to the event was made when the discrepancy was reported. Second, a review of models simulating the manufacturing lines presently being built by IE uncovered a major deficiency—they were failing to deal adequately with the reentrant flow characteristic. Third, we attended a **Cardinal Woolsey Religious Awakening** (Fordyce & Sullivan, 1983; Woolsey, 1991), where Gene Woolsey talked about ... where's the data ... I am now the voucher. A variety of interesting articles written by Gene Woolsey can be found in *Interfaces*.

In 1984, industrial engineering, with the help of manufacturing, reexamined its mission and the present decision support barriers to improved Burlington decision making and performance. The following was determined:

1. There was lack of real-time manufacturing floor status information.

2. There was insufficient integration of fact (knowledge) bases, real-time floor data, and tactical guidelines.

3. There were significant barriers to improving performance relying only on decision tier 2 and 3 modeling and human dispatch (decision tier 4).

These barriers involve controlling the timing and sequencing of lots through operations. The constantly changing nature of the floor meant the validity of daily or shift plans degenerated quickly. The combinatorial nature of the environment and the short decision intervals generate computational overload for traditional models and cognitive overload for a human. By controlling the dispatch decision with an automated system, AIE believed it could improve tool utilization and reduce cycle time (generally considered inversely related) at the same time by altering the arrival and/or service time curves and, therefore, shifting the trade-off curve (Chen *et al.*, 1988; Bitran & Tirupati, 1989; Fordyce & Sullivan, 1990); Miller, 1990.

As a result of this reexamination of mission, Industrial Engineering proposed building a dispatch system that would improve performance and would integrate a variety of decision technologies, including a new emerging technology called expert systems.

In 1984/85, having an industrial engineering group propose to build a sophisticated system with expert system components was "novel." In 1984/85, there were two primary groups that had to be sold on the idea: (1) immediate Burlington management and (2) the IBM Advanced Engineering and Manufacturing (AEM) Council. The AEM group is a corporate-wide group within IBM that provides seed money to sponsor high risk but leading edge applications within IBM that will benefit multiple manufacturing locations.

In 1984/85, Burlington manufacturing management intuitively felt they needed additional support, but they could not specify the exact nature of the type of support. AEM was receiving the request for better decision support from all the IBM plant managers. Therefore, both groups were open to proposals. AIE received limited but firm support from both groups to build LMS.

With five headcount, a few PCs, access to the general purpose 370/VM system, and a "commission" from the plant management and corporate manufacturing to produce something to help control manufacturing, AIE set out to build LMS.

17.2.2 Stage 1—Passive Support

To build LMS, AIE required developing or acquiring skills in transaction data gathering; knowledge (fact) base building; system integration; and a change in perspective from optimization to control and from tight coupling to loose coupling. These were not traditional IE skills in 1984 and 1985.

AIE choose APL2 Pascal, C, and Assembler as their toolkit of choice to build LMS. They believed LMS would need to combine different decision technologies, the KBS portion would be imbedded, and standard non-procedural rules would not be the appropriate form of knowledge representation. This kind of thinking is standard practise for AI leaders today (*Economist,* 1991) but "ran a bit against the grain" in 1985.

For knowledge engineers (an emerging term of distinction at that time), there was one young industrial engineer with manufacturing experience and one young ex-manufacturing lead technician being groomed for management. A more experienced IE accepted a dual role as knowledge engineer and network guru. Tom Henry offered access to some of his key manufacturing support people (including himself) to guide the direction of the project.

The first requirement was to obtain and maintain a real-time data base that contained the status or state of the manufacturing line: lot location, machine status (up, down, preventive maintenance, operation assigned to, ...), and an assessment of the quality of the status (a lot is so many days behind or ahead of schedule, the work in progress [WIP] built up in front of an operation is too small or too large, the tool has been down tool long, ...). To accomplish this required three items, real time access to the transactions collected by different Burlington floor control systems (FCS), integration of the real-time data with knowledge bases or fact bases, and a method to describe the desired form of the real-time status database.

After considerable coaxing, IS agreed to send electronically a copy of each transaction to the AIE's new acquired personal computer (PC). AIE then transferred this transaction from the PC to VM/370. After a little more coaxing, they sent a manual to help decipher the transactions. AIE then worked to translate all fields to character data, determine their meaning, delete the ones of no interest, and convert some into a more usable form. The conversion to a usable form generated the first use of knowledge bases—which AIE called a fact base and a translator (XLATOR). For example, it is important to characterize the type of transaction (is it a lot movement, a change in the status of a machine, or change in an order), characterize the lot type (is it a test lot from the lab, a test lot from manufacturing engineering, an express lot for an important order, etc.), and the priority of the lot (the transaction stream contains 50 priority codes, but operators convert those priority codes into four priority classes). When the transaction stream contains a record indicating a lot has entered an operation area, knowledge bases are accessed to identify setup time and preferred tools; when the lot is loaded on the tool, a fact base provides information about the process time.

Initially, the description and conversion of the transaction stream into an LMS status record was done with a combination of APL2 and fact bases. Some of the work was done by the programmer and some by the knowledge engineers. As the project progressed, this evolved into the BUILD TIME environment and the Gateway (described in the next section). The BUILD TIME environment enabled the knowledge engineer to describe the form of the database and build the required knowledge bases without programmer assistance. The GATEWAY took in each transaction from the FCS, made the conversions as described in the formatter generated in the BUILD TIME, and posted the information into the database.

This established the LMS approach: down and dirty code (get something working very quickly, and make it available to the users to try it out) and then patch/modify. When stability sets in, rewrite with an emphasis on an architecture that minimizes the need for a programmer and maximizes ease of adaptation. When prototype applications get bogged down by beauty too soon, they die from not providing what people want and then understanding what they need. Waiting too long to rewrite and freeze programming changes causes applications to die under the wait of endless user requests for change and spaghetti code.

AIE now had the best data in town and set out to use it effectively in three ways:

1. providing manufacturing people easy and real time access to the status of the floor on their PROFS machine

2. using it as a base to "simulate" and investigate different strategies for dispatch

3. supporting modeling efforts at decision tiers 3 and 2

AIE rapidly built the LMS component called MAT (Management Access Technique). MAT provided various users (managers, operators, planners, and AIE) a flexible and easy to use (pop up and nested windows, good use of color, blinking lights, pf key driven, etc.—leading edge in 1985 for IBM 370 machine) interface for requesting and displaying real-time views of the status of the manufacturing floor on their PROFS machine.

In the late 1970s and early 1980s, IBM made major strides in electronic mail and computer networks for internal use. By the early 1980s, electronic mail was ready to revolutionize communication. The missing link was an easy to use panel driven system to consolidated these advances and make them available to everyone. PROFS was the missing link. When MAT rolled out, people had soaked up

PROFS and become addicted to getting information from their terminal. Additionally, everybody now had a terminal. Timing is everything in life.

MAT is described in more detail in the next section, and example MAT screens can be found in Appendix 3. MAT was an instant success; manufacturing loved it. It put manufacturing into the decision support level of the support hierarchy. Usage of MAT went from 30 to start to over 400 in less than a year.

To exploit and satisfy the new found popularity of LMS, AIE did three things:

1. They acquired an IE with excellent programming skills to work full time at maintaining and improving MAT and one full time person to handle MAT training, etc.

2. They began exploring decision tier 2 and 3 models that would impact dispatch performance, for example, manpower planning (Fordyce, Sullivan, & Sullivan, 1990).

3. They required each manufacturing building (a major division of manufacturing in Burlington) to assign people (1–3) from their headcount to serve as the building representatives to LMS. They were responsible for MAT installation, training, etc., in their building.

About this time, the two original knowledge engineers moved on to bigger and better things, and they were replaced by three people—two who had good system skills and many years of experience in manufacturing and one who had been a successful process engineer and building superintendent.

Within a year, users were requesting LMS provide them alerts, that is, notify them when a specific situation or condition in the line existed. For example, a lot waited too long at an operation, a machine was down too long, the WIP levels for the feed operations dropped too low, WIP was too high in a sector, etc. AIE added the alert manager component. Users wrote "rules" describing the situations they wished to be alerted to and who should be alerted. This knowledge was added to the GATEWAY, and it would generate the alert when appropriate. The alerts were made operational in MAT through the addition of different colored blinking circles and squares to the information display. Later, people were notified of alert conditions by sending them a message through the electronic mail system—PROFS. The linkage to PROFS was considered a a technical first by some people (not the necessarily the authors). The ALERTS were a huge success. A common phrase to describe a successful line status meeting was "NO BLINKING LIGHTS."

17.2.3 Stage 2—ProActive Support

So far, LMS is helping manage the line, and improvements were already measurable, but the original goal was to dispatch the line. In 1987, business was booming, and Burlington needed to increase production. To accomplish this, throughput of a critical set of tools that were considered a production bottleneck or pinchpoint had to be improved. Ordering more tools was not an option because the lead time was one year. Again, timing is everything in life.

For the past two years, AIE had been exploring a number of dispatch strategies. It had become clear that there was no dispatch expert to codify, and traditional MS/OR heuristics were too simple and inadequate. What appeared to work was a combination of knowledge engineering, key manufacturing flow control people and traditional operational analysis.

AIE set out to improve throughput. They organized XSELL, or quality sessions with the operators of the bottleneck tools, and drew data and did analysis on the flow of lots through this part of the line.

The bottleneck tools had high production rates when they were running, but they were often down, and setup times were often long. Arrivals appeared to follow a Poisson process. The tools that fed the bottleneck tools had low production rates, were often up, were plentiful, and had short setup times. The strategy to improve the availability and utilization of the bottleneck machines was to build trains of lots that required the same setup and had different test requirements. This significantly reduced setup time and idle time and made the arrival of lots a more deterministic process.

Once strategy was worked out, heuristics were written to implement it. Some simple tests were run via a simple simulation, and then heuristics were implemented in LMS. Lot movements and dispatch decisions in that sector were then watched carefully on an hourly basis (using the LMS decision support and alert mode). Changes to the heuristics could and were made in a matter of minutes and immediately implemented. In less than a month, a stable set of heuristics was in place making dispatch decisions that improved throughput through this set of tools (IBM, 1988). It has been estimated this DDM improved product output about 35 percent and avoided a $10 million capital expenditure (Feigenbaum, McCorduck, & Nii, 1988, p. 63).

After this success, AIE was soon asked to help a building that had good throughput, but its serviceability measure needed improvement to meet new business requirements. Serviceability is on time delivery of lots—a lot that is 3 days ahead of schedule does not offset a lot that is 3 days behind schedule. Again, AIE had meetings with key manufacturing people and did analysis of the data. This investigation showed that the primary problem was ensuring that production energy was put into lots that were behind schedule as opposed to lots that were ahead of schedule. The implementation process was similar to that described above, The DDM was successful in improving the on time delivery of the product (IBM, 1989).

From these two successes, the dispatch decision making (DDM) structure (described in the next section) evolved.

After this second success, LMS's position as tactical (as opposed to strategic) component of Burlington's systems for controlling manufacturing floor operations was secure. AIE focused on the following:

1. existing Burlington implementations going in the face of constant change and LMS in new Burlington Fabs

2. more sophisticated DDM for LMS

3. extension to MAT and the Alert manager

4. generalization of the build time to link into any floor control system and the development of LMS's own FCS

5. better decision tier 3 and 2 models (for example, tool planning, alternate work schedules, manpower planning, daily output planning, and allowable resource modeling)

6. a few presentations describing LMS and related work

17.2.4 Stage 3—Post Survival

In the late 1980s the following events emerged that would shape LMS over the next few years:

1. an interest in successful KBS applications

2. the acceptance of KBS technology as one of many decision technologies

3. the establishment of a powerful IBM CIM (computer integrated manufacturing) competency center to ensure IBM remained a leader in manufacturing

4. a renewed interest on the part of IBM to participate in the manufacturing floor marketplace

5. a nationwide resurgence of interest in manufacturing and the decline in its fascination with finance

As a result of event 1 and a major stroke of luck, Ed Feigenbaum, a world renowned AI leader, choose to visit Burlington in 1987 as part of his research for his book *The Rise of the Expert Company: How Visionary Companies are Using Expert Systems to Make Huge Profits* (Times Books, 1988). After a very enjoyable (at least from Gary's point of view) visit, Ed devoted a few pages in his book to LMS. This gave LMS some outside (of IBM) exposure. Additionally, over the next two years, papers on LMS appeared in a number of other places.

The short term result of event 2 was a series of councils/task forces were put together to determine a strategic direction for scheduling/planning. Gary was

Burlington's representative on many of this councils. This provided an opportunity for AIE to increase its manufacturing knowledge and others inside of IBM to see the quality of their work.

The short term result of this interaction was LMS type features would be included in IBM's strategic floor control system product, Gary would provide advice to the development group, but LMS itself would remain tactical and would be replaced when the new product was completed. As this strategy evolved, it became clear the better approach was to put some LMS features (the build time capabilities and some of the queries) into the new floor control system and rework the rest of LMS (some of MAT and the dispatch decision maker) into a strategic new workstation based module that interacted with the new floor control system.

As a result of 3 and 4, IBM established a customer briefing center in Burlington where customer executives and key technical people would come to Burlington for CIM briefings and discussions and a return program where IBMers travel to customer cites. This provided AIE an opportunity to discuss manufacturing scheduling with executives and technical people from a wide range of industries (semiconductor, military, space shuttle, steel, chemicals, pharmaceuticals, etc).

The net result of the additional exposure LMS and AIE received from other IBM sites and IBM customers was a growing ground swell of demand for LMS to be installed outside Burlington.

A decision was made to make LMS software and consulting from AIE available to other IBM sites and IBM customers on a limited basis.

In June 1992, IBM entered an agreement with Professional Systems Corp. (PSC) (a business partner) giving ownership of the LMS software on the RS/6000 to PSC in return for a portion of future sales (see June 9, 1992 issue of *New York Times*). PSC is responsible for completing the interfaces between different floor control systems and LMS DDM—completing MAT, marketing LMS, and doing the LMS installs. The IBM Management Technologies consulting group is responsible for helping market LMS and the associated consulting that goes with an LMS implementation.

A number of customers and IBM internal cites have already been through the preliminary exploratory consultations and are planning to implement LMS soon.

Additionally, the research and manufacturing communities have become very focused on dispatch over the past few years and produced some very good work. As a result of an NSF workshop on scheduling in October 1992 and some prior meetings in 1992, it is likely some of the growing body of research on "dispatch algorithms" can be made available through the flexible LMS architecture.

AIE is still a small (six people), active, and dynamic group, continuing to pursue the ongoing goal of improving manufacturing performance. It is now focusing on capacity planning (Fordyce & Sullivan, 1993).

17.3 Technical Approach/LMS Components

LMS captures and stores in real-time all manufacturing transactions and maintains and provides access to knowledge bases and models. LMS provides the dispatch decision makers easy and flexible access to (1) relational databases that contain the latest manufacturing transactions, such as the status of a machine, the location of a lot, the due date of a lot, and the availability of an operator; (2) knowledge bases that contain such information such as the characterization of a transaction (is it a lot movement, a change in the status of a machine, or change in an order), the characterization of the lot type (is it a test lot from the lab, a test lot from manufacturing engineering, an express lot for an important order, etc.), the setup required for a lot, setup time, rework requirements, test requirements, alert conditions, product routing, throughput rates, preferred tools, operator training, operator schedules, average down time for a machine, and the calculation of elapsed time (elapsed time would be defined as the calculation present time minus elapsed time with adjustments; adjustments can be made for machine availability, second shift work, a holiday, etc.); (3) models that estimate how far ahead or behind schedule a lot is and the relative priority status of a lot, identify lots with the same setup requirements, determine daily output goals, establish global flow control levels (protective WIP, recommended output from a work cell for the day, and so forth) to guide production and avoid local optimization to the detriment of the global system, and assess the impact of machine dedication; and (4) heuristics to integrate the data, knowledge, and models to identify opportunities.

An overview of the LMS structure is presented in Figure 17-3. Each component is described in the rest of this section.

LMS is written in APL2, PASCAL, and C. Using APL2, AIE built XEN, which serves as the high level object orientated build time and knowledge representation/manipulation environment. For more information on APL2, see Brown, Polivka, & Pakin (1988), Reiter & Jones (1988), and Fordyce *et al.* (1991a, 1991b).

17.3.1 Floor Control Systems (FCS)

Transaction streams from various sources across the site are sent to LMS in real-time. These sources include process control, order booking, release scheduling, preventive maintenance, and engineering changes. Generally, each source has its own language and storage architecture; therefore, individual links and translators exist to each source. LMS ties into existing floor control systems or provides its own.

17.3.2 API/BUILD TIME

The API (application programming interface) is a structured set of minimum data requirements that must be provided to LMS to run the basic dispatch decision

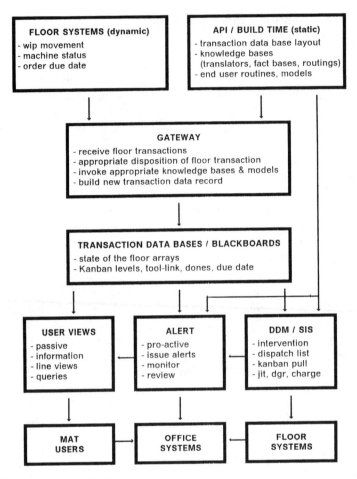

Figure 17-3: Overview of LMS structure

making (DDM) and user query (MAT) modules of LMS. The data required includes, but is not limited to, lot identification, quantity in LOT, report type, current operation, current KANBAN, next operation, next KANBAN, delta to schedule, and resources.

The data requirements can be handled entirely by the FCS or jointly by FCS and the LMS BUILD TIME. For example, the BUILD TIME would enable the user to build a fact base to describe which tools are assigned to which operations. This fact base would be invoked to pass to LMS the resources available to work on the lot that arrives at an operation. With the BUILD TIME, additional data elements can be added to the LMS state arrays.

The BUILD TIME environment provides an easy to use facility to permit the user to describe the information layout of the incoming transaction and "adjustments, additions, and deletions" to be made to the transaction before being stored in the Transaction Data Base. Additionally, BUILD TIME also provides the user an easy method to build knowledge bases (translators, fact bases, routings) and invoke the models needed to "adjust" the transaction and to be used in the INTERVENTION components. The BUILD TIME environment employs the concepts of functions, active variables, and data modeling that enable a change in the information layout to propagate through the entire system automatically.

Details on the API and the BUILD TIME can be found in the LMS/6000 documentation.

17.3.3 GATEWAY

The GATEWAY collects, screens, and categorizes the transaction received by LMS.

It then invokes the appropriate information layout, knowledge bases, and models to generate the appropriate record to store in the TRANSACTION DATA BASE and BLACKBOARDS. There is one transaction record for each lot and one for each machine.

For example, a transaction record indicating that lot 113 has been coated with photoresist is collected. from a knowledge base, LMS obtains information on the amount of time the lot might sit idle before the coating decays, the type of mask it requires, and the preferred photo tool. LMS might also recalculate whether the lot is behind or ahead of schedule.

17.3.4 Transaction Data Base/Blackboard

This component contains relational or tabular databases that contain the status of each tool and lot on the line. Additionally, blackboards for use by the INTERVENTION component are stored here. Examples of blackboard information are KANBAN (WIP) levels, total outs from an operation, and the prior status of a lot or a machine.

17.3.5 User Request (MAT)

MAT (Management Access Technique) provides decision makers with complete real-time visibility to events on the manufacturing floor (tool status, WIP buildup, lot status, due dates, process specifications, operator certification, and so forth). Individuals have the ability to build their own views of the data and penetrate from summary data to detailed data. Views are accessed and manipulated through an interactive and flexible nested window program function (PF) key-driven interface. Some simple examples of MAT are provided in Appendix 3.

Additionally, users can access the information in the transaction databases with an easy to use query-by-example–type query language or a programming language. Information generated in the intervention components ALERT and DDM can be displayed in MAT.

17.3.6 ALERT Manager

This module permits LMS users to write knowledge modules to specify what conditions they want to be alerted about or who they want alerted.

These knowledge modules define conditions requiring an alteration in manufacturing flow that will improve manufacturing performance.

For example, when the transaction record indicating that lot 113 has been coated with photoresist is received, an information record that includes the amount of time the lot might sit idle before the coating decays is put in the information base. A logical alert condition for the operator is to have a yellow flag flashed when half the permitted idle time has passed by. A manager might be very concerned that an important manufacturability test lot is not delayed. Therefore, he or she will ask to be alerted if this lot sits idle for more than 30 minutes at operation 1, 120 minutes at operation 2, ... and if it fails at any of the test points. Examples of other alert conditions are a machine down, a machine not being utilized, a lot behind schedule, a lot in the queue matching the present machine setup, and an express lot being held up.

Alert conditions are displayed through MAT or electronic mail.

17.3.7 Dispatch Decision Maker (DDM)

Having all the **status information** you desire about your manufacturing line does not necessarily imply you are running your operation more efficiently (*Economist,* 1991). To ensure this, the status information has to be used to generate better dispatch decisions.

In this section, we outline the paradigm used in the dispatch scheduling system or decision maker (DDM). Specific implementations vary based on the manufacturing specification.

DDM sets up a **zone of control** around a logical grouping or clustering of tool sets or individual tool sets. This zone of control includes an **IL-KANBAN** (I for intelligent and L for logical) for each level or pass a lot makes through a zone of control. IL-KANBANs exist logically in LMS, not physically on the floor.

In the manufacturing line depicted in Figure 17-4A, there is one product type that has three levels or layers and two zones of control (PHOTO and ION). Therefore, each lot must pass through the PHOTO and ION zones three times, and for each pass, the exact manipulations of the silicon are different. For a specific level, lots always are processed first by PHOTO and then by ION. All incoming WIP or

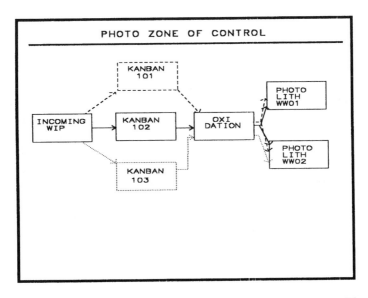

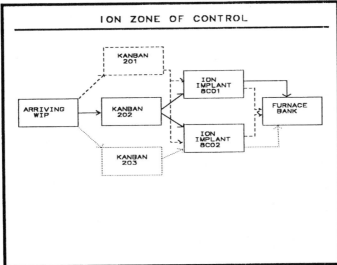

Figure 17-4:   DDM overview: A. Zones of control

lots to the PHOTO are "logically placed" into one of three KANBANs (101, 102, or 103). All incoming WIP or lots to the ION are "logically placed" into one of three KANBANs (201, 202, or 203).

Let's walk through the flow of lots in the example manufacturing line. When a lot is launched or started into our example line, it is processed by a number of non-bottleneck operations and then arrives at the PHOTO zone. Because this is their first pass through PHOTO, they are all "put" in KANBAN 101. Lots in KANBAN 101 are processed by the oxidation tool and then can be processed by either photolithography tool WW01 or WW02. When lots in KANBAN 101 leave PHOTO, they are processed by a number of non-zoned operations (typically, these have excess capacity, and therefore, a first in first out dispatch rule is fine) and then arrive at the ION zone. They are then placed in KANBAN 201. Note KANBAN 201 is fed by KANBAN 101.

Lots in KANBAN 201 are processed by either ion implant tool 8C01 or 8C02 and then processed by the furnace bank. When lots in KANBAN 201 leave ION they are processed by a number of non-zoned operations and then arrive at the PHOTO zone for their second pass through PHOTO. They are then placed in KANBAN 102. Note KANBAN 102 is fed by KANBAN 201. This means KANBAN 102 has a second order dependency in its sister KANBAN 101.

This flow pattern continues: KANBAN 102 into KANBAN 202 into KANBAN 103 into KANBAN 203 into inventory.

Each KANBAN maintains a knowledge base pertinent to the processing of its lots. Some of the information is global to all KANBANs. For example "it knows"

- process routing (for example, KANBAN 203 would know it can only use ION 8C02)
- process specifications' process time for each tool, cycle time multiplier, which is preferred tools, batch size, expiration times, setup costs, lot location, etc.
- changes in tool state (down, busy, available)
- changes in WIP state (into operation, out of operation, logical queue)
- tools presently working on lots from this KANBAN
- the daily outs goal for each KANBAN and the dones to date
- lot due dates and express lots
- strategic and tactical guidelines established by other decision tiers
- upper bound and lower bounds for WIP buildup

The information flow for the DDM is described in Figure 17-4B.

Each KANBAN has an upper control limit (**UCL**) and a lower control limit (**LCL**) for WIP levels based on batch size required for a machine run, the desire to reuse setups, starts, reliability characteristics of the machines, and protect WIP. Based on the WIP level, the KANBAN places a pull/stop signal on its upstream or feeder KANBAN. In our example, KANBAN 102 would place pull and stop signals on KANBAN 201, and KANBAN 201 would place pull and stop signals on

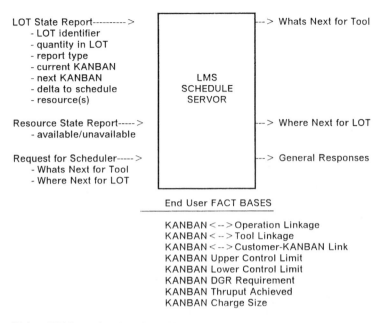

Figure 17-4: DDM overview: B. Information flow

KANBAN 101. As the WIP level approaches the lower bound, the pull signal increases in intensity until it puts out a must have message. As the WIP level approaches the upper bound, the pull signal decreases in intensity until it puts out a no more message. This signaling provides the loose coupling between zones of control.

DDM specifically recognizes four competing goals (on-time delivery, goal outs, downstream needs, and charge size) (Figure 17-4C), placing demands on the dispatch (what to do next) decision. Each of these goals is broken down into a set of transaction data requirements, calculations on that data, a set of fact bases or tables, and a set of heuristic function modules. This combination is called a **goal advocate**. The four advocates are:

Delta Schedule or Serviceability advocate is responsible for ensuring that the percentage of products delivered on time is as high as possible and that express lots move quickly through the line. Express lots are lots deemed by management to require special attention to minimize their process time. They might be lots from the development lab or manufacturing test lots.

To accomplish this, LMS requires that each LOT has a due date for leaving the line and an estimate of the lots XFACTOR. XFACTOR is the ratio between the amount of time the lot spends in the line and the actual raw process time.

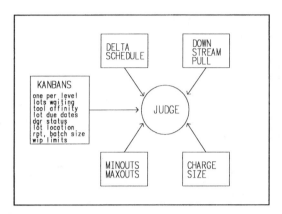

Figure 17-4:   DDM overview: C. Zone decision scheme

For lots made to order and express lots, a due date is given to the LOT when it enters the system and can be updated. For lots made so many out of the line each day, due dates can be assigned by working backward from the end of the line to the beginning to assign due dates to the lot to match required outs. From a pure LMS viewpoint, it does not matter how the due dates and XFACTORs are set, just that they exist. AIE uses models and statistical analysis to assess reasonable due dates and DGRs for LOTs based on manufacturing profile and available capacity. The DGR model is described in Fordyce *et al.* (1992).

LMS uses tables and productions to estimate whether they are ahead of schedule (plus lots) or behind schedule (minus lots). Lots change their plus/minus status because of changes in the lot order status, differences between estimated wait and process times, equipment availability, and the jump step nature of events. The Serviceability Advocate directs manufacturing resources away from those lots that are ahead of schedule to those lots that are behind schedule. It also provides advance notification when it becomes clear a lot will not be delivered by the due date. **It enables the manufacturing organization to move specific lots quickly through the line without bringing the cycle time for all lots down**.

Minimum, Maximum, and Goal Out.   Many semiconductor facilities like to establish a goal number of outs from an operation per day. This is often called a DGR (daily going rate) requirement. Others like to ensure that each operation does a minimum number of wafers each day or set of days. This advocate is concerned that the "outs" requirements are met.

Downstream Pull/Stop.   Each KANBAN sends a pull/stop signal to the zone of control that has its feeder KANBAN. This advocate urges attention to these needs.

For example, as the wafer level for KANBAN 201 drops toward its lower control limit, it increases the intensity of the pull signal it transmits to KANBAN 101. As the wafer level approaches the upper control limit, KANBAN 201 increases the intensity of its stop signal to KANBAN 101. The Pull/Stop advocate is concerned with meeting the needs of its downstream neighbor. This advocate provides the loose coupling coordination between zones of control.

In some implementations, it is necessary for the KANBAN advocate to do a look ahead. This is not to just look at the needs of the KANBAN it feeds but to take a look 3, 5, or 10 KANBANs ahead or at the average need of some downstream set of KANBANs.

With this advocate, one could implement the starvation avoidance concepts from Berkeley (Glassey & Lozinsky, 1988; Glassey & Petrakian, 1989); the release control strategies from Berkeley, MIT, and Stanford (Glassey & Resende, 1988; Wein, 1988; Wein & Chevalier, 1989; Wein, 1992); the hedging strategies from the control theory and dynamic programming community (Gershwin, Bai, & Srivatsan, 1992); or the CONWIP strategy from North Western (Spearman, Woodruff, & Hopp, 1990; Spearman & Hopp, 1991; Spearman & Zazanis, 1992).

The KANBANS serve as an AI vehicle to implement OR concepts (Fordyce, Norden, & Sullivan, 1987).

It also appears logical to have a KANBAN of KANBANs or instead of having the UCL and LCL fixed at a specific number have it specified by a formula that takes into account the total state of the system with emphasis on nearby neighbors (WIP levels and machine status).

Tool Charge, Characteristic, or Utilization Advocate (TUA) is responsible for improving throughput by increasing the availability of tools. This advocate concentrates on increasing machine availability or utilization on bottleneck operations by reducing setup time and exploiting the Weibull reliability characteristics of many pinchpoint machines by building build trains (series of lots that require the same tool setup) for the bottleneck operation in the operations that precede it. It also tries to package lots in the train that have different inspection requirements.

With this advocate, one could implement the dynamic batching concepts from Berkeley (Glassey & Weng, 1991) and others (Lee *et al.*, 1991; Lee, Uzsoy, & Martin-Vega, 1992).

Additionally, this TUA is concerned with avoiding requiring the robot to do two things at once. For example, if we dispatch Lot 1 to the oven, then 150 minutes from now, we will need the Robot to unload both Lot 101 (150 minutes left) and Lot 1 (10 minutes to load and 140 minutes to bake).

Goal advocates can be added and deleted as needed. For example, a fifth advocate might be Engineering Requirements. This advocate might be concerned with directing lots to those tools that engineering believes generate the best yields.

From the user's perspective, when a machine becomes available, each advocate develops an opinion about what action to take next to best achieve its goal. The opinion includes not just its wish about what to do next but the severity of the need and the impact of alternative choices. This opinion or view is communicated to the **Judge**. This judge makes a decision about what to do next that is in the best global interest of the facility.

The ultimate expression of each advocate is a numeric ranking or score for each lot queued in front of the available machine. Depending on the nature of the implementation, the advocate might provide a single summary score or a set of scores corresponding to categories of interest for each waiting lot.

A simplified example of processing or judging the rankings is as follows: Assume we have three advocates, a machine becomes available, and five lots are waiting to be serviced. Each advocate generates a ranking, or score, between 0 and 1. A 0 indicates a veto against assigning the lot to the machine. A 1 indicates a must-have situation. Values between 0 and 1 are of relative importance. This information can be stored in a 3×5 matrix called SCOREMAT (one row for each advocate, one column for each lot). The decision rules follow:

1. If a lot is vetoed (0) by one advocate, it is automatically dropped as a potential selection.
2. If a lot is designated a must (1), it is chosen, unless another lot is also designated a must.
3. If there are no must lots, then the lot with the highest average score is chosen.
4. If two or more lots are designated as must lots, then the lot with the highest average score is chosen.

The goal advocate approach or paradigm has very strong roots in adaptive cybernetic decision systems (Fordyce, Griesinger, & Sullivan, 1985), APL as a notation for thought (Iverson, 1962, 1980), the U.S. legal system, goal programming with or without pre-emptive priorities, and the integration of AI and OR decision technologies (Fordyce, Norden, & Sullivan, 1987; Simon, 1987). Aspects of this approach overlap with, and draw on, fuzzy sets and logic, game playing heuristics for Chess (Byrne, 1989) and Backgammon, multiattribute decision making, truth maintenance systems, blackboarding, and model based reasoning.

17.4 KNOWLEDGE REPRESENTATION AND USE IN LMS

The representation, storage, and manipulation of knowledge (see Fordyce, Norden, & Sullivan [1989] for our definition of knowledge and knowledge based systems) are an important part of each major component of LMS. Examples of the use of knowledge in the GATEWAY include characterizing a transaction (is it a lot movement, a change in status of a machine, a change in an order), converting a field stored in HEX to a character, and calculating elapsed time. Elapsed time would be defined as the calculation present time minus elapsed time with adjustments. Adjustments can be made for machine availability, second shift work, a holiday, etc. In MAT, knowledge about the relationships between operations is used to structure a view, and knowledge about the relationships between data fields is used provide assistance in making queries. In ALERT, knowledge is used to specify a situation that requires the attention of a decision maker. For example, if the machine xx is idle for more than 30 minutes during regular shift hours, then alert the floor supervisor. Examples of the use of knowledge in the LMS SCHEDULER include what the setup is that is required for a lot at a specific iteration, what the machine preferences are, how to calculate lower and upper bounds on the time needed to complete a wafer, how to identify lots requiring the same setup, and how to choose between conflicting goals.

In LMS, a variety of techniques are used to represent, store, and manipulate knowledge. In each case, the underlying theme is a function-object representation of knowledge (FORK) scheme. This approach uses the object orientated programming concepts of avoiding data type dependencies, linking data and procedure to generate a "natural" object, and being robust to change. Additionally, FORK draws on concepts from functional programming languages (such as APL2 and LISP) and mathematical function notation. A detailed description of FORK can be found in Fordyce *et al.* (1991a).

17.4.1 Fact Bases and Program Modules as Functions

Functions are a description of a mapping between one set of independent (input) variables and a dependent (output) variable. For each set of input variable values, there is a mapping into only one output variable value. Different input variable value sets can map into the same out variable value. The set of possible input variable value sets is called the domain. The set of possible output variable values is called the range. The reader is probably most familar with functions where the mapping description is expressed as an algebraic equation, and the domain and range are numbers; for example, $W = 2X + 4Y$.

Fact Bases or **Tables** represent a tabular representation of a functional relation between input and output variables, where the domains and ranges are a finite set of elements. **PMs** are small programming modules used to describe functional relationships that carry out standard conditional logic and computation on the input variables to generate the output variables. The linkages between functions represent composite function operations.

An example set of functions is

FACT BASE 1 (F1)

CHIPTYPE	STAGE	-> SETUP
tiger	1	3
tiger	2	2
lion	1	4
lion	2	4

FACT BASE 2 (F2)

SETUP	-> SETUP_TIME
2	20
3	20
4	50

FACT BASE 3 (F3)

CHIPTYPE	SETUP	-> PROCESS_TIME
tiger	2	60
tiger	3	50
tiger	4	NA
lion	2	NA
lion	3	NA
lion	4	60

PROCEDURE MODULE 1 (PM1)

```
∇PM1 [□]∇
    ∇
[0]    PM1
[1]    ⍝ THIS FUNCTION DETERMINES
[2]    ⍝ THE APPROPRIATE SETUP CONDITION
[3]    ⍝
[4]    ⍝ VALUE CALCULATED (OUTPUT VARIABLE):   SETUP_COND
[5]    ⍝
[6]    ⍝ POSSIBLE OPTIONS FOR OUTPUT VARIABLE: LONG
[7]    ⍝                                       SHORT
[8]    ⍝
[9]    ⍝ VALUES USED      ( INPUT VARIABLE): SETUP_TIME
[10]   ⍝                                     PROCESS_TIME
[11]   SETUP_COND←⊂'LONG'
[12]   CONDS←(SETUP_TIME<25),(SETUP_TIME<4×PROCESS_TIME)
[13]   →(∧/CONDS)/L010
[14]   →0
[15]   L010:
[16]   SETUP_COND←⊂'SHORT'
[17]   →0
```

Fact Base 1 is the mapping between the input variables CHIPTYPE and STAGE into the output variable SETUP. Fact Base 2 is the mapping between the input variable SETUP into the output variable SETUP_TIME. Fact Base 3 is the mapping between the input variables CHIPTYPE and SETUP into the output variable PROCESS_TIME. PM 1 is the mapping between the input variables SETUP_TIME and PROCESS_TIME into the output variable SETUP_COND.

These relationships can be written in the following functional notation:

```
SETUP = F1(CHIPTYPE, STAGE)
SETUP_TIME = F2(SETUP)
PROCESS_TIME = F3(CHIPTYPE,SETUP)
SETUP_COND = PM1(SETUP_TIME,PROCESS_TIME)
```

The concept of a composite function exists with our fact bases (table) and procedure module method of describing functions.

For example, the functional relationship between the input variables CHIPTYPE and STAGE and the output variable SETUP_TIME can be found using Fact Base 1 and Fact Base 2 and viewing the variable SETUP as an intermediate output variable:

```
SETUP_TIME = FC1(CHIPTYPE,STAGE) = F1 ° F2
```

The concept of "algebraic simplification" can sometimes be done by generating a new fact base. The composite function FC1 would result in the following table:

FACT BASE COMPOSITE 1 (FC1)

CHIPTYPE	STAGE	-> SETUP_TIME
tiger	1	20
tiger	2	20
lion	1	50
lion	2	50

In APL2, tables map directly into two dimensional general arrays. Fact Base 1 can be generated with the following statement:

```
F1← 4 3 ρ 'TIGER' 1 3 'TIGER' 2 2 'LION' 1 4 'LION' 2 4
```

F1 is a matrix with a shape (ρ) of four rows and three columns. The matrix is filled in row by row (row major).

APL2 provides indexing into any portion of the matrix and a variety of comparison operations. The following statement will access column 1 and check if any element in column 1 is equal to LION:

```
COL1← F1 [;1]
```

The variable COL1 is assigned the values in column 1 of F1. This statement stores the values in column 1 of F1 in the variable COL1. COL1 is a vector with four elements:

$$MATCH1 \leftarrow (\subset 'LION') \equiv COL1$$

This statement matches ($\equiv$) the character string LION against each element in the variable COL1. MATCH1 is a vector with four elements, one for each member of COL1. An element of MATCH1 gets a 1 if the corresponding element of COL1 has LION, else a 0. MATCH1 is 0 0 1 1

In APL2, a PM can be executed at any time with the execute primitive (ϕ). The commands $\Box_EA$ and $\Box_EC$ permit the "protected" execution of a PM.

17.4.2 The Network of Functions

Using the following two Boolean arrays and some Boolean array primitives in APL2, we can determine how the different functions relate to one another.

The *first item* generated is a Boolean matrix called INMATIP (IP is for INPUT). This matrix records which variables are input variables for which functions. INMATIP has one row for each variable and one column for each function (fact base or procedure module). A cell gets a 1 if the variable is in the "input portion" of a function, else a 0. For this example, INMATIP would be

	T1	T2	T3	P1
CHIPTYPE	1	0	1	0
STAGE	1	0	0	0
SETUP	0	1	1	0
SETUP_TIME	0	0	0	1
PROCESS_TIME	0	0	0	1
SETUP_COND	0	0	0	0

The *second item* generated is a Boolean matrix called INMATOP (OP is for OUTPUT). This matrix records which variables are output variables for which functions. INMATOP has one row for each variable and one column for each function (fact base or procedure module). A cell gets a 1 if the variable is in the "output portion" of a function, else a 0. For this example, INMATOP would be

	T1	T2	T3	P1
CHIPTYPE	0	0	0	0
STAGE	0	0	0	0
SETUP	1	0	0	0
SETUP_TIME	0	1	0	0
PROCESS_TIME	0	0	1	0
SETUP_COND	0	0	0	1

With these two arrays, we can determine that the variable SETUP_TIME is a function of the variables CHIPTYPE and STAGE through the intermediate variable SETUP. The following APL2 expression will give us this information:

```
INMATVAR ← INMATOP ∨.∧ ϕ INMATIP
W1 ← INMATVAR
W2← W1 ∨.∧ INMATVAR
```

The function ϕ generates a transposition of the matrix INMATIP. ϕ INMATIP:

```
1 1 0 0 0 0
0 0 1 0 0 0
1 0 1 0 0 0
0 0 0 1 1 0
```

INMATVAR is

	CHIP TYPE	STAGE	SETUP	SETUP _TIME	PROCESS _TIME	SETUP _COND
CHIPTYPE	0	0	0	0	0	0
STAGE	0	0	0	0	0	0
SETUP	1	1	0	0	0	0
SETUP_TIME	0	0	1	0	0	0
PROCESS_TIME	1	0	1	0	0	0
SETUP_COND	0	0	0	1	1	0

In INMATVAR, there is one row and one column for each variable in the system. Rows reference an out condition. Columns reference an input condition. INMATVAR shows "first order" dependencies between variables. If a variable is a direct input variable to an output variable, then that cell has the value 1. If not, the value is 0. For example, CHIPTYPE and STAGE are direct input variables to the variable SETUP through T1. Therefore, the cells (SETUP, CHIPTYPE) and (SETUP, STAGE) have the value 1.

The operator dot (.) carries out the inner product operation. The APL expression +.f is the primitive for matrix multiplication. The element in the first row and first column of W is obtained as follows:

```
The first row of INMATOP is:        0 0 0 0
The first column of ϕ INMATIP is:   1 0 1 0
We then "and"
   (∧) element by element.
This results in:                    0 0 0 0
```

We then "or" (∨) across the resulting vector. This results in a 0.

The element in the third row and first column of W is obtained as follows:

```
The third row of INMATOP is:        1 0 0 0
The first column of φ INMATIP is:    1 0 1 0
We then "and"
    (∧) element by element.
This results in:                     1 0 0 0
```

We then "or" (∨) across the resulting vector. This results in a 1.

W2 is

	CHIP TYPE	STAGE	SETUP	SETUP _TIME	PROCESS _TIME	SETUP _COND
CHIPTYPE	0	0	0	0	0	0
STAGE	0	0	0	0	0	0
SETUP	0	0	0	0	0	0
SETUP_TIME	1	1	0	0	0	0
PROCESS_TIME	1	1	0	0	0	0
SETUP_COND	1	0	1	0	0	0

In W2, there is one row and one column for each variable in the system. Rows reference an out condition. Columns reference an input condition. W2 shows "second order" dependencies between variables. If a variable is a second order input variable to an output variable, then that cell has the value 1. If not, the value is 0. For example, CHIPTYPE and STAGE are second order input variables to the variable SETUP_TIME. SETUP_TIME depends directly on SETUP (F2). SETUP depends directly on CHIPTYPE and STAGE (F1). Therefore, SETUP_TIME has a second order dependency on CHIPTYPE and STAGE (F2 to F1). Therefore, the cells (SETUP_TIME, CHIPTYPE) and (SETUP_TIME, STAGE) have the value 1.

Using a slightly more complicated set of Boolean operations, we can generate an ordering of the functions based on "relative independence." To explain "relative independence," let's look at an example. You have the equations

```
VOLUME = AREA x HT (eq 1)
PERIMETER = (2 x LENGTH) + (2 x WIDTH) (eq 2)
AREA = LENGTH x WIDTH (eq 3)
HEATING COST = 4 x VOLUME (eq 4)
```

You need to execute equation 1 before equation 4 and equation 3 before equation 1.

We could view equations 2 and 3 as making up the most independent group or class of rules because their input variables (LENGTH and WIDTH) are not calculated by any other equation. Equation 1 would be in the second group or class because its input variables are either not calculated by another equation (HT) or are calculated by an equation already ordered (AREA). Equation 4 would make up the third group.

For our example, the functions are ordered as follows:

```
CLASS 1: F1
CLASS 2: F2 F3
CLASS 3: PM1
```

This kind of information is particularly useful in debugging, firing more than one function per inference cycle, and resolving conflict.

17.4.3 Integrating FORK and Transactions

In the following example, we illustrate how FORKs are integrated with the LOT tracking database and the transaction stream.

In our manufacturing facility, we have lots that we process, operations that we do to the lots, and machines that carry out the operations. For each lot that is launched into the manufacturing stream, we keep the following information:

LOT TRACKING DATA BASE						
LOT_ID	LOT_FAMILY	OPR_FAMILY	PRIORITY	MASK	EST_LV	SETUP_TIME
11129	tiger	bend				
11130	tiger					
11132	lion					

When a lot is launched into production, the first two variables (LOT_ID and LOT_FAMILY) in the record are given values. The value for the variable OPR_FAMILY is changed in the record each time the lot enters a new manufacturing operation. All the other fields are generated from one of the following function-objects:

```
               FACT BASE 4 (F4)

       LOT_FAMILY   -> PRIORTY  -> MASK

           tiger              5     brown
           lion              10     blue
```

```
               FACT BASE 5 (F5)

       OPR_FAMILY     -> MACH_FAMILY

           bend                  xxx
           bake                  yyy
           test                  zzz
```

```
┌─────────────────────────────────────────────────┐
│                                                 │
│              FACT BASE 6 (F6)                   │
│                                                 │
│      MACH_FAMILY      -> SETUP_TIME             │
│      ─────────────────────────────             │
│             xxx             2                   │
│             yyy             1                   │
│             zzz             3                   │
│                                                 │
└─────────────────────────────────────────────────┘
```

```
┌─────────────────────────────────────────────────┐
│                                                 │
│                     PM2                         │
│                                                 │
│      output variable: EST_LV                    │
│                                                 │
│      input variable:   PRIORITY                 │
│                        OPR_FAMILY               │
│                                                 │
│      this procedure module                      │
│      estimates the expected time                │
│      the lot will leave the operation           │
│      where it is presently located              │
│                                                 │
└─────────────────────────────────────────────────┘
```

These relationships can be written in the following functional notation:

```
PRIORITY      = F4 (LOT_FAMILY)
MASK          = F4 (LOT_FAMILY)
EST_LV        = PM3 (PRIORITY, OPR_FAMILY)
MACH_FAMILY   = F5 (OPR_FAMILY)
SETUP_TIME    = F6 (MACH_FAMILY)
```

The values for **PRIORITY** and **MASK** are obtained from F4 when the lot is launched. Because lot 11129 belongs to the FAMILY tiger, it has a PRIORITY value 5 and a MASK value brown.

The value for SETUP_TIME is obtained from F5 and F6 each time the lot enters a new operation. From F5, we obtain the MACHINE used in the operation. Then we obtain the SETUP_TIME for that machine from F6. For lot 11129 entering the bend operation, MACHINE is xxx, and SETUP_TIME is 2.

The value for EST_LV is obtained from executing PM1.

The lot file now has the following record for LOT 11129:

LOT TRACKING DATA BASE						
LOT_ID	LOT_FAMILY	OPR_FAMILY	PRIORITY	MASK	EST_LV	SETUP_TIME
11129	tiger	bend	5	brown	300	2
11130	tiger					
11132	lion					

Notes and Observations. The production environment at Burlington is changing constantly. Tools are added, engineering places new requirements on production, product demand changes, new product families are phased in and old ones phased out, and so forth. To continue its success, LMS needs to be altered rapidly by users to stay current with the production environment. A static system or a system that relies on programmers to make changes stands no chance of success in dynamic production environments like the one at Burlington.

A team that varied between four and six people developed LMS over two years. Some of the team members had strong backgrounds in manufacturing, some were industrial engineers with only a few years of experience, and some were experienced in developing and implementing decision support systems for complex problems. Only two people did programming. During these two years, the system moved from a limited implementation with a few users to a full implementation with over 400 users.

Closed queuing systems like Burlington's will become as chaotic and disorderly as possible, subject only to the restraints imposed by their own structures (Chedzey, Holmes, & Soysal, 1976). LMS generates an additional level of structure or control at the dispatch level to improve performance by "reducing chaos" and shifting the cycle time/tool utilization curve. It makes no claim to optimize, and we do not consider optimization a legitimate goal.

Everyone, from the plant manager to the line technicians to IBM's CIM marketing group to IBM customers (Feigenbaum, McCorduck, & Nii, 1988; IBM, 1988, 1989, 1990; Wickman, 1989; Fordyce & Sullivan, 1990), considers LMS a success.

ACKNOWLEDGMENTS

Thanks to the LMS team: Ray Dunki-Jacobs, April Embree, Dick Sell, Steve Gaskins, Reggie Edwards, Rick Fletcher, Bill Frank, Marilyn Boyle, Barry Gerard, Gerald Sullivan, Kenneth Fordyce, Don Cobb, David DesRoches, Roy Jones, Rick Jesse, and Bill Ramus.

Thanks also to some significant others: Tom Henry, Bill Brueckner, Mary Ann Westover, Lee Dusa, Roger Riley, Nancy Murphy, Dave Domina, Dale Dalton Linda Chicoine, Maurice Gaboriault, Don Bradley, Norbie Lavigne, Jim Picciano, Bob Bray, Bob Wickman, and Ken Maynard.

References

Acock, M., and R. Zelmel. 1986. "DISPATCHER: AI Software for Automated Material Handling Systems," presented at ULTRATECH: Manufacturing Automation Protocol, Artificial Intelligence in Manufacturing, Automated Guided Vehicles, Long Beach, CA, 9/22–25.

Ahmadi, J., and R. Ahmadi. 1990. "Information and Optimization Problems of Electronic Board Assembly," IBM STD, Austin, TX.

Anderson, K., D. Coleman, R. Haill, A. Jaworski, P. Love, D. Spindler, and M. Simann. 1989. "Knowledge Based Statistical Process Control," *Innovative Applications of Artificial Intelligence*, edited by H. Schorr and A. Rappaport, pp. 169–182. AAAI Press, Menlo Park, CA.

Bitran, G., and D. Tirupati. 1989. "Tradeoff Curves, Targeting and Balancing in Manufacturing Networks," *Operations Research*, Vol. 37, No. 4, pp. 547–565.

Bobrow, D. 1991. "AAAI-90 Presidential Address: Dimensions of Interaction," *AI Magazine*, Vol. 12, No. 3, pp 64–80.

Brown, J., S. Pakin, and R. Polivka. 1988. *APL2 at a Glance*, Prentice-Hall, Englewood, NJ.

Byrne, R. 1989. "Chess Playing Computer Closing in on Champions," *New York Times*, Tuesday, September 26, Section 3 (Science) pp. 1, 12.

Chedzey, D., D. Holmes, and M. Soysal. 1976. "System Entropy of Markov Chains," *General Systems*, Vol. 21, pp. 73–85.

Chen, H., M. Harrison, A. Mandelbaum, A. Ackere, and L. Wein. 1988. "Empirical Evaluation of a Queuing Network Model for Semiconductor Wafer Fabrication," *Operations Research*, Vol. 36, No. 2, pp. 202–215.

Dayhoff, J., and R. Atherton. 1987. "A Model for Wafer Fabrication Dynamics in Integrated Circuit Manufacturing," *IEEE Transactions on Systems, Man, and Cybernetics*, Vol. SMC-17, No. 1, pp. 91–100.

Duchessi, P., S. Belardo, and J. Seagle. 1988. "Knowledge Enhancements to a Decision Support System for Vehicle Routing," *Interfaces*, Vol. 18, No. 2, pp. 29–36.

Economist. 1991a. "Artificial Intelligence—Brain Teasers," *Economist*, Vol. 320, No. 7720, pp. 62–63.

Economist. 1991b. "Too Many Computers Spoil the Broth," *Economist*, Vol. 320, No. 7721, pp. 30.

Economist. 1992. "High Cost of Late Deliveries—Manufacturing Management: I Want It Now," *Economist*, Vol. 323, No. 7763, pp. 78, 83.

Epp, H., M. Kalin, and D. Miller. 1989. "An Interactive Adaptive Real-time Scheduler for Steel Making," *Proceedings of the Third International Conference: Expert Systems and the Leading Edge in Production and Operations Management*, edited by K. Karwan and J. Swiegart, pp. 495–503.

Feigenbaum, E., P. McCorduck, and P. Nii. 1988. *The Rise of the Expert Company: How Visionary Companies Are Using Expert Systems to Make Huge Profits*, Times Books, New York.

Fordyce, K., and G. Sullivan. 1983. "A Self Programming Decision Support System," *Third IBM Manufacturing Modeling Conference*, June 3-5, 1983, Boulder, CO.

Fordyce, K., and G. Sullivan. 1989. "Logistics Management System (LMS): Implementing the Technology of Logistics with Knowledge Based Expert Systems," *Innovative Expert System Applications*, A. Schorr & A. Rappaport, (eds.) AAAI Press, Menlo Park, CA pp. 183–202.

Fordyce K., and G. Sullivan. 1990a. "Cycle Time versus Machine Utilization: Moving along the Curve versus Shifting the Curve," TR 21.1440, IBM, Kingston, NY.

Fordyce, K., and G. Sullivan. 1990b. "IBM Burlington's Logistics Management System (LMS)," *Interfaces*, Vol. 20, No. 1, pp. 43–61.

Fordyce, K., and G. Sullivan. 1993. "Capacity Planning with Goal Programming and Function Networks," Presented at Spring ORSA/TIMS meeting, Chicago, May.

Fordyce, K., D. Griesinger, and G. Sullivan. 1985. "ACDS: Adaptive Cybernetic Decision System," Working Paper, 34EA/284, IBM, Kingston, NY.

Fordyce, K., P. Norden, and G. Sullivan. 1987. "Links between Operations Research and Expert Systems," *Interfaces*, Vol. 17, No. 4, pp. 34–40.

Fordyce, K., P. Norden, and G. Sullivan. 1989. "Artificial Intelligence and the Management Science Practitioner: Expert Systems—One Definition of Knowledge Based Expert Systems," *Interfaces*, Vol. 19, No. 5, pp. 66–70.

Fordyce, K., G. Sullivan, and T. Sullivan. 1990. "The Two Penny Model for Man Power Planning or Non-linear and Discrete Function between Number of Operators and Production," *IBM POMS*, 33VA/284, Kingston, NY.

Fordyce, K., J. Jantzen, M. Morreale, and G. Sullivan. 1991. "Using Boolean Matrices or Integer Vectors to Analyze Networks," *APL Quote Quad*, Vol. 21, No. 4, pp. 174–185.

Fordyce, K., J. Jantzen, G. Sullivan, Sr., and G. Sullivan, Jr. 1989. "Representing Knowledge with Functions and Boolean Arrays," *IBM Journal of Research and Development*, Vol. 33, No. 6., pp. 627–646.

Fordyce, K., M. Morreale, J. McGrew, and G. Sullivan. 1991. "Knowledge Based Techniques in APL," *Encyclopedia of Computer Science and Technology*, edited by Allen Kent and James William, Marcus Decker, NY, pp. 345–378.

Fordyce, K., R. Dunki-Jacobs, B. Gerard, R. Sell, and G. Sullivan. 1992. "Logistics Management System (LMS): An Advanced Decision Support System for the Fourth Decision Tier Dispatch or Short Interval Scheduling," *Production and Operations Management*, Vol. 1, No. 1, pp. 70–86.

Fordyce, K., D. Dalton, B. Gerard, R. Jesse, R. Sell, and G. Sullivan. 1992. "Daily Output Planning: Integrating Operations Research, Artificial Intelligence, & Real-time Data with APL2," in *Expert Systems with Applications*, Vol. 5, pp. 245–256. Pergamon Press, NY.

Fowler, J. 1992. "Issues in Semiconductor MFG Scheduling," presented at Workshop on Hierarchical Control for Real-Time Scheduling and Manufacturing Systems, October 16–18, Lincoln, NH.

Galbraith, J. 1973. *Designing Complex Organizations*, Addison-Wesley, Reading, MA.

Gershwin, S., S. Bai, and N. Srivatsan. 1992. "Hierarchical Real-Time Integrated Scheduling of a Semiconductor Fabrication Facility," *Control and Dynamic Systems,* edited by C.T. Leondes. Academic Press, NY.

Glassey, C., and C. Lozinsky. 1988. "Bottleneck Starvation Indicators for Shop Floor Control," *IEEE Transactions on Semiconductor Manufacturing*, Vol. 1, No. 4, pp. 147–153.

Glassey, C., and R. Petrakian. 1989. "The Use of Bottleneck Starvation Avoidance with Queue Predictions in Shop Floor Control," *Proceedings of the 1989 Winter Simulation Conference*. The Society for Computer Simulation, San Diego, CA.

Glassey, C., and M. Resende. 1988. "Closed Loop Job Release Control for VLSI Circuit Manufacturing," *IEEE Transactions on Semiconductor Manufacturing*, Vol. 1, No. 1, pp. 36–46.

Glassey, C., and W. Weng. 1991. "Dynamic Batching Heuristic for Simultaneous Processing," *IEEE Transactions on Semiconductor Manufacturing*, Vol. 4, No. 2, pp. 77–82.

Graves, S., H. Meal, D. Stefek, and A. Zeghmi. 1983. "Scheduling of Re-entrant Flow Shops," *Journal of Operations Management*, Vol. 3, pp. 197–203.

Gribbin, J. 1984. "Chapter on the Mighty Micro," *In Search of Schrodinger's Cat,* pp. 137–142. Bantam Books, New York.

IBM. 1988a. "Burlington's 1987 Accomplishments," *IBM Burlington Closeup*, p. 3. IBM Communications Operations Department, General Technology Division, Essex Junction, VT.

IBM. 1988b. *From Sand to Semiconductors*, IBM Technology Marketing Support Center, General Technology Division, Essex Junction, VT.

IBM. 1989. "Burlington 1988 Key Achievements," *IBM Burlington Closeup*, p. 4. IBM Communications Operations Department, General Technology Division, Essex Junction, VT.

IBM. 1990. "Decision Making, Scheduling, and Running the Line (announcement of outstanding technical achievement awards)," *IBM Burlington Today*, p. 1. Communications Operations Department, General Technology Division, Essex Junction, VT.

Iverson, K. 1962. *A Programming Language*, John Wiley and Sons, NY.

Iverson, K. 1980. "1979 ACM Turing Award Lecture: Notation as a Tool for Thought," *Communications of the ACM*, Vol. 23, No. 8, pp. 444–465.

Jain, S., K. Barber, and D. Osterfeld. 1990. "Expert Simulation for On-line Scheduling," *Communications of the ACM*, Vol. 33, No. 10, pp. 54–62.

Kempf, K. 1989. "Manufacturing Scheduling: Intelligently Combining Existing Methods," *Working Notes of AAAI AI in Manfacturing Symposium*, edited by M. Fox, AAAI Press, Menlo Park, CA.

Kempf, K., Y. Chee, and G. Scott. 1988. "Artificial Intelligence and the Scheduling of Semiconductor Wafer Fabrication Facilities," *SIGMAN Newsletter*, Vol. 1, No. 1, pp. 2–3.

Leachman, R., and T. Carmon. 1992. "On Capacity Modeling for Production Planning with Alternative Machines," *Types*, *IEEE Transactions*, Vol. 24, No. 4, pp. 62–72. Berkeley, CA.

Lee C., R. Uzsoy, L. Martin-Vega, and P. Leonard. 1991. "Production Scheduling Algorithms for a Semiconductor Test Facility," *IEEE Transactions on Semiconductor Manufacturing*, Vol. 4, pp. 271–280.

Lee C., R. Uzsoy, and L. Martin-Vega. 1992. "Efficient Algorithms for Scheduling Semiconductor Burn-In Operations," *Operations Research*, Vol. 40, No. 4, pp. 764–775.

Miller, D. 1990. "Simulation of a Semiconductor Manufacturing Line," *Communications of the ACM*, Vol. 33, No. 10, pp. 98–108.

Minnich, H., and H. Bula. 1985. "Closeup: Manufacturing Control System at IBM Tracks Product Movement through Semiconductor Line," *Industrial Engineering*, Vol. 17, No. 11, pp. 82–90.

Morris, R., B. Ekroot, L. Rubin, B. Samadi, and W. Wong. 1989. "The Operations Assistant: A New Class of Resource Managment Tools for Manufacturing," AT&T Bell Laboratories, Holmdel, NJ.

Numao, M., and S. Morishita. 1989. "A Scheduling Environment for Steel-Making Processes," *Proceedings of the Fifth IEEE Conference on AI Applications*, pp. 279–286, IEEE Computer Society Press, Los Alamitos, CA.

Reiter, C., and W. Jones. 1988. *APL with a Mathematical Accent*, Wasworth & Brooks/Cole, Pacific Grove, CA.

Savell, D., R. Perez, and S. Koh. 1989. "Scheduling Semiconductor Wafer Production: An Expert System Implementation," *IEEE Expert*, Vol. 4, No. 3, pp. 9–15.

Sequeda, F. 1985. "Integrated Circuit Fabrication—A Process Overview," *Journal of Metals*, May, pp. 43–50.

Shortliffe, E., C. Langlotz, L. Fagan, S. Tu, B. Sikic, and E. Shortliffe. 1987. "A Therapy Planning Architecture That Combines Decision Theory and Artificial Intelligence Techniques," *Computers and Biomedical Research*, Vol. 20, pp. 279–303.

Simon, H. 1987. "Two Heads Are Better Than One: The Collaboration between Artificial Intelligence and Operations Research," Keynote and plenary address at National ORSA/TIMS meeting, October 27–29, Miami, Florida. Also in 1987, *Interfaces*, Vol. 17, No. 4, pp. 8–15.

Spearman, M., and W. Hopp. 1991. "Throughput of a Constant Work in Process Manufacturing Line Subject to Failures," *International Journal of Prod. Res.*, Vol. 29, No. 3, pp. 635–655.

Spearman, M., and M. Zazanis. 1992. "Push and Pull Production Systems—Issues and Comparisons," *Operations Research*, Vol. 40, No. 3, pp. 521–532.

Spearman, M., D. Woodruff, and W. Hopp. 1990. "CONWIP: A Pull Alternative to Kanban," *International Journal of Prod. Res.*, Vol. 28, No. 5, pp. 879–894.

Sze, S. 1988. *VLSI Technology,* Second Ed., McGraw-Hill, NY.

Thomson, N. 1990. "Short Term Scheduling in the Face of Uncertainty," Presented at IBM Manufacturing Symposium, September 4, 1990. Thornwood, NY.

Wein, L. 1988. "Scheduling Semiconductor Wafer Fabrication," *IEEE Transactions on Semiconductor Manufacturing*, Vol. 1, No. 3., pp. 115–130.

Wein, L. 1992. "Scheduling Networks of Queues: Heavy Traffic Analysis of a Multistation Network with Controllable Inputs," *Operations Research*, Vol. 40, No. 2 (supplement), pp. S312–S334.

Wein, L., and P. Chevalier. 1989. "A Broader View of the Job-Shop Scheduling Problem," Massachusetts Institute of Technology, Sloan School.

Wickman, R. 1989. "IBM Logistics Management System/DOS Announcement," IBM, Endicott, NY.

Woolsey, G. 1991. "On Inexpert Systems and Natural Intelligence in Military Operations," *Interfaces*, Vol. 21, No. 4, pp. 2–10.

APPENDIX 1: DECISION SUPPORT HIERARCHY

- **PASSIVE DATA**
  - No focus on the decisions being supported

- ○ Numerous and generic individual databases
- ○ No real-time retrieval
- ○ Only gross view available
- ○ Ad hoc paper fed deterministic models

- **MANAGMENT INFORMATION SYSTEM**
  - ○ Some focus on the decisions being supported
  - ○ Organized description of problem elements
  - ○ Some real-time retrieval
  - ○ Reasonably flexible batch reports generated by programs
  - ○ Better integration of deterministic models

- **DECISION SUPPORT SYSTEMS**
  - ○ Strong focus on the decisions being supported
  - ○ Decisions as the primary design guide for the data, the models, and their integration
  - ○ Real-time, flexible, and easy access to databases via user defined views
    - ○ logical relationships between data
    - ○ integration of different data sources
    - ○ status information
    - ○ penetration from summary to detail across some logical path
    - ○ flexible end user interface for queries
  - ○ Easy access to models that help evaluate alternative courses of action
    - ○ linkage between data and models
    - ○ linkage between models

- **PROACTIVE INTERVENTION ALERT**
  - ○ Automated watching of events and alerts based on analysis and priorities
  - ○ Ability of end user to specify alert conditions
  - ○ Explanations
  - ○ Dynamic and adaptive

- **PROACTIVE INTERVENTION ACTION**

- o Corrective action recommended or taken
- o Based on analysis and priorities
- o Generation of alternatives
- o Portrayal of consequences of alternatives
- o Judgments made
- o Explanations
- o Dynamic and adaptive

APPENDIX 2: OVEN DISPATCH EXAMPLE

This appendix and Figure 17-2 describe a simplified dispatch situation for semiconductor manufacturing that we use throughout the chapter.

Wafers move around in groups of 25 called a lot. All wafers in the lot are of the same type. Each lot must pass through the oven operation 10 times. Each Oven set is composed of four ovens or tubes and one robot to load and unload the oven. It takes about 10 minutes to load or unload an oven. The process time in the oven depends on the iteration. We will assume one lot to an oven at a time. Before a wafer enters the oven, it must be coated. The coating process takes 20 minutes. The coating expires in four hours. If the coating expires, the wafer must be stripped, cleaned, and recoated. This process takes four hours and often generates yield losses.

APPENDIX 3: EXAMPLES OF MAT VIEWS

In the following display, a user has loaded a view called DEVINSP and requested wafer and lot totals at each operation. The user inputs the name of the view he wants and then presses program function (PF) key 1. A view is a previously established description of the portion of the line of interest to the user. There is one window on the screen for each operation the user wanted information on. In this case, the view contains four operations: DEVELOP INSPECT, AMEX INSPECT, ANT INSPECT, and HOT LOT INSPECT. The user then presses PF key 6 to get wafer and lot totals:

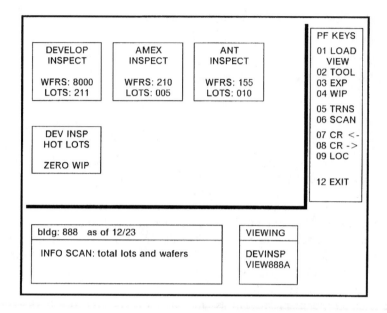

Seeing a high number of lots at the DEVELOP INSPECT operation, the user might then request the status of each machine in the DEVELOP INSPECT operation. The user makes this request by depressing PF KEY 2:

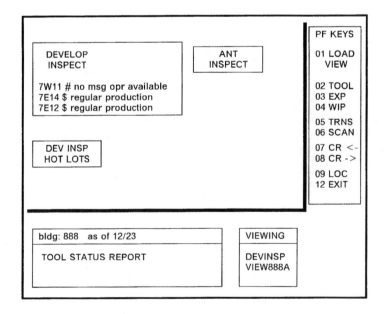

He or she might then request summary information on the status of each lot waiting for service at DEVELOP INSPECT. The user requests this information by depressing PF KEY 4:

```
DEVELOP
INSPECT
PRI    TECH  LOT        DATE      TIME      ETIME
444    AF1   W4001122   10/22     11:19     1.3
434    AF1   W5003311   10/21     22:31     6.7

---    ---   --------   -----     -----     ---
---    ---   --------   -----     -----     ---
---    ---   --------   -----     -----     ---

334    TW1   W5010001   10/20     12:31     100.3
```

```
bldg: 888   as of 12/23        VIEWING

  WIP REPORT                     DEVINSP
                                 VIEW888A
```

Alternatively, a user might want to track how particular levels, departments, or operations are doing in meeting their daily output requirements. The following MAT view tells the user the status of each operation in the CAT200 product at level TV:

```
Window: 15: CAT200 TV

GATE LVL TC DPT ENGLISH        OPN1  REQD DONE TODO  WIP ONTOOL TOPULL
0845 TV  C2 088 OXIDE P/C      M2X1  150   77   73    0          73
0845 TV  C2 062 RAINCHAMBER    M2X2  150   77   73    0          73
0845 TV  C2 063 NITRIDE DEP    M2X3  150   53   97   77    39    20
0845 TV  C2 064 PRE HMDS BAKE  M2X4  150   38  112    0         112
0845 TV  C2 076 ALIGN TV       M2X5  150  132   18   22    22     0
0845 TV  C2 088 DEV/ETCH       M2X6  150  131   19   16     0     3
```

This MAT view tells the user the status of each operation for CAT200 in department 062 by providing lot information about each lot waiting at the operations in department 062 and summary information about what is left to do to make its daily outs target:

```
Window:12 FSI *RADAR    (Lots: 142, Qty: 3352)

GATE LVL PRI DPT PC ENGLISH       OPN1  QTY  LOT       LJ TOOL ETIME
0377 RX  574 062 RM S/P CLEAN RX  M2Y1  025  J37094BS H2        0.1
0377 RX  587 062 RQ S/P CLEAN RX  M2Y2  025  J40L02AF H2        0.3
0377 RX  627 062 RQ S/P CLEAN RX  M2Y3  021  J36011AF U         1.2
0377 RX  637 062 RM S/P CLEAN RX  M2Y4  025  J39090BS UO        0.5

  REQD OUTS: 200, DONE: 75, TODO: 125, WIP: 096,  WIP NEEDED: 029


0567 CA  634 062 RM S/P CLEAN POS M2Z1  023  J34038BS UO        7.0

  REQD OUTS: 150, DONE: 141, TODO: 009, WIP: 023,  WIP NEEDED: 000
```

This MAT view allows the use to locate the lots best able to be pulled into operation M2P3 to enable it to meet its daily outs target:

```
Window:12  WIP PRIOR TO M2P3   (Lots: 9, Qty: 180)
GATE PRI PC DPT ENGLISH       OPN1 QTY  LOT       TOOL LJ CTIME ETIME
0567 631 RQ 063 DAMASCUS  8K  M2P1 024  J33032AF RLSE U   4.4   0.5
0567 631 RQ 063 DAMASCUS  8K  M2P2 023  J33040AF RLSE U   2.4   1.1
0567 631 RQ 063 DAMASCUS  8K  M2P2 024  J34100AF      U   2.4   1.8

REQD OUTS: 150, DONE: 004, WIP Needed: 146,  (WIP @ M2P3: 70)
```

This MAT view shows start and end WIP levels at two points in time.

LION START/END OPR FOR A LOT

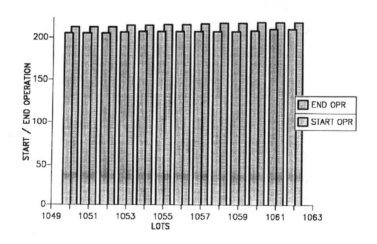

18

INTELLIGENTLY SCHEDULING SEMICONDUCTOR WAFER FABRICATION

Karl G. Kempf
(INTEL Corporation)

18.1 INTRODUCTION

Over the past several years, INTEL Corporation has addressed the problem of automating the scheduling of semiconductor wafer fabrication. After pursuing a variety of ideas and approaches and learning a number of hard lessons, an architecture has been devised and a number of its modules implemented and installed in production facilities. The technical aspects of the scheduling system are described here with motivations and results, as well as some novel concepts, but a more valuable contribution might be the discussion of the cultural issues encountered during the project. Capturing and holding the attention of the intended user community and gaining acceptance for the resulting system has been at least as difficult as solving the technical scheduling problem.

18.2 DESCRIBING THE WAFER FABRICATION SCHEDULING PROBLEM

18.2.1 Processing and Scheduling

Semiconductor devices are built upon thin wafers of silicon. These wafers are typically between 4 and 10 inches in diameter. The devices vary in complexity from a few thousand to a few million transistors and range in size from 1/8 to 1/2 inch on a side. This means that there can be from 50 to 1500 devices constructed on a single wafer. Wafers are transported around fabrication factories in lots of a few dozen and, once completed, are sent to assembly factories to be sawn apart so that the individual devices can be packaged for placement in consumer goods such as personal computers, automobiles, and video recorders.

The manufacturing process through which wafers flow is linear (with a few loops for rework) and contains a few hundred steps that require many weeks to complete from start to finish. The process builds layer after layer onto the wafer, the earlier steps building up the transistors, the later steps building up the electrical interconnects to form the micro-circuit. In a sense, the process is iterative because the steps involved in building up a given layer are similar to the steps involved in the preceding and subsequent layers. In fact, some of the same processing resources are used over and over, layer after layer.

A typical semiconductor factory contains hundreds of processing resources, including machines, personnel, and various tools such as lithography masks for projecting patterns onto wafers. The machines exhibit a wide variety of characteristics. Cycle times range from a few minutes to tens of hours. Load sizes vary from one wafer to a number of lots. There are machines that batch multiple lots together for processing, machines that require setup when switching from one step or one product to another, and machines that involve both batching and setups. Preventive maintenance schedules can be based on the number of wafers processed, on the amount of time spent processing, or simply on calendar time. Given the level of technology in the machines, emergency maintenance is common.

Scheduling of semiconductor manufacturing typically starts at some point in time when there are a number of lots of wafers positioned at specific steps in the process (some waiting, some in process) and a number of active resources (some idle, some processing, some under maintenance). The predictive part of scheduling produces a set of assignments of particular lots and specific steps to distinguished resources at future points in time over the scheduling period to advance the lots and make the resources busy. The reactive part of scheduling attempts to realize this set of assignments in the face of a variety of surprises that occur during execution on the manufacturing floor.

18.2.2 Predictive Scheduling Complexity

The predictive scheduling of wafer fabrication is difficult partly because of the number of decisions that must be made. A typical large factory can contain 750 resources running 2 or 3 processes with 150 steps each and a work-in-process inventory of 25,000 wafers bundled into 1,000 lots representing as many as 50 products. The equipment is assigned so that any given resource can be used for various steps (typically 3), and any given step can be executed on various resources (at least 2). Building a predictive schedule for the next 24 hours in this scenario is a serious undertaking.

The predictive task is made more difficult by the interactive nature of the assignments. With reference to Figure 18-1, the central oval represents a step:

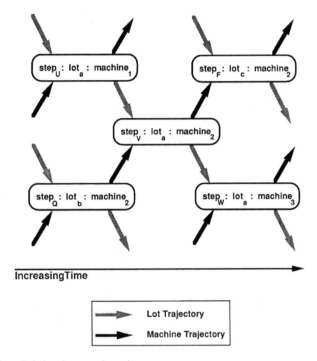

Figure 18-1: Relations between the assignments

lot:machine assignment with a start time and an end time on the time axis. A number of decisions had to be made to fix this assignment. The lot had to be selected from a number of candidates, as did the machine, as did the time slot. These selections are exclusive because the lot can only run on one machine at once, and each machine can only run one lot at a time (or a few lots at a time if a batching machine is involved). These decisions are strongly influenced by previous decisions and strongly influence subsequent decisions. For example, the machine selected in the central oval of Figure 18-1 was doing something prior to this assignment, as represented in the oval in the lower left of the figure, and will be doing something after this assignment, as represented in the upper right of the figure. Similarly, the lot selected in the central oval was doing something prior to this assignment, as represented in the oval in the upper left of the figure (unless the central oval contains the first step in the process), and will be doing something after this assignment, as represented in the lower right of the figure (unless the central oval contains the last step in the process). By expanding these concepts, the schedule can be seen as a network. Once it is realized that there are a finite number of machines, it is obvious that if the partial network shown in Figure 18-1 were expanded in the vertical direction to include all the machines, it would wrap around with the top joining the bottom. This provides a view of the schedule as a network on a cylindrical surface with time as the axis. From this view, it is clear that from any one assignment and its associated set of decisions, it is possible to interact with a very large number (in some cases all) of the subsequent assignments.

18.2.3 Reactive Scheduling Uncertainty

The reactive scheduling of wafer fabrication is difficult partly because of the inherent uncertainty in the execution environment. The predictive schedule invariably is built on a large number of assumptions, and the probability that all the assumptions will hold during execution is very small. Machines will break unexpectedly. Preventive maintenance will take longer (or shorter) than expected. Floor personnel expected to be present will be absent. Suppliers of tools or materials will deliver at times other than those expected. Automation systems will malfunction. Communication links will go down. Computing systems will need to be re-booted. The list could go on and on. The point is that the surprises possible during execution cannot even be enumerated, much less anticipated.

Most of the surprises listed thus far are based on something not being available when it was anticipated to be needed (and vice versa). The reactive task is also difficult because of prioritization changes that happen during execution. Because semiconductor devices cannot be tested fully until the last layer of interconnecting metal has been added (i.e., the full process has been run), it is sometimes the case that lower than expected yields of a particular product during end-of-line functional testing causes an emergency re-prioritization of work still in the manufacturing line to compensate for the loss. If the yields are especially low, it might be the case that highest priority diagnostic wafers must be inserted into various places in the process in attempts to discover the cause of the difficulty. Related priority adjustments can occur during the production ramp-up phase of a new process or new device or as a result of an emergency request from an important customer. Again, the number of surprises is innumerable, and each brings with it a disruption of schedule execution.

18.2.4 The Impact of Progress on Scheduling

The dynamics of scheduling semiconductor wafer fabrication are not limited to uncontrollable availability and prioritization surprises during execution. There are also changes that occur over a variety of longer time-scales. The skills pool changes as operational personnel are hired, retire, or leave, and further are trained. The equipment pool changes as old machines are retired, and new machines with improved or different functionality are added. The steps change as new processes are introduced, continuously improved, and retired in the technological quest for ever smaller devices. Devices are introduced and retired even more quickly in the steady march toward higher functionality. The metrics used at the corporate level to evaluate manufacturing organizations change with time, and of course, market demand indicates at regular intervals the quantities required of each existing product into the future. All these dynamics have their impact on the predictive and reactive phases of scheduling the semiconductor wafer fabrication process.

18.2.5 Personnel and Scheduling

A wide variety of personnel in a semiconductor wafer fabrication facility have an interest in scheduling. At the top of the organization is the factory manager, who is obviously graded to a large degree on the efficiency and effectiveness of schedule construction and execution. Reporting to the factory manager is a manufacturing staff, including managers for planning, maintenance, process engineering, industrial engineering, training, and production. Each of these managers has a different perspective on factory scheduling, impacting and being impacted by the scheduling process.

The planning manager serves as the interface to corporate headquarters where production goals are set. These goals are eventually broken down into small time buckets and are input into the scheduling process. The industrial engineering manager uses the corporate goals to determine the type and quantity of resources that should be available on the manufacturing floor that will be involved in scheduling. The maintenance manager is also involved with equipment but from the perspective of keeping the existing resources operational, including both preventive and emergency maintenance. The process engineering manager focuses on the health and improvement of each and every step in the processes that the factory performs. The training manager handles the skill set of personnel on the factory floor.

Last, but far from least, is the production manager for whom the scheduling tools described in this chapter were intended. This manager has four shift managers as direct reports (the factory runs 24 hours a day, 7 days a week, with 12-hour shifts), each of whom has four area supervisors as direct reports (one each for the lithography, etch, diffusion, and implantation areas), each of whom, in turn, has a number of production operators as direct reports. This is the team with the direct responsibility of building and executing schedules for the factory.

18.2.6 Personnel Interactions

There are at least three kinds of scheduling interaction between these personnel. The most frequent and intense interaction is that between the production manager's team members and their ongoing efforts to effectively operate on a shift to shift basis. Their problems are too much work for too few resources compounded by availability and prioritization surprises. This is predictive and reactive scheduling at its most detailed level.

A second type of scheduling interaction, only slightly less frequent and intense, occurs between the teams of the production, maintenance, process engineering, and training managers. This is a continuous competition for resource availability. The training personnel need the resources for enhancing the skill set of the factory floor personnel. The maintenance personnel need the resources on a regular basis to perform preventive maintenance and can never fix the resources that require emergency maintenance quickly enough. Process engineers need the resources for continuous improvement of the process and to track down and remedy processing problems. Although all these are vital to the manufacturing goals of the factory, they do reduce the short term capacity available to the production manager's team, which already perceives that there could never be enough capacity.

The third type of scheduling interaction is usually in the background and occurs between the teams of the production, planning, and industrial engineering managers. A part of the job of the planning personnel is the relay of the message from corporate headquarters to the manufacturing staff that output must be increased. A part of the job of the industrial engineering personnel is the relay of the message to the manufacturing staff from corporate headquarters that capital expenditures must be minimized. Because production personnel already perceive that there is too much work for too few resources, these interactions are not always welcomed.

18.3 DESCRIBING THE WAFER FABRICATION SCHEDULING SOLUTION

18.3.1 The Tools Indicated

These interactions provide an initial indication of three related scheduling tools that might be useful to the factory staff. The main differentiation between the tools has to do with the scheduling horizon that each addresses.

The first tool would support month-by-month interaction between planning, industrial engineering, and production to determine whether the equipment set of the factory is sufficient to achieve corporate production goals. Although we have built and installed a simulation-based scheduling tool to assist in solving this problem (Kempf, 1989c), it contains very little Artificial Intelligence (AI) technology and so is not discussed further here. The second tool would support shift-by-shift predictive scheduling to allocate capacity between production, maintenance, process engineering, and training as well as to direct activities on the factory floor. We have built and installed an AI-based tool to help address this need (Kempf, 1989b, 1989c; Kempf, Russell, 1991; Yu, Scott, & Kempf, 1988; Kempf, 1989, 1991), and it is the main focus of this chapter. The third tool would support minute-by-minute reactive scheduling by the production team on the factory floor as surprises occur.

Although we have designed and partially prototyped an AI-based tool to address this problem (Kempf, 1989c; Smith, Keng, & Kempf, 1990), it is not further discussed here.

18.3.2 Information Requirements

Whether the intelligent agent that is constructing or executing a schedule is a human being or a computer program, a minimal set of information is required to proceed (Kempf & Smith, 1991). Because the activity of scheduling is to assign lots and steps to resources in time, any scheduling agent must have access to information about lots, steps, and resources, especially from a temporal perspective.

In terms of reference information, it is important to know the steps that make up a process and the ordering of these steps as well as the catalog of resources available in the factory. It is important to know the mapping between steps and resources, including the kinds of resources required by each step, the resource instances that have been qualified for a particular step (many to one), and the steps that have been assigned to a particular resource (again many to one). Associated with each step:resource pair is a cycle time, the conditions under which setup must be changed and the time required, and the minimum and maximum sizes of batches as well as what products can be included in the same batch. Preventive maintenance guidelines and emergency maintenance statistics for each resource are also necessary as well as resource locations for considering transportation. These are the types of data that do not change very frequently (relative to the predictive scheduling period). The step data are usually available from the process engineers and the resource data from the industrial engineers, maintenance engineers, and trainers.

In terms of state information, it is important to know the status of the lots and resources at any point in time. The basic lot information includes the identity of lots currently active in the system (lots are differentiated from resources by the fact that they come and go rather quickly) and the process they are following as well as the product they represent and their start and due dates. The step in the process at which they are currently positioned is important as well as their status (waiting, running, or on hold) at that step. The status of resources is important (waiting, running, or undergoing maintenance) as well as the next time that they will be available (if running or being maintained). These are the types of data that do change very frequently (relative to the predictive scheduling period). It is usually possible to obtain this information only from a computerized data collection system given the amount of information involved.

18.3.3 Knowledge Requirements

For any intelligent scheduling agent in manufacturing, a minimal set of knowledge is also required (Kempf & Smith, 1991). Because the activity of scheduling is to assign lots and steps to resources in time, any scheduling agent must have access to knowledge about choosing between lots, steps, and resources and making trade-offs among the interacting goals of the factory and its staff. This knowledge can be segmented along lines similar to those used earlier to discuss the scheduling interactions between factory personnel.

One class of knowledge concerns the aggregate comparison between required capacity (the domain of the planning people in the factory) and available capacity (the domain of the industrial engineers). A number of complex trade-offs must be made here that influence the medium and long term effectiveness of the factory. How many instances of each type of resource are really needed to meet production goals without wasting capital? How much production can realistically be expected from the current resource set? How many instances of resources should be assigned to each step, and how many steps should be assigned to each resource? Where will the largest gains be realized for continuous improvement efforts on the equipment set?

Another set of knowledge focuses on the short term allocation of capacity. At the higher level, this involves making shift by shift trade-offs between the personnel concerned with production, equipment maintenance, process engineering, and training. At the lower level, this involves predictive scheduling by the production team, making trade-offs between products and steps competing for the available resources. Because the resolution of these questions is very situation dependent, requiring the overall machine availability and lot position status information at the beginning of the shift for resolution, it might be expected that this knowledge will be very rich and diverse.

A third class of knowledge concerns the detection, avoidance, and/or repair of surprises during schedule execution. This is knowledge of appropriate reaction and is the domain of the production staff on the manufacturing floor. When is execution sufficiently different from prediction that reaction is needed? Of the reactions possible, which is the best to invoke? Again, this requires situation dependent decision making based on large quantities of real time data and might be expected to involve rather complex knowledge.

18.3.4 Schedule Requirements

As noted previously, a detailed schedule consists of a set of resource assignments and a time for each step and lot to be processed. Generally, a schedule is intended to produce certain patterns of behavior in the manufacturing facility for which it was generated (Kempf & Smith, 1991). A predictive schedule is released to the floor at the beginning of a shift with the intention of guiding the basic behavior of the system over the duration of the shift. A reactive schedule is issued during the shift with the intention of guiding the recovery from some disruptive event. How strictly a schedule is adhered to will vary with the type of system to which it is passed. At one extreme, a schedule can be viewed as advice to the personnel on the manufacturing floor that they will follow to some degree. At the other extreme, a schedule can carry precise operational semantics that directly drive an automated manufacturing system. Transmitting the right level of scheduling instructions to the floor is an important issue.

18.3.5 Normal Practice

At the beginning of our work, there were no computational tools to help the manufacturing personnel address scheduling problems. This was clearly the motivation for our work. Fortunately, information gathering was not a source of much difficulty. Each of our manufacturing facilities had installed a database management system to handle the flood of information required for, and resulting from, factory operations. Although these systems were not set up to service automated scheduling tools, they certainly supported production personnel in this task and were easy enough to access for our requirements (more about difficulties here later).

Knowledge was a different story. At the beginning of our work, there was no clear methodology for codifying the knowledge necessary for building or executing schedules. It was not explicitly in the job description of any member of the manufacturing staff to develop, document, disseminate, or continuously improve operational knowledge about scheduling. This is not to say that there was no scheduling knowledge, but the knowledge was developed by the individuals on the manufacturing staff, not by the team. The knowledge was stored in the memories of individuals, not in a form available for inspection, and to a large degree, the knowledge concerned the handling of very specific circumstances that had been encountered in the past rather than abstracted general knowledge that could be applied more generally. These deficiencies had a profound effect on the way scheduling was done before we began tool development and on the course our efforts ultimately followed.

A normal shift scheduling session would begin with the "passdown" meeting involving the shift manager and area supervisors whose shift was ending and the shift manager and area supervisors whose shift was beginning. Status and problem reports would be explained. The incoming staff would next visit the database management system and the factory floor to confirm and expand their understanding of the status. Each area supervisor would then independently decide the basic approach for his or her area for the upcoming shift and do scheduling for each process step assigned to the area. The basic approach might contain personnel assignments to equipment bays; capacity allocations to training, engineering, and maintenance; and machine setup changes. Scheduling would involve mental capacity simulations to determine how many lots should run on each process step by mid-shift and by end-shift. Included here might be educated guesses on how many lots would come from upstream feeding operations and how many lots would be required by downstream fed operations. Next the shift manager and the area supervisors would meet to compare and confirm their guesses and assumptions and to compile the official "goaling sheet" of mid-shift and end-shift expectations step by step throughout the production processes. Finally, roughly 2 hours into the 12-hour shift, the goaling sheet would be transmitted to the floor manually with additional verbal instructions about lot and/or product prioritization. Detailed scheduling decisions about which specific lots to run through particular steps on individual machines at designated times were left to the operators on the floor, tempered by striving to meet the goals. The shift manager and area supervisors would have a mid-shift meeting to assess how things were going, but executional surprises were handled on an ad hoc basis by the operators and area supervisor involved. Seldom, if ever, was a shift graded by comparing its final results to the initial goaling sheet. Rather, total output by area and by shift was paramount.

Given the informality and incompleteness of the knowledge available, it should not be a surprise that this process yielded variable quality results at best. On any given shift, the area supervisors had their own ideas on how to optimize his or her own areas, perhaps in synergy, perhaps in conflict with the other areas on their shifts. In any given area, area supervisors across the four shifts had their own strategies, and even though they were operating the same equipment on the same steps, they would have serious disagreements at passdown. It was not uncommon for one shift to run very strongly but to leave the next shift a factory situation in which it was very difficult to do well. Operators on the floor striving to reach the issued goals, each with their own strategies, also caused integration problems. The quality of reaction on the floor depended strictly on the experience and insight of the operator performing the reaction. Sometimes excellent decisions were made, sometimes not. In any case, this predictive and reactive scheduling process led to performance that was suboptimal and unpredictable. This was the fundamental motivation for our work.

18.4 OUR TECHNICAL SOLUTION FOR WAFER FABRICATION SCHEDULING

18.4.1 Key Ideas in the Technical Approach

From the above description, it was obvious that the primary issue was the capture, utilization, and continuous improvement of the minimal complete and consistent set of knowledge necessary to run the factory efficiently. We call this set the "strategy" and recognize that it is dynamic. From our perspective, a good operational strategy is one of the keys to world-class manufacturing and provides considerable competitive advantage. A good operational strategy serves to integrate the activities of the areas and the shifts, improve predictive scheduling, simplify reactive scheduling, raise and stabilize the performance of the factory, and free manufacturing personnel for tasks other than scheduling. Three of the key ideas in our technical approach were driven by this concept of strategy and by a number of important ideas in the literature (Fox & Smith, 1984; Fox & Kempf, 1985, 1987; Smith & Ow, 1985).

We found the idea of a predictive-reactive scheduling system inescapable in our system design. To run only with a predictive scheduler did not make sense from at least two perspectives. First, because the scheduling problem described above is at least NP-hard, no system could produce schedules of such high quality that their precise execution should be mandated. Second, because of the frequency of availability and priority surprises during execution, no predictive schedule could survive for more than a fraction of a shift. We did not believe that we could build a system whose execution speed would permit complete predictive regeneration at every surprise (Kempf, 1989d). To run only with a reactive scheduler did not make sense either. We believed that any known purely reactive method could (and would) wander into grossly suboptimal sections of the solution space during execution in a problem of our complexity. We therefore decided on a collaborative pair. The predictor (Kempf, 1989b; Kempf & Russell, 1991) would produce a good schedule that would be used as a stake in the ground with full realization that it would not (in fact, could not) be executed in detail. However, staying as close as possible to the stake would be a good idea. The reactor (Smith, Keng, & Kempf, 1990) would be tethered computationally to the stake and respond to surprises within the boundary prescribed by the tether. At a point when the reactor could not function within that boundary, the stake would be uprooted, and the predictor would run again, restarting the process.

In the design of the predictive component, we made two complementary decisions about scheduling methods. At the higher level, we decided to pursue "importance-ordered" scheduling. Any serial scheduler must decide how to select the next job or resource to schedule. One popular approach is to use a forward-looking discrete event simulator at the core of the scheduler and to select the next entity to schedule as the next (in ordered time) resource and/or job to finish its current activity. The idea here is to make all possible assignments at time T, then all possible assignments at T+1, and so on. We followed this "time-ordered" scheduling approach in building a tool to support the long term capacity planning part of the scheduling problem mentioned previously (Kempf, 1989c). During this work, we found that such a scheduler tends to have only local information upon which to base its scheduling decisions, and this information is strictly about assignments made in the past relative to the assignment being considered. Hence, dispatching rules are typically the knowledge used to make decisions, and these had little to do with our conceptualization of operational strategies. (To clarify this point, consider a time-ordered scheduler stopped midway through a run. The Gantt chart representation of the intermediate result would have a scheduling frontier where assignments are being made, before which all assignments have been made irreversibly (from a practical perspective), after which no assignments have been made at all.)

Our approach is to choose the next job or resource to schedule based on its importance and to schedule it in its entirety (as far as possible). The idea here is to make all possible assignments for the most important entity in the problem, then all the assignments for the second most important, and so on. Such a scheduler tends to have global information upon which to base its scheduling decisions, and this information is typically about assignments made in the past and in the future relative to the assignment being considered. This fit much better with our idea of operational strategies. (To clarify this point, consider an importance-ordered scheduler stopped midway through a run. The Gantt chart representation of the intermediate result would have assignments throughout the scheduling period because some resources and/or jobs had been scheduled to exhaustion. It would be clear, however, that all the entities in the Gantt were of higher priority than those still to be scheduled.) Although we felt that this approach would produce superior schedules, it does require a prioritization scheme (that fits nicely into the concept of operational strategies) that will be discussed later.

At the lower level, we decided to pursue "multi-algorithm" scheduling. Although it is possible to build an importance-ordered scheduler that uses a machine-centered algorithm or a job-centered algorithm or any other single algorithm, we felt that a strong scheduler should be able to decompose a problem into its component parts and apply the most appropriate algorithm to each. Furthermore, this design decision is defensible from two practical perspectives. On one hand, the scheduling literature contains specific algorithms for machines with setups, machines that batch, lots with high priority, and so on. On the other hand, semiconductor wafer fabrication facilities contain machines with setups, machines that batch, lots with high priority, and so on. In other words, many specific algorithms are available, and many specific algorithms are required, and the design should incorporate them. This multi-algorithm decision is complementary with the high level decision to be importance-ordered.

Once we had conceptualized a predictive-reactive pair that could execute operational policies using a multi-method importance-ordered approach, we could see that it should be able to run in many modes (Figure 18-2). One would be strategy development mode for prediction (Figure 18-2, upper left). Here, predictive strategies could be evaluated over multiple runs from different starting states of the production facility covering the problem space. Another would be strategy development mode for reaction (Figure 18-2, upper middle). Here, reactive strategies could be evaluated over multiple runs with different difficulties in the execution environment covering the surprise space. Both of these development modes

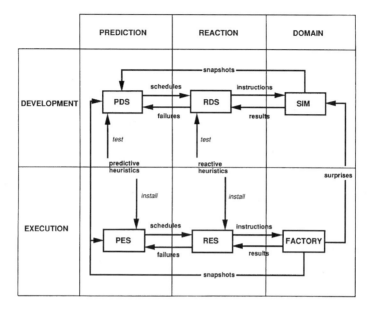

Figure 18-2: The solution architecture

would be coupled to a factory simulator (Figure 18.2, upper right). The third and fourth modes would include predictive strategy and reactive strategy execution (Figure 18-2, lower left and lower middle, respectively) coupled to the actual factory through the data base management system (Figure 18-2, lower right). It was thought that the reactive scheduler in execution mode might eventually be interfaced directly to production equipment and material handling systems to exercise real-time control.

18.4.2 The Scheduling Methodology and Modules

Based on input from our internal manufacturing customers, we began work on a predictive scheduler to run in execution mode (Figure 18-2, lower left). The objective was to provide a tool to support goaling meetings as described earlier, including the capture of a uniform operational strategy that all shifts and all areas could utilize. The outcome was hoped to be much less time spent to produce much

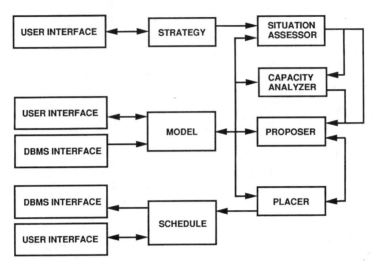

Figure 18-3:   The system modules and their interconnection

better goaling sheets supported by the predictive scheduling tool. The tool has been written in a very modular fashion to support continuous improvement of the software as well as testability and maintainability (Figure 18-3).

The MODEL module holds most of the resource information discussed in the earlier section on information requirements. It includes reference and status information for each lot, step, and resource (machines, workers, and lithography masks) in the factory as well as the mappings of lots onto steps and of resources onto steps.

Basic lot reference information includes lot, product, and process names and release date into and due date out of the factory. Status information for a lot is made up of number of wafers (because individual wafers can be destroyed in the process), priority class (because priority can change during the process), current step, and current status (busy, idle, hold). Name, position on the floor, and preventive maintenance requirements form the basic machine reference information. Name, shift, and machine training are the modelled reference attributes of the operators. Status information for machines and operators is simply current status (busy, idle, down) and the time when resources that are busy or down are expected to be available. Reference information for steps, beyond step name, centers on sequencing of the steps for the different processes in the factory.

Higher level information maps lots, steps, and resources together. The most important reference mapping is the "step:machine set," where machine qualifications and operating parameters are held. There are always multiple steps (min = 2, max = 12, ave = 3) and multiple machines (min = 2, max =16, ave = 4) in each set, with a normal factory having 50 to 100 such sets. Although a particular step can only be found in one set, and a particular machine can only be found in one set, it does not necessarily follow that each step runs on every machine in the set or that each machine runs every step in the set. However, every legal step:machine pair does have associated with it a cycle time, operator requirements, the conditions under which setup must be changed and the time required (if applicable), and minimum and maximum batch sizes and what products can be batched together (if applicable). The most important status mapping is the "step:lot set," where all the lots (busy, idle, and hold) associated with a particular step are held. Both the "step:machine" and "step:lot" sets are heavily used during scheduling to produce the "step:machine:lot" mapping, otherwise known as the schedule, which is held in the SCHEDULE module.

The USER INTERFACE to the MODEL is intended to supply all the reference information. This interface is designed to be used whenever anyone on the manufacturing staff makes a change in the basic parameters of the factory. This ranges from changes as large as an industrial engineer adding (or deleting) a machine to changes as small as a process engineer altering the cycle time of a step in the process or a trainer updating the qualifications of an operator. This editing module is currently available in prototype form. The DBMS INTERFACE to the MODEL supplies all the status information. This interface runs whenever a scheduling session is initiated and pulls from the mass of data that the database maintains the status of each lot and each machine required for scheduling. This interface module is currently available in a highly developed form, as is the MODEL module.

The STRATEGY module holds much of the scheduling knowledge discussed in the earlier section on knowledge requirements. Each individual strategy for a factory consists of four components.

The first component addresses the problem of putting all the lots, then all the machines, then all the steps into ordered lists by importance given a snapshot of factory status. In all three cases, there is a list of importance-ordering heuristics that can be used or not used as desired, and, if used, can be applied in a particular sequence. For example, the lot heuristics menu might include "product lots" given an importance-ordered list of products from the corporate level, "hot lots" as marked dynamically in the DBMS, and "critical ratio lots" as the ratio of cycle time required to calendar time available for completion. A strategy at this level could be "hot lots, critical ratio lots," which would later be interpreted as (1) build a more important set containing lots designated as hot in the DBMS and a less important set containing all other lots and (2) order the lots in each set by their critical ratio with the latest lots first. Machine examples might include "static bottleneck" machines, as determined by long term capacity calculations, and "instanta-neous bottleneck" machines, as determined by the position of current work-in-progress (WIP) and machine maintenance status. Step examples could have "under target" steps and "over target" steps (assuming a set of wip targets has been speci-fied in the MODEL) as well as "dry steps" with far too little WIP and "flooded steps" with far too much WIP.

The second component deals with dividing each of the three lists into two or more sub-problems. In some cases, this is easy, as exemplified by the "hot lots" above that always stand as an individual sub-problem. In other cases, parameters come into play. The "other lots" in (1) above, ordered by "critical ratio," might be divided into a number of manageable sub-problems by specification of ranges of critical ratios. Likewise for machines, "static bottlenecks" might always be first, with the rest of the machines segmented into sub-problems by ranges of "instanta-neous bottleneck" index. Ranges of "under target" and "over target" work in a similar fashion for steps.

The third component evaluates the three sets of sub-problems to build one importance-ordered list for the later modules of the scheduler to solve. The heuris-tics here are currently the most nebulous (Reece & Kempf, 1990). Suffice it to say that sometimes the "hot lots" are more important than the "static bottlenecks" and should be scheduled first, and other times, the reverse is true. Sometimes the most important set of "other lots" should be considered before the most important set of "over target" steps and sometimes not, and so on. The heuristics here are intended to explicitly state the conditions under which the three lists of ordered sub-prob-lems from the second strategy component can be merged into one ordered list of sub-problems to be passed along to the fourth strategy component.

The fourth component assigns scheduling algorithms to each of the sub-prob-lems. Currently, there are only three methods available, one each for lots, machines, and steps, so the mapping is trivial, but the system is designed so that there is an easy expansion for both the heuristics to identify specific problems and the algorithms to solve specific problems. Obviously, as new algorithms are incor-porated at the lower levels of the system, the strategies must exhibit the ability to recognize sub-problems that map appropriately.

At this point in time, any particular strategy in the STRATEGY module is hand-crafted by the developers after translation from user terms. Currently, the principal research goal of the development team is to understand the space of all operational strategies well enough that we can design and implement a strategy language. This goal reflects the concept that our scheduler might be thought of as a very intelligent interpreter of operational strategy language, with the manufacturing floor as its target machine (for which the interpreter has a MODEL). Although it will be vitally necessary when turning the entire system over to the users, the

USER INTERFACE to the STRATEGY has not yet been constructed. This module will be the editor for the forthcoming strategy language and will support the users in their continuous improvement process.

Assuming that the MODEL module has been provided with a lot and machine status update by the DBMS INTERFACE and that a strategy has been designated in the STRATEGY module, the SITUATION ASSESSOR executes the strategy on the status. As noted in the description of the STRATEGY module, the outcome is an ordered list of sub-problems with an indication of which scheduling method should be used on each. A prototype implementation of this module that takes less than 30 seconds to execute is currently available. Much more refined versions are expected once a formal strategy language has been designed and implemented.

The CAPACITY ANALYZER module accesses the MODEL module for the most current machine status information as well as information about preventive maintenance requirements during the shift and estimates of when currently broken machines will be back in service. It uses this collection of machine data to establish an available capacity for each machine in the scheduling problem. The CAPACITY ANALYZER then acquires sub-problems one at a time in importance order from the SITUATION ASSESSOR. The CAPACITY ANALYZER contains a rudimentary but focused simulator. Given a sub-problem with its associated scheduling method, it again accesses the MODEL to set up and execute the minimal simulation necessary. After each sub-problem is considered, the result is a capacity allocation of specific machines to particular steps. This module is available in a highly developed form and, to emphasize the rudimentary nature of the simulation, runs in under 60 seconds.

The minimal simulation that the CAPACITY ANALYZER constructs differs for lot-centered and machine-centered problems. For example, given the "hot lot" sub-problem described earlier, the CAPACITY ANALYZER would consider only the 10 to 15 lots included in the sub-problem, only the steps those lots could possibly reach in the scheduling horizon (by summing cycle times from their current positions), and only the machines that run those steps. For a "static bottleneck" sub-problem, it would consider only the 5 to 10 machines included in the sub-problem, only the steps that those machines run, and only the lots that could possibly reach those steps in the scheduling horizon, and so on. In doing its simulation, it simply allocates blocks of capacity until the scheduling horizon or the machine capacity is expended, records the capacity allocated, and goes on to the next sub-problem.

The majority of the computation involved in building a schedule is ready to begin at this point. The USER INTERFACEs to the MODEL and the STRATEGY are intended to be used outside the actual predictive scheduling cycle when modifications are indicated. The DBMS INTERFACE to the MODEL runs once per scheduling cycle but has become a regular function of the DBMS and runs on a separate computer. The SITUATION ASSESSMENT and CAPACITY ANALYSIS run for a total of less than 90 seconds, perform little if any search, and are intended to simplify the actual scheduling process by problem decomposition and rough capacity assignment, respectively. The PROPOSER and the PLACER modules now build the actual schedule in close communication with each other. Both modules have access to the MODEL. The PROPOSER accesses the SITUATION ASSESSOR, especially the sub-problem list, and the CAPACITY ANALYZER, especially the capacity allocation list. The PLACER accesses the SCHEDULE module where the current schedule is held.

The PROPOSER begins by getting the first sub-problem and tries to solve this sub-problem as completely as it can with the method attached. It first generates many possible permutations and combinations of plausible lot placements. Next it consults the capacity allocation list to refine its placements. Then it queries PLACER for information about resource availability and timing for the most promising possibilities. It finally uses the resulting information to select its best option. If it is dealing with a lot-centered problem, it evaluates the options on lot movement and picks the best. If it is dealing with a machine-centered problem, it evaluates the options on machine utilization and picks the best. Step-centered problems are evaluated on attainment of target WIP levels. PROPOSER tries to minimize the number of setups and maximize the size of batches in all cases. Once it has made its selection for assignment, it requests PLACER to install the result into the schedule and proceeds on to the next sub-problem on the list.

Over the course of one predictive scheduling run, the sub-problems are presented to PROPOSER in importance order. Over the course of solving one sub-problem, PROPOSER considers many possibilities. Averaging over a number of complete runs with a 12 hour horizon, PROPOSER built and evaluated roughly 100,000 possible assignments to realize a schedule with roughly 1,500 assignments (a ratio of 1 to 67). It should not be surprising under these conditions that PROPOSER never retracts an assignment once made, but PROPOSER might work on each sub-problem multiple times. It works through the list over and over, picking up the current status of the lots and machines from the schedule through PLACER and seeing if further progress can be made. This is done because, for example, the initial solution to sub-problem 2 might facilitate progress on the initial solution to sub-problem 1, and so on. This goes on until no progress is made for one complete pass through the sub-problem list.

The PLACER begins by accessing the MODEL to transfer the initial status of all resources into the empty schedule in the SCHEDULE module. It then responds to queries from PROPOSER about trial placements using both the MODEL and the SCHEDULE. It passes back the resources that could satisfy the placement request and the time block(s) during which they are available, the necessity (or not) of incurring a setup change if the trial placement was elected, and the presence (or not) of batches that are less than full that could accept some (or all) of the lots in question. It also accepts and instantiates in the schedule the assignments that PROPOSER finally decides.

In some cases, the search that PLACER must perform to find candidate resources is complex. Consider a placement that requires three different types of resources, and there are four instances of each type present, but they are each partially allocated already. Finding gaps of the correct (or greater) length for the trial placement for each resource where the gaps overlap correctly in time is difficult. PLACER is currently efficient enough to only look for gaps in the second resource type searched within the time bounds of gaps found for the first resource type searched and to search the third bounded by the combined results of the first two, but this is an area for future improvement.

PROPOSER and PLACER are both available in a highly developed form. However, for problems of the complexity described earlier over a 12-hour predictive horizon, these two modules required between 10 and 20 minutes to execute. Efforts to gain time efficiency are therefore focused on these modules. These efforts take the form of improved coding for both, improved scheduling method efficiency for PROPOSER, and improved gap searching algorithms for PLACER.

The schedule that results can be inspected and analyzed by the shift manager and the area supervisors using the USER INTERFACE to the SCHEDULE. This module supports inspection of the schedule by high-resolution mouse-driven bit-mapped graphics in a variety of different resources (Y) versus time (X) Gantt chart forms with bars indicating lot:step assignments. The possibilities include (1) all the machines in an area (for the area supervisor to assess load), (2) selected machines (usually bottlenecks), (3) selected lots (usually hot), (4) selected steps (usually high or low WIP), and (5) all the steps in the line in processing order (for the shift manager to assess flow). Some analysis is also possible through plots of WIP by area by hour and lots processed by area by hour.

If they agree with the resulting SCHEDULE, they can transmit it in one of two forms to the manufacturing floor through the DBMS INTERFACE. For continuity with the established procedure, the schedule can be reduced to a goaling sheet and transmitted by hand or electronically. For the future, the schedule can be converted in its entirety into a text file that can be distributed electronically to the appropriate places on the manufacturing floor. If the manager and supervisors disagree with the SCHEDULE, they can alter the input and make another run.

These modules were designed, implemented, tested, and installed over a 27-month period by a team that contained between 3 and 7 members at various times (averaging 5). The development work was done in Common LISP, CLOS, and

CLIM on Symbolics 1200 machines under GENERA (all execution times above are on this machine), although the delivery vehicle is the INTEL 80486 workstation.

18.5 OUR CULTURAL SOLUTION FOR WAFER FABRICATION SCHEDULING

18.5.1 Key Ideas in the Cultural Approach

Two different types of marketing were required to initiate and maintain the project (Meieran & Kempf, 1989). On one hand, there was the higher level management from the wafer fabrication facility up to the corporate level. We were interested to find that very few of these managers recognized the inherent or practical difficulty of the wafer fabrication scheduling problem. As a general rule (with a few notable exceptions), we found that the further removed the person was from the minute-to-minute operation of the factory floor, the more trivial the scheduling problem seemed. The interest that we were able to generate in this group was based on (1) the factory being better able to respond to corporate instructions on product due dates, (2) the possibility of increasing output with minimal (or no) capital expenditure because of better resource utilization, and (3) the possibility of using the automated scheduling tool to integrate other pieces of automation such as machine controllers and material handlers. The difficulties here were mainly getting across the message that the solution would not be simple and that a number of person-years would have to be invested to produce a strong result. The attempted solution to this set of marketing problems was intense communication with management. As successes were realized and difficulties further understood, messages were widely broadcast.

On the other hand, there were the manufacturing personnel from the shift managers down to the operators on the floor. Here we found a clear recognition of the practical difficulties, although (not surprisingly) few worried about the inherent theoretical ramifications of the problem. The main request was to provide a tool to foster (1) predictability of factory performance from week to week and (2) continuity of execution from shift to shift and area to area. The goals here were improving factory performance while easing the predictive and reactive scheduling workload. The difficulties were mainly responding to comments that although the system sounded wonderful in concept, it would be impossible to implement. One group based its arguments on the opinion that the manufacturing environment changed too rapidly to ever allow the model to be correct at a fine enough level of detail to be useful. Another group argued that the strategy was too complex to ever be captured sufficiently to allow automatic schedule generation. A third group pointed out that the manual goaling process described earlier was so ingrained that it would be very difficult to make the cultural changes necessary to adopt an automated system. Each argued that having been involved in a number of projects that promised software solutions to difficult manufacturing problems (some that delivered, more that didn't), there would be a time window of opportunity of finite duration in which a useful tool would have to be delivered, or interest and support would wane rapidly. The attempted solution to this set of marketing problems was intense involvement of the users. At every step along the way, the potential users were consulted, pulled into brainstorming sessions, shown intermediate prototypes, and generally involved in the design and development process. However, to varying degrees, each of the warnings of the critics were correct.

In the background of these difficulties were lessons learned by the larger factory automation group in which the scheduling research and development team resides. In the past, it has been our experience that new ways of doing things are difficult to adopt. Even if everyone agrees that the "standard way" (read: old way) of operating is inadequate and that the "automated way" (read: new way) is better, it is a major undertaking to implement the change. In addition to resistance to change being a recognized feature of human behavior, we believe that the tight teamwork among our manufacturing personnel is involved here as well. If there is a large team with a particularly integrated set of functions, changing the job of one person on the team changes (to some degree) the jobs of all the people on the team (Hilton & Kempf, 1988). If a shift manager is provided with a scheduling tool that changes a substantial part of his or her job, (1) the production manager will have to change the way the shift manager is graded to include how well he or she adapts to and employs the tool, (2) the area supervisors will have to get used to getting different instructions at a more detailed level in a more timely fashion, (3) the people who supply data to the shift manager will have to provide more data in a more accurate and timely manner, (4) the people who support the shift manager's hardware and software will have to expand their services, and (5) the people who train the whole manufacturing staff will have to expand their offerings as well. Therefore, change is slow to be implemented and is not often welcomed with open arms, even when the change is agreed to be valuable.

Furthermore, some changes are more difficult than others. Consider the problem: solution matrix shown in Table 18-1. As shown in the columns, manufacturing problems can roughly be characterized as those that engineers solve well today, ones that engineers struggle to solve poorly at this point in time, and those that engineers recognize but do not or cannot address currently. As the rows indicate, solutions to these problems can roughly be characterized as those that simply supply data (even if in large quantities), those that provide advice to the users, and ones that furnish control (possibly with minimal human intervention). In the upper left hand corner of the matrix, resistance to change can be minimized because the engineer is comfortable with the problem and is accustomed to looking at data. Automation, once throughly tested, can be viewed as a tool for saving time, and

Table 18-1: Increasing difficulty to gain customer acceptance.

	Problem Characterization		
Solution Characterization	Engineers Solve WELL	Engineers Solve POORLY	Engineers Do NOT Solve
Outputs Data	Relatively easy	Harder	Even harder
Provides Advice	Harder	Even harder	Very hard
Performs Control	Even harder	Very hard	Impossible?

this helps in making the required changes. In the lower right hand corner of the matrix, resistance is maximized. The engineer is clearly uncomfortable with the problem. It is not necessarily obvious what a good solution looks like, so testing is difficult. Because the engineering team will almost certainly still be responsible for the performance of the manufacturing system, turning control over to such a program will be extremely difficult.

Notice where the scheduling tools that we have proposed map onto this table. The capacity tool that goes well beyond spreadsheets and static models previously used is probably best placed in the middle column and the middle row. The reactive tool, because it tries to avoid and repair problems in real time with a global view of the factory and ultimately communicates directly to the machines and the material handling system to exercise control, should probably be placed in the lower right. The predictive tool, as described in this chapter, is somewhere between these two because it goes well beyond the "goaling meeting" model of predictive scheduling but stops short of directly controlling equipment.

18.5.2 Manageable Problems in Building Some of the Modules

Our initial approach to building the predictive execution tool attempted to directly confront some of these problems. We started our work with the USER INTERFACEs and the DBMS INTERFACEs. This was done under the rationale that the interfaces were the only things that most of the personnel and all the other computer programs in the factory would ever directly see of the scheduling system. Therefore, we believed that addressing these first would go some way toward answering the critics of the system.

The technical side of building the USER INTERFACEs contained some interesting software development problems (Holman, Hon, & Kempf, 1988; Kempf, 1989a), but these paled by comparison with the human acceptance difficulties. First, the users, from the shift managers to the floor operators, represented a wide spectrum of computer experience. At one extreme were a few people with advanced degrees in electrical engineering who had broad exposure to computation. At the other extreme was a larger population with very narrow computing experience, often with a negative connotation. Building an interface to satisfy all positions in this spectrum might well be impossible. The only practical way forward was to present straw men for refinement because few if any sound suggestions could be expected in the beginning from an audience with no notion of automated scheduling and little background in advanced graphics. After many iterations on the list of incremental improvements, we have a powerful USER INTERFACE to the SCHEDULE that seems natural to most users. Work continues on the USER INTERFACEs to the MODEL and the STRATEGY (more on both in a moment). Unfortunately, this approach to developing our set of USER INTERFACEs has opened a veritable floodgate, and none of the scheduling team now believes that the suggestions (and accompanying expectations) will ever run dry.

Construction of the DBMS INTERFACEs also caused an interesting set of technical and cultural difficulties. The technical problems stem from the fact that the commercial DBMS system that the factory employs was designed to interface to other applications in very restrictive ways. Getting it to serve an artificially intelligent scheduler has been a trying experience, but the cultural story is much more salient.

The MODEL made the broadest and most detailed status requests to which the DBMS had ever been subjected and, thereby, pointed out numerous inherent and configurational deficiencies. At the highest level, steps and resources that the manufacturing personnel considered trivial but that the scheduler needed to reason over were not tracked in the DBMS system. At the lowest level, discipline on the manufacturing floor was such that occasionally events on the floor were mislogged or not logged at all to the DBMS. Because the scheduler needed a complete, correct, and consistent snapshot of factory status on demand, all these flaws became painfully obvious. The DBMS support group quite correctly pointed out that as soon as the scheduling tool could be shown to provide its advertised advantages, the long and laborious process of modifying the system would be undertaken. The scheduling research and development group quite correctly took the position that as soon as the appropriate DBMS snapshot could be furnished, the strength of the scheduling system could be demonstrated. Only by showing that the DBMS deficiencies were also negatively impacting the reports that were being used to manually operate the factory was any progress made. However, the system development team still had to construct data sanitizing modules to protect the scheduling system in case new problems occurred. This problem lingers on today.

The reference side of the MODEL module provided some equally interesting but more tractable problems. Gathering the initial reference information was a challenge because each of the groups in the manufacturing domain had something to contribute, but keeping the model updated turned out to be a project in itself. Given the dynamics of the manufacturing facility described earlier, there was on average 1 change per day over the 27 months that this project has been active.

Considering the number of manufacturing staff from whom reference information must be gathered, the importance of the USER INTERFACE to the MODEL can be seen in a different light. But, however user friendly this editor can become, it remains to be proven that the model is valid and that the scheduler provides benefit before the manufacturing staff is willing to commit the effort required to maintain the correctness of the reference sections of the model. Hence, the system development team continues to shoulder the updating burden and to work the interfacing and validation issues.

Partial resolution of these problems allowed implementation of DBMS INTERFACEs to the MODEL and the SCHEDULE and a USER INTERFACE to the SCHEDULE. The SCHEDULE, represented as a Gantt chart, was not a point of contention nor was the internal structure of the MODEL. Therefore, implementation of the MODEL and SCHEDULE, as well as the CAPACITY ANALYZER, PROPOSER, and PLACER modules, progressed to supply a basic scheduler core. The MODEL and STRATEGY had to be maintained by the developers because no USER INTERFACEs were available, and the SITUATION ASSESSOR was hand simulated by the developers because there was no computational representation for the STRATEGY. However, predictive schedules could be built and sent to the floor for execution.

18.5.3 Unmanageable Problems in Building Other Modules

The development plan was to begin with the simplest approximation to the strategy used by the manufacturing staff, test it, use it, evaluate it, expand the strategy, and spiral on and on until the system could take over most, if not all, goaling and scheduling tasks. Although the users agreed that this was appropriate, our major cultural difficulties came from the inadequacy of this plan.

The plan was based on the assumption that the manufacturing staff could explicate a working operational strategy that, with refinement, would be agreed to by all concerned. During the initial rounds of brainstorming with the production manager, the 4 shift managers, and the 16 area supervisors, it did not seem surprising that we collected 21 related but different strategies, each rather incomplete in coverage, each rather devoid of substance from an algorithmic perspective. After all, this was not to be an expert system approach of modeling how they scheduled at that point in time but, a more general attempt to build a strategy engine. We pressed on to come to a strategy with which all felt comfortable enough.

The plan was further based on the assumption that if the execution of the strategy could be automated to produce plausible predictive schedules, the system would be used. In the time it took the scheduling team to implement each formally agreed strategy idea, the manufacturing staff, beginning to actually be convinced that a single well thought out strategy could be even better than we claimed, would have made another conceptual leap. Then the automated scheduling system couldn't be used until this new idea was incorporated. We pressed on believing that we were really getting to the heart of the matter.

The plan was finally based on the assumption that the results of the predictive scheduler could be measured (Gary et al., 1992), and the results of the measurement would trigger the next loop in the spiral of ever increasing understanding of strategies and ever more powerful scheduling systems. However, the users were accustomed to being graded on overall throughput, so extended evaluation of detailed, lot by lot, resource by resource, step by step Gantt charts showed only that each of the users didn't like something, and they were all different. We started to lose our way because lack of sound measurement of results inevitably means lack of sound development of functionality.

We had plans to implement the STRATEGY and SITUATION ASSESS-MENT modules as well as a USER INTERFACE to the STRATEGY module because it was immediately clear that the strategy would require continuous improvement by the user community. Furthermore, training and support plans were executed, resulting in comprehensive user and maintenance manuals and installation of field support staff. However, the creeping scope and enhancements to the STRATEGY and SITUATION ASSESSMENT modules and the lack of sound measurement criteria were too much of a handicap to maintain the project schedule. Although the predictive system has been used on and off in production (for roughly 6 months total) during the course of the last 27 months, management has wisely put the project on hold for redefinition and reorganization.

Although in a very real sense the software has failed because it is not in actual production use at this time, took at least double the originally scheduled period to complete, and is currently under management orders to be rethought, some of those involved judge the project as having succeeded in a limited sense based on two results.

The first is the qualitative change of mind-set exhibited by the manufacturing staff in the factory in which our development work was done. There are now regular meetings of a "strategy committee" that includes representatives from each shift and from the automated scheduling team, all of whom realize that there is a long exploration ahead in the space of operational strategies.

The second result is more qualitatively satisfying. There is now a complete (albeit very simple) operational strategy being uniformly executed by hand in the factory, with the results shown in Table 18-2. This strategy is the last one developed with the intention of being used with the predictive execution system and was tested prior to factory execution on the system. Because this is the primary factory producing INTEL 80486 microprocessors, these results paid for the predictive scheduler development effort within the first week of operational strategy execution. More progress should come from the committee and its continuous improvement efforts.

Table 18-2: Results of uniform execution of an operational policy.

Metric	% Improvement (first 26 weeks)
Wafer Starts	+ 10.3%
Water Finishes	+ 13.3%
Line Yield	+ 2.4%
Utilization of Key Resource #1	+ 7.8%
Utilization of Key Resource #2	+ 4.9%
WIP	+ 8.5%
Throughput Time	+ 9.2%

Plans for the immediate future are centered on building a predictive scheduler to be used in development mode (Figure 18-2, upper left) as a tool to support the understanding of strategies because this is where the root problem has been all along. However, the long term goal remains to be tools for capacity, predictive, and reactive problem solving to be used in both development mode and execution mode (all of Figure 18-2).

18.6 CONCLUSION

The efforts described here have convinced us that the techniques of Artificial Intelligence are appropriate in addressing the technical issues encountered in scheduling of semiconductor wafer fabrication. The architecture described here can rapidly provide high quality schedules. Although this is necessary to build a practical system, it is unfortunately not sufficient. Any development team must also rapidly provide high quality solutions to a large set of cultural problems. The most difficult for us proved to be scoping the project so that it could be delivered in pieces small enough to be adopted by the users but large enough to be useful, thereby generating pull for the next piece. The techniques of managing customer expectations and cultural change are at least as important as the techniques of AI in delivering practical scheduling systems.

ACKNOWLEDGMENTS

Three groups of people were instrumental in supporting the predictive scheduler project. G. Meieran, M. Balog, B. Giffin, D. Marsing, R. Null, and K. Thompson provided support at the management level. B. Sohn, B. Adams, F. Day, D. Dierke, F. Melkey, B. Orchard, J. Page, E. Sinnott, N. Teatsorth, R. Wiley, and D. Wormington served as collaborators in the manufacturing facility. K. Arvind, G.

Cleveland, D. Emme, K. Ho, J. Holman, N. Keng, C. Pickering, J. Sanborn, and S. P. Smith provided the software system design, implementation, and field support expertise.

References

Fox, B.R., and K.G. Kempf. 1985. "Opportunistic Scheduling for Robotic Assembly," *Proc. 2nd IEEE Inter. Conf. Robotics and Automation* (St. Louis), pp. 880–889. IEEE Computer Society Press, Los Alamitos, Calif.

Fox, B.R., and K.G. Kempf. 1987. "Reasoning about Opportunistic Schedules," *Proc. IEEE Inter. Conf. Robotics and Automation* (Raleigh), pp. 1876–1882. IEEE Computer Society Press, Los Alamitos, Calif.

Fox, M.S., and S.F. Smith. 1984. "ISIS—A Knowledge-based System for Factory Scheduling," *Expert Systems*, Vol. 1, No. 1, pp. 25–49.

Gary, K., R. Uzsoy, S.P. Smith, and K. Kempf. 1992. "Assessing the Quality of Production Schedules," *Intelligent Scheduling Systems*, eds. W. Scherer and D. Brown, Kluwer Academic Publishers, Norwell, Mass.

Hilton, C., and K. Kempf. 1989. "The Training Costs Associated with AI Applications in Manufacturing," *Proc. 2nd Inter. Conf., Expert Systems in Industry and Service* (Chicago), pp. 201–208. Elsevier Science Publishers, B.V., Amsterdam.

Holman, J., K. Ho, and K. Kempf. 1988. "Artificial Intelligence and Computer Interfaces for Manufacturing Personnel," *Proc. Intel Technology Conference* (Portland), pp. 177–180. Intel Press, Santa Clara, Calif.

Kempf, K. 1989a. "Intelligent Interfaces for Computer Integrated Manufacturing," *Proc. 3rd Inter. Conf. Expert Systems in Production Planning and Control* (Hilton Head, S.C.), pp. 269-279. University of South Carolina Press, Columbia, S.C.

Kempf, K. 1989b. "Manufacturing Scheduling—Intelligently Combining Existing Methods," *Proc. AAAI*, Stanford Spring Symposium, pp. 51–55. AAAI Press, Menlo Park, Calif.

Kempf, K. 1989c. "Scheduling Wafer Fabrication—The Intelligent Way," *SME Electronics in Manufacturing*, Vol. 4, No. 3, pp. 1–3.

Kempf, K. 1989d. "The Concepts of Chaos Applied to Manufacturing Production Scheduling," *Proc. AAAI/SIGMAN Workshop on Manufacturing Production Scheduling* (Detroit), Section 4, Paper 2, AAAI Press, Menlo Park, Calif.

Kempf, K., B. Russell, S. Sidhu, and S. Barrett. 1991. "Artificially Intelligent Schedulers in Manufacturing Practice," *AI Magazine*, Vol. 11, No. 5, pp. 46–56.

Kempf, K., S.F. Smith, B. Fox, and C. LePape. 1991. "Issues in the Design of Artificially Intelligent Manufacturing Schedulers," *AI Magazine*, Vol. 11, No. 5, pp. 37–45.

Meieran, E., and K. Kempf. 1989. "Applications of Artificial Intelligence in Factory Management," *Proc. 7th IEEE Inter. Electronics Mfg. Technology Symp.* (San Francisco), pp. 18–22. IEEE Computer Society Press, Los Alamitos, Calif.

Reece, G., and K. Kempf. 1990. "Designing a Multiagent Metaplanning Component for Intelligent Production Scheduling," *Proc. 2nd SIGMAN Workshop on Manufacturing Planning* (Boston), pp. 38–39.

Smith, S.F., and P.S. Ow. 1985. "The Use of Multiple Problem Decompositions in Time Constrained Planning Tasks," *Proc. IJCAI-85*, pp. 1013-1015. AAAI Press, Menlo Park, Calif.

Smith, S.F., N. Keng, and K. Kempf. 1990. "Exploiting Local Flexibility during Execution of Pre-Computed Schedules," *Proc. 2nd SIGMAN Workshop on Manufacturing Planning* (Boston), pp. 44–46. (See also Carnegie Mellon University, Robotics Institute Technical Report #90-13.) (See also *Artificial Intelligence Applications in Manufacturing*, ed. A. Famili, D. S. Nau, and S. H. Kim, pp. 277–293. AAAI Press, Menlo Park, Calif.)

Yu, C., G. Scott, and K. Kempf. 1988. "Artificial Intelligence and the Scheduling of Semiconductor Wafer Fabrication Facilities," *Proc. Intel Technology Conference* (Portland), pp. 135-138. Intel Press, Santa Clara, Calif.

19

PLANNING IN A FLEXIBLE SEMICONDUCTOR MANUFACTURING ENVIRONMENT

Hugh E. Fargher
Richard A. Smith
(Texas Instruments, Inc.)

19.1 INTRODUCTION

Texas Instruments (TI) has been contracted by the Air Force Wright Laboratory and the Defense Advanced Research Projects Agency (DARPA) to develop a next generation flexible semiconductor wafer fabrication system called Microelectronics Manufacturing Science & Technology (MMST). Several important areas have been addressed by MMST, including new single-wafer rapid thermal processes, in-situ sensors, cluster equipment, and advanced Computer Integrated Manufacturing (CIM) software. The objective of the project was to develop a manufacturing system capable of achieving an order of magnitude improvement in almost all aspects of wafer fabrication (McGehee, Johnson, & Mahaffey, 1991). TI was awarded the contract in October 1988 and completed development with a fabrication facility demonstration in April, 1993.

An important part of MMST was development of the CIM environment responsible for coordinating all parts of the system. The CIM architecture developed is based on a distributed object oriented framework made up of several cooperating subsystems. The software subsystems include Process Control for dynamic control of factory processes; Modular Processing System for controlling the processing equipment; Generic Equipment Model (GEM), which provides an interface between processing equipment and the rest of the factory; Specification System, which maintains factory documents and product specifications; Simulator for modeling the factory for analysis purposes; Scheduler for scheduling work on the factory floor; and Planner for planning and monitoring of work orders within the factory.

Semiconductor manufacturing broadly divides into three areas: material preparation and design (which involves designing the circuits to be fabricated, preparing photolithography masks, and making raw wafers); wafer processing (which involves constructing circuits onto the wafer); and assembly, packaging, and testing (which involves packaging and testing each individual circuit). Packaged circuits are referred to as *devices*. MMST is primarily focused on the wafer processing activity. Compared with most semiconductor manufacturing, MMST also aims at a low work in process (WIP) environment, with an emphasis on short cycle-time and high product mix. All Planner subsystem development has been made with such an environment in mind, with a WIP of around 250 wafers and machine groups numbering around 40. Wafer processing flows are on the order of 200 steps, with each step performed on one machine group. As with all semiconductor manufacturing, processing flows follow a *corkscrew* path, with the same machine groups (typically, photolithography or ion-implantation) used several times over in a flow.

Semiconductor manufacturing presents a challenging environment for planning and scheduling for several reasons. First, the requirements of the production manager change frequently, as new work is requested or priorities change. Second, the environment itself changes frequently in an unpredictable manner, as machines unexpectedly fail, or processing steps have to be reworked because of errors. Third, it is very difficult to define an evaluation function by which to judge a plan or schedule. Fourth, much of the data traditionally used for planning and scheduling is either unavailable (final processing flows for work might not be determined at work release) or uncertain (flow cycle-time data might be in the form of a distribution).

This chapter describes the MMST Planner in detail: the role it plays in semiconductor manufacturing, the algorithms it employs, and its performance in the manufacturing domain.

19.2 THE PLANNER VISION

The MMST planning system is designed to play the role of a *decision support tool*, available to a user experienced in the manufacturing domain. The system continually maintains an up-to-date plan, which determines work release and expected work completion dates and which is based on the current state of the factory. This dictates two overall properties of the system, first that it possesses a real-time interface to the rest of the manufacturing domain and second that it can determine the consequences of unexpected events, such as machine failure and the introduction of new work, very rapidly. Ideally, the system user could use the MMST Planner while he or she negotiates with a customer on the phone, determining whether requested work could be completed by a given delivery-date and, if not, exploring alternative scenarios.

19.2.1 Key Roles

The MMST Planner is designed to achieve the following six key roles:

1. Maintain a plan that determines when work should be released into the factory, and predict when that work will be completed: The plan does not determine precisely when wafers are processed by particular machines; instead, it determines that machine capacity will be available during the time the work is in the factory. All times are determined to within some *granularity*, typically, days or shifts. This supports the work release role shared between the MMST Planner and Scheduler, as illustrated in Figure 19-1. Although the Planner determines work that can be released during certain time intervals, the Scheduler determines when that work is released into the factory on a minute-by-minute basis. This reflects the level at which the two sub-systems model the manufacturing environment, the Planner using a high level processing capacity model and the Scheduler a detailed machine level model.

2. Enable continual and rapid plan updates, either to respond to user requests or to account for unexpected events such as machine breakdowns: User requests for planning new work are either *disruptive* (which allows existing planned work release and completion dates to be changed) or *non-disruptive* (which does not allow such changes). Typical disruptive requests for planning new work might be to *plan as soon as possible* or *plan by delivery date*, and typical non-disruptive requests might be to *plan when possible* or *plan by delivery-date if possible*.

3. Model uncertainty: This applies particularly to predicting work cycle-times once released into the factory. Very often, the best available data are in the form of a distribution of previously observed cycle-times for each processing flow. This implies that planned dates should have a confidence value associated with them.

4. Support the use of a planning strategy defined in terms of a hierarchy of factory goals.

5. Remain consistent with the current factory status and clock-time: This requires knowing work position and machine status as well as ensuring that the plan representation covers the current clock-time up to some predefined future plan horizon.

6. Enable *what-if* requests to be explored by a user of the system, with the option to *accept* or *reject* the resulting plan: Accepting the plan would elevate it to the status of the production plan used to determine work release into the

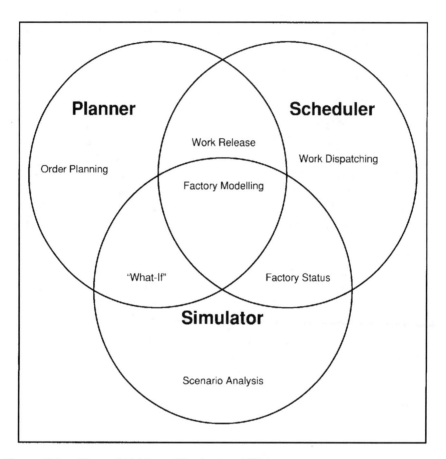

Figure 19-1:   Planner, Scheduler, and Simulator capabilities

factory. This ability supports the *what-if* role shared between the MMST Planner and Simulator, as illustrated in Figure 19-1. Planner *what-if* requests are used to explore the consequences of changes to the current state of the factory and demand immediate feedback to the system user. They cover, for example, what the consequences are of introducing a new piece of high priority work into a factory and how they might affect currently planned completion dates on existing work. This contrasts with the Simulator, which can perform several hundred simulations over a long period of time, using work input or machine failure distributions. Consequently, the Simulator could be used to determine more strategic decisions such as the purchase of a new machine.

19.2.2 Planning Approach

One of the key objectives for semiconductor manufacturing, especially in the Application Specific Integrated Circuit (ASIC) market for which MMST plays a role, is the reduction of product cycle-time. This has many proven benefits, including earlier detection of manufacturing problems and a faster time to market. The most effective way to reduce cycle-time is to reduce WIP, so that large queues do not form in front of bottleneck machines. There is considerable evidence to suggest that ensuring the correct work release rate and product mix is one of the most effective ways of achieving these objectives (Glassey & Resende, 1988). Consequently, one of the key roles for the MMST Planner is to determine work release into the factory. However, once work is actually released, it is the responsibility of the MMST Scheduler to ensure steady work processing. In effect, the Planner *challenges* the Scheduler to complete the work within an estimated cycle-time, based on the Planning system's model of the processing capacity available. If the Planner model were perfect, and no unexpected events occurred within the factory, then a work release algorithm could ensure machine queues of at most one piece of work. In this case, no Scheduler would be required. However because this is not possible or even desirable (if buffers in front of bottleneck machines are used for starvation avoidance), a Scheduler of some type is required.

This division of responsibility has been used within other planning work (Goldratt & Fox, 1988). In fact, there is evidence to suggest that once work is released, all scheduling decisions should be made entirely based on technology considerations and not on requested completion dates (Wein & Chevalier, 1992). This suggests that *priority* levels for work on the factory floor should not be used and that *first-in-first-out* (FIFO) is as good a dispatch rule as any. The fact that the *cost* of a top priority piece of work is often invisible (in terms of the detrimental effect it has on all other work) is probably the only reason that much high priority work exists at all (Fargher, Elleby, & Elleby, 1990).

19.2.3 Design Approach

All CIM subsystems have been designed and implemented within a distributed object-oriented environment. The resulting system is composed of a large number of cooperating *objects*, each of which is used to model the structure and behavior of key elements within the CIM system. The design methodology closely follows Booch (1991), and all implementation has been performed using Smalltalk. Design and code reviews were used to ensure that requirements were being met and that all subsystem interfaces were complete.

19.3 THE PLAN REPRESENTATION

19.3.1 Time-Phased Capacity Modeling

Figure 19-2 illustrates the plan representation which is based on the processing capacity of machine groups within the factory, divided into contiguous *time intervals*.

Processing capacity is the time a machine is available for work, taking into account measures such as mean-time-between-failure (MTBF) and mean-time-to-repair (MTTR). The time interval size can be arbitrary but typically corresponds to a single shift or day. All plan representation time intervals are of equal size and extend from the current clock-time to the plan horizon. Each machine group's processing capacity is represented in every plan time interval. A machine group has an associated set of processing capabilities that every member of the group is able to perform. Because a single semiconductor manufacturing machine can perform several different processes, a machine can be a member of several different machine groups.

Figure 19-2 illustrates two time intervals (T1 and T2) and three machine groups (MG1, MG2, and MG3). The shaded areas within each time interval represent the planned *utilization* of processing capacity for orders 1 and 2. For example, order 1 requires utilization of MG1 and MG2 during T1 and MG2 and MG3 during T2. Because processing capacity and utilization are divided between time intervals, the representation is referred to as a *time-phased capacity model*.

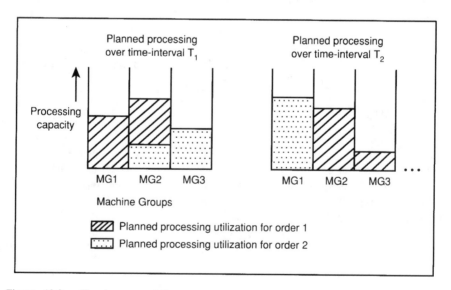

Figure   19-2:   The plan representation

The plan representation does not distinguish which machine within a group is planned to process a particular piece of work but simply commits processing time for the whole machine group to a particular piece of work. Also, the plan representation does not sequence processing within each time interval, only between time intervals. In this way, the level of detail modeled by the plan is a function of both machine groups and time interval sizes. If groups contained only one machine, and all time intervals were shorter than the shortest processing step, the plan representation would reduce to a Gantt chart describing the processing schedule for each machine. If, on the other hand, the entire plan were covered within a single time interval (such as a week), the representation would reduce to a simpler model that has been used for semiconductor manufacturing (Texas Instruments, 1989a). This simpler model determines work which can be released into the factory over the next week based on the total processing capacity available over that week. The time-phased representation outlined above lies somewhere between the two extremes.

The MMST Planner uses a work representation in which the required utilization for processing a group of wafers throughout their entire flow is divided into discrete *segments*. A segment represents the utilization of machine groups required during a time interval for a given order. Figure 19-2 includes two segments for order 1 and two segments for order 2. The first segment for order 1 requires utilization on MG1 and MG2 over T1. The second segment for order 1 requires utilization on MG2 and MG3 over T2. Division of required utilization for a given piece of work into segments is performed by calculating which segment each processing step would lie in if processing were distributed over the entire mean measured cycle-time. Because the cycle-time for the group of wafers is greater than the minimum theoretical processing time, such a representation models the expected queue time during wafer processing. For new processing flows, measurements might not be available; in which case, simulation could be used to estimate the mean cycle-time (which can be recorded as a function of production parameters such as the number of wafers per carrier). The planning problem then reduces to inserting segments into the time-phased model while satisfying all problem constraints.

The work representation must also be able to model yield. Yield is one of the most important measurables in semiconductor manufacturing because the number of devices that successfully pass final inspection might be considerably less than the number started. This is typically compensated for in ASIC production by starting more wafers than requested, so that the number of final working devices matches the customer demand. The MMST Planner uses a similar approach, calculating the number of wafers to start based on the estimated yield and the confidence to which the deliverable quantity is quoted (Texas Instruments, 1989a). The modeled processing step time is also reduced throughout the flow to account for expected loss because wafers are scrapped.

Finally, a load-sharing algorithm is employed to ensure that the estimated processing required by two or more machine groups, which share the same machine, is modeled properly (Texas Instruments, 1991). Not to be confused with balancing machine utilization (which is a planning goal), load-sharing models the fact that a machine shared between two groups will allocate its time between both groups, depending on the work load of each group. Each time the algorithm is *fired*, it iteratively re-distributes work between the groups until the loading is correct.

19.3.2 Modeling Uncertainty

The plan representation must be able to model the uncertainty inherent in cycle-times, which is recorded as the probability of completing all manufacturing steps on a wafer in a given time. Cycle-time and the two types of cycle-time distribution (CTD) used in the plan representation are defined as follows:

- *Cycle-time* is the total time required to complete a given set of processing steps (typically larger than the minimum theoretical processing time because of queue time, etc.)
- *Flow CTD* represents the frequency of observed cycle-times to complete all steps in a given flow. For example, 20% of the time, the flow requires 8 working days; 70% of the time, it requires 9 working days; and 10% of the time, it requires 10 working days.
- *Interval CTD* represents the frequency at which a particular cycle-time to complete a subset of steps in a given flow would be observed. The subset of steps are those expected to have completed by the end of the given time interval. For example, 10% of the time, the 50th step in a flow can be completed by the third time interval; 75% of the time, by the fourth time interval; and 15% of the time, by the 5th time interval. This would give the interval CTD for the fourth time interval.

This section describes how the MMST Planner models and uses these cycle-time distributions.

An objective of the MMST Planner is to predict work completion dates to within some given confidence, which can be used to negotiate with customers. For example, work can be represented within the plan so that it completes processing on Friday to within a 50% confidence level but on the following Monday to within an 80% confidence level.

Uncertainty is modeled within the Planner by reinterpreting the plan representation in terms of fuzzy sets (Kaufmann & Gupta, 1985). Machine group utilization for a given piece of work has a degree of membership within each time interval that reflects the expected utilization of machines for this work during the time interval. For example, the flow CTD for wafer processing can be interpreted as the probability distribution for completing the final processing step at a given time. This can be modeled within the plan representation by assigning degrees of membership between time intervals to match the given probability distribution for the final processing step. The advantage gained by this interpretation is two-fold. First, computation on fuzzy sets is much less expensive than on probability distributions. Second, cycle-time uncertainty within the time-phased representation means that machines committed to processing a given set of wafer steps within one time interval will very likely process some of those steps within other time intervals. This can be modeled using fuzzy set theory, where the set *member* corresponds to the wafer processing time required, and the member's *degree* describes the fraction of processing performed within different time intervals.

To enable the Planner to reason at this level of detail, knowledge of the flow CTD is required, as well as some estimate of the distributions required to complete each time interval's worth of processing. The flow CTD is available to the MMST Planner. However, interval CTDs might not be available. For this reason, the Planner uses an algorithm to estimate interval CTDs given the flow CTD. The algorithm attempts to decompose the flow CTD into interval CTDs for each successive time interval throughout a wafer's processing. This is done so that

- Interval CTD variance increases with successive intervals to reflect increasing future uncertainty.
- Interval CTD variance is bounded by the flow CTD variance.
- The final computed interval CTD matches the input flow CTD.

The algorithm represents distributions using fuzzy numbers and performs all calculations using fuzzy arithmetic. This approach is based on the job shop scheduling system FSS (Kerr & Walker, 1989), which also uses fuzzy arithmetic to model increasing uncertainty in generating future schedules. A key advantage with this approach is that calculations on distributions can be performed extremely rapidly. This approach is similar to that taken by Sadeh, who uses probability distributions to model uncertainty (Sadeh, 1991). The algorithm has been tested against simulated results, as described later.

Once interval CTDs have been calculated for a given wafer processing route, they are used to *fuzzify* the machine utilization (represented by segments) committed to processing steps during each time interval of the plan representation. This is achieved by using the fuzzification operator (defined for fuzzy set theory) and results in machine utilization being *smeared out* within the plan representation. This reflects the uncertainty in the time at which planned processing will actually take place in the factory. Once work has been planned for a wafer with a given processing route, the flow CTD is used to quote the completion date to within a given confidence level. For example, if 80% of the final time interval processing has been planned to complete by Friday, the wafer can be quoted to complete on Friday with an 80% confidence level. Alternatively, the confidence level can be set to some default value; in which case, completion dates are automatically planned to that level of confidence.

Finally, measured flow CTDs provide an important method for feedback to the Planner from the manufacturing environment. Recorded flow CTDs can be updated incrementally as wafers complete processing for each type of process flow, and the resulting cycle-times are measured. Furthermore, because cycle-times are closely related to current factory WIP and product mix, distributions used for planning should be chosen to reflect this.

19.3.3 Maintaining Model Consistency

An important role of the MMST Planner is to maintain a plan that is constantly up to date with the state of the factory and with the current clock-time. This requires maintaining an up to date capacity model, which is achieved in three ways: keeping track of machine status, regularly checking released work progress, and updating capacity model time intervals with passing clock-time.

Each machine status is tracked by the MMST GEM subsystem, which informs the Planner each time a machine goes down or comes up. Machine down information includes an estimated downtime, which is used to reduce available utilization within the capacity model. Information on machine up times is also required because machines that come up sooner than expected will make unexpected processing capacity available.

Work progress on the factory floor is tracked by the MMST Scheduler and the information made available to other subsystems as required. The Planner is designed to check work progress at the end of modeled time intervals (which are currently chosen to be one day in duration) and compare this with expected planned progress. If (within some tolerance) work progress on the factory floor is judged as falling behind plan, the work is replanned and the system user warned of any slippage in completion date.

Finally, the plan's capacity model time intervals must be updated with passing clock-time. This is achieved in three ways. First, all planned processing for the earliest time interval is removed from the capacity model when the clock time exceeds the time interval upper bound. This ensures that the plan represents only future processing capacity. Work corresponding to all removed processing is then checked for progress, as described previously. Second, each time this is done, processing capacity for a new time interval is appended to the end of the capacity model. This maintains a constant plan horizon, up to which all processing capacity is modeled. Third, the available capacity of machine groups within the first plan time interval is reduced linearly with clock-time to reflect the remaining hours in the day.

19.4 THE PLANNING ALGORITHM

19.4.1 Overview

The plan representation described in the previous section defines a set of manufacturing constraints that must be satisfied for a plan to be feasible (i.e., executable in the factory). Although much work has been done on constraint satisfaction algorithms (Nadel, 1987), the number of constraints found in real-life manufacturing typically dictates that optimal solutions cannot be generated. However, *good* sub-optimal solutions are very often acceptable, especially in manufacturing environments where determination of an optimal function is sometimes impossible (Elleby, Fargher, & Addis, 1988). Consequently, the approach taken by the MMST Planner is that of generating sub-optimal solutions that are considered *acceptable* by a user of the system who is experienced in the manufacturing domain.

This approach presupposes another property that is often true in manufacturing domains, namely, the existence of a large number of plans that satisfy all manufacturing constraints, even though the majority of such solutions would be considered *unacceptable* when judged by anyone experienced in the domain. For example, factories that perform poorly in terms of cycle-time and product quality (typically as a result of allowing too much WIP to accumulate) do nevertheless produce output, implying that a plan *solution* that has satisfied all manufacturing constraints has been found. This contrasts with planning problems found in other domains (e.g., theorem-proving [Charniak & McDermott, 1985]), where the generation of a plan solution can be extremely difficult.

Constraints on which time interval each segment can be planned into come from four distinct sources: the capacity model, the process flow for the work being planned, the user request used to plan the work, and the algorithm that controls the search space covered during planning. Capacity model constraints ensure that machines are not over-utilized given their estimated availability over each time interval. This also accounts for periods of time during which the factory might be completely down, with no machines available for use (e.g., an annual maintenance period). Process flow constraints ensure that segments of utilization for a given flow cannot be planned in the wrong chronological order into the capacity model. For example, in semiconductor manufacturing (as well as most other discrete manufacturing), processing steps must be executed in a strict sequence, which must not be violated when represented within the plan's capacity model (even though the model is not detailed enough to represent sequenced steps within a time interval).

Once the manufacturing problem has been defined as a set of constraints, several approaches can be taken to finding a solution. For example, Leachman (1992) has used a linear programming technique after first reducing the number of constraints (which are on the order of one half million in his example). The MMST Planner employs a beam search, using local and global heuristics during plan generation. Beam search has been used in other planners such as ISIS (Fox & Smith, 1984); however, unlike ISIS, the beam width grows with search depth and uses a simple back-tracking scheme to search within the beam. The advantage with this approach is two-fold. First, sub-optimal plans can be generated relatively quickly based on heuristics that experts in the domain can help to build. Second, once a plan has been generated, it can be updated incrementally by continuing the search process from the previous solution—a process that very often means only a small update to the existing plan. This is an important feature of the MMST Planner, which must provide continual and rapid plan updates if it is to play the role of a decision support tool. Constraints are not explicitly used to guide the MMST Planner search algorithm by ranking the set of plan choices (as is performed in ISIS) but are used to terminate search of a particular branch when any constraints are not satisfied.

The fundamental objective of the planning algorithm is to allocate utilization in the time-phased capacity model for work that is requested by the user of the system. This is done when the work representation has been divided into discrete segments as described previously, where each segment represents processing on resources that can be completed within one time interval of the plan representation. The result determines when work must be released into the factory and provides an estimate as to when work will be completed.

The load-sharing algorithm is used to balance utilization across machine groups within a single time interval. In principle, it should be *fired* after every insertion of a segment into the time interval because incorrect modeling of work shared between machine groups could distort the plan representation. However, *firing* after every insertion is computationally expensive. Another alternative is to fire the algorithm whenever a time interval processing capacity is exceeded because the resulting spread of utilization can reveal that further work might indeed be planned during the interval. However, this is not frequent enough and would mean that most planning decisions would be based on a distorted representation. Consequently, the approach used by the MMST Planner is to regulate the frequency at which the algorithm is *fired* by keeping account of the number of successful insertions into each plan time interval. When this reaches a predefined limit, the algorithm is *fired* on that particular interval. By choosing the limit carefully, the computation time required by the algorithm can be minimized while the distortion in the capacity model is limited as the plan is built up.

Work is released so as to utilize bottleneck machines as much as possible without exceeding their maximum available processing capacity. This requires estimating when released work will reach those bottlenecks. This is similar to the approach taken by OPT (Goldratt, 1988). If all utilization for a piece of work cannot be allocated in the capacity model within the plan horizon, the work will not be planned. The system user then has two options: to attempt to plan this work again when processing capacity becomes available or to use the Planner *what-if* capability to explore options (such as modifying other work priorities or due-dates) to improve the plan quality. The search algorithm is described in detail in the following three sections, which outline the implementation of a planning strategy (used to control the search process), initial plan generation, and incremental planning.

19.4.2 The Planning Strategy

It has been found that production managers, working in an MMST type of semiconductor manufacturing domain, can express their general production requirements as a priority list of goals and constraints. For example, the top requirement can be meeting all due-dates quoted to customers (while avoiding early completion of their work) followed by maximizing throughput with the constraint that WIP does not exceed a predefined level. Further down the list might be the requirement to balance work release and machine utilization or to reduce variance in yield found for each product.

Some of these goals are simply constraints (e.g., keeping WIP below a given level), but others require some heuristic mechanism to satisfy (e.g., meeting all due-dates or balancing machine utilization). Goals that can be represented by constraints are translated and stored within the Planner and are always satisfied during plan generation. Consequently, there is no concept of a *soft* constraint—if a constraint is to be relaxed, it is up to the system user to do this through *what-if* planning alternatives. Goals that require some heuristic mechanism are represented in the same way that AI heuristic evaluation functions are implemented—given a choice of alternative decisions (e.g., which work to next plan into the capacity model or which time interval to plan work for release into the factory), each decision is rated by its estimated benefit in achieving the given goal. This rating is given by a heuristic function associated with each goal. The heuristics are similar to those used in other systems (Baker, 1974). The result of each goal is therefore to either create more constraints (which is done once only, when the goal is instantiated) or to sequence a set of possible planning decisions (which is done many times over during the planning process).

Constraints are represented within the Planner by using Allen's temporal relations (Allen, 1983), or by setting planning *policy variables* that govern the algorithm behavior. For example, the maximum number of wafers allowed in one carrier is a *policy variable* constraint, which determines how work is divided up for release.

The planning strategy consists of a priority list of these goals, matching the priorities of the production manager. As well as creating the goal constraints, the strategy is used to make all Planner sequencing decisions by using the list of goals as a filter (*Strategy Manager*, 1989). First, the decisions are sequenced using the top level goal. However, if two or more possible decisions score equally using the goal's heuristic, the next level goal is used to try and sequence them using its own heuristic. This process continues iteratively through as many goal levels as required until a strict ordering on the planning decisions is achieved.

It is important to note that different goals can affect different parts of the planning process. For example, the goal to meet due-dates can affect which work is next planned out of a list because work with least slack to due-date (once cycle-time is taken into account) would take priority. However, balancing machine utilization is more influenced by the time interval in which work is released. The fact that goals affect different parts of the planning process is used to construct the global production strategy used by both the MMST Planner and Scheduler. The global production strategy is again composed of an ordered list of goals, some of which affect the Planner, some the Scheduler, and some both. The planning strategy is simply the subset of goals that affect the Planner, which might well overlap the subset of goals that affect the Scheduler. Each goal can have an associated heuristic function that can be used by the Planner as well as one that can be used by the Scheduler, although the two functions might require different implementations (reflecting the different levels of abstraction at which the Planner and Scheduler model the production environment). However, by guaranteeing that both the Planner and Scheduler use the same global strategy, some control can be achieved to ensure that the two systems *pull* in the same direction.

User requests provide a more local control over plan generation compared with the more global control provided by the planning strategy. Requests determine how each new piece of work is locally planned; for example, work might be required *as soon as possible* (which might require replanning existing work of a lower priority) or *by due-date if possible* (which means planning to complete on its due-date without disrupting existing planned work). The algorithm that controls the search space is described later in this section.

Finally, the Planner allows a trade-off between the computation time required to follow a given strategy and the closeness to which the strategy is adhered to. This is achieved by recomputing the strict ordering on planning decisions only after a given number of those decisions have been used in the planning process. For example, if the Planner needs a strict ordering on 10 new work items to plan, it might sequence these using its strategy, select the first 3 in the sequence and plan them, and then apply the strategy to produce another strict ordering on the remaining 7 work items. The Planner could then continue planning 3 work items at a time until all have been planned. The need to recompute the strict ordering of work items periodically stems from the fact that any updates to the existing plan can result in a different sequence, determined by the planning strategy that now sees an updated plan representation. In principle, strict orderings should be re-computed every time the Planner uses one of those decisions to update the plan representation. However, this is compromised to reduce the total computation time required for planning.

19.4.3 Initial Plan Generation

Initial plan generation is used to build a plan from scratch given the current state of the factory. In principle, this is performed only once, when the Planner is installed. After the initial plan is generated, all further updates are made incrementally. In both initial plan generation and incremental updating, plans are generated using a search based approach.

Each search *operation* during plan generation either inserts or removes discrete segments of utilization from the time-phased capacity model. Plan generation terminates when all required segments for processing the given work have been inserted or when no further processing capacity remains.

The Search Algorithm. The algorithm is divided into two distinct parts. The first part determines the time interval in which the first segment of a new piece of work's process flow is planned. This is described in the later section on incremental planning. However, once determined, the planner executes the second part of the algorithm, which inserts segments chronologically forward in time (in terms of the processing steps that each segment represents) into the capacity model. This is achieved using a modified beam search (Winston, 1984) with chronological backtracking.

Figure 19-3 illustrates the Planner search algorithm for three levels in the search tree. Each time interval that the search algorithm considers a possible candidate for inserting a segment is referred to as a *node*. In the example shown, the first segment cannot be inserted at time interval T0 without exceeding T0's maximum available processing capacity but can be inserted successfully at T1. The process flow's second segment is then successfully inserted at T2 and the third segment at T4. Note that the third segment cannot be inserted at T1 without violating the process flow sequence constraint, which says that processing steps must be executed in a strict sequence. Also, the third segment cannot be inserted at T5 without exceeding the beam width at level three in the search. The beam search is modified so that the beam width increases linearly with the search depth, where the linear factor is referred to as the beam *gradient*. For example, with a beam gradient of 1, the maximum number of nodes searched at the Nth level in the search tree is

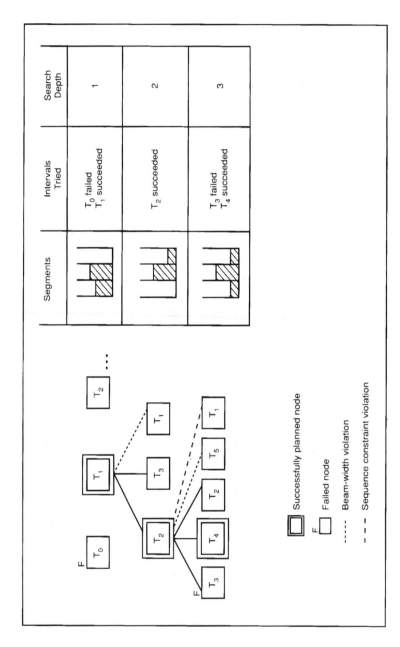

Figure 19-3: The Planner search algorithm

exactly N. The beam gradient used is based on the width of the flow CTD, such that a tighter flow CTD produces a more constrained search space. Search proceeds in a depth first manner with chronological backtracking and terminates when either all segments for the planned work have been inserted or when the search space has been exhausted. The beam width is further constrained by the ratio of the total measured process flow cycle-time to the minimum theoretical flow cycle-time. This ensures that when all segments for a process flow are inserted into the capacity model, they do not violate the constraint that each segment must be planned to occur after the first segment by a time at least equal to the minimum theoretical processing time up to that segment. For example, if all processing prior to the third segment in a process flow requires a minimum of two days, then that third segment must be planned to occur at least two days after the work is released.

Backtracking occurs when a segment cannot be planned for a time interval without exceeding the interval's maximum available processing capacity (referred to as a *failed* node) or when a node's children in the search space have all failed (referred to as a *backtracked* node). All nodes at each level of the search algorithm are sorted via a *straddle sequence* unless further constrained by the planning strategy. This sequences nodes so as to minimize the deviation from a uniform insertion of utilization into the capacity model. For example, if no backtracking occurs, all segments for a process flow will be inserted during contiguous time intervals. If backtracking is minimal, segments for a process flow will be inserted in *almost* contiguous time intervals.

Finally, the search algorithm has been adapted to account for *closed nodes*, corresponding to time intervals during which the factory, with all its machines, is unavailable for work. Although this is rare within semiconductor manufacturing, it is a condition that must be modeled. This is achieved by ensuring that the search algorithm never generates closed nodes during planning. The result is to prune parts of the search space that do not contain feasible solutions. However, flow processing can be planned around closed node time intervals. This reflects the common-sense notion that even though a factory might be down for a whole week, it can still contain WIP that is partially through its processing flow. The only exception to this might be work that contains inter-step time constraints. For example, some semiconductor processing steps must occur within a maximum time limit of each other to avoid the build up of oxides on the wafer surface. This approach also ensures that work can be planned during time periods that are normally unavailable by introducing *emergency shifts* because the capacity model still contains contiguous time intervals.

The beam search algorithm described has several benefits. First, it tends to concentrate computation in more promising areas of the search space. If backtracking occurs early on in the search process while new work is being planned, the algorithm will tend to give up early, compelling the algorithm to try planning that work for release during a different time interval. However, if backtracking occurs later in the search process (when more computation has already been committed to planning the new work for release during a given time period), the algorithm will explore a wider search space in an attempt to find available capacity. A second benefit of the algorithm is that it constrains the search space less tightly the further into the future segments are planned. This reflects the increasing uncertainty as to when planned processing will be executed the further into the future it is planned.

Search Behavior. The behavior of the search algorithm for initial plan generation has been examined in terms of three variables: the mean percentage of machine utilization committed over time in a plan, the number of machines planned, and the length of the plan horizon. As a result of this, several heuristics to reduce plan generation time have been explored. The behavior of the search algorithm, as well as the effectiveness of these heuristics, is described in this section.

Table 19-1 illustrates the search algorithm behavior as the mean percentage of planned machine utilization increases. In this example, the manufacturing model was chosen to enable plans, using artificially high machine utilization, to be generated. It illustrates the resulting percentage of successful search nodes (in which a segment was successfully inserted into the capacity model), failed nodes (in which the segment could not be inserted because it exceeded the maximum available processing capacity for that time interval), and backtracked nodes (which fail when all their children nodes fail) during plan generation. The results illustrate that for even a highly utilized factory (up to 80%), the percentage of successful nodes remains significant (80% utilization across all machines is artificially high for semiconductor manufacturing). However, no plan solution could be found for a machine utilization exceeding 80%, even though a large number of extra nodes were searched. This reflects the fact that an enormous increase in search is required to plan new work into a highly utilized factory once a threshold utilization has been met. This means that the time required to generate initial plans might largely be spent on planning in the last few pieces of work, which require considerable computation to find available processing capacity. In fact, examples were generated in which the next-to-last piece of planned work required a search of 63 nodes; the last piece of planned work required over 22,000 nodes; and thereafter, no more work could be planned.

This behavior has been observed in other planning systems (Sadeh, 1991), and has resulted in a simple heuristic that has been adopted independently by several groups. The heuristic sets an upper limit on the number of nodes searched while a piece of work is being planned. If the limit is reached, the search is terminated, concluding that the piece of work cannot be planned because of a lack of available processing capacity. The upper limit set is dependent on many factors, including the size of the search space and the response times considered acceptable

Table 19-1: Plan search behavior.

Committed Utilization (Percent)	Successful Node (Percent)	Failed Node (Percent)	Backtracked Node (Percent)
10	100	0	0
20	100	0	0
30	47	40	13
40	44	44	12
50	36	50	14
60	35	52	13
70	32	56	12
80	30	58	12

by the system user. However, results have shown up to a 97% reduction in total computation time to generate plans that include over 95% of the same work as the original plan. This heuristic has been used to significantly reduce computation time for the MMST Planner. Furthermore, a heuristic of this type has a justification based in the MMST manufacturing environment itself. Because of the uncertainties found in the environment, work that requires a large amount of search to include into an existing plan is often considered *unreliable* in terms of meeting the resulting planned completion date. This is because any small perturbation of the environment (such as a brief interruption in machine availability) will likely invalidate the work plan. However, such perturbations are less likely to affect work for which a plan solution was more easily found. This reiterates the point made earlier, which pre-supposes the existence of a large number of plan solutions in domains suitable for the MMST Planner.

Table 19-2 illustrates the search algorithm behavior as the number of modeled machines (which includes a mixture of both bottleneck and non-bottleneck) increases for a varying percentage of mean planned machine utilization and a plan horizon of 60 days. The table shows the total computation time required (in minutes) to generate an initial plan and demonstrates an exponential increase in computation time with the number of machines modeled. It is worth noting that even though initial plan generation can take some time (1.5 hours in the extreme case of 160 machines), incremental updates are still rapid (7 cpu seconds to plan the last piece of work in the case of 160 machines, where the committed utilization remains below the threshold at which an enormous increase in search is required).

The behavior suggests that reducing the number of machines modeled will always reduce the total planning time. However, when this was tried, an interesting observation was made. The planning time was only reduced when bottleneck machines were removed from the plan's capacity model. The removal of non-bottleneck machines gave almost no reduction in total planning time. This results from

Table 19-2: Plan generation time in minutes for increasing number of machines.

Committed Utilization (Percent)	Number of Machines			
	20	40	80	160
20	0.57	2.0	6.9	27.9
30	0.69	2.4	8.4	51.2
40	0.83	2.8	11.8	91.7

the fact that almost all plan computation time stems from the failed and back-tracked nodes explored during plan generation, and search nodes only fail when the maximum available processing capacity over a time interval is exceeded. Typically, only bottleneck machines have a planned utilization close to the maximum level; therefore, it is the bottlenecks that govern the entire search process. However, removing bottleneck machines from the capacity model would result in worthless plans.

As a consequence of this observation, all significant machines (whether they are judged as bottlenecks or not) are represented in the MMST Planner capacity model, even though semiconductor manufacturing contains very predictable bottlenecks (photo-lithography, ion-implantation, etc.). One benefit with this approach is that there is a reduced risk of omitting bottlenecks from the capacity model. Even though the variety of products manufactured in an MMST environment leads to *wandering* bottlenecks over time, all significant machines are modeled, so the bottleneck will always be considered in the planning process.

Table 19-3 illustrates the search algorithm behavior as the length of the plan horizon increases for a fixed percentage of mean planned machine utilization. The table shows the total computation time required (in minutes) to generate an initial plan and demonstrates an exponential increase in computation time with the length of plan horizon when using a total of 20 modeled machines.

The behavior suggests that as the scope for time intervals for planning work for release increases, the percentage of failed nodes searched also increases. As a result, heuristics that quickly eliminated time intervals for planning work release were found to be quite effective. One such simple heuristic was used to check that

Table 19-3: Plan generation time in minutes for increasing plan horizon.

Committed Utilization (Percent)	Plan Horizon in Days					
	10	30	60	120	240	365
20	0.09	0.26	0.57	1.3	3.2	7.1
30	0.10	0.29	0.69	1.7	4.7	10.2
40	0.11	0.34	0.83	2.2	6.0	13.6

work planned for release could completely be represented in the capacity model before the plan horizon. This ensured that the search algorithm did not spend fruitless computation on a piece of work only to find that the last few segments could not be planned to complete before the end of the plan horizon.

19.4.4 Incremental Planning

Incremental planning results from an unexpected change in the manufacturing environment: a newly requested piece of work, a change in machine status, or a change in requirements such as an already planned delivery date. Semiconductor manufacturing in general and MMST in particular present a manufacturing environment notorious for such unexpected events. Indeed, this is one reason why MMST planning and scheduling is so difficult and why incremental planning is essential. Ideally, the MMST Planner is required to generate an initial production plan from scratch once only. Thereafter, all planning will consist of incremental updates to the one production plan.

The Search Algorithm. The algorithm is divided into two distinct parts. The first part determines the time interval for which the first segment of a new piece of work's process flow is planned. The second part determines how existing planned work is replanned as a result of the change in available processing capacity. Other than this, the search algorithm that inserts segments into the capacity model is the same as that described in the previous section.

The time interval for planning a piece of work's first segment is determined by the plan request made by the user. A non-disruptive request such as *plan when possible* determines the time interval using the following simple algorithm, which attempts to plan the new work as early as possible, starting from the current time interval:

```
1. Set integer N equal to one.

2. Apply heuristic to check that the work can be planned for
release during the N'th time interval (without exceeding the
plan horizon).

If the work cannot be planned, abort the planning attempt. Other-
wise, continue.

3. Attempt to plan the work so that the first segment is
inserted into the N'th available time interval, using the beam-
search algorithm.

If the work cannot be planned, increment N by one and go to 2.
Otherwise, terminate because the work has successfully been
planned.
```

Algorithm 19-1:   Plan when possible.

```
1. Set integer N to index the latest time interval that the work
can be planned for release.

2. If N is less than one, abort the planning attempt.
Otherwise, continue.

3. Attempt to plan the work so that the first segment is
inserted into the N'th available time interval, using the beam-
search algorithm.

If the work cannot be planned, decrement N by one and go to 2.
Otherwise terminate, since the work has successfully been
planned.
```

Algorithm 19-2:   Plan by deliver-date if possible.

A non-disruptive request such as *plan by delivery-date if possible* determines the time interval using a similar algorithm, although N is initially calculated as the latest time interval that the work can be planned for release given that it must complete by its delivery-date within a given confidence level. N is then decremented (not incremented) so that plans that release work earlier than required but that still meet the requested delivery-date are explored. (See Algorithm 19-2.)

The second part of the planning algorithm determines how existing work is replanned. This results from a disruptive request such as *plan as soon as possible* and is more complicated because it potentially affects existing planned work. In this case, existing planned work of a lower priority is removed from the plan until the new work is planned to complete as soon as possible. All removed work is then planned back into the capacity model again.

There are two important features in Algorithm 19-3. First, only planned work that is currently unreleased into the factory can be replanned. This is in line with the overall approach that in planning new work, the Planner reshuffles work outside the factory door but, once released, does not replan work. Second, lower priority work that is removed during the algorithm can be planned back into the capacity model using any type of request. The MMST Planner uses the *plan when possible* request, which minimizes the number of pieces of work whose plan dates are changed, even though those changes might be large. This contrasts with the other approach, which can be to minimize the changes to plan dates, even though the number of pieces of work whose plan dates are changed might be large. The preference of one approach over the other depends on the requirements of the manufacturing domain. However, the approach taken by the MMST Planner does reduce the *domino* effect, in which one replanned piece of work leads to the replanning of several more, and so forth. Other disruptive requests such as *plan by delivery-date* use algorithms that are a mixture of those described above. Note that the

1. Set integer N equal to one.

2. Apply heuristic to check that the work can be planned for
release during the N'th time interval (without exceeding the
plan horizon).

If the work cannot be planned, abort the planning attempt.
Otherwise, continue.

3. Attempt to plan the work so that the first segment is
inserted into the N'th available time interval, using the beam-
search algorithm.

If required processing capacity is allocated to existing planned
work of lower priority, verify that the work can be planned if
the lower priority work were removed.

If the work cannot be planned, increment N by one, and go to 2.
Otherwise, remove and replan as much existing lower priority
work as required to plan in the new work.

Terminate.

Algorithm 19-3:   Plan as soon as possible

algorithms described are simplified to ignore the plan strategy, which is used when setting the value of N.

Finally, incremental planning can result from unexpected changes in machine status, which ultimately change the expected processing capacity available for planning. The MMST Planner is informed in real time of such events by the GEM subsystem, which provides the Planner with machine status information. GEM also provides estimates of how long each machine will be down for unexpected repair. The replanning algorithm used is similar to Algorithm 19-3, except that instead of planning in new work, a machine going down results in a predefined processing capacity being reduced within the capacity model over known time intervals. Furthermore, work that has already been released into the factory might well be affected because the work might require a machine that will not now be available. By replanning, the MMST Planner can warn system users of work, both unreleased and released, that will be affected. Unreleased work can be affected by a change in its planned release and completion date. However, work that has already been released might only be affected by a change in its planned completion date.

Search Behavior. The behavior of the search algorithm has been examined in terms of three possible causes of replanning: non-disruptive user requests, disruptive user requests, and unexpected changes in machine status. Typical replanning times were recorded for these requests based on a capacity model that represented the same WIP and number of machines anticipated in the MMST manufacturing environment.

Non-disruptive planning requests typically required the least computation time. For example, planning a piece of new work *when possible* required about 5 cpu seconds and affected 3% of the existing plan. Disruptive planning requests typically required more computation. For example, planning a piece of work *as soon as possible* required about 20 cpu seconds and affected 15% of the existing plan. Finally, replanning because of a change in machine status was highly dependent on the machine chosen and the period of time affected. Putting the ion implanter (a definite bottleneck machine) down for 12 hours required about 8 cpu seconds and affected 5% of the existing plan.

19.5 TESTING AND VALIDATION

The successful deployment of the MMST Planner depends on its ability to function properly under normal and abnormal conditions and to meet stated contract requirements, both of which can best be verified through formal testing. In the past, other potentially good manufacturing systems haved failed because of system bugs or the failure to conform to user requirements, both of which caused the loss of user confidence and eventual removal of the failed systems. The goal of testing of the MMST Planner is to prevent bugs and verify conformance to the stated user requirements in order to provide a working system that will gain the confidence of its users. Experience has shown that as much as half of the time spent creating working programs is spent testing the systems (Beizer, 1983). For this reason, a test methodology was implemented that allowed flexible test design, implementation, and execution of multiple test cases and that provided a systematic method for testing conformance to requirements as well as bug identification. When developing the formal testing procedure, some of the requirements considered were

- Tests will be run by non-developers.
- Each test must be repeatable for regression testing.
- Each test case must be documented.
- Tests should easily be configurable.
- Conformance to requirements must be verified.

The development of the test framework led to two ways of testing the MMST Planner: (1) to use programmatic testing to verify system performance under varied conditions (referred to as subsystem testing) and (2) to employ user testing as a way to verify conformance to user requirements and to collect feedback from future system users (referred to as user testing).

19.5.1 Approach to Subsystem Testing

Testing of the MMST Planner was broken into three categories, namely, unit tests, system tests, and integration tests. As a simplification, we will use the following definitions for the test categories:

- Unit tests verify the behavior of a single coded object.
- System tests verify behavior of multiple cooperating objects within a single subsystem.
- Integration tests verify behavior between cooperating subsystems.

Tests from each category are needed to completely verify system functionality.

Unit Tests. The first type of test performed within the MMST Planner is the unit test, which verifies that individual objects perform as designed. Typically, these tests are far simpler than the system tests (described later) and can be run in a short amount of time. As an example of how unit tests are implemented, we will review how such tests are implemented on the *machine* object.

The machine object is part of the capacity model and represents a single machine's processing time for a given time-interval. This object is responsible for maintaining the list of work expected to utilize the machine during the time-interval as well as the machine's current available capacity. Some of the operations that can be performed on this object include the inclusion of an additional piece of work, the removal of a selected piece of work, and the calculation of the current total utilization assigned to this machine. The unit tests designed for this object must verify that all the basic behavior is being performed correctly.

There are three ways of performing the first operation (inclusion of an additional piece of work):

1. Include work only if the maximum machine capacity level has not been exceeded.
2. Include work only if the goal machine capacity has not been exceeded.
3. Include work while you ignore maximum and goal capacity levels.

In each case, the machine will respond true if the utilization fits without violating any constraints and false otherwise. For number 1, the unit test sets the maximum capacity to a selected value, for example, 16 hours of available processing time, and tries to insert new work that requires utilization of less than, more than, and equal to the maximum capacity. When the new work value is less than or equal to the maximum capacity, the work should be inserted with the new value of assigned utilization equal to the value inserted, and the response true returned. When the new work leads to the maximum capacity being exceeded, the machine object should not allow the insertion and, therefore, respond by not updating the current assigned utilization and returning false. In the unit test, the returned value and the currently assigned utilization are compared to the expected results, and the test passes if all values match.

The tests described above are used to verify that the object performs correctly under normal operating conditions, but what happens under abnormal conditions? The unit tests must also verify that exceptional conditions are trapped and handled properly. An example of an exceptional condition would be an attempt to remove utilization for work that is not assigned within the given time-interval. In this case, the unit test would request that a machine object remove work that had not been assigned during the time-interval and verify that the result returned is correct and the exception handled properly.

Similar unit tests were designed for the basic behavior of all significant objects developed within the MMST Planner system.

System Tests.   Unit tests are sufficient for verifying that a single object operating alone or in concert with a small number of objects is working as designed, but a second more extensive type of testing is required for larger groups of cooperating objects. For this second type, called system tests, a hierarchy was designed that allowed testing of the MMST Planner at various levels. Figure 19-4 shows a portion of the hierarchy that was developed.

The test hierarchy can be viewed as being more general at the top of the hierarchy and more specific at the bottom. For instance, the top level Planner test supports all lower level tests, but the *Include When Possible Test* only supports tests related to the planning request *plan when possible*. However, because the tests are implemented as a hierarchy, all attributes and operations defined for the Planner Test are also available to the *Include When Possible Test*, thus allowing lower level tests to create an execution environment that can involve many different objects.

```
Planner Test
   Factory Output Commitments Test
      Order Creation Test
      Plan Order Item Test
         Include ASAP Test
         Include By DD If Possible Test
         Include By DD Test
         Include When Possible Test
```

Figure 19-4:   System tests hierarchy

To execute a single test, an environment must be selected and created and a particular test chosen and executed. Upon completion of the test run, the actual results are compared with the expected results, just as with unit tests. A typical system test would include the following steps:

1. Reset the environment—where environment and statistics variables are reinitialized.

2. Configure the environment—where parameters are set that will guide the creation of the environment for this test case.

3. Generate the new environment—where the objects needed to execute this test are actually created in preparation for the test run.

4. Execute the test and collect statistics—where the test is executed, and all selected statistics are collected.

5. Verify and display the results—where the test results are compared to expected values and displayed to the test administrator.

Item 1 resets all previous environment settings. For example, if the planning horizon is normally 60 days and is set to 10 days for a particular test, the procedure would reset the value to 60 days prior to the start of the next test. The details of items 2, 3, and 4 are discussed in the subsequent sections.

Item 5 is the step where system test verification is executed and the results formatted for user viewing. During a system test, verification routines can be run to ensure that the planning system is operating as expected. The verification tests do not assess the quality of the plan being generated; instead, they assess the consistency of the plan. An example verification routine is *verify release queue entries*. Each time interval in the system has an associated release queue that holds work planned for release during that time interval. As new work is planned, an expected release date is determined, and the work is placed in a specific time interval's release queue. The *verify release queue entries* routine checks the consistency of all work with respect to the set of release queues. This is done by iterating over all work in the plan and verifying that each piece of work that is not released appears in a single release queue. For each piece of work that has already been released, the routine verifies that the work does not appear in any release queue. Other items related to release queues are also verified during this process. Each test that is executed can include several verification routines. In addition, during system operation, the verification routines can be run at specified intervals to evaluate plan consistency over time. In this way, any inconsistency can be caught and corrected before a problem is encountered by a user.

Integration Tests. To complete the testing of the MMST Planner, integration tests are needed to verify that interactions between the MMST Planner and other MMST subsystems occur as expected. The interaction between two subsystems can be viewed as a producer/consumer relationship, with the *consumer* being responsible for designing and developing the integration tests. The MMST Planner is integrated with several other subsystems, including the Scheduler, Simulator, GEM, and Specification subsystems. This section will describe some of the integration tests developed to verify the interface between the MMST Planner and the Specification (SPEC) subsystem.

The SPEC subsystem provides the MMST Planner with all data related to product specifications, which will include the steps needed to manufacture a particular device and the flow CTD. During planning, the MMST Planner must query the SPEC subsystem for the steps in a product flow in order to allocate processing capacity to the required machine groups. In addition, the MMST Planner will use a flow CTD to determine the expected cycle time based on the selected confidence level. The MMST Planner is therefore the consumer of SPEC data and is responsible for designing and developing integration tests that will ensure that the interactions between the two systems are correct.

Integration tests for the product specification were designed using a 3-level approach, with each new test level verifying the interface in more detail. The level 1 test verifies that product specifications respond to queries such as *return flow distributions* or *return step planning data* and that each query is answered with the correct object type. The level 2 test verifies that the objects returned from queries contain objects of the correct type. For instance, the response to the query *return the flow distributions* should include both flow CTDs and yield distributions. The second level test verifies that this is true. Finally, the level 3 test verifies that all entries for the objects returned are of the correct object type. For instance, when flow CTDs are returned, the test verifies that each entry in the distribution is a number greater than 0. If any test fails, the remaining levels are not executed. Building tests of this type prevent many of the problems that typically occur during integration. The developers of the SPEC subsystem can use the Planner integration tests to ensure that their system is responding as required.

Configurable Test Framework. A large part of the effort involved in testing software goes into collecting or creating test data that are representative of the actual data that will be encountered when the system is installed in the manufacturing environment. The MMST Planner test framework provides the ability to configure tests that use either type of data (i.e., collected data and system created data). In the first case, data can be collected from the factory and used as input, and in the second case, the MMST test hierarchy can generate realistic data as input. In addition, combinations of the two are also possible.

Typical examples of data that are collected from the factory are process flows, process flow CTDs, and the availability of machines. The process flow data give the details of the steps that will be executed to produce a given product. The flow

CTDs provide data on cycle-times for each type of product that will be produced within the factory. Finally, the machine availability data give detailed information about what machines are in the factory as well as their typical availability given MTBF and MTTR. If some or no data are available, the test framework provides a facility for generating realistic data from a set of configuration specifications. In addition, a combination of collected and generated data can be used when creating a new test case. For example, the process flow, cycle-time, and machine availability data might be collected from the factory, but order information might not be available and, therefore, must be system generated.

The implementation of test data creation for collected data is simply a set of operations that read ASCII files and create the data from the information stored in these files. The test creator must specify the source of the data (i.e., the disk file name) from which the information will be read.

For the system generated data, the test case creator has more options to choose from and is therefore given the flexibility to design varied tests for the planning system in a short amount of time. As a test case designer, it is desirable to be able to generate data in many different forms. For instance, a test case might require that 100 orders, each for 2000 units of a specific product, be created with due dates that progress into the future for each new order created, or another test case might require that 200 orders be created, each for a randomly selected quantity and product type. For each type of test data that can be generated within the system, different methods of generating that data were implemented. Table 19-4 shows some of the options available when determining what type of order data can be created. The leftmost column lists the ways in which data can be generated, and the top row lists some of the data needed to place an order.

Option 1, *random from*, provides the ability to choose an item from a list of items at random. For instance, if a specific list of customers is known, and *random from* was chosen as the method for generating a customer, customer selection would occur by randomly choosing a name from the list of customer names. It is also possible to easily specify the distribution of the items selected. For example, in the case of customer, if desired, a distribution of customers could be specified with 20% of the orders for customer A, 30% for customer B, and 50% for customer C.

Table 19-4: Configuration options.

Option	Customer	Flow	Due-date	Priority	Qty.
Random from	X	X			X
Fixed	X	X		X	X
Progressive			X		X
Random between			X	X	X

Option 2, *fixed*, provides the ability to establish a single value that is used each time the selected piece of data is generated. For instance, the priority for all orders might be set to a default value by using this method. Option 3, *progressive*, allows creation of data based on the last piece of data created. For instance, order due dates could progressively be created, where the first order's due date is prior to the second, and so on. For this, a beginning date and end date are specified as well as an increment. If the end date is reached, then the progressive creation of data will circle back to the beginning date and start over. Option 4, *random between*, can be used to create data that are randomly selected between a lower and upper limit. This could be used to select quantity values for orders of 100 to 300 devices, for example. Table 19-4 illustrates how data are generated for orders, but other data within the system can be generated in a similar manner.

This configurable test framework allows varied tests to be configured and run easily, thus allowing more thorough testing of the MMST Planner. The system also allows for programmatic creation and execution of tests. Tests created and executed through software can systematically vary the configurations to cover as many cases as possible. The ability to programmatically create and execute tests provides the option to establish factory models and states that might not have been conceived by the system developers. This allows for testing of unusual cases that might or might not ever arise in the factory. In addition, a suite of tests can be defined that can be run each time updates have been made to the subsystem. This allows for thorough regression testing.

Test Suites. During the analysis phase of system development, a set of requirements were defined, which the MMST Planner needed to meet. In order to determine if these requirements had been met, individual test cases were created and executed to verify conformance to the stated requirements. Stringing an entire set of test cases together to verify conformance to a list of requirements is what we call a test suite. The configurable test framework allows for the creation and execution of these test suites. Typical examples of test suites would include system and stress tests. System tests are used to establish conformance to the stated requirements and stress tests are used to push the system beyond the normal intended limits of performance. Once a test suite is defined, the test administrator can select and execute the test, having all results displayed upon completion. A test suite can be made up of several test cases. If, during execution, a single test case fails or aborts, all remaining cases within the test suite will still execute. The error condition that caused the abort will be recorded and displayed. This provides the ability to run multiple tests without constant monitoring of the test executions.

For system tests, a suite of test cases were defined that thoroughly checked that the MMST Planner conformed to all stated requirements. In addition, tests were created to verify execution of system functions that were not specifically listed as requirements. Together, these made up the total set of system tests. Stress tests were designed to evaluate Planner performance under extreme conditions. For example, a set of stress tests were designed to determine computation time required by the MMST Planner when planning over longer and longer horizons. Several tests were designed that progressively increased the plan horizon from 10 days to 365 days (some results are shown in Table 19-3). Computation and memory utilization statistics were collected for each test and analyzed upon completion of the entire set of tests. A second example was to increase the number of machines modeled in the factory from 20 to 160 (some results are shown in Table 19-2). Similar statistics were collected and analyzed. In both cases, the test results provided the data for characterizing the MMST Planner performance.

For both test types (i.e., individual tests and test suites), part of the documentation required is a description or explanation of the test. For this reason, the test framework also included a method for explaining each test within the hierarchy. Each test case and test suite include an explanation that a user can view for details on what is being tested, the configuration needed, and the expected results.

Given that the tests were developed in a hierarchy, the top level test could be asked to execute all system tests; in which case, it would execute every system test from top to bottom. If a lower level test was selected and asked to execute all system tests, it would execute all system tests from itself down to the bottom of the hierarchy.

19.5.2 Approach to User Testing

For a system to be used, it must have the confidence of the end users. Confidence can only be gained by providing a functioning system that yields reasonable results and operates reliably. The previous sections outlined how the MMST planner functionality was tested to verify conformance to stated requirements. However, creating a complete set of tests that verify that a system conforms to requirements does not mean the users will use the system. Instead, the end users must be involved from the beginning of the project. Development of this type is sometimes termed *concurrent engineering*. During design of the MMST Planner, many hours were spent discussing planning and planning systems with manufacturing managers and software developers. In this way, we were able to learn and use terminology familiar to the end users as well as ensure that the MMST Planner addressed all important requirements. During system development, demonstrations of the system were presented to both groups of people, who were able to give feedback, resulting in upgrades to the Planner. As the system progressed further, user test sessions were designed and run to get feedback on how the system operated. These sessions allowed the end users to operate early versions of the Planner and make comments on what they did and did not like. In order to capture specific information from the users, a user task list was developed and used when administering the tests.

To accomplish a successful user test session, the following steps were followed:

1. Develop test scenario.
2. Develop initial training material and user task list.
3. Hold pilot test runs.
4. Update scenario training material and task list based on pilot runs.
5. Hold actual training and test run.
6. Analyze results.

Step 1 involved determining exactly what the user would see during the execution of the test. For example, the factory configuration and the products available for production would be determined during this step. The first part of step 2 involved creating the material that would be used to train the users on how to operate the system. The second part of step 2 involved creating a specific list of tasks the users would perform during their test session. The task list provided a means to test specific functionality and, therefore, get feedback on new or updated functionality. Step 3 was an optional step that could be used to verify the user testing material. For the MMST Planner, several members of other subsystems were used as test subjects and provided useful feedback, which was then used to update the user test material. In many cases, the future users of the MMST Planner were extremely busy and not able to spend a large amount of time with the system developers. Pilot runs helped to reduce the risk of wasting their time by pointing out obvious required updates before hand. Step 4 simply involved updating the user test material based on the pilot run subjects' feedback. Step 5 was used to train and test the future end users of the system. Finally, Step 6 involved analyzing comments and making notes of required changes based on the user feedback.

19.5.3 Approach to System Validation

System validation is used to ensure that both the model used and the plans generated are realistic when compared to detailed simulations of the manufacturing environment. The MMST Planner has been validated for both cases.

Model validation has been used to determine the accuracy of the Planner algorithm that decomposes flow CTDs into interval CTDs. This fuzzy arithmetic algorithm estimates interval CTDs for each modeled segment in the plan representation given the flow CTD. Table 19-5 illustrates the interval CTD mean and variance, for each modeled segment of a flow, calculated using both simulation and the proposed fuzzy arithmetic algorithm. The simulated cycle-time mean and variance were calculated by performing a series of simulations, forward in time, based on known interval CTDs. The resulting flow CTD (at time interval number 5) was then plugged into the fuzzy algorithm to generate the set of estimated intermediate

Table 19-5: Fuzzy algorithm comparison with simulation

Time Interval	Simulated Mean	Fuzzy Mean	Simulated Variance	Fuzzy Variance
1	1.11	1.00	0.10	0.00
2	2.21	2.04	0.20	0.04
3	3.30	3.10	0.28	0.16
4	4.40	4.07	0.37	0.37
5	5.48	5.48	0.45	0.45

interval CTDs. The algorithm estimated interval CTDs were then compared with the simulated distributions by measuring their mean and variance. Time units are measured in numbers of capacity model time intervals. Agreement between simulated and fuzzy means remains close, but agreement between simulated and fuzzy variance improves over several time intervals. Agreement improves as the number of time intervals increases because of the greater number of members in the fuzzy number used to represent the distribution. We are currently exploring possible variations on the algorithm in an attempt to improve agreement.

Plan validation was performed by comparing generated plans with low-level simulation results, both using the same data extracted from an MMST type factory. Simulation was used to estimate flow CTDs given the number of wafers per carrier and a mean wafer release rate. The flow CTDs were then used as part of the Planner model, which, in turn, was used to generate plans using a standard factory strategy. Agreement between the given simulated wafer release rate and the Planner generated wafer release rate remained within a few percent. Although further tuning is required, this indicates that the time-phased capacity model could be used to generate realistic plans that agree with detailed simulation.

19.6 CURRENT STATUS

A semiconductor fabrication facility was used to demonstrate MMST, including all integrated CIM subsystems, by using the system to produce processed wafers during the first quarter of 1993. The MMST planning system was installed in three staged *alpha* releases, each of which used steps 1 to 6 described in the user testing sub-section. The first alpha release covered the Planner order entry capability, and the second release covered the decision-support *what-if* capability. The third alpha release completed the required integration between the Planner and all related subsystems. Tests were run on an ongoing basis, and the results tracked along with other subsystem performance measures.

The MMST Planner is currently being offered as a product called PlanWORKS, which is part of the TI WORKS product line. PlanWORKS is currently in beta release, in preparation for release of version 1.0 in 1994. Future developments for the Planner include an improved search algorithm, which would dynamically manage planned utilization during plan generation. This would enable the plan representation to model time intervals of increasing duration, since near-term planning should be performed with finer granularity (e.g., daily time intervals) than long term planning (e.g., weekly or monthly time intervals). A further development includes generalizing the Planner to address worldwide planning for multiple factories.

19.7 CONCLUSION

Texas Instruments has developed a next-generation flexible semiconductor wafer fabrication system, contracted by the Air Force Wright Laboratory and DARPA, which was demonstrated in the first quarter of 1993. The system includes a CIM environment, which is designed around several integrated subsystems, including a Planner. The Planner provides a decision-support tool used to determine work release and completion times and is based on a high level time-phased capacity model of the factory.

Semiconductor manufacturing provides a challenging domain for planning because of the rapidly changing requirements and inherent uncertainty. The Planner tackles this by incrementally updating the existing plan (to keep up with the user requirements and factory conditions) and modeling uncertainty (represented by flow CTDs). In principle, the Planner need generate a plan from scratch only when it is installed in the factory.

The Planner uses a search-based approach to generating plans that satisfy all given constraints (resulting from both the manufacturing environment and the user defined production strategy). Plan computation time does not appear to rise sharply until a threshold machine utilization level is met; so, one heuristic used to cut down computation time is to terminate planning search after a predefined limit is met. However, reducing the number of non-bottleneck machines modeled in the plan does not significantly reduce computation time. The resulting Planner is able to replan for typical user *what-if* requests within a few seconds, which is essential for its role as a decision support tool.

All development on the Planner has been performed with close cooperation from the future CIM system users to ensure maximum benefit. This has greatly influenced the production strategies that the Planner is able to implement as well as the graphical user interface details.

A flexible testing framework has also been implemented to test the Planner performance on both simulated data and data extracted from a typical MMST-type manufacturing environment. This has proved crucial not only in stress-testing the implementation but also in validating the plans generated. Plan validation is performed by comparing generated plans with simulation based on precisely the same manufacturing data. Close agreement indicates that the high level capacity model used by the Planner is satisfactory when generating plans for execution in the factory.

ACKNOWLEDGMENTS

Thanks to Kathy Boys, Paul Kline, Steven Leeke, John McCollum, John McGehee, Darius Rohan, and Rick Wild for their comments and technical contribution to this work. We would also like to thank Wallace Martin, Darren McCosky, and David Reed for their valuable feedback during user tests and evaluation.

This work was sponsored in part by the Air Force Wright Laboratory and DARPA Defense Science Office under contract F33615-88-C-5448.

References

Allen, J. 1983. "Maintaining Knowledge about Temporal Intervals," *Communications of the ACM*, Vol. 28, No. 11, pp. 832–843.

Baker, K. 1974. *Introduction to Sequencing and Scheduling*, John Wiley & Sons, New York.

Beizer, B. 1983. *Software Testing Techniques*, Van Nostrand Reinhold Company, New York.

Booch, G. 1991. *Object Oriented Design with Applications*, Benjamin/Cummings Publishing Company, Inc., Menlo Park, Calif.

Charniak, E., & D. McDermott. 1985. *Introduction to Artificial Intelligence*, Addison-Wesley Publishing Company, Reading, Mass., pp. 360–369.

Elleby, P., H. Fargher, & T. Addis. 1988. Reactive Constraint Based Job-Shop Scheduling. *Expert Systems and Intelligent Manufacturing*, editor M. Oliff, North Holland, New York, pp. 1–10.

Fargher, H., P. Elleby, & A. Elleby. 1990. Knowledge-Based Applications: Avoiding the Mistakes, *Proc. of 4th Int. Con. on Expert Systems in Prod. and Operations Man*, pp. 440–446, University of South Carolina, Columbia, SC.

Fox, M., & S. Smith. 1984. "ISIS: A Knowledge-Based System for Factory Scheduling," *International Journal of Expert Systems*, Vol. 1, No. 1, pp. 25–49.

Glassey, C., & M. Resende. 1988. "Closed-Loop Job Release Control for VLSI Circuit Manufacturing," *IEEE Tran. on Semiconductor Manufacturing*, Vol. 1, No. 1, pp. 36–46

Goldratt, E. 1988. "Computerized Shop Floor Scheduling," *Int. J. Prod. Res.*, Vol. 26, No. 3, pp. 443-455.

Goldratt, E., & R. Fox. 1988. *The Race*, North River Press Inc., Croton-on-Hudson, New York.

Kaufmann, A., & M. Gupta. 1985. *Introduction to Fuzzy Arithmetic*, Van Nostrand Reinhold Company, New York.

Kerr. R., & R. Walker. 1989. "A Job Shop Scheduling System Based on Fuzzy Arithmetic," *Proc. of 3rd Int. Con. on Expert Systems and Leading Edge in Prod. & Operations Man*, pp. 433-450, University of South Carolina, Columbia, SC.

Leachman, R. 1989. "Modeling Techniques for Automated Production Planning in the Semiconductor Industry," Technical Report ESRC 92-7/RAMP 92-4, Engineering Systems Research Center, University of California, March 1992.

McGehee, J., D. Johnson, & J. Mahaffey. 1991. "Semiconductor Manufacturing: A Vision of the Future," *Texas Instruments Technical Journal*, Vol. 8, No. 4, pp. 14–26.

Nadel, B. 1987. "Constraint Satisfaction Algorithms," Technical Report, Computer Science Department, Wayne State University.

Sadeh, N. 1991. Look-Ahead Techniques for Micro-Opportunistic Job Shop Scheduling, Ph.D. Thesis, CMU-CS-91-102, School of Computer Science, Carnegie Mellon University.

Texas Instruments. 1989. Production Management Decision Systems, Technical Report CSC-TR89-004.

Texas Instruments. 1989. Documentation for Symbolic Spreadsheet Modules, Strategy Manager 2549313-0001*A, Texas Instruments Packaged Prototype.

Texas Instruments. 1991. CRA Technical Document PMDS Memo 91-DR-2.

Wein, L., & P. Chevalier: 1992. A Broader View of the Job-Shop Scheduling Problem, Private communication, January 1992.

Winston, P. 1984. Exploring Alternatives, *Artificial Intelligence*, Addison-Wesley Publishing Company, Reading, Mass., pp. 89–101.

20

ReDS:

A Real Time Production Scheduling System from Conception to Practice

Khosrow C. Hadavi
(Intellection, Inc.)

20.1 PROBLEM OVERVIEW

VLSI pilot lines are generally job shop environments except that the cycle times are relatively long. A typical pilot line is composed of many expensive pieces of machinery. Each lot is typically composed of 25 to 100 wafers, many of which are scrapped during the life cycle of the lot. If and when a lot, even with one wafer, makes it to the end of its recipe (process plan), that lot carries an enormous investment in terms of effort, expense, and depreciation. Many of the processing machines are duplicated. This duplication is done for many reasons: reduction of setup time, redundancy in case of break-downs, maintenance, quality, etc. For many lots, this duplication provides a choice of machines on which they can be processed. However, because the processes are re-entrant, the second or third time around this choice might no longer exist. This is done in order to eliminate discrepancy between machines that are supposed to be identical. Therefore, the initial choice of the machine dictates the future visits of the lot. The lots are introduced daily from a Management Information System (in this case Comets[1]); each lot is then released to the shop floor with a given recipe. The recipe describes the work centers (set of identical machines) and processing times. However, both of these can change without much advance notice. The recipes are dynamically defined and re-defined as the lot progresses through the shop floor. The processing times vary with a large variance. Processing times of twice that described originally are not

---

[1] Comets is a trademark of Consilium.

uncommon. Lot dependencies (the same concept as sub-assemblies) are a common occurrence. For example, test lots are introduced dynamically with only a few process steps in order to test the process before the main lot goes through. Needless to say, such test lots require capacity and time from resources that were not originally envisaged. There are also "forerunners," which means a portion of the lot, one or more wafers, might go ahead, with the rest of the lot waiting behind until a later time, depending on the outcome of the forerunners. Splitting of lots into smaller sub-lots and merging them at a later stage is also of common occurence. In the latter case, one would like to try and minimize the waiting time of the sub-lots. In many instances, the lots have to wait for inspection. Such inspections have to be carried out by engineers who are ordinarily not available on the shop floor. Timely inspection of these lots by the engineers can be a challenge. In some instances, the lots have to wait for a relatively long time before the specialist is available. This, of course, implies that the lot might end up being on hold for a long time before it is decided where it should go next and how the process should be modified. An interesting constraint is the so called *block factor*. A block factor in a recipe defines the maximum time allowed for a lot to go through a number of adjacent processes. If a lot does not make it within the prescribed time, then it has to go through rework. Reworks are very common for many reasons other than just the block factor. Reworks are generally undesired events as far as scheduling is concerned because they steal resources without much advance warning. In our case, the management had defined two classes of lot priorities: urgent and normal. They also expressed their own requirement of how they would like the urgent lots to be treated. For example, keeping the machine available when an urgent lot is coming from upstream was a requirement.

The machines also contribute to the uncertainties on the shop floor. Machine breakdowns are very common, the duration of which can be anything from minutes to days. Almost every machine goes through routine maintenance on a daily, weekly, monthly, and quarterly basis. In some cases, the maintenance depends on the usage of the machine. For example, every 500 times the machine is used, maintenance is required. Some machines, such as ovens could be loaded in parallel; i.e., more than one lot could be processed at the same time. Batching of the lots can be very critical in the sense that certain lots might have to wait for the arrival of upstream lots before they are loaded into the machine. However, too much waiting is undesirable because of the danger of starving certain bottlenecks downstream as well as missing the due dates. Therefore, loading the machine excessively by trying to form large batches has the obvious advantage of increasing machine utilization; however, the side-effects might not be desirable. The setup times vary from one machine to another. However, the setup times are not only a function of the machines but also depend on the sequencing of the lots. To this end, one has to measure the importance of machine utilization (reduction of setup time) against the meeting of the due dates.

At the time that the project was started, the scheduling of the fabrication line was performed manually, with some automated assistance from the Comets system. We were fortunate that a comprehensive data collection and order entry system was already in place. However, our scheduling system, ReDS (Hadavi, 1985; Hadavi, Shahraray, & Voight, 1990), required a lot more detail than was available in the existing system. Information such as statistical data for processing times of the lots, rework, and frequency of breakdowns and maintenance are just a few examples of missing detail. The number of steps or operations per lot varied from 10 to more than 100. On average, lots go through 200–300 steps. The average cycle times can vary from weeks to months depending on the priority of the lot. The management's first priority was to minimize the cycle times of lots. This was followed by machine utilization. Another interesting and rather unusual constraint was that the particular fab line was owned by a number of different divisions who were also customers of the fab line. Each division owned a certain percentage of the resources and the invested capital. This meant that the resources had to be allocated to each customer according to this ratio. If division X owned 20% of the fab line, then 20% of the total available resources had to be dedicated to products ordered by X. This was a very important and challenging constraint at the strategic level. The fab line operation was naturally subject to the rules and regulations of trade unions. This implied that one could not arbitrarily add shifts or change the working times without their prior knowledge and approval.

20.2 PREVIOUS APPROACHES

Numerous approaches have been suggested for solving factory scheduling problems by both operations research and artificial intelligence researchers. For decades, most of the scheduling literature took analytical approaches. These aproaches, aiming at seeking optimal solutions, proved to be applicable to only a small number of jobs and machines (Grant, 1986; Graves, 1981). Most often, schedules generated with these idealized assumptions turn out to be inadequate in reality. Problems dealt with in analytical literature are often restricted to a small number of jobs and machines. In the real world, these numbers are significantly larger, and standard techniques such as enumeration, integer programming, or branch and bound quickly become computationally impractical. However, the theoretical aspects of this type of research can still substantially contribute to the design of a scheduling system. This contribution includes determining the computational complexity of the problems and development of efficient algorithms. Some techniques derived from empirical research such as Apparent Tardiness Cost (ATC) heuristic (Vepsalainen & Morton, 1987) and the Shifting Bottleneck heuristic also influenced some later work done by AI researchers in manufacturing scheduling (Adams, Balas, & Zawack, 1988; Sadeh & Fox, 1989a).

In recent AI research, heuristics and rich domain knowledge have been used to find satisficing solutions to scheduling problems whose size and complexity are closer to reality (Mertens et al., 1986; Kanet & Adelsberger, 1987; Hadavi, Shahraray, & Voigt, 1990; Hsu & Lee, 1990). Constraint satisfaction has been a dominant issue among these methods. Systems such as ISIS view scheduling from a single order-based perspective (Fox, 1982, 1983, 1984) and employ knowledge-intensive search techniques along with a rich constraint representation. OPIS addresses the weakness identified within ISIS by providing multiple perspectives with the ability to dynamically shift between perspectives. OPIS outperformed schedulers that relied on a single perspective (Ow & Smith, 1988). However, by scheduling all the operations of a critical order or a critical resource, OPIS assumes that all these operations are critical (Sadeh & Fox, 1989a, 1989b). It is rarely the case that one entire job or resource remains remains critical indefinitely (Burke & Prosser, 1989; Sadeh & Fox, 1989a; Pinedo et al., 1991). Furthermore, at any given moment, OPIS only considers a single perspective. Even though the concept of a shifting bottleneck (Adams, Balas, & Zawack, 1988) was discussed in Smith et al (1986), it was never adressed in OPIS. In the Cortes project (Sadeh & Fox, 1989a), the activity-based approach was proposed. This approach employs multiple perspectives and considers shifting bottlenecks by lookahead techniques.

DAS (Burke & Prosser, 1989) is a planning and scheduling system formulated as a layered and distributed asynchronous system. It decomposes the scheduling problems across a hierarchy of communicating agents. DAS does not differentiate between prediction and reaction because one might consider scheduling a task that requires continuous reaction. Much of the problem solving effort focuses on conflict resolution. Meeting due dates is the primary scheduling objective and is treated as a preference constraint. Even though various dispatching strategies are included in DAS, the scheduling process does not pay much attention to other objectives such as machine utilization, inventories, and cycle times.

Finally, neither the AI nor the OR communities have paid much attention to order release control (Glassey & Resende, 1988). In most of the literature, no distinction is made between job arrival and job release, even though it has been proven that job release control plays a significant role in producing good schedules (Glassey & Resende, 1988). With good job release control, it is possible to reduce job waiting times, WIP, and finished goods inventory levels. Good job release control helps to shorten manufacturing cycle times but still meet due dates (Hadavi & Shahraray, 1989).

In ReDS, both predictive and reactive scheduling are incorporated along with a release control strategy named FORCE (Hadavi & Shahraray, 1989). ReDS also provides an order perspective and a resource perspective in real time. In the next sections, the principles employed by ReDS will be presented, and we shall discuss the evolution of ReDS from Requirements Driven Scheduling to Real-time Distributed Scheduling.

20.3 ARCHITECTURAL DESIGN

Before considering installation of ReDS, the management of the fab line had a few tools available to them for scheduling and planning the production. One such tool was Comets system's "Advanced Planning" module. The Comets' planning module is reminiscent of an MRP type of approach, namely, infinite capacity, batch mode, and pre-assigned job waiting times (fixed lead times). For an environment such as that described earlier, this was not dynamic and fast enough for reacting to these changes in real time. An alternative was to combine long term planning with a manual (expert-driven) approach. Thus, the use of a Gantt chart and other home-made charts to keep track of the production and related problems was not uncommon. However, because of the complexity of the processes and the large number of lots that were involved, it was not always possible to know where every lot was, how long it had been waiting, or when it was expected to arrive at a certain work area. This kind of privileged information was reserved for a handful of *express* lots that were critical to the development process. What was needed was a real time system that *actively* participated in scheduling of the lots. The use of simulation systems was also encouraged in order to remove bottlenecks and find out what the problem areas were. The latter approach was, at the time (and still is), a popular tool for planning and scheduling purposes. It is not a secret that the simulation systems are merely *passive* tools and, therefore, capable of performing little decision making.

ReDS offered the kind of functionality that the management needed. They were not as much interested in the optimality of the schedule as they were in having a reasonable control of the lot movements and some realistic prediction of the near future (hours-weeks) schedules. Another important factor is that a cluster of VAXes were being used on the site for Comets operation and other management information services. These VAXes[2] were generally overloaded because of the heavy demand both from the shop floor for data entry and acquisition as well as by the management for queries to the DBMS system and order entry. This left very little CPU time for other activities such as scheduling. The problem was even harder if one intended to perform scheduling in real time. Accessing DBMS in real time would potentially disrupt the users' access for queries and updating of the database.

---

[2] VAX is a trademark of Digital Equipment Corporation.

The DBMS problem changed the direction of our intended scheduling system. ReDS was originally intended to be a real time system, so that the events from the shop floor were received and processed in real time. After being processed by ReDS, the appropriate instructions would be sent to the shop floor where they would be executed by the operators and/or loading devices. However, getting the real time data from the shop floor through the DBMS system meant overloading the DBMS to the extent that the shop floor operation of the Comets system would have been degraded. That could have meant the machine operators had to wait longer than normal in order to get their desired data or to enter the events into DBMS. This problem was later overcome by intercepting data from the VAXes *before* they were entered into the DBMS.[3] Thus, because of the DBMS issue, it was decided by the management that instead of installing an event-driven version, as decided earlier, a time-driven system would be a more viable solution. That meant, the scheduler would refresh the schedule every so many hours. Thus, after X hours, the scheduler would record all the changes that had taken place since the previous run and based on this information form a new schedule. The new schedule would then be downloaded to the shop floor. The shop floor events that we were interested in were new orders entered, machine breakdowns, reworks, lot splittings, lots on hold, bottleneck areas, and a few others. Even though we were not quite satisfied that the time-driven version would be a good alternative, the management felt that it could be of value to them, and *they wanted it "yesterday."* In Section 20.3, we shall describe the time constraints and the role that they played in the development of the project.

Updating the schedule during the production run presented some unforeseen problems. We had initially anticipated getting the data in real time and extending the schedule in a more or less continuous manner. However, this approach implied a semi–real time operation. The discrepancy lies in the period between reading the DBMS and producing the schedule.[4] We had to predict what the status of the shop floor would be during this time period so that the resulting proposed schedule would be a realistic one; otherwise, the system would not be be of much value to the operators who were supposed to get instructions from ReDS for loading the machines. The instructions to the operators were intitially in the form of one sheet of paper per work center. The content of this sheet included the kind of information depicted in Table 20-1.

Obviously, if ReDS did not have up-to-date information, the content of such output would be meaningless. Then it would not be too long before the operators would refuse to use the listings because of their inaccurate content. For example,

---

[3] This was done for our second implementation of ReDS in a mask manufacturing facility.

[4] This period included getting the data from Comets across Ethernet to ReDS and then producing the schedule. The time needed was later improved to around 15 minutes.

Table 20-1: Loading instructions for work center 124.

Loading Time	Lot#	Coming from (previous WC)	Current Priority	Setup Info
6:00	XYZ111	123	66	apxt54zz
8:45	Maintenance			
10:30	XRT127	243	85	ghgdsj67s
2:45	GHT567	123	12	juzt22i

loading a lot that is not waiting or processing an absent lot that is going through rework or is already processed is a meaningless activity.

An important issue that is being raised here is that designing systems with the assumption that all the necessary data are available where and when they are desired is simply not a realistic one. It is essential to design systems that can challenge such imperfections of the real world, such as missing and fuzzy data. The outcome of all this was that we ended up with two architectures. One is the semi-real time architecture used initially, to which we refer to as the *time-driven* version, and the second one is the autonomous *event-driven* architecture working in real time that is capable of re-evaluating the schedule on a continuous basis and refreshing the instructions to the operator continuously. The following sub-sections will describe the basic architecture of the two approaches following a description of the heuristics that were deployed.

20.3.1 ReDS Architecture

The original ReDS architecture is what we refer to as a "shock absorber" architecture (Hadavi, 1985). This was basically a collection of modules that worked together at different levels of detail. Because it was intended to be a real time scheduling system, it was essential that the system not slow down the speed of the existing operations. Therefore, the lowest decision making level of the scheduler always reacted first, trying to remedy the situation. If there was a need for higher level strategies to intervene, then that was done later at "predefined" times. This architecture seemed to be effective for the kind of application that ReDS was going to be used for; however there was a serious problem. The system was not as dynamic and as up-to-date with the schedules as it could have been. To this end, a new architecture was designed based on functionally the same modules as before with the exception that each and every one of the modules were exposed to all messages, shop floor or otherwise, *all* the time. This architecture is now described in more detail.

Generally, it is hard to categorize systems in order to decide what class of architecture they fall into. Most systems have a hybrid architecture, and systems tend to exhibit different architectures depending on what aspect of the sytem is being examined. There are many systems that are, in theory, hierarchical but implemented in a distributed fashion. Even some supposedly novel architectures, such as the subsumption architecture (Brooks, 1986), have a very strong hierarchical tendency when used for control. In the case of the latter proposed architecture, certain modules have been endowed with the ability to exercise control over other modules. For example, on arrival of certain signals, different layers can make other layers virtually ineffective by inhibiting their actions as well as their input. This behavior, in addition to having hierarchical tendencies, implies that each module has to know the action of each and every module in response to various stimuli.

In order to be able to design complex control systems easier, it is essential that one subdivide the problem into independently smaller and less complex problems. In general, by doing so, one loses some measure of global optimality. Having smaller and independent modules (agents) is a good idea; however, even more desirable is the architectural uniformity of these modules, that is, having a "generic agent" design that can be used for different purposes. For example, consider the problem of designing "managers" for a factory. A manager at every level performs some function. The question is, Does a generic form of a manager exist that one can use for managing different areas of a factory? More specifically, let us look at the function of production control in factories. Some such functions are forecasting, production planning, scheduling, shop floor control, dispatching, and materials management. The purpose of our work has been to find a structure that can be used for designing production control systems. The structure proposed herein has many attributes; however, the most important aspect of the proposed architecture is that it is composed of recursively defined autonomous modules. Each module is referred to as a *planning agent*. Figure 20-1 depicts the structure of a Planning Agent (PA).

Each PA is composed of a *scheduling gene* and a number of input and output. A scheduling gene itself has two components: a *predictive* element and a *reactive* element. Ideally, a scheduling gene (SG) starts out as an almost reactive agent, and over time, it evolves into a more or less predictive element with some reactive component still left. An SG, therefore, has to go through an evolutionary process in

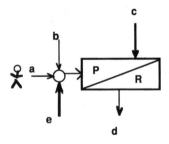

Figure 20-1:   A Planning Agent

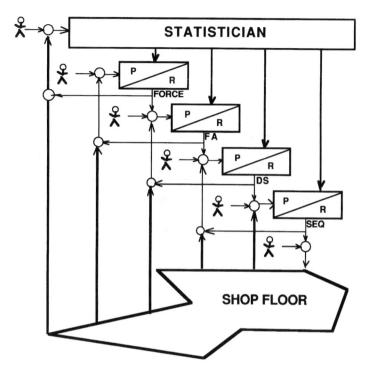

Figure 20-2:   Recursive architecture for production control

order to mold itself into the shape of the environment in which it is operating. The Statistician module (Hadavi, 1990d) depicted in Figure 20-2 aids the SGs in order to line up with each other so that desired results are achieved. Each PA is an independent and autonomous process. Each PA is "programmed" in order to perform a certain task, as best as it can, given to it by another agent. This implies that the agents are cooperative despite being locally greedy. The b-connection in Figure 20-1 is used for assigning tasks to the PA. The a-connection is intended for input from higher agents (i.e., having more global responsibilities) into the PA. This input can override or speed up the decision making process of the agent. It can also be used for teaching purposes. The e-connection tells the agent what is actually going on in the world it is trying to control. Based on such asynchronous events, each PA will make its decisions as to what its output should be. The latter is the d-connection. Finally, the c-connection is an input from an agent that tries to tell the PA how good his performance has been and if his assumptions about the real world are correct. In other words, we are concerned about two levels of feedback: (1) if the model of the world is correct and (2) if the reasoning model of the agent itself is adequate. The latter leads to evolving from a mostly reactive system into a mostly predictive one.

The architecture shown in Figure 20-2 is composed of a number of autonomous agents in the sense that each agent, based on the input from the shop floor, performs what it knows best. The action of each agent has implicitly been designed to cover a certain amount of time horizon. The same real world messages are broadcast to all PAs. Modules can elect to listen or not to listen to these messages. The coordination of PAs is perfomed not by one module controlling the other but by each module watching the performance and limitations of other modules. Furthermore, it should be noted that there is no central coordination module.

By watching each other's output, PAs will decide how much service they should request from other modules. We refer to this kind of approach as the *shock absorber* architecture. That is, like a shock absorber, each module independently tries to deal with the problem presented to it as best as it can. After a while, if the ride is not as smooth as expected, it is obvious that the shock absorbers cannot handle the road; therefore, other remedies are sought by the higher levels, namely, the driver of the vehicle, perhaps the automobile associations, local transportation authorities, Federal Government (DOT), and so on. By no means will any of the PAs refer to other modules in order to seek help in making their decision. The help will come automatically after it has been decided that a certain PA cannot handle the assigned job. In our analogy, the driver cannot change the road conditions. The automobile association can warn other drivers about the rough road conditions, and perhaps the transportation authorities can respond in their own time and improve the road. It should be noted that all these agents respond to the same problem in their *own way* and in their *own time*. This is essential if one is interested in delivering a certain level of performance with time constraints.

The function of each PA, as depicted in Figure 20-2, can be found in Hadavi, Shahraray, & Voigt (1990) and Hadavi (1990a). A brief description follows. The SEQ module is responsible for sequencing and dispatching issues. This is the fastest reacting module and is also the least generic module of the system. It deals with all the details of lot combining and setup information and customized rules of loading the machines and various disciplines needed around the shop floor. The DS or Detailed Scheduling module performs two basic functions. It takes care of the detailed scheduling of those orders that have passed the FA (Feasibility Analysis) phase by examining the more detailed requirements of the order, including capacity and inventory requirements; it also wakes up every x seconds and inspects the progress of the orders. In case certain orders are falling behind schedule, it will try to reconfigure the schedule in order to minimize the damage. The output of this module is then fed to the SEQ module without the latter having any knowledge of the changes that are being made by the DS module. The FA or Feasibility Analysis Module is responsible for "quick and dirty" analysis of the orders. It performs a qualitative checking of the feasibility of executing the orders on time. In the heart of FA, there exists a release algorithm, namely, FORCE (Hadavi & Shahraray, 1990). FORCE tries to find a suitable start time for incoming orders, so that when they are released, they will not spend too much time waiting for machines to become available. In addition, FORCE tries to make sure that machines are utilized at appropriate levels. In semiconductor industries, release of orders plays an important role for making sure that cycle times are reduced, and bottleneck work centers are utilized appropriately.

It should be noted that with this kind of design, one could easily plug in different PAs with different abilities. The better the performance of the PA, the more jobs that will be given to that PA. The contrary is also true. There are a number of interesting problems; for example, if the SEQ module is too slow, then a ripple effect will be created. That is, DS will have to do less, which means FA can do less, and FORCE will have to admit less jobs in the factory. This implies that such agents are expected to be very good performers, and if one of them is too slow, then this is because of the nature of the task rather than poor performance of the PA. It is obvious that picking the poor performers is not too hard. Once the poor performers are identified, this could imply either the others are too optimistic about the actual constraints of the real world, or the selected PA is simply a poor performer. The statistician module helps the modules in order to understand some of these issues as well as help the agents to do as best as they can. For further discussions on Statistician, the reader is referred to Hsu & Lee (1990). The Statistician module is responsible for three types of functions: monitoring data, detecting trends, and interpreting the events in the sense that the user and or the appropriate module of ReDS is informed accordingly. An example is breakdown patterns of a resource. In case there are too many breakdowns, such that the effective capacity of the resource deviates from the expected behavior, then Statistician will detect this and inform the users as well as fine tune the capacity profile of ReDS. The latter would result in more realistic schedules. Thus, the Statistician performs automatic model generation of the shop floor, i.e., continuous updating. Another simple and yet effective application of the Statistician module is detection of resources that frequently cause delays in the schedule. Detection of lateness patterns, as well as cycle times and work in process levels, is among other functions of the Statistician. The most complicated function of the statistician, an area where we have not yet made much progress, is detection of causes of trends. Examples of this are causes for tardiness of orders, causes of increased cycle times, and factors causing changes in throughput.

The basic philosophy of ReDS is based on release of orders. To this end, Feasibility Analysis module examines each incoming order in order to make sure that the start date is a realistic start date with respect to resource and material availability. In order to perform this phase, each process plan is examined, and its *essence* is generated. The essence of the process plan specifies all the critical needs of the process plan. The critical needs could be bottleneck resources, certain fixtures, or certan types of raw material. The essence of the order is then examined for release. The release is based on what is referred to as the *continuity index* of the order (Hadavi & Shahraray, 1990). The continuity index is a measure of the expected waiting time of the order based on current allocations. As an example, if a signal from the shop floor indicates that a resource might be down for two days, then the release of the orders requiring this resource might be put on hold pending the repair of the resource. The release is also a function of the priority of the order. In other words, higher priority orders face less resistance from the release module (FORCE) called by FA. FA can also interact with the users in order to resolve any issues, such as adding shifts and/or delays in due dates. After the FA phase is completed, an allocation of the order is made based on a least horizon planning principle. This means that the farther the expected execution time of the step in the process plan, the less the level of allocation. For example, steps that are expected to be performed next month are only scheduled at a monthly level, whereas steps for the next few days are scheduled at a daily or shift level. The representation of allocation steps is generic for all the subsequent modules. This implies that the allocations made by FA can be fine tuned by DS module, SEQ module, or any other module. DS will then examine the allocations made by FA and detail schedule the new orders on top of the existing orders. Because FA has already searched for a good start date based on the release algorithm, DS will try to detail schedule the allocation steps based on a first fit approach. Some changes and back-tracking might be needed based on more detailed knowledge of DS. In addition, DS would continuously examine the progress of the orders as executed by the lower modules (i.e., SEQ). If and when DS realizes that execution of some of the steps is impossible within the required due date, it will automatically re-schedule the order. Rescheduling implies preempting the remaining steps and finding the next best times for these steps to be executed. Needless to say, this process might require preemption of some other lower priority orders. Because such events happen frequently, future orders, as well as current orders, undergo frequent changes in schedule. The least commitment principle is a safeguard to reduce the amount of back-tracking needed. Finally, one has to consider the stability of the schedules. Too many changes in the schedule can cause organizational, as well as credibility, problems. Stability of the schedule was ensured primarily by giving all the started orders higher priority for the use of the resources. Thus, preemption was only in those cases where very high priority orders were entered. In order to avoid having too many high priority orders, the number of current high priority orders was monitored. If the users exceeded the accepted quotas, a warning was issued by the system, and a password was needed to enter the order at that priority. Finally, the SEQ takes the output of DS as its input and, based on pre-defined rules, tries to sequence as many steps as possible so that the steps defined by the higher modules are executed. The rules interpreted in DS are defined by the user based on his or her domain knowledge and can be changed dynamically.

The above procedure describes how new orders are treated. When events from the shop floor indicate problems such as machine breakdown, repairs in the schedule might be necessary. As soon as an event is detected, the SEQ module will respond to the event by resequencing some of the steps in order to avoid local congestion. DS module will examine the situation and might decide that because of the breakdown, not all the expected steps can be carried out. It, therefore, will preempt some of the prescribed steps, without the knowledge of the sequencer, and re-schedule them in the background. FA might also respond to the breakdown, as described earlier, and prevent further release of new orders. In this process, FA will look for other lots that avoid the problem resource. Thus, a balanced mix of orders is generated on the shop floor by avoiding bottlenecks and feeding the right mix so that the under-utilized resources are fed appropriately. For more detail, the reader is referred to Hadavi et al. (1992).

The communication between modules is based on a uniform representation of the tasks to be scheduled. In our first attempt, all the events were picked up by an *events interpreter* that decided which module(s) needed to respond to this event. Our next step was to broadcast messages so that each module could locally decide if it wanted to listen to the message or not and take appropriate actions. For example, a machine breakdown would alert the sequencer, possibly DS as well as FA. Statistician would also be interested in this event in order to monitor the trends and patterns of machine breakdowns on the shop floor.

20.4 DEVELOPMENT PROCESS

20.4.1 Planning

Transferring a new technology from a research laboratory into an actual production line is always a challenging problem. It is indeed a long and tedious process trying to convince the management that a novel system could be of benefit to them. In general, management and, in particular, middle management are not willing to take unnecessary risks. To this end, new systems are not always their first preference unless they have been used before, and the results are promising. Our initial strategy was to build a prototype of the system. This served two purposes: First, it could be used as a research vehicle in order to experiment with the ideas, and second, it could act as a means by which we could convey the ideas to management and show them what features the system offers. We were fortunate that from the beginning, the project was championed by senior management.

Our first stop was visiting the site in Germany in order to understand the details of the operation and formulate the desired features. After a few weeks of analysis, the project administration and milestones were decided. They asked us to make some minor changes to the existing prototype, which was written in Prolog on an Apollo workstation for a printed circuit board assembly line, and deliver the system to them in a few weeks. We promised them a prototype in six months. The development team was composed of a programmer from the site in Munich, Germany; a developer from a Siemens software house in Belgium; and a few of our developers in the Princeton Laboratory. The reason for choosing a programmer from the site was to facilitate technology transfer so that after installation, the users could take over the system administration. In a way, this minimized our effort in the future support of the project. The involvement of Siemens software house from Belgium was to ensure future support and maintenance of the system as well as future installations of the system in Europe.

Initially, all the developers were at the Princeton Laboratory for a few months. As the specification of the software became more and more clear, the necessity for all the developers to physically be present at the same site was reduced. Because the developers were separated in three countries, with a time difference of six hours, the problem of communication and coordination became a troubling issue. Because the project milestones were rushed, there was very little time for developing a software specification. As a result, frequent meetings were necessary, and individual developers played a major role in defining the functionality of the modules they developed. This, of course, led to more complications in integrating the different pieces. The bulk of the software was written in a customized Prolog language. We added object oriented capabilities to an existing commercial Prolog package.

During the development process, we kept the users informed of the kind of pre-requisites that were needed for deploying the scheduler at their site. This included communication packages such as Ethernet and TCP/IP, as well as system software and hardware, including database management systems and compilers. After about eight months of struggle, tension, travel, and many telephone calls, we were ready to take the system to the site and demonstrate it to the end users. The system was demonstrated to the end users using a simulation of the shop floor.

On arrival, the users expected a real system running in full power and controlling their major fabrication line in real time. What we had was a prototype that displayed most of the functionalities that were needed without any interfaces to the real world, such as data collection, and that was far from being robust enough to be used in a production environment. The source of this problem was inadequate communication between the developers and the users; their expectations and our understanding of their needs and urgencies did not match. This obviously led to some friction. We tried to deploy the prototype, as it was, for production use;

however, the Prolog system did not have adequate memory management capability. Therefore, it did not scale up for large process plans. As a result, we began with new deadlines and milestones in order to come up with a "working" system. The prototype acted as an excellent communication media between the developers and the end users in order to describe what functionalities were needed and which ones could be omitted. One surprise for us was that the users asked us to change the system from a real time operation to a semi–real time operation. In other words, they wanted us to run the scheduler periodically and produce listings for each work center describing the expected load sequence. As a result, we did not have to deal with real time events any more. Our task was reduced to capturing the events over a time interval and producing a schedule for the next few hours. However, this implied that the existing architecture of the prototype had to be altered, and the Prolog version, because of its performance, was no longer of value.

Thus, we started the second phase almost from scratch. In this phase, we also studied the existing data collection and MRP system at the site, viz., Comets. We needed to get process plans and new orders, as well as shop floor events, from these systems. The frequency of Comets data queries was a problem. Too many reads from DBMS system could jeopardize the response time of the system on the shop floor. This was simply not acceptable because it could be used as an excuse to reject the system's deployment. One alternative was to capture the data coming from the shop floor before it entered the Comets database, but this required a lot more work, and we did not have the time for it. The second alternative was to use Comets reporting facility in order to write into a file all the changes since the last query and then send this file over to ReDS residing on an Apollo workstation. This was a viable alternative. In our second installation, in a mask manufacturing shop where the events are handled in real time, we opted for the first alternative. The second phase was accomplished more smoothly because we had a much better understanding of the problem and the management's expectations. Furthermore, we had more experience and knowledge. Despite these favorable factors, we did not deliver on time. We were late in part because the debugging took longer than expected, in part because we had some interface surprises at the system level, and in part because the end user was not quite ready with all the prerequisites for ReDS to be deployed.

20.4.2 Development

While the development of the software was going on in Princeton, the end users in Munich were asked to make sure that all the supporting hardware and software were in place at the time of planned installation. However, a lot of complications developed because of the availability of different versions on the two sides of the Atlantic. Further, the end users had additional difficulties installing the appropriate prerequisite software because of the lack of personnel and trained individuals who were familiar with communication and systems software. The other important issue for the management of the fab line was to inform and explain the importance of using the scheduling system. They had to justify its use and explain the reasons why such software was needed. For example, one interesting use of the scheduler was explained to be that the machine operators would know ahead of time exactly when they were expected to be at their stations. This would give them a chance to get out of their rather uncomfortable clean room costumes. There was apparently very little objection to the introduction of the scheduler in the fab line. It was very clear that the proposed system could be of benefit to all levels of management and operations. The only minor problem in the process was to convince some of the local people that the proposed strategy of the scheduling system would be a valuable asset in managing the line. A certain few of the local MIS employees were convinced that the use of simulation, as they had been doing up to that point in time, was sufficient for scheduling purposes. Their strategy was deciding where the bottlenecks were and removing them. Of course, there is some merit to this approach. However, we argued that simulation is generally a static decision support system. To this end, it cannot deal with the dynamics of the shop floor, particularly when the bottlenecks are shifting, and the mix and the volume of lots, as well as the conditions of the shop floor, are constantly being changed. I don't think we could fully convince them that they needed a more powerful and active tool for their day-to-day decision making. However, the situation at the time was so delicate that upper management was very enthusiastic about trying any tool that had the potential to offer some extra control over the management of the line.

The interfacing with the existing VAX hardware was rather straightforward in design. As mentioned earlier, however, the issue was making sure that we access the existing Comets database, a DBMS, without degrading the performance of the system, particularly the response time of the system as far as the operators were concerned. Failing to do so would indeed jeopardize the chances of putting the system into operation. The system administrators of the Comets and the management were quite cooperative in making the necessary changes needed in order for ReDS to get the desired data. This included changing the process plans and adding extra fields for ReDS real time data needs. In addition, they had to make sure that machine downtime statistics were up-to-date, and accurate machine maintenance information was available. This kind of activity implied added work for the MIS staff, which was not welcome. However, having the consent of the upper management, as well as having a personal and good relationship between the developers and the MIS staff, were the two main factors that made the extra work tolerable. In this instance, we were faced with the problem of interacting with a more rigid business culture and expectations, which we later realized to be quite different from what we were accustomed to. Obviously, the language was an issue. Because both the users and developers worked for the same company, we had a rather informal relationship. That meant frequent changes in the demands of the end users and new features that we needed to cater to. Finally, we decided to freeze all changes until we had a reasonably stable system. Another added problem was that while we were developing the scheduling software, there were version changes going on in the related third party hardware and software systems. Very often we were faced with the question of either going ahead with the work as planned or changing the code and the design in order to incorporate some of the newly issued features of the related software systems and hardware platforms.

20.4.3 Deployment

Finally, we were ready to put the software into operation. The end users, having had one of their own programmers as part of the developing team, were confident that they could use and maintain the software on their own. Our first attempt to put the software into operation failed with many bugs, memory segmentation faults, and a few functionally undesirable features. After a few months of shuttling back and forth between New York and Munich, the system was finally stable enough to be used in parallel with the production line but only in a passive mode. This trial run lasted about six months. During this period, many more bugs and problems were discovered. However, the most important issue during this time period was to tune the system and the database in order to get a better performance as far as the reaction time of the scheduler was concerned. Furthermore, the management gained progressively more and more confidence in the decisions made by the system. The system was finally put into actual production use.

The use of the system by the shop floor operators and other users caused more changes and refinement to the user interface as well as functionality of the system. One of the interesting issues that resulted was that even though we had designed a user interface that would enable the management to directly interact with the system, they did not want to spend any time sitting at a workstation. They wanted the system to make all the decisions and report to an error log those problems or exceptions that the system could not handle. The user interface, however, was used occasionally in order to find out the kind of problems that the scheduler ran into as well as to prepare reports and check on the status of the lots. The scheduler, because of its real time capability, presented the management with a tool for monitoring the exact location of the lot "now" and in the future. With this capability, they could very closely monitor the movement of the lots and ask questions regarding the speed of progress. Needless to say, this made a few people on the shop floor rather nervous. If a lot was not moved for a long time, the management would be warned, and therefore, the problem would become very visible. This kind of *visibility* kept many of the machine operators and end-users on their toes and disciplined enough to make sure that the right data were entered at the right time and that the instructions coming from the system were followed as closely as possible.

During the first year of its deployment, the system was not as stable as the users expected. Many bugs and problems were discovered and corrected. However, sometimes too many bugs showed up all at the same time, to the extent that the users were questioning the use of the system. This made us very nervous. In particular, the operators had a lot of concerns and questions regarding the validity of some of the ReDS instructions to them. Many of these problems could be attributed to ReDS itself; many others were because of the inaccurate data in the data collection system or the wrong data entry by the users. For example, very often operators entered data regarding the movement of the lot at a later time than immediately after the lot was moved. This caused inconsistencies with ReDS instructions to other operators downstream. In other words, despite the lots' availability at the next resource for loading, the system did not instruct the operator to load the lot! The system also monitored the processing times of the lots on various resources. This was done by comparing the load-in time and move-out times. When both move-in and move-out were done at the same time, their difference did not account for their true processing times.

Major concerns of the users were reliability of the system and recovery after a crash. The crashes were not just because of ReDS but also because of the data collection system. On many occasions, because ReDS was the newcomer on the block, many of the problems were attributed to ReDS without knowing exactly what caused these problems. This presented the developers and system administrators of ReDS with a rather difficult situation. The developers, in particular, located in Princeton trying to support the system administrator in Munich, had a lot of frustrating telephone conversations trying to solve problems that were really caused by other related software systems working in conjunction with ReDS. Of course, the time difference of six hours did not help! However, the success of the system was a major incentive for all of us. This was a system just out of a research facility being tried for the first time. The success of the system could help to promote the reputation of the laboratory; the failure, on the other hand, would raise many questions regarding the real usefulness of the proposed theories. Consequently, we had to be very careful about making sure that the users' needs were satisfied, and the system was customized according to the users' requirements. This presented us with a dilemma. On one hand, we had to make sure that the users' needs were met; on the other hand, we believed in certain theoretical issues that we were very unwilling to make any compromises over. As an example, if the downstream machines are busy, i.e., presence of bottlenecks, ReDS release control, FORCE (Hadavi & Shahraray, 1990), would not allow new lots of normal priority to be released to the shop floor. On the other hand, management was of the opinion that all the lots should be released to the shop floor and be worked on as much as possible. One of their valid reasons was that if the lot is not processed on machine A because machine B downstream is busy, later on it might be the case that machine A goes down, therefore causing the lot to wait even longer! In certain cases, one could work around this problem by using machine A for those products not going to machine B, but this strategy is not always possible either because of the urgency of the lots going to B or simply because of the absence of having a product mix. On the other hand, there are cases where the management objective is to maximize the total number of steps performed per day. In this case, one would simply release lots into the system regardless of the nature of the bottlenecks at the time of release! It should be noted that increasing the total number of steps performed is in line with the idea that no bottlenecks should be starved. However, feeding bottlenecks excessively contributes to increase in cycle times, which is an undesirable side-effect.

This process was very educational for us in the sense that we were acquainted with a lot of problems and thought processes of the management, namely, what their reasoning was and why they performed certain tasks and made specific decisions. A simple conclusion was that the developers, as well as the management, had to educate themselves in order to understand each other's point of view and constraints. Management needed to know more about computers, their capabilities, their use, and their limitations. The developers should be able to know the kind of environments that management has to work in, the constraints, and the requirements. Most systems that are installed in real life have to be part of a bigger system that already exists. The cost prohibits installing systems that are revolutionary in nature. Incremental and compatible systems have the best chance of being used and accepted by the management. The new systems have to be able to communicate with the existing software systems and fit into the world in which the users are operating. Of course, the system has to make a difference; otherwise, what is the point of having a new system in the first place! This is where management education and open-mindedness play an important role. Managers have to be able to see the potential of the new systems and open the way for it to be successful.

20.5 STATUS AND BENEFITS

ReDS has been running for over four years in the VLSI fabrication line and more than two years at the mask manufacturing site. The system has been stable enough to operate for months without any major problems and/or crashes. The users are quite pleased with the system operation; in particular, the operators are so dependent on the output that when it is missing, they immediately call the system administrator and inquire about it. As expected however, the users have been asking for more functionality and new features. This is an on-going process that has been taken care of by our support group in Belgium.

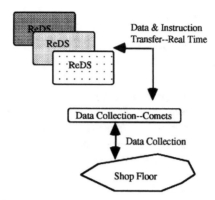

Figure 20-3:   Time-driven ReDS operation

The number of transactions handled by the system is on the order of hundreds of messages per shift from the shop floor. These messages are *move-in* and *move-out*, machine breakdowns, maintenance, rework, lots on hold, new lots, and split/join operations. The operators' loading lists are updated three times a day on their respective terminal monitors in the case of the time-driven version. For the event-driven version, the updating of the screens is in real-time depending on the event. In the former case, the main problem with refreshing these lists is the time needed for extraction of data from the data collection system Comets. The actual configuration between ReDS and Comets is shown in Figure 20-3.

The number of times that the dispatch lists are updated should be a function of the dynamics of the shop floor, i.e., the processing times, number of breakdowns, number of new lots, and so on. In the early phases of ReDS operation, the number of updates, i.e., once per day, seemed to be sufficient. However, as the size of the operation became bigger and the management expectation higher, more and more updates were needed. Later, there were two updates per day and, recently, three. However, management is of the opinion that the updates should be done on a continuous basis. This is the way ReDS event-driven version is implemented in the mask manufacturing shop also located in Munich. The event driven version handles on average over 100 events per hour. However, at certain times of day, the number of incoming events is a lot higher than this rate. In this version, the incoming data from the shop floor are intercepted before they get to the database of Comets. With this strategy, it is possible to monitor all the shop floor events; examine them; and, after filtering, take actions accordingly. The resulting instructions are then sent to the shop floor. This architecture is totally distributed.

Since the introduction of ReDS at the site, the productivity and cycle times have improved by a considerable amount. To what extent this improvement is attributable to ReDS is not quite known. During this period, the number of machines has changed, the product mix is different, the lot sizes and volume are higher, the operators are more skilled, and the number of shifts and some plant policies have been altered. In addition, because of ReDS and other factors, the management, engineers, and operators are more disciplined and prompt. Having all these changes going on in parallel makes it very difficult to quantify the direct benefits of ReDS or systems such as ReDS in such production environments. In general, as the systems get more and more intelligent, the evaluation of their performance in the work place becomes more and more challenging. One can make speculations that are at best subjective estimates. However, one way to judge the goodness of the system is to see how attached the end users are to the system. The use of simulation is of course another alternative for evaluating such systems. This tool can also be very biased depending on validity of the model as well as the experiments.

Our future research effort is improving the ReDS system both from the algorithmic point of view and the performance point of view. One of the interesting topics is the subject of merging lots and sub-assembly coordination. The objective is for the related lots to meet each other at their pre-specified merge points without too much waiting. Some preliminary results can be found in Hadavi et al. (1991). In addition, we are trying to expand the ReDS environment to that of a Decision Support System environment along with a number of other DSS systems, such as Inventory Manager, Forecasting system, Process Plan Definition System, and MRP systems. The issue of integrating these systems in a cooperative environment of DSS agents seems to offer many interesting challenges. Our current network is based on that of Contract Nets (Davis & Smith, 1983) and a broadcasting communication sub-system (Taft & Wolfson, 1989).

Our experience from conception to the actual realization of the system made us aware of some very important facts. The implementation proved to us that compared to the complexity of the real life problems and constraints, the theoretical design and prototyping of the system was relatively simple. Furthermore, it confirmed that the traditional approaches of operations research, having many simplistic assumptions and solutions that only fit the ideal situations, is far from the needs of the management. One has to understand the details of the problem and offer tools that can aid the process. AI has a long way to go as far as the needs of factory management are concerned, but it seems to be on the right track. As it appears, management is generally not just interested in having optimal solutions; it wants tools that can be *aids* in day-to-day decision making. Management is interested in tools that can provide guidance and direction as well as have the ability to correct (or give warning against) undesired moves. To this end, what we can presently offer management is an *environment* where the users are exposed to tools and can engage in a dialogue with the system so that Pareto optimal decisions can be obtained. Development of such environments will constitute a decision support system that can act as an *intelligent executive assistant* (consultant) to the managers and end users of the system. An important ingredient for this kind of environment is constraint representation and manipulation.

ACKNOWLEDGMENTS

I would like to thank the management of the sites where ReDS was implemented for their patience and understanding while we desperately tried to make the system stable enough for their production use. My thanks also to the Decision Support Systems Group and our Belgian colleagues who have loyally supported and made this project successful. Finally, I am indebted to John Gaylord who has always been a source of support and inspiration to all of us.

References

Adams, J., Balas, E, and Zawack, D. 1988. "The Shifting Bottleneck Procedure for Job Shop Scheduling," *Management Science* 34(3): 391–401.

Brooks, R. 1986. "A Robust Layered Control System for a Mobile Robot," *IEEE J. of Robotics and Automation* RA-2(1).

Burke, P., and P. Prosser. 1989. "A Distributed Asynchronous System for Predictive and Reactive Scheduling," Technical Report AISL-42, U. of Strathclyde.

Davis, R., and R. Smith. 1983. "Negotiation as a Metaphor for Distributed Problem Solving," *Artificial Intelligence* 20, pp. 63–109.

Fox, M.S. 1982. "Job-Shop Scheduling: An Investigation in Constraint-Directed Reasoning," Technical Report CMU-RI-82-11, Carnegie Mellon University.

Fox, M.S. 1983. "Constraint-Directed Search: A Case Study of Job-Shop Scheduling," CMU-RI-TR-83-22, Carnegie Mellon University.

Fox, M.S. 1984. "ISIS—A Knowledge-based System for Factory Scheduling," *Expert Systems* 1(1).

Glassey, C., and M. Resende. 1988. "Close-Loop Job Release Control for VLSI Circuit Manufacturing," *IEEE Trans. on Semiconductor Manufacturing,* 1(1): 36–46.

Grant, T.J. 1986. "Lessons for OR from AI: A Scheduling Case Study," *Journal of the Operational Research Society,* 37(1): 41–57.

Graves, S. 1981. "A Review of Production Scheduling," *Operations Research* 29(4): 646–675.

Hadavi, K. 1985. "Dynamic Scheduling for FMS," *AUTOFACT 85 Proceedings.* Society of Manufacturing Engineers, Detroit, MI.

Hadavi, K. 1990. "ReDS—A Real Time Scheduling System," *Proceedings of AAAI-90 Manufacturing Planning and Control Workshop*, AAAI Press, Menlo Park, Calif.

Hadavi, K. 1990. "ReDS—Statistician Overview," *Siemens Corporate Research Internal Memo.*

Hadavi, K., and M. Shahraray. 1989. "Release No Job Before Its Time," *Proceedings of the Third International Conference on Expert Systems and the Leading Edge in Production and Operations Management*, Production and Operations Management Society.

Hadavi, K., M. Shahraray, and K. Voigt. 1990. "An Environment for Planning, Scheduling, and Control of Factories," *Journal of Manufacturing Systems*, Vol. 9, No. 4.

Hadavi, K., and M. Shahraray. Forthcoming. "In Time Control of Factory Production via Global Feedback," Submitted to *Journal of Manufacturing and Operations Management.* Forthcoming.

Hadavi, K., T. Chen, W. Hsu, and C. Lee. 1992. "An Architecture for Real-time Distributed Scheduling," *Applications of AI in Manufacturing*, ed. D. Nau, AAAI Press, Menlo Park, Calif.

Hadavi, K., W. Hsu, M. Pinedo, and D. Levy. 1991. "Dispatching Issues for a Scheduling System in a Microelectronic Factory," *Joint US/German Conf. on New Directions for Operations Research in Manufacturing,* Jul. Hamburg, Germany.

Hsu W., and C.N. Lee. 1990. "Decision Support Agent Engineering Environment—De SAGE," *Siemens Corporate Research Internal Memo.*

Hsu, W., M. Prietula, and G. Thompson. 1990. "A Mix-Initiative Workbench: Integrating AI, OR, and HCI," *Proceedings of International Society of Decision Support Systems Conference.*

Kanet, J., and H. Adelsberger: 1987. "Expert Systems in Production Scheduling," *European Journal of Operations Research*, 29:51–59.

Mertens, P., and Kanet, J.J. 1986. "Expert Systems in Production Management: An Assessment," *Journal of Operations Management* 6(4):393–403.

Ow, P., and S. Smith. 1988. "Viewing Scheduling as an Opportunistic Problem-Solving Process," *Annals of Operations Research* 12:85–108.

Pinedo, M., D. Levy, K. Hadavi, W. Hsu, and R. Hou. 1991. "Dispatching Issues in Job Shop Scheduling," *Proceedings of Joint/German Conference on New Directions for Operations Research in Manufacturing*, Stuttgart, Germany.

Sadeh, N., and M. Fox. 1989. "CORTES: An Exploration into Micro-opportunistic Job-shop Scheduling," *IJCAI89 Workshop on Manufacturing Production Scheduling*, AAAI Press, Menlo Park, Calif.

Sadeh, N., and M. Fox. 1989. "Focus of Attention in an Activity-Based Scheduler," *Proceedings of the NASA Conference on Space Telerobotics.*

Smith, S., P. Ow, C. Le Pape, B. McLaren, and N. Muscettola. 1986. "Integrating Multiple Scheduling Perspectives to Generate Detailed Production Plans," *Proceedings of 1986 SME Conference on AI in Manufacturing. Society of Manufacturing Engineers*, Detroit, MI.

Taft, R., and D. Wolfson. 1989. "Conversation Tools Description," Technical Memo SCR-89-TM-221, Siemens Corporate Research, Princeton, NJ.

Vepsalainen, A., and T. Morton. 1987. "Priority Rules for Job Shops with Weighted Tardiness Costs," *Management Science* 33(8).

PART

TWO

APPLICATION CASE STUDIES
Heavy Manufacturing

21

DEVELOPMENT OF A COOPERATIVE SCHEDULING SYSTEM FOR THE STEEL-MAKING PROCESS

Masayuki Numao
(IBM Research, Tokyo, Japan)

21.1 INTRODUCTION

Japanese steel companies have been intensively promoting computerized production management and automated control of production processes to cope with market requirements for high-quality, value-added products manufactured in small quantities and with short production cycles. However, some tasks that have been difficult to adapt to conventional management techniques and control theories have hitherto been performed manually by human experts and have therefore relied heavily on these experts' knowledge and heuristics. One such task, operational scheduling, was difficult to automate because of the dynamically changing operational environment.

Scheduling problems have historically been studied in the field of operations research (OR). The various types of problems that arise in OR can be classified according to the difficulty of their solution. For a given objective, a typical job-shop scheduling task falls into the mathematical class of "NP-hard" problems, which means that it is difficult to solve computationally. In practice, however, an optimal solution is not necessarily needed if a "good" feasible solution is found. Human experts usually have knowledge or skills that can help them find such a solution, and this is why the expert system approach is effective.

Here. we propose a new approach called *cooperative scheduling*, in which three different factors, namely, procedures, rules, and the user, cooperate to make a schedule. Because interaction with the user is included in the system architecture, the purpose of this approach is not to replace the user and automatically produce an optimal solution to a problem that the user has formulated but to collaborate with the user in designing a feasible solution.

Then, as an actual application of the approach, we describe a system named *Scheplan* that assists in production scheduling for steel-making processes (Numao & Morishita, 1989). It was developed as a joint project by IBM Tokyo Research Laboratory (TRL), IBM marketing, Nippon Kokan Co. Ltd. (NKK), and NK-EXA. The resulting system was installed in NKK's Keihin plant for operational use.

In this chapter, we will describe the problems in the steel-making process; our approach, named *cooperative scheduling,* and its use in solving the problem; the technique for obtaining a feasible schedule efficiently; and the process by which the system was developed, paying special attention to the way in which the knowledge was extracted from experts and implemented in the system.

21.2 PROBLEM OVERVIEW

21.2.1 Steel-Making Processes

Figure 21-1 illustrates the steel-making process. It consists of three major steps. First, the converter (the basic oxygen furnace) refines pig iron into steel of the required composition by blowing oxygen into the hot metal to eliminate the impurities by oxidization. Ladle-refining equipment then eliminates impurities from molten steel or adds alloy ingredients to the molten steel in ladles to make high-grade steel. Finally, a continuous caster casts molten steel continuously into slabs, blooms, or billets.

In the NKK Keihin plant, there are three converters, which are used cyclically (two working while the other undergoes maintenance); nine different refining devices, which are applied according to the grade of the product; and five different continuous casters, which are applied according to the form of the product.

The amount of the molten steel from a converter to a ladle is about 300 tons, and this unit is called a *charge*. Between 40 and 50 *charges* are processed in a day.

21.2.2 Constraints

The objective of production scheduling is to determine the sequence of machine operations from the converting process to the continuous casting process for every *charge* in a day and the time and the length of the process in each machine. The problem is formalized as a variation of job-shop scheduling. However, some constraints are unique to steel-making processes because, for example, these processes have to deal with over 2000 kinds of steel products, and the temperature of the molten steel is over $1600°$ C. The following are examples of the constraints:

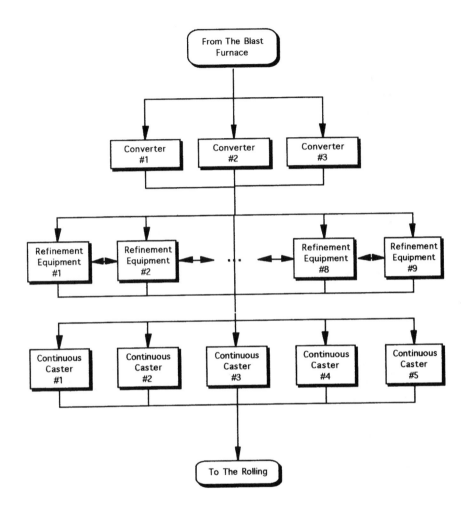

Figure 21-1: Steel-making process

1. Number of *charges*

   The production plan requires that a fixed number of charges should be scheduled in a day. This number is determined by the volume of the products, the due date, and the capacity of the converters.

2. Waiting time limitation

   The processes should be completed while the iron is still molten. Therefore, the sum of the waiting times in each charge is limited to less than 30 minutes.

3. Continuous process

   If the amount of the product exceeds the capacity of the converter (300 tons), it is divided into several *charges* for refining in the ladle. This set is called a *charge-set*, and all *charges* in the set end with some specific continuous caster, which must be operated continuously (with no resting time between operations) in order to maximize production yields. For this reason, the ladles should arrive at the casting machine before the previous casting process ends.

4. Order of the refinement process

   The refinement processes and their processing order are determined according to the kind of steel.

21.2.3 Evaluation Criteria

The following criteria are related to the quality of the schedule:

1. Minimization of waiting time

   The initial temperature of the iron is determined by the total waiting times of each charge. Therefore, the process waiting time should be as short as possible in order to reduce the heating cost.

2. Maximization of total charges

   The number of charges affects the productivity. Therefore, as many charges as possible should be scheduled.

These two criteria are considered objective functions of the schedule. However, they conflict with each other, and their priority is not static but varies according to the situation, the time, and the expert.

21.3 TECHNICAL APPROACH

21.3.1 Problems in the Conventional Approach

A scheduling problem is characterized by two difficulties. One is combinatorial explosion: an n-machine, m-job problem has $(m!)^n$ possible schedules, so that without elaborate and intelligent methods, a prohibitively large number of cases must be checked. The other is the diversity of conflicting constraints: a problem is usually constrained by due date, cost limits, production levels, machines, order characteristics, resources, and other factors.

Historically, scheduling problems have been studied extensively by OR, an analytical method for obtaining optimal solutions by modeling. However, because most job shop problems—for example, the *N-job-M-machine* problem, which assigns N different jobs to M equivalent machines and minimizes the total completion time—are NP-complete, recent theoretical research has shifted to developing algorithms that give a nearly optimal solution efficiently.

Recently, many complex problems have been investigated by using AI techniques: The AI approach considers scheduling as a search problem, which satisfies a given constraint and maximizes the evaluation function. To avoid combinatorial explosion, the system uses various kinds of "knowledge," but the major problem of knowledge-based systems is knowledge acquisition: how to get knowledge from an expert and put it into a system. Human experts often have difficulty conveying their expertise explicitly in words. They might not even be able to describe a given scheduling problem precisely because there are so many constraints, concerns, and objectives.

21.3.2 Cooperative Approach

We can avoid the problems described in the previous section by changing the viewpoint: In our *cooperative scheduling* approach, scheduling is regarded as a decision-making rather than a constraint-satisfaction problem. We designed the system as a type of decision support system.

The approach is supported by the following observation: Although it is hard to reduce an expert's knowledge to a set of explicit rules and propositions, it is much more straightforward for an expert, given a problematic schedule, to tell what constraints it violates. In addition to pointing out the constraint violations, an expert can describe how to improve a particular schedule and explain why it will be better. In this way, a schedule can be made by cooperation between a human expert and a computer.

We set the following criteria for the design of a system using such an approach:

1. Feasible solution
   The system efficiently generates feasible solutions, one of which the user selects according to the indices of the production activity, such as the bottleneck machine utilization, product cycle time, and the amount of stock.

2. Interactive environment
   The system offers a graphical interface through which the user can easily confirm the status of the scheduling and that reflects his decisions interactively.

3. Online re-scheduling
   The system generates a schedule in a short time so that it can handle real-time machine failure.

4. Modularity and compatibility
   The system is easily connected to existing systems and easily updated.

Our approach was to develop a system that helps the expert to make a schedule along with a bottom-up flow based on his heuristics and that solves local

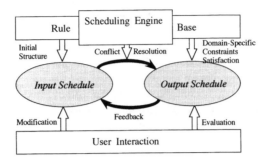

Figure 21-2:   Architecture for cooperative scheduling

constraints, which are difficult for humans to handle but easy for computer algorithms. The system generates a feasible solution efficiently and allows the user to review and improve it interactively. Evaluation of the total schedule is left to the user; the system simply helps him to make a global decision by maintaining the other local constraints.

21.3.3 Architecture of Cooperative Scheduling

Figure 21-2 illustrates the architecture of *cooperative scheduling*. There are three major components: a scheduling engine, a rule-base, and an interface. The scheduling engine works as a local constraint satisfier to solve general primitive constraints. Rules that represent domain-dependent knowledge then solve the domain-specific constraints by means of a pattern-matching function. Finally, the user evaluates the schedule and modifies it via a user-friendly interface with direct-manipulation functions. The user interaction is therefore included in the system architecture as a global constraint satisfier. The iteration of this cycle improves the schedule until it becomes feasible. The functions of each component are described below.

21.3.3.1 Interface

To allow a smooth and effective interaction, the system provides a full-screen–oriented interface, which displays a graphic diagram of the schedule and allows the user to modify it by direct manipulation.

Figure 21-3 is a diagrammatic representation of the schedule: Here, the horizontal axis is for time, and each line stands for the machine. A charge in a production process consists of the machine operations, represented by the thick horizontal lines on the machine lines, and the handling times, represented by the slanting lines

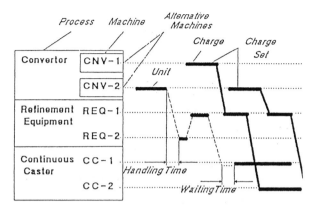

Figure 21-3:   Representation of scheduling terminology

connecting the operations. The waiting times are also shown by the dotted lines before the operations.

Any unit displayed on the screen is mouse-sensitive. The user can select a unit by using a mouse. He can then shift the unit or move it to an alternative machine. He can also select and shift the charge or charge-set as a whole as well as individual units.

The values of some evaluation functions are also displayed in the screen. For example, the color of the charge identifier stands for the total waiting time of the charge. The color turns from blue to red according to the waiting times, so the user can easily find which charge needs to be edited.

The user interface consists of two components: the display rule and the command interpreter. The display rule watches the working memory components and displays them on the screen in an appropriate form. A data-driven mechanism enables the rule to display only the modified part. The command interpreter interprets the user's operation as a working memory modification command, such as *make* or *modify*, whenever the user modifies part of the schedule by a mouse operation.

Figure 21-4 shows the data structure of the three major working memory components: *charge, unit,* and *machine.*

21.3.3.2 Scheduling Engine

The scheduling engine deals with two general local constraints: process conflict resolution and waiting time reduction. The engine receives a schedule that might violate these constraints and outputs a schedule that satisfies them. Figure 21-5 illustrates the conflict resolution process.

```
charge(
    id,                      : charge identifier
    charge-set-name,         : name of the charge set to which the
                               charge belongs
    charge-no,               : process order in the charge set
    top-unit,                : pointer to the first unit
    end-unit                 : pointer to the last unit
    )
unit(
    id,                      : identifier
    alternative-machines,    : a set of alternative machines
    selected-machine,        : a machine to operate the unit
    starting-time,           : the unit's starting time
    process-time,            : the unit's processing time
    previous-unit,           : pointer to the previous unit
    next-unit,               : pointer to the next unit
    mark                     : working tag for scheduling engine
    )
machine(
    id,                      : identifier
    available-time           : the time from which the machine is
                               available
    )
```

Figure 21-4:   Data structure of working memory elements

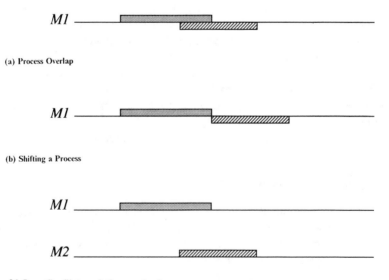

(a) Process Overlap

(b) Shifting a Process

Figure 21-5:   Conflict resolution mechanism

(a) If two processes are allocated to one machine at the same time, a process conflict occurs. There are two ways of resolving the conflict: (b) shift the later process to the end of the previous process, or (c) to move the later process to an alternative machine if there is any machine that performs the same function. Either way can introduce some waiting time, but the engine selects the one that introduces less waiting time.

The algorithm resolves the constraints efficiently but preserves the global structure of the input schedule. It is applied in one of two directions, according to the application: forward or backward. In the forward scheduling strategy, only the relative order of the process and the starting time of the first process in each charge are treated as input information, and the algorithm is applied according to the time sequence, like a simulator. In backward scheduling strategy, on the other hand, the ending time of the last process in each charge is treated as input, and the algorithm is applied backward.

The algorithm of the forward scheduling engine is shown in Figure 21-6. The input consists of *preset starting times* of all the units, which outline the rough frame of the schedule. The output consists of *revised starting time and selected machines* for all the units with no machine conflicts.

21.3.3.3 Rule Base

Rules are classified into two categories: those that represent domain-dependent knowledge solve domain-specific constraints by means of a pattern-matching function, and those that represent experts' heuristics improve the efficiency of the scheduling or the quality of the schedule.

Figure 21-7 shows examples of rules. Figure 21-7(a) represents the constraint of continuous casting:

If there are two continuous charges in the charge-set and if their final processes are not connected, then shift the earlier process so that it is connected to the next process.

This rule is applied backward, and the shifted units introduce some waiting time between the refining process and the continuous casting process.

Figure 21-7(b) represents the constraint of resting time requirements for convertors. Before invoking the rule, it is necessary to make a pseudo-unit at the beginning of the convertor process. This rule is applied forward.

If there is a pseudo-unit, then make another pseudo-unit with the necessary resting time, and place it at a specified time interval after the previous unit.

The pseudo-units represent resting times. After these units have been positioned, the scheduling engine is invoked to arrange them together with the normal

Input: Preset *starting times and a set of alternative machines* of all the units.

Output: Revised *starting times* and *selected machines* for all the units.

Procedure:

- **Initialization**
  - ○ Preset the *available time* of each machine to *0*.
  - ○ Select a top unit for each charge, and mark it *on*.
- **While any units are marked** *on*.
  - ○ Selection of the pair of a unit and a machine
    - ○ Select the unit marked *on* with the earliest *starting time*. Let *U* be the unit.
    - ○ Let *S* be a set of alternative machines for *U*. Select the machine with the earliest *available time* in the set *S*. Let *M* be the machine.
  - ○ Post-processing
    - ○ If the *starting time* of *U* is earlier than the *available time* of *M*, then reset the *starting time* to the *available time*. (Otherwise, the *starting time* of *U* is not changed.) Mark *U off*.
    - ○ Update the *available time* of *M* to the *ending time* of *U*.
    - ○ Mark the next unit after *U on*, and preset the *starting time* to the *ending time* of *U*.
- **End of while.**
- **End of procedure.**

Figure 21-6: Scheduling engine algorithm

units. They are then removed, and as a result, the convertor has resting times at regular intervals.

There are other rules for deciding the process path according to orders received. The scheduler receives a daily order for products; divides them into charge-sets; and decides the process path of each charge, namely, the machine operation sequence and the duration of each process. There are a total of 130 rules in the rule base component.

21.3.4 Scheduling Flow

The actual scheduling process consists of two steps: *subscheduling and merging* and *interactive refinement*. The system efficiently generates a schedule by the *subscheduling and merging* method, and the user evaluates and modifies it by

```
rule continuous-casting : -CN1 is
    charge( charge-set-name = CSN,
        charge-no = CN1,
        end-unit = EU1 ) &
    charge( charge-set-name = CSN,
        charge-no = CN2 : (CN2 = CN1 - 1),
        end-unit = EU2 ) &
    unit(  id = EU1,
        starting-time = ST1 ) &
    U = unit(  id = EU2,
        process-time = PT2,
        starting-time = ST2 ) &
    #( ST2 + PT2 < ST1 )
    =>
    modify( U, { starting-time := ST1 - PT2 }).
```

(a) Rule for Continuous Casting

```
rule convertor-resting-time is
    unit(  id = pseudo-unit,
        selected-machine = Id : ( Cnv1 | Cnv2 | Cnv3 ),
        starting-time = ST1 )
    resting-interval( Id, RInt ) &
    resting-time( Id,  RTime ) &
    =>
    ST2 := ST1 + RTime + Rint &
    make( unit(id := pseudo-unit,
            selected-machine := Id,
            starting-time := ST2,
            process-time := RTime ))
```

(b) Rule for Resting Time Requirements of Convertors

Figure 21-7:   Sample rules

interactive refinement. The iteration of modification by the user and revision by the system improves the schedule until it becomes feasible.

21.3.4.1 Subscheduling and Merging

The *subscheduling and merging* technique is formalized from experts' heuristics on making a complicated schedule in an efficient way. In steel-making processes, a series of charges is sequentially performed by a continuous caster in the final process: this group is called a charge-set. Human experts first decide the starting time of each member of the charge-set, so that the final process will be done on all the charges together. Meanwhile, they pay little attention to machine conflict. After all the charge-sets have been settled, they resolve the machine conflicts by shifting some of the units.

This heuristics utilizes the two characteristic constraints of the steel-making process: waiting time limitation and continuous casting.

- Waiting time limitation
  The sum of waiting time from the converter to the caster in each charge is limited to less than 30 minutes, which is shorter period than the process times. This suggests the possibility of the divide-and-conquer approach: If each charge is scheduled separately, then the total schedule can be obtained by arranging the separate schedules with a small modification because a large modification in a charge introduces a long waiting time.
- Continuous casting
  As shown in Figure 21-3, the final process of steel-making is continuous casting. All the final units of a charge-set should be connected there, and the continuous casting process naturally requires the longest processing time among the steel-making processes.
  This suggests that the unit of subscheduling should be charge-set and that subschedule is generated by backward scheduling.

Our approach to the efficient generation of a candidate schedule is modeled on the above know-how. The *subscheduling and merging* consists of the following three steps:

1. Divide a scheduling task into subscheduling tasks. Subscheduling is the scheduling of an individual charge-set; each member of a charge-set is scheduled backward, from the final process to the initial process. The subscheduling is easily performed without conflict resolutions. Because the final process is continuous casting, which has the longest processing time, if the final processes are aligned, other processes have no possibilities of overlapping with each other. Thus, the resulting subschedule is usually optimal because it has no waiting times between processes. Figure 21-8a shows an example of subschedules.

2. Overlap the subschedules. Because the quality of the total schedule depends on the global position of each subschedule, this step is very important. Determination of each position takes the following criteria into consideration:

   o Minimization of overlapping processes
     Because the resolution process for overlapping processes increases the waiting time (but not always), a small amount of overlapping processes is recommended.

○ Balancing the load over time

Balancing the load on the bottleneck machine is very important if average utilization of the machine is close to 1. Average density of the process in some time period should always be less than 1.

○ The positions cannot be determined uniquely and thus, the operation requires the heuristics of an expert. Many kinds of heuristic rules can be obtained from an expert to shift the subschedule to the appropriate position, but they are not infallible, and the user's refinement is still necessary. Figure 21-8b shows overlapping subschedules.

3. Merge the subschedules to get a total schedule. The overlapping subschedules are input to the scheduling engine, which then generates a schedule that satisfies the local constraints. The result is shown in Figure 21-8c. In this step, the waiting times can be increased in order to solve process conflicts. However, the total additional waiting times will be small if each subschedule has been allocated an appropriate position during the overlapping step.

21.3.4.2 Interactive Refinement

The user can interact at any time during the scheduling process to refine the schedule. He can modify any part of the schedule by shifting or reordering the units, moving them to alternative machines, and so on. While he is modifying the schedule, he need not take into account the local constraints. For example, he can even shift a unit onto another unit, violating the rule against process conflicts. Consequently, the modified schedule does not normally satisfy local constraints. The system, in turn, revises the schedule so that it does so, reflecting the intention behind the use's modification. This cooperative processing is iterated until the schedule satisfies the user's criteria.

The following example shows *interactive refinement* of the total schedule after *subscheduling and merging*. Figure 21-9a shows the part of the total schedule that needs to be edited by the user. In the figure, charges *h1, h2,* and *h3* have long waiting times. Charges *h1* and *h2* have to wait for the machine *REQ-2*, and charge *h3* has to wait for the machine *REQ-9*.

It seems that the machine *CNV-1* is a bottleneck. To reduce the load on this machine, the user selects the unit *m1* and transfers it from machine *CNV-1* to *CNV-2*. The result is shown in Figure 21-9b.

After this, the scheduling engine revises the schedule. The result is shown in Figure 21-9c. Now, there are no waiting times for charges *h1, h2,* and *h3*.

In the above example, the user is able to reduce the waiting times of a few parts without affecting the other parts of the schedule. However, if the schedule is dense, it is difficult to find the best operation, and editing can increase the waiting

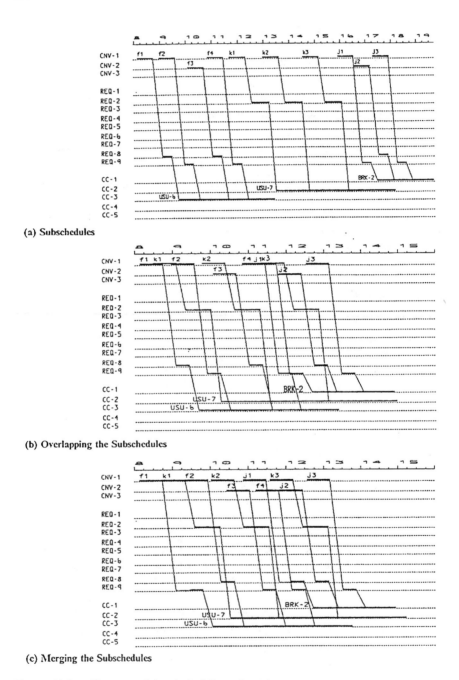

(a) Subschedules

(b) Overlapping the Subschedules

(c) Merging the Subschedules

Figure 21-8:   Three steps of the subscheduling and merging

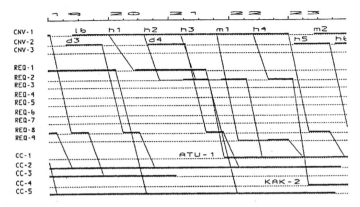

(a) Finding Units with Long Waiting Times

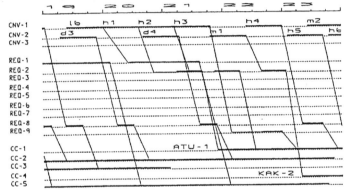

(b) Changing the Machine of the Unit

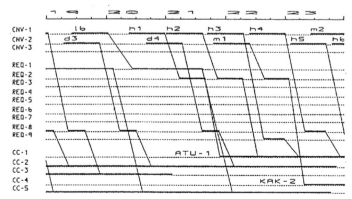

(c) Revising the Schedule

Figure 21-9:   Example processes of the interactive refinement

times in other parts of the schedule. In this case, it is necessary to iterate the editing and revision several times, until a satisfactory schedule is obtained.

21.4 DEVELOPMENT PROCESS

21.4.1 Planning

The project was planned to be completed in three steps: study, prototype development, and actual system development. At the end of each step, a review session was planned to evaluate the results and decide whether to proceed to the following step, to return to study, or to cancel the whole project. Therefore at the beginning, the expectation of developing actual system development was low, but that made the project research-oriented; we took time to identify the problems, to investigate the reasons for them, and to develop solutions. Consequently, the ideas and the heuristics were formulated as general techniques that could be used for other domains (Numao, 1994).

The study and the prototype development steps took about one year, starting in 1987. Ten people were involved in the prototype development: two researchers, six system engineers, and two scheduling experts. The important thing was that the user was involved in the project from the beginning. That made the development of the system, the installation in the plant, and the training in operating the system very easy.

21.4.2 Development

Knowledge acquisition and the system development process are illustrated in Figure 21-10.

21.4.2.1 Understanding the Domain

To gain a general understanding of the problem and to establish a relationship between the development team and the user, the development team visited the plant several times to observe the steel-making process and the actual scheduling environment in which the new system was to be installed. Here, we studied the process flow, machine configuration, and the function of each item of equipment to familiarize ourselves with the terminology of steel-making. We also consulted manuals, operation standards, and related documents in order to classify the knowledge.

21.4.2.2 Tracing and Analysis

To understand the scheduling process precisely, we held two tracing and analysis sessions with the expert. First, we recorded the whole scheduling process on videotape, which took three hours because it dealt with the actual data. Then, while

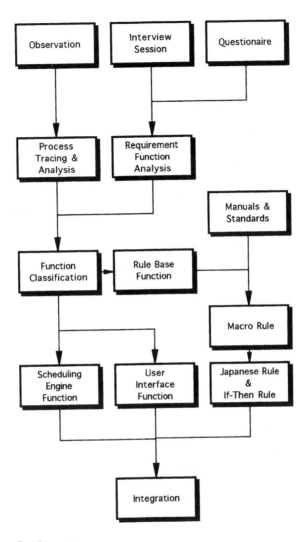

Figure 21-10: Development process

playing back the tape, we traced the process and asked the expert the reason for each of the decisions he made. Through this laborious work, we clarified the flow of scheduling and the related knowledge and heuristics.

For example, the *subscheduling and merging* technique was extracted and formalized from the current bottom-up approach. In steel-making processes, a series of charges in a charge-set is sequentially performed by a continuous caster in the final process. Human experts first decide the starting time of each converting process in the charge-set, so that the final process will be carried out on all the charges together. In the meantime, they pay little attention to process conflicts. After all the charge-sets have been settled, they resolve the process conflicts by shifting some of the units.

21.4.2.3 Functional Requirements and Analysis

Because the tracing and analysis session revealed only the current scheduling knowledge, it was necessary to investigate the problems in current scheduling and to elicit further requirements. We surveyed the requirements by giving a questionnaire to all the users, followed by interview sessions in which the reasons for the requirements were discussed and then classified according to priority. Through these sessions, the functional specifications of the system were defined and became the goal of the system development.

During the sessions, we discussed some of the problems in the current approach. For example, to simplify the scheduling, the current manual scheduling required the starting time of the charges to be set discretely at 15-minute intervals. However, the actual plant had no such limitations; it could start a charge at any time. Therefore, if the starting time could be set freely, the throughput of the total schedule would be increased. Of course, this was realized by the new system because in the backward scheduling strategy, the starting time is determined by the final process.

21.4.2.4 Division of the Functions

The required functions were divided into three categories—the scheduling engine functions, the rule functions, and the user interface functions—based on the architecture of *cooperative scheduling*. From this point, the development team divided into three groups, each of which developed one of the three components. We defined the interface between the components and set typical data based on the format of the interface to facilitate the individual development of each component.

21.4.2.5 Rule Encoding

Because there are over 2000 types of steel products, there are many standards describing the production processes for the specific products. These standards are updated whenever new equipment is introduced, or new production processes are developed. Therefore, rules should be written as closely as possible to the standards so that they can easily be revised to reflect updates in the standards. We defined four levels of representation, from an abstract level to a concrete one, to classify and manage these rules.

1. Rule class
   First, each rule is classified according to its function, such as "steel type definition rule" or "machine constraint rule."

2. Macro rule
   A macro rule defines the template for a specific rule, such as "the steel type is determined by the steel code and by the component."

3. Japanese rule
   A complete description is first written in Japanese stating that, for example, "If the first column of the steel code is 1 or 2, and the steel contains more than five percent of carbon, then the steel type is high-carbon steel."

4. If-then rule
   The description is then directly translated into an if-then rule:

```
rule high-carbon-steel is
   Ch = charge( steel-code = Code,
   steel-type = unknown )
   & #( substring( Code, 1, 1, 1 ) |
   substring( Code, 2, 1, 1 ))
   & #( component( Code, 'C', Percent) &
   Percent >= 5 )
=>
   modify( Ch, steel-type := high-carbon ).
```

21.4.2.6 Implementation

The prototype system was implemented in POPSYS (IBM, 1987b), which is a production system facility of Prolog, because the POPSYS rule format is easy to read and write and because Prolog is suitable for prototyping. However, there was a performance problem because both Prolog and POPSYS are interpreters. To resolve the problem and facilitate operational use, the second version was implemented in Knowledge Tool (IBM, 1987a), which is a rule-based language on top of PL/I. As a result, the performance of the scheduling engine was greatly improved, with a speed about 300 times that of the prototype version; this, in turn, contributed to a faster response time.

21.4.3 Deployment

21.4.3.1 Installation

The system was transferred to the Keihin plant of NKK as one component of a total system consisting of a central system and local systems. The central system makes a schedule and issues instructions through the local systems at the converter, continuous caster, rolling mill, and other sections of the plant. The actual data in these sections are then put into the local systems and fed back to the central system.

The central system consists of Scheplan and the existing production management system, which supplies all the necessary data to Scheplan: the production orders, including the kinds and volumes of the products and their due dates, which become the input data for Scheplan, and production process path and processing time master data, which become the referents for determining the sequence of operations for each charge.

21.4.3.2 Deployment

The actual daily operation consists of the following four steps:

1. Scheduling
   Scheplan is used to create several possible schedules.

2. Delivery
   One schedule is selected on the basis of the evaluation information and delivered to each section through the local systems.

3. Feedback
   Actual operation data are gathered by the local systems every eight hours and compared with the scheduling data.

4. Recovery
   If the actual data seriously differ from the scheduling data or if machine troubles occur, a new schedule is created to meet the situation.

Because the system was considered an assistant, it was readily accepted by the human experts and introduced into actual operation. When the project started, some schedulers were worried that the system would replace their current jobs, but because the major objective of the systematization is to improve the quality of the schedule and to stabilize the quality, which previously varied according to the schedulers, the time saved by the system is used to search for better alternative schedules and to improve the system. The schedulers are now satisfied with working in this new environment.

21.5 STATUS AND BENEFITS

Since 1989, the system has been used for daily production scheduling at NKK's Keihin Plant. The system has two major benefits. One is a reduction of the daily scheduling time from 3 hours to less than 30 minutes, which makes real-time re-scheduling possible when machine trouble occurs during operation. The other more important benefit is an improvement in the quality of the schedule: Figure

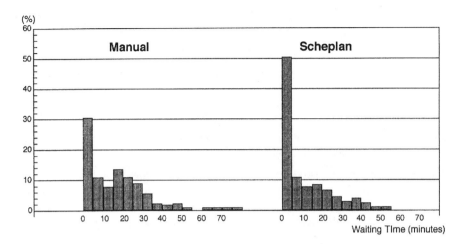

Figure 21-11:   Waiting time distribution

21-11 shows the waiting time distribution for manual scheduling and Scheplan. The average waiting time is reduced from 16 minutes to 8 minutes per charge, which contributes to a reduction in cost of the firebricks and other fireproof components and which will result in a saving of about 1 million dollars a year in production costs.

Another expected use of the system is for analysis of the plant itself: the system can be used to detect bottleneck machines in the current configuration and to advise on the effective operation of such machines. It can also be used to predict the effect of installing a new machine or replacing an existing one.

21.6 CONCLUDING REMARKS

NKK described this system in a press release on 18 February 1988 when the development of the prototype system was completed. Seven newspapers, including the *Nikkei Shinbun* and the *Asahi Shinbun*, carried the report. This press release had a strong impact on other Japanese industries, which came to understand that scheduling problems could be solved by applying the AI approach. The target area of expert system application in Japanese companies has now shifted from classification to planning and scheduling (Motoda, 1990).

The current survey on Japanese expert systems by Nikkei AI shows that the number of classification-type expert systems developed is still higher than that of other types, but in terms of the number of operationally used systems, planning-and-scheduling type systems rank first, which means that for Japanese companies, planning and scheduling are more important because they are closely related to daily business itself. Japanese company managers have began to think that the efficiency of the production flow and management flow can be promoted by using AI technologies.

References

IBM. 1987a. "IBM Knowledge Tool User's Guide and Reference—Release 1," IBM Corporation, Programming Publications Dept., Endicott, New York.

IBM. 1987b. "VM/Prolog Production System Program Description/Operations Manual," IBM Japan, Ltd., Tokyo.

Motoda, H. 1990. "The Current Status of Expert System Development and Related Technologies in Japan," *IEEE Expert*, Vol. 5, No. 4, pp. 3–11, IEEE Computer Society, Los Alamitos, Calif.

Numao, M. 1994. "An Integrated Scheduling/Planning Environment for Petrochemical Production Processes," *International Journal on Expert Systems with Applications*, Vol. 7, No. 4 (to appear), Pergamon Press, New York.

Numao, M., and S. Morishita. 1989. "A Scheduling Environment for Steel-Making Processes," *Proc. of the 5th Conference on Artificial Intelligence Applications*, pp. 279–286. IEEE Computer Society Press, Los Alamitos, Calif.

22

A FLOW SHOP WITH COMPATIBILITY CONSTRAINTS IN A STEELMAKING PLANT

Jürgen Dorn
Wolfgang Slany
*(Christian Doppler Laboratory for Expert Systems,
Technical University of Vienna)*

22.1 INTRODUCTION

Scheduling of factory processes is the allocation of required resources to jobs to be performed. Usually, a *job* is identified with a deliverable product that has to meet a certain quality. A job can have a *release* and a *due date*. Associated with each job is a formal specification of the product to be produced. *Resources* are typically those tools, units, materials, and personnel that are used or consumed in the production process. Associated with each resource is some formal specification of its characteristics and capabilities.

A *planner* considers the specifications of the jobs and the resources and generates a set of operations called a *process plan* that produces the desired result with a set of explicit ordering constraints on the operations and a set of resource requirements. Often these process plans are fixed for certain products. In contrast to a job shop, the sequence of operations is fixed in a *flow shop*.

When several jobs are to be executed together, the composition of their resource requirements implies additional ordering constraints that prohibit simultaneous demands on non-sharable resources. A *scheduler* must consider both the explicit ordering constraints imposed by the plans and the implicit ordering constraints derived from the availabilities of the resources. The scheduler also must consider release dates, expected due dates, set-up times, and maintenance intervals.

Scheduling or *resource allocation* is a problem that has been examined in the Operations Research (OR) literature since the early fifties (Conway, Maxwell, & Miller, 1967). Methods and theories developed are based on strong mathematical theories. Although the theoretical work brought several improvements over the years, it was never very successful in realistic applications. There are mainly three problems with these formal-analytical models from OR:

- The algorithms are too complex for real world applications.
- The models demand exact knowledge about durations and technical constraints.
- The effort to formalize a new scheduling problem is considerable.

Knowledge-based techniques promise a remedy because they offer solutions for the cited problems. First, in knowledge-based systems, it is easier to apply heuristics to reduce the inherent complexity. Second, knowledge-based systems offer the possibility of reasoning with incomplete, uncertain, vague, or probabilistic knowledge (Kerr & Walker, 1989; Berry, 1992). Finally, in knowledge-based systems, the existing knowledge is described explicitly, and therefore, it is easier to develop and maintain. The scheduling problem from the steelmaking industry described here can be used as a prototypical case to illustrate the advantages of knowledge-based techniques.

In this application, approximately 45 jobs have to be sequenced for one production line. In a mathematical model without using heuristics, the scheduler must check 45! possible sequences of jobs for constraint violations. It will be even more complex if conflicts between production lines are examined, or you consider arbitrary idle times between operations. The described methodology manages this complexity by applying heuristics that the human experts used too.

An important problem in the domain is the uncertainty and vagueness. The durations for operations are only known approximately, and constraints are often specified vaguely. Most mathematical approaches from OR could not address this problem. We solve this problem by applying qualitative reasoning based on fuzzy logic.

OR models assume a very idealistic view of scheduling problems. For example, for a number of machines M and a number of jobs N with a goal function "minimize makespan," a solution is computed. However, in most realistic domains, the devil is in the "nuts and bolts." If an additional constraint must be satisfied (e.g., machine m_1 should not operate simultaneously with machine m_2), a new model must be developed. In a knowledge-based model, an additional rule or constraint is added very easily.

22.2 THE PROBLEM

In a joint project between the *Alcatel Austria-ELIN Research Center* and the *Christian Doppler Laboratory for Expert Systems,* an expert system was developed for the *Böhler* company in Styria (Austria), one of the most important European producers of high-grade steel. The system supports the technical staff in the steelmaking plant in generating schedules for steel heats for one week (Dorn & Shams, 1991). The system was implemented with Pamela, a rule-based system developed by the *Alcatel Austria-ELIN Research Center* (Barachini & Theuretzbacher, 1988). Although this system works well, we generalize the problem and set the applied method on a firmer ground by making it robust with respect to the influence of uncertainty and vagueness.

22.2.1 Description of the Environment

The Böhler company is divided into several plants. The steelmaking plant is the first in the production process. The produced steel is delivered to plants, including the rolling mill or the forges. The steelmaking plant receives orders from these plants to produce slabs or ingots of a certain quality. The destination is important for the scheduling process because the working hours of these plants must be considered. Sometimes products are stored for several days in intermediate stock yards because the next plant cannot process the jobs in the same sequence as the steelmaking plant. The differing sequencing criteria of jobs cause considerable costs for the company. Moreover, because the steel cools down, it must be warmed up again in the next plant. To reduce costs and to improve the quality, some orders have due dates.

Wednesday morning, engineers of the different plants meet to discuss orders for the next week. Compatible orders that might have different destinations are used to form jobs. For each production line of the steelmaking plant, a list of jobs for one week is worked out manually. Usually, the first shift in the steelmaking plant starts Sunday evening, and the last shift ends Saturday. Sometimes fixed sequences for two or three jobs are given to facilitate the scheduling in the next plant. The task of the scheduler is to find a possible sequence for all jobs, violating as few compatibility constraints between jobs as possible, and to allocate resources over time without violating temporal and capacity constraints. The result of this scheduling process can be that some orders are rejected and shifted to the next week. To reduce the number of rejected orders, general rules that explain what combinations of orders might be produced in one week are given to the subsequent plants. Nevertheless, these constraining rules can be violated to produce important orders.

22.2.2 The Steelmaking Process

Pig iron produced in *blast furnaces* has usually more than 4% carbon and is, therefore, brittle. To get a deformable product, *steel* is produced by reducing carbon in pig iron down to 2%. For many high-tech products, the quality of steel must be even higher. *High-grade steel* is crude steel refined with *alloying metals* such as manganese, tungsten, and chromium. These alloying metals have desired effects such as compression strength and impact strength. High-grade steels are, for example, stainless steel, high-speed steel, tool steel, and structural steel. To reduce material costs, *scrap iron* with high percentages in the desired elements is used to obtain high-grade steel.

The steelmaking plant in Kapfenberg consists of three main production lines that share some aggregates. For every steel quality, there is a process plan that describes which operations must be performed on which aggregates to produce the quality. These operations and sequences must be replanned only when a failure occurs.

The steelmaking process starts with the charge of crude steel and scrap iron in one of the *electric arc furnaces* (EAF). The filling of one furnace is called a *heat* and already contains the main alloying elements. The furnaces have different capacities from 17 t to 55 t. The duration of the melting process depends on the ingredients but also on external causes. Because the furnaces consume much electric energy, they are sometimes switched off because of voltage peaks. As many as 5 hours can be required for the melting, but usually 2 to 2½ hours are enough. A fixed set-up and a maintenance interval of 20 minutes are included in this interval.

The melted steel is poured into *ladles* that are transported by a crane to a *ladle furnace* (LF). If the preceding heat has a long processing time in the ladle furnace, the current heat must wait. This slack time can not exceed two hours. The next step is a *heat treatment* in the ladle furnace, where the fine alloying takes place; the duration is usually about the same as the melting. Later, a special treatment may be performed in the *vacuum oxygen decarburation* (VOD) unit or in the *vacuum decarburation* (VD) unit. The VD-unit can be converted into a VOD-unit. This conversion takes about three to four hours.

The next step is the processing of the steel in a two-stranded *horizontal continuous caster* (HCC) to form *slabs* or the casting of it into *moulds* to form *ingots*. The teeming rate for the hcc is about 50 t/h. If the casting format must be altered, a set-up time must be considered too. For casting ingots, space in one of the four *teeming bays* (TB), where ingots can solidify in the moulds, is required. Normally, the solidification time for ingots in hours is half as much as the weight of the ingots in tons.

For example, a big ingot of 52t needs about 1 day. The storage places for big *forging grade ingots* (>19t) are limited. On the other hand, the effort for casting

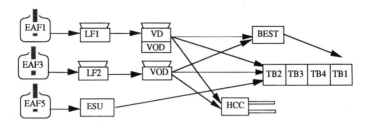

Figure 22-1:   Aggregates in the steelmaking plant

many small ingots is greater than for a few large ingots. About 70% of the jobs are cast into ingots.

The Böhler-Electro-Slag-Topping (BEST)-technology is a special casting technology for big ingots. These ingots are treated additionally in the best-unit, and for them, only one place in the teeming bays (TB1) exists. All aggregates and the routings for heats are shown in Figure 22-1.

22.2.3 Constraints in Scheduling

During the construction of a schedule, several constraints have to be considered. These constraints are often vague, and they conflict with each other. The engineer has no pretension to generate an optimal schedule because he knows that the uncertainty in the execution of his plan would break this optimality. The engineer can decide that some schedules are better than others but cannot give algorithms to construct the optimal schedule. The engineer considers the constraints discussed in the following subsections.

22.2.3.1 Compatibility Constraints

The main problem in scheduling is that residuals of one heat in the electric arc furnace can pollute the next heat. The engineers use, as a rule of thumb, that 3% of a chemical element in a heat remains in the wall of the electric arc furnace, and 3% of the difference of the elements in two consecutive heats will be assimilated by the second heat. Of course, the 3% is always on the safe side, and in some cases the expert relaxes this factor.

Assume a heat h_1 contains 20% nickel and a heat h_2 that is processed afterward in the furnace should have 4% nickel. The second heat will take approximately

$$\frac{20\% - 4\%}{100\%} \cdot 3\% = .48\% \text{ nickel from the wall}$$

When scrap iron is inserted in the furnace, this amount is considered, and only 3.52% of nickel is taken. If the second heat can contain only as much as .25% of nickel, then this sequence of heats is not allowed.

The rule is effective for 42 chemical elements, but usually only 8 main elements are considered. Because not all elements react uniformly, exceptions exist that must be handled separately. Because of the diversity of qualities, these constraints often cannot be met. Actually, eight to nine percent of all heats is destroyed. They must be melted again and can be reused for another less critical order. Besides avoiding such destructions, it is expensive to waste rare elements. If one job demands a high percentage of an expensive element such as cobalt, the next job should use as much of this residual as possible. Although these compatibility criteria hold for every aggregate in the production process (inclusive ladles), usually only the electric arc furnace constraints are observed.

22.2.3.2 Temporal Constraints

Because some steel qualities require the cast steel to be hot for the subsequent treatment, such as forging, there will be an appointment that must be held within a tolerance of ±2 hours between the steelmaking plant and the next plant. The average number of jobs with such due dates is about 10%. Of course, these constraints are not really hard because they can be relaxed through negotiations with the subsequent plant. However, it is desirable to hold these due dates to reduce the time needed for negotiations.

For some jobs, no appointments are made, although their subsequent treatment should be done immediately after casting. These jobs should not be scheduled at the end of the week because, usually, the subsequent plants are not working then. Some jobs with difficult treatments should be performed during day shifts because an engineer should supervise these jobs. Usually, the treatments in the aggregates behind the electric arc furnace are shorter than the duration of the melting. However, for very high qualities, the duration in the ladle furnace is longer. Finally, the scheduler must guarantee that waiting intervals between operations not exceed a certain limit. An objective for the production is to have these intervals as small as possible. This results in a minimization of the makespan, which will reduce production costs. However, this objective is only a secondary goal function. The main objective is always to have as few destroyed heats as possible. Because this objective cannot be determined exactly, the secondary goal function is seldom regarded.

22.2.3.3 Capacity Constraints

If a heat should be cast in many small ingots, the load for the workers that set up and strip off the moulds is larger than for few large ingots because the handling of every mould takes approximately the same time. The workers do not like to have many heats that are cast into small ingots during a short time period. One objective of the scheduler is to achieve a uniform load distribution over the planning horizon for the workers.

The solidification of big best-ingots (52t) takes about one day. Because only one slot exists for such big ingots, only one per day can be produced. The space for smaller forging grade ingots is also very limited. Because there is only one continuous casting unit, only one furnace can supply this unit during a certain period. If two subsequent heats of one furnace should be cast both on the continuous caster and have approximately the same steel quality, the caster should operate continuously. These jobs are called *serial castings*. As few delays as possible should occur between the consecutive jobs. If an amount of steel that does not make a full heat is ordered, it can be combined with another of compatible quality forming a *double-* or *triple-casting*. This means that only a part of the heat is poured in the refinement ladle. Durations of treatments in the refinement and casting process will be shorter in this case.

22.2.4 Heuristics Used by the Experts

The experts of the plant use heuristics to construct schedules. These are used to master the complexity of the construction, and they are not used to evaluate a constructed schedule. If no schedule is found, some constraints are relaxed because it is known that usually, there will be enough freedom during execution to correct the violated constraints. Again, this relaxation is controlled by heuristics.

Before the expert system project was started, an attempt was made to schedule the heats with traditional software methods. This project was canceled because the program handled the constraints too rigidly. It was not able to relax constraints. It scheduled a lot of jobs correctly that were easy to schedule, but some of the difficult jobs were always unscheduled.

22.2.4.1 Alloying Cycles

An important concept for the scheduling process is the *alloying cycle*. This is a series of heats in which the amount of a chemical element is decreasing. For example, the concentration of nickel could decrease over several heats from 26% to .5%. Several alloying cycles for one element can occur in sequence, and several alloying cycles for different elements can overlap in time. Heats should be scheduled in this order. Additionally, the quality that is produced at the end of a week affects the heats in the beginning of the next week. Figure 22-2 illustrates the overlapping alloying cycles. The figure visualizes the amount of nickel and chrome for the jobs of schedule 2-1 that was generated from the orders of Table 22-2.

One important task driven by heuristics is the recognition of possible alloying cycles. This is supported by the experience of the engineers in the plant: the

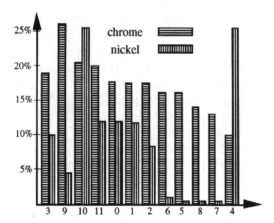

Figure 22-2:   Overlapping alloying cycles

amount of an element should decrease slowly over a sequence of heats but can increase very fast. Additionally, the number of peaks in this curve of a saw blade is kept to a minimum if possible.

22.2.4.2 Scheduling BEST-Ingots

BEST-ingots introduce some problems. Typically, there are groups of such jobs with all of them having the same chemical quality requirements. They are usually forging grade ingots; should be delivered hot to the forge; and are low-alloyed, which means their amount of alloying metals is very low. From the compatibility viewpoint, they should be produced in sequence. Unfortunately, they solidify slowly, and there is only one place for them in the teeming bay.

Therefore, BEST-ingots are scheduled at a rate of only one per day. Because they are low-alloyed, the furnaces will probably be high-alloyed in the intervening periods. Because they should be delivered hot, they cannot be scheduled before weekends or public holidays. Therefore, on weekends the furnaces shall be "high-alloyed," and as a consequence, these orders contain many small ingots.

22.2.4.3 Conflicts on the Continuous Caster

The HCC-unit is most economical if several heats with the same quality and format are cast continuously without breaks. In case that such a group of jobs exists, these jobs should be scheduled one after the other. However, all jobs of this group must be in time for their casting. After the processing of some jobs on the caster, a maintenance interval must be scheduled. Additionally, a set-up time of some hours must be reserved when a format conversion has to be performed.

Because the durations of the operations in the steelmaking process are very uncertain, the engineers prefer to charge the caster only with heats from one furnace. However, they sometimes change furnaces once per week. In this case, they decide when this change should take place before starting to schedule single jobs. Further, they accept only one format conversion. The expert schedules this conversion also a priori. Later, each job that requires the HCC-unit can be assigned to one part of the week.

22.3 THE METHODOLOGY

Our approach to solving the problems mentioned in the introduction is as follows: for a given planning horizon, a first schedule is generated by first considering very important jobs and those that are difficult to perform. To manage the given complexity, the schedule is constructed without chronological backtracking. The importance of jobs is dynamic, which means that the importance of one job can grow over time and is also dependent on the other jobs to be scheduled.

The preliminary schedule might not contain all jobs and still violate some constraints. In such a case, jobs in the schedule will be exchanged to find a proper schedule. A hill climbing search method controls this exchange.

To compare solutions, the system uses an evaluation function that is based on the given constraints. We use fuzzy set theory as defined in Negoita (1985) and Zadeh (1989) to model this evaluation. A fuzzy set is a set for which the boundary is non-sharp, with a gradual change from membership to non-membership. Fuzzy set theory is a more general form of normal set theory and is associated with fuzzy logic, a class of many-valued logic in which statements can have fuzzy-truth-values rather than be limited to the values *true* or *false*. Several formalisms have been proposed for the propagation of vague knowledge.

Motivation for this choice was the ease of formulating knowledge that reflects the complex non-linear behavior expressed by the human experts. Additionally, fuzzy-sets are well-suited to model knowledge containing vague human-like formulations. Such formulations can often be heard from human experts explaining their domain.

After introducing a small case from the application, we show how the constraints are represented by fuzzy sets and how an evaluation for a complete schedule can be computed. In the third subsection, we explain the generation of a preliminary schedule. The system generates the schedules iteratively; important jobs are scheduled first; gaps in the schedule are then filled; and finally, other jobs are scheduled. The schedule generated in this phase might violate constraints, and additionally, some jobs might exist that were not scheduled because of conflicting constraints.

Therefore, the last phase is a repair phase with a search for a proper schedule. This approach is similar to those in Minton *et al.* (1990) and Zweben *et al.* (1990). They have shown that the repair-based methods work well on large, real-world scheduling problems and are useful for optimization problems and over-constrained problems. Such schedules can only be found if constraints are relaxed because many constraints are antagonistic. This relaxation will be based on fuzzy sets.

22.3.1 Example

We take a small case study from the described application to illustrate the proposed technique (see Tables 22-1, 22-2). We restrict the case study to two furnaces and the planning horizon to one day. Additionally, we consider only a subset of the given constraints to reduce the complexity of the example. The input for the "scheduler" are two lists of jobs for the electric arc furnaces eaf1 and eaf3.

The name of each job identifies the quality of the steel. The column "time" gives the delivery date or the preferred time. The column "type" is used to give further information about the processing: 'C' stands for continuous casting, 'B' for BEST-technology, 'H' for hot delivering, and 'F' for fixed delivery. In the last column, the number and size of ingots are given. Each pair represents the number of ingots and the ingot's size in tons. For C-type jobs, the format of the produced slab is given.

22.3.2 Evaluation of Schedules

The knowledge of the application can be put into three main groups: knowledge about a particular job, temporal constraints, and constraints on the compatibility of jobs. All these are represented by fuzzy values.

22.3.2.1 Temporal Constraints

Temporal fuzzy values can be used to describe the duration of operations and job status, that is, whether jobs are too early or too late. The fuzzy value describes a degree of uncertainty in both directions. The following values can be identified: *very early*, *early*, *in time*, *late*, and *very late*. For the evaluation of a schedule, it makes no difference whether jobs are too early or too late. Therefore, the five values are mapped onto three values: *in time*, *nearly in time*, and *not in time*. From these values, a schedule can be evaluated with respect to its temporal constraints:

$$\text{timeliness}(S) = \bigwedge_{i=1}^{N} \text{timeliness}(H_i)$$

Since Prade (1979) and as recently as Bel *et al.* (1989), Dubois (1989), Dubois & Prade (1989), and Kerr & Walker (1989), fuzzy logic has been employed success-

Table 22-1: List for furnace EAF1.

No	Name	Time	Type	Ni	Cr	Co	Mn	Fe	V	W	Mo	Size
h_0	M100		H	.1	1.2	.0005	1.30	95	.10	.005	.005	34/1, 8/1.65
h_1	M200		H	.1	2.0	.0005	1.60	94	.10	.000	.230	2/24
h_2	M238		B	1.2	2.1	.0050	1.60	90	.10	.005	.250	1/52
h_3	M238		B	1.2	2.1	.0005	1.60	90	.10	.005	.250	1/52
h_4	K460		C	.1	.6	.0005	1.15	94	.15	.600	.005	157-13
h_5	K460		C	.1	.6	.0005	1.15	94	.15	.600	.005	157-13
h_6	K455		H	.1	1.2	.0005	.40	92	.20	2.100	.005	16/1, 18/1.6, 4/2
h_7	K600		H	4.2	1.4	.0005	.50	91	.10	.005	.300	33/1.6
h_8	S600	11 am	F	.2	4.3	.0005	.35	78	1.90	6.700	5.200	50/1
h_9	S600		F	.2	4.3	.0005	.35	78	1.90	6.700	5.200	50/1
h_{10}	W300		H	.2	5.2	.0005	.50	88	.50	.005	1.400	1/24, 1/1.1, 10/1.6
h_{11}	W302		H	.2	5.2	.0005	.50	89	1.10	.005	1.400	14/1, 17/1.6, 8/1.3

Table 22-2: List for furnace EAF3.

No	Name	Time	Type	Ni	Cr	Co	Mn	Fe	V	W	Mo	Size
h_0	A101		H	12.0	17.8	.0005	1.80	69	.10	.005	2.800	23/1.6
h_1	A300		K	11.5	17.5	.0005	1.50	67	.10	.005	2.300	3/1.31, 16/2
h_2	A506	morn.	K	8.5	17.5	.0005	2.00	69	.10	.005	.005	15/1, 16/1.6
h_3	A604		C	10.0	19.0	.0005	1.50	69	.10	.005	.005	65-20
h_4	A700		H	18.0	10.0	.0005	1.50	70	.10	.005	.100	1/33
h_5	N310		H	.5	16.5	.0005	1.50	81	.10	.005	.300	12/1.6, 21/1
h_6	N335		H	.9	16.5	.0005	.80	80	.10	.005	1.100	16/1, 15/1.6
h_7	N540		H	.5	13.5	.0005	.50	84	.10	.005	.500	13/3
h_8	N678		A	.5	14.0	.0005	.50	82	2.00	.000	.500	36/1
h_9	H304		H	4.5	26.0	.0005	1.30	65	.10	.005	.050	8/1.6, 24/1
h_{10}	H525		H	25.5	20.5	.0005	1.30	53	.10	.000	.000	27/1, 6/1.6
h_{11}	H550		H	12.0	20.0	.0005	1.30	66	.10	.000	.000	12/1, 16/1.6

fully to represent temporal constraints for knowledge-based scheduling. In those approaches, each crisp interval is preceded and followed by a slack time. For each moment of this slack time, there is an associated fuzzy membership grade defining the uncertainty that the corresponding slack time is correct. Thus, those systems can cope with small perturbations causing delays. The creation of robust schedules is facilitated because smaller intervals get higher scores and are considered identical to larger ones by systems not using fuzzy evaluation. Our approach generalizes the mentioned ones to include, beside such temporal constraints, other kinds, such as chemical or organizational fuzzy constraints.

22.3.2.2 Constraints between Jobs

The compatibility of two jobs integrates different chemical elements and the work load of workers. The compatibility between two jobs is calculated by first evaluating the compatibility for each factor separately to get restricted compatibility measures. Accordingly, six fuzzy sets for the global, as well as for each restricted, compatibility are defined: *very high, high, medium, low, very low*, and *no* compatibility. No combatability is a special case because a sequence being classified incompatible can never be scheduled in this order because of hard chemical constraints. In Table 22-3, some rules defining this compatibility measure for different factors are listed. The specifications of the ingredients are sometimes upper limits and sometimes nominal values. These rules can be interpreted directly as fuzzy inference rules.

The calculation of the nickel-compatibility is illustrated in Figure 22-3. In this case, only rules 5 and 6 contribute to the result. The condition parts of the rules contain statements about the percentage of a chemical element in the first heat compared to the following heat. In the example taken from Table 22.1, the heat h_3 must contain $h_3[Ni] = 1.2\%$ of the chemical element nickel, but heat h_4 should contain only $h_4[Ni] = .1\%$. The relative percentage of $h_3[Ni]$ is, therefore, 1200% of $h_4[Ni]$. With regard only to nickel, the question is whether the sequence h_3 preceding h_4 is allowed or not and, if yes, how good is this sequence compared to other

---

Table 22-3: Fuzzy compatibility rules for one element.

1. IF the percentage of chemical element E in heat H_0 is *less* than in heat H_1, THEN the E-compatibility of H_0 preceding H_1 is *medium*.

2. IF the percentage of chemical element E in heat H_0 is *slightly less* than in heat H_1, THEN the E-compatibility of H_0 preceding H_1 is *high*.

3. IF the percentage of chemical element E in heat H_0 is the *same* as in heat H_1, THEN the E-compatibility of H_0 preceding H_1 is *very high*.

4. IF the percentage of chemical element E in heat H_0 is *slightly more* than in heat H_1, THEN the E-compatibility of H_0 preceding H_1 is *high*.

5. IF the percentage of chemical element E in heat H_0 is *more* than in heat H_1, THEN the E-compatibility of H_0 preceding H_1 is *medium*.

6. IF the percentage of chemical element E in heat H_0 is *much more* than in heat H_1, THEN the E-compatibility of H_0 preceding H_1 is *low*.

7. IF the percentage of chemical element E in heat H_0 is *just below* the physical limit imposed by the element's presence in H_1, THEN the E-compatibility of H_0 preceding H_1 is *very low*.

8. IF the percentage of chemical element E in heat H_0 is *over* the physical limit imposed by the element's presence in H_1, THEN there is *no* compatibility for H_0 preceding H_1.

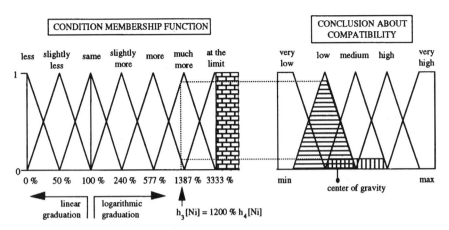

Figure 22-3: Computation of nickel-compatibility between heat h_3 and h_4 of Table 22-1

sequences. To decide this with the given fuzzy inference rules, somehow the vague linguistic variables and crisp but uncertain numeric values must be matched. This is done with fuzzy membership functions, as defined in Figure 22-3, both for the condition and for the conclusion part. Similar graphs representing the membership functions associated with fuzzy inference rules can be found, for example, in Maki *et al.* (1989) and Kanemoto *et al.* (1990), where the computations are done in a comparable way.

In our example, the numeric input of 1200% relates more or less with the linguistic variables *more* and *much more*. Follow the dotted lines to the conclusion membership functions for rules 5 and 6, and the two membership functions low $_{[Ni]}(h_3, h_4)$ and medium $_{[Ni]}(h_3, h_4)$ appear as a result of the calculation. Their combination

$$\text{comp}_{[Ni]}(h_3, h_4) = \text{low}_{[Ni]}(h_3, h_4) \vee \text{medium}_{[Ni]}(h_3, h_4)$$

is a new membership function defining the nickel-compatibility of h_3 preceding h_4, which is generally speaking more low than medium. The fuzzy-or operator represents the maximum of both arguments. We obtain as a result that the nickel-compatibility for h_3 preceding h_4 is more *low* than *medium*.

The conditions of the fuzzy inference rules consider only relative values for the percentage of elements such as nickel in the two compared heats. Absolute values are, for the compatibility problem, of minor interest but could easily be modeled by introducing more complex three dimensional membership functions. We chose a half-logarithmic graduation to be able to handle those relative values. Because the compatibility rule is asymmetric and only restricts the second heat to a minimal value for a certain chemical element that must be at least present in this heat, the graduation is asymmetric, too, and only logarithmic on the right half.

Beside simplifying the visualization, this logarithmic scale has an additional positive effect because positions on the right side of the 100% mark that are still near the center are preferred and get more attention per unit than positions more close to the physical limit on the far right. This reinforces the natural meaning of the fuzzy linguistic variables positively.

The fuzzy inference rules such as those in Table 22-3 give several fuzzy judgments about the compatibility between heats. These judgments are in the form of membership functions and can be simplified to the linguistic variable to which the judgment mainly pertains. The resulting fuzzy values can all be combined by computing a weighted mean of the membership functions for each component to get one overall value for the two heats:

$$\text{comp}(H_i, H_j) = \sum_{E \in \{Wl, Ni, Cr, \ldots\}} g(E) \, \text{comp}_{[E]}(H_i, H_j)$$

In this formula, $g(E)$ is the normalized weight of a rule, and E is a member of the set of all factors influencing the compatibility, namely, work load (Wl) and the eight chemical elements such as nickel or chromium. The compatibility can also be defuzzified by calculating the center of gravity of the surface and then taking the value of its x-coordinate as the result. This value can be computed by the following formula:

$$\text{defuzzy}(\text{comp}(H_i, H_j)) = \frac{\int_{x=min}^{max} x \, \text{comp}(H_i, H_j)(x) \, dx}{\int_{x=min}^{max} \text{comp}(H_i, H_j)(x) \, dx}$$

This computation is done for every pair of jobs that can be scheduled. The result is a matrix of defuzzyfied values, where the value of one cell describes how compatible the sequence of the job of a column after the job in a row is according to all rules. Table 22-4 shows this matrix for our example. It will be used for the construction of the preliminary schedule and during the improvement process. The values in the table are the previously used linguistic variables because for the sake of understandability, we have replaced the defuzzyfied values with the name of the fuzzy set to which the defuzzyfied value mainly belongs.

To evaluate schedules during improvement steps, an evaluation value for the compatibility of the entire schedule must be computed. This can be achieved with a fuzzy and-operator. For a given schedule S with N jobs, the evaluation function is given by

$$\text{comp}(S) = \bigwedge_{i=1}^{N} \text{comp}(H_i, H_{i+1})$$

Table 22-4   Compatibility matrix for heats on furnace EAF1.

H_0\H_1	h_0	h_1	h_2	h_3	h_4	h_5	h_6	h_7	h_8	h_9	h_{10}	h_{11}
h_0	-	high	high	high	high	high	high	medium	medium	medium	high	high
h_1	medium	-	high	high	medium	medium	medium	medium	medium	medium	medium	high
h_2	low	medium	-	very high	low	low	low	high	medium	medium	medium	medium
h_3	low	medium	very high	-	low	low	low	high	medium	medium	medium	medium
h_4	high	medium	medium	medium	-	very high	medium	medium	high	high	medium	medium
h_5	high	medium	medium	medium	very high	-	medium	medium	high	high	medium	medium
h_6	medium	low	medium	medium	medium	medium	-	low	high	high	low	low
h_7	very low	very low	high	high	very low	very low	very low	-	low	low	low	low
h_8	low	low	very low	very low	low	low	medium	low	-	very high	medium	high
h_9	low	low	very low	very low	low	low	medium	low	very high	-	medium	high
h_{10}	medium	medium	medium	medium	low	low	medium	low	high	high	-	high
h_{11}	medium	low	low	low	very low	very low	low	low	very high	very high	very high	-

22.3.2.3 Classification of Jobs

In a real-world application such as scheduling a steelmaking plant, many optimization criteria compete with each other. Chen, Pan, & Xue (1987) describe one approach to handle multi-objective scheduling using fuzzy sets. Similarly, the system presented in this chapter uses operators from fuzzy set theory to compound those conflicting objectives. Each different objective is introduced through the calculation of an importance measure for jobs.

The importance of jobs is used to control the generation of a schedule by scheduling the most important jobs first. In this context, the importance is a combination of the difficulty to schedule a job in general and the importance to schedule it for the actual planning horizon.

A job that requires a bottleneck resource such as the continuous caster or the teeming bay for a BEST-ingot is usually difficult to schedule. However, the difficulty depends on the number of jobs with such characteristics. If only one job has to be performed on the continuous caster, then this job is not difficult.

A job with a certain delivery date is urgent because it must be scheduled in the planning horizon in which the delivery date falls. Jobs that are not that important can be shifted to the next planning horizon. To get such a shifted job scheduled, it is necessary that the importance of the job increase over time. The range of fuzzy

Table 22-5: Classification of jobs.

urgent	$\{h_8\}$
very-important	$\{h_2, h_3, h_4, h_5\}$
important	$\{h_7, h_9\}$
medium	$\{h_6, h_{10}, h_{11}\}$
not-important	$\{h_0, h_1\}$

values to represent this importance is *urgent, very important, important, medium,* and *not important.*

The classification of jobs in the list is dependent on the situation in the actual planning horizon. If many large ingots are produced, these orders are difficult to schedule because there is not enough space for the solidification process. If many heats are to be scheduled that are cast into small ingots, these are difficult jobs because of the objective to achieve a uniform distribution of work load.

The inverse evaluation is necessary for chemical ingredients: if for the actual planning horizon many jobs with a high chromium-nickel-alloy exist, as it is in Table 22-2, then a high percentage of chromium (Cr) is no problem. On the other hand, when there are only few jobs with high nickel (Ni) percentages, these jobs can be difficult to schedule. Job h_7 in Table 22-1 has a disproportionate amount of nickel in relation to the other jobs in the list and must be scheduled early. For the jobs of Table 22-1, we obtain the classification of jobs shown in Table 22-5.

One objective of our strategy is to schedule as many jobs as possible. However, in order not to forget the difficult jobs, these are scheduled first. Furthermore, the evaluation function for an entire schedule must contain a factor representing the importance of jobs. Hence, an evaluation function is defined to assign an importance value to a schedule, with N the number of jobs:

$$\text{importance}(S) = \bigwedge_{i=1}^{N} \text{importance}(H_i)$$

22.3.3 Generating a Preliminary Schedule

To generate a preliminary schedule, the jobs are classified according to their importance. Then they are scheduled in the sequence of their importance. The *urgent* and *very important* jobs are scheduled first. To be scheduled means that a temporal interval is assigned to them that describes the time when a job is in the electric arc furnace. The assigned intervals can spread over the entire planning horizon because of temporal and resource constraints. To simplify our example, we assume slots with a duration of two hours in the schedule. In reality, the duration of jobs varies as much as five hours, and this variation must be considered by the system too.

During this scheduling process, empty intervals can remain between scheduled jobs. The compatibilities with the jobs before and after these empty intervals are not considered. If empty intervals with a duration of approximately one job remain, they are filled with compatible jobs as soon as possible. During this scheduling process, the compatibility matrix, as shown in Table 22-4, is used.

A special strategy is applied to prune the search space. It is comparable with preprocessing techniques in constraint satisfaction problems (CSP), as described in Dechter & Meiri (1989). The objects in our CSP are the heats, and for every heat, a set of possible successors exists. With constraint propagation, the set of successors can be reduced. If one job is the only possible successor of a job, it cannot be any more the successor of another job. If for a heat H_0, only one heat H_1 has a good compatibility value, then the two heats can be interpreted as one job consisting of two heats. H_1 is the definitive successor of H_0. If one of these heats is scheduled, the other one is scheduled automatically too. If a heat H_0 has two possible successors, H_1 and H_2, and H_1 is scheduled after another heat, the heat H_2 will be assigned as the definitive successor of H_0. Jobs with *no* sequence-compatibility are not scheduled one after the other.

To illustrate the generation, we explain the generation of a schedule from the orders given in Table 22-1. We use the classification of jobs given in Table 22-5. The whole schedule for both furnaces is shown in Table 22-6. The system considers the jobs in the following sequence:

h_8:   In the list of jobs given in Table 22-1, job h_8 has a delivery date and is compatible with only a few jobs. Therefore, it was classified urgent and must be scheduled first. It is scheduled at 11am.

h_2, h_3:   Next, jobs h_2 and h_3 are scheduled because they are very important jobs. They need a long time span between each other because they are cast into BEST-ingots. One is placed in the first and the other in the last slot of the schedule.

h_4, h_5:   Jobs h_4 and h_5 should be scheduled one after the other because they are cast with the same format on the HCC-unit. In the list for the second furnace, there is another job that will be produced on the caster. Because this job is cast with a different format, a maintenance interval between these jobs is necessary. The single job should be scheduled as early as possible and the two jobs of the first list as late as possible. Consequently, h_4 and h_5 are scheduled before the last slot.

h_7:   The urgent and very important jobs are scheduled. No small intervals exist, so the system can proceed with the important job h_7. This job is difficult to schedule because it has only a few compatible

Table 22-6: Intermediate schedule for example heats.

schedule 1-1:	med	med	low	v. high	high	v. high	med	med	high	v. high	med
EAF1	h_2	h_1	h_7	h_8	h_9	h_{11}	h_{10}	h_6	h_0	h_4	h_5	h_3

schedule 2-1:	high	high	high	high	high	low	med	high	high	low	high
EAF3	h_3	h_9	h_{10}	h_{11}	h_0	h_1	h_2	h_6	h_5	h_8	h_7	h_4

time: 5am   7am   9am 11am 1pm 3pm 5pm 7pm 9pm 11pm 1am 3am 5am

successors. The two best fitting jobs, h_2 and h_3, are not possible. There are four potential successors with low compatibility. To generate fewer small intervals, job h_7 is scheduled before h_8.

h_9:   Job h_9 is then scheduled optimally after h_8.

h_1:   At that time, the strategy is changed, and a job that fits best in the slot between h_2 and h_7 is sought. Job h_1 is a good candidate.

h_{11}:   Four jobs remain for two empty intervals. Because job h_{11} has a request time "day shift," it should be scheduled as early as possible. It is placed after h_9.

h_{10}:   Because h_{10} is a very good successor, it is scheduled thereafter.

h_0, h_6:   Job h_0 should be scheduled before h_4 because h_6 does not fit well.

The resulting schedule is illustrated in the first part of Table 22-6. The compatibilities are shown in the line above the heat sequence. We assume that schedule 2-1 was constructed for the second furnace. The problems in the list for the second furnace are the molybdenum- and manganese-compatibilities. The algorithm (Algorithm 22-1) to generate this schedule is simple.

22.3.4 Improving the Schedule by Relaxation of Constraints

Usually, some jobs cannot be scheduled because they will always violate some compatibility constraints. In addition, some empty intervals can remain in the schedule, and the compatibility between the jobs adjacent to these intervals is usually poor. Instead of taking back the last scheduling decisions by backtracking, we try to repair or improve such a preliminary schedule. In our example, no empty intervals exist, and no jobs remain. However, there are some ways to improve this preliminary schedule.

To improve a schedule, an evaluation function is required. One potential evaluation is the sum of violated constraints minus the correctly scheduled jobs. Unfortunately, the violation of constraints can have far-reaching consequences. The vio-

```
s := {};
list-of-jobs := classify(list-of-jobs);
matrix := classify(list-of-jobs);
repeat
    job := get-most-important(list-of-jobs);
    s := schedule(job);
    list-of-jobs := reclassify(list-of-jobs);
until very-important(job) ∉ list-of-job;
repeat
    while gaps-exist(s)
        s := fill-gap(s);
    repeat
        job := get-most-important(list-of-jobs);
        s := schedule(job);
        list-of-jobs := reclassify(list-of-jobs);
    until gap-exists(s) or empty(list-of-jobs)
        or full(s);
until empty(list-of-jobs) or full(s);
```

Algorithm 22-1: Generation of schedule

lation of a temporal constraint can cause more resources, such as additional energy, to be consumed or can require rescheduling in the next plants. The violation of a chemical constraint can result in the loss of a heat that would be an important financial damage. On one hand, hard constraints that cannot be relaxed must be considered, and on the other hand, constraints can be relaxed to a certain degree to get a feasible schedule with as many jobs as possible. To evaluate these antagonistic constraints, an evaluation function based on the fuzzy values seems to be more adequate because the grade of the satisfaction of a constraint is evaluated too.

We have defined a repair strategy based on these fuzzy values. The actual schedule is called the "currently best schedule." This schedule can usually be improved. To improve it, the system looks for a constraint being insufficiently satisfied. For the first furnace, such a violation is found between heat h_7 and h_8. Therefore, one of them is taken out of the schedule. There are two reasons to remove h_7: heat h_8 has a delivery date, and h_7 probably causes the conflict because it is a very difficult job to schedule. A better place is sought, such as before h_3.

There are two possibilities to clear this slot. All jobs between h_1 and h_3 could be shifted by one place, or h_5 could be taken out of the schedule. The first alternative is easier to do. The result is shown in Schedule 1-2 in Table 22-7. The disadvantage of this schedule is that the delivery date cannot be met exactly. However, it is better than the first schedule.

Table 22-7: Intermediate schedule for example heats.

schedule 1-2:	med	med	v. high	high	v. high	med	med	high	v. high	med	high
EAF1	h_2	h_1	h_8	h_9	h_{11}	h_1	h_6	h_0	h_4	h_5	h_7	h_3

schedule 1-3:	med	med	med	v. high	high	v. high	med	med	high	v. high	med
EAF1	h_2	h_1	h_0	h_8	h_9	h_{11}	h_{10}	h_6	h_5	h_4	h_7	h_3

time: 5am 7am 9am 11am 1pm 3pm 5pm 7pm 9pm 11pm 1am 3am 5am

With the second strategy, a better schedule cannot be found straight away because it is not possible to schedule h_5 in the morning. Job h_5 should be scheduled before h_4. To achieve this, heat h_0 can be scheduled into the old slot of h_7. The result is shown in Schedule 1-3. It will become the "currently best schedule" that can be improved further. Especially if we consider the aspect of the load of the workers, more improvements are possible.

Every exchange of jobs in the schedule, every exchange between jobs in the schedule and jobs in the list, and each shift of jobs can be interpreted as an operator in a search process. The search for better schedules is guided by heuristics based on our evaluation function. This heuristic search is a kind of hill climbing method. Unfortunately, the disadvantage of such a method is that it can be caught in local maxima. Glover (1989, 1990) describes a technique called TABU-search that can be used to overcome this problem. This technique allows the system to choose a slightly worse schedule as "current best schedule" to escape the local maxima. However, to restrict the search, a tabu list describing which operations can not be performed anymore in the search process is used.

If no further constraint violation can be detected or no further improvement is achievable, the search for the best schedule ends. Judging whether a further improvement can be achieved is generally difficult. It makes sense to define a distance function between an optimal schedule where all compatibilities would be very high, and all the other constraints would be satisfied too. Thus, the distance function is the summation of the deviation of all constraints from their optimum. If such a function is available, one can restrict the search effort by a ratio between distance and search effort. It would be fruitless to invest much more search effort if only a small distance exists, or with great effort, only small improvements are achieved. On the other hand, if the distance is large, one should search longer for a better schedule. A simplified version of this repair algorithm is given as Algorithm 22-2.

```
tabu-list := {};
s := current-best-schedule;
search-effort := 0;
repeat
    job1 := find-violation(s, tabu-list);
    op := choose-best-repair-operator(job1, s);
    case op:
        1:  s := shift(job1, s);
        2:  find(job2, list-of-jobs);
            s := exchange(s, job1, job2);
        3:  find(job2, s);
            s := exchange(s, job1, job2);
    end case;
    if better(s, current-best-schedule)
        then current-best-schedule := s
        else tabu-list := add(tabu-list, {job1, op});
    search-effort := search-effort + 1;
until distance(s) / search-effort < limit;
```

Algorithm 22-2: Repair of schedule

22.4 COMPARISON TO RELATED SYSTEMS

In other projects, it was shown that steel production is a worthy domain for the application of knowledge-based scheduling systems (Numao & Morishita, 1989; Shah, Damian, & Silverman, 1990; Stohl et al., 1991). In contrast to our application, these systems are used in plants for mass steel production where steel qualities do not vary as much as in our application. The main problem and bottle-neck resource in these applications are the continuous casters. Because the casting process should be continuous, heats must be ready in time for casting. On the other hand, heats should not wait too long because the steel would consolidate. A backward scheduling strategy is applied in these systems, reasoning temporally from the last operation in the process plan of one job to the first operation.

In contrast, we apply a kind of forward reasoning because most jobs do not use the continuous caster, and the main problem is the chemical constraints in the first unit, the electric arc furnace. In the described systems, the required resources are always the same. Only one of several equal units can be chosen. In our application, there are different process plans for different steel qualities.

In Shah, Damian, & Silverman (1990), a minimization of waiting time is given as an evaluation criterion for schedules. In our application, this would not be appropriate because the execution is uncertain, and the minimization would only be theoretical. This is also the case for other applications (Kerr & Walker, 1989; Smith, Fox, & Ow, 1986). Therefore, no optimal schedule is computable. The goal function of our system is simply to find a feasible schedule violating as few constraints as possible and optimizing the schedule by local improvements.

In handling the problem of scheduling under uncertainty, the main difference with other approaches, such as probability calculus (Berry, 1992), is our pragmatic focus on simple modeling. One difficulty with probabilistic approaches is that they usually require judgmental estimates of many parameters for which little or no empirical support is available and are very tedious computationally. A further problem lies in the contentious conceptual basis for manipulating subjectively derived probabilities in the same way as classical probabilities obtained from empirically observed frequency distributions (Kerr & Walker, 1989). Fuzzy set theory, on the other hand, has had a considerable degree of success in capturing human ability to reason in terms of vague quantities. In fact, it was even designed to this very end, i.e., to allow an easy formulation of subjective fuzzy rules. Additionally, fuzzy logic is a well-grounded mathematical theory derived from fuzzy set theory that does not lead to conceptual problems such as certainty factors (Kruse, Schwecker, & Heinsohn, 1991). Nevertheless, we must concede that some membership function tuning is required to really get an application right. Especially, the overlapping of membership functions has been shown by Boverie, Demaya, & Titli (1991) to be a major influence factor, whereas their number or exact shape seem to be of minor importance.

Woodyatt *et al.* (1992) have used fuzzy set theory to successfully satisfy collections of customer orders yet minimize the number of steel qualities actually produced. They assign metallurgical grades to steel to select the specific applicable grades and then dress the customer orders according to the likelihood of a grade meeting the customer's specifications. Finally, they combine orders with matching fuzzy grades to optimize the productivity and yield of a continuous caster. Their approach is similar to ours because in both cases, fuzzy set theory is used to identify compatible orders. We nevertheless go further by applying fuzzy techniques to a much broader set of constraints used to actually schedule all orders available.

22.5 CONCLUSION

Because of the highly unreliable data, the vague knowledge formulation, and the conflicting objectives in scheduling applications, mathematical-analytical methods as used in OR are often insufficient. We have illustrated this problem for a steelmaking plant. To overcome this deficiency, we have developed a solution that combines two sound AI-techniques for problem solving: approximate reasoning and constraint relaxation. Our knowledge representation technique covers the

uncertainty of problem domain knowledge and supports the straightforward generation of a schedule based on the importance of the jobs considered. However,
because of this ad hoc generation of schedules, some jobs usually remain unscheduled. We have proposed a "repair-based" control strategy that deals with several
types of constraints (temporal, spatial, and chemical) and supports the dynamic
relaxation of conflicting constraints. Although we have not compared this strategy
with other approaches, we believe that this is the most simple and efficient way to
regard antagonistic constraints that have no clear hierarchical order.

Additionally, the generation of robust schedules is stimulated by using fuzzy
sets. The heats that are cast on the continuous casters were scheduled on different
ends of the schedule because this improves the robustness of the schedule. We
describe the duration between both heats with a temporal fuzzy set that evaluates
the schedule better in which the interval between both heats is longer.

The presented control strategy can be used to also handle emergency cases. If
some event such as a delay occurs, the schedule is evaluated again. In case that this
value is worse than a specified level of quality, a repair is necessary. By applying
the repair strategy, reactive scheduling is achieved, and it becomes possible to react
dynamically to events during job execution.

Additionally, improper conditions for consecutive jobs require immediate and
dynamic adaptation. We have supported this adaptation by providing the human
expert assistance in relaxing constraints. With this approach, it becomes possible to
evaluate different scenarios before actual activities are performed. We call this kind
of problem solving "what-if" games. Such a simulation prevents human experts
from causing troubles with improper decision-making. Finally, the decision process
is more transparent. However, to support the evaluation and experimentation with
chemical element constellations, as well as production constraints, we have to
develop a sophisticated human-computer interaction concept. In particular, the condition membership functions for inference rules, as shown in Figure 22-3, should
remain under the control of the human expert. The compatibility rule, element
constellation, shape of the membership functions, and the weights of the fuzzy
inference rules should be considered during what-if games with the schedule to
support estimates of schedule modifications. The condition membership functions
in Figure 22-3, for example, can be adapted for each element in two ways. First,
their general shape can be altered to get sharper or softer transitions from one
linguistic variable to the next. Second, the compatibility rule can be changed for
one element from 3% to 2.5%, which would mean that this latter element does not
remain in the furnace as a residual to the same extent as the others. Additionally,
the relative weights of the fuzzy inference rules can be adapted to the relative
importance of the playing factors; e.g., the work load constraint could be classified
more important and, thus, receive higher weights than chemical constraints. These
adaptations need a lot of fine tuning; therefore, the engineers should have the

opportunity to experiment with the system to be able to match their own way of decision making more accurately. An enriched, spreadsheet-like environment is the proper interaction technique for this type of correlated information. In such an environment, the change of one dimension can be traced simultaneously with the remaining dimensions. This immediate feedback enhances the way the engineers can experiment with their assumptions to find better values for the system's parameters.

The idea behind our methodology is to allow easier modeling of the activities of human scheduling experts. Our prototype is successful in simulating the human performance. We believe that using the described techniques, the development cycle for scheduling systems becomes shorter and the knowledge representation easier. Whether the solutions of our system or those of the previously developed expert system are better cannot be decided definitively. However, we assume that with the given techniques, better schedules can be generated because the human expert can easily tune the problem solving process.

The described methodology was implemented in a prototype for the described application. We deploy this methodology at the moment for another steelmaking plant with different production characteristics and constraints. Later on, we intend to develop a reusable tool for different applications ranging over the whole steelmaking process.

ACKNOWLEDGMENTS

We would like to acknowledge the work in knowledge acquisition done by Dorothea Czedik and Alexandra Eder; the helpfulness of the experts Ing. Pauker and Ing. Gromann; the frankness about new techniques of Dr. Meyer; the head of the steelmaking plant, Reza Shams for his work in the implementation of the expert system that has influenced our work heavily; and Rainhard Steindl for his implementation and critique of our fuzzy constraint based approach. Thanks also to Monte Zweben for careful review of this chapter.

References

Barachini, F., and N. Theuretzbacher. 1988. The Challenge of Real-time Process Control for Production Systems. *Proceedings of the 7th National Conference on Artificial Intelligence*, pp. 705–709. AAAI Press, Menlo Park, Calif.

Bel, G., E. Bensana, D. Dubois, J. Erschler, and P. Esquirol. 1989. A Knowledge-based Approach to Industrial Job-shop Scheduling. *Knowledge-Based Systems in Manufacturing*, Andrew Kusiak (ed.), Taylor & Francis, pp. 207–246. London.

Berry, P.M. 1992. Scheduling: A Problem of Decision-Making under Uncertainty. *Proceedings of the 10th European Conference on Artificial Intelligence*, pp. 638–642. John Wiley, Chichester.

Boverie, S., B. Demaya, and A. Titli. 1991. Fuzzy Logic Control Compared with Other Automatic Control Approaches. *Proceedings of the 30th IEEE Conference on Decision and Control*. IEEE Computer Society Press, Los Alamitos, Calif.

Chen, D., Y. Pan, and J. Xue. 1987. A Fuzzy Production System with Backtracking Control Strategy for Multiobjective Scheduling to a One-machine-n-parts Problem. *Modern Production Management Systems*, Andrew Kusiak (ed.), pp. 135–145. Elsevier, Amsterdam.

Conway, R.W., W.L. Maxwell, and L.W. Miller. 1967. *Theory of Scheduling*. Addison Wesley, Reading, Mass.

Dechter, R., and L. Meiri. 1989. Experimental Evaluation of Preprocessing Techniques in Constraint Satisfaction Problems. *Proceedings of the 11th International Joint Conference on Artificial Intelligence*, pp. 271–277. AAAI Press, Menlo Park, Calif.

Dorn, J., and R. Shams. 1991. An Expert System for Scheduling in a Steelmaking Plant. *Proceedings of the World Congress on Expert Systems*, pp. 395–404. Pergamon Press, New York.

Dubois, D. 1989. Fuzzy Knowledge in an Artificial Intelligence System for Job-Shop Scheduling. *Applications of Fuzzy Set Methodologies in Industrial Engineering*, Gerald W. Evans et al. (eds.), pp. 73–89. Elsevier, New York.

Dubois, D., and H. Prade. 1989. Processing Fuzzy Temporal Knowledge. *IEEE Transactions on Systems, Man, and Cybernetics*, Vol. 19, No. 4, pp. 729–744.

Glover, F. 1990. Tabu Search Part II. *ORSA Journal on Computing*, Vol. 2, No. 1, p. 432.

Glover, F. 1989. Tabu Search Part I. *ORSA Journal on Computing*, Vol. 1, No. 3, pp. 190–206.

Kanemoto, M., H. Yamane, T. Yoshida, and H. Tottori. 1990. An Application of Expert Systems to LD Converter Processes. *Journal of the Iron and Steel Institute of Japan*, ISIJ International, Vol. 30, No. 2, pp. 128–135.

Kerr, R.M., and R.N. Walker. 1989. A Job Shop Scheduling System Based on Fuzzy Arithmetic. *Proceedings of the 2nd International Conference on Expert Systems and Leading Edge in Production and Operations Management*, pp. 433–450.

Kruse, R., E. Schwecke, and J. Heinsohn. 1991. *Uncertainty and Vagueness in Knowledge Based Systems—Numerical Methods*. Springer, New York.

Maki, Y., Y. Masuda, T. Sawada, T. Matsumoto, H. Obata, and N. Takashima. 1989. Application of Fuzzy Theory for Automatic Control of Hot Stove Combustion Gas Flow. *Proceedings of the 6th IFAC Symposium on Automation in Mining, Mineral, and Metal Processing*, pp. 278–284.

Minton, S., M. Johnston, A. Philips, and P. Laird. 1989. Solving Large-scale Constraint Satisfaction and Scheduling Problems Using a Heuristic Repair Method. *Proceedings of the 8th National Conference on Artificial Intelligence*, pp. 17–24. AAAI Press, Menlo Park, Calif.

Negoita, C.V. 1985. *Expert Systems and Fuzzy Systems*. Benjamin/Cummings, Redwood City, Calif.

Numao, M., and S. Morishita. 1989. A Scheduling Environment for Steel-making Processes. *Proceedings of the 5th International Conference on Artificial Intelligence for Industrial Applications*, pp. 279–286. IEEE Computer Society Press, Los Alamitos, Calif.

Prade, H. 1979. Using Fuzzy Set Theory in a Scheduling Problem: A Case Study. *Fuzzy Sets and Systems*, Vol. 2, No. 2, pp. 153–165.

Shah, M.J., R. Damian, and J. Silverman. 1990. Knowledge Based Dynamic Scheduling in a Steel Plant. *Proceedings of the 6th International Conference on Artificial Intelligence for Industrial Applications*, pp. 108–113. IEEE Computer Society Press, Los Alamitos, Calif.

Smith, S.F., M.S. Fox, and P.S. Ow. 1986. Constructing and Maintaining Detailed Construction Plans: Investigations into the Development of Knowledge-Based Factory Scheduling Systems. *AI Magazine*, Vol. 7, No. 4, pp. 45–61.

Stohl, K., W. Snopek, T. Weigert, and T. Moritz. 1991. Development of a Scheduling Expert System for a Steelplant. *Proceedings of the IFIP Conference on Experts Systems in Mineral and Metallurgy*.

Woodyatt, L.R., K.L. Stott, F.E. Wolf, and F.J. Vasko. 1992. Using Fuzzy Sets to Assign Metallurgical Grades to Steel. *Journal of Metallurgy*, February.

Zadeh, L.A. 1989. Knowledge Representation in Fuzzy Logic. *IEEE Transactions on Knowledge and Data Engineering*, Vol. 1, No. 1, pp. 89–100.

Zweben, M., M. Deale, and R. Gargan. 1990. Anytime Rescheduling. *Proceedings of the DARPA Workshop on Innovative Approaches to Planning and Scheduling*, pp. 251–262.

23

MACMERL:

Mixed-Initiative Scheduling with Coincident Problem Spaces

Michael J. Prietula
(Carnegie Mellon University)

Wen-Ling Hsu
(Carnegie Mellon University)

Peng Si Ow
(IBM, Austin, TX)

Gerald L. Thompson
(Carnegie Mellon University)

23.1 INTRODUCTION

The scheduling of work on machines is one of the most important aspects of a manufacturing enterprise because in most cases, no schedule means no output, and a bad schedule means high costs. Although much research has been and continues to be conducted on solving versions of the "scheduling problem," there is often a distinct difference between the theory and the practice of scheduling (Graves 1981; McKay, Buzacott, & Safayeni, 1988; Ow & Smith, 1988). When one considers the primary goal of scheduling *theory*, the scheduling problem is characterized in an abstract form, stylized by simplifying assumptions, in order to bring to bear the tools appropriate to the analysis of the problem as presented—most typically in an analytical form. On the other hand, when one considers the primary goal of scheduling *practice*, the scheduling problem is usually embedded in a context that does not permit the relaxation of certain constraints or invalidates assumptions on which existing solutions rest. Rather, the scheduling problem is "solved" in a context that

655

includes other corporate considerations and constraints that require a schedule to be generated: within a time frame, within a budget, with specific software, on a particular machine, with fluctuating demands, and so forth. What is important to scheduling theory is the solution to an abstractly specified *scheduling* problem. What is important to scheduling practice is the solution to an actual *organizational* problem.

Scheduling theory yields a solution that is stable and expressed in terms of the context (assumptions, constraints) within which it was formulated; that is, the solution is proved to be correct within the context described. Scheduling practice generally yields a solution that is relatively good; that is, it is good only to the extent that the organizational context within which it was formulated remains stable. For either case, one way of assigning value to the solution is the generality of the results. In practice, value is often also discovered in the *process* by which the solution was achieved—creating a solution to the organizational scheduling problem provides insights into the organizational context within which the problem was defined.

In this chapter, we describe a real company's organizational scheduling problem, a solution technique that we created, and the process by which we achieved it. The organizational problem is a familiar one:

- Scheduling was done in the plant for many years by a small group of individuals (two in particular).
- Changes in the nature of the competitive environment have increased the importance of the scheduling task.
- The firm wishes to incorporate computer technology to facilitate the task of the schedulers.
- There is no documentation on how the schedulers do what they do so well.
- The individuals who do the scheduling are nearing retirement age.

Thus, the lack of specific organizational knowledge (of the scheduling practice) placed the organization at risk. The solution to the company's problem involved discovering and embodying the relevant organizational knowledge in a computer program, called *MacMerl*. The approach used a cognitive perspective in solving the (organizational) scheduling problem. Specifically, the problem was viewed as "understanding and supporting scheduling from the perspective of the human expert scheduler." Thus, the role of the human expert was central to the problem description and, consequently, to the design of the system. Note that *understanding* the expert's perspective does not necessarily mean *implementing* the expert's methods—the intent generally espoused in "traditional" expert systems development (Hayes-Roth, Waterman, & Lenat, 1983). Methods are developed by an expert to achieve goals. Although an expert's goals might be insightful and appropriate for expressing a solution to the organizational problem, the severely restricted attention and computation abilities of a human expert serve to inhibit the quality of the solutions generated. For these human schedulers, as the complexity of the scheduling task increases, their primary goal shifts from one of producing good schedules to one of avoiding obviously poor ones.

If a system could be designed to somehow work within the framework used by the expert scheduler, then the (presumably appropriate) goals of the expert could be supported in computational form. In the parlance of cognitive psychology, problem solving—by any intelligent agent—can be characterized as *search* conducted through a problem space of alternatives, where a problem space is basically a representation of specific (and relevant) aspects of the task. The primary objective for the design of an interactive scheduler then was seen to be one of permitting the human and the machine to be operating in *coincident problem spaces,* where search by the human scheduler could be augmented with search by the machine. The key was to discover the decision horizon where the methods of the human scheduler would fail, but the methods of the machine could succeed. This was accomplished by forming a "backbone" system design based on the primary methods used by the human scheduler and supporting the achievement of critical scheduling *goals* and *operators* (to achieve those goals) with strong, computationally based search mechanisms. However, the design also had to support a cooperative approach to generating and reviewing schedules because the system could not anticipate the entire set of parameters that define acceptable solutions. Therefore, we incorporated a design that permitted a *mixed-initiative approach* to scheduling—schedule alternatives and critiques could be offered by both the user and the system. MacMerl, then, is a system in which the human and the machine interact in a coherent and cooperative manner to solve complex production scheduling.

We first describe the scheduling task environment, the process by which we defined the critical aspects of the task, and the general goals and constraints driving the solution design. Next we summarize the general design approach and explain the characterization of coincident problem spaces. Following this, we present the detailed design of MacMerl and show the solution of an example. We conclude with a discussion of the implementation issues and the implications for the development of related systems.

23.2 ANALYSIS OF THE SCHEDULING TASK

The company produces replacement windshields for automobiles, trucks, and recreational vehicles. The general production process is summarized in Figure 23-1. The primary raw materials for producing windshields are glass and vinyl, where each windshield consists of two pieces of bent glass and one piece of vinyl. The glass must be cut, screened (edging added by a silkscreen process), and bent, and the vinyl must be stretched and cut before the two can be put together. Further

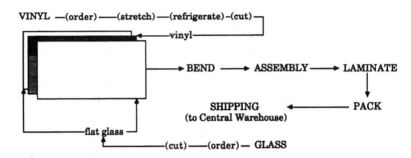

Figure 23-1:   Flow diagram of the manufacturing process

operations such as deairing, laminating, and attaching the ancillary parts (e.g., rear-view mirror attachments) are completed before the finished products can be added to the inventory. The most critical phase of production is the bending process, where two pieces of matched automotive glass are placed on a special rack-holder, called an *iron*, and moved through a large oven, called a *lehr*. As the glass is heated, it softens and bends into the required shape by the interaction between the profile of the iron and the force of gravity, the placement of counterweights on the iron, the particular heating pattern imposed on it by the lehr, the speed of its route through the lehr, and attributes of the glass itself (e.g., thickness, composition). It continues on the conveyer out of the oven and around the plant to cool before any further assembly can be done. In the plant, the task of scheduling jobs to the lehr for bending the raw glass is the bottleneck activity. This particular scheduling task includes deciding which type of windshield glass should be bent at what time and for how long (the length of the time determines the quantity of glass to be bent as well). The scheduling task itself involves the determination of when a part is to be run on which lehr and for what duration. The human scheduler constructs these schedules on a rolling horizon: each week a new five-week schedule is generated, which makes use of the last four weeks of the five-week schedule constructed in the previous week together with an up-to-date windshield inventory report. Although the bending process is the primary concern, considerations are also given to other required operations (such as materials ordering and preparation) as well as scheduling labor. There is a distinction between the sets of *constraints* that define admissible schedule options and *preferences* that reflect concerns that are "softer" but are essential in determining relevant precedence ordering over a set of admissible schedules. The total number of different kinds of parts the plant produces is on the order of several hundred.

At the plant, scheduling of the lehrs has been accomplished by two employees who have more than 30 years of experience between them. Throughout those years, they have developed and relied on effective heuristic methods and tactics to schedule lehr production runs. For the development of MacMerl, the most experienced of the two schedulers (who, in fact, now has primary responsibility for the generation of the schedules) was selected to serve as the referent expert.

23.3 DESIGN APPROACH: DEFINING COINCIDENT PROBLEM SPACES

Critical to the design approach is the concept of coincident problem spaces, and critical to the coincident problem space perspective is the concept of expertise. Expertise is viewed as a psychological construct involving task environments and problem spaces. A *task environment* refers to "an environment coupled with a goal, problem or task—one for which the motivation of the subject is assumed" (Newell and Simon, 1972, p. 55). A task environment is the problem as presented to the problem solver and viewed by an omniscient observer (Simon, 1978). The task environment includes the knowledge of the problem solver as well as the knowledge of the devices at his or her and other problem solvers' disposal (e.g., computer terminal, supporting documentation, or other problem solvers). To solve a problem, the problem solver must create internalized representations of the task environment in the form of problem spaces. A *problem space* can be viewed as a set of nodes (symbol structures) representing various attainable knowledge states (i.e., that which the problem solver "knows" in the state), with one or more distinguished states representing the solution to the problem—the goal. Implicit in the problem space formulation is the form of the state-representation, that is, the particular way the state space is represented in terms of interpretable symbol structures. *Operators* are knowledge that change the internal structural state in search for the goal state(s). For example, in a scheduling problem, one type of operator might be "swap two jobs (x,y)," and another might be "determine the next available machine." Problem solving is therefore realized as search for the correct (or reasonable) sequence of operators to apply to the problem space that achieve a scheduling goal.

Expertise, as a construct, depends on task-specific adaptations within a constrained cognitive architecture (Newell & Simon, 1972). The flexibility admitted by the cognitive mechanisms permits differential adaptations in the form of knowledge to occur that reduce the problem solving effort by more efficient search through better task representations, better search control knowledge, or both (these two alternatives, however, are not entirely independent) in the form of problem space formulations. Thus, we get better at a repetitive, complex cognitive task because, in part, we both augment existing representations and generate (develop) new representations and knowledge that permit more effective and efficient problem space searches (Anderson, 1985). Such adaptations are influenced by the specific perceptions of the task environment, the task environment itself, and the (prior) knowledge of the problem solver. As a consequence, expert adaptation serves as a "barometer" to the key regularities and potentially important aspects of the task environment (Prietula, Feltovich, & Marchak, 1989). Although the *performance* (i.e., the relative worth of the final schedule generated) of the human scheduler might be sub-optimal, the *behavior* (i.e., the knowledge, goals, and tactics brought to bear) can provide insights into the scheduling shop task environment.

From the perspective of scheduling, an expert human scheduler might have established a quite plausible set of situation-specific sub-goals to achieve but might not have the computational capacity to optimally realize them. Therefore, the human expert can employ severely sub-optimal heuristics or methods for the task. On the other hand, a scheduler can be quite effective at making judgment calls when modifying a schedule or the scheduling process (e.g., constraint or preference specifications); that is, there are aspects to the expert's reasoning processes that are quite flexible and can adjust (via efficient search mechanisms) to situation-specific event variability. Thus, the premise of our approach rests on the value of examining the underlying form and substance of expertise in a particular scheduling domain where the task is computationally intractable (see also, McKay, Buzacott, Charness & Safayeni, 1991).

Specifically, we offer the following proposition:

> To configure effectively a support system that can exploit the knowledge of the sched-
> uling expert, it is important to direct the behavior of the system to function in a
> manner that is consistent with the key problem spaces of the scheduler; that is, the
> system and the scheduler should be problem solving in *coincident problem spaces*.

This proposition has appeared implicitly in various forms when addressing human-computer interaction and knowledge engineering, such as the use of mental models (Carroll & Olson, 1988), GOMS (Card, Moran, & Newell, 1983), shared frames of reference (Woods & Roth, 1988), or different embodiments of task analysis (Diaper, 1989). Our approach simplifies the characterization of the interaction to "search in common problem spaces through operator selection and application," reflecting Newell's view of the problem space as a fundamental category in problem solving (Newell, 1990). Therefore, by determining the dominant goals (and operators) that the human scheduler invokes, we can gain insight into the problem representation and constraints as perceived by the expert (Yost & Newell, 1989). These goals and operators are reviewed to assess their role in the problem solving process and the extent to which system design should attend to them.

It is important to identify the critical goals and operators that are essential to the expert's performance because it is those goals and operators that become candidates for inclusion into the system. The reason for this is to have the system implement an operator (in service to a goal) and generate a state in the system's problem space that is also *admissible* to (i.e., could have been generated within) the expert scheduler's own problem space. The admissibility condition refers to the extent that the generated state is one that the human scheduler's operators "should have" produced under ideal computational conditions (full information, sufficient time and power). This is critical because admissibility permits the generated state to be subsumed within the entire set of states that the human could have generated and, consequently, permits the engagement of expert knowledge. In the context of our scheduling system, the schedules produced by the system must be sufficiently close to those that the scheduler *tries* to produce that they "make sense" to the human expert. If we could represent the methods of scheduling that the expert employs and if the expert were perfectly aware of those methods, then the system would not only produce schedules that were similar to the expert's but would also produce them, at some level of specificity, in the *same way*. Thus, the problem space for the human scheduler is functionally expanded by aspects of the machine's problem space that are "coincident with" the human's. In the parlance of cognition, the human scheduler *understands* the schedules generated by the system.

A coincident problem space can be viewed as consisting of three primary components: (1) the expert's problem solving methods in the given domain, (2) an underlying causal model of the expert's problem solving methods, and (3) generic problem solving methods to support the expert's methods. The methods of the expert are the goals and operators (search mechanisms) that are employed to solve aspects of the problem. These are made up of task-specific knowledge that is brought to bear in problem solving. The general form and substance of these methods are heavily influenced by an underlying (causal) model of how (and why) the task environment "behaves" as it does. Finally, the generic problem solving methods are the more mechanistic search and representation components reflecting the computational techniques to support the expert's problem solving methods and are guided by the underlying causal model.

The intent of the coincident problem space perspective is to define a mechanistic problem solving procedure that can generate admissible states that permit and support the engagement of task-specific, human expertise. The intent is not to produce a functionally equivalent cognitive model because that implies an unacceptable level of performance. Despite the fact that experts DO have special knowledge of, and insight to, the problem (and relevant representations and heuristics), they sometimes cannot APPLY all that knowledge to effectively deal with the complexity of the task (Reason, 1990). Rather, the goal is to effectively characterize and distribute the problem solving process between the human and the machine so that they can coordinate their efforts. The goals and operators not distributed to the machine form the complementary knowledge of the human expert that provides the flexible and judgmental components of scheduling that cannot easily be realized in mechanistic form.

The task of creating the coincident problem space for MacMerl was divided into three phases: (1) understanding the task and representing the expert's methods,

(2) creating initial computational mechanisms to support or realize those methods, and (3) iterating review and refinement of the computational forms (and representations) by having the expert use the system. In other words, cloning the expert, improving the clone, and letting the expert improve the clone.

23.3.1 Analysis and Representation of Expert's Methods

In the first phase, we studied in detail what the expert's view of the scheduling problem was, the expert's scheduling behavior (i.e., problem solving methods), and the reasoning process behind the expert's actions. This was done by a variety of techniques, including direct questioning, *in situ* protocol analysis as the expert developed schedules, post-task interviews, and an extended apprenticeship involving our learning to do the task in a rudimentary manner. The purpose was to ensure that the eventual operators and goals supplied and addressed by MacMerl would be consistent with those used by the human scheduler; therefore, information about problem representation, problem solving methods, and causal reasoning was collected. The goal of identifying aspects of the scheduler's *problem representation* required learning how the scheduler characterized the particular task environment. This involved lengthy sessions of monitoring and interviewing the expert to determine the goals and heuristics used to build schedules. The results indicated that the expert characterized the scheduling goals as those that minimize stock-out costs, reduce setup costs, optimize the use of resources (such as machine and labor), and minimize the complaints from the shop floor. From the expert's perspective, the primary scheduling goal was to determine which part to schedule next, how long to schedule it for, and what machine to schedule it on.

Some of the subproblems the human scheduler handled were in the category of NP-hard problems. One was an integer programming problem of grouping together several jobs that each had less than 40 irons and had the same heat patterns in such a way that they would fit into a lehr during the same run. Other scheduling problems include proper reactive adjustments to situation changes and occasional feedback from the factory floor (generally when running new types of jobs). A significant discovery during this phase was the expert's extensive memory of the characteristics of parts and part compatibilities. Such accumulated information enabled the expert to generate sections of a schedule (relatively) quickly as well as recognize sections of the schedule that violated various types of constraints.

The expert's knowledge of part characteristics and constraints served to reduce search in two ways. First, infeasible combinations of parts were seldom generated; rather, groups of possible parts that could be run together without incurring a machine setup were associatively grouped in memory (as evidenced by the situation-specific contexts in which they were generated and as they were discussed by the expert). These various association structures were referred to as *family-groups*; the specific set of parts scheduled to run together without a setup was referred to as a *reservation-group*. Second, the expert would review a section of an already produced schedule in order to check for higher-level constraint or preference violations (e.g., between-machine constraint violations or excessive setup time). The patterns of knowledge tuned to specific constraint and preference violations affected both the *generation* of schedules as well as the *review* of generated schedules.

We determined that the expert used a general algorithm that was dominated by three scheduling goals: (1) to reduce the total number of machine setups generating reservation-groups (setup collapsing), (2) to minimize stock-outs, and (3) to set a higher priority for scheduling high-volume sales parts than for scheduling low-volume sales parts (which can dominate stock-out considerations). Achieving these goals was handled with a simple two-pass procedure. First, an "urgent" part (that is, a part having zero or low inventory, a part carried over from a previous week, an unfinished part, a low-inventory high-volume part) was selected to be scheduled as the *driving part*. The expert then generated a reservation-group around the driving part based on the associated knowledge of family groups. It was found that heuristics for determining the duration of each part made use of the optimal order quantity determined by the Material Planning department (along with a few other constraints, such as delivered raw material lot size).

The determination of the causal model was made by continually asking the expert to explain and justify the decisions made. The model consisted of a series of descriptions underlying expressed constraints and preferences. Specifics of a particular constraint- or preference-model characterize the reasoning that led to the form, function, and elasticity (i.e., degree of permitted relaxation) of the constraint or preference. To the extent that a particular model changes (as a representation of relevant aspects of the task environment), the role of the constraint or preference changes. Furthermore, certain constraints and preferences had shared models, that is, equivalence in the underlying descriptions. It was possible to determine (and predict) the role of certain constraints and preferences based on the nature of the model. For example, during holidays, the supply of available personnel was altered in a manner that affected the scheduling of certain types of parts that required additional laborers. The underlying models served as powerful augmentations to the more "schedule-specific and part-specific" constraints and preferences.

23.3.2 Development of Computational Analogs

Once a detailed understanding of the key aspects of the expert's problem solving representations and methods was achieved, we designed a fundamental data structure that was compatible with those representations and methods. Every part is associated with two linked lists: a family list and a compatibility list. Both provide the potential compatible parts for generating reservation-groups. This data structure affords search efficiency and emulates the accumulated (and chunked) knowledge of the expert. Ancillary structures and support routines to implement the goals and operators were designed based on the basic data structure.

The basic system emulating the expert's approach generates a schedule in two passes: a preprocessing pass and a detail schedule generation. Preprocessing builds the basic data structure and prepares a preliminary schedule. The preliminary schedule is generated according to the most important goal, minimize stock-outs, and considers only inventory levels and stock-out costs (relaxing all the other constraints). In essence, preprocessing coincides with the expert's initial pass in scheduling—seeking out the important, urgent tasks to consider first. After preprocessing, the detail schedule generation code is divided into the following three steps (which are equivalent to the primary goals in the expert's approach): (1) select a lehr to schedule, (2) select a driving part, and (3) form a reservation-group given a driving part. Heuristic rules used for each step include both heuristics used by the expert as well as program-specific heuristics that attempt to improve the speed and quality of schedule generation. For example, we incorporated two different heuristics, first-fit and best-fit, for forming reservation-groups.

23.3.3 Expert-Based Iterative Refinement

This phase involved multiple interactions with the expert in reviewing the generated schedules and the operators incorporating scheduling adjustments. When there were discrepancies, the code of MacMerl was altered to make its decisions in closer agreement with those of the expert's. Although the completed schedule was presented on the computer as a Gantt chart, another way of displaying it, called the "Merl chart," was also available because that was the way the expert was used to looking at it. By this technique, we were able to maintain the coincidence of problem spaces. The main purposes of this phase were (1) to concentrate on generating admissible schedules and (2) to complete an interface that permitted acceptable communication between the human and the machine (i.e., tuning the interface and the schedule generator to permit coincident problem space development). The nature of the scheduling environment permitted the development of a stable, goal-oriented "generator" that implemented the key schedule-generation operators that collectively produced admissible schedules. However, the environment also included many context-dependent scheduling exceptions that were primarily associated with particular parts or part-combinations. These were rare events that were deemed to be best handled manually because of their unique nature. The resulting set of key scheduler goals and supporting MacMerl operators is summarized in the Table 23-1.

Table 23-1: Key scheduler operators implemented by MacMerl.

Task	Human Expert's Goals	MacMerl's Operators
Problem specification and goal recognition	1. Review starting conditions. 2. Determine critical constraints and preferences. 3. Determine scheduling goals.	1. Display schedule & parts list. 2. Set constraint/preference switches. 3. Adjust weights on terms in the objective function.
Schedule generation	1. Devise rough-cut capacity plan (expert's initial pass). 2. Generate reservation-groups. 3. Generate detailed schedule.	1. Generate schedule. 2. Construct family & compatibility lists for each part. 3. Execute scheduling algorithm.
Schedule evaluation	1. Evaluate schedule quality.	1. Display Critiquer & other supporting reports, charts (e.g., Merl-Chart).
Schedule modification	1. Address special cases. 2. Adjust schedule.	1. Pin parts to schedule & reinvoke scheduler to schedule around them. 2. Manually add/modify/delete jobs.

23.4 SYSTEM ARCHITECTURE[1]

The general system architecture for MacMerl is shown in Figure 23-2. MacMerl is written in Think C™ (from Symantec™), which, when compiled, occupies approximately 300 Kbytes on an Apple Macintosh computer. The Scheduling Kernel and the Manual Scheduler are the main components of MacMerl. All the system routines were integrated in an icon-based, interactive graphical user interface environment that served to primarily support the Manual Scheduler routines. The graphical user interface permits manual manipulation of the schedule and incorporates the Critiquer facility. All routines in the Scheduling Kernel are invocable from the Manual Scheduler.

23.4.1 Scheduling Kernel

As was discussed, the development of the Generative Scheduler was based on the analysis of the expert. The goal was to clone the methods of the expert and create a system that is capable of generating schedules similar to those generated by the human scheduler. Two basic general heuristics for both revising and creating a five-week schedule were incorporated by the expert:

---

[1] This section is drawn from the primary description of MacMerl as presented in Hsu, Prietula, Thompson, & Ow (1993).

- Schedule parts with lowest inventory first to avoid stock-outs. (The expert also took into account the priorities of the parts—parts with a high stock-out cost have high priority.)

- Schedule as many as possible of the parts in a reservation-group close together in order to reduce set-up time.

The first is commonly used by "made to stock" manufacturers when no actual due-dates are assigned to parts, and the second heuristic is commonly used to reduce set-up costs. Recall that a *reservation-group* refers to a set of jobs that can be run sequentially on the same machine without changing machine settings, which involves a setup cost. A mapping is required from any given part to a set of other

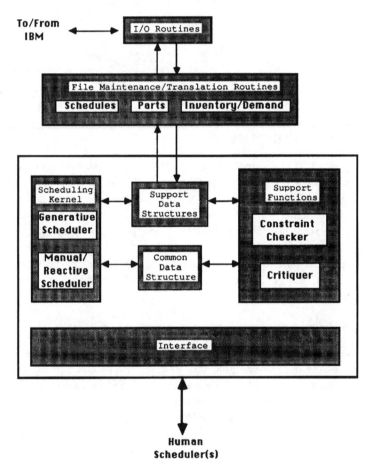

Figure 23-2:   Overall architecture of MacMerl

parts that are "reservation-compatible." Although some parts can form a better reservation-group than others, the quality of a reservation-group (and sometimes even membership) is quite difficult to specify analytically. No general rules could be articulated to determine whether parts are reservation-compatible; however, the determination that one part is "more compatible" than another had to be left to an explicit enumeration of cases. The *compatibility* concept is embedded in a data structure that permits the rapid generation of those parts that are compatible with a particular part. Compatibility data are important knowledge pieces that can be explicitly stored and maintained by the firm as institutionalized memory (Waterman, 1986).

Other preferences were expressed by the expert when constructing a schedule, such as avoiding scheduling difficult parts at the beginning and end of the week (when absenteeism is highest) and avoiding scheduling large parts back-to-back (to avoid the continued lifting of heavy windshields, which caused workers to occasionally drop them). Whether this breakage occurred because of physical strain or served as editorial comments on the quality of the schedule could not be determined. Regardless, it was a rule that was rarely ignored. The overall approach to scheduling by the expert was mostly constraint-driven rather than an attempt at optimizing an objective function; therefore, it was possible to improve the performance of MacMerl by improving the search rules. These improvements included reducing schedule conflicts, satisfying more preferences, and reducing stockouts.

Generative Scheduler. The expert's approach to forming schedules is incorporated in the Generative Scheduler. The problem is decomposed into three subproblems within the Generative Scheduler: (1) selecting a lehr to schedule, (2) selecting a part to schedule on the lehr, and (3) scheduling additional parts along with the selected parts in the same reservation-group so that no machine setups are required. Each subproblem is iteratively invoked by a Search Control Manager that conducts the search for scheduling alternatives according to the criteria set by the subproblems. The algorithm is as follows:

1. **GenerateList**. Produce *PartsList* by sorting downloaded Inventory File according to inventory level and stockout cost.
2. **SelectNextLehr(L)**. Choose the lehr **L** with the earliest available start time as the lehr to focus on next for scheduling.
3. **SelectDrivingWindshield(ws)**. From the *PartsList*, get the next unscheduled windshield **ws** as the driving part for scheduling lehr **L**.
4. **SelectFamilyGroup(ws,F)**. Identify the set of parts **F** that can be run with the same settings and the same set of irons (i.e., racks) based on the properties of **ws**.

5. **Schedule(ws,F)**. Try to schedule the driving part **ws** as well as all of **F** guided by the component economic run lengths.

6. *If* Step 5 fails, *then* **SwapParts(ws, ws_{next})**, GOTO Step 4, *else* Add the resulting reservation-group to lehr **L**, GOTO Step 2.

The algorithm begins by generating an ordered Parts-List from a two-key sort based on the weekly-supply and reorder point of an inventory file download from the firm's primary database. The inventory level and possible stock-outs are shown in the weekly supply figures, whereas the reorder point reflects the batch size and the popularity of the part. The master production schedule by the material planning department is the source of the downloaded file data. The earliest available lehr to schedule is selected by the Generative Scheduler, and then a part to schedule on that lehr is chosen. Because one of the most important objectives is to minimize stock-outs, a heuristic is used that chooses the part having the highest priority cost. Once the windshield is chosen, it is called the "driving-windshield" because this windshield basically drives the formation of its reservation-group. Forming a reservation-group involves the scheduling of several compatible parts sequentially in time that collectively require only a single, initial setup. Because the number of windshields to be scheduled is quite large (i.e., hundreds of parts and increasing in size every year), windshields with high weekly-supplies are not included to prevent the formation of too large a group. The search for compatible parts in the formation of a reservation-group can also lead to an excessively large grouping. A stopping rule (determined by interaction with the expert) is applied in order to avoid both situations.

Given a driving-windshield, reservation-groups are formed by selecting parts that are "compatible." There are three types of parts that are compatible: (1) parts from the same family-group (i.e., they can be processed with the same iron/rack but require different composite material combinations), (2) parts that can be processed in the same lehr setting (i.e., they use different irons but rely on the same oven temperatures and processing speed), and (3) twin-parts (i.e., parts that must be processed in pairs, typically large windshields for buses, recreational vehicles, or trucks, that are composed of separately produced left and right components). Compatible parts from the same family-group are scheduled to run either sequentially (when one part type batch is completed, the next part type batch is run) or in parallel (two part types are run through the machine in the same batch) in a time interval (as constraints permit) and with only one machine setup required for the entire group. In forming a reservation-group, two heuristics are available. The first heuristic looks for a compatible part with the lowest weekly-supply and forms the reservation-group. A "cut-and-patch" procedure is used to form the group.[2] If this heuristic fails, a second heuristic looks for the "best fit" to form a reservation-group in order to minimize machine idle time, after which the cut-and-patch procedure is applied.

Once the reservation-group is formed, it is added to the schedule at the appropriate time on the appropriate lehr. If there are difficulties encountered (i.e., constraint violations), heuristics (actually, Reactive Scheduling operators) are applied to try to resolve the violations. If these adjustments cannot resolve the problem, then the driving windshield is removed from the schedule (its affiliated reservation-group is undone), it is returned to its appropriate place on the Parts-List, and the next part in the Parts-List (which has not been scheduled yet) is selected as the driving windshield to be applied to the schedule. If the newly selected part succeeds, then the originally selected part is the next one to be tried (because it is back on its original place in the Parts-List). Thus far, most schedules we have encountered have required only one or two such "part swaps" to solve the problem.

Constraint Checker. The primary function of the Constraint Checker is to check the feasibility of a given schedule or schedule fragment. It is used by the Generative Scheduler, the Reactive Scheduler components in the Scheduling Kernel, and the Critiquer as well as invoked by the human scheduler via the Manual Scheduler at the interface. The Constraint Checker inputs a schedule or schedule fragment and returns information on detected violations (if any): (1) the type of constraint violated (such as assigning too wide a piece of glass to a small lehr), (2) the time location in the schedule of the violation, (3) the lehr on which the violation occurred, and (4) the specific part that caused the violation. The human scheduler has the option of selecting specific constraints to enforce or ignore when invoking the Constraint Checker from the Manual Scheduler interface.

Reactive Scheduler. The Reactive Scheduler consists of a set of components that facilitate the schedule generation process. When a potential reservation-group is formed by the Generative Scheduler, the Constraint Checker is called. If no violations occur, the reservation-group is assigned to the schedule. However, if violations are detected, the Reactive Scheduler is invoked to possibly resolve the conflict. The Reactive Scheduler comprises an embedded Search Manager and several Reactive Operators. Reactive Operators are independent of each other, so additional Operators can be added or dropped, and existing ones can be modified. Each Reactive Operator inputs a schedule with a reservation-group violation and tries to resolve the conflict in its own manner. Currently, there are six Reactive Operators:

---

[2] This is a procedure to ensure the quantity of jobs scheduled is in multiples of its supplied (i.e., shipped) quantity of glass sheets, so that small quantities of sheet glass will not be left over.

(1) insert idle time on a lehr, (2) insert a reservation-group, (3) delete a reservation-group, (4) swap parts within a specific reservation-group, (5) swap two reservation-groups (on the same lehr or across lehrs), and (6) regenerate a schedule starting at a particular time. In the present version, the Search Manager stops when the first Reactive Operator resolves the conflict, but testing is being conducted to examine the effects of alternative search strategies and Reactive Operators on the efficiency and effectiveness of reactive scheduling.

Manual Scheduler. The Manual Scheduler is the unifying structure within which all the components can operate. The Manual Scheduler supplies both form and function consistent with the methods and perspectives of the human but supportive of the underlying computational search strategies provided. This permits a distribution of effort between the machine and the human in a manner that permits both agents to engage in cooperative problem solving. Although the machine might be directed to generate a schedule on its own, it is possible for the human to augment the process in an iterative manner in which both agents can initiate problem solving, thus allowing a mixed initiative approach between the human and the machine.

Interface and Manipulation Routines. When running the Manual Scheduler, the user has a variety of options that affect scheduling procedures or simply review scheduling results. A summary of the options can be given as

- Choose the number of days to schedule beginning at an arbitrary initial date.
- Invoke the Generative Scheduler (perhaps with a list of priority parts to schedule first).
- Add, delete, or modify scheduled parts by clicking and dragging part icons.
- Select a schedule (or portion of a schedule) to be checked by the Constraint Checker.
- Manually alter the preference matrix that gives priority/stockout trade-offs prior to generating a schedule.
- Upload/download data and schedules from the IBM mainframe.
- Examine a variety of output reports from Generative Scheduler (e.g., load analysis, critique report).
- Add/delete/modify setup times to the schedule.
- Select parts (i.e., scheduled jobs) from an already generated schedule to save as high-priority items to schedule first in the next iteration (their position on the new schedule might vary).
- Select parts (i.e., scheduled jobs) from an already generated schedule to save at their exact position, and invoke the scheduler to "schedule around" them (their position on the new schedule is fixed).

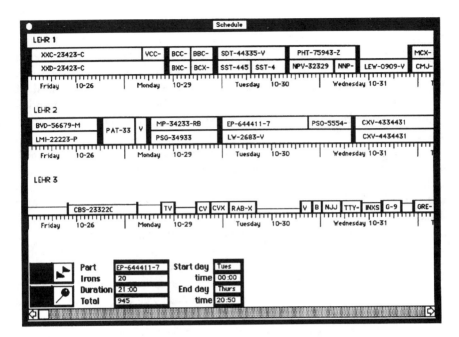

Figure 23-3: Icon (click and drag) Gantt chart of a generated schedule

At the interface, a schedule is represented by a Gantt Chart, which is a time line for each machine on which rectangular icons depict specific jobs (see Figure 23-3). The length of a rectangle reflects the duration of the job, and the height of the rectangle indicates the number of parts running in the lehr. When a job (i.e., rectangle) is "clicked on" by the user, it changes color, and all the relevant information regarding that particular job is displayed at the bottom of the screen. The user can choose the pin icon to select individual or multiple parts within or across lehrs (1) to check against the Critiquer; (2) to check against the Constraint Checker; or (3) to save in a file as a priority set of parts that must be scheduled first and then reinvoke the Generative Scheduler to produce a new, slightly modified schedule. The user can drag and view the generated schedule to any point in the time line of the schedule.

Critiquer. The goal of the Critiquer is to generate a critique of a schedule proposed by a human or by MacMerl's Generative Scheduler. The Critiquer does not attempt to simulate an expert's decision making processes in order to provide good answers; rather, the Critiquer seeks to review a plan of action (in this case, a schedule) and present a concise discussion of its important and, possibly, erroneous aspects. The user can select which aspects of the schedule the critiquer should check. The unique nature of all these applications is the significant amount of subjective judgment involved. As a consequence, the advice suggested by the Critiquer might be appropriate, or it might not given (the perhaps unique or unspecifiable) exogenous parameters relevant to a particular scheduling context. For example, the Critiquer checks (1) to see if the selected constraints are satisfied, (2) to see how many preferences are satisfied, and (3) to see how many high-priority jobs have not been scheduled. The report simply notes violations of such preferences.

Once the schedule has been generated, a Critiquer scans the generated schedule and produces several reports that *summarize* various aspects of the generated schedule (e.g., machine load statistics, weekly part productions) and *identifies* potential difficulties as reflected by specific preference violations (e.g., scheduling of large parts back-to-back). An interesting note is that the primary (and well-accepted) interface between user and computer is the direct manipulation of an icon-based Gantt chart. The Critiquer also produces (per the expert's request) a text-based depiction of the schedule, called the Merl-Chart, that replicates the original representation the expert used. The role of the Critiquer directly addresses several goals that the scheduler attempts to perform as well as those that he would like to perform in a post-generation review of a schedule.

A schedule that has been produced by the generative scheduling component can subsequently be modified by the human based on additional information or, perhaps, simply the scheduler's interest in testing alternative configurations (e.g., lehr loadings, product mixes). In addition, the scheduler might wish to specify and examine partially specified schedules. The Critiquer supports the ensuing analyses of such schedule modifications/specifications by permitting multiple perspectives to be brought to bear on the schedule. These perspectives are defined by allowing or disallowing the testing of classes of constraints or preferences. Essentially, the user simply selects a schedule or indicates a specific part of a schedule and invokes the Critiquer. When MacMerl has generated a schedule on its own, the Critiquer is automatically invoked, and the resulting report is available for review. Originally developed to critique anesthetic management plans in medicine (Miller, 1984, 1986), variations of the technique have subsequently been applied in many other domains (e.g., Silverman & Mazher, 1992).

23.5 A SCHEDULING EXAMPLE

We will illustrate the capabilities of MacMerl with an example. The data used are real, but the displayed values and identifiers have been altered for purposes of confidentiality. With MacMerl, the user has the option of enforcing any or all of eight scheduling constraints (e.g., no simultaneous setups; attention to specific resource capacities) and four preference options (e.g., minimize large jobs sched-

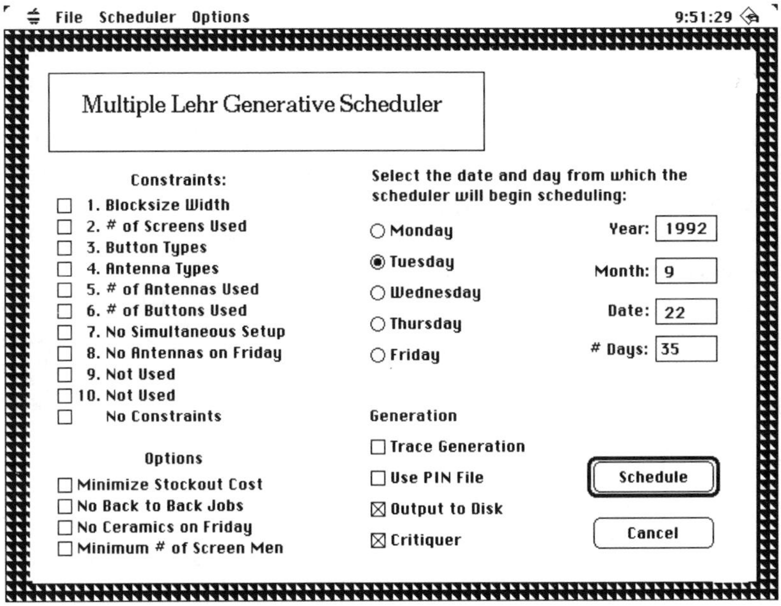

```
 ⬌  File  Scheduler  Options                              9:51:29 ⬟
```

Multiple Lehr Generative Scheduler

Constraints:
☐ 1. Blocksize Width
☐ 2. # of Screens Used
☐ 3. Button Types
☐ 4. Antenna Types
☐ 5. # of Antennas Used
☐ 6. # of Buttons Used
☐ 7. No Simultaneous Setup
☐ 8. No Antennas on Friday
☐ 9. Not Used
☐ 10. Not Used
☐   No Constraints

Options
☐ Minimize Stockout Cost
☐ No Back to Back Jobs
☐ No Ceramics on Friday
☐ Minimum # of Screen Men

Select the date and day from which the scheduler will begin scheduling:

○ Monday   Year: 1992
◉ Tuesday   Month: 9
○ Wednesday
○ Thursday   Date: 22
○ Friday   # Days: 35

Generation
☐ Trace Generation
☐ Use PIN File
☒ Output to Disk   [**Schedule**]
☒ Critiquer
                       [Cancel]

Figure 23-4:   Initial MacMerl screen with scheduling options

uled back-to-back, minimize stockout costs). We will compare and contrast two scheduling runs. The difference will be the selection of constraints to enforce: one run will involve no enforcement, and the second will involve the enforcement of all constraints. The scheduling problem contains 241 parts to be scheduled on three machines. Two output are relevant to understanding the generated schedule. First, there is the Critiquer output that was explained previously. Second, there is a Trace Facility that, in effect, is a reflection of the scheduling deliberation unfolding dur-

Table 23-2:   Comparison of a job set run with no constraints and a job set run with all constraints.

	No Constraints	All Constraints
Time (sec)	15	20
Days scheduled	37	37
Constraint violations	25	1
Idle time (min)	0	500
Groups scheduled	110	112
Solo groups	6	8
Compatible groups	30	29
Detours	0	14

ing processing. Selection of constraint, preference, and tracing options is offered at the initial screen shown in Figure 23-4. Parameters comparing both runs are presented in Table 23-2.

The time it takes to schedule both job sets is roughly equivalent, 15–20 sec, which yields a 5-week schedule. Although the No Constraint run minimized idle time, there were 25 violations detected. On the other hand, enabling Constraints dramatically reduced constraint violations but caused the idle time to grow. "Detours" are the number of trial searches needed to overcome a detected constraint violation. In essence, detours reflect deeper searches for schedule fragments when initial trial solutions are found to be infeasible. These might or might not terminate with satisfactory solutions. Groups scheduled are the number of job sets scheduled between setups. Of those, some sets consist of only one type of job (Solo Groups), jobs that can use different irons but the same lehr settings (Compatible Jobs), or jobs that can use the same irons and compatible lehr settings (the rest of the Groups scheduled). Once a schedule is generated, the Trace was helpful interpreting the schedule generation process. For example, consider the following trace for the Constraint run:

```
START REACTIVE SCHEDULER
SELECT XXR0653V195K
0 GROUPS ALREADY SCHEDULED
SCHEDULE PART ON LEHR 3
SETUP NO VIOLATION FOUND
    PILING XXR0653V195K ONTO STACK
    GET PART XXR0653V195K FROM STACK
        MAKE SCHEDULE
        QUANTITY = 750
lehr: 3 year:1992 date:217 day 2 start: 52 dur: 750 irons:18
part:XXR0653V195K
```

In this section, part XXR0653V195K was selected to be scheduled on Lehr 3, and it is placed on a stack of "schedulable" parts. No constraints are violated, so it is popped from the stack and added to the schedule at a particular start time, duration (750 hours), and machine loading (18 irons). A second part is selected (XXC0452T190) and scheduled to be placed on Lehr 2. There is an observation made that this would result in Lehr 2 being below capacity, so a detour is made to find parts compatible with the initial "driving" part. A set of compatible parts was found and placed on a stack. Each is then examined for potential constraint violations (none were found) and scheduled:

```
SCHEDULING SUCCESSFUL
PART SUCCESSFULLY SCHEDULED
SELECT XXC0452T190_
1 GROUPS ALREADY SCHEDULED
```

```
SCHEDULE PART ON LEHR 2
SETUP NO VIOLATION FOUND
(SCHEDULE BELOW CAPACITY)
   DRIVER XXC0452T190_
   COMP XXC0375T290_
   PILING XXC0452T190_ ONTO STACK
   PILING XXC0452T185_ ONTO STACK
   PILING XXC0375T290_ ONTO STACK
   PILING XXC0375T285_ ONTO STACK
   GET PART XXC0452T185_ FROM STACK
           ADD PART TO SCHEDULE
           QUANTITY = 1100
lehr:2 year:1992 date:217 day 2 start:102 dur:1100 irons:20
part:XXC0452T185_
        NO VIOLATION FOUND
   GET PART XXC0375T285_ FROM STACK
           ADD PART TO SCHEDULE
           QUANTITY = 1650
lehr:2 year:1992 date:217 day 2 start:102 dur:1650 irons:20
part:XXC0375T285_
        NO VIOLATION FOUND
   GET PART XXC0452T190_ FROM STACK
           ADD PART TO SCHEDULE
           QUANTITY = 1100
lehr:2 year:1992 date:217 day 2 start:1203 dur:1100 irons:20
part:XXC0452T190_
        NO VIOLATION FOUND
   GET PART XXC0375T290_ FROM STACK
           ADD PART TO SCHEDULE
           QUANTITY = 550
lehr:2 year:1992 date:217 day 2 start:1753 dur:550 irons:20
        NO VIOLATION FOUND
```

Every schedule can be associated with a specific explanation (trace) file. In addition, the Critiquer output help provide insight into potential problems with preferences (not constraints). A portion of the Critiquer output for the above run is

```
THE FOLLOWING IS A LIST OF UNSCHEDULED LARGE PARTS WHOSE WEEK SUPPLY
IS LESS THAN 5.4 WEEKS:
   XXC0583V185K WEEK SUPPLY = 4.500000
   MM-2381T195M WEEK SUPPLY = 4.600000
      .
      .
```

THE FOLLOWING IS A LIST OF UNSCHEDULED SMALL PARTS WHOSE WEEK
SUPPLY IS LESS THAN 5.4 WEEKS:
        .
        .
        .

THE FOLLOWING IS A LIST OF LARGE PARTS THAT HAVE BEEN
SCHEDULED BACK TO BACK.
        .
        .

THE FOLLOWING IS A LIST OF THE STOCKOUT COSTS FOR EACH
PART SCHEDULED UP TO WEEK 5.
        LEHR 1 MM-1946T195C WEEK SCHED 2 WEEK SUPPLY 1.9 C COST=6
        LEHR 1 CH-1263T195_ WEEK SCHED 3 WEEK SUPPLY 2.8 D COST=5
        LEHR 1 DD-0998T194_ WEEK SCHED 3 WEEK SUPPLY 2.9 D COST=5
        .
        .
        .

        SUM COST FOR WEEK 1 OF LEHR 1 = 6
        SUM COST FOR WEEK 2 OF LEHR 1 = 13
        .
        .
        .

        TOTAL COST FOR FIRST 5 WEEKS OF LEHR 1 = 49
        AVERAGE WEEKLY COST FOR LEHR 1 = 9.800000
        .
        .
        .

        TOTAL COST FOR FIRST 5 WEEKS OF ALL LEHRS = 90
        AVERAGE WEEKLY COST = 18.000000

In addition to possible preference violations (e.g., scheduling large parts back-to-back, stock outs for parts), cost information is also available. Although the cost data presented are artificial, the user has the option to define cost values that reflect trade-offs between types of parts and tardiness (in terms of weeks). Comparative analysis between schedule costs is, thus, possible.

In summary, we have briefly shown an example scheduling run together with the supporting trace documentation and analysis. MacMerl permits much more interaction with the generation process, as we have described earlier. In fact, the user could "pin" a section of the schedule and elect to either keep those selected parts in the same place in the schedule or simply request that the scheduler place that set at the top of the stack and schedule them first (which might move them from their original slots but is computationally easier). Thus, MacMerl affords a true mixed-initiative scheduling environment, exploiting the power of the machine and the experience (or ability to handle uncertainty) of the human.

23.6 DEPLOYMENT ISSUES

Communication is essential to the success of this type of project. We considered the start of the project as the starting point of deployment. Our target organization received our idea on the design and development of the system as the project proceeded. On one hand, we continuously observed and recorded our understanding of the expert's knowledge, scheduling activities, and role in the organization business process. The observations and understanding of the organization were constant input to the design of the software system. On the other hand, the organization was also constantly informed with the current research design, software architecture, and progress on implementation. Feedback from the organization was crucial as guidance to proper design such that the final product can be used and maintained by the organization. Such communication requires efforts from both research team and representatives (in specific, the primary user of the system and the primary maintenance staff) from the organization. The communication channel is primarily maintained in the following two ways: (1) constant knowledge acquisition from the expert scheduler and (2) use of one of the MIS representatives from the organization as technical liaison to facilitate technological transfer.

At the beginning of the project, the researchers shadowed the expert and obtained fundamental skills in accordance with the expert's job (i.e., familiarity with business jargon and observing and recording of the expert scheduler's activities, tools used, and related business processes). This acquired knowledge served as building blocks of the software system. Many expert systems have historically attempted to replicate complete sequences of expert performance in a task, such as diagnosing diseases, debugging malfunctioning systems, or analyzing financial events, with human adjustments permitted at the end. Problem space characterizations help define the fundamental representations of the knowledge structures underlying expert and, hence, system performance. In some tasks, the complete task sequences cannot be automated totally, although the entire task itself can still be described within the context of a problem space perspective. The coincident problem space perspective described here afforded various degrees of freedom in crafting a system to augment human judgment on such a task. For example, with schedule generation, the system attempted to match the human's goals and methods for generating a schedule but applied them in a manner that would *exceed* the level of performance of the expert. However, adjustments to the schedule solution might be needed, so simplistic schedule manipulation operators were provided. Altered schedules had to be rechecked but not after every direct manipulation to the schedule and perhaps not to all parts of the schedule; therefore, flexible operators for critiquing (check hard and soft constraints) were made available. Finally, alternative representations of the schedule and its properties were provided to allow different perspectives to be viewed by the human scheduler. Thus, many operators were provided, but there was a heterogeneity in form, and much of the application sequencing was under the control of the user to search the particular problem space at hand.

Throughout the design and implementation phase of the scheduling system, the researchers periodically visited the shop floor, meeting with the expert scheduler to verify the design and obtain feedback from the scheduler. In order to keep the organization informed of the progress of the design and development of the system, one representative from the MIS department, which will take charge of maintaining the system when transferred, participated at various times throughout the project. Such arrangement turned out to be very beneficial for both parties; however, both time and budget constraints on the firm severely limited the level of participation of this person.

In addition to understanding the expert's problem solving methods, knowledge of related business processes within the organization is crucial. Detailed understanding of how data flowed, were structured, and were maintained was important to the design of interface to other existing systems. Such an interface design included a method for downloading data from the mainframe as input to MacMerl and a method for generating output that the mainframe can use to modify and maintain its database. The evaluation of scheduling system performance prior to transferring the system to the company was primarily based on the following factors: speed, quality, and user friendliness. The speed was very fast because we were able to generate the schedules quickly (about 20–30 seconds for the generation of a 5-week schedule). As for the quality and friendliness of the user interface, we relied on the expert's feedback and made changes until the expert was satisfied. As we have noted, the coincident problem space approach relies, in part, on having the system generate a schedule that "makes sense" to the expert. Again, this aspect of the schedule generation process was successful as judged by the expert.

At the final phase of implementation, meetings were held with the expert over a course of three months. These were possible because of the coincident problem spaces that were used by both the expert and the computer program. The expert went through the schedules generated by our scheduling system thoroughly and pointed out every detail with which he did not agree. Such meetings were frequently time consuming but were worthwhile and were used to fine tune the system. Eventually, the computer generated schedule became almost indistinguishable from those generated by the expert except that a computer generated schedule was more accurate and more consistent and guaranteed no (avoidable) constraint violations. However, fluctuations in materials flow, orders, and other types of events still necessitate many manual adjustments to the schedule, making the strong support of interactive manipulation to the schedule a critical component for adoption. A "partially correct" schedule is essentially useless if subsequent adjustments cannot be made, with relative ease, to craft and test an acceptable one. Although no attempts to quantify the benefits of MacMerl have been made, MacMerl is used daily by the human scheduler, who believes that MacMerl is now an essential component of the scheduling effort. In addition, MacMerl has also been used as a training device for new personnel brought into the scheduling group to learn about the process. Because no written procedures exist to describe the detailed nature of the scheduling task, MacMerl provides a mechanism to help an employee develop the requisite problem space perspective for plant scheduling. Furthermore, continual changes in the competive environment have necessitated downsizing and austerity measures for the organization, making scheduling an even more important task for the firm's performance goals of quality, availability and timeliness.

As a scheduling tool, MacMerl provides usable solutions to very difficult and commonly encountered scheduling problems as well as gives new perspectives on interface development. A tool such as MacMerl is designed to be used in a very specific organizational context. Consequently, it must be able to change as the organization changes. If an organization cannot acquire or produce the knowledge to support such change, then the tool (and, to some extent, the organization) is at risk. Although a tool such as MacMerl solves the current problem of the organization, its long term value will be determined by how the organization can exploit the work done to date in developing the tool, internalize the knowledge gained in that development, coordinate tool change with organizational change, and disseminate the knowledge to other parts of the organization. Again, the key issue is in recognizing that MacMerl represents a solution to an organizational problem, and organizations and their problems are in constant flux, which requires constant responsiveness to a very uncertain world.

23.7 CONCLUSION

Control of production scheduling can reduce production costs, which is essential for a firm to be able to compete in the emerging global marketplace. Despite the advances in theoretical scheduling theory, many actual scheduling problems are too complex to yield analytic solutions, so organizations must rely on the use, to a greater or lesser extent, of the wisdom and the experience of human schedulers. Research in artificial intelligence has begun to address the scheduling problem (Fox & Smith, 1984; Glover & McMillan, 1986; Ow & Smith, 1988; Shaw & Whinston, 1989; Sycara et al., 1991). Through the use of symbolic computation and an infusion of flexible symbolic structures, new ways are being proposed for specifying alternative methods for representing the scheduling problem (e.g., Hadavi et al., 1992). The representation and scheduling logic in these approaches are generally not modeled after the methods of the human (McKay, Safayeni, & Buzacott, 1988).

For certain scheduling problems, an approach of value can be one that integrates operations research, artificial intelligence, and human-computer interaction techniques based, to some extent, on the analysis of expertise to improve the problem solving capacity of the human-machines scheduling component (Hsu et al., in press). This view, in part, is reflected in systems that address complex, interactive scheduling tasks (e.g., van Vliet, Boender, & Kan, 1992). Although reviews of research in human scheduling exist (Sanderson, 1989), the disparate natures of the studies have not converged to provide guidance. It is useful to turn to the analysis of the human problem solving mechanism itself.

In this chapter, we have presented an overview to a system called MacMerl, which provides a set of computer-based scheduling tools for the user in a mixed-initiative interactive form. The primary design of MacMerl was driven both by a detailed analysis of the task and a detailed analysis of an expert's adaptation to the task. The scheduling code was constructed so that its problem space and that of the expert were coincident, which made it possible for the expert's scheduling ideas to easily be implemented in the code. The examination of the expert's strategies not only provided insight into the design of the interface but suggested interesting ways to generate and modify schedules. By augmenting these strategies with algorithmic approaches, schedules that once took hours to generate now take seconds.

The current theory of scheduling in operations research is concentrated mainly on scheduling of products to a single machine, and essentially the only scheduling constraints that are considered are the release dates and due dates of the products. Only a few papers have been written that involve scheduling of multiple machines, and those do not involve difficult cross-machine constraints of the kinds addressed by MacMerl. Accordingly, it can be concluded that the theory of scheduling has not yet reached a state at which it could begin to attack these problems with optimal procedures. Until such a time that these difficult constraints can be included in a theoretical model, only heuristic approaches, such as the one described by MacMerl, are appropriate.

ACKNOWLEDGMENTS

This work was funded through an external corporate grant to the Center for the Management of Technology, Graduate School of Industrial Administration, Carnegie Mellon University. We would like to express our appreciation to the Center's director, Paul Goodman, for his guidance and advice on this project. We would also like to thank the corporate participants for their time and effort. Cameron Long and Sandi Kwee were the primary programmers for the project. This chapter benefited from discussions at the *Fourth International Symposium on Artificial Intelligence* held in Cancun, Mexico, November 13–16, 1991, and some of the material in this chapter is based on the paper presented there (Prietula, Hsu, & Ow, 1991).

References

Anderson, J. 1985. *Cognitive Psychology and Its Implications,* 2nd Edition. New York: Freeman.

Card, S., T. Moran, and A. Newell. 1983. *The Psychology of Human-Computer Interaction.* Hillsdale, NJ: Lawrence Erlbaum.

Carroll, J., and J. Olson. 1988. Mental models in human-computer interaction. *Handbook of Human-Computer Interaction,* M. Helander (ed.). New York: Elsevier Science Publishers.

Diaper, D. 1989. *Task Analysis for Human-Computer Interaction.* New York: Halsted Press.

Fox, M., and S. Smith. 1984. ISIS: A knowledge-based system for factory scheduling. *Expert Systems,* 1(1), 25–49.

Glover, F., and C. McMillan. 1986. The general employee scheduling problem: An integration of MS and AI. *Computers and Operations Research,* 13, 563–573.

Graves, S. 1981. A review of production scheduling. *Operations Research,* 29(4), 646–675.

Hadavi, K., W.L. Hsu, T. Chen, and C. Lee. 1992. An architecture for real-time distributed scheduling. *AI Magazine,* 13(3), 46–56.

Hayes-Roth, F., D. Waterman, and D. Lenat. 1983. *Building Expert Systems.* Reading, MA: Addison-Wesley.

Hsu, W.L., M. Prietula, G. Thompson, and P.S. Ow. 1993. A mixed-initiative scheduling workbench: Integrating AI, OR, and HCI. *Journal of Decision Support Systems,* 9(3), 245–247.

McKay, K., J. Buzacott, and F. Safayeni. 1988. The scheduler's knowledge of uncertainty: The missing link. Paper presented at the IFIP Working Conference on Knowledge-based Production Mangement, Galway, Ireland, August.

McKay, K., N. Buzacott, N. Charness, and F. Safayeni. 1991. The Scheduler's predictive expertise: An interdisciplinary perspective. *Artificial Intelligence in Operations Research,* R. Paul (ed.). New York: MacMillan.

McKay, K., F. Safayeni, and J. Buzacott. 1991. Common sense realities of planning and scheduling in printed circuit board production. Paper submitted for publication.

Miller, P. 1984. *A Critiquing Approach to Expert Computer Advice: Attending.* London: Pitman, and San Francisco: Morgan Kaufmann.

Miller, P. 1986. *Expert Critiquing Systems.* New York: Springer-Verlag.

Newell, A. 1990. *Unified Theories of Cognition.* Cambridge, MA: Harvard University Press.

Newell, A., and H. Simon. 1972. *Human Problem Solving.* Englewood Cliffs, NJ: Prentice Hall.

Ow, P.S., and S. Smith. 1988. Viewing scheduling as an opportunistic problem-solving process. *Annals of Operations Research,* 12, 85–108.

Prietula, M., P. Feltovich, and F. Marchak. 1989. A heuristic framework for assessing factors influencing knowledge acquisition. *Proceedings of the Twenty-second Hawaii International Conference on Systems Sciences,* Los Alamitos, CA: IEEE Society Press, pp. 419–426.

Prietula, M., W.L. Hsu, and P.S. Ow. 1991. A coincident problem space perspective to scheduling support. *Proceedings of the Fourth International Symposium on AI,* F. Cantú-Ortiz & H. Tavashima-Marin (eds.), Cancún, Mexico, pp. 113–119.

Reason, J. 1990. *Human Error.* Cambridge, UK: Cambridge University Press.

Sanderson, P. 1989. The human planning and scheduling role in advanced manufacturing systems: A critical review of field and laboratory research. *Human Factors,* 31(6), 635–666.

Shaw, M., and A. Whinston. 1989. An artificial intelligence approach to the scheduling of flexible manufacturing systems. *IEEE Transactions,* 21(2), 170–183.

Silverman, B., and T. Mazher. 1992. Expert critics in engineering design: Lessons learned and research needs. *AI Magazine,* 13(1), 45–62.

Simon, H. 1978. Information processing theory of human problem solving. *Handbook of Learning and Cognitive Processes, Volume 5: Human Information Processing,* W. Chase (ed.). Hillsdale, NJ: Lawrence Erlbaum.

Sycara, K., S. Roth, N. Sadeh, and M. Fox. 1991. Resource allocation in distributed factory scheduling. *IEEE Expert,* February, 29–40.

van Vlient, A., C.G.E. Boender, and A.H.G. Rinnooy Kan. 1992. Interactive optimization of bulk sugar deliveries. *Interfaces,* 22(3), 4–14.

Waterman, D. 1986. *A Guide to Expert Systems.* Reading, MA: Addison-Wesley.

Woods, D., and E. Roth. 1988. Cognitive systems engineering. *Handbook of Human-Computer Interaction,* M. Helander (ed.). New York: Elsevier Science Publishers.

Yost, G., and A. Newell. 1989. A problem space approach to expert systems development. *Proceedings of 11th International Joint Conference on Artificial Intelligence,* Menlo Park, Calif.: AAAI Press, pp. 621–627.

PART

TWO

APPLICATION CASE STUDIES
Defense Logistics

24

APPLYING AN AI PLANNER TO
MILITARY OPERATIONS PLANNING

David E. Wilkins
Roberto V. Desimone
(SRI International)

24.1 INTRODUCTION

This chapter describes the cooperative work taking place under two projects in the ARPA/RL Planning Initiative to produce a prototype system for quickly developing joint military courses of action. One project, at the Artificial Intelligence Center of SRI International (SRI), developed a novel planning and execution system based on several high-performance artificial intelligence (AI) technologies. Another project, at SRI's Information and Telecommunications Sciences Center, is applying these technologies to planning problems of the U.S. Central Command (CENTCOM).

As a result of this collaboration, SRI developed SOCAP (System for Operations Crisis Action Planning). It combines a newly extended version of an AI planning system, SIPE-2 (System for Interactive Planning and Execution), with a color map display and applies this technology to military operations planning. SOCAP was connected to the Dynamic Analysis and Replanning Tool (DART) via FMERG [1] to constitute the second Integrated Feasibility Demonstration (IFD-2) for the Planning Initiative. FMERG elaborates in more detail the SOCAP transportation plans and then uses DART to run a simulation to determine their transportation feasibility.

---

[1] FMERG (Force Module Expanded Requirements Generator) was developed by BBN and ISX under the DARPA/RL Planning Initiative to bridge the gap between the description of major forces in a course of action and the description of their corresponding TPFDD-level components required for DART, which is in operational use and tests a TPFDD (see Section 24.2) on a transportation feasibility model.

IFD-2 was demonstrated in early 1992 both at CENTCOM and at the Pentagon. The aim was to demonstrate the feasibility of applying the SIPE-2 technology for the generation of large-scale military operations plans (OPLANs).

The objective of the SOCAP research effort is to develop decision aids to enable military planners to produce more flexible and accurate joint military courses of action in less time when responding to a crisis. To develop prototypes that can have a provable impact in an operational environment, it is necessary for them to be tested by the military community. Thus, SOCAP was developed by consulting with military operation planners at CENTCOM to elicit their requirements and their knowledge of the planning process. In addition, information from other sources and publically available texts was used to develop this application. SOCAP successfully generated employment plans for dealing with specific enemy COAs and expanded deployment plans for getting the relevant combat forces, supporting forces, and their equipment and supplies to their destinations in time for the successful completion of their mission. Input to the system includes threat assessments, terrain analysis, apportioned forces, transport capabilities, planning goals, key assumptions, and operational constraints.

This chapter describes the SOCAP problem domain, the ways in which SIPE-2 was used to address this problem, and the strengths and weaknesses of our approach. The cooperative aspect of the work is important: the domain requirements of the application are driving some of the research in developing AI planning technologies, and these evolving AI tools and techniques are being transferred to the application as rapidly as possible.

24.2 MILITARY OPERATIONS CRISIS ACTION PLANNING

This section briefly describes the SOCAP problem domain. The military must manage crises. Good crisis management is characterized by quick response, decisive action, and flexibility to adapt to the changing situation. Developing a good course of action (COA) and modifying it as necessary must take into account a number of factors: approaches used in past cases that have worked well, novel features of the new situation, differing priorities for subparts of the crisis, and feasibility of suggested COAs. A COA should describe an *employment* plan for dealing with one or more enemy COAs and should identify a *deployment* plan for moving the relevant combat forces, supporting forces, and their equipment and supplies to their destinations in time for the successful completion of their mission.

Currently, the military crisis action planning process involves several phases. When a crisis occurs that requires a military option to be considered, the crisis is assessed and the situation reviewed to determine if military action is required. If it is, then tentative COAs are generated based on doctrine, past exercises, and existing concept and operations plans. Various estimates are developed for personnel

(J1), intelligence (J2), operations (J3), logistics (J4), and command and control (J6). The estimates and recommendations are presented for approval, and the commanders' estimate is constructed from these. Final approval is required before a complete OPLAN is generated.

Next, the force composition, logistics to support the mission, and all the transportation needs are defined, planned, synthesized, and simulated. Time-phased force deployment lists are generated based on force module libraries or previously developed deployment lists. These are routed for a detailed transportation feasibility analysis. The refined TPFDD (Time-phased Force Deployment Data) is approved for both operational and transportation feasibility, and operation orders are developed. Finally, the operation orders are executed and monitored.

The crisis action planning process is a distributed, interactive process. Accurate, timely, and secure exchange of information among geographically separated commanders is required to produce the best plans in the shortest time. Also, the planning process, as defined above, provides for the maximum reuse of plans where possible. Uncertainty is inherent in planning a response to a developing crisis and must be handled adequately if plans are to be robust. Other requirements for automating the joint military operations planning process are given elsewhere (Bienkowski, 1992).

A typical OPLAN contains approximately a few hundred actions, describing the employment and deployment of force modules chosen to deter or counter the enemy threat. A typical TPFDD contains a few thousand entries, each describing which unit, or part of a force module, is being deployed; where and when it arrives at its destinations; and which means of transportation it uses. Each enemy threat can be deterred or countered with a wide variety of operations that apply differing levels of aggression. These operations can vary from a show of force to a blockade or quarantine to a complete defensive or offensive operation. There is also a wide variety of units that have differing capabilities suitable for many different operations.

The number of possible COAs is enormous: developing a COA involves choosing operations at many levels of detail, military units and resources, and locations and times of these operations. In addition, rules of engagement need to be observed; operational constraints (e.g., troop limits) need to be satisfied; permissions for overflight of Allied airspace must be observed; and key assumptions need to be made explicit, such as the nonintervention of third-party forces. Most of these conditions are provided either in the mission statement or as planning guidance.

For demonstration purposes, SOCAP encodes a typical scenario that involves the use of U.S. forces to protect the territorial integrity of a friendly country from a neighboring enemy. A joint force is chosen that has significant defensive, rather than offensive, capability. The mission statement normally identifies a D-day by which date the ground forces should be deployed and a further date by which the defensive operations should have been completed. Associated with each action is an estimate of its duration, estimates of the appropriate size of unit it requires, and the location and region where it takes place. This information is required to "source" the military units in the plan (i.e., identify actual units); later, this information helps to determine the effects of deployment delays on subsequent actions.

The primary role of the ground forces is to provide a defensive screen near the border with the enemy and to secure key terrain in this border region. The role of the Navy is to secure sea lines of communication between the friendly territory and its trading neighbors and to protect major seaports. The role of the Air Force is to provide air defense over the territory. In addition, the Navy and Air Force have subsidiary roles to protect the deployment of ground forces and to support some of their operations, as with amphibious landings and close air support. Such interdependencies between actions make it possible to predict the impact of various changes in the situation or the reduced availability of specific units.

24.3 THE SIPE-2 PLANNING SYSTEM

SRI's AI Center has been conducting research into planning and problem-solving systems for the past three decades. SIPE-2 (System for Interactive Planning and Execution)[2] is the most advanced of SRI's planning systems and provides the core reasoning engine for plan generation in SOCAP. This section briefly describes the features of SIPE-2 that are most important to SOCAP; the system has been described in detail elsewhere (Wilkins, 1988, 1990, 1992).

SIPE-2 provides a formalism for describing actions and utilizes the knowledge encoded in this formalism, together with its heuristics for handling the combinatorics of the problem, to generate plans for achieving given goals. Given an arbitrary initial situation, the system either automatically or under interactive control generates plans, possibly containing conditionals, to achieve the prescribed goals. The generated plans include causal information so that during plan execution, the system can accept descriptions of arbitrary unexpected occurrences and modify its plans to take these into account. Unlike expert systems, SIPE-2 is capable of generating a novel sequence of actions that responds precisely to the situation at hand.

SIPE-2 is a nonlinear AI planning system that plans at different levels of abstraction. Because this technology is generic and domain-independent, it has the potential to affect a large variety of problems in fields as diverse as manufacturing, construction, and the military. Unlike most AI planning research, heuristic adequacy (efficiency) has been one of the primary goals in the design of SIPE-2. This has enabled its application to many domains, including the blocks world, the

---

[2] SIPE-2 is a trademark of SRI International.

actions of a mobile robot, the movement of aircraft on a carrier deck, travel planning, construction tasks, the problem of producing products from raw materials on process lines under production and resource constraints, and the military operations planning described in this chapter.

SIPE-2 has implemented several extensions of previous planning systems, including the use of constraints for the partial description of objects, the incorporation of heuristics for reasoning about resources, and replanning techniques. The planning formalism allows description of planning and simple scheduling problems in terms of the goals to be attained and the various activities that can be undertaken to achieve these goals. One of the most powerful heuristics for avoiding combinatorics in SIPE-2 is the ability to avoid frequent consistency checks by temporarily producing invalid plans. The system relies on *plan critics* that check for and correct problems in these plans at certain intervals.

24.3.1 Describing the Domain in SIPE-2

The input and output of SIPE-2 are depicted in Figure 24-1. Although the input to the planner attempt to model the "real world," current AI techniques cannot handle the full complexity of our everyday world, and generally it is an abstraction of the real world that is represented. The vertical arrows in the figure indicate the relationship of representation by which entities in the world are encoded internally in the planning system. The output is a plan—a partially ordered set of *primitive* actions and conditions to be carried out. Conditions the plan expects to be true at certain times are also included in the plan. A plan can be represented as a directed, acyclic graph in which each node is an action or condition, and each edge represents a temporal ordering.

SIPE-2 takes as input a description of the initial state, a description of a set of actions, a problem descriptor, and a set of rules describing the domain. The initial state consists of a *sort hierarchy*, a *world model*, and a set of deductive rules. The sort hierarchy represents invariant properties of perpetual objects, describes the classes to which an object belongs, and allows for inheritance of properties. In SOCAP, the sort hierarchy is used to encode information such as terrain analysis, the attributes of the combat forces available, and transport capabilities. The world model is a set of predicates that hold over objects in the sort hierarchy. Some predicates are given explicitly in the database, and others are deduced by applying deductive rules to the database. Predicates encode information such as operational constraints, assumptions, and intelligence reports.

An *operator* is the planner's representation of actions or abstractions of actions that can be performed in the domain. In SOCAP, operators vary from abstract strategies to specific military operations that can achieve employment or deployment goals. An operator is input in the system's formalism and specifies the conditions under which an action is appropriate, the constraints on the objects in

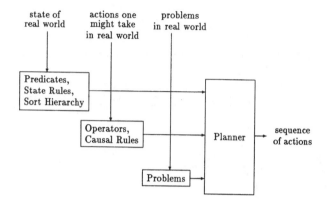

Figure 24-1:   SIPE-2's view of the planning problem

the action, a set of instructions for performing the action, and the main effects accomplished by the action (additional context-dependent effects are deduced by the system from deductive rules).

To produce a plan, the planner instantiates operators by binding their variables, combines these instantiations by ordering them, and then adds additional constraints to avoid problematic interactions between actions. For example, if a potential resource conflict is detected between two actions, the planner can order the actions to execute sequentially or can constrain the action to use different resources. The left side of Figure 24-2 depicts SIPE-2 choosing one of a set of operators for each goal in an abstract plan. This produces the more detailed plan on the right to which the planner has added an ordering link to avoid a problem it has detected (e.g., a resource conflict). The graphs in the figure represent plans where each rectangle is a goal or action, and the edges are temporal ordering links run-

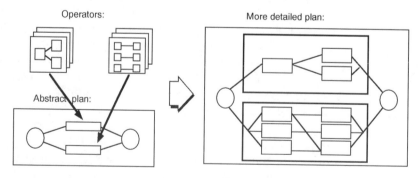

Figure 24-2:   Using operators to expand a plan

ning from left to right. Section 24.5 describes a SOCAP operator and its application during plan generation.

24.3.2 The User Interface in SIPE-2

Because of the size and complexity of the SOCAP problem domain and the plans produced, the user interface is critically important. It proved necessary to have two different interfaces—one for system engineers developing the implementation (the SIPE-2 interface) and another for the military users (the SOCAP interface). The map-based SOCAP interface is described in Section 24.5; the SIPE-2 graphical user interface (GUI) is described here.

Several new interface capabilities were needed to cope with the size of the military planning problem. For example, the sort hierarchy needed to be displayed graphically as a tree to help ensure its correctness. The world model, operators, and objects also needed to be displayed graphically. With commands to aid in generating plans, viewing complex plans and other information as graphs on the screen, and following and controlling the planning process, it was necessary to provide easy access to all the commands. To support this, we carried out a complete redesign and reimplementation of the SIPE-2 GUI as part of this research. The new interface is built on Grasper-CL[3] and uses a set of noun menus, each of which brings up a verb menu. The new interface provides many new capabilities and makes them more easily accessible through the noun/verb menus. Figure 24-3 shows the functionality of the new SIPE-2 interface by depicting the various menus of the GUI (the five nouns are at the top of each menu, and the verbs for the selected noun are below).

The five nouns let the user choose the level at which the verbs (commands) will operate. The PROFILE noun activates commands for setting defaults that allow the user to customize the behavior of the planner. The DOMAIN noun activates commands that apply to the problem domain as a whole, e.g., inputing and inspecting a domain or solving a problem. The PLAN noun activates commands that apply to a specific plan, including executing a plan and solving a problem to produce a plan. The DRAWINGS noun activates commands that draw various data structures. Objects that can be drawn include plans, operators, the sort hierarchy, the initial world model, and problems. Finally, the NODE noun activates commands that apply to specific nodes in the currently drawn plan. Each action and goal in a plan is represented as a node in the graphical drawing of the plan.

---

[3] Grasper-CL is a trademark of SRI International. Grasper-CL is a programming-language extension to Lisp that introduces graphs—arbitrarily connected networks—as a primitive data type. It includes procedures for graph construction, modification, and queries as well as a menu-driven, interactive display package that allows graphs to be constructed, modified, and viewed through direct pictorial manipulation.

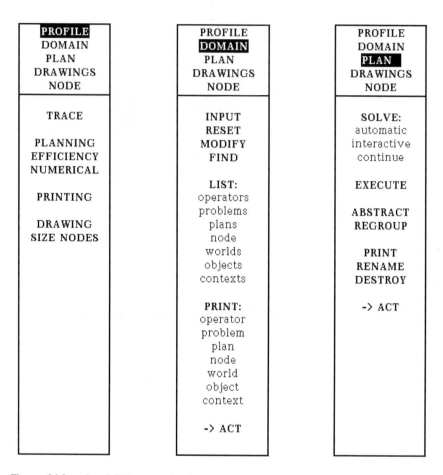

Figure 24-3:   Sipe-2 GUI noun and verb menus

The commands in the NODE menu are particularly helpful when analyzing large plans that can be difficult to interpret. These commands are used to find and modify nodes; to find resources and predicates at nodes; and to view, by highlighting nodes, various properties of a plan. The modification options are useful for customizing the appearance of the drawing on the screen—the user can move nodes around with the mouse to make the drawing look exactly as desired. An example of using highlighting of nodes effectively is the *Resource* command, which can be used to highlight all the nodes that mention Fennario Port, effectively showing the schedule for that port (as in Figure 24-4). Although only a part of the plan is shown in the figure, the GUI provides powerful capabilities for panning over the entire plan, locating a particular part of the plan, or looking at a bird's-eye view of the entire plan.

```
┌─────────────────┐        ┌─────────────────┐
│     PROFILE     │        │     PROFILE     │
│     DOMAIN      │        │     DOMAIN      │
│      PLAN       │        │      PLAN       │
│ ▐DRAWINGS▌      │        │    DRAWINGS     │
│      NODE       │        │    ▐NODE▌       │
├─────────────────┤        ├─────────────────┤
│     DRAW:       │        │      FIND       │
│    operator     │        │      PRINT      │
│    problem      │        │                 │
│      plan       │        │  PREDECESSORS   │
│     world       │        │   SUCCESSORS    │
│    objects      │        │    PARALLEL     │
│                 │        │                 │
│    SELECT       │        │    RESOURCE     │
│    DESTROY      │        │    ARGUMENT     │
│                 │        │   PREDICATE     │
│   NEW VIEW      │        │                 │
│   RENAME        │        │    RESHAPE      │
│   REDRAW        │        │     MOVE        │
│                 │        │    ALIGN        │
│   BACKUP        │        │                 │
│   REVERT        │        │                 │
│   RESCALE       │        │                 │
│   HARDCOPY      │        │                 │
│                 │        │                 │
│   GRAPH:        │        │                 │
│    select       │        │                 │
│    create       │        │                 │
│    destroy      │        │                 │
│    input        │        │                 │
│    output       │        │                 │
└─────────────────┘        └─────────────────┘
```

Figure 24-3:   Continued

24.3.3 Interactive Planning

Although SIPE-2 can generate plans autonomously, it also permits the user to interact with and control the planning process. In military operations planning, this feature is critical because the plans are large and complex, and there are many experienced human planners whose expertise can be used. Because of this, a new and more powerful interactive search algorithm was designed and implemented. In particular, the interactive search is now tightly integrated with the GUI.

The GUI allows the user to control, when desired, many aspects of the planning process during joint military operations planning. The user can decide when to apply certain planning algorithms (known as *plan critics*), can choose which opera-

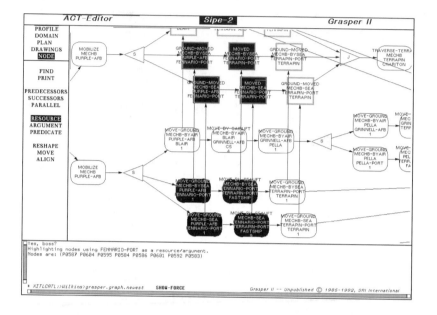

Figure 24-4: SOCAP plan highlighting resource: Fennario Port

tor to apply after the system has determined which ones are applicable, and can choose which object (e.g., a military unit or location) to use for a particular action. At any of these choice points, the complete power of the GUI is available for inspecting data structures (e.g., an operator can be drawn before choosing it). The option of planning automatically for either one abstraction level or for the rest of the plan is available. All choices are kept so that different alternative plans can be developed simultaneously. The ability to understand what SIPE-2 is doing is enhanced by the ability to highlight a node on the screen whenever the system is making a decision about that node, e.g., planning for the node, choosing an operator for the node, or choosing instantiations for the variables at that node.

The combination of these features allows the user to understand and effectively control the planning process in domains as large as military operations planning.

24.3.4 Scheduling

Robust solutions to complex, real-world problems require both planning and scheduling. In this section, we describe how SIPE-2 differs from most scheduling systems and why it is necessary to combine planning and scheduling. If the set of actions that must be performed, i.e., the process network, is known beforehand, then it is a scheduling problem to assign resources and times to these actions. On the other hand, if the set of actions must be generated based on the current situation and the current goals, then the problem solution also involves planning which requires that the system reason about how the world changes as scheduled events occur. This is the situation in military operations planning.

Other features of a scheduling problem can require planning; in fact, problems are often not separable into distinct planning and scheduling problems. For example, if some subset of the constraints in a scheduling problem will change depending on how another subset is satisfied, e.g., if the constraints on the afternoon's schedule will change depending on how the constraints on the morning's schedule were satisfied, then such a scheduling problem becomes a planning problem. Similarly, if a system is to modify an existing plan or schedule in response to unexpected occurrences during execution, then reasoning about the effects of actions and the causal relationships between actions becomes necessary to determine which subplans remain valid or are amenable to modification. In most real-world situations, unexpected occurrences are the norm during operations, and it is important to modify plans quickly in response to these occurrences.

In SIPE-2, time is treated as a consumable resource that can be consumed but not produced and whose consumption over parallel tasks is nonadditive (Wilkins, 1988, 1990). The numerical value can be a list of numbers customized for the problem. For example, time can be represented as **(days hours minutes seconds)**. Each action specification can have *start-time* and *duration* slots containing variables with numerical constraints on them that are satisfied by the planner. In particular, a variable can be constrained to be the value computed by a Lisp function, which is generally how durations are computed.

SIPE-2 will calculate specific values for time variables only when the constraints force a particular value; otherwise, the allowable range is computed. When several such variables have ranges, it is a scheduling problem to determine optimal or desirable times for each variable. The planner does not have built in algorithms for doing this—good algorithms often require tailoring to a specific domain. SIPE-2 does have hooks built in so that external scheduling modules can assign these times. We are currently working on developing such a tie with the scheduling systems being developed at Carnegie Mellon University (CMU) (Smith, 1987). However, many research issues must be addressed to maximize the benefit from such an integration (see Section 24.6).

SIPE-2 has several techniques for establishing relative orderings of actions. These techniques include inserting ordering links to avoid resource conflicts, using one action to meet several different requirements by ordering them after the action, and coordinating separate subplans by adding ordering links to goals that have been declared as *external*. SOCAP makes heavy use of the latter two techniques; in fact,

SIPE-2 was extended to do more sophisticated reasoning about when and how to achieve several different requirements by one action in order to support SOCAP.

From the scheduling viewpoint, SIPE-2 creates the project network that must be scheduled. In addition, it does the part of the scheduling that can be determined from its hard constraints and also uses heuristics for adding relative ordering links. Depending on the specific circumstances, this can do much of the work of establishing a schedule (as in SOCAP), or it can leave considerable work to be done by another scheduling module. As described in Section 24.6, we would ideally like to have a scheduler interact with the planner during planning, providing values for its time variables based on scheduling algorithms.

24.4 SOCAP—SYSTEM FOR OPERATIONS CRISIS ACTION PLANNING

The objective of the IFD-2 version of SOCAP was to demonstrate the feasibility of applying the SIPE-2 technology to the generation of large-scale military OPLANs. This was accomplished by developing decision aids for the generation of more flexible and accurate joint military COAs. To date, no research or development activity has integrated a generative AI planning system into an operational environment. Although SOCAP stresses the demonstration of generative planning techniques, subsequent phases of this research will emphasize replanning techniques.

SOCAP includes an application of SIPE-2 to military operations planning together with a user interface tailored to this domain using a situation-map display system. Figure 24-5 shows the architecture, highlighting the necessary input for the generation of COAs and OPLANs, the available output, and the user interaction. The following input should be fed into the SOCAP database from available military databases:

> **Threat assessment:** list of enemy threats, locations, and dates
>
> **Terrain analysis:** information on terrain features affecting mobility and observability
>
> **Apportioned forces:** list of combat forces available for planning purposes
>
> **Transport capabilities:** list of available assets

Other input would come from the mission commander or his/her joint staff:

> **Planning goals:** list of goals that match mission statement
>
> **Key assumptions:** e.g., rules of engagement, non-intervention of third party forces
>
> **Operational constraints:** e.g., overflight privileges, troop limits in country

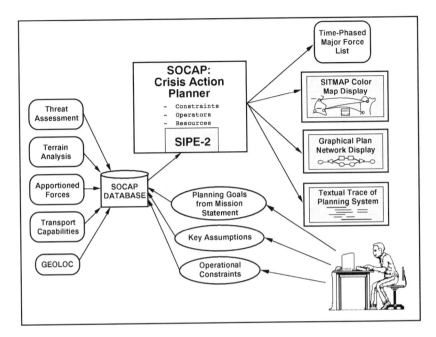

Figure 24-5: SOCAP architecture

Most of the above information is inherently dynamic and is best represented in SIPE-2 as first-order statements, such as `(threat-enemy 1stArmBde route-A 25)`, which states that there is an enemy threat unit, the 1st Armored Brigade, whose avenue of approach is denoted by `route-A`, and that the enemy unit should be countered by Day 25. There are over 2100 predicate statements in the SOCAP knowledge base. However, a great deal of the available data are static (i.e., they do not change over time as actions are executed) and, for efficiency reasons, are represented in the sort hierarchy and not as predicate statements.

The major (parent) classes represented in the static database are

Forces: including combat, combat support, and combat service support

Transports: including air, sea, and ground

Territory: including land, sea, and air

All other entities, such as cargo, equipment, aircraft, ships, routes, regions, and urban areas, are either subclasses derived from the above three classes or are properties of classes. For example, cargo requirements and combat capabilities for specific combat forces should be denoted as properties of these forces. There are over 200 classes and 500 objects in the IFD-2 knowledge base. For efficiency reasons, it is important to represent static information using the sort hierarchy whenever possible. This is discussed in Section 24.5.

SOCAP requires a large set of operators to describe military operations that can achieve specific employment or deployment goals. For instance, there are a variety of military operations for deterring an enemy army, navy, or air force. Each of these operations can be represented by a different SIPE-2 operator, which all have the common effect of deterring an enemy force. However, they can have different sets of preconditions or different resource requirements that need to be satisfied before they can be used in a plan.

There are operators at every level of abstraction. The ability of SIPE-2 to plan at different levels of abstraction naturally maps onto the following levels of the operations planning process:

Level 1: Select mission type.

Level 2: Identify threats and their locations.

Level 3: Select employment operations, major forces, and deployment destinations.

Level 4: Add deployment actions.

Section 24.5 describes how important the hierarchical nature of the planning process is to the success of SOCAP.

24.4.1 Applying Operators

It is the operators that capture most of the domain-specific planning capability. There are currently around 70 SIPE-2 operators in the SOCAP knowledge base. Each operator brings into the plan an appropriate network of military actions and subgoals that together achieve the purpose of the operator. We have made use of these subgoals to highlight dependencies on other parts of the plan to provide supporting military actions such as resupply, close air support, or artillery support.

Figure 24-6 shows a typical operator for deterring an enemy ground threat as drawn by the GUI. Here we briefly describe how this ground-patrol operator is used to generate a more detailed plan by the process depicted in Figure 24-2. Figure 24-7 shows an abstract plan produced after the second level of planning, during which enemy threats are detected. This plan is a subset of the plan developed for IFD-2 and has four parallel goals of deterring each of four immediate enemy threats. The second goal, (immediate-threat enemy-army-B coa-1 26), requires the enemy army to be deterred by Day 26. The operator shown in Figure 24-6 is one of four operators applicable to this goal because its *purpose* matches the goal. The planner chooses this ground-patrol operator to expand the plan to level 3 and binds enemy-army-B to the army.2 variable in the operator. The expansion succeeds because the precondition of the operator is true. Matching the precondition constrains variables; e.g., urban.2 is constrained to be

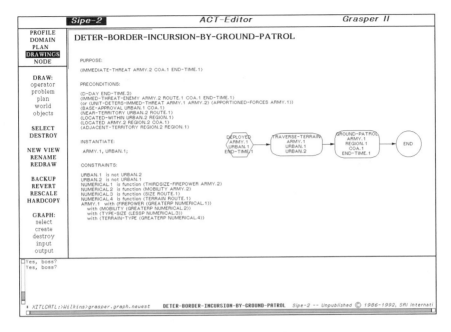

Figure 24-6:   Deter Border Incursion Operator in SIPE-2 Interface

near `route.1` and within `region.1`. Additional constraints (shown in Figure 24-6) are posted by application of this operator; e.g., `army.1` must have appropriate firepower and mobility.

The graph on the right side of Figure 24-6 depicts the instructions for achieving deterrence at the next level of detail, which consists of the subgoal (a hexagonal node) of deploying `army.1`, followed by the action (a capsule node) of tra-

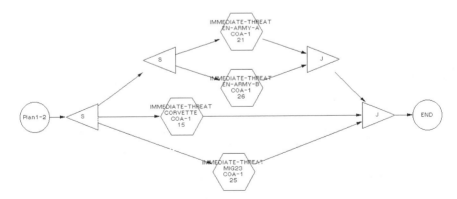

Figure 24-7:   Plan after threat identification (level 2)

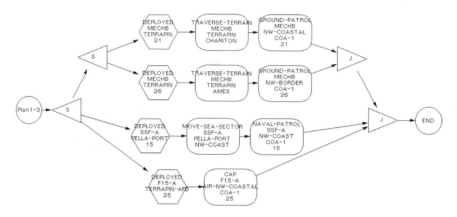

Figure 24-8:   Plan after deterring threats (level 3)

versing from **urban.1** to **urban.2**, followed by the action of doing ground patrols in **region.1**. Figure 24-8 shows the plan at the next level when all threats have been countered. Both the first and second threats have been countered by the ground-patrol operator, but the third and fourth threats have been countered by other operators. In both applications of the ground-patrol operator, **army.1** was instantiated to be the particular mechanized unit, **mechb**, because this unit met the constraints on firepower, mobility, location, etc. The plan requires the **mechb** to do ground patrols simultaneously in the NW-Coastal region and the NW-Border region (because **region.1** was instantiated differently in the two operator applications). The planner ensures there are no conflicts in the plan and then plans another level by a similar application of operators to the newly produced plan. The next planning level will use deployment operators to solve the deployment subgoals that are now in the plan.

24.4.2 The User Interface in SOCAP

The SOCAP interface provides facilities for guiding the user through the plan generation process. The amount of user interaction can be varied during the planning process. It can range from being fully automated, in which case a plan is generated with no human interaction, to semiautomated, in which the user makes some choices, to fully manual, where the user makes all the choices. At each goal in the plan, the user can request the relevant operators that achieve the goal to be displayed. Likewise, when attempting to bind a variable associated with an argument of an operator, the possible bindings can be displayed. For instance, the user can be presented with the set of military units that have the appropriate capabilities to deter an enemy threat or a list of suitable locations for the military operation.

Table 24-1: Size of knowledge base for current SOCAP and operational SOCAP.

Data Structure	IFD-2	Operational
Classes/objects	500	2,500
Properties per object	5 to 15	50 to 100
Predicates	1,500	15,000
Operators	50 to 70	500 to 1,000

This set can be constrained by the preconditions and other constraints associated with the arguments of the relevant SIPE-2 operator. At the end of each plan level, the plan is checked for logical consistency and then progresses to the next level until there are no more goals to be satisfied or actions to be decomposed further.

The plan can be displayed at each plan level, either as a partially ordered network of actions and goals or on a time-based map display. The map display shows the actions that are occurring on different days during the mission. The temporal information for the map display is derived from durations associated with each action and from the dates when the enemy threats should be deterred or countered. Clicking the mouse on a token on the map display will bring up a window describing the military operation represented by the token and the location, times, and units of the operation. A second mouse click can be used to bring up another window with further information about a specified military unit, e.g., its current military status or mobilization status.

Section 24.5 describes more of the techniques used to encode information. The plans generated so far have 100 to 200 executable actions in the final plan. (The entire plan has many times this number of nodes, because some nodes are conditions that help record the rationale behind the plan and information for repairing it.) The major forces identified in the plan are then further decomposed by FMERG to their TPFDD-level components, resulting in 2,500 entries in the TPFDD. For a large-scale military operation, such as in the Gulf crisis, the number of TPFDD-level entries would probably be an order of magnitude larger. The IFD-2 knowledge base is by no means complete. It has fleshed out the skeleton of a much larger set of plan operators, including predicates for describing the current situation and classes and objects for capturing static information. A rough estimate for an operational SOCAP knowledge base is given in Table 24-1.

24.5 LESSONS LEARNED

The lessons learned from applying SIPE-2 to military crisis action planning can be divided into three sections: successes in applying the existing technology, difficulties, and future research.

24.5.1 Successes

The SIPE-2 hierarchical planning process maps well to the military operations planning process. As a result, it was relatively easy to group sets of operators according to the various phases/levels of the operations planning process described earlier. The hierarchical structure of the operators also encourages a similar structure for the predicates that describe the world. Hence, the preconditions of operators are an excellent means of bringing situational data and information to bear at the relevant planning level and at the appropriate level of detail. For instance, general locations of enemy threats and high-level geographic features are appropriate for the identify-threats level of the planning process, but more detailed threat assessment, e.g., force composition, strength, and terrain analysis, is required for the employment planning phase. Furthermore, the hierarchical structure maps well to the chain of command, described in Section 24.2.

The sort hierarchy provides a clear representation of static information within SOCAP. This static information is captured in the properties of classes and objects that are often used in posting constraints on the arguments of operators. For instance, the choice of an airfield for a deployment action might rely on having the property `runway-length` be long enough for available air transports, such as C-5s, C-141s, and C-130s. There is a clear distinction between static information, represented in the sort hierarchy and as predicate statements, and dynamic information, represented only by predicate statements. This distinction is important for two reasons: (1) the retrieval of static information is more efficient than the retrieval of dynamic information because the system does not need to reason about the effects of actions and (2) the validation of static information is helped by the tree structure of the sort hierarchy.

The arguments of operators and preconditions are represented as planning variables with constraints. This provides a means of delaying the binding of specific instances to these variables until the constraints select the most appropriate instance. This least-commitment approach to variable binding is an important capability provided by SIPE-2 that is heavily used in SOCAP. SOCAP also makes use of the planner's ability to force the binding of these variables with user guidance. For instance, this facility can be used to force the selection of favored military units for specific operations.

SIPE-2 provides a mechanism for permitting situational knowledge to determine the number of specific subgoals introduced into a plan. For instance, in order to determine how many enemy threats to counter, the system checks the number of enemy threat units identified in the threat assessment database and generates a subgoal for each. This mechanism permits iteration where the number of iterations is determined by the situational data rather than provided in advance. There are a variety of these iterative operators that search for different types of enemy threats, whether ground, sea, or air. Section 24.5.2 discusses problems concerning the number and choice of subgoals introduced by this mechanism.

SIPE-2 permits a great deal of information to be presented to the user at a variety of levels of detail. As a result, the GUI has many menus that can be called to access this information, and using it effectively requires some knowledge of the workings of the planner. The GUI is thus better suited for developing applications than for using an application operationally. The SOCAP interface, on the other hand, is tailored to the military crisis action planning environment. In particular, it stresses the interactive nature of the planning process and extracts appropriate details during the planning process and presents them to the user. Thus, when a user is viewing the possible choices of military units for an operation, SOCAP presents the constraints that led to these choices. It is possible to view all the possible instantiations of a planning variable given the constraints associated with the variable, whether it represents a military unit, resource, location, or time. Operator choices for extending the plan are displayed, and the plan structure produced is highlighted, including the effects achieved and the preconditions that must be satisfied. The ability of the SIPE-2 GUI to highlight specific information about the plan or its structure is particularly useful in the SOCAP interface. This includes highlighting nodes that contain certain predicates or arguments and highlighting the predecessors, successors, and actions in parallel for a given action.

A time-based map display provides another means of displaying the plan that is particularly appealing to military planners. This map display is currently being developed to display situation data or overlays on a digitized map. It is possible to show the operations that occur on each day of the mission and display appropriate information about the type of military operation, the units involved, and the boundary of the operation. In this way, the user can query what is going on, where and when, in the context of map information. We have used this map display to represent both the employment plan on a detailed map of the area of interest and the deployment plan on a coarser-grained map.

24.5.2 Difficulties

SOCAP did not extensively use the SIPE-2 resource reasoning capability for three reasons. First, dealing effectively with resource conflicts involves balancing various trade-offs. This requires complex representations of hard and soft constraints and mechanisms for constraint relaxation. Most AI planning systems (including SIPE-2) do not have these capabilities and instead rely on the representation of hard constraints and constraint satisfaction algorithms. Second, an algorithm tailored to this particular domain would be necessary to intelligently assign resources. For instance, when choosing military units for operations, in order to minimize the number of troops involved in the operation, it is often wise to choose units already involved in the plan, except when they have been overused. In addition, there must be information to allow balancing such a desire with other conflicting heuristics.

Finally, although SIPE-2 does have a mechanism for representing shareable resources, it must be determined in advance how such resources might be shared. This is too inflexible for military operations planning. For instance, a large military unit, such as a division, can be employed in several operations simultaneously, where each operation uses some of the division's capabilities. The number of operations over which the division can be shared depends on the amount of resources required for each operation. Thus, the only way to reason about the shared resource is to consider the capabilities of the division as a consumable resource purely for this specific set of operations. However, a recent extension to SIPE-2 is dynamic calculation of resource sharing.

Each of these three problems is difficult and best addressed with technology that relaxes soft constraints in search of an optimal solution, e.g., the scheduling technology at CMU. An integration of planning and scheduling, as described in Section 24.6, is needed to address these problems.

Another difficulty is the limited temporal reasoning in SIPE-2. Two SIPE-2 actions are either ordered with respect to each other, or they are unordered. If the latter, the planner considers it possible to order them in either order or execute them simultaneously. Information about start times and durations is only used when it can be deduced that two actions should be ordered based on this information. This is limiting; for example, one cannot model when during the execution of an action, its various effects become true, nor can one model actions that *must* occur simultaneously. Allen's 13 temporal relations (Allen, 1982) would have been useful. This would have permitted more versatile operations with explicit representation of actions starting or finishing at the same time, overlapping each other, or one occurring during another. Many dependencies between different military actions could have been represented in this way. For instance, cargo offload teams should arrive at the same time as the first air or sea transport arrives at the air or sea port, the deployment of troops to their destination should overlap the deployment of supplies and equipment, and close air support should take place during a ground offensive operation.

Another useful capability is the serendipitous combination of subgoals. For instance, at present, for every enemy threat identified, a friendly unit is identified to deter or counter it. If several small enemy forces are located close to each other, SOCAP attempts to deal with each threat individually rather than consider them as an aggregate threat that might be countered with a single, larger, friendly force. Whether the aggregation is done by the user or by some algorithm, it is important that the original subgoals be replaced by a new subgoal.

Currently, it is cumbersome to represent the notion of a task force whose composition is determined dynamically by whichever military units were assigned to lower-level actions. It is possible to represent a class of objects of type `task-force` and make use of a `part-of` predicate to relate specific military units to a specific task force, but this is not perspicuous. This notion of a higher-level term used to describe the combination of lower-level objects is an important aspect of military planning. For instance, a military brigade that comprises three battalions can be split into two or more battalion task forces that could make use of the battalions within the brigade or additional units and resources from other brigades or divisions. It is important to make reference to the battalion task force at higher levels of the plan, especially when coordinating with other task forces or higher-level units. It is also necessary to ensure that the capabilities of the task force are explicitly represented so that they are not overutilized.

Another problem involves the lack of an explicit mechanism for reasoning about the order in which goals should be achieved. SIPE-2 supports operators that delay solving of a goal for one planning level when the preconditions of the operator are true. For instance, one might decide to achieve all employment goals first and only start on the deployment goals when the employment goals have been satisfied. However, having to encapsulate such a heuristic in the preconditions of an operator is not ideal. One solution is to permit the developer to specify an algorithm to weigh trade-offs between several heuristics that determine which goals to satisfy next. This would allow expansion of some parts of the plan down to a detailed level, but other parts of the plan might be kept at a higher planning level, thus allowing details associated with one part of the plan to be specified before another part of the plan, which depends on these details, is formulated. The O-Plan architecture provides a framework for doing this type of reasoning (Currie & Tate, 1991).

24.6 FUTURE WORK

This section describes the important issues that SRI plans to address in the future in conjunction with other research groups in the Planning Initiative. During the planning process, many decisions have to be made concerning the choice of operations, military forces, resources, locations, and times. To reason about the various possibilities requires using a variety of simulators, case-based reasoners, and decision-theoretic and uncertain reasoning aids for guiding such choices. The simulators might perform feasibility analyses for combat, logistics, transportation, command and control, and the like. Case-based reasoners would explore the similarity between the current situation and previous examples (or cases) of missions that employed specific operations, forces, and resources at certain locations and times. Decision-theoretic aids and uncertain reasoning techniques can be applied to determine the utility of specific choices and to provide probabilistic measures of success that could be used to determine the alternatives to be explored and enumerated. The above techniques could be applied during the planning process to guide choices or afterward to evaluate the plan(s) developed. Such techniques could also provide metrics for identifying qualitatively different COAs.

During the SOCAP project, a simple simulator was used as a postprocess to determine the transportation feasibility of the COA. The output of the simulator included a list of the number of military forces that were predicted to arrive late at their destinations. The input to this simulator required specific times to be associated with the movement actions in the deployment plan. Ideally, a TPFDD is the proper input to the simulator. The Planning Initiative includes work on simulation and scheduling systems that could be used for determining transportation feasibility.

24.6.1 Replanning and Knowledge Acquisition

During IFD-2, the emphasis was on demonstrating the feasibility of applying plan generation techniques to the crisis action planning process. By stressing the generation of plans, it was possible to focus attention on describing the different types of military operations, forces, and their capabilities and using situational data to guide the necessary choices during planning. However, in a crisis, the situation is changing rapidly. Previous decisions need to be revised, and new goals need to be satisfied. Replanning techniques are required to reuse as much as possible of the existing plan but modify it appropriately.

To complicate matters further, not only is the situation changing rapidly, but the environment is also uncertain. It will be necessary to develop techniques to reason about how the uncertainty in the situational data affects the planning choices. This is important both for selecting operators, which might now have uncertain effects, and for selecting units for use in the plan. Exploring the use of uncertainty measures to determine the robustness of plans or the sensitivity of plans to changes is also important. An ongoing effort at SRI is investigating planning and executing in uncertain environments.

Military operations planners who viewed SOCAP often asked about support facilities for updating and writing new operators. This involves providing facilities for checking that the preconditions and effects are syntactically and semantically correct. An ongoing effort at SRI (Wilkins et al., 1992) has specified the ACT formalism and developed an interactive editor for inputing operators in this formalism that can be translated to SIPE-2. However, algorithms to ensure that the revised or new operators do not adversely affect other existing operators would also be needed. This is a difficult problem that might provide an excellent domain for machine learning techniques.

24.6.2 Integrating Planning and Scheduling

Another important research area is the relationship between, and integration of, planning and scheduling techniques. Current research work (involving SRI and CMU) is investigating the integration of SIPE-2 with the OPIS (Opportunistic Intelligent Scheduler) scheduling technology developed at CMU. This research will be conducted in several phases.

The first phase will provide a SIPE-2 plan as input to the OPIS system and send feedback to the planner concerning resource conflicts that present difficulties to OPIS. The second phase will examine the integration of capacity planning techniques during the plan generation and replanning processes to aid the early assignment of resources based on projections of predicted resource bottlenecks. The third stage will investigate more closely the guidance to the scheduling process that can be provided by the dependency structure of the plan, the choices made during the plan generation process, and the alternative choices that are recorded in the plan state.

We will examine how information from the scheduling process might be used to guide replanning. For example, the scheduler might provide information that suggests which alternative miltary actions should not be considered because they make use of over-utilized resources. Providing such information during the replanning process would reduce resource conflicts during the subsequent re-scheduling process. Controlling the planning and scheduling processes poses some difficult questions, such as, when should the system stop plan generation and run the scheduler, or can they run simultaneously? When can the scheduler repair a plan, and when must the planner be used for plan repair? When should the system simulate the execution of the plan, and how should the simulation interact with the planner and scheduler?

24.7 CONCLUSIONS

SOCAP successfully demonstrated that AI planning techniques can be used for the generation of large-scale military OPLANs. It provides the first steps toward an operational prototype that can be tested on real military crises, although it has so far been tested on only one scenario. It shows how the domain requirements of the application drive research in AI planning technologies and how rapidly these evolving tools and techniques can be transferred to the application.

SIPE-2 supported efficient plan generation for this scenario. The effectiveness and efficiency stemmed from its hierarchical planning process (which naturally fit the hierarchical structure of the domain), extensive use of its sort hierarchy for encoding military databases, the ability to place constraints on planning variables, its powerful graphical interface for viewing plans and data, and the interactive planning capabilities. Several difficulties were identified, however, including the inability to reason about complex temporal information, lack of an ability for encoding a domain-specific algorithm for assigning resources to actions, an inability to combine subgoals, and lack of a mechanism for reasoning about when goals should be achieved.

Producing decision aids that will help military planners in an operational setting will involve the integration of several ongoing research areas in the Planning Initiative. These include machine learning, scheduling, plan repair, case-based reasoning, simulation, and uncertain reasoning techniques.

ACKNOWLEDGMENTS

The research described in this chapter was supported by the ARPA/Rome Laboratory Planning Initiative under contracts F30602-91-C-0039 and F30602-90-C-0086. The research underlying the initial SIPE system was supported by the Air Force Office of Scientific Research. The development of SIPE-2 was supported by SRI International, the Australian AI Institute, and the above DARPA/Rome Laboratory contracts. Grasper-CL and SIPE-2 are trademarks of SRI International. Our thanks to the people involved in the SOCAP implementation: Marie Bienkowski, Marie desJardins, Jeff Decurtins, Peter Karp, Mabry Tyson, and John Lowrance.

References

Allen, J.F. 1982. "Maintaining Knowledge about Temporal Intervals," *Communications Association for Computing Machinery*, 26:832–843.

Bienkowski, M.A. 1992. "Initial Requirements Analysis for Automation in Support of Joint Military Planning," Technical Report ITAD-2062-TR-92-40, SRI International Artificial Intelligence Center, Menlo Park, CA.

Currie, K., and A. Tate. 1991. "O-plan: The Open Planning Architecture," *Artificial Intelligence*, 52(1):49–86.

Smith, S.F. 1987. "A Constraint-based Framework for Reactive Management of Factory Schedules," *Proceedings of the International Conference on Expert Systems and the Leading Edge in Production Planning and Control*, M. Oliff (ed.). Charleston, SC. Benjamin Cummings Publishing, Redwood City, CA, pp. 113–130.

Wilkins, David E., *et al.* 1992. "Planning in Dynamic and Uncertain Environments," Annual Report, SRI International Artificial Intelligence Center, Menlo Park, CA.

Wilkins, David E. 1988. *Practical Planning: Extending the Classical AI Planning Paradigm.* Morgan Kaufmann Publishers Inc., San Francisco, CA.

Wilkins, David E. 1990. "Can AI Planners Solve Practical Problems?" *Computational Intelligence*, 6(4):232–246.

Wilkins, David E. 1992. *Using the SIPE Planning System: A Manual.* SRI International Artificial Intelligence Center, Menlo Park, CA.

25

DART:

Applying Knowledge Based Planning and Scheduling to Crisis Action Planning

Lt. Col. Stephen E. Cross, USAF
(Advanced Research Projects Agency)

Edward Walker
(Bolt Beranek and Newman Inc.)

25.1 INTRODUCTION

This chapter discusses the design, development, and impact of DART, the Dynamic Analysis and Replanning Tool. DART resulted from a demonstration project undertaken by ARPA, Rome Laboratory, and the United States Transportation Command in early 1990. The prototype originally was intended to provide a means for demonstrating and evaluating the usefulness of knowledge based planning and scheduling technology supported by a ARPA/Rome R&D program. However, during the Persian Gulf crisis, an operationally usable version of DART was developed in only eight weeks. This hasty prototype was used for planning and analysis during Desert Shield and Desert Storm. DART has been enhanced since then and is used regularly at USTRANSCOM and several other field sites.

DART is just the first product of the two-way flow of requirements and technology that the ARPA and Rome Laboratory Planning Initiative was designed to provide. DART's architecture and that of a companion Common Prototyping Environment provide the substrate for creating, evaluating, and fielding additional decision aids for planners. Software components and data from DART are being shared among researchers in the Planning Initiative in order to facilitate research and increase the interoperability of research software.

DART also represents the first steps toward establishing the shared concurrent reasoning infrastructure for collaborative plan generation and analysis that is the ultimate goal of the Initiative. Although the technical goals of DART itself were modest, it has been used to evaluate the effectiveness and performance of a client-server architecture in the operational domain. A follow-on project uses DART as the basis for an integrated modeling environment, and components of the system are being used to support demonstrations of distributed collaborative planning. Other means for inserting newly developed planning technology, conducting evaluation exercises, and testing the operational utility of research products will become available, but the DART system constitutes a concrete platform and practical bridge between application and research projects in the crisis planning domain.

25.1.1 Historical Overview

Based on a staff college white paper by the first author, Rome Laboratory (RL) funded Carnegie Mellon University and the MITRE Corporation, to conduct a requirements analysis of the transportation planning problem. The Proud Eagle Exercise conducted by the DoD in November 1989 demonstrated bottlenecks and inadequacies in the currently fielded automated support for crisis action planning. An ARPA Planning Workshop held in December 1989 defined a research and technology demonstration program to overcome these limitations. By July 1990, BBN Systems and Technologies and Ascent Technologies, Inc. had installed RAPIDSIM, a transportation model, onto a UNIX workstation and demonstrated interfaces for downloading and modifying data as well as for conducting transportation analysis.

These initial capabilities were demonstrated to the Desert Shield Crisis Action Team (CAT) at USTRANSCOM, and shortly thereafter, ARPA was tasked to accelerate the development of the prototype. Operational personnel were reassigned from the CAT to work on the project. A development team led by BBN and Ascent and including personnel from SRA Corporation, MITRE Corporation, and ISX Corporation began an intense night and day development effort. In two weeks, an initial DART system was being used for Desert Shield transportation analysis. Improvements to DART continued, and after eight weeks, a second system was installed in Europe, where it contributed to the successful deployment of forces from there to the Persian Gulf.

In 1991, a second phase of development was undertaken to fix known problems with the prototype and improve the user interface. The system also was hardened against user induced errors, and more graceful error recovery was provided. Functional enhancements allowed better access to details of transportation data, improved the model running environment, and made new output of the model available. Better access to related models and data sources also was provided, and the system was installed at two beta sites.

Between November 1991 and January 1992, DART hardware and software were installed at more than a dozen additional commands and several evaluation sites. A build cycle and user training, hotline support, and configuration management were undertaken. In June 1992, an extensive evaluation of the DART system's hardware and software architecture capability as a multi-user client server for use by all operational planning sites was successfully concluded. Formal fielding and maintenance of DART is under way.

25.2 THE CRISIS PLANNING PROBLEM

Crisis action planning generally begins with assessing the situation at hand and establishing the high level objectives of the plan. General constraints on the means and methods available for accomplishing those objectives led to specific mission objectives and planning constraints, which are passed to plan generation, scheduling, and analysis stages. In the initial stages of developing a plan, stereotypic forces and supporting resources are allocated to one or more candidate courses of action. The feasibility of these candidate plans is analyzed from several perspectives, including the mobilization of personnel and equipment, their movement to the theater of operations, their use in the mission at hand, and the sustainment of forces during the course of the mission.

A feasible course of action results from analysis and negotiation among the many participants in the planning process, during which actual personnel and equipment are designated, actual schedules are constructed, and the detailed orders necessary for executing the plan are produced. Of course, unexpected events occur; the situation changes; and the plan must be modified by iterating the process described above, even as it is being completed.

The components of DART now are being used to address many aspects of planning and scheduling; however, the specific initial concern of the system as a whole was with transportation planning and scheduling. Several aspects of this domain are technically challenging. The first challenge is scale. There can be 10,000 to 50,000 individually scheduled records in a typical transportation database, each describing the parameters for moving either a military unit (with equipment) or supporting cargo. These records describe the origin, destination, and intermediate ports to be used for moving the cargo and people involved and specify the date they are available for movement. Earliest and latest dates for their arrival at the port of debarkation and at their final destination are provided as well. Each database record embodies one or several individually schedulable movements because there can be intermediate stops and multiple modes of transportation (air, sea travel) in moving from an origin to one or several ports (airports and/or seaports), stops enroute, and a variety of means for traveling from a port in the theater of operation to a staging area. A careful scheduler would also take into account loading and unloading activities at each port and the variety of capacity constraints implied by docking, landing or parking space, onloading, offloading and local transport equipment, and storage.

The second problem to be addressed when developing automated scheduling tools in this domain is the need for responsiveness to changes in the plan or its surrounding circumstances. The alternate plans developed in response to a crisis are best viewed as plans for different kinds of contingencies, but the size and detail required for accurate scheduling and simulation mean that only one plan typically is fully developed for a situation at any given time. Usually this plan is for a worst case scenario that would involve moving the largest number of troops and materials. Smaller "options" are developed by rearranging elements of this large plan, that is, by scheduling their deployment earlier than in the worst case option. Because this kind of rescheduling is generally done under great time pressure, planners would like to change the time and relative order of deployment of only the salient elements of a plan, then have all the capacity and resource constraints applied automatically to produce the details of the revised schedule.

The third problem in automating planning and scheduling for this domain is that of representing explicitly the temporal constraints and resource conflicts among possible actions. Indeed, it can be difficult to acquire the needed information at all because only a fraction of the constraints can be specified much in advance of the crisis. Good graphical interfaces that make it easy to obtain, create, or modify this kind of information interactively must be available so planners can describe the structure of the plan to the machine quickly and naturally.

The sequential process and hierarchical organization of details implied in the description above conforms with the doctrinal view of plan generation and analysis, but it does not convey adequately the extent of concurrent information processing and collaborative problem solving that occurs in military planning. As in other planning contexts, informal communication and data sharing among levels of command and across areas of responsibility are commonplace. Many elements of the plan are developed and evaluated simultaneously. The current electronic product of the manual planning process, the so-called Time Phased Force and Deployment Database, or TPFDD, results from work by a large number of people in various organizations at a variety of sites. Each participant develops the portion of the TPFDD that specifies the set of ports to use and acceptable arrival times for the units for which he or she is responsible, attending primarily to the requirements of the plan from the perspective of the military service and command for which they work and only secondarily to guidelines about which transportation resources are available to the command.

Either explicitly or mentally, each participant compares several alternative planning options. In the absence of direct communication and collaboration, planners actively model or estimate the potential decision making or data input of other participants. Complex constraints derived from prior experience and from the planning process, however, are expressed only in the dates specified for the arrival of units, and there is no way to convey a rationale for deciding the arrival times for particular units. Indeed, it is a major challenge to discover what those constraints are and to determine which kinds of constraints could be maintained in a form that relieves users of the tremendous burden of modifying or reiterating every constraint when a new plan is built.

A fourth problem arises at the boundary between planning and scheduling. A typical transportation plan involves operational forces, whose primary goal is the performance of the offensive, defensive, or humanitarian mission raised by the crisis; Combat Support elements, which provide direct support such as artillery and air cover; Combat Service Support elements, which include engineering units, port handling units, truck and other land transport units, medical, and food; and a variety of other support units. However, much of the planning for Combat Service Support is based on the size of the operation in terms of numbers of people and/or cargo arriving at or based in different locations. This circularity is a problem for the modular decomposition of the planning process and, in particular, for the separation of scheduling from other functions.

25.2.1 Summary of Technical Challenges

From a technical point of view, the following features of the crisis action planning domain present significant R&D challenges:

- Planning problems can involve very large numbers of resources, activities, constraints, and planners.
- Plans generally are created concurrently by multiple agents who are geographically and temporally dispersed.
- Information is incomplete, uncertain, distributed, and dynamic.
- Guidance, assumptions, and constraints on the plan as a whole, as well as the rationale for individual elements of the plan, are difficult to express and maintain in electronic form.
- Retrieval and evaluation of prior plans are difficult.
- Creating and modifying existing and ongoing plans is difficult without a highly interactive graphical environment.
- Several crisis situations can occur simultaneously, and plans always are made in the context of ongoing activities.
- Time to plan before execution must begin typically is short.
- Planning tools must function as embedded systems in existing but changeable computing, communications, and staff environments.

25.3 THE PLANNING PROCESS BEFORE DART

Before DART was developed, there was a great deal of room for improvement in the basic computer tools and communications resources available to operation planners and analysts. Room remains. A brief list of tasks and current capabilities is shown in Figure 25-1.

It should be evident from the list of challenges in the preceding section that DART was directed at relieving only a few specific bottlenecks in the larger context of the overall planning process. The deployment data associated with a plan (which units must move from where to where and when) must be analyzed with one or more transportation models in order to estimate the gross feasibility of the movement of forces entailed. This analysis contributes to a refinement process in which the forces involved, the dates they are moved, and transportation assets are adjusted until a feasible plan for accomplishing a given set of objectives is derived. Before DART, transportation analysis was a manually controlled, terminal-oriented batch data processing, and paper and pencil process that seriously slowed the process of refinement. DART made the process faster and more interactive by putting

Planning Function	Current Operational Practice	Initiative Goals
Data storage	Off-line tapes Sequential flat files	On-line disks Rel and/or obj databases
Data interpretation	Human 1 database E 500 records/8 hours	Knowledge-based 100 databases 40,000 records/hour
Plan representation	Single perspective Static, syntactic 1 COA	User def multiple perspectives Temporarily rich, semantic >5 COAs
Plan effectiveness	"TLAR"	Multiple intelligent simulation models
Plan feasibility	Single monolithic models Batch processing 24 hours	Hierarchical space of models <10 minutes
Plan reuse	Non-existent	Library of 1000 partial plans Rapid on-line adaptation
Scheduling	Single black box models 24 hours	Interactive setup and analysis <30 minutes
Sensitivity analysis	Non-existent	"What-if" capability automatic choke point explanation
Plan analysis	Manual 21–28 days	Interactive on-line tools <4 hours
Deliberate planning	2 years	<1 week
Crisis action planning	3 weeks	8 hours

Figure 25-1: Planning capabilities before DART

the input data and a standard model on a workstation with a graphical interface. Answers and recommendations about transportation can now be produced within the decision cycle of other planners. DART produced this improvement by addressing four specific problems of the transportation planning and analysis process.

The Toothache of Data Visualization. Each TPFDD record identifies a unit or item of material and specifies a required movement of personnel or equipment. These data are fundamental to military planning. MITRE personnel identified the difficulty that experts had in locating and modifying data about the units to be deployed as a compelling "toothache" that had to be fixed before underlying scheduling and planning problems could be addressed.

Manual Links between Tools. To the obvious data visualization problem, the USTRANSCOM analysts added the equally obvious difficulty of moving data between software tools to run transportation models. The primarily manual links between data sources and models significantly slowed the analysts' response to new plans and severely constrained the number of modify and test cycles used to refine or alter plans.

Aggregation, Access to Real-Time Data. It quickly became apparent that the obvious editing and integration problems concealed more challenging endemic difficulties with the data processing environment of planners and analysts. These experts not only needed to view and modify individual unit data and run models but also wanted to aggregate data into arbitrary force modules, which have characteristic structure and capabilities, or group data by attributes of concern to the analysis at hand. Furthermore, plans built and analyzed with standard unit characteristics and rule of thumb planning factors were poor substitutes for actual data values and realistic estimates for the critical attributes of units.

Collaborative Refinement. Finally, providing the many planners and analysts who work together to create the final form of a given plan with consistent tools, ways to share data, and common computing resources is a logical next step after providing the individuals involved with integrated workstation capabilities. In fact, making sure that the necessary software links among separated planners exist is just the logical next step after linking an individual planner's tools to one another.

25.4 PLANNING AND SCHEDULING WITH DART

DART is merely an integrated set of data processing tools and a database management system, together with a graphical viewing and editing environment for rapidly modifying and analyzing operational plans for transportation feasibility.

From the user's perspective, DART's primary improvements over prior systems are a major reduction in analysis time, the window interface, and an underlying architecture that allows fairly straightforward integration of related functional capabilities. DART also is quickly understood by new users and modifiable to meet new requirements. Taken together, these improvements make it possible for planners to consider more alternative plans and to produce a feasible plan faster. The speedup contributes to more rapid decision making and more thorough analysis throughout the planning process.

DART exploits interactive interfaces to display complex information in such visual formats as GANTT charts, world maps, flow diagrams, summary tables, and analysis graphs. Software, rather than the user, integrates familiar feasibility estimation models with easy to use record editing and model setup tools. An interactive environment is used to retrieve data, edit records, parameterize models, and produce summary reports of model results. Commercial software and standard open systems technology are used to make the system a good partner in a variety of system environments.

The prototype is hosted on the same desktop workstation used at USTRANS-COM and commonly available throughout the DoD. An Oracle relational database system is used as a blackboard for communication among software modules and as means for providing local storage. The interface used for database access and record editing is adapted from commercial resource allocation software developed by Ascent Technology. A simple outline map interface displays such relevant information as the location of points of origin, air and sea ports, destinations, and routes involved in a deployment. A Motif-style model setup interface provides for flexible parameterization of model input. A detailed visualization of the results of a model run is displayed and edited with a general purpose scientific graphing package. Data input to the model and storage of results data were handled by the relational database system.

25.4.1 Before/After Comparisons

DART achieved a high level of interest and approval from planners and analysts because it compares so favorably with previous planning tools. The system reduced USTRANSCOM's key analysis task from four days to four hours, and it was critical to deployment planning during the second phase of deployment in Desert Shield. Because the TPFDD modification capability incorporated in DART was guided by the requirements of planners, as well as transportation analysts, it provides significant capability for manual plan generation and refinement. Field tests demonstrated that this capability reduces significantly both plan generation time and plan refinement time. Planners who are not transportation experts also can use these DART tools and interfaces to build or modify a plan as well as perform an initial transportation feasibility analysis. Because planners and transportation

Test	System		
	JDS	**JOPS**	**DART**
1. Acquire and load	4 hrs	5 min	30 min
2. Cut, copy, paste old—>new TPPFDD	120 min	30 min	27 min
3. Modify by force module	30 min	N/A	12.3 min
4. Add ULN data	1 min	N/A	1 min
5. First pass feasibility est.	N/A	8 hrs	13 min
6. TPFDD iteration	N/A	6 hrs	20 min
7. Asset iteration	N/A	5 hrs	18 min
8. Histories	N/A	Run log	Analysis
9. Download	4 hrs	5 min	3 min

Figure 25-2:   Comparison of DART with other planning systems

analysts can use the same set of tools, they can collaborate to develop multiple options and refine plans in less time than it formerly took to create and analyze a single candidate plan. Perhaps the most dramatic form of approval by users is that operational command centers funded the distribution of the system to joint command centers and selected component commands from discretionary funds.

A number of quantifiable comparisons between DART and previous systems are summarized in Figure 25-2.

25.5 DISTRIBUTED COLLABORATIVE PLANNING

Besides speeding up the planning process, the installation of DART in several command centers enabled paradigm shifts in deliberate and crisis action planning. Planners and analysts can evaluate a plan in less time than it previously took to run a single scenario, so multiple courses of action can be proposed and compared interactively using a variety of analytic techniques. Because the modules of the system can be distributed across local or wide area networks, the planners and analysts involved in producing a plan can participate in a distributed planning process, regardless of their organizational or geographic location.

DART and the hardware on which it is hosted are designed to interoperate with other systems and software modules in the application computing environment. The DART system's open, evolvable hardware and software architecture provides an excellent basis for future command and control computing environments. An experiment to test the ability of DART, hosted on a multiprocessor UNIX system equipped with appropriate memory and storage capacity, demonstrated that up to eight simultaneous users can be supported without limiting loss of system performance. Successful demonstrations of the capability of DART systems to interoperate with one another and with other command and control software

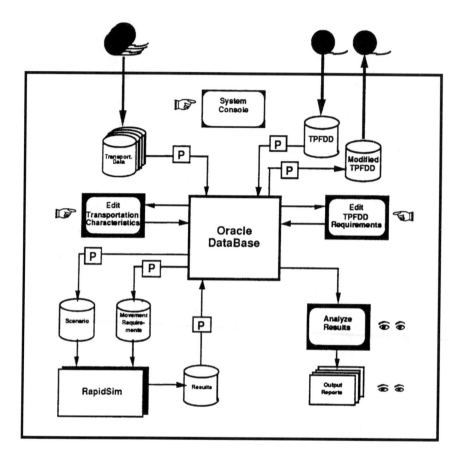

Figure 25-3: Updated DART architecture

resources to support both simultaneous and time-distributed collaboration over wide area networks took place during 1993.

25.5.1 System Design

DART's top-level software architecture is shown in Figure 25-3. The foundation of the system is the Oracle relational database, which is used to store multiple TPFDDs and related reference data during DART operations. The main software component is the application module, which connects to the Oracle Database and performs all the application-specific processing associated with DART. Copies of TPFDDs and other data maintained in the Oracle database are shared between two LISP applications: TPEDIT and the main DART application. TPEDIT provides the icon based editor for retrieving and manipulating TPFDD data. The DART applica-

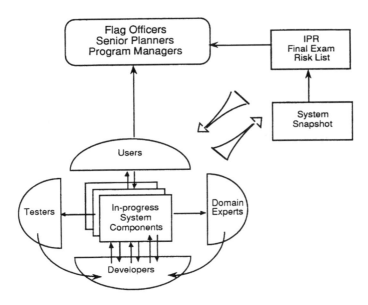

Figure 25-4: DART continuous management

tion handles other operations required to set up and run models in order to analyze transportation feasibility.

The information product of the planning process is generated concurrently by a large number of planners at a variety of sites and refined iteratively in collaborative conferences among these planners. The DART application software and database can be distributed over a local network of UNIX machines. Multiple users at a site can be supported by machines for running the Oracle software and DART application and small workstations used as X-Terminals. Each cluster of users who will share TPFDD information has a database server machine running Oracle. A large DART installation can have one or more application servers for running multiple copies of the DART application. This distributable client-server architecture is fundamental to providing support for the distributed collaborative planning process required to meet evolving military needs.

25.6 LESSONS LEARNED FROM DEVELOPING DART

The chief lesson learned from DART has been the utility and effectiveness for all aspects of development of early, intensive, and continuous involvement of a committed team representing funder, user, developer, and project management points of view. The general organization and management process used in DART is illustrated in Figure 25-4. During the Desert Shield effort, such a team collaboratively developed and managed a detailed project schedule using virtually continuous In Progress Reviews and over-the-shoulder demonstrations to surface problems and measure both functional and development status. A high proportion of the development effort took place on site. The resulting close involvement of users and other experts in the development process served to focus them on the most compelling operational requirements. It also provided for concurrent design review and performance evaluation of the system by all participants. The same overall management and development style has been followed, at a slower pace, in subsequent phases of DART development, and effective use has been made of telecommunications capabilities to reduce the earlier need for simultaneous and face to face interaction.

25.6.1 Risk Management

DART development efforts were directed toward aggressive goals and pursued at a brisk pace. To protect these efforts from foreseeable disruption, risks were identified at the start of each effort and intensively managed. The high priority risks identified in the initial development were

1. creeping requirements growth because of extreme operational need
2. inadequate development facilities or limited access to resources
3. delays or barriers because of security considerations
4. lack of connectivity to required data sources
5. requirements for participation by operational personnel
6. inadequate funding or managerial support for transition of developed capability to operational use
7. technical constraints imposed by existing systems and equipment

25.6.2 Knowledge Acquisition

Many members of the development team were current or former military planners, and the project management and development staff had participated in studies of the military planning process conducted during the initial phases of the ARPA/Rome Laboratory program. This "rich" knowledge acquisition environment was critical to the breadth of user knowledge incorporated in DART and the speed with which it was identified and developed.

Equally critical was the use of the developing system itself as an effective medium for knowledge acquisition and design throughout the project. With its familiar interface and close coupling to the operating environment, the initial prototype created a concrete, realistic "system" and "features" familiar to all parties. DART soon had sufficient functionality and a short enough response time to support frequent impromptu knowledge acquisition sessions between planners and developers that involved active use of the system on realistic problem-solving tasks. Furthermore, the intense pace of development meant there was a very short time lag between user feedback and the appearance of new or modified features in the system.

25.6.3 Testing

Besides serving as a knowledge acquisition tool and medium for communication between developer and user, the prototype provided a means to isolate and refine metrics for performance and quality. In-house testing of the system components developed at contractor sites was supplemented with everyday user involvement and feedback at USTRANSCOM. Expert planners from other commands were given extended demonstrations during the development to ensure that DART's capabilities were not tuned to idiosyncratic requirements.

Third party testers conducted a formal evaluation of the system functionality. Each DART build was tested by this independent test group, which followed a System Test Plan and issued a Test Analysis Report on the results of the testing. In addition, a Final Exam was constructed at the beginning of the project and used as the standard for intermediate review and project completion. This final exam was keyed to a functional specification for DART and driven by a problem-solving scenario. Results were recorded for comparison to existing systems and to project goals. The final exam for the 10-week effort is shown in Figure 25-5.

25.6.4 Concurrent Configuration Control

DART software is now under configuration management at USTRANSCOM. Software Incident Reports (IRs) and System Change Proposals (SCPs) are kept in a database and are analyzed by the development contractors. A DART Configuration Control Board decides which IR/SCPs are to be addressed and when the improvements should be released. Feedback to the IR/SCP submitter is always provided.

This description of DART configuration management, although correct, conceals the process that is key to DART's success from a management perspective. DART's formal configuration management was merely the result of concurrent configuration management by a team of users, developers, testers, and domain experts, who literally worked together in a collaborative development project. Not only during the 10-week project but also in follow-up phases of DART, all these constituencies participated on a day-to-day basis, often on-site, in a process by which the DART system evolved incrementally. *The process also included an active review of its functional requirements, test plan, training materials, and connectivity to other systems and procedures.* Concurrent configuration management is

Week 1 C+32 8-Sep-90
- Add/Delete Assets—Edit Scenario File
- "One-button" run RapidSim—Get 4 plots
- CAT Graphics on MAC
- Display Mtons or Stons—Use cargo categories
- Documentation & Training

Week 2 C+39 15-Sep-90
- Change 1PFDD—write out a TPFDD file
- Generate multiple run graphics displays
- Documentation & Training

Week 3 C+46 22-Sep-90
- Manually define/undefine known Force Modules

Week 4 C+53 29-Sep-90
- Change dates of a defined Force Module
- Change ports of a ULN
[CheckPoint—Replan]

Week 5 C+60 6-Oct-90
- Force Module Editor/Viewer (Release 1)
- Delete/Add Existing Force Modules

Week 6 C+67 13-Oct-90
- Scenario Builder (Release 1)
- Build new Force Module
- Ready to talk to people at CENTCOM
[Format in Process Review]

Week 7 C+74 20-Oct-90
- Make it easier. Make it better

Week 8 C+81 27-Oct-90
- Make it easier, Make it better
[CheckPoint—Replan]
- Consider and Propose
  Systems and networks for AOR fielding
  Actual scheduling solutions:
  Ascent/CMU/MitreB

Week 9 C+88 3-Nov-90
- Make it easier. Make it better.

Week 10 C+95 10-Nov-90
- Scenario Builder (Release 2)
- Hard proposal for continuation
- Presentation/Demonstration

All Weeks
Every Saturday: IPR & Demo

Figure 25-5:   Final Exam chart

a critical management practice required to take advantage of the speed and flexibility of modern software development environments and system capabilities.

25.6.5 Support

During the Desert Shield project, little effort was available for cleaning up the residue of pandemonium development and deployment or for enhancing or modifying system capabilities that were not essential to the immediate operational problem. Enormous progress in incorporating core functionality was made during this period; however, beginning in January 1991, a "toxic waste cleanup" was undertaken to prepare the system for long term use at TRANSCOM and potential deployment to other sites.

The initial deployment placed a single SPARC2 workstation in a stand-alone configuration in each selected site with installed and tested DART software. The procedures followed in the installation were established at beta distribution sites. Before the installations began, a site survey identified the existing electronic infrastructure and individual site needs. The hardware and software for each installation were checked and tested at the contractor's facility before shipment and then tested again after its installation on site. Up to seven days of on-site training were provided as a part of each site installation. Centralized training courses gave more in-depth training to site personnel who can train other users. A User's Manual and a System Administrator's manual were provided to each site and upgraded as DART software was enhanced. System documentation has been written to allow transition of DART functions and architecture to the Joint Command and Control ADP environment.

The DART program maintains a hotline at TRANSCOM for user problems. A log is kept of all incoming calls and requests. The hotline operator will hand off the problem to the appropriate contractor or government staff member.

25.6.6 Software Engineering Methodology

Much of the power of DART came from integrating AI technology with relational database, networking, distributed system, and user interface technology. DART's speed of construction and fielding was attained by matching and modifying user needs to available component capabilities (rather than by building custom code to satisfy a previously fixed requirements specification). The system architecture was exploited as a "software bridge" to link software components. The DART development represents the use of early forms of such megaprogramming methods. When these methods are fully developed, the components of such a development strategy will allow software applications to be built component-by-component rather than instruction-by-instruction. The required technology will include component definitions, development tools, and environments that support composition, component libraries, and associated capabilities for software commerce based on components.

Practical Total Quality Management principles, such as adopting a total process approach, involving all the stakeholders, using end-user needs to drive priorities, and identifying high-leverage actions, were fundamental guiding principles for managing the development effort. DART's rapid acceptance by planners was a direct result of specifically involving users in defining initial prototype capabilities, refining the prototype into the initial operational DART system, and incrementally examining elapsed planning and analysis times to focus on major sources of improvement.

DART used modern computing and communications to manage prototyping and evolutionary development rather than rely on paper documents for capturing user requirements, configuration management, etc. This allowed DART to evolve rapidly through a series of increasingly more robust prototypes that were increasingly well matched to user needs over a time scale of weeks and months. The DART development did uncover shortfalls in the technology needed to support such prototyping and acquisition techniques, and the risks associated with these vulnerabilities were discussed and managed aggressively at each design review.

At any given time, a "snapshot" of the science and technology base shows projects using mature technology, projects proceeding from earlier science investments into maturing technology, and current science investments focused on new long-range concepts or "missing science" identified by the use of current technology. The DART projects' requirements were closely matched to the state of the art by the project members' awareness of the state of maturity of previous DoD investments in AI planning, relational databases, user interfaces, workstations, and networking technology.

DART benefited strongly from the commercial software technology that has been stimulated by previous DoD investments in software technology. The existence of this software reduced the acquisition and maintenance bill for the resulting prototype and has allowed it to "ride the commercial technology curves" for fast-moving hardware and component software technology in order to capture increased capability without expensive porting efforts.

25.7 FUTURE DIRECTIONS FOR PLANNING SYSTEMS

The DART system fixes yesterday's computing problems. DART's open architecture permitted relatively low-risk use of off-the-shelf technology and commercial software, and the development team used an incremental integration strategy with short development cycles in order to provide for regular review of technical progress and direction. The incremental development effort struck a balance between formality and flexibility in order to adapt to rapidly changing computer technology and user needs but be comprehensive and formal enough to provide continuing support for the system and its users. Specific site tailoring and expansion was not undertaken, but the DART system has been expanded and tailored in response to site feedback as the capabilities of the system have grown.

The real goal of the DART project was to implant an evolutionary development methodology, which included posing concrete and interesting research problems and setting a high standard for the abstract architectural basis of hardware, software, and human resources used to explore such problems. Crisis action planning encompasses a number of enduring technical challenges. In addition to its primary engineering objectives, the DART system was conceived as a practical foundation for research, a platform for technology transition, and a starting point for a successive application development that would rapidly leave behind the "old school" of planning problems that DART addressed.

Eventually, automated planning systems will help commanders and their staffs evaluate proposed courses of action using decision metrics and qualitative criteria, use descriptions of situations to assess the applicability of existing plans, and conduct interactive simulations to address the implications of underlying assumptions or dynamically changing constraints. Robust and flexible plans will facilitate rapid response to unforeseen changes in external conditions, unexpected

AI/Planning Research	Crisis Planning and Operations
Generative planning	Mission objectives, courses of action, major force assignments
Constraint-based scheduling	Resource constraints, feasibility analysis, time-phasing, etc.
Case-based planning	Force analysis, plan library development, failure analysis, plan revision techniques
Intelligent databases	Distributed, Heterogeneous Intelligence and status databases
Interactive graphical displays and editing environments	Data acquisition, situation analysis, plan refinement, briefing, and order production

Figure 25-6: Specific connections between planning research issues and operation planners' tasks

outcomes of actions, or evolving mission objectives. Intelligent database systems will help generate and maintain force and deployment databases to provide an accessible shared repository and systematic organizing structure for the extensive qualitative and quantitative information developed in the planning process. In addition, sophisticated computer-human interaction will permit clear, natural communication among its many machine and human participants.

The utility of improvements in planning and scheduling technology is self-evident, and the generation and execution of crisis action plans provide many opportunities for creating and applying AI technology, for accelerating the software acquisition process by which technical capabilities are transitioned to practice, and for solving planning and scheduling problems that have dual use in military and commercial domains. The everyday nature of the domain produces a wealth of test cases and examples as well as readily accessible test-bed opportunities focused on difficult practical problems. Furthermore, the domain lends itself to exploiting incremental improvements from on-going research in individual technical components. Some specific correlations between operation planning requirements and knowledge-based scheduling and planning technology are shown below. (See Figure 25-6.)

Individual research projects and a variety of Technology Integration Experiments are being undertaken in the ARPA/RL program to integrate planning and scheduling components and analyze the trade-offs among approaches to the organization of planning systems. It is anticipated that in order to behave effectively in this domain, classical plan generation methods will have to incorporate reasoning under uncertainty, decision theory, and plan justification methods. Constraint directed scheduling techniques will have to be integrated with current transportation scheduling and combat analysis programs to provide execution monitoring and replanning support. Case-based planning methods will have to be applied to plan assembly and subplan reuse to support planning with force module libraries. In addition, these methods all will have to be made available in a concurrent environment that provides uniform intelligent access to multiple, distributed sources of planning knowledge and allows simulations of plans to be composed from constituent models and executed to test and evaluate planning options.

A sequence of Integrated Feasibility Demonstrations (IFDs) is the Initiative's mechanism for bringing together component planning and scheduling technologies and demonstrating how the results of these individual efforts apply to critical military planning and scheduling problems. These demonstrations contribute to evaluating the progress of the research program and elicit feedback from the target user community on the applicability and effectiveness of new technology. The early prototype that led to the development of DART was the first such demonstration, and a second, which took place in January 1992, highlighted the use of generative planning technology (SIPE-2) as a semi-automated plan generation capability for developing and refining a TPFDD that could be analyzed using DART. A third demonstration is focusing on distributed collaborative planning for highly variable non-combatant evacuation operations.

The sequence of experiments and demonstrations forms a rapid prototyping process for a future joint planning system. Feasibility Demonstrations also take advantage of new technologies from outside the Initiative proper as they become available, and they have gradually expanded in scope to address new technical and operational challenges. Thus, although the focus of the early DART development was on assembling existing software and procedures, it represents the first operational impact of a long range program to develop technical components for a shared concurrent reasoning infrastructure that enables all participants to collaborate actively and continuously in the planning process.

ACKNOWLEDGMENTS

DART, the Dynamic Analysis and Replanning Tool, initially was developed by ARPA, in partnership with Rome Laboratory and USTRANSCOM, under Contract No. MDA972-90-C-0074. DART was built by a team of government and contractor personnel from ARPA; Rome Laboratory; USTRANSCOM; BBN Systems and Technologies; Ascent Technology, Inc.; The MITRE Corporation; SRA Corporation; Carnegie Mellon University; and ISX Corporation. In addition to those directly involved in the development project, many other government and contractor participants in the ARPA–Rome Laboratory Planning Initiative are contributing to the ongoing improvement and exploitation of DART.

References

Baerson, K. 1991. Pentagon Sun/Mac System Tracks Global Hot Spots, *Federal Computer Week*, 4 November.

Boehm, B.W. 1991. Information Science Technology Office, Defense Advanced Research Projects Agency, Arlington, VA. Private Communication to S. Cross.

Burstein, M.H. 1990. A Quick Introduction to the Military Transportation Planning Process, BBN Technical Report No. 7495, Bolt Baranek and Newman, Cambridge, MA.

Burstein, M.H., and D. Kosy. PFE, The Prototype Feasibility Estimator: A Transportation Simulator for the Common Prototyping Environment, BBN Technical Report No. 7598, Bolt Beranek and Newman, Cambridge, MA.

Cross, S.E. 1989. "Applications of Artificial Intelligence to Crisis Action Planning." Unpublished paper, Air Command and Staff College, Maxwell AFB, AL.

Cross, S.E. 1990. A Proposed Initiative in Crisis Action Planning, DARPA, Arlington, VA.

Cross, S.E. 1991. Knowledge Based Tools for Deliberate and Crisis Action Planning: The DARPA–Rome Laboratory Planning Initiative, DARPA, Arlington, VA.

Cross, S.E., and M. Fox. 1989. DARPA Knowledge-Based Planning Workshop, Clearwater, Florida, December.

Martin, R., R. Lowe, and R. Estrada. 1991. DARPA/Rome Laboratory Planning and Scheduling Initiative: Product Transition Plan (DRAFT), Joint Net Military Assessment.

Martin, R. and N. Weiderman. 1992. DARPA/RL Planning Initiative Standards, Conventions, and Specifications, Software Engineering Institute, Pittsburgh, PA.

Reis, V. 1991. Congressional Testimony, April.

INDEX